Praise for *Jewish-Christianity and the History of Judaism*

"This landmark book of essays by an enormously influential scholar challenges us to question our most traditional terminology—Judaism/Christianity/religion—and invites us to creatively rethink the complex history of our shared identity."

—Elaine Pagels, Harrington Spear Paine
Professor of Religion, Princeton University

"In *Jewish-Christianity and the History of Judaism*, Annette Yoshiko Reed enacts her mastery of enormous ancient corpora: canonical, noncanonical, and especially para-biblical, those writings of indeterminate identity where no meaningful distinctions can be made. And she dances on the numinous edge, engaging with garrulous angels and demons, with 'magicians,' divinatory experts, and charisma-infused individuals, as well as with 'the suits': those theologians, bishops, rabbis, and emperors who monopolize our historical investigations. By retrieving marginalized texts and by renouncing the anachronism of scholarship's comfortable identity bins—Judaism, Christianity, orthodoxy, monotheism—Reed summons us to rethink and to redraw our academic map of ancient Mediterranean relations between heaven and earth."

—Paula Fredriksen, The Hebrew University of Jerusalem

"In this groundbreaking study, the brilliant scholar of Judaism and Christianity Annette Yoshiko Reed transforms our understanding of both religions. Based on careful research and close readings of ancient evidence, she gives us a fascinating portrayal of the birth and growth of Jewish-Christianity. Rather than a heretical event in the emergence of Christianity and its split with Judaism, Jewish-Christianity, Reed demonstrates, is an important moment in the emergence of Judaism and the profound influence of each religion on the other."

—Susannah Heschel, author of *The Aryan Jesus:
Christian Theologians and the Bible in Nazi Germany*

"In this rich and learned collection of essays, Annette Yoshiko Reed shows how scholarship's ongoing attachment to the unsatisfactory category 'Jewish Christian' gives voice, in often unnoticed ways, to a set of problems which cluster round previous ways of discussing Jewish-Christian relations. Reflecting, in often original and arresting ways, shifts in the intellectual climate of the past forty or so years, Reed's work is a strikingly original, always challenging, and multifaceted contribution to the ongoing question of Jews and Christians in antiquity and the many significant questions which relate to this much-discussed subject."

—James Carleton Paget, Peterhouse College, University of Cambridge

Annette Yoshiko Reed

Jewish-Christianity and the History of Judaism

Fortress Press
Minneapolis

JEWISH-CHRISTIANITY AND THE HISTORY OF JUDAISM

Cover image: Photo © Zev Radovan / Bridgeman Images. Mosaic floor from the Samaritan synagogue at El-Khirbe, West Bank, 4th century AD (mosaic)

Cover design by Laurie Ingraham

Print ISBN: 978-1-5064-8207-1

For KunKun
(Alexander Reed Fleming)

Table of Contents

Part II

"Jewish-Christianity" in Jewish History and Jewish Studies

Abbreviations

AGJU	Arbeiten zur Geschichte des antiken Judentums und des Urchristentums
AJS Review	*Association for Jewish Studies Review*
Apoc	*Apocrypha*
BJS	Brown Judaic Studies
CBQ	*Catholic Biblical Quarterly*
CBR	*Currents in Biblical Research*
CH	*Church History*
CSCO	Corpus Scriptorum Christianorum Orientalium
DSD	*Dead Sea Discoveries*
GCS	Die Griechischen Christlichen Schriftsteller
Hen	*Henoch*
HT	*History and Theory*
HTR	*Harvard Theological Review*
HUCA	*Hebrew Union College Annual*
HUT	Hermeneutische Untersuchungen zur Theologie
JAAR	*Journal of the American Academy of Religion*
JAJ	*Journal of Ancient Judaism*
JBL	*Journal of Biblical Literature*
JECS	*Journal of Early Christian Studies*
JJS	*Journal of Jewish Studies*
JJTP	*Journal of Jewish Thought and Philosophy*
JNES	*Journal of Near Eastern Studies*
JPS	Jewish Publication Society
JQR	*Jewish Quarterly Review*
JR	*Journal of Religion*
JRS	*Journal of Roman Studies*
JSJ	*Journal for the Study of Judaism*
JSJSup	Supplements to the Journal for the Study of Judaism
JSNT	*Journal for the Study of the New Testament*
JSP	*Journal for the Study of the Pseudepigrapha*
JSQ	*Jewish Studies Quarterly*
JSS	*Jewish Social Studies*
JTS	*Journal of Theological Studies*
JTSA	Jewish Theological Seminary of America
MTSR	*Method & Theory in the Study of Religion*
NovT	*Novum Testamentum*
NovTSup	Supplements to Novum Testamentum
NTA	*New Testament Apocrypha*
NTS	*New Testament Studies*
PL	Patrologia Latina
PT	*Poetics Today*
RÉJ	*Revue des Études Juives*
RevQ	*Revue de Qumran*
RSR	*Recherches de Science Religieuse*

SBL	Society of Biblical Literature
SBLSymS	SBL Symposium Series
SR	*Studies in Religion/Sciences Religieuses*
STDJ	Studies on the Texts of the Desert of Judah
StPB	Studia Post-biblica
SUNY	State University of New York
TSAJ	Texts and Studies in Ancient Judaism
TSMJ	Texts and Studies in Medieval and Early Modern Judaism
TU	Texte und Untersuchungen zur Geschichte der altchristlichen Literatur
VC	*Vigiliae Christianae*
VCSup	Supplements to Vigiliae Christianae
WUNT	Wissenschaftliche Untersuchungen zum Neuen Testament
ZAC	*Zeitschrift für Antikes Christentum*
ZNW	*Zeitschrift für die Neutestamentliche Wissenschaft*

Primary Sources

1 Apol.	Justin, *1 Apology*
1 Clem.	*1 Clement*
Adv. haer.	Irenaeus, *Adversus Haereses*
Adv. Jud.	Tertullian, *Adversus Judaeos*
Adv. Marc.	Tertullian, *Adversus Marcionem*
Alm.	Ptolemy, *Almagest*
Apoc. Pet.	*Apocalypse of Peter*
Barn.	*Epistle of Barnabus*
Cels.	Origen, *Contra Celsum*
Comm. Jo.	Origen, *Commentarii in evangelium Joannis*
Comm. Matt.	Origen, *Commentarium in evangelium Matthaei*
De mens.	Epiphanius, *De mensuris*
De myst.	Iamblichus, *De Mysteriis Aegyptiorum*
Dial.	Justin, *Dialogus cum Tryphone*
Did. apost.	*Didascalia apostolorum*
Did.	*Didache*
Ep. Pet.	*Epistle of Peter to James*
Ep.	Augustine, *Epistles*
Epist.	Jerome, *Epistulae*
Haer.	Hippolytus, *Refutatio omnium haeresium*
Hist. eccl.	Eusebius, *Historia Ecclesiastica*
Hist. Rom.	Cassius Dio, *Historia Romana*
Hist.	Tacitus, *Histories*
Hom. Cant.	Origen, *Homiliae in Canticum*
Hom. Matt.	John Chrysostom, *Homiliae in Matthaeum*
Hom.	Pseudo-Clementine *Homilies*
Magn.	Ignatius, *Letter to the Magnesians*
Mon.	Tertullian, *De monogamia*
Odes Sol.	*Odes of Solomon*
Or.	Tertullian, *De oration*
Paed.	Clement, *Paedagogus*
Pan.	Epiphanius, *Panarion*
Phil.	Ignatius, *Letter to the Philadelphians*
Praep. ev.	Eusebius, *Praeparatio evangelica*
Praescr.	Tertullian, *De praescriptione haereticorum*
Prot. Jas.	*Protevangelium of James*
Ps.-Clem.	Pseudo-Clementine
Ptol.	Ptolemy
Rec.	Pseudo-Clementine *Recognitions*
Res. mort.	Tertullian, *De resurrectione mortuorum*
Rom.	Ignatius, *Letter to the Romans*
Sat.	Juvenal, *Satires*
Strom.	Clement of Alexandria, *Stromateis*
Vir. ill.	Jerome, *De viris illustribus*

Introduction

Historicizing "Jewish-Christianity"

The term "Jewish-Christianity" is a modern invention.[1] Unlike "Jew," "Christian," "heretic," or "Judaizing," the adjective "Jewish-Christian" finds no ancient counterpart as a self-claimed identity-label or even as a term of accusation.[2] Today, it is commonly used to denote premodern texts, sects, and figures that cultivated messianic beliefs in Jesus while maintaining some meaningfully central commitment to Jewish practice and the people Israel.[3] This phenomenon is

---

* Parts of this argument were first presented at Fordham University as "Problems in Defining 'Jewish-Christianity': Taxonomy and Terminology before 'Religion' and beyond 'Identity,'" 30 November 2016. I am grateful to James Carleton Paget, Andrew S. Jacobs, Jae Han, and Shaul Magid for comments and critiques.

[1] See further F. Stanley Jones, ed., *Rediscovery of Jewish Christianity: From Toland to Baur* (History of Biblical Studies 5; Atlanta: Society of Biblical Literature, 2012).

[2] An argument for a possible precedent in Jerome, *Comm. Zech.* 3.14.19 is made by Simon Claude Mimouni, *Le judéo-christianisme ancien* (Paris: Cerf, 1998), 62; that this is based in a misinterpretation of the passage, however, has been shown by James Carleton Paget, *Jews, Christians, and Jewish-Christians* (WUNT 251; Tübingen: Mohr, 2010), 289. Oskar Skarsaune argues for some precedents for the term in references to "Jewish believers" (Origen, *Cels.* 2.1), "believing Jews" (Eusebius, *Hist. eccl.* 4.5.2), and related designations (John 8:31; Eusebius, *Hist. eccl.* 4.22.8; 6.25.4); "Jewish Believers in Antiquity," in *Jewish Believers in Jesus: The Early Centuries*, ed. Oskar Skarsaune and Reidar Hvalvik (Peabody, MA: Hendrickson, 2007), 3–6. Even if we were to grant a maximalist reading to this handful of examples as reflecting some set terminology with an established taxonomic sense in ancient times, it remains that – as Edwin Broadhead notes – "we have no examples of the term used as a self-reference in antiquity"; *Jewish Ways of Following Jesus: Redrawing the Religious Map of Antiquity* (WUNT 266; Tübingen: Mohr Siebeck, 2010), 29. To be sure, early scholarship on "Jewish-Christianity" often used the term interchangeably with "Ebionism," but this usage has been abandoned since it imposes an overly monolithic reading on the diverse relevant sources. There are no surviving sources, moreover, that use "Ebionite" as a term of self-definition.

[3] Many such definitions treat Torah observance as a necessary condition. Mimouni, for instance, defines the term as denoting those Jews who believe in Jesus as messiah and continue to live by the laws of the Torah; "Pour une définition nouvelle du judeo-christianisme ancien," *NTS* 38 (1992): 161–86. So too for Patricia Crone: "'Jewish Christianity' is a modern term for the beliefs of those followers of Jesus who saw devotion to Jesus as part of God's covenant with Israel, not as a transfer of God's promise of salvation from the Jews to the gentiles. Some of them regarded Jesus as a prophet, others saw him as a heavenly power, but all retained their Jewish identity and continued to observe the law"; "Jewish Christianity and the Qur'ān (Part One)," *JNES* 74 (2015): 225. Contrast the more open-ended formulation by Edwin Broadhead: "persons and groups in antiquity whose historical profile suggests that they both follow Jesus and maintain Jewishness and that they do so as a continuation of God's covenant with Israel" (*Jewish Ways of Following Jesus*, 56).

typically associated with the very earliest stages of Christian history, most proximate to the Jewish origins of Christianity. Appeals to "Jewish-Christianity" often conjure the possibility of recovering something of the Jesus Movement when it still remained culturally and demographically close to its roots in the Land of Israel – prior to the construction of "Christian" identities in contradistinction from "Jewish" identities. Thereafter, "Jewish-Christianity" is figured as a marginal position: those whom late antique Christian heresiologists condemned as *too* "Jewish" to count as *really* "Christian" (e. g., Ebionites; Nazarenes/Nazoraeans) are also those deemed "dangerous ones in between" by modern scholars who wish to retell the early history of Christianity as the tale of its emergence as a "religion" distinct from "Judaism."[4]

The present volume is not a comprehensive synthesis or survey of the data for "Jewish-Christianity."[5] It is shaped, rather, by three specific aims. First is to bring further attention to a cluster of fascinating but understudied late antique texts and traditions that do not fit neatly into present-day notions of "Christianity" as distinct from "Judaism." Second is to help lay the textual, historiographical, theoretical, and bibliographical groundwork for their further integration into the study of Late Antiquity, on the one hand, and into Jewish Studies, on the other. Third is to use the very rubric of "Jewish-Christianity" as a lens through which to probe the power and limits of our own scholarly practices of sorting and studying "religions."

Recent insights into the continued fluidity and overlaps of "Christian" and "Jewish" identities have sparked new debates about how best to define "Jewish-Christianity" and whether to reject the term altogether.[6] Scholarship on Christian Origins now emphasizes connections to Jewishness across the entire continuum of the Jesus Movement, thus raising questions about whether the designation is simply superfluous for the early period. The decline in the use of this term in New Testament Studies, in turn, has served to expose some an-

---

[4] The relevant heresiological and other Patristic evidence is handily collected in Albertus Frederik Johannes Klijn and Gerrit J. Reinink, *Patristic Evidence for Jewish Christian Sects* (NovTSup 36; Leiden: Brill, 1973), 95–281. The parallel with modern scholarly practice is made already by John G. Gager, "Jews, Christians, and the Dangerous Ones in Between," in *Interpretation in Religion*, ed. Shlomo Biderman and Ben-Ami Scharfstein (Philosophy and Religion 2; Leiden: Brill, 1992), 249–57. It is in this sense, moreover, that Daniel Boyarin more recently mounts his argument for dismissing the term "Jewish-Christianity" as irredeemably heresiological in "Rethinking Jewish Christianity: An Argument for Dismantling a Dubious Category (to Which Is Appended a Correction of My *Border Lines*)," *JQR* 99 (2009): 7–36 – on which see further below.

[5] For a comprehensive survey, see most recently Dominique Bernard, *Les disciples juifs de Jésus du Ier siècle à Mahomet: Recherches sur le mouvement ébionite* (Paris: Cerf, 2017).

[6] See further James Carleton Paget, "Jewish Christianity," in *The Cambridge History of Judaism*, vol. 3: *The Early Roman Period*, ed. William Horbury, W. D. Davies, and John Sturdy (Cambridge: Cambridge University Press, 1999), 733–42; Carleton Paget, "The Definition of the Terms Jewish Christian and Jewish Christianity in the History of Research," in Skarsaune and Hvalvik, *Jewish Believers in Jesus*, 22–54.

alytical difficulties in its traditional application to later materials as well. For instance, as common as it has been to read the Jewishness of "Jewish-Christian" as denoting ethnicity, it remains – as Charlotte Fonrobert reminds us – that our texts are rarely forthcoming on issues of genealogical lineage, thus leaving scholars to speculate on the somewhat problematic basis of their own assumptions of the beliefs or practices to which this or that ethnic group might have been more predisposed.[7] Likewise, as common as it is to tie the Jewishness of "Jewish-Christianity" to Torah-observance, it remains – as James Carleton Paget reminds us – "unclear which parts of the law should be kept in order to make someone a Jewish Christian."[8] To set a singular definition of the Jewishness of "Jewish-Christianity," moreover, is to identify a single feature as "the hard core of a given class of religion" in a manner that denies it "change over time" – as Matt Jackson-McCabe has noted.[9] And to do so for Jewishness, in particular, bears problematic resonance with longstanding scholarly habits of studying Judaism as the purportedly static background to an evolving Christianity.

Despite these difficulties, Fonrobert has suggested that "our understanding of the formation of Jewish and Christian collective identities as separate identities depends on developing an intelligible way of discussing the phenomenon called 'Jewish Christianity,' one that is not marred by Christian theological prejudices, nor by unexamined assumptions about either 'Jewish' identity formation or its 'Christian' counterpart."[10] If this task has proved difficult in practice, it is perhaps for reasons that are themselves quite revealing. Scholars have tended to reconstruct the beliefs and practices of "Jewish-Christians" primarily from the New Testament when discussing the early period. For the later period, however, they depend largely on secondhand Patristic reports that denounce such positions to promote their own visions of what should properly be deemed "Christian."[11]

---

[7] Charlotte Fonrobert, "The *Didascalia Apostolorum*: A Mishnah for the Disciples of Jesus," *JECS* 9 (2001): 483–509 at 499–502. See also Carleton Paget, *Jews, Christians, and Jewish Christians*, 26–28.

[8] Carleton Paget, *Jews, Christians, and Jewish Christians*, 25.

[9] Matt Jackson-McCabe, "What's in a Name," in *Jewish Christianity Reconsidered: Rethinking Ancient Groups and Texts*, ed. Jackson-McCabe (Minneapolis: Fortress, 2007), 7–38 at 36.

[10] Fonrobert, "*Didascalia Apostolorum*," 484.

[11] My point about heresiology here refers to the narrower definitions of "Jewish-Christianity" which have tended to predominate particularly within studies that include its late antique expressions and which most shape the current discussion. Notably, there is also another line of definition and discussion – from Albert Schwegler in the nineteenth century to Jean Daniélou in the twentieth century – that adopts a more expansive sense of "Jewish-Christianity," not limited to heresiological tropes but encompassing a broad variety of "thought-forms" as well as practices. This line of research, however, tends to be focused on the first two centuries CE and on claims about the Jewishness of "primitive" Christianity. Accordingly, it has been less influential in recent decades as Christianity's originary Jewishness has increasingly become a matter of consensus within New Testament Studies. For further examples, see Appendix B below. I thank James Carleton Paget for pushing me on this point.

Normative concerns can be thereby imported unintentionally, together with the crypto-heresiological presumption that "Jewish-Christianity" is ultimately an improper expression of the Jewish heritage of the Church – potentially authentic in the early period but self-evidently anachronistic thereafter. The very selectivity of sources conventionally privileged in the study of "Jewish-Christianity" thus transposes normative claims into historical assertions and predetermines the conclusion of Christianity's diminishing Jewishness. Partly as a result, moreover, even the *Jewishness* of "Jewish-Christianity" has been defined almost wholly from a Christian perspective and in terms of Christian history – typically centered on the depiction of Peter, James, the Jerusalem Church, and "circumcision party" in the New Testament, on the one hand, and the depiction of Ebionites and Nazarenes/Nazoraeans by Epiphanius and other late antique heresiologists, on the other.[12]

The proliferation of publications on the topic attests a renewed interest in "Jewish-Christianity," variously defined.[13] But it remains that the topic is almost always discussed as part of the diversity or dynamics of Christianity.[14] The vast majority of specialist studies on "Jewish-Christianity" have been penned by and for those trained in the specialist study of the New Testament – and under the assumption that the significance of "Jewish-Christianity" is largely limited to the period of Christian Origins, prior to a presumed "Parting of the Ways" with Judaism in late first or early second century CE.[15] Even the fascinating new lines

---

[12] That one of the factors that distinguishes "Jewish-Christianity," for instance from "Judaizing," is the continuity with Peter, James, and the Jerusalem Church of the apostolic age is assumed in the conventional narrative of its rise and fall. This narrative is nicely summarized by Georg Strecker: "Jewish Christianity, according to the witness of the New Testament, stands at the beginning of the development of church history, so that it is not the gentile Christian 'ecclesiastical doctrine' that represents what is primary, but rather a Jewish Christian theology. This fact was forgotten quite early in the ecclesiastical heresiological tradition. The Jewish Christians usually were classified as 'Ebionites' in the ecclesiastical catalogues of sects or else, in a highly one-sided presentation, they were deprecated as an insignificant minority by comparison with the 'great church.' Thus implicitly the idea of apostasy from the ecclesiastical doctrine also was applied to them"; "Appendix 1: On the Problem of Jewish Christianity," in Walter Bauer, *Orthodoxy and Heresy in Earliest Christianity*, ed. and trans. Robert A. Kraft and Gerhard Kroedel (Philadelphia: Fortress, 1971), 245. Joan Taylor demonstrates the problems with assuming that such continuity is necessary for the Jewishness of "Jewish-Christianity" to be authentic, and she makes a case for extricating them: "There is no doubt that Jewish-Christians, defined as Christian Jews and their Gentile converts who maintained Jewish praxis, existed throughout the first four centuries of the Christian Church, and indeed, for all we know, for many centuries afterward." Taylor argues nonetheless that "Jewish-Christianity was not ... a multi-fibrous strand of heterodox sectarianism unravelling from the Jerusalem community via Pella"; "The Phenomenon of Jewish Christianity," *VC* 44 (1990): 314–15.

[13] See further Appendix B below.

[14] On the language of "diversity" and what hides and conveys, see Karen King, "Factions, Variety, Diversity, Multiplicity: Representing Early Christian Differences for the 21st Century," *MTSR* 23 (2011): 216–37, as well as my discussion in the Epilogue below.

[15] For a particularly sophisticated example, see Jackson-McCabe, *Jewish Christianity Re-*

of research on the modern genealogy of current scholarship on "Jewish-Christianity" have focused almost wholly on Christian thinkers. Surprisingly rare, by comparison, is any sustained engagement with Jewish comparanda and the discourses about identity, history, and difference therein.[16]

The present volume collects and extends the results of over a decade of my experiments in reorienting research on "Jewish-Christianity" so as to relativize and recontextualize the representation of Jews and Jewishness in Patristic literature, while also engaging Jewish sources, trajectories of Jewish history, and questions from and about Jewish Studies. I thus set aside the scholarly habit of privileging the secondhand reports about Ebionites and Nazoraeans by late antique heresiologists like Epiphanius.[17] I focus instead on the firsthand witness of those writings that have been traditionally studied under the rubric of "Jewish-Christianity." Instead of assuming the New Testament as my primary reference point for assessing "Jewish-Christianity," I here raise questions about possible links to Rabbinic, Hekhalot, and other Jewish literature as well. Rather than framing my questions solely in terms set by Ferdinand Christian Baur, Adolph von Harnack, and other formative figures for New Testament Studies and Church History, I look also to Heinrich Graetz, Kauffman Kohler, Gershom Scholem, and other formative figures in Jewish Studies.

Foremost among these firsthand sources are the Pseudo-Clementines – a corpus of Greek novels and epistles from fourth-century Syria that have long been studied as the main source for firsthand expressions of "Jewish-Christianity."[18]

---

considered. An important exception to the typical orientation toward "origins," however, is the work of F. Stanley Jones, who has increasingly looked to third-century Syro-Mesopotamia as a locus for the development of "Jewish-Christian" perspectives, especially in tension with Marcionism; see especially now *Pseudoclementina Elchasaiticaque inter Judaeochristiana: Collected Studies* (Orientalia Lovaniensia Analecta 203; Leuven: Peeters, 2012), 152–71, 359–52.

[16] Charlotte Fonrobert and Burton Visotzky are important exceptions to this general pattern – and much of the inspiration for the present volume. See esp. Visotzky, "Prolegomenon to the Study of Jewish-Christianities in Rabbinic Literature," in Visotzky, *Fathers of the World: Essays in Rabbinic and Patristic Literatures* (WUNT 80; Tübingen: Mohr Siebeck, 1995), 129–49; Fonrobert, "*Didascalia Apostolorum*," 484–87; Fonrobert, "Jewish Christians, Judaizers, and Christian Anti-Judaism," in *A People's History of Christianity*, volume 2: *Late Ancient Christianity*, ed. Virginia Burrus and Rebecca Lyman (Minneapolis: Fortress, 2005), 234–55. As noted below in Chapters Seven, Eight, and Eleven, however, there are a number of precedents in nineteenth- and early twentieth-century research. For more on this dynamic and its ramifications, see my discussion in the Epilogue below.

[17] On Ebionites, see further Carleton Paget, *Jews, Christians, and Jewish Christians*, 325–82; Jones, *Pseudoclementina*, 513–16.

[18] Strecker is representative in noting that the focus has conventionally fallen on "the legalistic Jewish Christianity situated in Greek-speaking Syria," as attested by "[1] the indirect witness of the *Didascalia* and then [2] the Jewish Christian *Kerygmata Petrou* ('Proclamations' or 'Sermons of Peter'; abbreviated KP) source of the Pseudo-Clementines, and compare our results with [3] the so-called ecclesiastical position, which in this instance means with the statements about Ebionitism made by the ecclesiastical heresiologists"; "On the Problem of Jewish Christianity," 245. Here, I focus on the Pseudo-Clementines in their received forms,

Instead of culling them for clues about the apostolic age, I situate them in Late Antiquity, and I investigate their representations of Jews, Jewishness, and Christianity's Jewish past. I seek to bring them into conversation with Rabbinic and other Jewish sources from Late Antiquity, and I also ask whether these and other "Jewish-Christian apocrypha"[19] might shed light on topics of enduring interest within Jewish Studies – ranging from messianism, mysticism, and Rabbinization to the politics of the past in *Wissenschaft des Judentums*. In the process, I use a focus on these sources to expose the degree to which past scholarly narratives about Jewish/Christian relations have been structured and constrained by Christian authors – from Eusebius and Epiphanius to Baur and Harnack.

Perhaps precisely because "Jewish-Christianity" is an anachronistic, clumsy, fraught, and contested category, I propose that it proves useful as a site for reassessing some of the interpretative habits that we take most for granted. Its definition has been much debated. Even the perceived need for such a hybrid term points powerfully to the limits of modern taxonomies of "religions" for describing all of our premodern data. Just as the heresiological discourse surrounding Ebionites in Late Antiquity aided in the initial construction of an ideal of a pure "Christianity" separate from "Judaism,"[20] so the modern practice of labeling sources as "Jewish-Christian" often permits scholars to marginalize those very sources that most expose the anachronism of our current notions of "Christian" identities and "Jewish" identities as always and inevitably mutually exclusive.

Precisely as a result of this modern marginalization, the premodern materials commonly compartmentalized under the rubric of "Jewish-Christianity" provide an especially powerful reservoir of resources for complicating our modern labeling and sorting of premodern religious identities. Almost by definition, after all, these materials resist reduction to our scholarly narratives about religions as distinct, commensurable, and bounded entities with discrete histories that interact only in moments of conflict, reaction, or influence. Attention to the theorization of identity, history, and difference *within* these sources can thus help to relativize the Christian heresiological and other Patristic discourses of difference-making that presaged the modern Western category of "religion" –

---

and I also draw upon more recent studies expanding the category to include works like the *Didache* as well as so-called "Old Testament pseudepigrapha" like the *Testaments of the Twelve Patriarchs*, *Ascension of Isaiah*, *5 Ezra*, and *6 Ezra*, and "NT apocrypha" like the *Apocalypse of Peter*, *Protevangelium of James*, and Ethiopian *Book of the Cock*. See Chapter Three below.

[19] On the category of "NT/Christian apocrypha" – which, like "Jewish-Christianity," is in essence a modern category – see my discussion of its genealogy in "The Afterlives of New Testament Apocrypha," *JBL* 134 (2015): 401–25. On "Jewish-Christian apocrypha," see Chapters Three and Eight below.

[20] See especially Jerome's description of Ebionites as *semi-christianus* and *semi-iudaeus* in *Comm. Gal.* 3.13–14.

not least by drawing attention to their overwriting of Jewish and other discourses of difference-making.[21]

As a classificatory rubric, the category of "Jewish-Christian" is problematic in many ways. But it is problematic – I here suggest – in some ways that enable its special utility as a heuristic irritant: those premodern sources that most defy our modern notions of "Christianity" as separate, by definition, from "Judaism" can push us to think out and beyond some of the systems and practices of classification that we most take for granted. Even its anachronism may bear some analytical utility, serving as an invitation to revisit the geneologies of the modern notions of "Christianity" and "Judaism" that structure and constrain our current historiographies of "religion(s)."

The Strategic Heurism of "Jewish-Christianity"?

For the purposes of the present volume, I choose to retain the term "Jewish-Christianity" as strategically useful for our current scholarly moment – at least when used with a sharp awareness of its power and limits for our own scholarly practices of [1] reading, writing, and categorizing sources, [2] deciding which sources are representative or otherwise worthy of attention, [3] delimiting which sources do and do not count as relevant contextualizing comparanda for others, and [4] selecting which sources to use as dots to connect in our scholarly narratives about trajectories of change and development (and which to dismiss as outliers). It is critical – as Joan Taylor reminds us – not to imagine the contours of our modern category as mapping directly upon a single unified ancient group or movement.[22] And it is also critical – as David Frankfurter stresses – not to use the term as a way to avoid or isolate evidence for the broad range of different types of ways that features of identity that we now deem "Christian" do and do not overlap or draw upon features of identity that we now deem "Jewish."[23] Likewise – with Daniel Boyarin – we must be wary of the apologetic work that this (and other such) categories can *do*.[24]

Inasmuch as the term presumes a need to mark certain expressions of "Christianity" as *too* "Jewish" to be called *just* "Christian," it functions to naturalize

---

[21] This issue is taken up in more detail in my Epilogue below.

[22] Taylor, "Phenomenon of Early Jewish-Christianity."

[23] David Frankfurter, "Beyond 'Jewish-Christianity': Continuing Religious Sub-cultures of the Second and Third Centuries," in *The Ways That Never Parted: Jews and Christians in Late Antiquity and the Early Middle Ages*, ed. Adam H. Becker and Annette Yoshiko Reed (TSAJ 95; Tübingen: Mohr Siebeck, 2003), 134–35.

[24] So especially Daniel Boyarin, *Judaism* (Key Words in Jewish Studies; New Brunswick: Rutgers University Press, forthcoming). Note also my comments in "Categorization, Collection, and the Construction of Continuity: 1 Enoch and 3 Enoch in and beyond 'Apocalypticism' and 'Mysticism,'" *MTSR* 29 (2017): 268–311.

an understanding of "Christianity" as essentially or inevitably distinct from "Judaism." Since the development of academic research on the topic in nineteenth- and early twentieth-century German Protestant scholarship, the term has thus served, in practice, either to mark off a distinct "party" and a certain early era in which an overlap could nevertheless "still" exist (e. g., as for F. C. Baur)[25] and/or to bracket certain texts, figures, or groups as isolated from a mainstream of development and as irrelevant for understanding the history of "Christianity" *per se* (e. g., as for Adolf Harnack).[26]

But the more scholars in the later twentieth century came to emphasize that "everyone in the first generation of Christianity was Jewish-Christian" (e. g., as Helmut Koester put it),[27] the more postapostolic "Jewish-Christianity" came to be perceived as a "problem" (e. g., as Georg Strecker put it).[28] To deploy the term in the context of the scholarly discussion of Christianity is therefore to make a normative judgment about what constitutes the Jewishness that goes beyond the bounds of what *should* be called "Christian" – and *when*.

---

[25] Ferdinand Christian Baur, "Die Christuspartei in der korinthischen Gemeide, der Gegensatz des petrinischen und paulischen Christentums in der alten Kirche, der Apostel Petrus in Rom," *Tübinger Zeitschrift für Theologie* 4 (1831): 61–206. See further David Lincicum, "F. C. Baur's Place in the Study of Jewish Christianity," in Jones, *Rediscovery of Jewish Christianity*, 137–66.

[26] Harnack argues as follows: "[1] Original Christianity was in appearance Christian Judaism, the creation of a universal religion on Old Testament soil …. The heritage which Christianity took over from Judaism, shews itself on Gentile Christian soil, in fainter or distincter form, in proportion as the philosophic mode of thought already prevails, or recedes into the background. To describe the appearance of the Jewish, Old Testament, heritage in the Christian faith, so far as it is a religious one, by the name 'Jewish Christianity' … must therefore necessarily lead to error, and it has done so to a very great extent …. [A]ll Christianity, insofar as something alien is not foisted into it, appears as the religion of Israel perfected and spiritualized …. There is no boundary here; for Christianity took possession of the whole of Judaism as religion …. Wherever the universalism of Christianity is not violated in favor of the Jewish nation, we have to recognize every appropriation of the Old Testament as Christian …. [2] But the Jewish religion is a national religion, and Christianity burst the bounds of nationality, though not for all who recognized Jesus and Messiah. This gives the point at which the introduction of the term 'Jewish Christianity' is appropriate. It should be applied exclusively to those Christians who really maintained in their whole extent, or in some measure, even if it were to a minimum degree, the national and political forms of Judaism and the observance of Mosaic law in its literary sense, as essential to Christianity, at least to the Christianity of born Jews, or who, though rejecting these forms, nevertheless assumed a prerogative of the Jewish people even in Christianity (*Hom.* 11:26). To this Jewish Christianity is opposite, not Gentile Christianity, but the Christian religion … that is, the main body of Christendom insofar as it has freed itself from Judaism as a nation …. A history of Jewish Christianity and its doctrines does not, therefore, belong to the history of dogma"; "Appendix: The Christianity of the Jewish Christians," in *History of Dogma*, vol. 1, trans. Neil Buchanan (Boston: Roberts Brothers, 1895 [1885]), 287–317.

[27] Helmut Koester, "ΓΝΩΜΑΙ ΔΙΑΦΟΡΟΙ: The Origin and Nature of Diversification in the History of the Early Church," *HTR* 53 (1965): 380.

[28] I.e., in the title to his Appendix to the 1964 revised edition of Walter Bauer, *Rechtgläubigkeit und Ketzerei im ältesten Christentum* (Tübingen: Mohr, 1934), published in English as "On the Problem of Jewish Christianity."

As noted above, this pattern in the modern usage of "Jewish-Christianity" thus recalls the function of "Ebionites" in late antique Christian heresiology: when Epiphanius and others discuss Ebionites, their task is not descriptively ethnographical, but rather – as Andrew Jacobs has shown – "the question of incorporation and exclusion is paramount: What part of Judaism remains in Christianity?"[29] Largely because of this parallel, Boyarin makes a compelling argument to abandon the term "Jewish-Christianity" altogether:

"Jewish Christianity" always functions as a term of art in a modernist heresiology: It is a marker of the too Jewish side of the Goldilocks fairytale that is "ordinary" Christianity …. I propose that any definition of "Jewish Christianity" implies an entire theory of the development of early Christianity and Judaism …. My case for abandoning this term is an argument in three movements. In the first movement, I will present evidence and discuss evidence already given for the claim that there is never in premodern times a term that non-Christian Jews use to refer to their "religion," that *Ioudaismos* is, indeed, not a religion … and that consequently it cannot be hyphenated in any meaningful way. In the second movement, I will try to show that the self-understanding of Christians of Christianity as a religion was slow developing as well and that a term such as "Jewish Christian" (or rather its ancient equivalents, Nazorean, Ebionite) was part and parcel of that development itself and thus *eo ipso*, and not merely factitiously, a heresiological term of art. In the third movement, I will try to show that even the most critical, modern, and best-willed usages of the term in scholarship devolve willy-nilly to heresiology.[30]

I will return to discuss his argument about "Judaism," "Christianity," and "religion" in more detail in the Epilogue to this volume. For now, it suffices to note that I find the conceptual issues surrounding "Jewish-Christianity" to be especially productive for the same reasons that Boyarin finds them especially problematic.

My concern here is with the range of ways that the term *functions*. Boyarin is certainly correct in describing and diagnosing its most common uses, as we have seen above. And to the degree that these are articulated from within Christian frameworks of difference-making, they may well be fated to "devolve willy-nilly to heresiology." I would like to suggest, however, that the past and potential functions of the term "Jewish-Christianity" are not necessary limited to this particular set. When one takes a broader purview on the history of research – looking before Baur and beyond the bounds of nineteenth-century German Protestant NT scholarship and its secular academic heirs – one can glimpse some other possibilities. Accordingly, I would like to make a case for its continued usefulness (at least for the present moment) with reference to the different ways that the category functions in three quite different contexts: [1] early eighteenth-century

---

[29] Andrew S. Jacobs, *Epiphanius of Cyprus: A Cultural Biography of Late Antiquity* (Berkeley: University of California Press, 2016), 91.

[30] Boyarin, "Rethinking Jewish Christianity," 8.

English Deism, [2] *Wissenschaft des Judentums* in nineteenth-century Germany, and [3] Jewish Studies and Reform Judaism in early twentieth-century America.

The first is exemplified by John Toland, who invented the term.[31] Significantly, he did not do so for heresiological aims or with secondhand reports about Ebionites as his structuring analytical framework. Rather, he privileged the positions in newly-published "apocrypha" at his time like the *Epistle of Peter to James*, Pseudo-Clementine *Homilies*, and *Gospel of Barnabas*, and he was especially attuned to their blurring of those very boundaries that so concerned the Church Fathers. His coinage of the term was thus intended precisely to destabilize Christianity as a distinct "religion" – and especially to undermine the authority of those late antique ecclesiarchs and early modern clerics who gained power from policing distinctions like "apocrypha"/Scripture, "heresy"/"orthodoxy," and "Christian"/"Muslim"/"Jew."[32] Toland did so, moreover, at a pivotal moment for the construction of what we now take for granted as the taxonomy of "religions."[33]

It is in this sense that we might look back to Toland for a poignant example of what this category can *do* – and take inspiration to return to rethink the results of the imposition of modern notions of "religion" on our understanding of pre-modern sources. I explore this possibility further in the Epilogue to this volume. For now, it suffices to note that my argument for retaining the term is therefore both complimentary and inverse to Boyarin's argument to jettison it: whereas he makes the case that "Jewish-Christianity" should be abandoned because "Judaism" is anachronistic, I here suggest that the debate about "Jewish-Christianity" can help us to see some of what is effaced by the imposition of modern senses of "Judaism" and "Christianity" on the full range of our ancient sources – and what is also occluded by the very privileging of classification as an explanatory act. Furthermore, "Jewish-Christianity" was invented at an important modern moment for the construction and naturalization of the very notion of "religions." Attention to its genealogy may thus prove especially promising as a means by which to revisit and reassess our present presumptions and practices.

The second is exemplified by Heinrich Graetz.[34] For his massive and influential *History of the Jewish People*, he drew upon the discussion of "Jewish-Christians" among Baur and other nineteenth-century German Protestant scholars. He did so, however, largely as an entry-point for appropriating early Christian sources for writing Jewish history and reinterpreting Christianity – even beyond

---

[31] See the discussion of Toland in Chapters Eight and Eleven below.

[32] This aim is not incompatible, in my view, with his aim to recover authentic Christianity from antiquity; see Matt Jackson-McCabe, "The Invention of Jewish Christianity in John Toland's *Nazarenus*," in Jones, *Rediscovery of Jewish Christianity*, 69–90, and discussion in Chapters Eight and Eleven below.

[33] See further Peter Harrison, *"Religion" and the Religions in the English Enlightenment* (Cambridge: Cambridge University Press, 1990).

[34] See the discussion of Graetz in Chapters Seven and Eleven below.

Jesus and after Paul – from within a Jewish framework and perspective. For Graetz, "Jewish-Christians" serve to remap the Jewish people as encompassing some of what Baur et al. took for granted as belonging to Christian Origins and Church History. What "Jewish-Christianity" *does* for Graetz, thus, provides an interesting precedent and model as well. Just as Toland's invention of the term "Jewish-Christianity" subverts the distinction of "religions" at a key moment in their modern reification, so too Graetz writes about "Jewish-Christians" as part of the Jewish people at a key moment for the importation of Christian ideas about "Judaism" into an ostensibly neutral and objective scholarly discourse about the history of "religions." It is perhaps not coincidental that Graetz's use of this hybrid category resists the reduction of Jewishness merely to what was deemed "religious" by analogy to Christianity – not least by turning the tables and retelling parts of the story of Christian Origins as actually a story about the Jewish people.

The third is exemplified by Kaufmann Kohler, who went even further in this direction.[35] Whereas Graetz was writing in the wake of Baur, Kohler was writing after Baur's positions had been marginalized by Adolph von Harnack's pointed exclusion of "Jewish-Christianity" from the study of Church History. To the degree that Harnack laid the groundwork for repurposing "Jewish-Christian" as a label for marking, collecting, and isolating those sources that express more or different affiliations to Jewish traditions than those that deemed properly "Christian," he thus facilitated the consultation and use of these very sources by Jewish scholars interested in using Christian sources to fill the gaps in the history of Jewish thought and practice – as did Kohler for the *Didache, Didascalia apostolorum*, and the Pseudo-Clementines (and, by extension and most famously, the *Apostolic Constitutions*). And as for Kohler, so too today: the very label "Jewish-Christian" does the opposite work for Jewish Studies than it does for Church History – functioning not as a term of *exclusion* but rather a term signaling those Christian sources that bear the most potential for *inclusion* in the historiography of Jews and Judaism.

I have no aim to define "Jewish-Christianity" in any sense meant to suggest a direct one-on-one correlation to an ancient group or movement. I quite agree with those scholars who have argued against the accuracy of "Jewish-Christianity" as a *descriptive* category. My suggestion, rather, is that it may remain useful as a *redescriptive* category – at least for some purposes. For the purposes of this particular volume, I thus adopt a definition that is oriented toward maximizing its usefulness for reassessing the history of early Jewish/Christian relations, on the one hand, and for rethinking modern scholarly practices and presumptions about "Judaism" and "Christianity," on the other. In what follows, "Jewish-Christian" is used to denote those premodern figures, sects, and sources which can be mean-

---

[35] See the discussion of Kohler and further references in Chapter Eight.

ingfully defined as both "Jewish" and "Christian" and which thus do not fit into a modern taxonomic system that treats "Judaism" and "Christianity" as mutually exclusive. By virtue of this definition, I set aside the task of telling any singular history of "Jewish-Christianity," and I attend instead to the potential of these sources to unsettle the narrowly presentist narratives commonly told of the Jewish and Christian past. In this, my ultimate aim is to try to tell a more capacious tale about identity and difference in Late Antiquity – a tale which is not limited to those particular Patristic perspectives that have most shaped research on Jewish/Christian relations, but which also encompasses other Christian as well as other Jewish perspectives, in part by attending to their overlaps.[36]

Accordingly, I would not wish to defend my definition of "Jewish-Christianity" as globally applicable or apt for every inquiry. My suggestion, rather, is that the term proves provisionally useful at our present moment precisely due to its status as metalanguage. "Jewish-Christianity" is a term that makes sense and meaning in one specific system of language about language – that is: scholarly discourse about the retrospectively "religious" past.[37] It is a modern analytical category defined by its place, function, and interrelation within an academic system of studying the past, as shaped by and within conceptual frameworks that make sense and meaning within those German, British, and American cultures that most shaped scholarship on "religions."[38] In using the term, then, I make no claim for any direct one-to-one correspondence to any discrete social group or movement in the premodern eras here under analysis, nor even to any clear-cut discourse surrounding a self-claimed identity in the relevant premodern literature. What I claim, rather, is that a focus on "Jewish-Christianity" may be useful as a lens through which to reconsider the theorization of identity within late antique literature and especially to highlight some cases where premodern data and discourses differ strikingly from those modern modes of theorizing identity now naturalized in our very notions of "Judaism," "Christianity," and "religions." Precisely due to its clumsy hybridity, "Jewish-Christianity" can provide a focus to help us to identify materials conventionally *omitted* in the modern study of the Jewish and Christian past, while also pushing us to ask how premodern conceptualizations of identity might differ from our own.

When we take seriously its modern construction, the category of "Jewish-Christianity" invites reflection on our own historiographical habits: what we choose to see as connected and why, what we compare, what we contrast,

---

[36] I.e., James Carleton Paget is thus quite correct to note my interest in the topic "has less to do with creating a clear definition of the word 'Jewish Christian' and more with seeking to raise questions about older models of Jewish-Christian engagement and interaction in the period following Bar Kokhba"; *Jews, Christians, and Jewish Christians*, 31. I owe the honing of this point to his insightful summary of my work there as well as further conversations with him.

[37] I here use this term in the manner suggested by Carsten Colpe, *Das Siegel der Propheten* (Berlin: Institut Kirche und Judentum, 1989).

[38] Francophone scholarship has a somewhat different trajectory; see Appendix B.

and how and why we draw lines of continuity to our present. In the process, it may open a productive space for experimenting with more integrative ways to intertwine the historiography of Judaism with historiography of Christianity in a manner not just limited to Jesus or ending with Paul. Inasmuch as this particular category has been used in the past to cordon off a variety of materials deemed *too* "Jewish" to be called "Christian," moreover, "Jewish-Christianity" can also be used to expose the biases embedded within current research and to identify those materials that are perhaps especially useful for rooting constructive correctives. And inasmuch as these materials include late antique sources that have been imagined to be "too Jewish" to be more than a "survival" within Christianity after the second century CE, they include materials that have been ignored in scholarship on Late Antiquity but might contribute much to the study of this period – perhaps also facilitating the direly needed integration of Jewish materials into discussions of Late Antiquity more broadly.

Chapter Summary and Acknowledgements

The present volume includes revised and updated versions of nine previously published articles, together with three previously unpublished articles, a Timeline and Annotated Bibliography on "Jewish-Christianity," and an Epilogue reflecting further on the methodological and theoretical issues raised here and below.

I intend the title of this volume in two senses, one of which is explored by the articles in the first section, and the other by the articles in the second. In the essays in the first section, I focus on "Jewish-Christianity and the History of Judaism" in historiographical terms, showing how "Jewish-Christian" sources can help to expose the predominantly Christian frameworks (and peculiarly Patristic lenses) through which Jewish/Christian relations and post-Christian Judaism have been commonly studied. The first two chapters use "Jewish-Christianity" to question the "Parting of the Ways" and experiment with other approaches to our evidence – the first does so with a focus on self-definition within the Pseudo-Clementine literature, while the second surveys Jewish and "Jewish-Christian" sources from Syro-Palestine that map difference with the rites and rhetorics of blood and water. The third chapter turns to survey a variety of "apocrypha" that have been posited as possibly "Jewish-Christian," asking how the early history of Jewish/Christian relations might look different if seen through these sources. The fourth and fifth chapters focus on the modes of theorizing difference in the Pseudo-Clementines in particular: one looks to their extension of older Jewish ideas about "Hellenism" and "Judaism," and the other to their double-pronged participation in Rabbinic and Patristic discourses about *minut* and "heresy" respectively. The sixth chapter compares the treatment of Jewish and apostolic history in Pseudo-Clementines with that in Eusebius' *Ecclesias-tical History*, using the former to relativize the latter, while also opening more connections with Rabbinic traditions, especially in relation to succession from Moses and the transmission of (Oral) Torah.

In the second section, I experiment with bringing "Jewish-Christian" sources to bear on Jewish Studies, looking more closely, in the process, at nineteenth- and early twentieth-century precedents for more integrative approaches. Chapter Seven integrates "Jewish-Christian" sources into a discussion of messianism as seen from the perspective of Jewish thought and history. Chapter Eight traces ideas about the secrecy and suppression of the Jewishness of Christian Origins in relation to the *Epistle of Peter to James* and its reception by Toland, Baur, Graetz, and Kohler. Chapter Nine brings "Jewish-Christian" sources to bear on questions about Rabbinization and the representation of Pharisees in relation to Rabbis, while Chapter Ten focuses on parallels with Hekhalot literature and their place in the study of Jewish mysticism. In the eleventh chapter, I extend recent insights into the early modern invention of "Jewish-Christianity" by focusing on its modern Jewish reception, attending especially to Graetz but also recovering the influence of Augustus Neander, a Jewish convert to Christianity who was also a prominent scholar of both *Gnosis* and Church History.

The end of the volume includes an Epilogue discussing "Jewish-Christianity" as an example of the limits of the heurism of categories of "religions," on the one hand, and modern scholarly discourses about identity and alterity, on the other. Appendix A is a timeline of the major figures, texts, and events mentioned in this volume, and Appendix B is an annotated bibliography that surveys some of the larger discussion surrounding "Jewish-Christianity," from the apostolic age to early Islam. Appendices C and D reprint two brief online essays on the terms *Ioudaios* and "Jew."

At various points when preparing this volume, I considered compiling a sep-arate chapter cataloguing Rabbinic parallels to the Pseudo-Clementine *Homilies* and other "Jewish-Christian" literature. Such an approach would fit the usual practice whereby non-Jewish texts or corpora are typically argued to be relevant to Jewish Studies. In the end, however, I decided instead to try to model here a more integrative approach. Rather than addressing the question of the relation-ship of "Jewish-Christianity" and Rabbinic Judaism in isolation, I here attempt to showcase what I see as the potential value of "Jewish-Christian" texts and traditions for aiding in the integration of Rabbinic and other late antique Jewish texts and traditions into the study of Late Antiquity more broadly. Accordingly, Chapter Two considers ritual purity in "Jewish-Christian" writings in conversa-tion with the Mishnah but also in context of "pagan" and other uses of water in Roman Syria; Chapter Five analyzes "Jewish-Christian" heresiology in triangu-lation with Epiphanius' *Panarion* and Rabbinic disputation tales about *minim*; and Chapter Six treats the theme of succession in the Pseudo-Clementines in contrast with Eusebius' depiction of apostolic succession but in comparison with early Rabbinic ideas about the Oral Torah. Much of my argument for the late antique context of the Pseudo-Clementines throughout this volume, moreover, rests on their connections to distinctively Rabbinic traditions. Chapter Two similarly stresses the special relevance of Rabbinic texts and traditions for understanding the *Didascalia apostolorum* as well as the Pseudo-Clementines, while Chapters Nine and Ten suggest, in turn, that these "Jewish-Christian" works might help us to contextualize Rabbinic and Hekhalot traditions respectively. In addition, in Chapters Eight and Eleven, I point to precedents among nineteenth- and early twentieth-century scholars of Jewish Studies for reading "Jewish-Christian" and Rabbinic materials in concert, prior to trends in the mid- and late twentieth century towards modes of academic specialization that have fostered more isolationist reading practices. Attention to such precedents, in turn, may help us to look ahead – not least to recover the relevance of both "Jewish-Christian" and non-Christian Jewish materials for the study of Late Antiquity.

* * *

Research for this volume was generously supported by grants from the Social Science and Humanities Research Council of Canada and the National Endowment for the Humanities. Substantial portions were completed during two fellowship years at the Katz Center for Advanced Judaic Studies (2007–2008, 2014–2015). I am grateful to Henning Ziebritzki, Peter Schäfer, and the current editorial board of TSAJ for the opportunity to publish this volume as well as to the publishers that granted permission for reprinting articles herein: Mohr Siebeck, Éditions du Cerf, Éditions du Zèbre, Indiana University Press, Oxford University Press, and Marginalia Review of Books.

I benefited much from delivering related lectures at Duke University, Fordham University, Indiana University Bloomington, New York University, Princeton University, Université François-Rabelais de Tours, Université de Lausanne, University of California Los Angeles, University of Ottawa, University of Pennsylvania, and Yale University. Over the years, I have had the pleasure of discussing this project with many generous intellectual interlocutors there and elsewhere, whom I acknowledge in specific chapters below. I would be remiss, however, not also to express my special appreciation for those who have helped to shape the project as a whole through their continued support and continued challenges: John G. Gager, Peter Schäfer, Daniel Boyarin, Adam H. Becker, James Carleton Paget, Andrew S. Jacobs, David Stern, F. Stanley Jones, Natalie Dohrmann, Dominique Côté, Pierluigi Piovanelli, and Bob Kraft.

I wrote these materials while at Princeton University, McMaster University, and the University of Pennsylvania, and I hope that the results bear some imprint of my deep intellectual debts to each institution. In particular, the ideas and arguments herein have been forged and honed in the crucible of conversations with my graduate students, especially Karl Shuve, Lily Vuong, and Susan Wendel at McMaster and Matthew Chalmers, Phillip Fackler, Jae Han, Alex Ramos, Jillian Stinchcomb, and Phillip Webster at Penn. To Alex, I am further indebted for the gleeful perfectionism with which he proofread this volume. For indexing, I am grateful to Patrick Angiolillo at NYU. Special thanks also to Coach Kate Allen-Cottone, Coach Mary Bee, Coach Neal Santos, Coach Zachary Ferris, and our "dawn patrol" crew at VIII Limbs Academy for providing the perfect writing breaks.

For many varieties of inspiration during the final stages of this project, I remain ever grateful to Shaul Magid. I dedicate this volume to my son, KunKun (Alexander Reed Fleming), who never ceases to remind me – as he likes to put it – that "Life is just so interesting all the time ..."

Christian Origins as Jewish History*

Do Christian sources have a place within the study of Jews and Judaism? Aren't Christian sects and sources by definition not Jewish? And isn't part of the point of Jewish Studies, as a discipline, to create a space for the study of the history, literature, and religion of Jews apart from the dominant Christian frameworks that have informed so much of what universities teach as "religion," "ethics," "history," "literature," etc.?

Throughout most of the twentieth century, the answers to such questions seemed obvious. A popular sense of the mutual exclusivity of "Jewish" and "Christian" identities was mirrored by a disciplinary separation even in secular academic scholarship on their ancient sources and histories. Among scholars of both Judaism and Christianity, it was common to treat Jesus as the founder of a new "religion" that was essentially and inevitably distinct from Judaism. And if not Jesus, then certainly Paul. Consistent with the Christian theological training of most early twentieth-century scholars of the New Testament, their studies typically took for granted a supersessionist model of history: the rise of Christianity was read as the restoration of the religion of ancient Israel from the corruption of postbiblical/postexilic Judaism.[1]

More recent trends in research have inspired a renewed understanding of the Jesus Movement as an integrated (and perhaps even integral) part of the history of the Jews.[2] Whether Jesus himself is termed a Jewish wisdom teacher, political

---

* An earlier and much shorter Hebrew version of this essay appeared in Yirmiyahu Yovel, ed., *A New Jewish Time – Jewish Culture in a Secular Age: An Encyclopedic View* (Jerusalem: Keter, 2007), 200–4.

[1] This position is exemplified by the older practice in New Testament Studies of periodizing post-exilic Jewish history as *Spätjudentum* ("Late Judaism"), especially as outlined by Wilhelm Bousset. See, e. g., Bousset, *Die Religion des Judentums in neutestamentlichen Zeitalter* (Berlin: Ruether and Reichard, 1903); Anders Gerdmar, *Roots of Theological Anti-Semitism: German Biblical Interpretation and the Jews from Herder and Semler to Kittel and Bultmann* (Studies in Jewish History and Culture 20; Leiden: Brill, 2009), 146–61; also Susannah Heschel, "The Image of Judaism in Nineteenth Century New Testament Scholarship in Germany," in *Jewish–Christian Encounters over the Centuries; Symbiosis, Prejudice, Holocaust, Dialogue*, ed. Marvin Perry and Frederick M. Schweitzer (New York: Peter Lang, 1994), 215–40. There were early critiques even among Christian scholars – most notably: George Foot Moore, "Christian Writers on Judaism," *HTR* 14 (1921): 197–254 – but this pattern nevertheless predominated well into the 1960s.

[2] I stress "renewed" here because there are ample precedents in the nineteenth century and into the early twentieth century, on which see below. Shaul Magid notes that "Jewish writing

revolutionary, or apocalyptic prophet, there is now a scholarly consensus that the Jesus Movement was one of many similar Jewish movements in the first century CE.[3] Studies have even reconsidered the Jewishness of Paul, reassessing the image of this apostle as the founder of Gentile Christianity and the author of Christian anti-Judaism.[4]

Particularly in North America, the emergence of these new approaches was enabled both by a paradigm shift in research on the New Testament since World War II and by concurrent changes in the dominant institutional settings in which Judaism and Christianity are studied.[5] A number of Christian historians and theologians responded to the horrors of the Holocaust by grappling with the images of Jews and Judaism in the New Testament and by addressing the possible place of these texts in the prehistory of modern anti-Semitism.[6] The last half of the twentieth century also saw the establishment of departments of Religious Studies in secular universities across the United States and Canada, facilitating the non-confessional study of Christianity as well as the growing participation

---

about Jesus in America, with a few exceptions, ended after the 'Jesus Controversy' in 1925," which was sparked by Joseph Klausner's *Yeshu ha-Notsri* (Jerusalem: Shtibl, 1922). It was only "toward the end of the twentieth century," Magid further notes, that "numerous Jewish scholars and theologians, mostly in North America, came to articulate new approaches to the question of a Jewish Jesus"; *American Post-Judaism: Identity and Renewal in a Postethnic Society* (Bloomington: Indiana University Press, 2013), 134–35. On the shifting place of Jewishness in American ideas about Jesus, see also Stephen Prothero, *American Jesus: How the Son of God Became a National Icon* (New York: Macmillan, 2003), 229–66.

[3] For the latter point, see Richard A. Horsley with John S. Hanson, *Bandits, Prophets, and Messiahs: Popular Movements at the Time of Jesus* (2nd ed.; Harrisburg: Trinity, 1999). On key elements in the ample discussion on the Jewish Jesus, see Zev Garber, ed., *The Jewish Jesus: Revelation, Reflection, Reclamation* (West Lafayette, IN: Purdue University Press, 2011).

[4] E. g., Daniel Boyarin, *A Radical Jew: Paul and the Politics of Identity* (Berkeley: University of California Press, 1994); Mark D. Nanos and Magnus Zetterholm, eds., *Paul Within Judaism: Restoring the First-Century Context to the Apostle* (Minneapolis: Fortress, 2015); Nanos, *The Mystery of Romans: The Jewish Context of Paul's Letter* (Minneapolis: Fortress, 1996); Jacob Taubes, *The Political Theology of Paul* (Stanford: Stanford University Press, 2004). For a survey of premodern and early modern precedents, see now John G. Gager, *Who Made Early Christianity? The Jewish Lives of the Apostle Paul* (New York: Columbia University Press, 2015), 37–52.

[5] On these shifts, see esp. John G. Gager, *The Origins of Anti-Semitism: Attitudes toward Judaism in Pagan and Christian Antiquity* (Oxford: Oxford University Press, 1983).

[6] E. g., Gager, *Origins of Anti-Semitism*, 11–34; Marcel Simon, *Verus Israel: Étude sur les relations entre Chrétiens et Juifs dans l'Empire Romain (135–42)* (Bibliothèque des Écoles Françaises d'Athènes et de Rome 166; Paris: Editions de Boccard, 1948); Jules Isaac, *Jésus et Israël* (Paris: A. Michel, 1948); Isaac, *Genèse de l'antisémitisme: Essai historique* (Paris: Calmann-Levy, 1956); Isaac, *L'enseignement du mépris: vérité historique et mythes théologiques* (Paris: Fasquelle, 1962); Rosemary Radford Ruether, *Faith and Fratricide: The Theological Roots of Anti-Semitism* (New York: Seabury, 1974); Alan Davies, ed., *Anti-Semitism and the Foundations of Christianity* (New York: Paulist, 1979). Note also the parallel discussion among Christian theologians such as Paul Van Buren; see, e. g., *Discerning the Way: A Theology of the Jewish-Christian Reality* (New York: Seabury, 1980) and the review-essay by David Novak in *Judaism* 31 (1982): 112–20.

of Jewish and other non-Christian scholars in New Testament Studies.[7] Together, these developments have helped to foster a scholarly discourse that is more attuned to the biases of the past and seeks further to situate the New Testament in its historical and cultural contexts, as distinct from its status for Christians as Scripture.[8]

New institutional settings have also helped to inspire further experimentation with models and approaches from disciplines ranging from Classics to Sociology, thereby opening fresh perspectives on the history of Christianity in relation to Jews and Judaism.[9] Statements about Jews in the New Testament, for instance, have been reassessed in light of more sophisticated understandings of identity, alterity, and the anachronism of our modern sense of "religions": not only have philological studies destabilized any solely "religious" interpretation of the Greek term *Ioudaioi* ("Jews," "Judaeans"),[10] but even its polemical usage has been increasingly reread in terms of the ambivalent rhetorics of communal identity-formation and the complex sociocultural dynamics of self-definition. Among the results has been a recognition of the *inner*-Jewish orientation of some of the seemingly *anti*-Jewish statements about Pharisees, Sadducees, scribes, and other Jews in the NT Gospels.[11]

The past fifty years have also been marked by the emergence of a new awareness and appreciation of the diversity of Judaism in the Second Temple period (536 BCE–70 CE), catalyzed in large part by the discovery of the Dead Sea

---

[7] As much as recent trends in the history of research on ancient Judaism, ancient Christianity, and Jewish/Christian relations are often discussion in terms of the inclusion of "*both* Jews *and* Christians," it is worth remembering that these disciplinary and institutional shifts have also resulted in the participation of others, including some scholars (like me) with no cultural or confessional connection to *either* tradition.

[8] These shifts are discussed in more detail in Annette Yoshiko Reed and Adam H. Becker, "Introduction: Traditional Models and New Directions," in *The Ways That Never Parted: Jews and Christians in Late Antiquity and the Middle Ages*, ed. Becker and Reed (TSAJ 95; Tubingen: Mohr Siebeck, 2003), 1–34.

[9] See esp. John G. Gager, *Kingdom and Community: The Social World of Early Christianity* (New York: Prentice-Hall, 1975). As Helmut Koester notes, postwar German scholarship on the historical Jesus and the NT has taken a somewhat different trajectory, due in part to the enduring influence of Rudolf Bultmann; "Epilogue: Current Issues in New Testament Scholarship," in *The Future of Early Christianity: Essays in Honor of Helmut Koester*, ed. Birger Pearson (Minneapolis: Fortress, 1991), esp. 469–73.

[10] See esp. Steve Mason, "Jews, Judaeans, Judaizing, Judaism: Problems of Categorization in Ancient History," *JSJ* 38 (2007): 457–512; see also the contributions by myself and others in Timothy Michael Law and Charles Halton, eds., *Jew and Judean: A Forum on Politics and Historiography in the Translation of Ancient Texts* (Los Angeles: Marginalia Review of Books, 2014), http://marginalia.lareviewofbooks.org/jew-judean-forum/.

[11] E.g., Douglas Hare, "The Rejection of the Jews in the Synoptic Gospels and Acts," in *Anti-Semitism and the Foundations of Christianity*, ed. Alan Davies (Eugene, OR: Wipf and Stock, 2004), 27–46.

Scrolls.[12] The publication of these long-lost texts helped to highlight the rich multiplicity of pre-Rabbinic Judaism. In the process, research on Second Temple Judaism has shed doubt on the traditional image of the Pharisees as the *de facto* leaders of the Jewish people prior to the destruction of the Temple.[13] Far from being proto-Rabbis with authority ratified by popular support, Pharisees are now seen as one of many sects. Together with the adoption of more critical approaches for studying the classical Rabbinic literature, this new emphasis on the diversity in Second Temple Judaism has largely undermined the notion of a single, "mainstream" Judaism that led directly to the Rabbis.[14] At present, our picture of pre-Rabbinic Judaism is more like a tapestry made up of many different, intersecting strands. Partly as a result, the story of the Rabbis' rise to power is now told as a more prolonged process.[15]

The ramifications of such insights have rippled through the study of Judaism, but the effects on the study of Christianity are no less marked. Scholars of Jewish history and Christian Origins were long complicit in asserting a monolithic Judaism from which Christianity sprung and with which it could make a clean break.[16] But this is no longer the case. The recovery of a multiform Second Temple Judaism has opened our eyes to the broad continuum of biblically-based belief and practice of which Jesus and his followers formed a part. Accordingly, historical inquiries into the Jewish "background" of Christianity have gradually led to the recognition that the Jesus Movement fits surprisingly well *within* what we know as Second Temple Judaism. Increasingly, the New Testament is thus consulted by historians and archaeologists – alongside the writings of Philo and Josephus, the Dead Sea Scrolls, "pseudepigrapha," etc. – for information about Judaism and the Land of Israel in the late Second Temple period.[17]

---

[12] See further Annette Yoshiko Reed, "Second Temple Judaism," *Oxford Bibliographies Online*, 2012 [DOI: 10.1093/OBO/9780195393361-0087].

[13] See Chapter Nine below.

[14] Peter Schäfer, "Die sogenannte Synode von Jabne: Zur Trennung von Juden und Christen im ersten/zweiten Jahrhundert n. Chr.," *Judaica* 31 (1975): 54–64, 116–24; Schäfer, "Der vorrabbinische Pharisäismus," in *Paulus und das antike Judentum: Tübingen-Durham-Symposium im Gedenken an den 50. Todestag Adolf Schlatters*, ed. Martin Hengel and Ulrich Heckel (WUNT 58; Tübingen: Mohr Siebeck, 1991), esp. 172–75; also, Shaye J. D. Cohen, "The Significance of Yavneh: Pharisees, Rabbis, and the End of Jewish Sectarianism," *HUCA* 55 (1984): 36–38. Note already Jacob Neusner's notion of "Judaisms," e. g., in "Jewish Studies in the American University," *Journal of General Education* 13 (1961): 160–66; cf. Seth Schwartz, "How Many Judaisms Were There? A Critique of Neusner and Smith on Definition and Mason and Boyarin on Categorization," *JAJ* 2 (2011): 208–38.

[15] See, e. g., Seth Schwartz, *Imperialism and Jewish Society, 200 BCE to 640 CE* (Princeton: Princeton University Press, 2001); Hayim Lapin, *Rabbis as Romans: The Rabbinic Movement in Palestine, 100–400 CE* (Oxford: Oxford University Press, 2012).

[16] See further Reed and Becker, "Introduction."

[17] This project of rereading the New Testament in terms of Jewish history and literature is exemplified – and many of its results synthesized – by Marc Brettler and Amy-Jill Levine, eds., *The Jewish Annotated New Testament* (Oxford: Oxford University Press, 2011).

The task of rereading the New Testament as a source for Jewish Studies has been most popular in relation to Jesus himself. Jewish thinkers at least since Abraham Geiger have been interested in Jesus from a specifically Jewish perspective.[18] These Jewish approaches to Jesus were founded on a sharp distinction between the Jesus of history and the Christ of faith: the former a Galilean Jew whose actions and teachings during life shed light on the history and culture of the Jews, the latter a figure whose significance is tied to faith-claims about his resurrection and divine status.[19] The two tend to be inextricable in older writings about Jesus penned from a confessional Christian perspective. With the maturation of the study of Christianity within Religious Studies, however, their distinction has come to shape historical scholarship on the New Testament by Christians, Jews, and others. Jewish scholars, from David Flusser to Amy Jill Levine, have written celebrated studies of the historical Jesus in his Jewish context.[20] And, especially in recent years, even Christian scholars have been surprisingly open to the idea of a Jewish Jesus.[21] William Arnal, in fact, suggests that the Jewishness of Jesus is now so much of a matter of consensus that "the non-Jewish historical Jesus is a straw man."[22]

Much about this ostensibly "new" realization of the Jewishness of Christianity's messiah was already anticipated by nineteenth-century Jewish thinkers like Geiger.[23] It is certainly the case, as Shaul Magid notes, that the first wave

---

[18] Especially in Abraham Geiger, *Das Judentum und Seine Geschichte* (3 vols.; Breslau: Schletter, 1864–1871); see further Susannah Heschel, *Abraham Geiger and the Jewish Jesus* (Chicago: Universiy of Chicago Press, 1998). Other early and influential examples include Claude Montefiore, *The Synoptic Gospels* (2 vols.; London: Macmillan, 1909); Israel Abraham, *Studies in Pharisaism and the Gospels* (2 vols.; Cambridge: Cambridge University Press, 1917–1924); Joseph Klausner, *Yeshu ha-Notsri* (Jerusalem: Shtibl, 1922). Shaul Magid notes a precedent already in Baruch Spinoza, albeit flowering especially in the nineteenth century concurrent "with the rise of the search for the historical Jesus among liberal Protestants"; *Hasidism Incarnate: Hasidism, Christianity, and the Construction of Modern Judaism* (Stanford: Stanford University Press, 2015), 113–14.

[19] This formulation is typically credited to Martin Kähler, *Der sogenannte historische Jesus und der geschichtliche, biblische Christ* (Leipzig: A. Deichert, 1892). For reflections on its context, heurism, and limits in relation to academic research on the historical Jesus, see John P. Meier, "The Historical Jesus: Rethinking Some Concepts," *Theological Studies* 51 (1990): 3–24.

[20] E.g., David Flusser, *Jesus in Selbstzeugnissen und Bilddokumenten* (Reinbek bei Hamburg: Rowohlt, 1968); Amy-Jill Levine, *The Misunderstood Jew: The Church and the Scandal of the Jewish Jesus* (New York: Harper Collins, 2009).

[21] E.g., Bruce Chilton, *Rabbi Jesus: An Intimate Biography* (New York: Random House, 2002).

[22] William Arnal, *The Symbolic Jesus: Historical Scholarship, Judaism and the Construction of Contemporary Identity* (New York: Equinox, 2005), 19.

[23] That said, the intervening period was marked in part by efforts to interpret Jesus as not Jewish, sometimes appealing to his Galilean roots; see further Susannah Heschel, *The Aryan Jesus: Christian Theologians and the Bible in Nazi Germany* (Princeton: Princeton University Press, 2010).

of Jewish efforts at rereading Jesus from within Judaism often aimed "to separate Jesus *from* Christianity" or to assert "Judaism as the religion *of* Jesus while Christianity is the religion *about* him."[24] For Geiger, Claude Montefiore, Kaufmann Kohler, and others, moreover, this apologetic aim vis-à-vis Christianity was coupled with an appeal to Jesus as a precedent for their own efforts to reform Judaism in the nineteenth and early twentieth centuries.[25] Nevertheless, it remains that there is a wealth of evidence in our ancient sources for Jesus' Jewishness, to which their writings helped to draw sustained scholarly attention.[26]

In the earliest accounts of his life in the NT Gospels, we find no hint that Jesus saw himself as anything other than a Jew. The Gospels themselves were written decades after Jesus' death, at a time when some members of the Jesus Movement were attempting to distinguish themselves from their Jewish contemporaries. Nevertheless, these texts preserve traditions about Jesus as preaching in synagogues, visiting the Temple, celebrating Passover, interpreting the Hebrew Bible, and debating halakhic issues with Pharisees. Furthermore, Jesus teaches by means of parables that recall in form and content the *meshalim* of the Jewish Wisdom literature and Rabbinic Midrash.[27] Even his apocalyptic and messianic pronouncements fit well within the Judaism of his time, an age of uncertainty and upheaval when many charismatics worked wonders and warned of impending Eschaton.[28] We also find hints that he may have understood his message as oriented solely towards his fellow Jews: according to the Gospel of Matthew, for instance, he notes that he was sent "only to the lost sheep of Israel" (15:24; also 10:6).

Jesus' Jewishness is evident even in the Sermon on the Mount (Matt 5–7), a set of teachings traditionally seen by Christians as exemplifying his break from Judaism. Yet, here too, we find exhortations to observe the whole of the Torah (5:17–20). Such statements shed an interesting perspective on his fierce polemics against the Pharisees, raising the possibility that he and his followers saw themselves as engaged in inner-Jewish debates akin to the arguments between

---

[24] So Magid, *Hasidism Incarnate*, 114.

[25] See further Donald Hagner, *The Jewish Reclamation of Jesus* (Eugene, OR: Wipf and Stock, 1997); Matthew B. Hoffman, *From Rebel to Rabbi: Reclaiming Jesus and the Making of Modern Jewish Culture* (Stanford: Stanford University Press, 2007).

[26] Likewise, even despite the apologetic force of assertions about the necessity of training in Rabbinics for studying the New Testament, the results contributed greatly to the compilation of relevant Jewish intertexts that help to contextualize Jesus and earliest Christianity.

[27] David Stern, "Midrash and Parables in the New Testament," in Brettler and Levine, *Jewish Annotated New Testament*, 565–68.

[28] See, e.g., Horsley and Hanson, *Bandits, Prophets, and Messiahs*; Martha Himmelfarb, "Afterlife and Resurrection," in Brettler and Levine, *Jewish Annotated New Testament*, 549–51; Geza Vermes, "Jewish Miracle Workers in the Late Second Temple Period," in Brettler and Levine, *Jewish Annotated New Testament*, 536–37; Matthew V. Novenson, *Christ among the Messiahs* (Oxford: Oxford University Pres, 2012). See also discussion and further references in Chapter Seven in this volume.

other sects in Second Temple times. We also find parallels between his teachings and later Rabbinic traditions. Most famously, the Gospels attribute to Jesus a version of the "Golden Rule" (Matt 7:12) that parallels a saying that the Talmud attributes to Hillel (*b. Shabbat* 31a).[29]

By separating the Jesus of history from the Christ of faith, a surprising number of Jewish thinkers have been able to embrace Jesus as a part of Judaism's history and heritage. Martin Buber could call him a brother;[30] Joseph Klausner could term him the "most Jewish of Jews."[31] For modern Jewish thought as well as secular academic scholarship in Jewish Studies, however, it has proved more challenging to integrate Paul.[32] Paul's own letters tell us of the vision of the resurrected Christ that prompted this Pharisee to change his name from Saul to Paul and to proclaim himself the "apostle to the Gentiles." Although remembered as a student of Rabban Gamaliel the Elder (Acts 22:3), it was Paul who first argued that Gentiles can be saved through faith in Christ apart from observance of the Torah (e. g., Rom 1–9; Gal 1–3), and he is often thus credited with inaugurating the Christian negation of the requirements of Jewish law and the Church's rejection of the chosenness of the Jewish people. Both within scholarship and within modern Jewish thought, those who accept a Jewish Jesus thus often do so with appeal to Paul's alleged apostasy, which is touted as the real catalyst for Christianity's break with Judaism.[33]

One line of recent research, however, has proposed that Paul's approach to the Torah and Judaism may have been more positive. Even after his self-claimed commission to be "apostle to the Gentiles," the apostle still considers himself a Jew and a Pharisee (Gal 2:15; Phil 3:5; Acts 22:3; 26:4–5). According to scholars like Lloyd Gaston and John G. Gager, Paul may maintain the chosenness of the Jews and the efficacy of Torah observance for them, even as he charts a separate path for Gentiles that does not entail circumcision or Torah observance.[34] Scholarly debates about Paul's attitudes towards the Torah and Jewish salvation have

---

[29] P. S. Alexander, "Jesus and the Golden Rule," in *Hillel and Jesus: Comparisons of Two Major Religious Leaders*, ed. James H. Charlesworth and Loren L. Johns (Minneapolis: Fortress, 1997), 363–88.

[30] Martin Buber, *Two Types of Faith*, trans. Norman P. Goldhawk (New York: Macmillan, 1951), 12. See further Magid, *Hasidism Incarnate*, 113–36; Magid, "Defining Christianity and Judaism from the Perspective of Religious Anarchy: Martin Buber on Jesus and the Ba'al Shem Tov," *JJTP* 25 (2017): 36–58.

[31] Joseph Klausner, *Jesus of Nazareth: His Life, Times, and Teaching* (New York: Macmilolan, 1925), 363.

[32] See further Daniel R. Langton, "Modern Jewish Identity and the Apostle Paul: Pauline Studies as an Intra-Jewish Ideological Battleground," *JSNT* 28 (2005): 217–58; Langton, "The Myth of the 'Traditional Jewish View of Paul' and the Role of the Apostle in Modern Jewish–Christian Polemics," *JSNT* 28 (2005): 69–104; Langton, *The Apostle Paul in the Jewish Imagination* (Cambridge: Cambridge University Press, 2010).

[33] On this pattern and its genealogy, see Chapter Eight in this volume.

[34] Lloyd Gaston, *Paul and the Torah* (Vancouver: University of British Columbia Press, 1987); John G. Gager, *Reinventing Paul* (Oxford: Oxford University Press, 2002). This posi-

thus served to highlight the surprisingly broad range of Second Temple Jewish approaches to the question of the fate of Gentile/Jewish difference in the messianic age.[35] In the process, such debates have also helped to open the way for the study of other NT texts in terms of a continuing relationship with Judaism – or even an ongoing place within it.[36]

Much of the New Testament focuses on the issue of Gentile salvation. It also contains fiercely polemical statements about Jews that served to fuel later forms of anti-Semitism. The medieval demonization of Jews was buttressed, for instance, by the Gospel of John's statement that the Devil is their father (8:44) and by Revelation's references to the "synagogue of Satan" (2:9; 3:9). Likewise, the notion of Jewish collective guilt for the death of Jesus found precedent in the account of the crucifixion in the Gospel of Matthew, at which the crowd cries out: "His blood be upon us and our children!" (27:25; also 1 Thes 2:14–16).[37]

When one reads the New Testament only in light of later developments in Christianity, however, one misses the degree to which concerns among Jesus' followers resonated with concerns among Jews in Second Temple times and beyond. Commonalities can be found on topics ranging from purity to eschatology, halakhic observance to biblical interpretation.[38] Early debates in the Jesus Movement, moreover, were not framed in terms of the relationship between "Christianity" and "Judaism." What is later reread in those terms, in fact, is a debate about the practical challenges of including Gentiles in a Jewish messianic movement. Best remembered are those Jewish followers of Jesus, like Paul, who took the opportunity to rethink the meaning of Torah for Gentiles in what they saw to be the messianic age. But the New Testament also preserves some clues

---

tion is partly presaged already in E. P. Sanders, *Paul and Palestinian Judaism* (Philadelphia: Fortress, 1977).

[35] E. g., Paula Fredriksen, "Judaism, the Circumcision of Gentiles, and Apocalyptic Hope: Another Look at Galatians 1 and 2," *JTS* 42 (1991): 532–64; Terence Donaldson, "Proselytes or 'Righteous Gentiles'? The Status of Gentiles in Eschatological Pilgrimage Patterns of Thought," *JSP* 7 (1990): 3–27; Donaldson, *Judaism and the Gentiles: Jewish Patterns of Universalism (to 135 CE)* (Waco, TX: Baylor University Press, 2007); Michael E. Fuller, *The Restoration of Israel: Israel's Re-Gathering and the Fate of the Nations in Early Jewish Literature and Luke-Acts* (Berlin: de Gruyter, 2006).

[36] Most notably for Revelation; see above and John W. Marshall, "John's Jewish (Christian?) Apocalypse," in *Jewish Christianity Reconsidered: Rethinking Ancient Groups and Texts*, ed. Matt Jackson-McCabe (Minneapolis: Fortress, 2007), 233–56.

[37] As noted above, recent literary studies of the New Tesament have suggested that many of these statements refer only to specific groups of Jews at the time, hold different meanings when read in context, and/or make sense when framed as inner-Jewish debate. On the challenges of keeping both Jewish origins and anti-Jewish reception in view, see Paula Fredriksen and Adele Reinhartz, eds., *Jesus, Judaism, and Christian Anti-Judaism: Reading the New Testament after the Holocaust* (Louisville: Westminster John Knox, 2002).

[38] Recent examples include Nina Collins, *Jesus, the Sabbath and the Jewish Debate: Healing on the Sabbath in the First and Second Centuries CE* (London: T&T Clark, 2014); Cecilia Wassen, "The Jewishness of Jesus and Ritual Purity," *Scripta Instituti Donneriani Aboensis* 27 (2016): 11–36.

about other Jewish followers of Jesus, who conceptualized Gentile inclusion as necessarily predicated on circumcision and some degree of Torah-observance (e. g., Gal 2:12; Acts 15:1–5).

Nor is this situation limited to pre-70 materials that speak to the era in which the Jerusalem Church remained dominant. Across the NT literature, in fact, one finds a range of representations of Jewishness. Among the Gospels, Matthew exhibits the strongest and most explicit connections with Judaism.[39] Jesus is there defended as the Jewish messiah, and there is a persistent interest in the Torah and the Jewish people. But the other Gospels also contain clues about the Jesus Movement's complex relationships to its Jewish cultural contexts and literary heritage. Luke is often deemed most "Hellenized," and it is largely concerned with Gentile inclusion and a horizon toward the Roman Empire; nevertheless, its language and form exhibit striking parallels with Hellenistic Jewish literature.[40] John is infamous for its virulent anti-Jewish statements, but even these may reflect a break with a Jewish community of which its own group was originally a part.[41] As for the rest of the New Testament, a nascent supersessionism may be apparent in some texts, such as the Epistle to the Hebrews. But others articulate devotion to Christ in a manner that overlaps in different ways with a distinctively Jewish self-definition, as with Revelation's coupling of apocalyptic Christology with a commitment to ritual purity.[42]

It is perhaps not surprisingly, then, that so much of the New Testament can be profitably read alongside Jewish intertexts. Hence, conversely, a good case can be made for reading at least some of the New Testament as direct evidence for the Jewish thought and culture of its time.[43] Whatever their precise relationship with Jews and Judaism, many NT texts also remain rich sources for Jewish history. Paul's letters provide interesting clues about the cultural assumptions of first-century Jews. In the course of telling the story of Jesus' life, the Gospels of-

---

[39] E. g., Anthony J. Saldarini, *Matthew's Christian-Jewish Community* (Chicago: University of Chicago Press, 1994); Donald Hagner, "Matthew: Christian Judaism or Jewish Christianity?" in *The Face of New Testament Studies: A Survey of Recent Research*, ed. S. McKnight and G. Osborne (Grand Rapids: Baker Academic, 2004), 263–82.

[40] E. g., Gregory Sterling, *Historiography and Self-Definition: Josephos, Luke-Acts, and Apologetic Historiography* (NovTSup 64; Leiden: Brill, 1992).

[41] On this approach to John – and its challenges – see Adele Reinhartz, *Befriending the Beloved Disciple: A Jewish Reading of the Gospel of John* (New York: Continuum, 2005); cf. Raimo Hakola, "The Johannine Community as Jewish Christians? Some Problems in Current Scholarly Consensus," in Jackson-McCabe, *Jewish Christianity Reconsidered*, 181–201.

[42] David Frankfurter, "Jews or Not? Reconstructing the 'Other' in Rev 2:9 and 3:9," *HTR* 94 (2001): 414–16; John W. Marshall, *Parables of the War: Reading John's Jewish Apocalypse* (Waterloo: Wilfrid Laurier University Press, 2001).

[43] Most recently: Daniel Boyarin, *The Jewish Gospels* (New York: New Press, 2012). Note also, e. g., the inclusion of the Gospel of Matthew in George Nickelsburg, *Jewish Literature between the Bible and the Mishnah* (Philadelphia: Fortress, 1981), 303–5, and the treatment of Revelation in Martha Himmelfarb "'A Kingdom of Priests': The Democratization of the Priesthood in the Literature of Second Temple Judaism," *JJTP* 6 (1997): 89–104 at 90.

fer a wealth of information about the Land of Israel in the first century. Likewise, the Book of Acts tells us much about the Diaspora Jewish communities whose synagogues were visited by the earliest Christian missionaries.

In the decades after Jesus' death – and especially after the failure of the first Jewish Revolt against Rome – the Jesus Movement became more geographically and demographically displaced from its original Galilean and Judaean settings. Nevertheless, the beliefs and practices of his followers (whether ethnic Jews or Gentile converts) continued to be infused by the diverse forms of Jewish belief and practice that flourished in the Land of Israel and the Diaspora. In the New Testament and Patristic literature, one can discern the first traces of a long process by which some of Jesus' followers distinguished themselves first from other Jewish groups and progressively from what they thereby constructed as "Judaism." Nevertheless, a profound continuity often served as the very ground for these innovations, thus opening potential lines for contact, conflict, and competition for centuries thereafter.

The overlaps remain notable enough into Late Antiquity, moreover, that it is impossible to pinpoint any single, decisive, or irreversible moment at which the study of Jewish sources and self-definition becomes globally irrelevant for understanding Christian sources and self-definition.[44] Those interested in teleologically constructing an origin myth for our current sense of the mutual exclusivity of "Judaism" and "Christianity" can certainly find a set of sources to tell that presentist story. It has been common, in fact, to pluck NT and Patristic sources from diverse locales to create a globalized and monolithic image of the "Parting of the Ways" – from Paul's mission as "apostle to the Gentiles," to Ignatius' coining of "Christianity" as an term distinct from "Judaism," to Justin Martyr's argument for the church as the new Israel, to John Chrysostom's rabidly anti-Jewish/anti-Judaizing sermons. But such selectivity hides as much as it reveals, not least through its erasure of local difference and its imposition of a unilinear chronology.

Even seemingly unequivocal evidence for "Parting," for instance, occurs side-by-side with evidence for continued connection, blurring, or overlap. Paul's argument about Gentile salvation apart from the Torah is attested in precisely the same sources that bear witness to the "circumcision party" within the Jesus Movement and its association with James, Peter, and the Jerusalem Church; Justin innovates a supersessionist reading of the Torah but also knows and accepts Jews who believe in Jesus and remain Torah-observant, as long as they don't compel Gentiles to do the same (*Dial.* 47); Ignatius and Chrysostom both hail from Syria, the very region in which one also finds the greatest density of writings that scholars label "Jewish-Christian" (e.g., *Didascalia apostolorum*;

---

[44] See further Becker and Reed, *The Ways That Never Parted*, as well as discussion below in Chapter Two.

Pseudo-Clementines).[45] Nor is there a clear chronology of increasing Christian distance from Jews or disinterest in Judaism. Just as Ignatius frets about the temptations posed by "Judaizing" in the early second century, so too with Chrysostom in the fourth century. The latter's lament about Christian interest in Jewish festivals and synagogues, moreover, echoes Origen's complaints in the third but, if anything, answers a situation that is far more extensive.[46] Likewise, far from diminishing as time goes on, our evidence for "Jewish-Christianity" – both firsthand and secondhand – clusters in the fourth and fifth centuries CE.

The majority of scholars continue to study Judaism and Christianity in isolation, sometimes even in the early period. There is a case to be made, however, for experimenting with rereading some Christian sources as evidence for Jewish history even into Late Antiquity, extending the same trends that are now increasingly common for the New Testament. For doing so, moreover, "Jewish-Christianity" may have a special utility: these are the very sources, after all, which have most frustrated modern Christian scholarly narratives about the church's universalistic "transcendence" of its particularistic Jewish roots and which have therefore been compartmentalized and marginalized in research on Christian thought and history precisely through this labeling as "Jewish-Christian."[47]

As with the recovery of a Jewish Jesus, one finds precedents for this too among nineteenth- and early twentieth-century Jewish thinkers: for his history of the Jewish people, for instance, Heinrich Graetz did not just mine the New Testament to discuss Jesus and Paul, but he also culled information about Peter from the Pseudo-Clementines and information about Ebionites from the writings of Irenaeus, Origen, and Epiphanius.[48] In this, Graetz continued a practice already begun in his dissertation on Judaism and *Gnosis*, wherein he cited materials from Pseudo-Clementines alongside the Mishnah, Talmud, Sefer Yetzirah, and the Zohar.[49] Nor was this pattern limited just to nineteenth-century Germany. Kaufman Kohler, writing in America in the early twentieth century, took an even more

---

[45] See further Judith Lieu, *Image and Reality: The Jews in the World of the Christians in the Second Century* (Edinburgh: T&T Clark, 1996), esp. 39–56; Robert Louis Wilken, *John Chrysostom and the Jews: Rhetoric and Reality in the Late Fourth Century* (Berkeley: University of California Press, 1983), esp. 66–94; John G. Gager, "Jews, Christians, and the Dangerous Ones in Between," in *Interpretation in Religion*, ed. Shlomo Biderman and Ben-Ami Scharfstein (Philosophy and Religion 2; Leiden: Brill, 1992), 249–57; Dominique Côté, "Le problème de l'identité religieuse dans la Syrie du IVe siècle: Le cas des Pseudo-Clémentines et de l'*Adversus Judaeos* de S. Jean Chrysostome," in *La croisée des chemins revisitée: Quand l'Église et la Synagogue se sont-elles distinguées?*, ed. Simon Claude Mimouni and Bernard Pouderon (Patrimoines Judaïsme antique; Paris: Cerf, 2012), 339–70.

[46] E.g., Origen, *Homilies on Leviticus* 5.8; Chrysostom, *Homilies Against the Jews*.

[47] This pattern is clearest – and most influential – in the case of Adolph von Harnack, on whom see the discussion above in the Introduction.

[48] See Chapter Seven in this volume.

[49] See Chapter Ten in this volume.

expansive approach, lamenting Paul as the founder of a non-Jewish Christianity but asserting the post-Pauline continuance of more Jewish approaches among Elchasites and Ebionites. Kohler did so, moreover, by re-appropriating "Jewish-Christian apocrypha" like the *Didache, Didascalia apostolorum*, and Pseudo-Clementines as resources for recovering the full history of ancient Judaism.[50] As with the New Testament, thus, perhaps so too for Late Antiquity: rereading some retrospectively "Christian" or "Jewish-Christian" materials as sources for Jewish history may help to open up new perspectives for the study of Judaism and Christianity alike.

---

[50] See Chapter Eight in this volume.

Part I

"Jewish-Christians" and the Historiography of Early Jewish/Christian Relations

Chapter One

"Jewish-Christianity" after the "Parting of the Ways"*

What is "Jewish-Christianity," and how do we know a "Jewish-Christian" text when we see one? Our answers to these questions may tell us as much about our own assumptions concerning the definition, development, and interrelation of Judaism and Christianity as about the broad continuum of biblically-based approaches to belief and worship in Late Antiquity.

From our literary and archaeological evidence,[1] we know of a variety of texts and groups that cannot be readily categorized as either "Jewish" or "Christian" – or, at least not by a modern schema that treats the two as different by definition and uses Rabbinic Judaism and Western Christian orthodoxy as the standards for judging "Jewishness" and "Christianness." Contrary to our common understanding of early Christian self-definition as inextricably tied to supersessionism, triumphalism, and antinomianism, some late antique authors and communities appear to have accepted Jesus as a special figure in salvation-history, without seeing this belief as inconsistent with Torah observance and/or the continued validity of God's eternal covenant with the Jews.[2] And, contrary to the tendency to treat the Rabbis as the sole arbiters of halakhah in late antique Judaism, some

---

* An earlier version of this chapter appeared in 2003 as "'Jewish-Christianity' after the 'Parting of the Ways': Approaches to Historiography and Self-Definition in the Pseudo-Clementines," in *The Ways That Never Parted: Jews and Christians in Late Antiquity and the Early Middle Ages*, ed. Adam H. Becker and Annette Yoshiko Reed (TSAJ 95; Tübingen: Mohr Siebeck, 2003; revised paperback reprint: Minneapolis: Fortress, 2007), 188–231. Earlier versions were presented at the 2001 workshop and 2002 conference on "The Ways That Never Parted" at Princeton University; it was much shaped by feedback in these fora, especially from Adam H. Becker, John G. Gager, Martha Himmelfarb, Bob Kraft, and Peter Schäfer. It is reprinted here with permission from Mohr Siebeck. This version has been revised and updated.

[1] The bulk of our evidence for postapostolic "Jewish-Christianity" has been surveyed in Simon Claude Mimouni's weighty volume *Le Judéo-christianisme ancien: Essais historiques* (Paris: Cerf, 1998); see esp. his treatment of non-literary sources on pp. 317–452. For the relevant Patristic references, see Albertus Frederik Johannes Klijn and Gerrit J. Reinink, *Patristic Evidence for Jewish-Christian Sects* (NTSup 36; Leiden: Brill, 1973), 95–281. For a more recent survey and synthesis of the potentially relevant data, see Edwin K. Broadhead, *Jewish Ways of Following Jesus: Redrawing the Religious Map of Antiquity* (WUNT 266; Tübingen: Mohr, 2010). See also Appendix B below.

[2] See below for examples from the Pseudo-Clementine literature.

of these same individuals seem to have been no less preoccupied with matters such as dietary restrictions and ritual purification.[3]

Scholars most often use the label "Jewish-Christian" (as opposed, for instance, to "Judaizing" Christian or just "Christian") to designate ethnically Jewish and/or Torah-observant Christ-believers[4] – albeit with varying degrees of sensitivity to the problematic presupposition that the two categories are coterminous, as well as to the difficulties involved in defining "Christian."[5] For our present pur-

---

[3] Note, for instance, the instructions in the Pseudo-Clementine *Hom.* 7.8 for Gentiles not only "to be baptized for the remission of sins," but also "to abstain from the table of devils – that is, from food offered to idols – from dead carcasses, from animals that have been suffocated or caught by wild beasts, and from blood" and "not to live any longer impurely; to wash after intercourse; that the women on their part should keep the law of purification [i.e., after menstruation]." For other examples from the Pseudo-Clementine literature, see, e.g., *Ep. Pet.* 4.1–2; *Rec.* 2.71–72; 6.9–11; 7.29, 34; 8.68; *Hom.* 11.28–30; 13.4, 9, 19. See further Chapter Two in this volume.

[4] A handy survey of scholarly attempts at definition can be found, together with analysis and bibliography, in James Carleton Paget, "Jewish Christianity," in *The Cambridge History of Judaism*, vol. 3: *The Early Roman Period*, ed. William Horbury, W. D. Davies, and John Sturdy (Cambridge: Cambridge University Press, 1999), 733–42. To summarize, "Jewish-Christian" has been typically taken to mean: [1] a Christ-believing Jew (i.e., using the adjective "Jewish" primarily in an ethnic sense, although usually with a qualification to include Jews by conversion); [2] a person of any ethnicity who combined elements of Judaism and Christianity (most frequently with the former consisting of Torah observance and the latter of belief in Jesus as the Messiah – "Jewish" in practice and "Christian" in belief – so as to distinguish this approach from the combinations thereof accepted as "orthodox" in the "Great Church"); and/or [3] a person who articulates his/her Christianity in Jewish cultural or literary forms (a category that encompasses Jean Daniélou's radically broad definition of "Jewish-Christianity" as "l'expression de christianisme dans les formes du *Spätjudentum*" in *Théologie du Judéo-Christianisme* [Paris: Desclée & Cie, 1958], 19, but also more widespread views, such as the notion that to be "Jewishly" Christian is to have a low Christology). Most often, we find combinations and conflations of the three (esp. due to the often unquestioned assumption, in much research on the New Testament and early Christianity that only an ethnic Jew would voluntarily choose to keep the precepts of the Torah). Each of these three modes of definition, as Carleton Paget and others have shown, is methodologically problematic in its own way – not least because #1 is the only criteria that clearly distinguishes these "Jewish-Christians" from Judaizers (esp. #2) or Christians in general (esp. #3). For important developments in the debate on definition since 2003, see Daniel Boyarin, "Rethinking Jewish Christianity: An Argument for Dismantling a Dubious Category (To Which is Appended a Correction of My Border Lines)," *JQR* 99 (2009): 7–36; Oskar Skarsaune and Reidar Hvalvik, eds., *Jewish Believers in Jesus: The Early Centuries* (Peabody, MA: Hendrickson, 2007), esp. James Carleton Paget, "The Definition of the Terms Jewish Christian and Jewish Christianity in the History of Research," 22–54; Matt Jackson-McCabe, ed., *Jewish Christianity Reconsidered: Rethinking Ancient Groups and Texts* (Minneapolis: Fortress, 2007), esp. Jackson-McCabe, "What's in a Name," 7–38.

[5] Accordingly, some scholars have eschewed the use of the term "Jewish-Christianity," citing both its vagueness and its problematic use as a rubric under which to conflate a broad variety of different groups, texts, and figures, primarily on the basis of our own inability to fit them into (our own) categories of "Jew" and "Christian"; see, e.g., Joan Taylor, "The Phenomenon of Early Jewish-Christianity: Reality or Scholarly Invention?" *VC* 44 (1990): 313–34; David Frankfurter, "Beyond 'Jewish Christianity': Continuing Religious Sub-cultures of the Second and Third Centuries and Their Documents," in Becker and Reed, *The Ways That Never Parted*,

poses, the vexed question of definition proves less pressing than the fact that, by their very existence, these texts, groups, and figures complicate commonplace assumptions about Christianity's so-called "Parting of the Ways" from Judaism. Whether we speak of "Jewish-Christianity" or "Jewish-Christianities,"[6] distinguish the former from "Christian Judaism,"[7] or limit our discussions to specific groups like Nazarenes/Nazoraeans and Ebionites,[8] it remains that the sources traditionally studied under the rubric of "Jewish-Christianity" shed doubt on any tidy narrative about an unavoidable, mutual, and final split between Christianity and Judaism in the first or second century CE.

The "Parting of the Ways" is typically depicted as an inexorable development from Jesus' revolutionary teachings, Paul's preaching of a law-free Gospel for the Gentiles, and/or the de-Judaization of the church's base of converts in the wake of the Jewish revolts against Rome. To these proposed catalysts for the purported "Parting," many add the alleged demise of "Jewish-Christianity,"[9]

131–43. There is no doubt a problem in using this label to denote a cohesive movement or phenomenon, as made clear by the reception of Jean Daniélou's *Théologie du Judéo-Christianisme*, particular after its translation into English (*The Theology of Jewish Christianity* [trans. J. Baker; London: Darton, Longman & Todd, 1964]); see esp. Albertus Frederik Johannes Klijn, "The Study of Jewish Christianity," *NTS* 20 (1973–1974): 419–31; Robert A. Kraft, "In Search of 'Jewish Christianity' and Its 'Theology': Problems of Definition and Methodology," *Recherches de Sciences Religieuse* 60 (1972): 81–96. Personally, I am not quite ready to jettison the term. I feel that it still holds some value, not least of all as a heuristic irritant; for, when read with some awareness of the scholarly debate about "Jewish-Christianity," the term serves to disturb – literally by definition – any unquestioned assumptions that we might harbor about the essential incompatibility and inevitable "parting" of Judaism and Christianity, while also reminding us that we have yet to settle some basic definitional issues about "Judaism" and "Christianity" and that our scholarly categories (even the ones with ancient counterparts) are exactly that: categories shaped by our scholarly aims and modern experiences that we choose to impose, for better or worse, on our ancient evidence. See discussion above in the Introduction to this volume as well as Chapter Two.

[6] See, e.g., Marcel Simon, *Verus Israel: A Study of the Relations between Christians and Jews in the Roman Empire, AD 135–425* (trans. H. McKeating; London: Littman Library of Jewish Civilization, 1996), 240; Burton Visotzky, "Prolegomenon to the Study of Jewish-Christianities in Rabbinic Literature" in *Fathers of the World: Essays in Rabbinic and Patristic Literatures* (WUNT 80; Tübingen: Mohr Siebeck, 1995), 130.

[7] See, e.g., Bruce Malina, "Jewish Christianity or Christian Judaism: Toward a Hypothetical Definition," *JJS* 7 (1976): 46–50.

[8] This approach is admirably sensitive to the fact that the term "Jewish-Christianity" is a wholly modern invention, whereas our ancient accounts speak of specific groups. Yet, the task of reconstruction proves difficult, due to the tendentious, muddled, and inconsistent nature of our secondhand testimonies to these groups (i.e., writings of Christian heresiologists), from which it proves difficult to draw any concrete conclusions; see discussion in Klijn and Reinink, *Patristic Evidence*, 67–73, and more recently and in more depth, Boyarin, "Rethinking Jewish Christianity."

[9] Interestingly, this is especially the case in accounts of the "Parting of the Ways" as approached from the Jewish perspective. See, e.g., Gedalia Alon's chapter on this theme – aptly entitled: "Jewish Christians: The Parting of the Ways" – in *The Jews in their Land in the Talmudic Age, 70–640 CE* (trans. G. Levi; Jerusalem: Magnes, 1980–1984), 1:288–307; Lawrence

opining that this movement lost its single stronghold either during the first Jewish Revolt (66–70 CE), when members of the Jerusalem Church reportedly fled to Pella,[10] or after the Bar Kokhba Revolt (132–135 CE), when a defeated Jewish Jerusalem became a pagan city closed to all Jews.[11] Some go on to speculate that the "Jewish-Christian" message was simply rendered obsolete with the establishment of the mutual exclusivity of Christ-belief and Judaism, as allegedly proclaimed from both sides (i.e., by proto-orthodox Christians and early Rabbinic Sages, each of whom are presumed to speak for all of their respective coreligionists).[12] Others go even further, suggesting that, by the close of the first century, "Jewish-Christianity" had already ceased to be a viable and vital religious option that could compete with the Rabbinic movement for Jewish adherents or, for Gentile converts, with the law-free forms of Christianity proclaimed in the name of Paul.[13]

Schiffman, "At the Crossroads: Tannaitic Perspectives on the Jewish–Christian Schism," in *Jewish and Christian Self-Definition*, vol. 2: *Aspects of Judaism in the Graeco-Roman Period*, ed. E. P. Sanders, Albert I. Baumgarten, and Alan Mendelson (Philadelphia: Fortress, 1981), 156; P. S. Alexander, "'The Parting of the Ways' from the Perspective of Rabbinic Judaism," in *Jews and Christians: The Parting of the Ways, AD 70 to 135*, ed. J. Dunn (Grand Rapids: Eerdmans, 1992), 3, 20–24. For a recent iteration from a Christian perspective, see James D. G. Dunn, *Christianity in the Making*, vol. 3: *Neither Jew nor Greek: A Contested Identity* (Grand Rapids: Eerdmans, 2015), esp. 509–74.

[10] The notion of a flight to Pella is based on Eusebius, *Hist. eccl.*, 3.5.3; Epiphanius, *Pan.* 1.29.7–30.7; *De mens.* 15. Although this tradition has long been a mainstay of scholarly reconstructions of the history of "Jewish-Christianity," some scholars question its historicity; e.g., Gerd Lüdemann, "The Successors of Pre-70 Jerusalem Christianity: A Critical Evaluation of the Pella Tradition," in *Jewish and Christian Self-Definition*, vol. 1: *The Shaping of Christianity in the Second and Third Centuries*, ed. E. P. Sanders (Philadelphia: Fortress, 1980), 161–73, Lüdemann, *Opposition to Paul in Jewish Christianity* (trans. E. Boring; Minneapolis: Fortress, 1989), 200–12; J. Verheyden, "The Flight of Christians to Pella," *Ephemerides theologicae lovanienses* 66 (1990): 368–84; Taylor, "Phenomenon of Early Jewish-Christianity," 315–16; Johannes Munck, "Jewish Christianity in Post-Apostolic Times," *NTS* 6 (1959): 103–4. Cf. Marcel Simon, "La migration à Pella: Légende ou réalité?" *RSR* 60 (1972): 37–54; Jürgen Wehnert, "Die Auswanderung der Jerusalemer Christen nach Pella – historische Faktum oder theologische Konstruktion?" *Zeitschrift für Kirchengeschichte* 102 (1991): 231–55; Carleton Paget, "Jewish Christianity," 746–48.

[11] So Schiffman, "At the Crossroads," 155–56.

[12] See, e.g., Carleton Paget, "Jewish Christianity," 750. Here, when concluding his summary of our evidence for "Jewish-Christianity" (see pp. 742–50), Carleton Paget admits that "we know little about the historic fate of Jewish Christianity," notes that proto-orthodox/orthodox Christian heresiological comments are "not, of course, proof positive that they were perceived in such a way [i.e., as 'heretics'] everywhere," and even allows for the possibility that groups like the Nazarenes "might in certain quarters have been regarded as orthodox [i.e., orthodox Christians] even up to the middle of the fourth century." It is thus particularly striking that he goes on to assert: "What is clear is that, excluded from both Church and synagogue … it [i.e., 'Jewish-Christianity'] declined dramatically" – and, moreover, associates this decline with "the late second century onwards" (or, as he further specifies on p. 752: "by the 160s").

[13] E. g., Simon, *Verus Israel*, 268–69.

Our extant evidence for so-called "Jewish-Christianity," however, frustrates scholarly attempts to tell the story of Christian origins as simply a tale of the inevitable separation of Christianity (in all its varieties) from its theological, social, and cultural ties to Judaism (both without and within). Following the "Parting" model, for instance, one would expect a proto-orthodox Christian like Justin Martyr – who wrote so soon after the Bar Kokhba Revolt and who so strenuously argued the church's supersession of the "old" Israel – to denounce those who retained Jewish observance alongside a belief in Christ, as part of his own construction of a Christianity in radical distinction from Judaism. Justin, however, readily embraces such individuals as authentic Christians (*Dial.* 47).[14] However tempting it is to imagine that early Christian polemics against Judaism were accompanied by equally strident efforts to purge the church of "Jewish-Christianity," our sources make clear that the situation was not so simple.[15]

Modern theories about the early split between Christianity and Judaism might also lead us to imagine that our evidence for "Jewish-Christian" groups should be strongest for the first two centuries of Christianity and then progressively peter off, as Christ-believing Jews were replaced by new Gentile converts to an increasingly dominant orthodoxy and as "living" forms of Judaism were allegedly rendered irrelevant for the Christians of all stripes. This, indeed, is the story told by most historians.[16] It remains the case, however, that much of our extant data about "Jewish-Christians" – both firsthand and secondhand – comes from the third, fourth, and fifth centuries CE.[17]

---

[14] Notably, Justin here expresses concern that some Christ-believing Jews wish to convert Gentiles to a Torah-observant Christianity.

[15] Indeed, in the second and third centuries CE, it seems that Marcion's complete rejection of Christianity's Jewish heritage was perceived as much more of a threat by proto-orthodox Christian authors than so-called "Jewish-Christians"; see e. g., Justin, *1 Apol.* 26.5–8; 58.1; *Dial.* 38.6 (also Irenaeus, *Adv. haer.* 4.6.9, on Justin's no longer extant treatise against Marcion); Irenaeus, *Adv. haer.* 1.1.2–4, 3, 23, 30.9; 3.3.4, 4.3, 11.2; 4.8–13, 29–34; Tertullian, *Adv. Marc.* See now F. Stanley Jones, *Pseudoclementina Elchasaiticaque inter Judaeochristiana: Collected Studies* (Orientalia Lovaniensia Analecta 203; Leuven: Peeters, 2012), esp. 152–71, on the importance of Marcionism for understanding "Jewish-Christianity" in Syria in particular.

[16] Not surprisingly, the classical formulation of this perspective can be found in Adolf von Harnack's influential works (see, e. g., *The Mission and Expansion of Christianity in the First Three Centuries* [Gloucester: Smith, 1972], 44–72). For a summary of the history of scholarship on "Jewish-Christianity," see, e. g., Carleton Paget, "Jewish Christianity," 731–75; Klijn, "Study of Jewish-Christianity," 419–26; Simon Claude Mimouni, "Le Judéo-Christianisme ancien dans l'historiographie du XIXème et du XXème siècle," *REJ* 151 (1992): 419–28; Lüdemann, *Opposition to Paul in Jewish Christianity*, 1–34. For more recent interventions, which point to the precedents already in the eighteenth century, see F. Stanley Jones, ed., *Rediscovery of Jewish Christianity: From Toland to Baur* (History of Biblical Studies 5; Atlanta: Society of Biblical Literature, 2012), as well as Chapter Eleven below.

[17] From even a glance at the collection of Klijn and Reinink (*Patristic Evidence*), it is clear that our secondhand data cluster in these centuries. It is notable that the first author to mention the Nazoraeans/Nazarenes is Epiphanius (*Pan.* 29); it is no less striking that authors of his time seem far more preoccupied with the Ebionites than their heresiological predecessors (note,

This makes it especially ironic that regnant assumptions about the "Parting of the Ways" are perhaps nowhere more evident than in research on "Jewish-Christianity." Most striking is the contrast between scholarly approaches to "Jewish-Christian" tendencies in the New Testament literature and approaches to postapostolic evidence exhibiting the same tendencies.[18] When dealing with the pre-"Parting" period, scholars (now, at least) see "Jewish-Christian" characteristics as authentic, widespread, and even normative, viewing them as important evidence for the Jewish heritage of the church and the vibrant diversity of the earliest Christ-believing communities. After the second century CE, however, "Jewish-Christianity" becomes a problem for the church historian: a phenome-

e. g., Irenaeus' very brief comments about this group at *Adv. haer.* 1.26.2; 3.11.7, 21.1; 4.33.4; 5.1.3, in contrast to his copious comments about Marcionites, Valentinians, etc.). Moreover, the *Didascalia apostolorum* appears to date from the third century, whereas the Pseudo-Clementine *Homilies* and *Recognitions* are both from the fourth (see discussion below).

The three "Jewish-Christian gospels" that scholars have reconstructed from comments of proto-orthodox/orthodox Christian authors – the so-called *Gospel of the Nazoraeans*, *Gospel of the Ebionites*, and *Gospel of the Hebrews* – are all commonly dated to the first half of the second century (so Philip Vielhauer and Georg Strecker, "Jewish-Christian Gospels," in *NTA* 1:134–78, esp. 159, 169, 176). But, as with the evidence for these gospels in general, their early dating is based on a very particular reading of a set of data that admits multiple explanations and enables very little certainty (as clear from the summary in Vielhauer and Strecker, "Jewish-Christian Gospels," 1:136–151). For instance, the second-century dating of the *Gospel of the Ebionites* is based on the statements of Irenaeus (ca. 180 CE) about the Ebionites' use of a Hebrew version of the Gospel of Matthew redacted to fit their own beliefs (*Adv. haer.* 1.26.2; 3.11.7, 21.1; 5.1.3). Arguments about a similarly early date for the *Gospel of the Nazoraeans* and the *Gospel of the Hebrews* are based on Eusebius' statement that Hegesippus (ca. 180) must be a convert from Judaism since "he quotes from both the Gospel according to the Hebrews and the Syriac" (*Hist. eccl.* 4.22.8). In light of the widespread traditions about Matthew composing his gospel in Hebrew and the early Christian application of the label "Gospel of/according to the Hebrews" to a broad variety of works – including the Gospel of Matthew itself (Epiphanius, *Pan.*, 30.3.7) and Tatian's *Diatesseron* (Epiphanius, *Pan.* 46.1) – none of these arguments prove terribly persuasive, particularly if we follow Klijn, Reinink, and others in questioning the overconfidence with which some scholars reconstruct the beliefs and practices of the Ebionites and the Nazoraeans/Nazorenes from our heresiological witnesses (see *Patristic Evidence*, esp. 67–73). Rather, what is striking about the secondhand evidence adduced by Vielhauer and Strecker is that so many Christian authors in the centuries following the so-called "Parting of the Ways" (i. e., especially the fourth and fifth centuries, but even well into the Middle Ages) seem to know of gospels written in Hebrew or Hebrew letters (i. e., Hebrew or Aramaic), gospels circulated among "the Jews," and gospels that generally strike them as τὸ Ἰουδαϊκόν. For a more recent attempt to recover early strata from these materials, however, see now Petri Luomanen, *Recovering Jewish-Christian Sects and Gospels* (VCSup 110; Leiden: Brill, 2011).

[18] This is perhaps most clear in the work of Jean Daniélou. As mentioned above, Daniélou offers a very broad definition of "Jewish-Christianity." Nevertheless, he still remains firm in limiting this phenomenon to the period before mid-second century CE. Afterwards, in his view, there could only be "secondary contributions, Jewish traditions incorporated into a whole that was no longer Jewish" (*Theology of Jewish Christianity*, 8–10). Hence, he treats the evidence for later attempts to combine Jewish and Christian elements under the title "Heterodox Jewish-Christianity," and he deems these efforts significant only insofar as they "preserve certain elements which they had in common with Jewish-Christianity (i. e., the earlier, orthodox variety)" (p. 55).

non in need of explanation, whose spread and influence can ideally be limited to a narrow geographical scope or constrained into tiny "heretical" sects huddled on the periphery of the "Great Church."[19]

Within most modern studies of "Jewish-Christianity" after the "Parting of the Ways," one detects a notable sense of disbelief at the possibility that, after the second century CE, anyone might be attracted to varieties of Christianity that still "clung" to Jewish observance – let alone the possibility that there could be varieties of Judaism that granted some special role to Jesus.[20] Even Marcel Simon – who so incisively critiqued the tendency to see "Jewish-Christianity" as "an aberrant manifestation of early Christianity" and who stressed the diversity of "Jewish-Christian" groups and the diversity of the Judaism from which they drew – described late antique "Jewish-Christianity" as a "fossilized form of Christianity," a stunted "survival" left in the wake of the decisive evolution of the church away from its Jewish origins.[21] The implications are striking: Christianity's early "Parting" from Judaism was allegedly so decisive as to transform certain normative variations in biblically-based belief and practice into bizarre anachronisms, at best, and pernicious heresies, at worst. In other words, the narratives told in modern research echo proto-orthodox/orthodox Christian historiography in asserting that "Jewish-Christian" forms of belief and worship should have never survived – let alone thrived – long beyond the apostolic age. Accordingly, scholars largely follow the lead of the heresiologists, by minimizing, marginalizing, and explaining away the evidence to the contrary.

Insofar as the "Problem of Jewish-Christianity" resonates with very basic questions about how assumptions about religious identity shape the modern categorization of ancient groups (as well as the scholarly reconstruction of the relationships between them), this issue proves particularly relevant for experimenting with approaches to Judaism and Christianity as "Ways that Never Parted."

---

[19] On the traditional tendency to insist upon the limited regional scope of "Jewish-Christian" tendencies and their complete lack of influence on orthodox Christianity, see Klijn, "Study of Jewish-Christianity," esp. 421–25. Here too we can discern the influence of Harnack, who accepted the existence of a variety of "Jewish-Christian" groups in both the apostolic and postapostolic periods, but stridently emphasized that they had no impact on the "Great Church" (see, e. g., *Lehrbuch der Dogmengeschichte* [repr. ed.; Darmstadt: Wissenschaftliche Buchgesellschaft, 1965], 317).

[20] It should be noted that "Jewish-Christianity" has usually been studied as a variety of Christianity, rather than a variety of Judaism; an important exception is Charlotte Fonrobert, "The *Didascalia Apostolorum*: A Mishnah for the Disciples of Jesus," *JECS* 9 (2001): 483–509. See further Visotzky, "Prolegomenon to the Study of Jewish-Christianities," 129–49, and studies of Rabbinic traditions about *minim* ("heretics" or "sectarians" – a category that sometimes includes "Jewish-Christians"), particularly: Daniel Boyarin, "A Tale of Two Synods: Nicaea, Yavneh, and Rabbinic Ecclesiology," *Exemplaria* 12 (2000): 55–60; Boyarin, "Justin Martyr Invents Judaism," *CH* 70 (2001): 438–49; Boyarin, *Border Lines: The Partition of Judaeo-Christianity* (Divinations; Philadelphia: University of Pennsylvania Press, 2004); also Richard Kalmin, "Christians and Heretics in Rabbinic Literature of Late Antiquity," *HTR* 87 (1994): 155–69, esp. 163–65.

[21] Simon, *Verus Israel*, 238–44.

Towards this goal, I will here focus on the Pseudo-Clementine *Homilies* and *Recognitions*, two fourth-century texts widely recognized as our most important and extensive sources for reconstructing a first-hand account of "Jewish-Christianity."[22] I will begin by considering how assumptions about the "Parting of the Ways" have shaped modern scholarship on the Pseudo-Clementines. Then, I will turn to examine three selections from the *Homilies* and *Recognitions* (*Rec.* 1.27–71; 4–6; *Hom.* 8–11), attempting to elucidate the self-understanding of their final authors/redactors. Finally, I will try to locate these texts in their late antique context, offering some tentative suggestions about their broader significance for our understanding of the history of Jewish/Christian relations more broadly.

Due to the complex literary history of the Pseudo-Clementines, this inquiry will raise more questions that it can answer. Nevertheless, I here hope to highlight the diversity of viewpoints that the modern category of "Jewish-Christianity" conflates, by drawing attention to the range of perspectives expressed and preserved, even within a single corpus. In the process, I hope to show the special value of so-called "Jewish-Christian" sources – and the Pseudo-Clementines in particular – for a fresh approach to the relationship between Judaism and Christianity in Late Antiquity, pursued apart from traditional assumptions about their allegedly "parted ways." New approaches, I will argue, are nowhere more needed than in the study of late antique "Jewish-Christianity," due to the dissonance between our ancient evidence and the modern frameworks used to interpret it. And, for precisely this reason, the sources studied under the rubric of "Jewish-Christianity" may provide particularly heuristic foci for forging and testing fresh approaches to the interactions between Jews and Christians – and the continuing ambiguities in "Jewish" and "Christian" identities – in the multiple geographical, social, intellectual, and political worlds of Late Antiquity.[23]

The "Parting of the Ways" and the History of Scholarship
on the Pseudo-Clementines

In form, the Pseudo-Clementine *Homilies* and *Recognitions* are composite texts that integrate ample material from earlier sources. Insofar as the *Homilies* and *Recognitions* share the same basic structure and contain many parallels, most

---

[22] For an extensive, accessible, and generally invaluable survey of the scholarship on this literature, see F. Stanley Jones, "The Pseudo-Clementines: A History of Research," *Second Century* 2 (1982): 1–33, 63–96 – now extended in Jones, ed., *Rediscovery of Jewish Christianity*.

[23] This potential is tapped to brilliant effect in Fonrobert, "*Didascalia Apostolorum*" (see esp. her comments on pp. 484–87, 508–9). As Fonrobert rightly stresses there, "Our understanding of the formation of Jewish and Christian collective identities as separate identities depends on developing an intelligible way of discussing the phenomenon called 'Jewish Christianity,' one that is not marred by Christian theological prejudices, nor by unexamined assumptions about either 'Jewish' identity formation or its 'Christian' counterpart" (p. 484).

scholars accept that they rework the same Basic Source (or *Grundschrift*), which most scholars date to the early third century CE.[24] The earlier of the two appears to be the *Homilies* (ca. 300–320 CE), for which the original Greek is still extant.[25] The *Recognitions* is commonly dated to the middle of the fourth century, but it only survives in full in Rufinus' Latin translation (ca. 407 CE).[26] The Syriac version of the Pseudo-Clementines integrates selections from both (i.e., *Rec.* 1–4.1.4; *Hom.* 10–14) and is extant in a manuscript from 411 CE.[27] In addition, we have later epitomes of the *Homilies* and/or *Recognitions* in many languages, including Greek, Arabic, Georgian, and Armenian, as well as fragments in Slavonic and Ethiopic.[28]

Both the *Homilies* and *Recognitions* legitimize their teachings by means of an overarching narrative about the conversion and early career of Clement of Rome. In both, exhortations and instructions are attributed to Clement's distinguished mentor, the apostle Peter. Among these are statements emphasizing the importance of Moses, the Torah, and halakhic observance (especially ritual purity and dietary laws), asserting the continued chosenness of the Jews, and depicting the Mosaic Torah and the teachings of Jesus as equal sources of salvific knowledge.[29] In addition, the *Homilies* and *Recognitions* appeal to the authority of this apostle to promote an account of early church history that counters the epistles

---

[24] See further Jones, "Pseudo-Clementines," 8–14. This source is generally dated to before 220 CE, due to its apparent dependence on Bardaisan. Jones' many insights into this source are handily collected now in *Pseudoclementina*, esp. 114–206.

[25] For the text of the Pseudo-Clementine *Homilies*: Bernhard Rehm, *Die Pseudoklementinen*, vol. 1: *Homilien* (GCS 42; Berlin: Akademie-Verlag, 1969), on which all citations in this article are based. The edition is prefaced with a discussion of its date and provenance, the relationship between the two extant Greek MSS ("P" and "O") and the two Greek Epitomes ("e" and "E"), and its text-history (pp. vii–xxiii).

[26] For the text of the Pseudo-Clementine *Recognitions*: Bernhard Rehm, *Die Pseudoklementinen*, vol. 2: *Rekognitionen in Rufinus Übersetzung* (GCS 51; Berlin: Akademie-Verlag, 1969), on which all citations in this article are based. Notably, *Recognitions* is extant in a greater number of MSS than is *Homilies* (i.e., over a hundred, dating from the fifth to fifteenth centuries; see pp. xvii–xcv, cix–cxi).

[27] I.e., British Museum add. 12150. For a preliminary edition of the Syriac of this and a later MS, together with reconstructed Greek, see Wilhelm Frankenberg, *Die syrischen Clementinen mit griechischem Paralleltext: Eine Vorarbeit zu dem literargeschichtlichen Problem der Sammlung* (TU 48.3; Leipzig: Henrichs, 1937). It is notable that the selections from *Rec.* 1–4 in this version seem to come from a different translator than the selections from *Hom.* 10–14 (pp. viii–ix). On the importance of this understudied version for our knowledge about the Greek *Vorlage* of Rufinus' Latin *Rec.*, see F. Stanley Jones, *An Ancient Jewish Christian Source on the History of Christianity: Pseudo-Clementine Recognitions 1.27–71* (Atlanta: Scholars Press, 1995), 39–49. See now Jones, *Pseudoclementina*, 207–305; Jones, trans., *The Syriac Pseudo-Clementines: An Early Version of the First Christian Novel* (Apocryphes 14; Turnhout: Brepols, 2014), a translation based on Jones' forthcoming edition.

[28] See Jones, "Pseudo-Clementines," 6–7, 80–84, and references there.

[29] See discussion below.

of Paul and the Book of Acts.[30] Most notably, they exalt James and Peter as the true guardians of Jesus' message and the authentic leaders of the apostolic community, while condemning Paul and the law-free mission associated with him.[31]

Although the literary history of the Pseudo-Clementines is notoriously complex, almost all scholars thus acknowledge that some "Jewish-Christian," or specifically Ebionite, strata are imbricated therein.[32] Different scholars, however, have identified these strata and have reconstructed their sources (and the sources for their sources) in different ways,[33] depending in large part on their assumptions about the development of Judaism, Christianity, and "Jewish-Christianity" after the "Parting of the Ways." In judging the "Jewish-Christianity" of the Pseudo-Clementines and reconstructing the "Jewish-Christian" stages in their redaction history, most scholars have imposed external criteria upon the *Homilies* and *Recognitions* either from [1] heresiological comments about the Ebionites (especially Epiphanius, *Pan.* 30)[34] or [2] scholarly reconstructions of the history of "Jewish-Christianity," such as the theory that late antique "Jewish-Christian" groups are remnants of the Jerusalem Church which, after the flight to Pella, regrouped into small sects in Syria and Palestine.[35]

The former has led some scholars to follow the heresiologists in determining the "Jewish-Christianity" of different strata primarily on the basis of doctrinal issues, such as christology,[36] and perhaps to overstate the importance of Epiphanius' comments about the Ebionites for our understanding of the Pseudo-Clementine literature (and "Jewish-Christianity" in general).[37] The latter helps to explain the inordinate amount of attention given to the material about James, Peter, Paul, and the Jerusalem church in scholarship on the *Homilies* and *Recog-*

---

[30] This is most obvious in the *Epistle of Peter to James*, commonly affixed to the *Homilies*, in which Peter purportedly writes to James to complain against those who "pervert my words by various interpretations, as though I taught the abolition of the Law" (2.4; cf. Acts 11:4–17; Gal 2). *Rec.* 1.27–71 is also notable; on its literary relationship to Acts, see F. Stanley Jones in *Pseudoclementina*, 207–29.

[31] See Lüdemann, *Opposition to Paul*, 171–94.

[32] For the history of scholarship on this issue, see Georg Strecker, *Das Judenchristentum in den Pseudoklementinen* (TU 702; Berlin: Akademie-Verlag, 1981), 1–34; Jones, "Pseudo-Clementines," 84–96. On the Pseudo-Clementines and the Ebionites, see esp. Hans Joachim Schoeps, *Theologie und Geschichte des Judenchristentums* (Tübingen: Mohr, 1949) and the revised English version of this work, *Jewish Christianity: Factional Disputes in the Early Church* (trans. D. Hare; Philadelphia: Fortress, 1969).

[33] See discussion in Jones, "Pseudo-Clementines," 84–96

[34] For a survey of the other Patristic evidence concerning the Ebionites, see Klijn and Reinink, *Patristic Evidence,* 19–43.

[35] See, e. g., Schoeps, *Jewish Christianity*, 18–37. See above.

[36] So Schoeps, *Jewish Christianity*, 59–73.

[37] See discussion in Jones, *Ancient Jewish Christian Source*, 35–37. Although the attempt to correlate the literary history of the Pseudo-Clementines with Epiphanius' description of the Ebionites has dominated both source-critical and textual scholarship on this corpus, the result has been an almost total lack of unanimity.

nitions.[38] Although this research has proved invaluable for supplementing (and interrogating) the canonical depiction of the apostolic age found in Acts, it has often been pursued with the assumption that the scholarly value and religious authenticity of the "Jewish-Christian" material in the *Homilies* and *Recognitions* stands contingent on proof for its continuity with a form of Christianity that existed prior to the "Parting of the Ways."

In this sense, the influence of Ferdinand Christian Baur still looms large. Baur first brought the Pseudo-Clementines to popular prominence as a neglected source for the conflicts of the apostolic age. Not coincidentally, he was also largely responsible for popularizing the concept of "Jewish-Christianity" as we now know it.[39] Baur's reconstruction of apostolic history revolved around the dichotomy between the "Jewish-Christianity" of James, Peter, and the Jerusalem Church, and the "Gentile Christianity" of Paul and the Diaspora communities that he founded.[40] His interests in recovering the former led him to draw attention to later heresiological comments about "Jewish-Christian" groups, but also to the *Homilies* and *Recognitions*. Just as he traced a straight trajectory of (d)volution from the Jerusalem Church to the Ebionites mentioned by Irenaeus and Epiphanius, so he posited that the *Homilies* and *Recognitions* were second-century texts, which preserve precious remnants of the "Jewish-Christianity" that was soon doomed to be usurped by the "Gentile Christianity" at the heart of the "Great Church."[41]

In short, the modern study of the Pseudo-Clementine literature and the very concept of "Jewish-Christianity" emerged hand-in-hand on the scholarly scene, and at least since the nineteenth century, they have been paired within discussions about early apostolic history. Now, nearly two hundred years later, it seems almost superfluous to speak of "Jewish-Christianity" in the first century CE, and it seems strange to limit "Jewishness" to only one group or stream of the Jesus

---

[38] See, e.g., Schoeps, *Jewish Christianity*, 38–58; Robert E. Van Voorst, *The Ascents of James: History and Theology of a Jewish-Christian Community* (SBL Dissertation Series 112; Atlanta: Scholars Press, 1989).

[39] Although the term was used prior to Baur, he is widely credited as the father of the modern study of "Jewish-Christianity" (see, e.g., Stanley K. Riegel, "Jewish Christianity: Definitions and Terminology," *NTS* 24 (1978): 411; Mimouni, *Judéo-christianisme ancien*, 419; Klijn, "Study of Jewish-Christianity," 419; Carleton Paget, "Jewish Christianity," 731). For more recent reassessments of Baur's influence, see David Lincicum, "F. C. Baur's Place in the Study of Jewish Christianity," in Jones, *Rediscovery of Jewish Christianity*, 137–66, and more broadly, Martin Bauspieß, Christof Landmesser, and David Lincicum, eds., *Ferdinand Christian Baur und die Geschichte des frühen Christentums* (WUNT 333; Tübingen: Mohr Siebeck, 2014). See also Terence L. Donaldson, "'Gentile Christianity' as a Category in the Study of Christian Origins," *HTR* 106 (2013): 433–58, on the understudied other half of this dichotomy (i.e., *Heidenchristentums*).

[40] See esp. Ferdinand Christian Baur, "Die Christuspartei in der korinthischen Gemeide, der Gegensatz des petrinischen und paulischen Christentums in der alten Kirche, der Apostel Petrus in Rom," *Tübinger Zeitschrift für Theologie* 4 (1831): 61–206.

[41] Baur, "Die Christuspartei in der korinthischen Gemeide," 114–17.

Movement: in Helmut Koester's words, "Everyone in the first generation of Christianity was Jewish-Christian."[42] Furthermore, scholars have since sought to move beyond Baur's simple dichotomy between "Jewish-Christianity" and "Gentile Christianity," turning instead to recover from the New Testament literature a range of attitudes towards the Torah and Jewish chosenness, as espoused by multiple groups of Christ-believing Jews and their Gentile converts.[43] As a result, some scholars now reserve the label "Jewish-Christian" only for texts and groups in the postapostolic period, when Christianity had purportedly "parted" from Judaism, thus becoming non-Jewish enough in orientation and self-definition that the designation actually proves meaningful.[44]

Although the *Homilies* and *Recognitions* are now known to date from this later period, scholarship on the Pseudo-Clementine literature still operates largely within the parameters set by Baur back in the 1830s. Most notably, it is still widely assumed that the "Jewish-Christian" material in the *Homilies* and *Recognitions* is only worthy of study insofar as it can tell us something about the primitive church.[45] Indeed, it is perhaps not coincidental that, after scholars such as Charles Biggs and Hans Waitz demonstrated the fourth-century dates of both the *Homilies* and *Recognitions*,[46] research on these texts has been dominated by source-critical inquiries. Rather than studying the *Homilies* and *Recognitions* for their own sake, scholars have focused their efforts on reconstructing the early sources that may lie *behind* their (also nonextant) Basic Source.[47] In effect, those

---

[42] Helmut Koester, "ΓΝΩΜΑΙ ΔΙΑΦΟΡΟΙ: The Origin and Nature of Diversification in the History of the Early Church," *HTR* 53 (1965): 380.

[43] See esp. Raymond E. Brown, "Not Jewish Christianity and Gentile Christianity but Types of Jewish/Gentile Christianity," *CBQ* 45 (1983): 74–79.

[44] Mimouni, for instance, reserves the term "Jewish-Christian" for groups after 135 CE (*Judéo-christianisme ancien*, 475–93).

[45] Jones describes two tendencies in scholarship on the "Jewish-Christianity" of the Pseudo-Clementines: "[1] the tendency to maintain Baur's evaluation by dating the Jewish Christian element early in the literary history of PsCl and by emphasizing the importance of Jewish Christianity for the history of the church and [2] the tendency to refute Baur's evaluation of the PsCl either by denying the Jewish Christian element in the PsCl or by relativizing its importance through the assignment of a late date to the Jewish Christian influence or through denial of the seriousness of this influence" ("Pseudo-Clementines," 86).

[46] The fourth-century dating, which is now commonly accepted, was argued by Charles Biggs on the basis of the *Homilies'* apparent familiarity with the Arian controversy and the occurrence of certain Syriac words therein ("The Clementine Homilies," in *Studia biblica et ecclesiastica*, vol. 2 (Oxford: Clarendon, 1890), 191–92, 368–69). On *Recognitions*, see Hans Waitz, *Die Pseudoklementinen: Homilien und Rekognitionem: Eine quellen-kritische Untersuchung* (TU 10.4; Leipzig: Hinrichs, 1904), 372.

[47] Proposed sources of the Pseudo-Clementine Basic Source include: a *Kerygma Petrou* or *Kerygmata Petrou* related to the text of that name quoted by Heracleon; a *Praxeis Petrou* somehow related to the extant Acts of Peter; a version of *Anabathmoi Jakobou* related to the text mentioned by Epiphanius in *Pan.* 3.16; and Bardaisan's *Book of the Laws of the Countries* (esp. *Rec.* 9.19–29). In this endeavor, modern scholarship on the Pseudo-Clementines has been inextricably shaped by the foundational work of Georg Strecker (see further Jones, "Pseudo-

who take seriously the "Jewish-Christianity" of the *Homilies* and *Recognitions* still search, like Baur, for second-century heirs to the Jerusalem Church of James and Peter.

Accordingly, critics of this approach, who deny any continuity between the Pseudo-Clementines and apostolic "Jewish-Christianity," tend either to downplay these texts' "Jewish-Christian" elements or to dismiss them as late, "heretical"/"heterodox" accretions that prove largely irrelevant to our understanding of this literature and the late antique church more broadly.[48] In both cases, the scholarly approach to the "Jewish-Christianity" of the Pseudo-Clementine literature has been inextricably shaped by the broader tendency to treat the post-70/post-135 survival of "Jewish-Christianity" as merely a footnote to a narrative about early Christian history in which its alleged demise functions as a necessary contrast to the triumphant rise of "Gentile Christianity" and as a necessary corollary to the "Parting of the Ways" with Judaism.

Historiography and Identity in the Pseudo-Clementines

Here, I will approach the Pseudo-Clementine *Homilies* and *Recognitions* with a different set of assumptions. In my opinion, the notion of an early and decisive "Parting" between Christianity and Judaism is neither plausible nor heuristic, due to our evidence for the continually complex and charged relationships between Jews, Christians, and "Jewish-Christians" in the centuries that followed. This model fits with the assertions of some proto-orthodox Christians and Rabbinic Jews, but it errs in reading the rhetoric, polemics, and normative claims of these groups as historical statements. In light of recent research on the early Rabbinic movement and new perspectives on "orthodoxy" and "heresy" in early Christianity, we can no longer write the history of Jews and Christians

---

Clementines," 14–33, and Jones, *Ancient Jewish Christian Source*, 20–36). Some scholars, however, have expressed their doubts about how methodologically sound it is to, in Gerd Lüdemann's words, "reconstruct a source used by a document [i.e., Basic Source] that itself must be reconstructed as a source for our existing documents" (*Opposition to Paul*, 169–70).

[48] An important example is Johannes Munck, "Primitive Jewish Christianity and Late Jewish Christianity: Continuation or Rupture?" in *Aspects du Judéo-Christianisme: Colloque de Strasbourg, 23–25 avril 1964* (Paris: Presse Universitaires de France, 1965), 77–94. Munck here observes that, "In the case of the Pseudo-Clementine writings, we have to try to make our way back to the second century – if we can – by means of a complicated classification of sources, about which no two scholars are in complete agreement" (p. 106). Together with his judgment that "fragments of the so-called Jewish-Christian gospels ... do not contain Jewish-Christian features linking them with primitive Christianity," this leads him to conclude that [1] we cannot "learn anything about primitive Jewish Christianity from sources other than the New Testament writings," [2] "primitive Jewish Christianity ceased to exist at the destruction of Jerusalem," and [3] "all later Jewish Christianity [which he terms 'heretical Jewish Christianity'] has its origin in the Gentile-Christian Church of the post-apostolic period" (pp. 107, 114).

in Late Antiquity as merely a tale about the triumphant emergence of these twin "orthodoxies" out of the ashes of the Second Temple. It is now clear that, even in the second and third centuries CE, neither group held the authority that they so vociferously claimed for themselves. And, just as we cannot assume that their writings are representative of "Judaism" and "Christianity" more globally, so we should be wary of the attractive but simplistic image of an early "Parting" between two "religions," conceived in monolithic terms.[49]

Furthermore, recent research has suggested that the elite authors of these "orthodoxies" remained so preoccupied with, and so vehement about, the boundaries between "Judaism" and "Christianity" precisely because these boundaries were still being constructed, negotiated, contested, and blurred "on the ground" – not only in the second century CE, but also, with growing intensity, in the third and fourth centuries (and even beyond, particularly in some locales). If we can no longer presume that "Jew" and "Christian" were firmly established as mutually-exclusive religious identities by the close of the second century CE, then we also cannot assume as a matter of course that the so-called "Jewish-Christians" of Late Antiquity were transgressing a clear-cut boundary between "normative" Judaism and "normative" Christianity or forging a hybrid identity based on universally accepted notions of "Jew" and "Christian."[50]

Some scholars now point to the fourth century as the critical era for the establishment of these identities as socially, religiously, and definitionally distinct (at least in the Roman Empire).[51] This raises the intriguing possibility that the authors/redactors of the *Homilies* and *Recognitions* were participating in a broader discourse about the relationship between "Christianity" and "Judaism," rather than simply deviating from a set norm. Consequently, it is perhaps most prudent to revisit the question of the "Jewish-Christianity" of the Pseudo-Clementines, reconsidering these sources in light of the new scholarly sensitivity to the diversity of biblically-based forms of religiosity well into Late Antiquity. Towards this goal, I will here focus on the fourth-century authors/redactors of this literature, exploring the efforts at self-definition found within the *Homilies* and *Recognitions* in their extant, redacted forms.[52] Rather than judging their

---

[49] Adam H. Becker and I discuss these issues in more detail in "Introduction: Traditional Models and New Directions," in Becker and Reed, *The Ways That Never Parted*, 1–24.

[50] On the methodological problems involved in treating "Jewish-Christianity" as simply the "middle ground" between two well-defined entities, see Visotzky, "Prolegomenon to the Study of Jewish-Christianities," 129–30.

[51] See esp. Daniel Boyarin, *Dying for God: Martyrdom and the Making of Christianity and Judaism* (Stanford: Stanford University Press, 1999), 18.

[52] I here follow Jones' approach in *Ancient Jewish Christian Source*, where he attempts to move beyond the multiplication of hypothetical sources (and conflicting scholarly hypothesis about them) in previous research on the Pseudo-Clementines by focusing upon the internal literary features of the text itself, rather than emphasizing its hypothetical relationship to the nonextant texts mentioned by Epiphanius, Hegesippus, and others (see esp. pp. 35–37).

"Jewish-Christianity" in terms of modern models or other external criteria, I will attempt to highlight the texts' own attempts to define proper belief and practice, by focusing on their accounts of the origins of both proper and improper modes of worship.[53]

Like Gentile Christian writers from Luke to Justin Martyr to Eusebius, the fourth-century authors/redactors of the *Homilies* and *Recognitions* use biblically-based historiography to situate the true believer in relation to Jews and Gentiles, the Torah and the Gospel, the demonic and the divine. Within the *Homilies* and *Recognitions*, we find three passages that use the early history of humankind to expound the origins of sin and the path(s) to salvation. The *Recognitions* addresses this theme twice, first in the context of Peter's initial instructions to Clement (*Rec.* 1.27–71) and then in the context of their sojourn at Tripolis (*Rec.* 4–6). In the *Homilies*, the theme occurs once, in the parallel to *Rec.* 4–6 at *Hom.* 8–11.

In light of the large quantity of shared material between *Hom.* 8–11 and *Rec.* 4–6, it is probable that both of them recast the corresponding section of their shared third-century Basic Source. By contrast, there is no counterpart in the *Homilies* to *Rec.* 1.27–71. Since this unit also contains many divergences from the *Homilies* and the rest of *Recognitions*,[54] it has been widely recognized as preserving a special source of either the Basic Source or the *Recognitions*.[55] From an analysis of internal criteria, F. Stanley Jones has argued that *Rec.* 1.27–71 reflects a source that the Basic Source integrated *en bloc*, with only minor revisions and additions, and that this source was written by a "Jewish-Christian" living in Judaea around the year 200 CE.[56] Whatever the precise date and provenance of *Rec.* 1.27–71, we here have a discrete unit that can be labeled "Jewish-Christian," but – as we will see – differs notably from the *Homilies* and the rest of the *Recognitions* on key issues pertaining to the relationship between the Torah, the Gospel, and Jesus' place in salvation history.

To illuminate the historiographical construction of religious identity in these passages, this inquiry will consider their attitudes towards three key issues: [1] the status of Jesus in comparison to Moses, [2] the status of Gentiles in

---

[53] Fonrobert similarly stresses that "In each case, we need to question what 'Christian' and 'Jewish' means to the author(s) of such 'Jewish-Christian' texts, since 'Christian' is not a stable category until late into the period of the Christianization of the Roman imperial power and the consolidation of political-institutional Christian power" ("*Didascalia Apostolorum*," 485).

[54] See Jones, *Ancient Jewish-Christian Source*, 129–31.

[55] Portions of *Rec.* 1.27–71 have been identified with a variety of nonextant sources, most notably the *Kerygma Petrou* or *Kerygmata Petrou* (e.g., Waitz, Cullman) and *Anabathmoi Jakobou* (e.g., Bousset, Schoeps, Strecker, Lüdemann, Van Voorst). For a summary of the history of scholarship on this issue, see Jones, *Ancient Jewish-Christian Source*, 4–33. A handy table listing the major theories about this unit can be found in Van Voorst, *Ascents of James*, 25 (Table 1).

[56] See Jones, *Ancient Jewish Christian Source*, 157–68.

comparison to Jews, and [3] the path(s) to salvation. We will begin with *Rec.* 1.27–71, which uses a summary of Jewish history from Creation to the death of James to argue that Jesus' teachings fulfill and correct those of Moses. Then, we will proceed to examine the Gentile-oriented histories in *Rec.* 4–6 and *Hom.* 8–11. After analyzing two parallel passages that assert the absolute equality of the Torah and the Gospel (*Rec.* 4.5; *Hom.* 8.5–7), we will explore the ways in which *Rec.* 4–6 and *Hom.* 8–11 rework their shared source material, thereby expressing strikingly different attitudes towards the relationship between Jews, Gentiles, and those who follow the teachings of Jesus.

Jews, Gentiles, and Salvation-History in Rec. 1.27–71

The review of history attributed to Peter in *Rec.* 1.27–71 presents an apt starting point for our inquiry.[57] This unit appears to embody two criteria that scholars sometimes use to define texts or persons as "Jewish-Christian": [1] the notion of the "Jewish-Christian" as an ethnic Jew who believes in Jesus and [2] the idea that "Jewish-Christianity" can be identified with the type of Christianity first promulgated among Jews in the Jerusalem Church, in contrast to the type commonly associated with Paul and his mission to the Gentiles.

As for the first criterion, the pseudepigraphy of this source frustrates any certainty about the identity of its author. It is notable, however, that the Pseudo-Peter of *Rec.* 1.27–71 stresses his own Jewish ethnicity (*Rec.* 1.32.1) and exalts Hebrew as the original tongue of humankind and the language "pleasing to God" (Syriac *Rec.* 1.30.5) or "divinely given" (Latin *Rec.* 1.30.5). Moreover, the author of this text depicts the Christian community as one of a number of competing Jewish sects that debate questions of belief amongst themselves (e. g., resurrection, the identity of the Messiah), but he makes no mention of any variance with regard to practice. In fact, the author explicitly states that there is only one difference between Christians and other Jews: the Christians identify Jesus as the Messiah, whereas some Jews think John the Baptist is the Messiah, and other Jews are still waiting for this savior to appear (*Rec.* 1.43.2; 1.50.3; also 1.44.2; 1.60; 1.62.4). Although it is impossible to be certain, these features suggest that the author himself self-identified as Jewish.

At the very least, *Rec.* 1.27–71 has been shaped by a concern to depict the followers of Jesus as a group *within* Judaism, akin to the Pharisees, the Sadducees, and the followers of John the Baptist.[58] As in many pre-Rabbinic and

---

[57] All English translations of *Rec.* 1.27–71 follow Jones' parallel translations of the Syriac and Latin versions, as well as Armenian fragments, in *Ancient Jewish-Christian Source*, 51–109.

[58] Notably, the contrast is not between "Christian" and "Jew" but between true Judaism and Jewish "sects" (i. e., parallel to the role of *minim* [lit. "kinds"] in the Sages' promotion of Rabbinic Judaism as simply "Judaism"). The author even offers an aetiology of Second Temple

Rabbinic Jewish sources, the Sadducees and Samaritans are the main objects of the author's criticism.[59] The former receive condemnation on the basis of their rejection of resurrection (1.54.2–3; 1.56.1; see Matt 22:23/Mark 12:18/Luke 20:27), and the latter are said to share this terrible error, which is compounded by their claims about the primacy of Mt. Gerizim (1.54.4–5; 1.57.1). The depiction of the Pharisees is more complex – but also more intriguing. Whereas the Sadducees and Samaritans are paired by means of their rejection of resurrection and their links to Dositheus (1.54.3, 5),[60] the Pharisees are associated with the followers of John the Baptist (1.54.7–8). They are credited with being baptized by John (cf. Matt 3:7–10) and with possessing "the word of truth received from Moses' tradition" (*verbum veritas tenentes ex Moysi traditione*) that is "the key to the kingdom of heaven."[61] Even though they are critiqued for hiding this key (cf. Matt 23:13), the latter – as Albert Baumgarten notes – is a surprising affirmation of one of the most radical and controversial characteristics of Pharisees and/or early Rabbis: their claim to preserve a tradition no less ancient than the (written) Torah itself.[62]

Similarly ambivalent is the portrayal of their relationship with Jesus' followers. Consistent with the Pharisees' special connection to Moses, it is a Pharisee who here contests the equality of Moses and Jesus (*Rec.* 1.59.1; see below). Yet R. Gamaliel is portrayed positively as the leader of the nation and as a secret be-

---

sectarianism: when "the Slanderer" saw that the Messiah would soon be coming, he "created sects and division" to frustrate his acceptance by his own people (*Rec.* 1.54.1, see also 1.54.9). Consistent with this view, the Syriac version stresses that "the gospel will be made known to the nation as a witness for the healing of the schisms that have arisen so that also your separation [from them] will occur" (*Rec.* 1.64.2; contrast the Latin version: "so that your unbelief may be judged on the basis of their belief").

[59] On the Rabbinic parallels and their significance, see Albert I. Baumgarten, "Literary Evidence for Jewish Christianity in the Galilee," in *The Galilee in Late Antiquity*, ed. Lee I. Levine (New York: JTSA, 1992), 42–43. On Sadducees and John the Baptist more specifically, see now Jones, *Pseudoclementina*, 267–78; Jones, "John the Baptist and his Disciples in the Pseudo-Clementines: A Reappraisal," in *Rediscovering the Apocryphal Continent: New Perspectives on Early Christian and Late Antique Apocryphal Texts and Traditions*, ed. Pierluigi Piovanelli and Tony Burke (WUNT 349; Tübingen: Mohr, 2015), 317–36.

[60] Interestingly, both Dositheus and Simon Magus are here said to have been Sadducees, thus evoking the treatment of Sadducees as a paradigmatic group of *minim* in early Rabbinic sources (see esp. *m. Niddah* 4.2; also *Avot de Rabbi Nathan*A 5); note also the polemics against those who deny resurrection (e. g., *m. Sanhedrin* 10.1; *Bereshit Rabbah* 53.12).

[61] In both cases, the author integrates traditions from the Gospel of Matthew, but revises them towards a more positive characterization of the Pharisees. In Matt 3:7–10, John turns away the "scribes and Pharisees" who wish to be baptized by him; here, they are baptized. In place of the enigmatic reference to the Pharisees "sitting on the seat of Moses" (Matt 23:1) and the accusation that they shut "the kingdom of heaven against humankind" (Matt 23:13) – which, in Matthew, is followed by a series of increasingly fierce denunciations (vv. 15–32) – it is here stressed that they truly possess "the word of truth received from Moses' tradition," and their concealment thereof does not occasion further condemnations.

[62] I.e., the claims at the heart of the later distinction between the Oral Torah and the Written Torah. See Baumgarten, "Literary Evidence," 42; also Chapter Nine in this volume.

liever in Jesus, working behind the scenes to aid James and his community (*Rec.* 1.65.2–68.2).[63] Even as the author appeals to the apostolic heritage cherished by other Christians, he may also, as Baumgarten suggests, view "the Jewish past in much the same way as the Pharisees and/or their Rabbinic heirs did."[64]

The second criterion – continuity (real or claimed) with the Jerusalem Church – is unquestionably present in *Rec.* 1.27–71. In his statements about Jesus and early apostolic history, the author counters the narrative in Acts by depicting James as the true leader of the authentic community of Christians (see, e. g., *Rec.* 1.66). Moreover, the martyrdom of the Jewish James here replaces the martyrdom of the Gentile Stephen in Acts 7, with notable ramifications for the place of Jew and Gentile in Christian salvation history.[65] In this, the anti-Paulism that many scholars associate with "Jewish-Christianity" plays a key role: not only is Paul held responsible for the martyrdom of James, but he is blamed for the failure of the Christian mission among the Jews.[66] After a seven-day sermon defending the authenticity of Jesus' claim to be the Messiah to his fellow Jews, James had finally succeeded in persuading "all the people together with the high priest" to be baptized (*Rec.* 1.69.8). At that very moment, however, the "enemy" Paul violently burst into Temple, accused James of being a magician, and provoked the priests into joining him in slaughtering James and many of his followers (*Rec.* 1.70). This necessitates the Christian mission to the Gentiles, since the number of the chosen remains unfilled (see *Rec.* 1.50). Rather than aetiologizing the Gentile mission with reference to the Jews' "hard-heartedness" or their perennial persecution of prophets, the author here points to the alleged scheming of a figure celebrated in proto-orthodox Christian circles as "The Apostle" and, perhaps more importantly, embraced by Marcion.

The message is clear: the real enemy of Jesus' followers is not the Jewish nation that now remains unconvinced, but rather Paul. The end of this unit poignantly describes Paul promising the high priest Caiaphas to "massacre all those who believe in Jesus" and then setting off "for Damascus, to go as one carrying letters from them, so that when he got there the nonbelievers might help him and might destroy those who believe" (*Rec.* 1.71.3). Although this passage echoes

---

[63] Cf. Acts 5:34; 22:3. On late antique Christian traditions about R. Gamaliel – e. g., the tale about the discovery of Gamaliel's tomb in 415 CE in *Epistula Luciani* (PL 41.807ff) and the fifth-/sixth-century *Gospel of Gamaliel* – and their possible link to "Jewish-Christian" traditions, see Günter Stemberger, *Jews and Christians in the Holy Land: Palestine in the Fourth Century* (trans. R. Tuschling; Edinburgh: T&T Clark, 2000), 108–12; M.-A. van den Oudenrijn, "The Gospel of Gamaliel," in *NTA* 1:558–60.

[64] Baumgarten, "Literary Evidence," 43. Notably, Baumgarten does not here distinguish between *Homilies* and *Recognitions*, let alone any strata therein. His evidence for this assertion, however, comes from only two units: *Rec.* 1.27–71 (esp. 54) and *Hom.* 11 (esp. 28; on which see below).

[65] On *Rec.* 1 and Acts 7, see Jones, *Pseudoclementina*, 211–12.

[66] Cf. Eusebius, *Hist. eccl.* 2.9. See Lüdemann, *Opposition to Paul*, 183–85.

Acts 9:1–2 (also 22:5), we here find no hint of Paul's subsequent vision of the risen Christ or his commission as the "apostle of the Gentiles" (Acts 9:3–22; 22:6–16). In fact, the narrative setting – Peter's account of apostolic history to Clement, well after these events took place – serves to imply that Paul is *still* "the enemy" of James and the authentic Christian community, thereby suggesting that Paul's apostleship and preaching are the deceptive continuation of his failed efforts to destroy them through violence.

Are these features sufficient to make *Rec.* 1.27–71 "Jewish-Christian" (as opposed, for instance, to merely anti-Pauline)? It is hardly a coincidence that, by a certain definition, the material about Jesus and the apostles at the end of this review of history (i.e., *Rec.* 1.39–71) is paradigmatically "Jewish-Christian," since these very passages proved central to Baur's reconstruction of apostolic "Jewish-Christianity." Consequently, we must further ask whether this unit's description of the rest of human history depicts the ideal believer as simultaneously Jewish and Christian in a sense that differs from the negotiation of these identities that is usually accepted as "Christian."

Does the preceding treatment of early human history (i.e., *Rec.* 1.24–38) depart notably from similar accounts in other early Christian sources? The author here begins by enumerating the twenty-one generations before Abraham and recounts the progressive decline of humankind with special appeal to the spread of nonmonotheistic worship. Here, the first transgression was not the sin of Adam but rather the unnamed sins promulgated by the "sons of God" of Gen 6:1–4, here interpreted euhemeristically as righteous men who became corrupted by lust (*Rec.* 1.29). This leads to the Flood, from which only Noah and his family were saved, and it prompts God's "first commandment": the prohibition against eating blood (1.30). The subsequent degradation of humankind is marked by the spread of fire-worship and idolatry (see esp. *Rec.* 1.30), and this moral decline continues unhindered until the birth of Abraham, the father of "our race, the Hebrews, who are also called the Jews" (Syriac *Rec.* 1.32.1).[67] The assertion that the "prophet of truth" revealed "everything" to Abraham (*Rec.* 1.33) represents the only possible clue to the "Christian" nature of this narrative,[68] which otherwise resembles – and draws heavily from – Second Temple Jewish writings like *Jubilees*.[69]

---

[67] Latin *Rec.* 1.32.1: "Abraham, from whom the race of us Hebrews is descended."

[68] I say "possible" because the designation "true prophet"/"prophet of truth" is not quite as clear as we might wish. We can readily interpret this "true prophet"/"prophet of truth" as Jesus (1.44.6), who appears first to Abraham (1.33.1) and then to Moses (1.34.3 in Latin and Armenian). The Syriac version of the latter, however, refers to Moses too as the "prophet of truth" (see also Syriac 1.34.6 in contrast to Armenian and Latin), thus evoking the doctrine of a single "true prophet" who entered into a succession of figures (e.g., Adam, Moses, Jesus) in *Hom.* 1.19, 3.17–28; on the latter, see further Strecker, *Judenchristentum*, 145–53.

[69] On the use of *Jubilees* in this unit, see Jones, *Ancient Jewish Christian Source*, 138–39. See further now Eibert Tigchelaar, "Manna-Eaters and Man-Eaters: Food of Giants and Men in

The material that follows, however, is dominated by one main theme: the polemic against animal sacrifice. The author achieves this goal through a careful argument that distances the biblical precepts related to the Temple cult from the rest of the Torah given by God at Mount Sinai.[70] Moses himself is exalted as a prophet (*Rec.* 1.34.4; 1.36.2),[71] but he is here held responsible for the institution of sacrifice among the Jews – albeit begrudgingly and for solely pragmatic aims: after the incident with the Golden Calf,[72] Moses realizes that the Jews must be distracted at all costs from the desire to practice the idolatry that tainted them in Egypt (*Rec.* 1.35–36), and he therefore sets aside a single place for his people to sacrifice to the one God (*Rec.* 1.36–37, 39). The author sees the rest of Jewish history as God's attempt to wean the Jews off of sacrifice, by periodically exiling them to other lands in order to encourage their adoption of other forms of monotheistic worship (*Rec.* 1.37.3–4).

Notably, this argument recalls the proto-orthodox/orthodox polemic against the Jewish sacrificial cult, albeit with important distinctions: rather than singling out the Jews as a "hard-hearted," disobedient, and sinful people who are particularly prone to the idolatrous worship of demons (e. g., Justin, *Dial.* 19; 22; 92; Irenaeus, *Adv. haer.* 4.15.2; Tertullian, *Adv. Marc.* 2.18),[73] the author here takes pains to associate these practices with the Canaanites and Babylonians (*Rec.* 1.30.2, 4, 7) and to depict the Jews' temptations to idolatry as a result of their "evil upbringing with the Egyptians" (Syriac *Rec.* 1.36.1; see also 1.35.1, 5–6).[74] Furthermore, the polemic against sacrifice in *Rec.* 1.27–71 is pursued apart from any broader denigration of Jewish Torah observance.[75]

---

the Pseudo-Clementine *Homilies* 8," in *The Pseudo-Clementines*, ed. Jan N. Bremmer (Studies on Early Christian Apocrypha 10; Leuven: Peeters, 2010), 92–114; Kelley Coblentz Bautch, "The Pseudo-Clementine Homilies' Use of Jewish Pseudepigrapha," in Piovanelli and Burke, eds., *Rediscovering the Apocryphal Continent*, 337–50; Annette Yoshiko Reed, "Retelling Biblical Retellings: Epiphanius, the Pseudo-Clementines, and the Reception History of *Jubilees*," in *Tradition, Transmission, and Transformation from Second Temple Literature through Judaism and Christianity in Late Antiquity*, ed. Menahem Kister, Hillel Newman, Michael Segal, and Ruth Clements (STDJ 113; Leiden: Brill, 2015), 304–21.

[70] Notably, the author also privileges the Ten Commandments over the rest of the Torah (*Rec.* 1.35.2).

[71] See parallel comparison of Syriac, Armenian, and Latin translations in Jones, *Ancient Jewish Christian Source*, 61.

[72] Cf. Stephen's speech in Acts 7, for which the Golden Calf incident also serves as the key turning point – in this case, the point at which "God turned away from them and handed them over to worship the host of heaven" (7:42). See Pier Cesare Bori, *The Golden Calf and the Origins of the Anti-Jewish Controversy* (trans. D. Ward; Atlanta: Scholars Press, 1990).

[73] See further Simon, *Verus Israel*, 167–69.

[74] The gist of the Latin is the same, although its rhetoric is softer: "When Moses, that faithful and wise steward, perceived that the vice of sacrificing to idols had been deeply ingrained into the people *from their association with the Egyptians* ..."

[75] Cf. Justin's argument that the laws about sacrifice, circumcision, food, festivals, and Shabbat are only in the Torah because God used these measures to punish the Jewish people and to set them apart as a pariah among the nations (*Dial.* 16–22).

Nevertheless, the issue of sacrifice proves central to the author's assertion that Jesus' teachings are the fulfillment and completion of those of Moses. In his view, this is the main reason that God sent the "true prophet" Jesus: to abolish sacrifice and to preach, in its place, baptism for the remission of sins (see esp. *Rec.* 1.39.1). According to this retelling of Jewish history, Moses himself anticipated the coming of a second prophet when he instituted the Temple and sacrificial laws (1.37); he took on the first half of the task of instituting proper worship among his people (i. e., cleansing his people of Egyptian idolatry), with full knowledge that a "prophet like me" would come in the future to complete the second half (i. e., the abolishment of sacrifice and promulgation of baptism).

Within the account of apostolic history, Jesus' superiority to Moses is stated explicitly, in the context of debates between his followers and other Jews (*Rec.* 1.59.1–3):

Hearing this, a certain Pharisee chided Philip because he put Jesus on a level with Moses. Answering him, Bartholomew boldly declared that we do not only say that Jesus was equal to Moses, but that he was greater than him (*quidam non dicimus Iesum aequalem Moysi, sed maiorem*),[76] because Moses was indeed a prophet – as Jesus was also – but Moses was not the Messiah/Christ, as Jesus was. And therefore he is doubtless greater who is both a prophet and the Messiah/Christ, as opposed to he who is only a prophet.

Just as the polemic against sacrifice can be read as a pro-Jewish variant of an anti-Jewish trope of proto-orthodox/orthodox Christian historiography (see esp. Justin, *Dial.* 19; 22),[77] so this statement about Moses and Jesus evokes the supersessionist attitudes common among proto-orthodox Christians.[78]

---

[76] In light of *Rec.* 1.60 (discussed below), it may be significant that Bartholomew here frames the superiority of Jesus to Moses as something that "we say," rather than simply asserting it.

[77] Oskar Skarsaune has argued that Justin draws this and other traditions from a "Jewish-Christian" source related to the Pseudo-Clementines (*The Proof from Prophecy: A Study in Justin Martyr's Proof-text Tradition: Text-type, Provenance, Theological Profile* [NTSup 56; Leiden: Brill, 1987], 316–20; so too David Rokéah, *Justin Martyr and the Jews* [Hebrew] [Jerusalem: Dinur Center, 1998], 34–39). We should not, however, close off the possibility that this author may instead be dependent on Justin's writings and rework his arguments in order to paint a different picture of the Jews – just as he recasts traditions from Acts to counter its account of early apostolic history.

[78] This becomes even clearer as the passage continues: "After following out this train of argument, he [i. e., Bartholomew] stopped. After him, James the son of Alphaeus gave an address to the people, with the aim of showing that we are not to believe in Jesus on the ground that the prophets foretold concerning him, but rather that we are to believe that the prophets were really prophets, because the Messiah/Christ bears testimony to them; for it is the presence and coming of Christ that shows that they are truly prophets, since testimony must be borne by the superior to his inferiors, not by the inferiors to their superior." Interestingly, this passage has many parallels with *Rec.* 1.60, which records a debate on the relative status of John the Baptist and Jesus: "And, behold, one of the disciples of John asserted that John was the Christ, and not Jesus, inasmuch as Jesus himself declared that John was greater than all men and all prophets. 'If,' he said, 'he is greater than all, then he must be held to be greater than Moses and than Jesus himself. And, if he is the greatest of all, then must he be the Messiah/Christ.'" For the surprising conclusion to this debate, see below.

Yet it is significant that the author consistently describes and defends Jesus as "the image of Moses that had previously been announced by Moses" (see *Rec.* 1.36.2, 1.40.4–41.1) and, moreover, makes no attempt to argue that God has disowned His chosen nation in favor of the Gentiles. In fact, he paints a surprisingly sympathetic portrait of non-Christian Jews. The priests – those who benefit most from the Jewish sacrificial cult – are said to have recognized how much they stood to lose if "the entire people came to our faith" (*Rec.* 1.43.1), and they thus scheme against both Jesus and his followers. By contrast, the majority of the Jewish people did not recognize the truth of Jesus' teachings simply because "they had been educated to believe these things [about the Temple and sacrifice] for so long" (Latin *Rec.* 1.40.2).[79] Even in the course of describing the Jews' rejection of Jesus, the author makes efforts to stress that belief in Jesus is the only difference between Christians and other Jews (*Rec.* 1.43.2). Moreover, non-Jews are here granted the chance for salvation because Paul undermined the Jews' acceptance of the inheritance that was rightly theirs. And, even as the text describes the failure of James' (almost successful) conversion of the Jewish people in its entirety, it refrains from suggesting that individual Jews cannot or will not number among the chosen.[80]

Seen from an inner-Christian perspective, *Rec.* 1.27–71's review of history can be read as an attempt to articulate a vision of Christianity that is not predicated on the denigration of Jews or the severing of the church's traditional ties to Judaism. Is it also possible, then, to read this source as a Jewish text? Most significant in this regard is the primacy of the author's polemic against animal sacrifice. In its emphasis on this particular issue, *Rec.* 1.27–71 fits well in the context of Jewish attempts to come to terms with the tragic events of 70 and 135 CE (e. g., *4 Ezra, 2 Baruch*).[81] Furthermore, the polemic in *Rec.* 1.27–71 not only presupposes that the Gentiles' idolatrous and polytheistic worship is far worse, but it also chooses to critique the Jews for something that they – at the time of the author – simply no longer do.

---

[79] Contrast the Syriac version, which here states: "For they are people who are more wretched than any, who are willing to believe neither good nor bad for the sake of virtue." That both versions go on to condemn the nonbelieving majority without condemning "the Jews" *en tout* (see esp. *Rec.* 1.40.3) suggests that the Latin is closer to the original Greek.

[80] See also the Syriac version of *Rec.* 1.64.2, as discussed above.

[81] Whereas proto-orthodox Christian authors like Justin connect the Roman destruction of the Temple and the establishment of Aelia Capitolina to the Jews' alleged violence against Jesus (e. g., Justin, *Dial.* 25.5; 26.1; 92; 108.3; *1 Apol.* 32.4–6; 47–49; 53.2–3), this source associates these tragedies with their "sacrificing after the end of the time for sacrificing" (e. g., *Rec.* 1.64.1–2). Accordingly, the blame for the Jews' refusal to listen to Jesus' message is placed particularly on the priests, as is clear from the account of Peter's prediction of the destruction of the Temple and the erection of an "abomination of desolation in its place" in *Rec.* 1.64–65. The priests grow quite irate after Peter's statements, but R. Gamaliel calms them, saying: "Leave these men alone, for if this matter is of human origin, it will come to nothing. But if it is of God, why are you transgressing in vain and achieving nothing?"

Although the author's argument about sacrifice rests on a reading of the Torah as a combination of God's eternal precepts and Moses' own attempts to guide his people,[82] his choice to depict *this* issue as the primary area in which Jesus corrects the Mosaic covenant ironically has the effect of downplaying the differences between him and his non-Christian Jewish contemporaries. Inasmuch as the author repeatedly stresses that Christ-belief is the only thing distinguishing James' community from other Jews, it is difficult to imagine any radical differences in praxis existed between them;[83] indeed, even the addition of baptism can be readily situated in a broader Jewish discourse about purity and piety in the absence of the Temple, particularly since *Rec.* 1.27–71 promotes this practice as a substitute for sacrifice (see esp. *Rec.* 1.39.2).

Also notable is the attitude implied in *Rec.* 1.60, which depicts Jesus' followers and other Jews arguing about the identity of the Messiah. One might expect the argument to end with the unquestioned victory of Jesus' followers, but the author portrays the groups as coming to an absolute impasse. To this, Barnabas offers a surprisingly tolerant solution:

Barnabas … began to exhort the people that they should not regard Jesus with hatred, nor speak evil of him. For it is much more proper for the one who does not know Jesus, or is in doubt concerning him, to love rather than hate him (*multo enim esse rectius, etiam ignoranti vel dubitanti de Iesu, amare eum quam odisse*). Latin *Rec.* 1.60.6

Although the author is firm in his opinion that Jesus is the Messiah, he appears to understand why some Jews might not think so – not only on the grounds of ignorance, but also because of doubt.[84] Rather than condemning them outright, he encourages them to embrace Jesus in a more limited capacity (i. e., like the

---

[82] Cf. the doctrine of the false pericopes found elsewhere in the Pseudo-Clementines (e. g., *Hom.* 2.38), which posits that the Torah contains some later emendations; see further Strecker, *Judenchristentum*, 166–86. For the *Homilies'* approach to Torah exegesis, see now Donald H. Carlson, *Jewish-Christian Interpretation of the Pentateuch in the Pseudo-Clementine Homilies* (Minneapolis: Fortress, 2013).

[83] Notably, the author is not forthcoming on the question of primary concern for modern scholars: must the Gentile converts undergo circumcision? Strecker tentatively posits a positive answer with appeal to *Rec.* 1.33.5, which – in the context of explaining how the practice of circumcision amongst "some of the Indians and the Egyptians" was the result of the travels of Abraham's progeny – calls circumcision "the proof and sign of purity" (*Judenchristentum*, 251). Jones, however, downplays its significance: he identifies *Rec.* 1.33.5 as part of the Basic Source's additions to the original source (*Ancient Jewish Christian Source*, 160) and goes on to speculate that "the very notion of calling the nations to complete the number shown to Abraham (*Rec.* 1.42; compare *Rec.* 1.63.2, 64.2) contradicts the view that these Gentiles should first have to convert to Judaism (e. g., submission to circumcision) before entering Christianity" (p. 164). Even if we accept Jones' text-critical argument, the latter proves problematic; we know too little to conflate so confidently the support of a Gentile mission with the acceptance of non-circumcised Christ-believers, especially since the Gentile mission accepted by the author is so firmly distinguished from the Pauline one. Although the text's own lack of interest in this issue precludes any certainty on our part, Strecker's view strikes me as more plausible.

[84] Interestingly, the latter option is omitted in the Syriac version of this verse.

followers of John, who are said to accept him as a prophet).[85] Seen from this perspective, the author's Christian supersessionism looks a lot like Jewish messianism, and his viewpoint does indeed seem both "Jewish" and "Christian," insofar as he portrays the ideal Christian as a Jew who accepts Jesus as the Messiah, without wholly condemning those Jews who do not.

Two Teachers of Truth: Moses and Jesus in Hom. 8.5–7 and Rec. 4.5

Many of the same issues are addressed by the parallel accounts of Peter's sojourn in Tripolis in *Hom.* 8–11 and *Rec.* 4–6. Here, however, we find very different explanations of the relationship between the Torah and the Gospel, which fit different modern definitions of "Jewish-Christianity."

Both accounts can be divided according to the different audiences depicted therein. In each, Peter first speaks to his followers about the equality of Moses and Jesus (*Hom.* 8.5–7 = *Rec.* 4.5) and then proceeds to preach a series of sermons to gathered crowds of Gentiles. In *Hom.* 8–11 and *Rec.* 4–6 alike, Peter's initial words to his Jewish and Gentile followers function to contextualize his public preaching to nonbelieving Gentiles by offering a broader perspective on the relationship between Jewish and Gentile paths to salvation. Here, both the *Homilies* and *Recognitions* articulate a soteriology that can be termed "Jewish-Christian" insofar as it appeals to the equality of Moses, Jesus, and their respective teachings to assert the equality of the Torah and the Gospel as paths to salvation.[86]

In *Rec.* 4.5 and *Hom.* 8.5–7, Peter first cites the Jews' special dispensation through Moses, as a "teacher of truth." In *Rec.* 4.5.1–5, the apostle uses this assertion as the basis for his argument that Gentiles too have now been given the chance for salvation, through their very own "teacher of truth":

For so also it was given to the people of the Hebrews from the beginning, that they should love Moses and believe his word, as it is written: "the people believed God and His servant

---

[85] It is notable that the negative exemplar is the high priest Caiaphas, who is here portrayed as hating Jesus (*Rec.* 1.61–62).

[86] Especially since scholars are often tempted to see "universalism" as a "Christian" characteristic and "particularism" as a "Jewish" characteristic, we should note that the concept of two different paths to salvation fits far better with Jewish tradition than with Christian tradition. Within the former, we find some affirmations that righteous Gentiles will have a place in the World to Come, as well as discussions about the more limited requirements for righteousness (i.e., the Noachite commandments) that God places upon Gentiles (see, e.g., *t. Avodah Zarah* end; *t. Sanhedrin* 13.2). By contrast, the vast majority of Christian soteriological traditions are emphatically "one way": peoples of different ethnicity can be saved, but only if they follow the one, single path opened by Jesus. Seen from this perspective, Christianity is much more "particularistic" and Judaism more "universalistic," thereby underlining the profoundly problematic nature of the dichotomy. See further Anders Runesson, "Particularistic Judaism and Universalistic Christianity? Some Critical Remarks on Terminology and Theology," *Journal of Greco-Roman Christianity and Judaism* 1 (2000): 120–44, esp. 125–27.

Moses" (Exod 14:31). What was therefore a special gift from God toward the nation of the Hebrews, we see now to be given also to those who are called from among the Gentiles to the faith (*quod ergo fuit proprii muneris a deo erga Hebraeorum gentum, hoc nunc videmus dari etiam his qui ex gentibus convocantur ad fidem*). The method of works is put into the power and will of everyone, and this is their own. But to have an affection towards a teacher of truth, this is a gift of the heavenly Father (*desiderium vero habere erga doctorem veritatis, hoc a patre caelesti donatum est*). And, salvation is in this: that you do the will of one whom you have conceived a love and affection through the gift of God; lest that saying of his, which he spoke, be addressed to you: "Why do call you me 'lord, lord,' and do not what I say?" (Luke 6:46). It is thus the special gift bestowed by God upon the Hebrews that they believe Moses, and the special gift bestowed upon the Gentiles is that they value Jesus (*est ergo proprii muneris a deo concessi Hebraeis, ut Moysi credant, gentibus autem, ut Iesum diligant*).

The contrast with *Rec.* 1.27–71 is striking. This passage does not exalt Jesus over Moses, but neither does it depict Jesus as the true Messiah of the Jews. Instead, Jesus is portrayed as the teacher of the Gentiles, just as Moses is the teacher of the Jews.

The parallel passage in the *Homilies* focuses on the issue of proper praxis. In *Hom.* 8.5, the assertion of the Jews' special dispensation through Moses functions as the basis for Pseudo-Peter's argument that the salvation of the Gentiles is dependent on their good works:

For even the Hebrews who believe Moses but do not observe the things spoken by him are not saved, unless they observe the things that were spoken to them ... Since, therefore, both for the Hebrews and for those who are called from the nations (Ἐβραίοις τε καὶ τοῖς ἀπὸ ἐθνῶν κεκλημένοις), to believe in teachers of truth is from God, while good deeds are left to each one to do by his own judgment, the reward is justly bestowed upon those who act well. For there would have been no need of Moses or of the coming of Jesus, if they would have understood of themselves what is reasonable (οὔτε γὰρ ἂν Μωυσέως οὔτε τῆς τοῦ Ἰησοῦ παρουσίας χρεία ἦν, εἴπερ ἀφ' ἑαυτῶν τὸ εὔλογον νοεῖν ἐβούλοντο). Neither is there salvation in believing in teachers and calling them "lords." (cf. Matt 7:21; Luke 6:46)

Interestingly, the version in the *Homilies* emphasizes proper praxis to such a degree that *this* Pseudo-Peter even downplays the importance of Moses and Jesus. For, according to the *Homilies'* authors/redactors, God sent both teachers to reassert what human beings should have already known to be true and rational. As a result, mere faith in these teachers as exalted figures is sorely misguided, as *Hom.* 8.5 asserts by alluding to the saying of Jesus quoted in *Rec.* 4.5.4 (i.e., Luke 6:46).

In both cases, the example of Moses is used to explain the importance of Jesus for the Gentiles. Interestingly, however, *Hom.* 8.5 appears to presuppose what *Rec.* 4.5 must assert with a scriptural prooftext, namely, that the Jews were granted long ago the salvation now accessible to Gentiles. In arguing that the Gentiles who believe in Jesus should follow the example of the Jews in following their "teacher of truth" through their actions and in seeing this teacher as a pedagogical figure, instead of a soteriological one, the authors/redactors of the *Homilies* assume that its audience already accepts the (continued) chosenness of the Jews and, moreover, sees them as a model for monotheistic piety.

Both the *Recognitions* and the *Homilies* then turn to the topic of Jewish and Gentile salvation. In *Rec.* 4.5.5–6, Pseudo-Peter cites another saying of Jesus to expand on its "two-ways" model of salvation:

For this also the master (*magister*) intimated when he said, "I will confess to you, O Father, Lord of heaven and earth, because you have concealed these things from the wise and prudent, and you have revealed them to babes" (Matt 11:25/Luke 10:21). By which it is certainly declared that the people of the Hebrews, who were instructed out of the Law, did not know him (*per quod utique declaratur, quia Hebraeorum populus qui ex lege eruditus est, ignoravit eum*).[87] But the people of the Gentiles have acknowledged Jesus and venerate him, on which account they too will be saved (*populus autem gentium agnovit Iesum et venerator, propter quod et salvabitur*), not only by acknowledging him, but also by doing his will.

Although the ignorant "wise and prudent" of Matt 11:25/Luke 10:21 are here identified with the Jews and the knowing "babes" with the Gentiles, the authors/ redactors of the *Recognitions* do not use this saying to critique non-Christian Jews, nor to depict them as dispossessed heirs to God's promises. Rather, *Rec.* 4.5.6 explains this saying to mean simply that "the people of the Hebrews, who were instructed out of the Law, did not know him (i.e., Jesus), but the people of the Gentiles have acknowledged Jesus and venerate him." The text goes on to assert that believers – among both the Jews and the Gentiles – should strive to accept both teachers:

But he who is of the Gentiles and who has it from God to value Jesus should also have it of his own purpose to believe Moses too (*debet autem is qui ex gentibus est et ex deo habet, ut diligat Iesum, proprii habere propositi, ut credat et Moysi*). And again, the Hebrew, who has it from God to believe Moses, should have it also of his own purpose to believe in Jesus (*et rursus Hebraeus qui ex deo habet, ut credat Moysi, habere debet ex proposito suo, ut credat in Iesum*) – so that each of them, having in himself something of the divine gift and something of his own exertion, may be perfect by both (*sit ex utroque perfectus*). For concerning such a one our lord (*dominus noster*) spoke, as of a rich man, who brings forth from his treasures things new and old. (*Rec.* 4.5.7–9; cf. Matt 13:52)

By distinguishing between the divine gift of salvation and human efforts at perfection, *Rec.* 4.5 deftly avoids condemning either Jews who do not accept Jesus or Gentiles who do not accept Moses. Nevertheless, *Rec.* here encourages both Jew and Gentile to recognize the two as equally "teachers of truth" – and clearly asserts the superiority of those who do.

---

[87] Cf. Paul's critique of those Jews who "rely on the Law and boast of your relation to God, and know his will, and determine what is best because you are instructed from the Law (κατηχούμενος ἐκ τοῦ νόμου)" in Rom 2:17–19.

The parallel passage in *Hom.* 8.6 also expounds on the relationship between Jews, Gentiles, Moses, and Jesus with appeal to Matt 11:25/Luke 10:21, albeit with different results:

For this reason, Jesus is concealed from the Hebrews who have taken Moses as their teacher (ἀπὸ μὲν Ἑβραίων τὸν Μωυσῆν διδάσκαλον εἰληφότων καλύπτεται ὁ Ἰησοῦς), and Moses is hidden from those who have believed Jesus (ἀπὸ δὲ τῶν Ἰησοῦ πεπιστευκότων ὁ Μωυσῆς ἀποκρύπτεται). For, since there is a single teaching by both (μιᾶς γὰρ δι' ἀμφοτέρων διδασκαλίας), God accepts (ἀποδέχεται) one who has believed either of these. But, to believe a teacher (τὸ πιστεύειν διδασκάλῳ) is for the sake of doing (ἕνεκα τοῦ ποιεῖν) the things spoken by God. And our lord himself says that this is so: "I thank you, Father of heaven and earth, because you have concealed these things from the wise and prudent, and you have revealed them to sucking babes" (Matt 11:25/Luke 10:21). Thus God Himself (αὐτὸς ὁ θεὸς) has concealed a teacher from some, who foreknew what they should do (τοῖς μὲν ἔκρυψεν διδάσκαλον ὡς προεγνωκόσιν ἃ δεῖ πράττειν), and He has revealed [him] to others, who are ignorant about what they should do (τοῖς δὲ ἀπεκάλυψεν ὡς ἀγνοοῦσιν ἃ χρὴ ποιεῖν).

Jesus' saying about the "wise" and "ignorant" (Matt 11:25/Luke 10:21) is here interpreted to mean that God concealed Jesus from the Jews precisely because they already know "what they ought to do." When considered in light of the *Homilies'* previous assertion that neither Moses nor Jesus would have been sent if humans had simply done what they know to be rational, the ramifications are striking. Above, we noted that *Rec.* 1.27–74 excuses those Jews who do not recognize Jesus as Messiah by placing the blame on the evil Paul. The *Homilies* here goes even further, explaining the rejection of Jesus by Jews as the result of God's own choice to hide him from this people and send him only to the Gentiles.

The version in the *Homilies* then goes on to explain its theory of concealment. First, it stresses that neither Jews nor Gentiles are condemned for their ignorance of the "teacher" of the other, since this division of labor conforms with God's will; "God accepts one who believes in either," so neither is superior to the other. The authors/redactors add, however, two important qualifications: [1] all must do the things commanded by their own teacher, and [2] they must not "hate him whom they do not know" (*Hom.* 8.7.1–2).[88] The *Homilies* then comments on each qualification with appeal to a saying of Jesus.

On the topic of proper practice, the *Homilies'* Pseudo-Peter appeals to the same saying quoted in *Rec.* 4.5.4 (i. e., Luke 6:46) to stress that "it is not saying that will profit anyone, but doing; by all means, therefore, is there need of good works!" (*Hom.* 8.7.4). On the value of recognizing both the Torah and the Gos-

---

[88] Does this mean that Jews must accept Jesus as the Messiah? Interestingly, the theme of "hating" is not present in *Rec.* 4 and thus likely not present at this point in their shared source. Here, *Homilies* appears to have integrated a portion of *Rec.* 1.27–71, which it otherwise omits: Bartholomew's statements in *Rec.* 1.60 (see above).

pel, *Hom.* then alludes to Matt 13:52 (as quoted in *Rec.* 4.5.8) and concludes by exalting the one who "has been thought worthy to recognize by himself both as preaching one doctrine" (καταξιωθείη τοὺς ἀμφοτέρους ἐπιγνῶναι ὡς μιᾶς διδασκαλίας ὑπ' αὐτῶν κεκηρυγμένης) and who thus "has been counted rich in God, understanding both the old things as new in time, and the new things as old" (*Hom.* 8.7.5). Whereas the parallel in *Rec.* 4.5 encourages Jews and Gentiles to perfect themselves by supplementing the knowledge of their own teacher with knowledge about that of the other, *Hom.* 8.7 implies that few are worthy enough to realize that the two teachings, new and old, are really the same.

Both *Hom.* 8 and *Rec.* 4 exalt those whom some scholars might call "Jewish-Christians" (or even "Christian Jews"),[89] in the sense of people who view the Torah and the Gospel as equal in soteriological value. In this, both *Hom.* 8 and *Rec.* 4 depart from *Rec.* 1.27–71, which depicts Jesus as the Jewish messiah, Christianity as the correct sect of Judaism, and Gentile believers as filling the slots for the saved left empty by unbelieving Jews (a point that remains significant, even if it is a result of the malicious mechanizations of Paul). Nevertheless, the two parallel texts themselves express different perspective on the relationship between the followers of Moses ("Hebrews"/"Jews") and the followers of Jesus (whom we might, although the text does not, call "Christians").

For both the *Homilies* and *Recognitions*, any exaltation or worship of a teacher is misplaced, since God's purpose lies in the encouragement of good works among his creatures. Of the two, *Homilies* develops the more coherent (and more radical) argument. Whereas *Recognitions* proposes that Moses and Jesus opened two separate paths to salvation through praxis, *Homilies* asserts that the teachings of the two are essentially the same and, moreover, consist of the proclamation of principles that are inherent to all humankind. Within the *Homilies*, this means that neither Jew nor Gentile can be condemned for not knowing the teacher meant for the other – not only because God has chosen to conceal Jesus from the Jews, but also because Moses and Jesus are really two messengers with the exact same message.

Demons, Jews, and Gentiles in Hom. 8–11 and Rec. 4–6

The differences between *Hom.* 8–11 and *Rec.* 4–6 become even more apparent when we consider their subsequent descriptions of Peter's public preaching to nonbelieving Gentiles. In contrast to *Rec.* 1.27–71's account of the history of

---

[89] Bruce Malina, for instance, suggests that from a purely terminological standpoint, the label "Jewish-Christian" more aptly describes proto-orthodox and orthodox Christianity, which (in contrast to Christians like Marcion) actively integrates Jewish elements into their Christian belief. Those who saw the Torah and the Gospel as two equal parts of the same message, without subordinating the former to the latter or claiming that the church superseded Israel, are – in his view – better termed "Christian Jews" ("Jewish Christianity or Christian Judaism," 46–50).

the Jews, these units focus on the history of the Gentiles and the demons that enslave them. In both, Peter attempts to correct the Gentiles' ignorance about the supernatural influence that guides them and the illnesses that infect them by describing the origins, spread, and methods of the demons. Towards this goal, the apostle associates the demons with the fallen angels (*Hom.* 8.7ff; *Rec.* 4.26; cf. *Rec.* 4.8); recounts the long history of their corruption of humankind through innovations in improper worship (e. g., *Hom.* 9.2–7); and explains how they infiltrate the human mind by pretending to be gods (*Hom.* 9.13, 9.16; *Rec.* 4.19) and how they sneak into the body through the wine and meat that has been consecrated to the idols of these false gods (*Hom.* 8.20, 9.8–10; *Rec.* 4.16), thereby causing suffering and disease (e. g., *Hom.* 9.12). Both texts depict that idolatry as the root cause of all human wickedness and suffering (*Rec.* 4.31, 5.2–4; *Hom.* 9.14, 11.15), and they proclaim baptism and monotheism as the ways for Gentiles to free themselves from the demons (*Rec.* 4.17–18; *Hom.* 8.22, 9.11, 9.19) and thereby return to their original state as the "image of God" (e. g., *Hom.* 10.6, 11.7).

In light of the ample thematic and linguistic parallels, it is likely that the two units are both based on the same parts of the Basic Source. It is notable, however, that these sections are marked by formal and structural differences between the *Homilies* and *Recognitions*.[90] As such, the two versions of Peter's Tripolis sermons provide us with an ideal opportunity to see how each set of fourth-century authors/redactors recast, reshaped, and supplemented their shared Basic Source according to their own views about the "pagan" past, the salvation of the Gentiles, and the relative status of Gentiles and Jews after the earthly sojourn of the "true prophet."[91]

Their distinct approaches to Gentile salvation are perhaps most evident in their demonologies. The *Homilies*, consistent with its earlier assertion that the teachings of Moses and Jesus are one, depicts baptism and the abandonment of idols as the means by which Gentiles can become more like Jews, who are not enslaved by demons. In *Hom.* 9.16, for instance, Peter argues for the causal connection between idolatry and demonic possession by citing the "fact" that

---

[90] E. g., the *Homilies* structures the material into four sermons, whereas the *Recognitions* has only three. See further Strecker, *Judenchristentum*, 70–75, and esp. the chart on p. 75.

[91] Source-critical inquiries into the *Homilies* and *Recognitions* are often based on the tacit assumption that the authors/redactors responsible for composing them are mere tradents and compilers of earlier material. In my view, this proves problematic, due to the nature of Jewish and Christian literary production in Late Antiquity. Contrary to our modern concept of the "author" as an autonomous creative agent and the resultant tendency to view all later literary hands as only adulterating the purity of the "original" text, the literary practices of authorship, redaction, collection, and reproduction were not always so clear-cut prior to the invention of the printing press; just as the named authors of premodern times often integrated large selections from earlier texts and drew heavily from source-collections, so redactors, compilers, and anthologists often displayed an "authorial" creativity that significantly shaped the meaning of texts in their final form.

the demons "do not appear to the Jews." After explaining to the Gentile crowds how baptism can empower them against these evil creatures (*Hom.* 9.19), this Pseudo-Peter assures them:

Do not then suppose that we do not fear demons on this account, that we are of a different nature. For we are of the same nature (φύσεως), but not of the same worship (θρησκείας). Therefore – being not only much but altogether superior to you – we do not begrudge you becoming like us (ὄντες καὶ ὑμᾶς τοιούτους γενέσθαι οὐ φθονοῦμεν). Rather, we counsel you, knowing that all these [demons] honor and fear beyond measure those who are reconciled to God. (*Hom.* 9.20.1–2)

From the comment in *Hom.* 9.16, it is clear that Peter's "we" refers to "we Jews." In stark contrast to the proto-orthodox/orthodox Christian demonization of the Jews, the authors/redactors here exalt them as the only ones from whom the demons cower, due to their superior mode of worship. Accordingly, baptism[92] is presented as a means by which Gentiles can "become like us," free from demons and reconciled to the one God.

When the text later returns to this argument (*Hom.* 11.16), Pseudo-Peter admits that there are some exceptions. He explains them by clarifying his definition of "Jew," a category that, for him, encompasses the Gentile "God-fearer":

But no one of us can suffer such a thing; they themselves are punished by us, when, having entered into anyone, they entreat us so that they may go out slowly. Yet, someone will perhaps say: "Even some of the God-fearers (θεοσεβῶν)[93] fall under such sufferings [i. e., diseases caused by demons]." I say that is impossible! For I speak of the God-fearer who is truly God-fearing, not one who is such only in name, but one who really fulfills the commandments of the Law that has been given him (ὁ δὲ ὄντως ὢν τοῦ δοθέντος αὐτῷ νόμου ἐκτελεῖ ταῖς προστάξεις). If anyone acts impiously, he is not pious. And, hence, if a foreigner keeps the Law, he is a Jew, but he who does not is a Greek (ἐὰν ὁ ἀλλόφυλος τὸν νόμον πράξῃ, Ἰουδαῖός ἐστιν, μὴ πράξας δε Ἕλλην). For the Jew, believing in God,

---

[92] Notably, "baptism" is here conceived as regular ritual ablutions, both for the remission of sins and for the purification of the body after defilement; see *Hom.* 11.26–30. See further discussion in Chapter Two below.

[93] The term θεοσεβής can simply denote any pious person (including Jews), but it is also used in a more technical sense to designate those Gentiles who affiliate themselves with Judaism without undergoing full conversion (i. e., like the Hebrew equivalent יראי שמים – "those who fear Heaven [= God]"; e. g., *Mekhilta Nezikin* 18; *Bereshit Rabbah* 53.9). The latter is particularly fitting in the present context: Peter's attempts to persuade the Gentile crowds to give up idolatry and turn to the one God, so that they can become more like Jews. See discussion in Joyce Reynolds and Robert Tannebaum, *Jews and God-Fearers at Aphrodisias: Greek Inscriptions with Commentary* (Cambridge: Cambridge Philological Society, 1987), 48–66. For recent reassessments, see Dietrich-Alex Koch, "The God-Fearers between Facts and Fiction: Two *theosebeis*-Inscriptions from Aphrodisias and Their Bearing for the New Testament," *Studia Theologica – Nordic Journal of Theology* 60 (2006): 62–90; Ross Kraemer, "Giving Up the Godfearers," *JAJ* 5 (2014): 61–87; Paula Fredriksen, "If It Looks like a Duck, and It Quacks like a Duck …": On Not Giving Up the Godfearers," in *A Most Reliable Witness: Essays in Honor of Ross Shepard Kraemer*, ed. Susan Ashbrook Harvey et al. (BJS 358; Providence: Brown University Press, 2015), 25–34.

keeps the Law (ὁ γὰρ Ἰουδαῖος πιστεύων ποιεῖ τὸν νόμον). But he who does not keep the Law is manifestly a deserter through not believing God. And thus – as no Jew, but a sinner (ἁμαρτωλὸς) – he is on account of his sin brought into subjection to those sufferings that are ordained for the punishment of sinners. (*Hom.* 11.16.1–4)

The authors/redactors go on to explain how the "punishment of sinners" differs from God's punishment of the Jews (and, by extension, of Gentile "God-fearers"): the latter is simply a "settlement of accounts" by which God mercifully permits Jews to be "set free of eternal punishments" (*Rec.* 11.16.5–6).[94]

Here, the *Homilies* redefines the category of "Jews" to include Torah-observant monotheists of non-Jewish ethnicity and, accordingly, condemns idolatrous and nonobservant Gentiles as "sinners," together with nonobservant Jews. It is unclear, however, whether the former category (i. e., true "Jews") can be simply mapped onto our category of "Christian"; for instance, the authors/redactors tie freedom from demonic possession not to belief in Jesus as Christ but rather to worship of the one God. This is consistent with the rest of *Hom.* 8–11, which repeatedly stresses the need for faith in God as the only God, while treating Jesus as a "teacher" (e. g., *Hom.* 11.20) and as the "prophet of truth" whom God sent to tell Gentiles what to do and believe (e. g., *Hom.* 10.3–4, 11.19).

By contrast, the *Recognitions* has reworked the material in the Basic Source to express a different demonology, historiography, and soteriology, based on different ideas about those who are free from demonic influence. There is no parallel to *Hom.* 9.16, and the smug "we" in the parallel to *Hom.* 9.20 at *Rec.* 4.33 appears to refer to those who believe in Jesus as Christ. For instance, the statements about "our" freedom from the demons are directly followed by a description of the temptation of Jesus by the Devil (i. e., *Rec.* 4.34). The *Homilies* treats this theme in another context (see *Hom.* 8.21), introducing the incident as an instructive example (see *Hom.* 8.20) and concluding with Jesus' assertion that "You shall fear the Lord your God, and you shall serve *only Him*" (cf. Matt 4:10/Luke 4:8). Although *Rec.*'s version also integrates this saying, its authors/redactors stress that Jesus is the one through whom the Devil will be destroyed –

---

[94] In effect, the Pseudo-Clementine *Homilies* here outlines a principle for the interpretation of Jewish history that differs markedly from the proto-orthodox/orthodox Christian approach; following this theodical principle, the historical tragedies of the Jewish nation are not signs of God's abandonment of an allegedly sinful and "hard-hearted" people, but rather emblems of their righteousness, continued chosenness, and their inheritance in the World to Come. Cf. *Bereshit Rabbah* 33.1, which attributes to R. Akiva the statement, "He [God] deals strictly with the righteous, calling them to account for the few wrongs that they commit in this world, in order to lavish bliss upon and give them a fine reward in the World to Come; He grants ease to the wicked and rewards them for the few good deeds that they have performed in this world in order to punish them in the future world" (see also *b. Qiddushin* 40b; *b. Ta'anit* 11a). On God's punishment of the Jews as distinct from the nations, see also 2 Macc 6:12–17; *Ekha Rabbah* 1.35; *b. Yevamot* 63a.

thereby expressing a demonology more consonant with that of proto-orthodox/ orthodox Christians.

Likewise, the *Recognitions'* parallel to *Hom.* 11.16 does not focus on the meaning of being a true "Jew," but rather what it means to be a "worshipper of God" (*dei cultor*):

But someone will say, "These passions sometimes befall even those who worship God." It is not true! For we say that he is a worshipper of God who does the will of God and observes the precepts of His Law (*etenim nos illum dei dicimus esse cultorem, qui voluntatem dei facit et legis praecepta custodit*). For in God's estimation he is not a Jew who is called a Jew among men, nor is he a Gentile who is called a Gentile, but he who, believing in God, fulfils His Law and does His will, even though he is not circumcised (*etiamsi non sit circumcisus*). He is the true worshipper of God (*verus dei cultor*),[95] who not only is himself free from passions but also sets others free from them; although they are so heavy that they are like mountains, he removes them by means of the faith with which he believes in God .... Yet he who seems to worship God, but is neither fortified by a full faith nor by obedience to the commandments, is only a sinner ... (*Rec.* 5.34)

The *Recognitions* here dismisses both "Jew" and "Gentile" as meaningless categories – and adds that circumcision is not a precondition for adherence to God's Law and will. And, even as this passage retains some of the emphasis on proper praxis that we have seen above in *Rec.* 4.5, it also stresses the need for "a full faith" and freedom from the passions. Accordingly, this passage ends with a treatment of the theme of different kinds of punishment, which revolves around the contrast between believers and unbelievers, with no reference to the Jews or their special status in the eyes of God.

Furthermore, *Rec.* 4–6 is marked by an exaltation of Jesus' soteriological role that is absent in *Hom.*'s version of the Tripolis sermons. This is most evident in *Rec.* 5.10–13, which has no parallel in the *Homilies*. Here, the authors/redactors describe Jesus as the "true prophet in all that he spoke," but then states that "the sayings of the Law ... were fulfilled in him; and the figures of Moses and of the patriarch Jacob before him bore in all respects a type of him" (*Rec.* 5.10). Through the mouth of Peter, he goes on to contrast the Jews, who still wait for the Messiah, with the Gentiles, to whom "all things which are declared concerning him are to be transferred" (*Rec.* 5.11.3):

The Jews from the beginning had understood by a most certain tradition that this man should at some time come, the one by whom all things should be restored. And they are meditating daily and looking out for his coming. However, when they saw him amongst them, accomplishing the signs and miracles – as had been written of him – they were blinded with envy and could not recognize him (*ubi adesse eum viderunt et signa ac prodigia, sicut de eo scriptum fuerat, adimplentem, invidia excaecati agnoscere nequiverunt praesentem, in cuius spe laetabantur absentis*; *Rec.* 5.11.4)

---

[95] Note that Rufinus does not use the Latin equivalent of θεοσεβεῖς, in the sense of a Gentile affiliated with Judaism (i.e., *metuentes*), but rather chooses a rendering based on its more generic denotation of piety.

The *Recognitions'* Pseudo-Peter concludes with a qualification: "Nevertheless, the few of us who were chosen by him understood it" (*intelleximus tamen pauci nos qui ab eo electi sumus*; *Rec.* 5.11.4). The context, however, suggests that this statement refers primarily to the Jewish disciples selected by Jesus, rather than to the Jews of its own time. Even as the authors/redactors remain acutely aware of the apostle Peter's own Jewishness, he here equates the Gentiles' salvation through Jesus with the disinheritance of the Jews.

The subtle difference between their references to James may also prove significant. In the parallel units in which both the *Recognitions* and *Homilies* warn their audiences about the demonically-inspired forgeries of the Gospel, the *Recognitions'* Pseudo-Peter asserts that one should only believe those who bring the testimonial of either "James, the brother of Jesus" or those in his line of succession (*Rec.* 4.35). The version in the *Homilies* is more expansive. Here, James is not only called "the brother of my Lord," but also the one "to whom was entrusted to administer the *church of the Hebrews* in Jerusalem" (*Hom.* 11.35). In effect, the *Homilies* takes this opportunity to emphasize that all true followers of Jesus stem from his Jewish disciples.

That *Hom.* 8–11 views the close connections between Jews and Jesus' Gentile followers as not merely artifacts from the apostolic age is also suggested by its treatment of the Pharisees. In the course of stressing the need for both moral and physical purity (*Hom.* 11.28–30), the text quotes a saying of Jesus that critiques this group for their preoccupation with only outer purity (i.e., Matt 23:25). Rather than reading this as a blanket denunciation of the Pharisees (or of the Jews more broadly), the *Homilies'* authors/redactors specify that Jesus spoke "the truth with respect to 'the hypocrites' among them, *not with respect to all of them*," and he stresses that "to some, he said that obedience should be rendered, because they were entrusted with 'the chair of Moses'" (*Hom.* 11.29 on Matt 23:2).

Interestingly, the main point of the passage is not the importance of moral purity, but rather the need for converted idolaters to partake in regular ritual ablutions with water, particularly after intercourse, and to avoid copulation with women rendered impure by menstruation, "for thus the Law of God commands" (*Hom.* 11.28, 30). As Baumgarten notes, these passages may reveal familiarity with, and respect for, Rabbinic culture.[96] To this, we might add that the authors/redactors of the *Homilies* self-consciously participate in a Jewish discourse about halakhah, even as the focus here falls on issues pertaining to Gentile impurity and purification.[97]

---

[96] Baumgarten, "Literary Evidence," 47.

[97] On Rabbinic attitudes towards Gentile impurity, see Christine Hayes, *Gentile Impurities and Jewish Identities: Intermarriage and Conversion from the Bible to the Talmud* (Oxford: Oxford University Press, 2002), 107–98, esp. the discussion on pp. 107–44 concerning the ritual impurity of Gentiles and Rabbinic debates about the defilement associated with idolatry, on

"Jewish-Christianity" in Hom. 8–11 and Rec. 4–6

Insofar as the soteriology of *Hom.* 8–11 is more consistent with the shared material about Moses and Jesus (i.e., *Rec.* 4.5 = *Hom.* 8.5–7), it is possible that the *Recognitions'* version of the Tripolis sermons reflects redaction of their shared Basic Source towards consonance with proto-orthodox/orthodox Christian traditions. Comparison with this shared material also suggests that the authors/redactors of the *Homilies* enhanced and developed those very features of the Basic Source that those of the *Recognitions* chose to downplay. If the authors/redactors of *Rec.* 4–6 did indeed seek to neutralize the "Jewishness" of the Basic Source, then those responsible for the *Homilies* seem to have done the opposite.

Of course, all such theories remain speculative in the absence of the Basic Source, and no firm source-critical conclusions can be drawn only from the Tripolis material alone. Moreover, for our present purposes, the precise relationship of *Homilies* and *Recognitions* to the Basic Source proves less significant than the contrast between their final forms, which attests the divergent concerns of different fourth-century authors/redactors. As we have seen, *Hom.* 8–11 and *Rec.* 4–6 both fit the label "Jewish-Christian," albeit in different ways. The authors/redactors of *Hom.* 8–11 appear to conceptualize Christianity as essentially the transformation of "pagans" into God-fearers and/or Jews, as made possible by Jesus' (re)revelation of the same teachings as Moses. Here, it proves significant that *Hom.* 8–11 defines a "Jew" as one from any ethnicity who "keeps the Law" and describes "baptism" as the first step in a continual process of purification by washing, both for the remission of sins and for the removal of physical defilement (*Hom.* 11.28–29). In this sense, one could call *Hom.* 8–11 "Jewish-Christian," but one could also call it a Jewish missionary text that uses the sayings of Jesus to encourage Gentiles to abandon their idolatry, free themselves of the impurity that clings to "pagans," and adopt a praxis that serves the one, true God.

It proves more challenging to characterize *Rec.* 4–6. As we have seen, Peter's sermons are here prefaced by his assertion of the equality of the Torah and the Gospel as paths to salvation. What follows, however, is a series of sermons in which Jesus is described as necessary for salvation and the Gentiles are said to be the true heirs of God's biblical promise to the Jews. Nevertheless, it proves significant that *Rec.* 4–6 requires from Gentile Christ-believers a level of Torah observance similar to the *Homilies* (see, e.g., *Rec.* 4.36), thus evoking yet another common scholarly criterion of "Jewish-Christianity": the combination of Jewish practice with Christian belief.

One could thus characterize *Rec.* 4–6 as a "catholicizing" redaction of "Jewish-Christian" material that chooses to retain a critique of the antinomianism associated with Paul. This, however, evades a more puzzling question: if

----

the one hand, and the seminal and menstrual emissions of non-Jews, on the other. See further Chapter Two in this volume.

"Jewish-Christianity" was – as many scholars believe – so marginalized after the "Parting of the Ways" and thus so irrelevant to the majority of Christians, why would a fourth-century Christian wish to rework and transmit this material in the first place? And, more puzzling still, why would Rufinus translate it into Latin?

The Pseudo-Clementines in Their Late Antique Contexts

These questions, in my view, may be the key to determining the significance of the so-called "Jewish-Christian" material in the Pseudo-Clementine *Homilies* and *Recognitions* for our understanding of Judaism and Christianity as "Ways that Never Parted." As noted above, most research into the Pseudo-Clementines has been devoted not to understanding the *Homilies* or *Recognitions* but rather to reconstructing the sources of their hypothetical Basic Source; instead of considering the fourth-century context in which the texts were composed, scholars have focused on the nonextant sources that allegedly stand *behind* their nonextant third-century source. Even if we accept the historical and text-critical value of using hypothetical sources to fill the gap between our New Testament evidence for "Jewish-Christianity" and our Patristic evidence for "Jewish-Christian" groups,[98] we can still question the heurism of using the latter only to reconstruct the former. As noted above, source-critical inquiries into the *Homilies* and *Recognitions* serve to neutralize the tension between this late antique evidence for "Jewish-Christianity" and the modern scholarly model of the "Parting of the Ways," either by projecting the "Jewish-Christian" elements of the *Homilies* and *Recognitions* into an earlier era or by dismissing them as later "heretical"/"heterodox" accretions to an originally "orthodox"/"catholic" core. In the process, such studies evade important questions about the function of "Jewish-Christian" material in the final forms of these texts: as fourth-century products of creative acts of composition, compilation, and redaction (shaped by choices about the inclusion of material, no less than choices about excision and supplementation); and as books that proved surprisingly popular with a late antique Christian readership.[99]

Whatever the validity of the dazzling variety of hypotheses about sources of the hypothetical Pseudo-Clementine Basic Source,[100] it remains that the *Hom-*

---

[98] Note also J. Wehnhar's critique of this approach on linguistic grounds in "Literarkritik und Sprachanalyse: Kritische Anmerkungen zum gegenwärtigen Stand der Pseudoklementinen-Forschung," *ZNW* 74 (1983): 268–301.

[99] Did these books also reach a Jewish readership? This idea should not be dismissed out of hand, and further inquiries into their parallels with Rabbinic literature (see below) should also leave open the possibility that these texts may have influenced Jewish traditions, whether by written or oral channels.

[100] See further Jones, "Pseudo-Clementines," 14–33; Jones, *Ancient Jewish Christian Source*, 20–36.

ilies and *Recognitions* both date from the fourth century, and they were transmitted, read, epitomized, and translated in the fifth century and following.[101] If these texts do indeed integrate very early "Jewish-Christian" material, then they also serve as important evidence for the continuous preservation of such traditions, for centuries after the "Parting of the Ways" allegedly rendered "Jewish-Christianity" irrelevant for both Christians and Jews.

Although it is difficult to make sense of this data using the "Parting" model, new approaches to Jewish/Christian relations in Late Antiquity may prove more helpful. Eschewing the sociological and methodological simplicity of the idea of a single, early separation between the two religions, scholars such as Daniel Boyarin, John Gager, Judith Lieu, and Israel Yuval have stressed the need for a more critical reading of our sources, one which is sensitive both to the elite status of their literate authors and to the gaps between their rhetoric and the social realities "on the ground."[102] In the process, these and other scholars have demonstrated that Jewish and Christian efforts at self-definition remained intimately interconnected, charged with ambivalence, and surprisingly fluid, long after the so-called "Parting of the Ways." Contrary to traditional assumptions about the complete independence and isolation of late antique Christianity from post-Christian Judaism and vice versa, it seems that interactions between Jews and Christians hardly ceased in the second century; accordingly, the relationship between Judaism and Christianity was negotiated in different ways in different social contexts, intellectual discourses, and geographical milieux – including but not limited to the nascent academies of the Rabbinic movement and the proto-orthodox/orthodox Christian churches of the Roman Empire. In short, both were still in the process of formation, usually in a generative tension with one another, even (and perhaps especially) in the fourth century.

For our purposes, these insights prove consequential insofar as they may point the way to a fresh approach to the *Homilies* and *Recognitions*, which recovers the significance of the texts' final forms by exploring the significance of their composition/compilation, transmission, translation, and reception for our under-

---

[101] Interestingly, the third-century *Didascalia apostolorum* was similarly translated into both Syriac and Latin in the fourth century CE.

[102] See, e.g., Boyarin, *Dying for God*, esp. 6–19, and articles cited above, as well as Boyarin, "Semantic Differences; or, 'Judaism'/'Christianity,'" in Becker and Reed, *The Ways That Never Parted*, 65–86; John G. Gager, "Jews, Christians, and the Dangerous Ones in Between," in *Interpretation in Religion*, ed. S. Biderman and B. Scharfstein (Philosophy and Religion 2; Leiden: Brill, 1992), 249–57; Gager, "The Parting of the Ways: A View from the Perspective of Early Christianity," in *Interwoven Destinies: Jews and Christians through the Ages*, ed. Eugene J. Fisher (New York: Paulist, 1993), 62–73; Judith M. Lieu, "'The Parting of the Ways': Theological Construct or Historical Reality?" *JSNT* 56 (1994): 101–19; Israel Yuval, "Easter and Passover as Early Jewish–Christian Dialogue," in *Passover and Easter: Origin and History to Modern Times*, ed. Paul F. Bradshaw and Lawrence A. Hoffman (Notre Dame: University of Notre Dame Press, 1999), 98–124; Yuval, *Two Nations in Your Womb: Dual Perceptions of the Jews and of Christians* [Hebrew] (Tel Aviv: Am Oved, 2000).

standing of the ongoing discourse about Christian and Jewish identities in Late Antiquity. Needless to say, time and space do not permit a detailed investigation of these issues. For now, I would like to offer several suggestions about potentially fruitful directions for future investigation.

Foremost is the need to integrate the study of the Pseudo-Clementines, together with other so-called "Jewish-Christian" sources, more fully into research on late antique Judaism and Christianity. Within modern scholarship, the label "Jewish-Christian" too often functions to marginalize texts like the Pseudo-Clementines and to ensure that they are studied in relative isolation from broader discussions. Simply stated, such works are treated as evidence for "Jewish-Christianity," but not for Christianity or Judaism. This selectivity is inculcated by the traditional view of the former as a monolithic phenomenon with no real relevance for our understanding of post-70 developments in the "mainstream" of either religion. Yet, as Stephen Wilson observes, "The evidence seems to point neither to their rapid marginalization nor to their continuing dominance after 70 CE but rather to their survival as a significant minority."[103]

Likewise, theories about the post-70/post-135 decline of "Jewish-Christianity" are insufficient to explain the integration of such viewpoints in both the *Homilies* and *Recognitions*[104] – let alone the widespread circulation of these and other Pseudo-Clementine compositions in the centuries that followed. A different approach to the question of the "Jewish-Christianity" of this literature is suggested by Georg Strecker's characterization of their shared source:

Noch nachdem die Orthodoxie den Sieg über die Häretiker endgültig errungen hatte, mußte Johannes Chrysostomus die Homilien „Adversus Judaeos" halten, um die Christen seiner Gemeinde von dem Besuch der jüdischen Synagogen (PG 48 Sp. 850) und dem Feiern der jüdischen Fast- und Festtage (ebd. Sp. 844. 849) zurückzuhalten. Dies – das ungeklärte Verhältnis zwischen Judentum und Christentum – ist das Milieu, in dem ein Buch wie die pseudoklementinische Grundschrift entstehen und gelesen werden konnte.[105]

Strecker limits this conclusion to the third-century Basic Source and to the Syrian cultural context in which this source likely originated. In light of recent research on Judaism and Christianity in the fourth century, Strecker's observations about the Basic Source – as reflecting not "Jewish-Christianity" *per se* but rather the unresolved relationship between Judaism and Christianity – may prove no less relevant for our understanding of the *Homilies* and *Recognitions*, as

---

[103] Stephen G. Wilson, *Related Strangers: Jews and Christians, 70–170 CE* (Minneapolis: Fortress, 1995), 158.

[104] Schoeps, for instance, uses the Pseudo-Clementines and its hypothetical sources (in this case, the *Kerygmata Petrou* and the *Anabathmoi Jakobou*) to reconstruct the Ebionites' "Jewish-Christianity." Yet, even by his calculation, a specifically Ebionite origin can only be proposed for about 25 % of this corpus (*Jewish Christianity,* 17).

[105] Strecker, *Judenchristentum,* 260.

well as the subsequent circulation of both (especially the *Recognitions* in Latin translation) far beyond the bounds of Syria.

With regard to the early history of Jewish/Christian relations, Daniel Boyarin has proposed that our data are best approached, not in terms of a simple contrast between a "Judaism" derived from the classical Rabbinic literature and a "Christianity" derived from the writings of the Church Fathers, but rather in terms of a continuum, marked on one end by Marcion's construction of a Christianity severed of all connections to Judaism and, on the other, by Jews for whom Jesus was similarly irrelevant.[106] Following this approach, Western Christian orthodoxy represents only one of the many possible solutions to mapping a middle ground between these two poles. The various churches of the East articulate other solutions, which would prove no less theologically and practically feasible. Likewise, so-called "Jewish-Christian" sources may attest to the continued existence (and ongoing emergence) of a variety of groups, which offered still other answers to the same questions in the centuries before political and social developments enabled a more final resolution.[107]

There are reasons to believe that these ambiguities persisted into the fourth century,[108] forming an important part of the cultural landscape from which both the *Homilies* and *Recognitions* emerged. The debates about the place of Judaism and Jewish praxis in Christian identity may have even intensified, concurrent with the beginning of the Christianization of the Roman Empire and the (possibly resultant) consolidation of Rabbinic power in Roman Palestine.[109] The former would eventually empower orthodox ecclesiarchs to promote, institutionalize, and legislate their own particular concept of Christianity as a religion that had co-opted the biblical heritage from the Jews and thus stood in absolute conflict with post-Christian forms of Judaism. This, however, seems to have been a rather challenging task, which encountered not a little resistance.

In the fourth and fifth centuries, we find an increase in orthodox Christian polemics against Judaizers and so-called "Jewish-Christian" sects, as well as a rise in the violent tenor of Christian anti-Judaism.[110] This evidence likely speaks

---

[106] Boyarin, *Dying for God*, 8.

[107] This occurred in different places at different times and paces; see Adam H. Becker, "Beyond the Spatial and Temporal Limes: Questioning the 'Parting of the Ways' Outside the Roman Empire," in Becker and Reed, *The Ways That Never Parted*, 373–92.

[108] See Paula Fredriksen, "What 'Parting of the Ways'? Jews, Gentiles, and the Ancient Mediterranean City," in Becker and Reed, *The Ways That Never Parted*, 35–64. On the archeological evidence for ongoing interactions, see Leonard Victor Rutgers, "Archaeological Evidence for the Interaction of Jews and non-Jews in Antiquity," *American Journal of Archaeology* 96 (1992): 110–15.

[109] On the latter, see Seth Schwartz, *Imperialism and Jewish Society, 200 BCE to 640 CE* (Princeton: Princeton University Press, 2001), 179–289.

[110] See Robert Louis Wilken, *John Chrysostom and the Jews: Rhetoric and Reality in the Late Fourth Century* (Berkeley: University of California Press, 1983), 66–94; Gager, "Jews, Christians, and the Dangerous Ones in Between," 249–57.

to orthodox Christian efforts to establish the mutual exclusivity of Judaism and Christianity, but it may also hint at the reception of such efforts: Joan Taylor, for instance, suggests that the fourth century was also marked by "widespread interest in Jewish praxis by Gentile members of the church and a variety of groups exhibiting 'Jewish-Christian' characteristics."[111] If so, then it is possible that some Christians reacted to these ecclesiastical efforts by articulating and defending different approaches to Christianity's Jewish heritage vis-à-vis Christian praxis, based both on the Old Testament and on contacts with their Jewish contemporaries (not to mention the New Testament accounts of Jesus and his own observance of Torah).

When we locate the *Homilies* and *Recognitions* within this broader context, their so-called "Jewish-Christian" features take on a new significance. Studies of the *Homilies* and *Recognitions* have shown that their authors/redactors actively engaged in the Christological debates that raged during the fourth century and culminated in the denunciation of Arianism at the Council of Nicaea (325 CE). Through their integration and reworking of "Jewish-Christian" material, they may also participate in the no less heated discussions concerning Christianity's relationship with pre-Christian and post-Christian Judaism – as also evinced by the decision, at the same council, to calculate the date of Easter independently from the Jewish festival of Pesach and to condemn all Quartodecimani as "heretics."[112]

In the case of the *Homilies*, the authors/redactors appear to promote a vision of Judaism and Christianity as two equal paths to salvation, acknowledging and accepting those who view these religions as different by definition. This proves particularly intriguing insofar as they are clearly familiar with proto-orthodox/ orthodox Christian traditions and may also be in close cultural contact with Rabbinic Jews. With regard to the latter, further research is needed and to determine the precise scope and nature of his familiarity with contemporary form(s) of Judaism and to confirm that the Jews with whom he seems to interact can indeed be identified with the Rabbis. Notably, this task is facilitated by the *Homilies*' fourth-century context, which makes inquiries into its parallels with Rabbinic sources like the Tosefta, Talmud Yerushalmi, and *Bereshit Rabbah* far less problematic than the usual scholarly attempts to correlate early Christian references to Jews with statements from the classical Rabbinic literature.[113]

---

[111] Taylor, "Phenomenon of Early Jewish-Christianity," 327.

[112] See Wolfgang Heber, *Passa und Ostern: Untersuchungen zur Osterfeier der alten Kirche* (Berlin: Töpelmann, 1969), esp. 1–88.

[113] It is indeed an apt time to take another look at the parallels between the Pseudo-Clementines and the classical Rabbinic literature compiled by earlier scholars such as J. Bergman ("Les éléments juifs dans les Pseudo-clementines," *REJ* 46 [1903]: 89–98) and A. Marmorstein ("Judaism and Christianity in the Middle of the Third Century," *HUCA* 10 [1935]: 223–63). As noted above, Baumgarten has made an important contribution to this task ("Liter-

If we can in fact draw such connections, then the *Homilies'* theories about the concealment of Jesus from the Jews may function as an aetiology of the assertion of the mutual exclusivity of Judaism and Christianity by Rabbinic Jews and Christian ecclesiarchs in the Roman Empire – the two groups to whom we owe our modern conceptions about the "Parting of the Ways." Even as the authors/redactors of the *Homilies* stress that both will be saved and explains their perception of difference with reference to God's will, he critiques both of them alike by promoting the combination of the two as superior to either alone; for him, the ideal Gentile Christian is a Torah-observant God-fearer, whereas the ideal Jew is one who recognizes Jesus as a teacher of the same divine precepts revealed to Moses. If these authors/redactors are responding to Rabbinic Jewish and proto-orthodox Christian efforts to "part" Christianity from Judaism, he does so with a poignant combination of acceptance and resistance, which hints at his participation (or desire for participation) in both religious spheres.

By contrast, the *Recognitions* couples its claims about the equality of the Torah and the Gospel with supersessionist statements about Gentiles and Christ. That the *Recognitions* incorporates material that expresses different stances towards the relationship between Judaism and Christianity is also demonstrated by its inclusion of *Rec.* 1.27–71, which the authors/redactors of the *Homilies* evidently chose to exclude from his Clementine pseudepigraphon. In the *Recognitions'* final form, this unit functions as Peter's initial explanation to Clement concerning how the Christians came to proselytize among the Gentiles, whereas *Rec.* 4–6 is set in the context of Clement's travels with Peter on this mission. In effect, the account of Jewish history in *Rec.* 1.27–71 is juxtaposed with the exploration of Gentile history in *Rec.* 4–6, such that the Jewish heritage of the church is positively affirmed even as the focus falls on the Gentile mission. Together, they offer an alternative account of Christianity's separation and supersession of Judaism that eschews the fierce denigration of Jews, Judaism, and Jewish Law found in contemporaneous treatments of this theme in favor of a stress on the sinfulness of "pagans" and on the continuity between authentic Christianity and its Jewish heritage, both pre-Christian and apostolic.

Unlike the *Homilies*, the *Recognitions* appears to operate mainly in a Christian cultural context. Yet this text can also be read as a critique of other fourth-century Christian approaches to the relationship between Judaism and Christianity. The authors/redactors not only chose to include both *Rec.* 1.27–71 and Peter's discussion of the equality of the Torah and the Gospel in *Rec.* 4.5, but he consistently stresses the need for good works and articulates the ideal Christian praxis as a combination of moral and ritual purity. In the process, he promotes his own synthesis of Judaism and Christianity as the only authentically apostolic way to

---

ary Evidence," 39–51), but his conflation of evidence from *Homilies* and *Recognitions* makes his findings preliminary.

adhere to Jesus' teachings. The result is a text that challenges the importance of Paul for proto-orthodox/orthodox articulations of the church's relationship to Judaism, while simultaneously severing, with varying degrees of success, the assertion of the truth of Christianity from the antinomianism and anti-Judaism of the nascent orthodoxy.

Rufinus' translation of this book may have been motivated primarily by its status as "proof" for Clement's close connections with Peter and, hence, of the authentic apostolicity of the Roman church. Nevertheless, it is striking that he was not more troubled by its anti-Pauline stance and its refutation of the apostolic history in the Book of Acts, nor (despite his notorious abhorrence of Judaizing) by the so-called "Jewish-Christian" features discussed above. We might speculate that Rufinus viewed these characteristics merely in terms of historical verisimilitude, as a faithful record of the opinions of the Jewish apostle Peter and perhaps also of the important place of ethnically Jewish-Christians in the early Roman church.[114] But, in any case, Rufinus ironically ensured that the so-called "Jewish-Christian" material therein would circulate widely in the Roman Empire for many centuries to follow, presented as the words of Peter himself. An understanding of the influence of this material on the later readers must await further research into the reception history of the *Recognitions*.

To conclude, I would like to pose a variation of the question with which I began: how should we define "Jewish-Christianity" in light of new perspectives on Judaism and Christianity? In our analysis of selections from the *Homilies* and *Recognitions*, we have seen how the variety of viewpoints that can be fit under this rubric strains the heurism of the category. Rather than seeking a single "Jewish-Christianity" that stands in a direct line of development from the Jerusalem Church, it may be more prudent to view the persistence of so-called "Jewish-Christian" modes of belief and worship as a natural extension of Christianity's origins within Judaism, Christians' continued contacts with Jews, and the church's use of the Jewish Scriptures, as well as the long and rich tradition of messianic speculation within Judaism itself.[115]

Likewise, our discussion of the history of scholarship has shed doubt on the traditional approach to "Jewish-Christianity" as a self-contained phenomenon, distinct from all varieties of "Gentile Christianity." As Albertus Frederik Johannes Klijn notes, our term "Jewish-Christian" encompasses all those who combined Judaism and Christianity in ways that differed from the combination(s) that ecclesiarchs in the Roman Empire eventually succeeded in pro-

---

[114] The latter is discussed by Daniel Stökl Ben Ezra in "Whose Fast Is It? The Ember Day of September and Yom Kippur," in Becker and Reed, *The Ways That Never Parted*, 259–82.

[115] See, e.g., Patricia Crone, "Islam, Judeo-Christianity, and Byzantine Iconoclasm," *Jerusalem Studies in Arabic and Islam* 2 (1980): 93, and John G. Gager's discussion thereof in "Did Jewish Christians See the Rise of Islam?," in Becker and Reed, *The Ways That Never Parted*, 361–72.

moting as "Christian."[116] This, however, may tell us more about the formation of Western Christian orthodoxy than about the phenomenon that we term "Jewish-Christianity." Just as the notion of "heresy" was a product of efforts to construct "orthodoxy" and never remained a static category, so the idea that some Christ-believers were too "Jewish" to be "Christian" arose in the course of discussions about the precise nature of the Jewish heritage of the church and its exact ramifications for Christian practice. As with other modes of heresiology, the critique of "too Jewish" Christian groups has roots in the first and second centuries but appears to reach an apex in the fourth and fifth. Far from evincing the marginalization of "Jewish-Christian" viewpoints after 70 or 135 CE, the evidence traditionally studied under this rubric may instead help us to illuminate their relevance for a broader discourse about Christianity's relationship to Judaism, which continued to shape Christian self-definition for centuries after the so-called "Parting of the Ways."

---

[116] Klijn asserts that we can only "speak of the 'Jewish Christianity' of a particular writing or of a particular group of Christians" in the sense that "we can detect ideas having a Jewish background and which were not accepted by the established Church" ("Study of Jewish-Christianity," 431). When commenting on Daniélou's efforts to reconstruct a single, coherent "theology of Jewish Christianity," Klijn similarly emphasizes that "we are dealing with one Christian movement in which the Jewish ideas and practices and the Jews themselves play a part in Jerusalem and Rome, Ephesus and Alexandria. For this reason it is impossible to define the term 'Jewish Christian' because it proved to be a name that can readily be replaced by 'Christian'" (426).

Chapter Two

Beyond "Judaism" and "Christianity" in the Roman Near East*

Central to the scholarly discussion of the "Parting of the Ways" has been the question of *when* "Christianity" emerged as a "religion" distinct from "Judaism." With the increased emphasis on the Jewishness of Jesus and the diversity of Second Temple Judaism in the wake of World War II, the theological triumphalism of earlier research has been largely purged from the historical study of Christian Origins. What was once described as Israel's supposedly inevitable replacement by the "Great Church" became commonly reframed in terms of the relationship between "religions." At the same time, studies of the Jesus movement and New Testament increasingly engaged the full history of Judaism, as well as the history of interactions between Jews and Christians from Late Antiquity to the present. Especially since the 1970s, fresh efforts were thus made to replace the supersessionist rhetoric of older research with more ecumenical metaphors – with "Judaism" and "Christianity" reconceived as two equal and active entities.[1]

Perhaps most prominent was the model of the "Parting of the Ways," which was popularized particularly in the 1980s and 1990s as an ostensibly more neutral counterpart to older supersessionist approaches.[2] Despite its more ecumenical emphasis, however, the "Parting" model retained some of the problems

---

* This chapter originally appeared in 2012 as "Parting Ways over Blood and Water? Beyond 'Judaism' and 'Christianity' in the Roman Near East," in *La croisée des chemins revisitée: Quand l'Église et la Synagogue se sont-elles distinguées?*, ed. Simon Claude Mimouni and Bernard Pouderon (Paris: Cerf, 2012), 227–59; it is reprinted here with permission from Les éditions du Cerf. Earlier versions were presented at the conference on "La croisée des chemins revisitée" on 18–19 June 2010 at Université François-Rabelais de Tours and in the Classical Studies Colloquium at the University of Pennsylvania on 28 October 2010; it benefited much from questions and comments at both events. My gratitude to Simon Claude Mimouni, Bernard Pouderon, Yair Furstenberg, Nicholas Harris, Ralph Rosen, Sarah Scullin, Paola Tartakoff, and Phillip Webster for bibliographical and other suggestions. This version has been revised and updated.

[1] For the history of research, see Annette Yoshiko Reed and Adam H. Becker, "Introduction: Traditional Models and New Directions," in *The Ways That Never Parted: Jews and Christians in Late Antiquity and the Early Middle Ages* (TSAJ 95; Tübingen: Mohr Siebeck, 2003), 1–24.

[2] Among the most widely-cited articulations of the model are James G. D. Dunn, *The Partings of the Ways: Between Christianity and Judaism and Their Significance for the Character of Christianity* (London: SCM, 1991); Dunn, ed., *Jews and Christians: The Parting of the Ways, AD 70 to 135* (Grand Rapids: Eerdmans, 1992). See also now Dunn, *Neither Jew nor Greek: A Contested Identity* (Grand Rapids: Eerdmans, 2015), esp. 509–74.

and assumptions of its precedents. The focus on the question of timing, for instance, took for granted the presumption that processes of identity-formation are unilinear in character and global in scope. Whether one argued for situating the so-called "Parting" in the first century with Paul, in the second century with the Bar Kokhba Revolt, or in the fourth century with Constantine and the Christianization of the Roman Empire, the search for one pivotal moment of change thus served to foreclose the analysis of the different paces and dynamics of developments in different locales.

To tell the story of Christian self-definition as a singular tale about the separation of "Judaism" and "Christianity" as two "religions," moreover, entails the scholarly act of collapsing the local and geographical diversity of our sources into a series of points, selected for the ease of their plotting onto one thin line of globalized teleology.[3] Partly as a result, the discussion of the "Parting of the Ways" largely assumed the categories produced by the very processes under analysis: it tended to proceed as if categories like "Judaism" and "Christianity" were natural, inevitable, self-evident, or neutral, rather than concepts themselves created through efforts at parting cult from culture, *ethos* from *ethnos*, "religion" from peoplehood and place.[4]

For these and related reasons, scholars have increasingly questioned the heurism of the "Parting of the Ways" as a model for understanding the formation of Christian identities.[5] Critiques of the model have spread almost as rapidly as the

---

[3] On the ways in which selectivity vis-à-vis sources has often served to shore up conventional scholarly narratives about "Christianity" and "Judaism," see Ra'anan S. Boustan and Annette Yoshiko Reed, "Blood and Atonement in the Pseudo-Clementines and *The Story of the Ten Martyrs*," *Hen* 20 (2008): 333–64.

[4] For Late Antiquity, the seminal articulation of this point remains Daniel Boyarin, "Semantic Differences; or, 'Judaism'/'Christianity,'" in Becker and Reed, *The Ways That Never Parted*, 65–86. On the European colonial contexts that shaped the modern meaning and significance of "religion(s)," see Talal Asad, *Genealogies of Religion: Discipline and Reasons of Power in Christianity and Islam* (Baltimore: Johns Hopkins University Press, 1993); Daniel Dubuisson, *L'Occident et la religion: Mythes, science, et idéologie* (Paris: Editions Complexe, 1998). The relationship between late antique and modern developments is well described in Adam H. Becker, "Martyrdom, Religious Difference, and 'Fear' as a Category of Piety in the in the Sasanian Empire," *Journal of Late Antiquity* 2 (2009): 302–3; cf. Brent Nongbri, "Dislodging 'Embedded' Religion: A Brief Note on a Scholarly Trope," *Numen* 55 (2008): 440–60. See further now Nongbri, *Before Religion: A History of A Modern Concept* (New Haven: Yale University Press, 2013); Russell T. McCutcheon, "The Category 'Religion' in Recent Publications: Twenty Years Later," *Numen* 62 (2015): 119–41.

[5] For surveys and assessments of critiques of the model, see e.g. Becker and Reed, eds., *The Ways That Never Parted*; Mimouni and Pouderon, eds., *La croisée des chemins revisitée*; Anders Klostergaard Petersen, "At the End of the Road – Reflections on a Popular Scholarly Metaphor," in *The Formation of the Early Church*, ed. Jostein Ådna (WUNT 183; Tübingen: Mohr, 2005), 45–72; Adele Reinhartz, "A Fork in the Road or a Multi-Lane Highway? New Perspectives on 'The Parting of the Ways' Between Judaism and Christianity," in *The Changing Face of Judaism, Christianity, and Other Greco-Roman Religions in Antiquity*, ed. Ian H. Henderson and Gerbern S. Oegama (Gütersloh: Gütersloher, 2006), 278–93; Paula Fredriksen,

model itself. The past two decades have seen such a flurry of talks, conferences, and volumes on its problems, in fact, that its interrogation has been a major catalyst for scholarly conversation, drawing specialists from disparate subfields into productive conversation over issues of "religion," identity, and difference.[6]

The conversation has also yielded helpful insights into the construction of collective identities and the power of categorization as practice in its own right.[7] In a 2009 review essay on critiques of the "Parting" model, for instance, Megan Hale Williams makes the helpful observation that the relevant data allow for two different levels of analysis: [1] "the story of the interactions of actual Jews and Christians" and [2] "a history of the conceptual systems within which categories like Judaism and Christianity were [made and] used."[8] The former encompasses all those who call themselves "Jews" and "Christians," whereas the latter is more narrowly concerned with those among them who were "engaged in *constructing* conceptual frameworks in which these categories and their relation to each other in turn serve to configure reality in new ways."[9] What has become clear in the wake of critiques of the "Parting" model is just how critical it is not to conflate the two, especially before Constantine – lest the social histories of Jews and Christians, in their localities and specificities, become elided with the account of how certain elites innovated the terminologies and taxonomic systems that

---

"Mandatory Retirement: Ideas in the Study of Christian Origins Whose Time Has Come to Go," *SR* 35 (2006): 231–46; Simon Claude Mimouni, "Les origines du Christianisme: Nouveaux paradigmes ou paradigmes paradoxaux?" *Revue biblique* 115 (2008): 360–82; Megan Hale Williams, "No More Clever Titles: Observations on Some Recent Studies of Jewish–Christian Relations in the Roman World," *JQR* 99 (2009): 37–55; James Carleton Paget, *Jews, Christians, and Jewish Christians in Antiquity* (WUNT 251; Tübingen: Mohr Siebeck, 2010).

[6] For critiques, see above and below, as well as Steven T. Katz, "Issues in the Separation of Judaism and Christianity after 70 CE: A Reconsideration," *JBL* 103 (1984): 43–76; W. Kinzig, "Non-Separatists: Closeness and Co-operation between Jews and Christians in the Fourth Century," *VC* 45 (1991): 27–53; Philip S. Alexander, "'The Parting of the Ways' from the Perspective of Rabbinic Judaism," in Dunn, *Jews and Christians*, 1–25; Martha Himmelfarb, "The Parting of the Ways Reconsidered: Diversity in Judaism and Jewish–Christian Relations in the Roman Empire, 'A Jewish Perspective,'" in *Interwoven Destinies: Jews and Christians Through the Ages*, ed. Eugene J. Fisher (New York: Paulist, 1993), 47–61; John G. Gager, "Jews, Christians, and the Dangerous Ones in Between," in *Interpretation in Religion*, ed. Schlomo Biderman and Ben-Ami Scharfstein (Philosophy and Religion 2; Leiden: Brill, 1992), 249–57; Gager, "The Parting of the Ways: A View from the Perspective of Early Christianity," in *Interwoven Destinies: Jews and Christians through the Ages*, ed. Eugene J. Fisher (New York: Paulist, 1993), 62–73; Judith M. Lieu, "'The Parting of the Ways': Theological Construct or Historical Reality?" *JSNT* 56 (1994): 101–19; Daniel Boyarin, *Dying for God: Martyrdom and the Making of Christianity and Judaism* (Stanford: Stanford University Press, 1999).

[7] On the latter, see now Todd Berzon, *Classifying Christians: Ethnography, Heresiology, and the Limits of Knowledge in Late Antiquity* (Berkeley: University of California Press, 2016).

[8] Williams, "No More Clever Titles," 41–43. On the broader historiographical problem of which this issue forms a part, see Michael Werner and Bénédicte Zimmermann, "Beyond Comparison: *Histoire Croisée* and the Challenge of Reflexivity," *HT* 45 (2006): 30–50, esp. 42–44.

[9] Williams, "No More Clever Titles," 42; also Carleton Paget, *Jews, Christians, and Jewish Christians in Antiquity*, 12.

ultimately lie behind our modern notions of "Judaism," "Christianity," and perhaps even "religion."

The 2010 Tours conference on "La croisée des chemins revisitée" honed in upon the second level of analysis: rather than speaking in terms of the "parting" of "religions," Simon Claude Mimouni proposed that we might better reframe the discussion in terms of processes of "distinction" – stressing, moreover, the initial involvement only of certain Jews (i.e., Rabbinic) and Christians.[10] Mimouni thus offers an alternate framework within which to consider the key figures, texts, and events in earlier discussions about the "Parting of the Ways." Pragmatically sound, this proposal enables us to retain the insights produced within the earlier discussions, while sidestepping the trenchant problems with the "Parting" model (e.g., the conflation of rhetoric with reality, the generalization of some perspectives into descriptions of the interactions of supposedly monolithic "religions," the resultant effacing of local and other differences within traditions). He and others at the 2010 Tours conference thus pushed for a renewed focus on discursive and other practices of differentiation and for the limitation of scholarly claims concerning the initial scope and influence of elite speech and writing.

In this spirit of moving ahead, I am here less concerned with critiquing the much-maligned model of the "Parting of the Ways," and more with exploring the questions made newly pressing by its deflation.[11] Studies pursued within the framework of the "Parting" model, for instance, have largely presumed the inevitability of the processes in question,[12] and they have thus tended to proceed as if finding *even one* example of something seemingly akin to modern views of "Christianity" and "Judaism" would suffice to prove that the entire process was already complete – whether at the time of Paul, Matthew, John, Ignatius, or Justin. With new insights and perspectives now in hand, however, we are now able to historicize and contextualize our current notions of "Judaism" and "Christianity" in new ways, more attuned to the variety (and the limits) of our evidence for Jews and Christians in Late Antiquity.

If the production of Jewish and Christian difference was initiated solely among small sets of "separatists," for instance, how did their ideas come to take hold? When and why did Patristic rhetoric, in particular, persuade? And if this process was as gradual as some scholars now surmise,[13] might it be possible to glimpse some of the alternative visions that were current in Late Antiquity? Can

---

[10] See Mimouni and Pouderon, ed., *La Croisée des chemins revisitée*, esp. Mimouni, "Introduction: Sur la question de la séparation entre 'jumeaux' et 'ennemis' aux ier et iie siècles," 7–20.

[11] In this, I have been influenced especially by Carleton Paget, *Jews, Christians, and Jewish Christians in Antiquity*, 12–15.

[12] Or, at least, the claim that there was some moment at which it *became* inevitable; see, e.g., Dunn, *Jews and Christians*, 367–68.

[13] That the process was "bitty" is admitted even in Dunn, *Jews and Christians*, 367.

we recover any of the *other* ways in which late antique Jews and Christians partitioned their identities, drew lines of distinction around and among themselves, and constructed conceptual frameworks to understand and reimagine their local realities?

In what follows, I tentatively explore these questions with a focus on the Roman Near East. In the first half of this chapter I begin by reflecting upon how some of the local urban cultures in this region contributed to the creation of categories that were exported throughout the Roman Empire, eventually shaping imperial ideologies, as well as communal identities and modern scholarship about them in the West. Then, in the second half, I turn to explore some of the older and alternate approaches that persisted in Late Antiquity by focusing on blood, water, and the boundaries of identities as reflected in Jewish and Christian writings from Syria and Palestine. Such a focus, I shall suggest, might enable us to trace some relevant concepts and concerns between and beyond "Judaism" and "Christianity." Consequently, it may help us to bring the prehistory of the creation of such categories into sharper relief, while also highlighting a bit of the broader range of perspectives on identity and difference that circulated within a particularly potent set of interconnected late antique cultures.

Exporting "Christianity" and Other Local Identities

Already in 1994, Judith Lieu sharply articulated some of the base problems with the model of the "Parting of the Ways," in a widely-cited call for attention to the multiple local contexts in which Christian identities were forged:

The problem with the model of the "parting of the ways" is that, no less than its predecessors on the pages of Harnack or Origen, it operates essentially with the *abstract* or *universal* conception of each religion, Judaism and Christianity, whereas what we know about is the *specific* and the *local* …. Yet as soon as one asks the questions of time and place appropriate to a historical account, the model becomes increasingly vague …. The problem is exacerbated when we find that geography equally resists the scheme and we are forced to speak of considerable variation in time and place.[14]

In the introduction to our 2003 volume, *The Ways That Never Parted*, Adam H. Becker and I similarly noted the paucity of the "Parting" model to account for the richness of our evidence. Accordingly, we stressed the need to return to the specificity of our sources, and their local and social contexts – setting aside questions about "Judaism" and "Christianity," in order to grapple anew with what our evidence might tell us about late antique Jews and Christians.[15]

---

[14] Judith M. Lieu, "'The Parting of the Ways': Theological Construct or Historical Reality?," *JSNT* 56 (1994): 108; italics mine.

[15] Becker and Reed, "Introduction: Traditional Models and New Directions," 24. We reiterate this point in the new Preface to the paperback reprint (Minneapolis: Fortress, 2007), stressing

Since Lieu's 1994 essay, a number of studies have heeded her call to focus on the local, albeit sometimes in ways that have failed to escape the problems that she associates with abstraction.[16] In his 2004 *Border Lines* and related articles, however, Daniel Boyarin has shown how the creation of abstract categories like "Christianity" and "Judaism" is an important story in its own right – not merely an accretion for the modern scholar to clear away, look beyond, or read "against the grain."[17] The historiographical ramifications are significant: in a postmodern age in which metanarratives and totalizing discourses are increasingly subject to suspicion, it is comforting to seek refuge in the local and microhistorical. Yet some of the local stories told by Jews and Christians in Late Antiquity reflect their own efforts at universalizing and abstractifying, with specific events and circumstances recast in global, total, or even cosmic terms.[18]

Furthermore, in the case of many of the late antique writings that survived the centuries to come down to us today, something of this translocal orientation became actualized through their transmission and reception, far beyond their original local settings – sometimes with conceptual or taxonomic consequences that still reverberate today. Although the modern model of the "Parting of the Ways" may be misleading in its conflation of literary rhetoric with social reality in Late Antiquity, something is also missed if a focus on the local leads us to overlook the potential social power of totalizing and differentiating rhetoric;[19]

"the inadequacy of any monolithic model that seeks to theorize the relationships between 'Judaism' and 'Christianity' without considering the socio-cultural and discursive specificities that shaped interactions between Jews and Christians in different cultural contexts, geographical locales, and social strata" (p. vi).

[16] For a recent example relevant for the below discussion, which effectively emphasizes local and social contexts, see Magnus Zetterholm, *The Formation of Christianity in Antioch: A Social-Scientific Approach to the Separation between Judaism and Christianity* (London: Routledge, 2003). Contrast, however, Thomas Arthur Robinson, *Ignatius of Antioch and the Parting of the Ways: Early Jewish–Christian Relations* (Peabody: Hendrickson, 2009), where the evidence of Ignatius is cited in support of the claim that the "Parting of the Ways" was not a matter of perception or representation but rather "real" (e.g., p. 241).

[17] See esp., Boyarin "Semantic Differences"; Boyarin, *Border Lines: The Partition of Judaeo-Christianity* (Divinations; Philadelphia: University of Pennsylvania Press, 2004); Boyarin, "Apartheid Comparative Religion in the Second Century: Some Theory and a Case Study," *Journal of Medieval and Early Modern Studies* 36 (2006): 3–34; Boyarin, "Rethinking Jewish Christianity: An Argument for Dismantling a Dubious Category (to Which Is Appended a Correction of My Border Lines)," *JQR* 99 (2009): 7–36. The present essay also owes much to our conversations during the 2010 Tours colloquium.

[18] Indeed, as Arjun Appadurai (*Modernity at Large: Cultural Dimensions of Globalization.* [Minneapolis: University of Minnesota Press, 1996], 13) reminds us, "locality is itself a historical product." The borders of local cultures, moreover, are often – like the borders of "religions" – much less natural than they appear at first sight, and we might best understand the cities and provinces of the Roman Empire, in particular, not as border-bounded spaces akin to those in modern nation-states, but rather as nodes in overlapping networks, along which elements from multiple local cultures were exported, universalized, and transformed (see further below).

[19] I.e., insofar as the analysis of rhetoric might disclose its own set of narratives about the past, which can neither be reduced to reflections or projections of what we imagine, in contrast,

it was, after all, by expressing local and lived experiences in such terms that certain late antique authors articulated visions of reality that came to reshape social circumstances, beyond their own lifetimes and locales.[20]

Here, as elsewhere, the local microhistory is perhaps not the only (or most effective) antidote to the problems of the abstract metanarrative. If we limit ourselves to local spaces, we may run the risk of myopia, foreclosing the investigation of the transmission and transformation of local identities, along the many roads and rivers which Jews and Christians traveled in Late Antiquity, together with their letters, texts, liturgies, and rituals.[21] Accordingly, the challenge of moving beyond the model of the "Parting of the Ways" may involve much more than the rejection of the abstract in favor of a focus on the local. Rather, it may call us to create new approaches that are more attuned *both* to the specificities of local cultures and their social histories (as often constituted by intercredal crossings) *and* to the ways in which certain locales could become crucibles for the creation of texts and categories that were exported far beyond their original local contexts (sometimes with long-standing transregional consequences).

For this, Roman Syria and Palestine offer an apt test case. Despite their peripheral place on the eastern buffers and borders of the Roman Empire, the local cultures of these regions played a puzzlingly disproportionate role in creating the transregional identities and idioms that eventually came to shape the ideologies of the Roman Empire, and its medieval and modern European heirs in Western Christendom. From Palestine, one might cite the shift from "Judaean" to "Jew"

---

to constitute lived experiences "on the ground," nor completely severed from these realities. Together with the much-cited calls to distinguish the "rhetoric" and "reality" of Jewish and Christian self-definition – esp., Judith M. Lieu, *Image and Reality: The Jews in the World of the Christians in the Second Century* (Edinburgh: T&T Clark, 1996); Paula Fredriksen, "What 'Parting of the Ways'? Jews, Gentiles, and the Ancient Mediterranean City," in Becker and Reed, *The Ways That Never Parted*, 35–64; Fredriksen, "Roman Christianity and the Post-Roman West: The Social Correlates of the *Contra Iudaeos* Tradition," in *Jews, Christians, and the Roman Empire: The Poetics of Power in Late Antiquity*, ed. Natalie B. Dohrmann and Annette Yoshiko Reed (Philadelphia: University of Pennsylvania Press, 2013), 249–66 – note the more recent attempts to interrogate and enrich the "rhetoric" side of this dichotomy, such as the essays in Willi Braun, ed., *Rhetoric and Reality in Early Christianities* (Waterloo: Wilfrid Laurier University Press, 2005), esp. Laurence Broadhurst, "Melito of Sardis, the Second Sophistic, and Israel," 49–74. On the challenges of navigating between these approaches, see also Carleton Paget, *Jews, Christians, and Jewish Christians in Antiquity*, 12–13, 43–76.

[20] A concern for the reception of these ideas also points us to the asymmetry of power that became central for the mapping of such concepts onto social realities; see further, e.g., Williams, "No More Clever Titles," 49, and below.

[21] This point has arisen most sharply in scholarship on early modernity, etc., in the recent turn away from national histories towards transnational approaches. My reflections here are part of an experiment in bringing insights from these historiographical discussions to bear on the study of Late Antiquity; for an initial attempt, see Annette Yoshiko Reed, "Beyond the Land of Nod: Syriac Images of Asia and the Historiography of the West," *History of Religions* 49 (2009): 48–87. Here too, I draw particularly on the insights in Werner and Zimmerman, "Beyond Comparison."

in the meaning of Ἰουδαῖος or the articulation of "Judaism" (Ἰουδαϊσμός) in contrast to "Hellenism" (Ἑλληνισμός),[22] or the emergence of "Israel" as a utopian ideal and emblem of election, potentially abstracted from geography and genealogy alike.[23] Syria too served as a crucible for the creation of concepts and categories that became exported throughout the Roman Empire, as well as eastward into its Parthian and Persian counterparts.[24] It is to Antioch, for instance, that we owe the term "Christian" from the first century (i. e., Χριστιανός in Acts 11:26), as well as "Christianity" from the second.[25] When Ignatius of Antioch articulates the latter, moreover, he does so with a distinct note of Syrian pride about the origins of the former in his native city – even when writing from Smyrna and articulating this new notion of Χριστιανισμός with a universalizing horizon, in explicit opposition to Ἰουδαϊσμός (*Magn.* 10.1–3; see also *Rom.* 3.3; *Phil.* 6.1).

To be sure, Ignatius' famous contrast of Ἰουδαϊσμός and Χριστιανισμός is not quite the clear sign of "Parting" that some scholars have hoped to find, nor the pure moment of "invention" that others have sought to pinpoint. Rather, it retains something of the juxtaposition of two actions (i. e., "Judaizing" and "Christianizing"), both of which are credited to those whom *we* would call "Christians."[26] The limits of the immediate influence of Ignatius' "invention," moreover, are clear from the writings of Justin Martyr. Scholars commonly point to Justin as the key figure in delineating "Christianity" as distinct from "Judaism," and even perhaps for the very concept of "Judaism" as "religion." Yet Justin nowhere uses Ignatius' novel terminology.[27]

---

[22] See further Martha Himmelfarb, "Judaism and Hellenism in 2 Maccabees," *PT* 19 (1998): 19–40; Shaye J. D. Cohen, *The Beginnings of Jewishness: Boundaries, Varieties, Uncertainties* (Berkeley: University of California Press, 1999), esp. 69–130; Steve Mason, "Jews, Judaeans, Judaizing, Judaism: Problems of Categorization in Ancient History," *JSJ* 38 (2007): 457–512; David M. Miller "The Meaning of *Ioudaios* and its Relationship to Other Group Labels in Ancient Judaism," *CBR* 9 (2010): 98–126. For a recent and accessible summary of the debate, see the essays in Timothy Michael Law and Charles Halton, eds., *Jew and Judean: A Forum on Politics and Historiography in the Translation of Ancient Texts* (Los Angeles: Marginalia Review of Books, 2014), http://marginalia.lareviewofbooks.org/jew-judean-forum/.

[23] E. g., perhaps most famously, Justin's claim of the church as truly "Israel," but perhaps no less the contemporaneous Rabbinic conception of what is aptly termed "Utopian Israel" by Sacha Stern, *Jewish Identity in Early Rabbinic Writings* (AGJU 23; Leiden: Brill, 1994), 128–30.

[24] I here use the language of "exportation" to signal a possible parallel (however broad) with the European origins and colonial spread of the term "religion" in the early modern period, as charted in Dubuisson, *L'Occident et la religion*, 272–75; Dubuisson, "Exporting the Local: Recent Perspectives on 'Religion' as a Cultural Category," *Religion Compass* 1 (2007): 787–800.

[25] For a survey of the relevant early evidence, see Annette Yoshiko Reed and Lily Vuong, "Christianity in Antioch: Partings in Roman Syria," in *Partings: How Judaism and Christianity Became Two*, ed. Hershel Shanks (Washington, DC: Biblical Archaeological Society, 2013), 105–32.

[26] Mason, "Jews, Judaeans, Judaizing, Judaism," 470.

[27] I owe this point to Carleton Paget, *Jews, Christians, and Jewish Christians in Antiquity*, 12–13.

In fact, as Steve Mason has deftly demonstrated, it is not until the third century that Ignatius' usage begins to be adopted:

That Ἰουδαϊσμός did not yet [for Ignatius] mean "Judaism" as a comprehensive system and way of life (an English *-ism*) seems clear because throughout the first two centuries no other Christian text used the term: not the gospels of Matthew, Mark, Luke, or John, the letter to the Hebrews, Justin (even in the *Dialogue with Trypho, a Ioudaios*), Melito (even in the *Paschal Homily*), Irenaeus, the apologists, or Clement of Alexandria – though the issue was often precisely what we incline to call "Judaism." Late-antique Christian and modern-critical scholarly commentaries to these texts are *filled* with references to "Judaism," but there is no corresponding term in the Greek texts. From the early third century, things begin to change dramatically among Christian writers. To the church fathers Tertullian (24 occurrences), Origen (30), Eusebius (19), Epiphanius (36 occurrences in the *Panarion* alone), John Chrysostom (36), Victorinus (about 40), Ambrosiaster (21), and Augustine (27), we owe a new use of Ἰουδαϊσμός and *Iudaismus*, now indeed to indicate the whole belief system and regimen of the *Ioudaioi*: a true "*-ism*," abstracted from concrete conditions in a living state.[28]

For the evolution of this pair of terms towards meaning something like "Judaism" and "Christianity" as we now know them, their exportation, translation, and recontextualization appears to have been pivotal. The reification of "Judaism" and "Christianity" in further abstraction from Jews and Christians seems to have resulted (at least in part) from Tertullian's rendering of the pair into Latin as *Iudaismus* and *Christianismus*, in a North African milieu shaped more by the struggle with Marcion than with any concern for Jews of his own time.[29] Tertullian's *Iudaismus* and *Christianismus*, however, are still not quite "religions." They serve, rather, as a temporally-inflected pair – as inseparable as past and present, Torah and Gospel, prophetic prediction and messianic actualization. What Tertullian argues, against Marcion, that "Judaism" is the necessary first stage; it is not the living "religion" of the Jews, so much as the corpse revivified at the Jesus' resurrection as "Christianity."

Yet even if the evidence from Ignatius, Justin, and Tertullian does not quite satisfy a contemporizing desire to pinpoint the "origins" or "invention" of the categories familiar to us today, it does signal the place of category-creation as an important social practice for the articulation of early Christian identities. It remains significant that, in the course of trying to determine what it might mean to be "Christian" (e. g., whether as a participant in a kind of *paideia*, piety, politic, or philosophy; or as a member of an *ethnos*, *genos*, or *laos*), some Patristic authors reversed the Roman imperial gaze to reconfigure existing binaries and

---

[28] Mason, "Jews, Judaeans, Judaizing, Judaism," 471; italics in original. Cf. Seth Schwartz, "How Many Judaisms Were There? A Critique of Neusner and Smith on Definition and Mason and Boyarin on Categorization," *JAJ* 2 (2011): 208–38, presented in an earlier form at the 48th Philadelphia Seminar on Christian Origins, University of Pennsylvania, 21 October 2010.

[29] Mason, "Jews, Judaeans, Judaizing, Judaism," 471–474; Boyarin, "Rethinking Jewish Christianity," 10–11.

taxonomies of collective identity in startling new ways. Insofar as Roman Syria and Palestine served as crucibles for some of the most lasting results of this creativity, their local cultures contributed to "constructing conceptual frameworks" that – in Williams' formulation – "in turn serve to configure reality in new ways," especially once "Imperial Christianity … had the power to construct a Judaism that reflected its own self-image, not only within its literature but in Roman society as well."[30]

But what is no less significant, for our present purposes, is that Roman Syria and Palestine are also especially rich in evidence for the *limits* of category-creation to shape local and lived experiences. It is also from precisely these same regions that we find those sources that most unsettle modern scholarly claims about "Christianity" as categorically distinct from "Judaism" already in Late Antiquity.[31] By the third and fourth centuries, there is mounting evidence for the successful exportation of Ignatius' notion of a reified "Judaism" and "Christianity," as a conceptual pair, far beyond Antioch (and perhaps even back again). Yet on the Syrian ground from which terms like Χριστιανός and Χριστιανισμός first sprung, there is also evidence for resistance – from the third century and well into the fourth.[32] This evidence includes works such as the *Didascalia apostolorum* and the Pseudo-Clementine literature,[33] in relation to which modern scholars have been forced to coin clumsy categories such as "Jewish-

---

[30] Williams, "No More Clever Titles," 42, 49; see also Carleton Paget, *Jews, Christians, and Jewish Christians in* Antiquity, 12.

[31] Some of these sources, moreover, simultaneously unsettle any conceptualization of "Israel" as ontological distinct from "the nations"; see, e.g., Ps.-Clem. *Hom.* 11.16, and note also the assumption in some of the Pseudo-Clementine materials that Gentiles are susceptible to ritual impurity and thus subject to rules concerning menstrual separation, etc. See discussion below.

[32] Our literary evidence for late antique Palestine yields some evidence for this as well – that is, within Patristic polemics that puzzle precisely over the persistence of these older or alternate approaches. It seems, e.g., that for fourth- and fifth-century authors such as Eusebius, Epiphanius, and Jerome, it was becoming so natural to partition the world into "Christianity" and its abject "Judaism" that any alternative was deemed monstrous – the stuff of hybrids and hydra-headed "heresies." Less clear is the degree to which these Patristic reports can be used for historical reconstruction. Accordingly, I here focus on the Syrian evidence, rather than chasing after Ebionites, etc. For the relevant Patristic passages, see Albertus Frederik Johannes Klijn and Gerrit J. Reinink, *Patristic Evidence for Jewish-Christian Sects* (NTSup 36; Leiden: Brill, 1973), 95–281, and on the fuller range of relevant evidence, see Simon Claude Mimouni, *Le Judéo-christianisme ancien: Essais historiques* (Patrimoines; Paris: Cerf, 1998).

[33] Perhaps most sensitive to the Syrian contexts of these works is Georg Strecker, *Das Judenchristentum in den Pseudoklementinen* (TU 70; 2nd ed; Berlin: Akademie-Verlag, 1981), and Strecker, "On the Problem of Jewish Christianity," in Walter Bauer, *Orthodoxy and Heresy in Earliest Christianity*, ed. and trans. Robert A. Kraft and Gerhard A. Kroedel (2nd ed.; Philadelphia: Fortress, 1971), 244–57. On the value of situating the Pseudo-Clementine literature in the fourth-century Syrian contexts of their redactional formation, see Chapters One, Five, and Six in this volume; Nicole Kelley, *Knowledge and Religious Authority in the Pseudo-Clementines: Situating the* Recognitions *in Fourth-Century Syria* (WUNT[2] 213; Tübingen: Mohr Siebeck, 2006), 179–212; Kelley, "On Recycling Texts and Traditions: The Pseudo-Clementine Recognitions and Religious Life in Fourth-Century Syria," in *The Levant: Crossroads of Late Antiquity*,

Christianity."[34] If such works resist easy categorization as *either* "Christian" *or* "Jewish," however, it is perhaps not because they combine or hybridize two already stable identities. What I would like to suggest, rather, is that they may preserve evidence for the persistence of older or alternate approaches to categorizing identity and difference (e. g., "Israel" vs. "the nations," "Jew" vs. "Greek," "Greek" vs. "barbarian").

Modern studies pursued within the model of "Parting of the Ways," with its teleological thrust, have largely ignored the persistence of any other perspectives besides those that lead directly to our own. Newer lines of discussion, however, have made the analysis of late antique alternatives perhaps quite pressing. It is all too tempting – as Carleton Paget has cautioned – to counter a simplistic notion of "Parting" by contrasting the elite "separatists" responsible for our literature with an imagined popular and undifferentiated ecumenism "on the ground."[35] Yet it is clearly not enough to read "separatist" sources "against the grain" in order to posit "popular" views as simply their opposite.

Water, Blood, Purity, and Boundaries

Is it possible, then, to reorient our analyses so as to glimpse some of these other perspectives? For this, I suggest that a focus on blood and water may provide one interesting way to see the mapping of Jewish and Christian identities, as if sideways, in a manner that might help to expose something of what is lost in the privileging of Patristic practices of differentiation and their discursive disembodiments of difference as doctrine.[36] Practices, liturgies, and beliefs involving blood and water were common in early Christian efforts at distinguishing their own communities, histories, and practices from Jewish and other "Others," and they also feature in early Rabbinic efforts at reconfiguring "Israel" and its boundaries, in the wake of the Roman destruction of the Second Temple in

---

ed. Ellen Bradshaw Aitken and John M. Fosey (McGill University Monographs in Classical Archaeology and History 22; Leiden: Brill, 2013), 105–12.

[34] On the history of research (including the discussion prior to Ferdinand Christian Baur), see references and discussion in Carleton Paget, *Jews, Christians, and Jewish Christians in Antiquity*, 289–324. Major critiques of the terminology include Boyarin, "Rethinking Jewish Christianity"; Joan Taylor, The Phenomenon of Early Jewish-Christianity: Reality or Scholarly Invention?" *VC* 44 (1990): 313–34. See also Chapter Three and Appendix B in this volume.

[35] Carleton Paget, *Jews, Christians, and Jewish Christians in Antiquity*, 12–13.

[36] That the categorization of difference through heresiology was itself something perhaps shared, at least between proto-orthodox Christians and some Rabbinic Jews, is argued by Boyarin, *Border Lines*, 112–47. I suggest something similar with respect to the fourth-century authors/redactors responsible for the Pseudo-Clementine *Homilies* in Chapter Five in this volume. See also F. Stanley Jones, *Pseudoclementina Elchasaiticaque inter Judaeochristiana: Collected Studies* (Orientalia Lovaniensia Analecta 203; Leuven: Peeters, 2012), 516–31.

70 CE.[37] Within Jewish and Christian traditions, these fluids could function as literary and liturgical symbols on the level of language, but also within laws, prayers, and practices that inscribe identity and difference onto individual bodies (particularly those of converts and women) and, with them, onto the body politic of the communities thereby cohered and constructed. Perhaps precisely because these two fluids seem like such paradigmatically *natural* symbols, they seem to have been powerful for articulating and naturalizing identities within and beyond "religions" (e. g., with appeal to the blood of birth, menstruation, or death; or to that which connects fathers to sons; or that which spills in sacrifice and martyrdom; or to the water that washes them, for purification, initiation, healing, or exorcism).

Particularly in the Roman Near East, we find a rich body of late antique evidence for debates surrounding the proper management and ritual manipulation of the blood of animals and humans alike, as well as for an array of practices of varying degrees of what we might call "religious" power, centered on washing, bathing, and water. These encompass Jews, Christians, and so-called "pagans," but also those who do not fit within this typicalized triangle – such as Samaritans, Ebionites, Elchaasites, Manichees, and a seemingly constant stream of local baptismal movements that resist categorization.[38] Accordingly, a focus on the Jewish and Christian traditions surrounding these fluids in Roman Syria and Palestine may help to illumine a bit of the broader context for the processes of category-formation and differentiation discussed by Boyarin, Mimouni, and others, while also helping us to attend to the insights of Lieu, Williams, and others vis-à-vis the importance of bringing the local, specific, and social to bear on the abstract and discursive.

It shall suffice to reflect upon three examples, which span the period from the late second to mid-fourth centuries CE: [1] the Mishnah, a Hebrew halakhic work that scholars place firmly within "Judaism," as the foundational document of the Rabbinic movement, [2] the *Didascalia apostolorum*, a community-rule

---

[37] For the relevant references, see David Biale, *Blood and Belief: The Circulation of a Symbol between Jews and Christians* (Berkeley: University of California Press, 2007); Raʿanan S. Boustan and Annette Yoshiko Reed, "Introduction to Theme-Issue: Blood and the Boundaries of Jewish and Christian Identities in Late Antiquity," *Hen* 30 (2008): 229–42. The potential of purity discourse for social history is richly shown by Yair Furstenberg, "Outsider Impurity: Trajectories of Second Temple Separation Traditions in Tannaitic Literature," in *Tradition, Transmission, and Transformation from Second Temple Literature through Judaism and Christianity in Late Antiquity*, ed. Menahem Kister et al. (STDJ 113; Leiden: Brill, 2015), 40–68.

[38] See further, e. g., Joseph Thomas, *Le mouvement baptiste: Palestine et Syrie* (Gembloux: Duculot, 1935); Kurt Rudolph, "The Baptist Sects," in *The Cambridge History of Judaism*, vol. 3: *The Early Roman Period*, ed. William Horbury, W. D. Davies, and John Sturdy (Cambridge: Cambridge University Press, 1999), 471–500; Simon Claude Mimouni, "Les elkasaïtes: États des questions et des recherché," in *The Image of the Judaeo-Christians in Ancient Jewish and Christian Literature*, ed. Peter J. Tomson and Doris Lambers-Petry (WUNT 158; Tübingen: Mohr Siebeck, 2003), 209–29.

text written in Greek in the third century and translated into Syriac in the early fourth, which is usually placed within "Christianity" from a religious perspective, albeit in genealogical and cultural connection to "Judaism," and [3] the Pseudo-Clementine *Homilies*, a Greek novel redacted in the fourth century and translated into Syriac in the late fourth or early fifth, which has long served as a major source for reconstructing what might have flourished in between "Christianity" and "Judaism." The three – I shall suggest – preserve perspectives of those who claimed identities in continuity with the Torah and biblical "Israel," and who thus faced the common challenge of articulating postsacrificial ideologies from scriptures deeply steeped in sacrificial imagery and ideals.[39] They also reflect three different (and possibly competing) efforts to appropriate priestly prerogatives and prestige, by rereading ritual purity in absence of the Jerusalem Temple.[40] Each of these sources articulates its own ideals of piety and pedagogy in part through its positions on whether the blood of sacrifice atones, and whether and for whom the blood of menstruation pollutes.[41] And, within each, an assessment concerning the power of water to purify plays an important part in remapping the borders and peripheries of the chosen.[42]

Mishnah Niddah

In tractate *Niddah* of the Mishnah, we find early evidence for the intensive Rabbinic Jewish efforts to retheorize the meanings of blood. Such efforts, as Charlotte Fonrobert has shown, are exemplary of the Rabbinic repurposing of the purity system of the Torah as a conceptual matrix for mapping a continuum

---

[39] As Guy Stroumsa (*The End of Sacrifice: Religious Transformations in Late Antiquity* [trans. Susan Emanuel; Chicago: Chicago University Press, 2009]) has noted, "To a certain extent Rabbinic Judaism and Christianity would both remain sacrificial religions, but very special sacrificial religions because they functioned without blood sacrifice" (pp. 63–64). See further Annette Yoshiko Reed, "From Sacrifice to the Slaughterhouse: Ancient and Modern Perspectives on Meat, Ritual, and Civilization," *Method and Theory in the Study of Religion* 26 (2014): 111–58.

[40] For pre-70 precedents, see, e.g., Beate Ego et al., eds. *Gemeinde ohne Tempel* (WUNT 118; Tübingen: Mohr Siebeck, 1999), esp. 267–84; Eyal Regev, Abominated Temple and a Holy Community: The Formation of the Notions of Purity and Impurity in Qumran," *Dead Sea Discoveries* 10 (2003): 24–78; Jonathan Klawans, *Purity, Sacrifice, and the Temple: Symbolism and Supersessionism in the Study of Ancient Judaism* (Oxford: Oxford University Press, 2006), 134–38, 145–74.

[41] Some mention should also be made of the blood of circumcision, which is sometimes cited as emblematic of the defining difference between Jew and Gentile by late antique Jews and Christians alike. In Roman Syria and Palestine, however, circumcision may not have been quite the differentiating mark that it was elsewhere, due not only to the case of Samaritans, but also to the circumcision of some "pagan" Syrian priests – perhaps most famously, the Roman emperor Elagabalus (on whom see below).

[42] For the broader context of the development of Christian baptism, see now Everett Ferguson, *Baptism in the Early Church: History, Theology, and Liturgy in the First Five Centuries* (Grand Rapids: Eerdmans, 2009).

of identities.[43] In contrast to the priestly focus on the blood of sacrifice, much of the Rabbinic focus fell on the blood of menstruation.[44] Perhaps not coincidentally, this choice allowed for broader horizon of authority – encompassing both women and men, while also enabling the naturalization of a new reconfiguration of "Israel" in relation to "the nations."[45] According to the Levitical laws of the Torah (esp. Lev 12–15), Gentiles are neither capable of ritual purity, nor susceptible to ritual pollution – the two states that define "Israel" in their capacity as a "kingdom of priests," set apart by the possibility of approaching God through sacrifice in the Jerusalem Temple. In its early Rabbinic reception and reinterpretation,[46] this Pentateuchal principle seems to have served as one means for renewed reflection on "Israel" and its boundaries, with the possibility of ritual impurity marking the potential inclusion of a body within the body politic.

In *m. Niddah* 7.3, for instance, the problem of the boundaries of Israel is posed with reference to the ritual status of fabric with blood stains from Rekem – a town on the border of Israel (cf. *m. Gittin* 1.1), the inhabitants of which are doubly border-dwellers inasmuch as they also claim to be converts. Here, an anonymous statement that "all menstrual bloodstains that come from Rekem are ritually pure" occasions a discussion that explores the Rekemites' status as converts and border-dwellers, on the fluid peripheries of postsacrificial "Israel." First is R. Yehudah's ruling that their blood stains are impure since the Rekemites are converts who err; they are placed within Israel, inasmuch as they are capable of ritually impurity, but their exegesis and practice is questioned: they cannot be trusted to observe purity laws properly (or, at least by Rabbinic standards). R. Meir's ruling, by contrast, seems to be predicated on the dismissal of the validity of their conversion; his ruling suggests that the status of their blood

---

[43] On Rabbinic "genres" of blood, see Charlotte Elisheva Fonrobert, "The *Didascalia Apostolorum*: A Mishnah for the Disciples of Jesus," *JECS* 9 (2001): 483–509, esp. 244–45. As shall become obvious below, this essay is deeply indebted to her entire corpus of studies on menstrual purity.

[44] Cf. Nancy Jay, *Throughout Your Generations Forever: Sacrifice, Religion, and Paternity* (Chicago: University of Chicago Press, 1992) – if she is correct to suggest that the power of sacrificial blood is itself rooted in the (male) redeployment and supersession of the power of (female) reproductive blood as a locus for lineage and descent, the Rabbinic focus on menstrual impurity proves all the more poignant. On the generative tension between sacrificial blood and reproductive blood as it continued into Late Antiquity, see also Joan R. Branham, "Blutige Frauen und blutige Räume: Menstruation und Eucharistie in Spätantike und Mittelalter," *Vorträge aus dem Warburg-Haus* 3 (1999): 129–61.

[45] Or, rather, "Israel" as Rabbinic reconceived, with Rabbis at the center and priests pushed to the periphery, precisely through Rabbinic claims to the traditionally priestly domains of reading blood and Scripture. On the promotion of priestly authority as a factor in the very emergence of blood as a locus for religious expertise, see William K. Gilders, *Blood Ritual in the Hebrew Bible: Meaning and Power* (Baltimore: Johns Hopkins University Press, 2004).

[46] See further Christine Hayes, *Gentile Impurities and Jewish Identities: Intermarriage and Conversion from the Bible to the Talmud* (Oxford: Oxford University Press, 2002), 19–44, and below.

stains reverts to what it would otherwise be on the basis of genealogy. The blood stains of the Gentiles among them are thus unquestionably pure (i. e., since those who are not part of Israel and not susceptible to ritual impurity). This leaves, then, the problem of the status of the blood stains of those of the Rekemites who belong to "Israel" by birth. With respect to them, R. Meir – for reasons unstated – judges them suspect in their observance of purity and thus deems their blood stains as impure.

The discussion concludes with the statement that "The Sages, however, declare them pure, since they are not suspect with regard to their blood stains." This conclusion picks up and confirms the anonymous statement at the outset. Yet there are different ways in which we could interpret it in relation to the intervening rulings by R. Yehuda and R. Meir.[47] On the one hand, the reference to those who are not suspect, in the judgment of the Sages, could be taken to refer simply to the Jewish-born Rekemites whose blood stains were deemed impure by R. Meir; if so, the Sages' statement would counter R. Meir's judgment, while seemingly accepting his assessment of the invalid conversion of the other Rekemites. Yet the concluding statement of the Sages can also be read in relation to R. Yehuda's ruling, as accepting his assessment of the Rekemites as valid converts but countering his judgment about their error.

What is highlighted, then, is the seemingly paradoxical fact that the results in either case are exactly the same. Following the logics of Levitical purity laws, menstrual blood stains could be treated as pure *either* from those who are deemed to be trustworthy Jews, clearly within Israel in genealogy and practice, *or* from those who are Gentiles, clearly outside. Impurity is at issue for those otherwise within Israel, by genealogy or conversion, who do not practice as they should. Through the border-dwelling Rekemites is thus signaled a tension (ultimately unresolved) about whether "Israel" is constituted primarily through blood, in the sense of genealogical descent, or through the proper management of blood, as in the pollution of menstruation, which here emblematizes proper exegesis and practice. What makes it possible to explore these and other fluidities at the borders of Israel, moreover, is the stable state of the Gentile woman, whose place outside of the system enables her to function as a static reference point – a pole star for the Rabbinic navigation of identity.

One finds something similar in *m. Niddah* 4.1–3, perhaps the passage that has been most discussed in the context of the place of menstrual purity in the Rabbinic rethinking of "Israel."[48] Here, the blood of the Gentile woman and the Jewish

---

[47] My reading here departs from the usual interpretation of this passage, particularly in raising the possibility of some unresolved tension; contrast, thus, Hayes, *Gentile Impurities and Jewish Identities*, 111, who sees the issue addressed as a demographic one.

[48] See esp. Hayes, *Gentile Impurities and Jewish Identities*, 122–31; Boyarin, *Border Lines*, 58–63; Charlotte Elisheva Fonrobert, "Blood and Law: Uterine Fluids and Rabbinic Maps of Identity," *Hen* 30 (2008): 243–66; also Fonrobert, "When Women Walk in the Way of Their

woman are juxtaposed with those of the two groups that are thereby situated in between, namely, Samaritans and Sadducees. The very pairing of the two raises the possibility of determining the bounds of "Israel" through different criteria. That Samaritans stand in an ambivalent relationship to Jewishness due to their ancestry and uncertain motives for conversion is polemically claimed already in 2 Kings 17. Sadducees, by contrast, can be excluded from "Israel" only heresiologically (e.g., by virtue of claimed deviance from beliefs that Rabbis deem proper, such as in the case of resurrection).[49]

Here, however, the shared commitment to Torah law seems to allow for the partial inclusion of both Sadducees and Samaritans – whose menstrual blood, unlike those of Gentiles, at least bears the possibility of ritual impurity. Sadducees can, through choices about "the ways" to follow in interpreting blood and choices about washing with water, move in and out of the boundaries of "Israel," as here Rabbinically redefined. Samaritans, by contrast, are placed firmly on the outer boundary within. They are capable of impurity, unlike Gentiles, but incapable of purity, unlike Jews; they are said to be "like non-Jews" but also "like Israel" (*t. Terumot* 4.12; also *Massekhet Kutim* 1.1).[50] In a sense, the early Rabbinic pairing of Samaritans and Sadducees, as doubled foils for the articulation of identity, thus recalls the place of Jews and "heretics" in the early Christian imagination, even as the status of the Samaritan in the early Rabbinic imagination also evokes the status that a number of early Christians claim for themselves, namely, as "neither Jew nor Greek" but also something of both.

The Mishnah is notoriously silent about Christians, and nowhere in Rabbinic literature do we find anything akin to the explicit discussions of Jewish and Christian difference so common in the writings of their Patristic contemporaries. The possibilities of inclusion and exclusion here mapped by laws about menstrual blood, however, may open the way for some imaginative speculation as to which features of various types of Christians may or may not have seemed like meaningful differences and commonalities, when viewed from the perspective

---

Fathers: On Gendering the Rabbinic Claim for Authority," *Journal of the History of Sexuality* 10 (2001): 398–416.

[49] I.e., as presumably in the doctrinal mapping of "all Israel" in *m. Sanhedrin* 10.1, which serves to exclude Sadducees alongside Samaritans by virtue of their denial that the doctrine of resurrection can be found in the Torah. See further Boyarin, *Border Lines*, 58–63.

[50] Notably, Samaritans here serve a role akin to that "the Jews" in Christian literature – namely, as figures and foils for exploring the identities of those who claim to be the true "Israel"; the discussion, in other words, is less about Samaritans than about the boundaries of "Israel" or "Jew." See further below as well as Stern, *Jewish Identity in Early Rabbinic Writings*, 99; Laurence Schiffman, "The Samaritans in Tannaitic Halakhah," *JQR* 75 (1985): 323–50; Andreas Lehnhardt, "The Samaritans (*Kutim*) in the Talmud Yerushalmi," in *The Talmud Yerushalmi and Graeco Roman Culture III*, ed. Peter Schäfer (TSAJ 93; Tübingen: Mohr Siebeck, 2003), 139–60. For an account of the history of Roman Palestine that seeks to do justice to the place of Samaritans, alongside Jews, Christians, etc., in the religious, physical, and political landscape, see now Hagith Sivan, *Palestine in Late Antiquity* (Oxford: Oxford University Press, 2008).

of early Rabbis in Roman Palestine. Like Rekemites, for instance, Christian communities in the area included both Jews and Gentiles by birth. Unlike Sadducees and Samaritans, most Christians believed in resurrection. With Rabbis, Sadducees, and Samaritans, many shared a commitment to the exegesis and extension of Torah law. And some in nearby Syria – as we shall see – also shared a conviction of the need to maintain ritual purity even apart from the Temple, for which the management of the pollution of menstrual blood could prove paradigmatic.[51]

Didascalia apostolorum

The third-century *Didascalia apostolorum* provides indirect evidence of shared practices and perspectives between Rabbis and Syrian Christians on menstrual purity.[52] Its authors, in fact, engage in an extended polemic against those Christians of Jewish lineage who continue such practices. Some of those who, in their words, "have been converted from the People [i.e., Israel]" are here said to continue in practicing "purifications and sprinklings and baptisms and distinction of meats," and the authors argue against these practices as "keep[ing] vain bonds" (*Did. apost.* 26). For this, the problem of menstrual purity is paradigmatic and discussed in the most detail.

As in the Mishnah, the Torah and its laws still serve in the *Didascalia apostolorum* as the primary source for redrawing the borders of postsacrificial "Israel" with water, blood, and purity providing a focus for anxieties about the fluidity at its peripheries. In the case of the *Didascalia apostolorum*, the focus falls largely on water, consistent with the reimagining of "Israel" as a post-Temple ideal of a people never shaped by the blood of sacrifice, nor bound by Levitical law. The Temple, animal sacrifice, and the attendant purity laws are here associated with what the text calls "the People" or "the former People," in contrast to whom "the People" is said to have been constituted by the sprinkling of the atoning blood of the death of Jesus, in service to whom is a new bloodless priesthood of bishops. Just as the blood sacrifice of Jesus is here distinguished by its singularity from animal sacrifices, so the locus for the transformative, ritual efficacy of water is

---

[51] Of course, within Christian traditions, concerns about menstrual impurity are hardly limited to Syria, and also cannot be dismissed as solely the concern of "Jewish-Christians," Jewish converts, etc. – nor does this concern necessarily tied to Torah exegesis (as it is in the case of the *Didascalia apostolorum*). See further Shaye J.D. Cohen, "Menstruants and the Sacred in Judaism and Christianity," in *Women's History, Ancient History*, ed. S.B. Pomeroy (Chapel Hill: University of North Carolina Press, 1991), 273–99; Lesley Dean-Jones, *Women's Bodies in Classical Greek Science* (Oxford: Clarendon, 1994), esp. 225–47; and Helen King, *Hippocrates' Woman: Reading the Female Body in Ancient Greece* (London: Routledge, 1998), esp. 75–98.

[52] See esp. Fonrobert, "*Didascalia Apostolorum*," 483–509.

shifted to a single, initiatory baptism, the fragility of which is fiercely defended against the temptation to repetition.

Despite exhibiting some of what we are accustomed to reading as markers of the distinction of "Christianity" from "Judaism," then, the *Didascalia apostolorum* bears striking discursive and exegetical overlaps with the Mishnah and Tosefta; Fonrobert, in fact, goes so far as to call it a "counter-mishnah," proposing that both its authors and their opponents can be meaningfully placed on a continuum of Jewish identities no less than Christian ones.[53] Fonrobert posits, moreover, that some awareness of early Rabbinic legal discourse is signaled by its references to δευτέρωσις," a Greek term equivalent to Hebrew *mishnah* (although rendered in the Syriac translation, as *tinyan nimosa,* or "second law"). If she is correct, this work represents our earliest evidence for the exportation of distinctively *Rabbinic* Jewish traditions outside of Roman Palestine.[54] And, if so, it proves particularly poignant that the authors counter the continued commitment to this "second legislation" by some within their own community, by reenacting a past moment in the interactions between Syria and Palestine – namely, the incident at Antioch and the "apostolic decree" from Jerusalem, as described in Galatians 2 and Acts 15. It is in this context that the authors of the *Didascalia apostolorum* take up the problem of the post-Temple/postsacrificial exegesis of the Torah.[55]

Much attention has been given to statements therein that seem to fit the modes of supersessionism associated with Justin Martyr and the *Contra Iudaeos* tradition. After all, the *Didascalia apostolorum* does include the assertion that "all the workings of the Lord our God has passed from the People [i. e., Israel] to the Church through us apostles; and He has withdrawn Himself and left the People" (*Did. apost.* 198). This point is also underlined by references to Israel as "the former People" (e. g., 85). A closer look, however, shows its own framing of identities to be a more complex. *Didascalia apostolorum* does use the term "Christian" at times, but it is not in binary contrast with "Jew": rather, it occurs primarily in discussions of the hypocrisy of those who claim the name "Christian" while not acting in accordance with it (e. g., 39, 102, 142, 162–63). For much of the text, moreover, the operant binary is between "the People" and "the nations." The church is thus described as consisting of "those who have believed, from the People and from the Gentiles" (213) – that is, as a combination of what we might call "Jewish-Christians" and "Gentile Christians." Nor is

---

[53] Fonrobert, "*Didascalia Apostolorum*"; cf. Joseph G. Mueller, "The Ancient Church Order Literature: Genre or Tradition?" *JECS* 15 (2007): 337–80.

[54] See further discussion in Chapter Nine below.

[55] Indeed, it is perhaps telling that the issue of the "second legislation," etc., first arises in the course of a discussion of proper and improper reading – i. e., an exhortation to avoid the "books of the heathens" and to turn instead to the biblical books of Kings for histories, biblical prophets for wisdom and philosophy, Psalms for songs, Genesis for cosmogony, and the Torah for law (*Did. apost.* 2; CSCO 402:14–15).

this distinction only demographic. Jesus' task is correspondingly described as a doubled one: he is said to have come to earth so that "he might redeem us, who are of the People, from the bonds of the Second Legislation (i. e., δευτέρωσις) ... and might redeem you also, who are of the Gentiles, from the worship of idols and from all ungodliness, and get you for an inheritance" (164). Even as the ultimate hope and horizon of its instructions is a single church with a single Law, the *Didascalia apostolorum* does not construct "Judaism" in contrast with "Christianity." Rather, it attends to how the coming of the Jewish messiah has also affected the people Israel. Far from treating Judaism as merely a figure of Christianity's superseded past, the *Didascalia apostolorum* is quite explicit in describing a post-Christian distinction within Israel – between "the People who did not believe in him" and "the People who have believed in Jesus" (i. e., what we might call "non-Christian Jews" and "Christian Jews"; 185–86).

To the degree that the *Didascalia apostolorum* appeals to any past moment of "Parting," moreover, it is within the prehistory of the people Israel, as catalyzed by the worship of the Golden Calf in Exod 32.[56] It is here argued that the first and true Law was that given prior to the Calf; this is the Law of Moses, the Ten Commandments, which speak nothing of sacrifice, blood, or ritual purity. The "second legislation" (i. e., δευτέρωσις), by contrast, is that which was given as punishment "for the making of the calf and for idolatry"; this Law that encompasses blood sacrifice and its purity regulations, and defines those of "the former People" not redeemed from it through belief in Jesus (*Did. apost.* 26).[57]

Interestingly, the Jew who is baptized into belief in Jesus as messiah/Christ is thus imagined in much the same terms as the Gentile of Levitical purity laws of the Torah: as a person who stands outside of the sacrificial system, no longer bound by purity laws, nor subject to ritual pollution. According to the authors of the *Didascalia apostolorum*, the water rite of baptism replaces the blood rites of sacrifice and thus frees the baptized Jew from the requirement of further water rites for purification. Baptism, by this logic, effectively transforms a Jew into a Gentile.

With this appeal to the transformative power of water, however, the authors are forced to explain how the water rite of baptism differs from the water rites for purification from menstrual and other impurities. The difference between what we might call "Christian" baptism and "Jewish" ritual ablution is described with language that signals anxieties of similarity: it is a difference between baptism and baptisms.

---

[56] Cf. Exod 32; Acts 7:39; *Barn.* 4.6–8; 14.1–4; Justin, *Dial.* 20.

[57] In effect, "Israel" is thus bifurcated – into [1] one people under the burden of a Law and Temple imposed for a past sin of idolatry and [2] another that can return to the older, pre-Temple Law in a post-Temple age, through the water of baptism and the retrospective rejection of the blood of sacrifice.

The power of this seemingly small difference is explored through the case of the baptized Jewish woman who misreads her menstrual blood as impure – not recognizing that the one baptism of the church has removed her from the bounds of sacrificial Israel. What is most striking is the suggestion that her practices of purification through water serve to "undo [her] baptism." By these multiple baptisms, she regains the capacity for ritual impurity and thus the need to maintain ritual purity, losing the benefits of the one baptism; in the belief that she needs to wash again to keep the Holy Spirit, she loses it.[58] Just as a *single* baptism, here, can effectively turn a Jew into a Gentile, so one can be turned back into a Jew, at least Levitically-speaking, by *too many* baptisms.[59] And hence the "former People" with the second Law, with its priesthood of sacrificial blood and peoplehood of genealogical blood, remains fluidly at the borders of the new *ekklesia* constituted by the singular sacrifice of the blood of Christ and by a singular baptism.

Pseudo-Clementine Homilies

Within the Pseudo-Clementine literature, we find traditions that voice views of blood and water similar to those that the *Didascalia apostolorum* appears to contest. Here, it shall suffice to limit ourselves to the Pseudo-Clementine *Homilies*, where engagement with Rabbinic traditions is most clearly attested and where the concern with blood, water, and ritual purity is developed in most detail.[60] The theorization of blood and water is so extensive in the *Homilies* as to encompass cosmogony and genesis, the origins of demons and disease, the genealogy of false worship, the polemic against animal sacrifice, the defense of dietary regulations, the proposal of false pericopes in the Torah, the partial ac-

---

[58] I.e., just as the water rites of initiatory baptism are here imagined as exempting the Jew from the purity requirements of Levitical law, so the practice of Levitical rites of washing functions to "undo baptism," thereby transforming a Christian of Jewish descent back into a Jew. In light of the debates at the time concerning whether women could baptize, it is interesting that the implication here is that a woman might be able to "unbaptize" herself!

[59] Compare the place of water in later rituals of reconversion to Judaism, on which see, e. g., Ephraim Kanarfogel, "Returning to the Jewish Community in Medieval Ashkenaz: History and *Halakhah*," in *Turim: Studies in Jewish History and Literature Presented to Dr. Bernard Lander*, ed. Michael A. Shmidman (New York: Touro College Press, 2007), 69–97.

[60] I have argued elsewhere that the *Homilies* are even more irenic towards Judaism than other strands of the Pseudo-Clementine tradition and that its fourth-century authors/redactors appear to have made efforts to enhance precisely those elements of their received tradition that modern thinkers have tended to associate more with "Judaism" than with "Christianity" – and to have done so, moreover, with reference to Rabbinic traditions of their own time; see Chapters One, Three, Five, Six, and Nine in this volume. On Rabbinic parallels to material in the Pseudo-Clementine literature, see also J. Bergman, "Les éléments juifs dans les Pseudo-Clementines," *REJ* 46 (1903): 89–98; Albert I. Baumgarten, "Literary Evidence for Jewish Christianity in the Galilee," in *The Galilee in Late Antiquity*, ed. Lee I. Levine (New York: Jewish Theological Seminary of America, 1992), 39–50.

ceptance of Pharisaic authority, and the outlining of proper practices for Gentile converts to shed the impurity of their former lives of idolatry and "Hellenism."[61]

We have seen how the third-century authors of the *Didascalia apostolorum* place both the Gentile and the Christian completely outside of the bounds of ritual impurity, consistent with the inextricability of sacrificial Israel, the Temple, and Levitical purity in the Torah. By contrast, the fourth-century authors/redactors of the *Homilies* proceed from a position more similar to later Rabbinic innovations on Torah law, wherein the Gentile is functionally granted some degree of ritual impurity, potentially contagious to the Jew.[62] It is perhaps telling, moreover, that the authors/redactors of the *Homilies* are therefore concerned, not with the misuse of water by baptized Jews, but rather with the misuse of blood by their Gentile counterparts.

In the *Homilies*, baptism is not a one-time water rite that exempts the believer from further need for purification. It is, in fact, perhaps the opposite. Baptism cleanses the Gentile of the impurity caused by the idolatry, sexual impieties, and demon-worship that are imagined to characterize all non-Jewish life. Consequently, baptism is here presented as the first of many washings needed to maintain purity in an impure world. It is part of a process whereby the Gentile takes on elements of Levitical law: observing menstrual separation, washing after intercourse and seminal emissions, exercising caution in meat-eating to avoid consuming blood, carrion, or the meat of animals offered to idols, and so on.[63] The *Homilies*, in effect, promote belief in Jesus as a way for Gentiles to join Israel in maintaining purity and monotheism in a world polluted by polytheism, idolatry, and bloodshed.[64]

In contrast to their Rabbinic contemporaries, and in continuity with the *Didascalia apostolorum*, the authors/redactors of the *Homilies* denounce all sacrifice, and they reject those portions of the Torah that describe the power of animal

---

[61] See Boustan and Reed, "Introduction to Theme-Issue," 336–49, for more detailed discussion of the relevant themes and passages.

[62] I.e., the Gentile defiles like a *zav*. I here follow the view of Hayes, *Gentile Impurities and Jewish Identities*, 107, that the Mishnah and Tosefta maintain this view of Gentiles as not subject to purity regulations (and, hence, not capable of being either pure or impure) as Torah law, even while introducing this notion of Gentile impurity as Rabbinic law. The broader point of the usefulness of Rabbinic purity discourse for understanding some Syrian Christian sources may still hold, however, even if one does not follow Hayes' reading of a difference between early and later Rabbinic sources regarding the impurity of Gentiles.

[63] For the practices incumbent on the baptized Gentile, see Ps.-Clem. *Hom.* 7.4, 8; 11.28–30; 13.4, 9, 19; cf. *Rec.* 2.71–72; 6.9–11; 7.29, 34; 8.68.

[64] In the *Homilies*, Jews and Pharisees are both painted in surprisingly positive terms, apparently shaped by some awareness of Rabbinic movement and some acceptance of the authority of their Oral Torah. See Ps.-Clem. *Hom.* 2.38; 3.18–19, 47, 51–52; 70; 11.29; cf. *Sifre Deuteronomy* § 351; *y. Megillah* 4.1; *y. Pe'ah* 2.6; *Pesiqta Rabbati* 14b; *b. Shabbat* 13a; Baumgarten, "Literary Evidence for Jewish Christianity in the Galilee," 42–43.

blood to atone.[65] Within the *Homilies*, this forms part of a broader argument about blood as polluted and polluting. Blood here stands at the origins of false prophesy and polytheism, with the menstrual pollution of Eve, as connected to the blood of both sacrifice and war:

She, not only presuming to say and to hear that there are many gods, but also believing herself to be one … as a female in her menses at the offering of sacrifices, she is stained with blood, and thus she pollutes those who touch her (cf. Lev 15:19). When she conceives and brings forth temporary kings, she stirs up wars pouring out blood. With respect to those who desire to learn truth from her, she keeps them always seeking and finding nothing, even until death, by telling them all things contrary and by presenting many and various services. From the beginning a cause of death lies upon blind men. Prophesying deceit, and ambiguities, and obliquities, she deceives those who believe her. (Ps.-Clem., *Hom.* 3.24)[66]

The origins of demons and disease are also tied to blood improperly shed, namely, by the Giants in the days before the Flood, who are said to have been the first to engage in meat-eating and war, and who, in their postdiluvian demonic forms, are also set at the origins of animal sacrifice.[67]

It is in this broader context that the text mounts its polemics against the priesthood of the Jerusalem Temple,[68] whereby Aaron is condemned as a false

---

[65] Ps.-Clem. *Hom.* 3.45–46; 18.1. Compare the first book of the Pseudo-Clementine *Recognitions* (e.g., 1.36–39) where Jewish sacrifice is presented as an innovation by Moses, aimed at weaning his people from the idolatry to which they had become addicted in Egypt. Notably, in their antisacrificial polemics, the *Didascalia apostolorum* and Pseudo-Clementine *Homilies* are preceded by, and largely echo, Justin Martyr's arguments about the origins of Jewish Temple sacrifice. Such parallels have led some scholars to suggest that Justin draws from a "Jewish-Christian" source somehow related to the Pseudo-Clementines; e.g., Oskar Skarsaune, *The Proof from Prophecy: A Study in Justin Martyr's Proof-Text Tradition: Text-Type, Provenance, Theological Profile* (NTSup 56; Leiden: Brill, 1987), 316–20; David Rokéah, *Justin Martyr and the Jews* [Hebrew] (Jerusalem: Dinur Center, 1998), 34–39. What is significant for our purposes is that the authors/redactors of the *Homilies* seem to make special efforts to extricate such traditions from their potentially anti-Jewish implications – in contrast both to Justin and to the *Didascalia apostolorum*. See further Boustan and Reed, "Introduction to Theme-Issue," 338–42.

[66] Some Rabbinic traditions also pair menstrual blood and the blood of death in discussions of Eve; see discussion in Charlotte Elisheva Fonrobert, *Menstrual Purity: Rabbinic and Christian Reconstructions of Biblical Gender* (Contraversions; Stanford: Stanford University Press, 2000), 30–31.

[67] Ps.-Clem. *Hom.* 8.13–20; 9.14; cf. *Rec.* 1.29; 2.71; 4.29; 5.32. Porphyry similarly links the origins of meat-eating, animal sacrifice, and the bloodshed of war in *De abstinentia* 2.7, citing Theophrastus.

[68] For an analysis of how the *Homilies*' polemics against sacrifice relate to the treatment of the same theme in the *Recognitions* and for a summary of scholarly interpretations of antisacrificial statements in the Pseudo-Clementine literature, see Nicole Kelley, "Pseudo-Clementine Polemics against Sacrifice: A Window onto Religious Life in the Fourth Century?," in *Rediscovering the Apocryphal Continent: New Perspectives on Early Christian and Late Antique Apocryphal Texts and Traditions*, ed. Pierluigi Piovanelli and Tony Burke (WUNT 349; Tübingen: Mohr Siebeck, 2015), 391–400. Kelley notes, for instance, that "the *Recognitions* likewise contains much of the same negative attitude toward sacrifice, which demonstrates that the Pseudo-Clementines' anti-sacrificial stance goes at least as far back as the third-century

prophet.[69] In the process, however, Moses, the true Torah, and Israel are distanced from the Temple and animal sacrifice.[70] Hence, the authors/redactors of the *Homilies* are able to affirm the continuance of God's covenant with the Jews even after its destruction of the Temple: they redefine "Judaism," past and present, as a religion without blood. Here, the teaching of Moses to the Pharisees and other Jews consist instead of monotheism, piety, and rites of water. It is opposed to the *paideia* of the Greeks, but continuous with the teaching of Jesus as preached by the apostle Peter, for which labels like "Christian" and "Christianity" seem deliberately resisted. In the *Homilies*, rather, Gentile followers of Jesus are called "God-fearers" and an argument is even made that they could be termed "Jews" (with Ἰουδαῖοι redefined as those who follow the Law; *Hom.* 11.16).[71] The paradigm of the righteous Gentile – the pseudonymous author, Clement of Rome – is even described as abandoning the Greek wisdom of his education and the ancestral customs of his Roman lineage to embrace the "barbarian" teachings and ethics of the God of Israel.[72]

The authors/redactors, in other words, seem strikingly *unconcerned* with mapping "Christianity" and "Judaism" – the difference so pressing for some other Syrians, such as Ignatius before them and John Chrysostom contemporaneous with them.[73] Their concern, rather, appears to have been with promoting piety in a world in which the choice between "Jew" and "Greek" was imagined to be a choice between the divine and the demonic, true and false prophecy, the purity of water and the pollution of blood.

Blood and Water, Between and Beyond "Religion(s)"

For our purposes, the Pseudo-Clementine *Homilies* thus prove helpful inasmuch as they point us beyond the bounds of "Judaism" and "Christianity." Although scholars have been long preoccupied with the question of where the text fits between the two, the text's own overarching concern is not with the differences

---

Grundschrift (the hypothetical common ancestor of the *Homilies* and *Recognitions*)." Much of the treatment about sacrifice in the *Recognitions*, however, occurs in the material in the first book that is unparalleled in the *Homilies* (esp. *Rec.* 1.30, 36–39, 64); compare, however, *Rec.* 2.71; 4.19; 5.30–32.

[69] See esp. *Hom.* 2.16, 34; 20.9; note also the polemics against Sadducees in 3.50, 54.

[70] This approach also allows the authors/redactors of the *Homilies* to stress that the True Prophet "hates sacrifice, bloodshed, and libations" (3.26), while also emphasizing that Jesus "did not come to destroy the Law" (*Hom.* 3.51; cf. Matt 5:17).

[71] The Pseudo-Clementine *Recognitions* differ in this regard, such that it is unclear whether or not this terminology – and the resistance of the label "Christian," etc. – reflects earlier sources. See further Chapter One in this volume.

[72] See Ps.-Clem, *Hom.* 4.7, 13, and my discussion in Chapter Four below.

[73] On the latter, see Dominique Côté, "Le problème de l'identité religieuse dans la Syrie du IVe siècle: Le cas des Pseudo-Clémentines et de l'*Adversus Judaeos* de S. Jean Chrysostome," in Mimouni and Pouderon, *La croisée des chemins revisitée*, 339–70.

between Jews and Christians. It is rather with the dangers of "Hellenism." And even as its authors describe the struggle between Hellenistic and Jewish pedagogies in cosmic terms, they situate the abstract and the global firmly in local perspective – not least by means of the trope of the travels of Peter and Clement to a chain of cities on the eastern coast of the Mediterranean, on the move from Judaea towards Antioch.[74]

Accordingly, the example of the Pseudo-Clementine *Homilies* serves to remind us that the discussions about blood and water in the Mishnah and *Didascalia apostolorum*, too, form part of a continuum with so-called "pagan" concerns in the region – from Porphyry's Tyre to Iamblichus' Apamea. Just as Christians and Jews shared the challenge of reinterpreting purity, peoplehood, and the Torah in the absence of a physical Temple, some learned "pagans" in the Roman Near East were also struggling anew with questions about blood, animal sacrifice, and ritual efficacy.[75] During these centuries, moreover, monuments to the control of water – in the form of aqueducts, water wheels, and public baths – were becoming an increasingly visible emblem of Roman imperial power in Syria and Palestine, and perhaps partly as a result, there seems to have been a surge in the popularity of baths, sacred springs, hydrotherapy, and baptismal movements alike.[76]

Propriety with respect to mixed-sex mingling in public baths, as Hayim Lapin notes, was claimed by Rabbis as a distinctive to "the Jews," but also by the authors of the *Didascalia apostolorum* as a characteristically "Christian" value, and by Romans as characteristically "Roman" as well – thus serving simultaneously as a shared trope and a self-claimed point of distinction.[77] So too, perhaps, with water rites. We have seen how the Christian authors of the *Didascalia apostorolum* voiced their anxieties about the repetition of baptism in relation to "the former People." Although typically read in terms of a Christian rejection of Jewish ritualism or legalism, the concern for repeated washing is also paralleled among some Rabbis of their time (e. g., *t. Yadaim* 2.20). Even the authors/redactors of the Pseudo-Clementine *Homilies*, who promote repeated baptisms, critique those whom they call "Day-Baptists" for repeating such rites *too often*, thus even condemning John the Baptist as a false prophet.[78]

---

[74] E.g., Tyre, Sidon, Beyrout, Byblos, Tripolis, Orthasia, Antaradus, Aradus.

[75] On the Neoplatonic defense of animal sacrifice, see esp. book 5 of Iamblichus' *De Mysteriis* and discussion in John Dillon, "Iamblichus' Defence of Theurgy: Some Reflections," *International Journal of the Platonic Tradition* 1 (2007): 30–41.

[76] See further, e. g., Estée Dvorjetski, *Leisure, Pleasure, and Healing: Spa Culture and Medicine in Ancient Eastern Mediterranean* (JSJSup 116; Leiden: Brill, 2007); A. de Miranda, *Water Architecture in the Lands of Syria: The Water-Wheels* (Rome: L'Erma di Bretschneider, 2007).

[77] Hayim Lapin, "Law of Moses and the Jews," in Dohrmann and Reed, *Jews, Christians, and the Roman Empire*, 79–97.

[78] See, e. g., Ps.-Clem., *Hom.*, 2.23. On ritual repetition, see further Jorunn Jacobsen Buckley, "Why Once Is Not Enough: Mandaean Baptism (Maṣbuta) as an Example of a Repeated Ritual," *History of Religions* 29 (1989): 23–34.

If such anxieties might further signal something of a shared discourse about water in the Roman Near East, it is perhaps significant that they resonate across imperial as well as religious borders in late antique Syro-Mesopotamia – from Mani's critiques of the Elchaasites, to the Zoroastrian discourse on menstrual and other impurities, to Christian and later Muslim reports about the seemingly perennial problem of baptismal movements in the area that blurred the boundaries of "religions."[79]

Beyond "Judaism" and "Christianity"

Categories like "Judaism" and "Christianity" are so commonly used in research on local and imperial identities in the Roman Empire, it is easy to forget that they did not originate as simply neutral or descriptive terms.[80] To treat this pair as natural – or at least in some way that pairs like "Greek" and "barbarian," or "Israel" and "the nations," are assumed *not* to be – is to read our sources through the lens of certain (peculiarly Patristic) perspectives. Moreover, the modern scholarly categories that can be pressed without too much violence upon the writings of retrospectively "orthodox" Christian authors like Ignatius, Justin, and Tertullian can be fit only with difficulty on other late antique sources, including those texts and traditions of their Rabbinic contemporaries (i.e., those typically credited with effecting the "Parting of the Ways" from the other side).[81]

It remains to be seen whether the recent scholarly preoccupation with issues of "identity" and the power of language has led us to overstate the importance of

---

[79] See above, as well as Scott John McDonough, "We and Those Waters of the Sea Are One: Baptism, Bathing, and the Construction of Identity in Late Ancient Babylonia," in *The Nature and Function of Water, Baths, Bathing, and Hygiene: From Antiquity through the Renaissance,* ed. Cynthia Kosso and Anne Scott (Technology and Change in History 11. Leiden: Brill, 2009), 263–76; Samuel Israel Secunda, "*Dashtana – Ki Derekh Nashim Li*: A Study of the Babylonian Rabbinic Laws of Menstruation in Relation to Corresponding Zoroastrian Texts" (PhD dissertation, Yeshiva University, 2007); T. Fahd, "Ṣābi'a," in *The Encyclopaedia of Islam*, ed. Peri Bearman et al. (Leiden: Brill, 2010).

[80] Lieu, *Christian Identity in the Jewish and Greco-Roman World*, 306–7, for instance, thus stresses the dangers of slippage: "Although rooted in the language of (a very small minority of) our texts, the conceptual baggage these terms carry belongs rather more to our contemporary agenda. Far too frequently recent scholarly discussion has forgotten this, and slips … from speaking of 'Jews' and 'Christians,' to conceptualizing and fixing 'Judaism' and 'Christianity,' as if these, at least, required no further definition"; cf. Carleton Paget, *Jews, Christians, and Jewish Christians in Antiquity*, 12. See now Cynthia Baker, *Jew* (Key Words in Jewish Studies; New Brunswick: Rutgers University Press, 2016); Daniel Boyarin, *Judaism* (Key Words in Jewish Studies; New Brunswick: Rutgers University Press, forthcoming).

[81] To do so is not just to give the false impression that Rabbinic approaches to collective identity mirror their Patristic contemporaries, but also – Boyarin suggests (see esp. "Rethinking Jewish Christianity") – to credit the two sets of elites with producing the only stable or "pure" identities, from which other biblically-based forms of religiosity can be only interpreted as hybrids or "heresies."

those late antique authors who so happen to share our preoccupations, while imposing their systems of distinction upon those writings that do not.[82] In a recent article, Ra'anan Boustan and I noted how these and other tendencies of scholarly selectivity have shaped our understanding of "Judaism" and "Christianity" alike:

> Partly due to practical necessity, most scholarship on early Jewish–Christian relations has built on the distinctions drawn in those polemical sources in which the boundaries between Jews and Christians are most explicitly outlined, catalogued, and discussed. Faced with few late antique examples of explicit Jewish polemics against Christians, necessity has also pressed scholars to depend heavily on the witness of church fathers, reading the comparably ambiguous references in the classical rabbinic literature in light of the more lengthy and detailed comments in patristic literature. To what degree, however, are the representations of Jewish and Christian difference in patristic literature really so representative?[83]

What I have tried to suggest in the present essay is that, at the very least, the literature of Roman Syria and Palestine offer a rich reservoir of sources for alternate visions for the creation and categorization of identities – some of which may have remained vital in Late Antiquity in ways that our own modern interests, assumptions, and contexts may have led us to neglect. The perspectives of the *Didascalia apostolorum* and Pseudo-Clementines, for instance, do not fit so neatly *either* into the unilinear trajectories of modern scholarly accounts of the "Parting of the Ways" *or* into the modern mapping of identities as personal or communal expressions of stable, reified, and distinct "religions."

If such sources point us to the need to engage a broader range of perspectives (including those effaced by any simple binary contrasts between "Judaism" and "Christianity"), then they also may help to clear the way for rethinking the place of the local and the abstract even in the production of these "religions."[84] Not long after Ignatius, for instance, we find intriguing clues as to possible efforts to export and universalize yet another aniconic Near Eastern monotheism from one

---

[82] For suggestions that the "Parting" model reflects a distinctly Christian perspective, and theological concerns shaped by it, see Lieu, "The Parting of the Ways"; Himmelfarb, "The Parting of the Ways Reconsidered," 47.

[83] Boustan and Reed, "Blood and Atonement," 349–50.

[84] Compare the conclusions vis-à-vis "westernization" and early modern literature in Laura Doyle, "Notes Toward a Dialectical Method: Modernities, Modernisms, and the Crossings of Empire," *Literature Compass* 7 (2010): 205–6: "If there is something we would call 'westernization' that has spread in the last few centuries, then we would have to call the underlying historical formations of this westernness something like 'ottomanization' or 'easternization.' But all of these names are too simple, and indeed reflect the lingering influence of empires, their power to direct our vocabulary, which thus divides the world into parts, especially binaries, and speaks only of invasion, domination, and spheres of influence. The key point is rather that there are multiple empires jockeying all at once, not always calling themselves empires, and also multiple movements of dissent, insurgency, and anti-coloniality, not always with shared values or targets. And all of these interact to shape the production, migration, and styles of literature." It remains to see whether something similar might be posited for earlier phenomena such as "Christianization," particularly in relation to the local cultures of the Near East.

of its local cultures, namely, the cult of the Syrian sun god from Emesa. Roughly around the same time as *Didascalia apostolorum* was taking form, the Roman emperor Elagabalus seems to have mounted some attempt to export the sun god's worship westward to Rome.[85] That the emperor was himself a circumcised Syrian priest in the lineage of this god is, at the very least, a poignant reminder of the limits of categories like "Judaism," "Christianity," and "paganism" to describe the interactions between Roman center and Near Eastern periphery in the Roman Near East in this period. Elagabalus' move, furthermore, presages Constantine's embrace of the "barbarian wisdom" of Christianity in the fourth century, roughly around the same time that the Pseudo-Clementines were taking their present forms.

Constantine, of course, succeeded where Elagabalus had failed, and his embrace of universalizing traditions from the Roman empire's Near Eastern peripheries eventually reshaped the culture and society of the Roman center. The earlier developments, however, stand as reminders that the story of the emergence of the ideas of "Christianity" and "Judaism" is also a story about how "Hellenism" and the Roman Empire were changing in the second, third, and fourth centuries CE, perhaps in part because of developments in the Roman Near East.[86] When ideas from Jerusalem and Antioch became universalized and totalized under the imperial banner of Rome, it was due in part to changes also evident in (and exported from) local cultures forged in cities like Caesarea, Emesa, Apamea, and Edessa.

Looking back at late antique Syria from a present purview in the modern West, it proves challenging even to describe these epochal events apart from the later changes that they helped to catalyze, the later categories that they helped to create, and the modern identities that their remembrance now helps to naturalize. It seem natural to read our late antique sources in terms of their consequences, using categories common today (e.g., "Christianity," "Judaism," "religion"). This naturalization is itself a witness to just how influential such category-creation has been. In the circulation of ideas about blood and water, however, we

---

[85] This is most starkly asserted – with an intriguing reference to Jews and Christians – in the problematic but suggestive account in *Scriptores Historia Augusta, Vita Heliogabali*, 13.4–5.

[86] For the former point, see also Williams, "No More Clever Titles," 51, where she notes how recent critiques of the "Parting" model make clear that "the relations between Judaism and Christianity in the Roman world cannot be understood in isolation from the relation of each to categories such as Hellenism or Romanitas. It is not sufficient to treat the Roman empire merely as a context or backdrop against which the intertwined histories of Judaism and Christianity played out. Rather, the two terms central to this essay intersected with other systems of categories: Jew/gentile, Greek/barbarian, Roman/Greek, and so on." On the latter point note also the elegant articulation of the issue in Fergus Millar, "Redrawing the Map," in *Rome, the Greek World, and the East*, vol. 3: *The Greek World, the Jews, and the East*, ed. Hannah M. Cotton and Guy M. Rogers (Chapel Hill: University of North Carolina Press, 2006), esp. 505–8. See further now Dohrmann and Reed, *Jews, Christians, and the Roman Empire*, especially the bibliography and discussion in our introduction on "Rethinking Romanness, Provincializing Christendom," 1–22.

might glimpse something of the other perspectives cultivated in Late Antiquity, as sometimes connecting that which the rhetoric of others sought to distinguish and divide.

Chapter Three

"Jewish-Christian" Apocrypha
and Jewish/Christian Relations*

Recent Anglo-American scholarship on early and late antique Christianity has
been marked by concerted efforts to supplement, enrich, and interrogate the
Eusebian account of church history that dominated past research.[1] Earlier work
largely progressed from the framework laid out in Eusebius's *Historia ecclesiastica*,[2] telling the history of Christianity's first four centuries in terms of a series

---

* This chapter was originally prepared for precirculation at the 2006 workshop on "Christian Apocrypha for the New Millennium: Achievements, Prospects and Challenges" at the
University of Ottawa and published in 2015 as "'Jewish-Christian' Apocrypha and the History
of Jewish/Christian Relations," in *Rediscovering the Apocryphal Continent: New Perspectives
on Early Christian and Late Antique Apocryphal Texts and Traditions*, ed. Pierluigi Piovanelli
and Tony Burke (WUNT 349; Tübingen: Mohr Siebeck, 2015), 87–116; It is reprinted here
with permission from Mohr Siebeck. I would like to thank Pierluigi Piovenelli for the idea for
this paper, which was sparked by our discussions in Lausanne and Geneva during the 2006
Association pour l'Étude de la Littérature Apocryphe Chrétienne conference on "Le roman
Pseudo-clémentin." It benefited much from questions, comments, and conversation at the
Ottawa workshop as well, especially from F. Stanley Jones. The research for this chapter was
supported by a grant from the Social Science and Humanities Research Council of Canada. The
present version has been updated and revised.

[1] By no means do I mean to suggest that such corrective concerns are unique to Anglo-American scholarship! Here, however, I am specifically concerned to trace a trajectory of research
reflected in English-language studies since the mid-1960s. Although obviously related to its
continental counterparts in many meaningful ways, Anglo-American scholarship has progressed at a different pace and with different points of focus (note, e.g., the relative lack of
attention granted to the creation of scholarly editions of Christian apocrypha compared to
German- and French-language scholarship; the North American context, in particular, may be
characterized by more suspicion towards text- and source-critical approaches, more concern
for sociocultural issues, and a more pointed interest in experimenting with sociological and
anthropological models). On some differences of definition, e.g., see my discussion in Reed,
"The Afterlives of New Testament Apocrypha," *JBL* 134 (2015) 401–25.

[2] Eusebius's role in shaping the dominant scholarly understanding of early church history was noted already by Walter Bauer, whose alternative account was founded on a highly
suspicious reading of the *Historia ecclesiastica* as a selective and apologetic account with
many purposive omissions; *Rechtgläubigkeit und Ketzerei im ältesten Christentum* (Tübingen:
Mohr, 1934; rev. ed. by Georg Strecker, 1964), e.g., 135–49. See further Arthur J. Droge, "The
Apologetic Dimensions of the Ecclesiastical History," in *Eusebius, Christianity, and Judaism*,
ed. Harold W. Attridge and Gohei Hata (StPB 42; Detroit: Wayne State University Press,
1992), 492–509; and Glenn F. Chesnut, "Eusebius, Augustine, Orosius, and the Late Patristic
and Medieval Church Historians," in Attridge and Hata, *Eusebius, Christianity, and Judaism*,
687–713. For recent reassessments of Eusebius, see Sabrina Inowlocki and Claudio Zamagni,

of figures retrospectively deemed "Church Fathers." Having purportedly shed the influence of Judaism, authors such as Clement, Ignatius, Justin, Ireneaus, and Tertullian have been celebrated as those who fought to maintain authentic apostolic traditions in the face of the manifold challenges posed by "heresy," on the one hand, and "paganism," on the other. Their story, moreover, has been told in teleological terms: from the struggle with "heresy," they set Christian theology on the path to Nicaea, and from the struggle with "paganism," their vision of Christianity emerged victorious, rising from a persecuted sect to the religion of the Roman Empire.

This familiar "master narrative" was long reflected and reinforced by the dominant disciplinary contexts of research and teaching on early and late antique Christianity in North America. Until the 1970s, early and late antique Christianity was studied under the twin rubrics of Patristics and ecclesiastical history in relative isolation from scholarship on Second Temple and Rabbinic Judaism, late antique history and society, comparative religion, Classics, and even – to some degree – New Testament Studies. Accordingly, past research on postapostolic literature was largely limited to the doctrines of Church Fathers writing in Greek and Latin. Attention focused, almost wholly, on developments within the Roman Empire.[3]

The move towards more integrative, interdisciplinary, and expansive perspectives responds to a variety of factors. Precipitants include the discovery of the Nag Hammadi codices,[4] the discussion sparked by Walter Bauer's *Rechtgläubigkeit und Ketzerei im ältesten Christentum*,[5] and the emergence of Late Antiquity as

---

eds., *Reconsidering Eusebius: Collected Papers on Literary, Historical, and Theological Issues* (VCSup 107; Leiden: Brill, 2011); Aaron P. Johnson and Jeremy Schott, eds., *Eusebius of Caesarea: Tradition and Innovations* (Cambridge: Harvard University Press, 2013).

[3] Eusebius, for instance, is largely blamed for the modern scholarly neglect of Syriac Christian literature by Sebastian Brock, "Eusebius and Syriac Christianity," in Attridge and Hata, *Eusebius, Christianity, and Judaism*, 212; Adam H. Becker, "Beyond the Spatial and Temporal Limes: Questioning the 'Parting of the Ways' Outside the Roman Empire," in *The Ways That Never Parted: Jews and Christians in Late Antiquity and the Early Middle Ages*, ed. Adam H. Becker and Annette Yoshiko Reed (TSAJ 95; Tübingen: Mohr Siebeck, 2003), 373–74.

[4] E.g., John D. Turner and Anne MacGuire, eds., *The Nag Hammadi Library after Fifty Years* (Nag Hammadi and Manichaean Studies 44; Leiden: Brill, 1997); and the review by Kurt Rudolph (trans. Donald Dale Walker) in *JR* 79 (1999): 452–57.

[5] Although first published in 1934, the importance of the book was not widely recognized until the 1960s, with the publication of the second German edition (1964) and the discussion of Bauer's findings in H. Koester's seminal article "ΓΝΩΜΑΙ ΔΙΑΦΟΡΟΙ: The Origin and Nature of Diversification in the History of Early Christianity," *HTR* 58 (1964): 279–318. In Anglo-American scholarship, full engagement with Bauer's work awaited its English translation (*Orthodoxy and Heresy in Earliest Christianity* [ed. and trans. Robert A. Kraft and Gerhard Kroedel; Philadelphia: Fortress, 1971]). On the reception of Bauer's work, see pp. 286–316; and Daniel J. Harrington, "The Reception of Walter Bauer's *Orthodoxy and Heresy in Earliest Christianity* during the Last Decade," *HTR* 73 (1980): 289–98.

a vibrant subfield of History.[6] New perspectives have been facilitated also by the diversification in the backgrounds and institutional settings of research and graduate training in early and late antique Christianity.[7] This diversification, in turn, has fostered a new openness towards experimentation with methodologies from fields such as sociology, anthropology, literary criticism, gender studies, and critical theory.[8] Perhaps above all, the shift away from Eusebian models reflects a broader growth of interest in noncanonical materials – including newly discovered texts (e. g., Dead Sea Scrolls, Nag Hammadi literature) but also familiar texts too long neglected (e. g., Old Testament pseudepigrapha, Christian apocrypha, Hekhalot literature, *piyyutim*, Graeco-Roman magical materials).

What happens when we tell the history of early and late antique Christianity apart from the traditional focus on Church Fathers, doctrinal concerns, and retrospectively normative metanarratives? For the forging of new perspectives on the beliefs, practices, and experiences of early and late antique Christians, the evidence of Christian apocrypha has been critical.[9] Apocryphal gospels and acts

---

[6] In particular, the work of Peter Brown helped to spark the new interest in the "postclassical" era within the field of History; see especially Brown, "The Rise and Function of the Holy Man in Late Antiquity," *JRS* 61 (1971): 80–101; Brown, *The Making of Late Antiquity* (Cambridge, MA: Harvard University Press, 1978). For reflections on the fate of "Late Antiquity" in the last thirty years, see Peter Brown, "The Study of Élites in Late Antiquity," *Arethusa* 33 (2000): 321–46; James Joseph O'Donnell, "Late Antiquity: Before and After," *Transactions of the American Philological Association* 134 (2004): 203–13; and the articles in *JECS* 6.3 (1998) and *Journal of Late Antiquity* 1.1 (2008) as well as further discussion and bibliography in Natalie B. Dohrmann and Annette Yoshiko Reed, eds., *Jews, Christians, and the Roman Empire: The Poetics of Power in Late Antiquity* (Philadelphia: University of Pennsylvania Press, 2013), esp. 9–14.

[7] The recovery of the "postclassical" period from scholarly neglect has facilitated the study of late antique Christianity in departments of History and Classics. Since the 1960s, in North America in particular, the study of early and late antique Christianity in Divinity Schools and departments of Theology has also been increasingly supplemented by its study in departments of Religious Studies in secular universities. For the institutional history of Religious Studies in North America, see, e. g., Claude Welch, "Identity Crisis in the Study of Religion? A First Report from the ACLS Study," *JAAR* 39 (1971): 3–18, esp. 3–7; D. G. Hart, "The Troubled Soul of the Academy: American Learning and the Problem of Religious Studies," *Religion and American Culture* 2 (1992): 41–77.

[8] Discussions of the profits and pitfalls of such approaches include Elizabeth Anne Castelli, "Gender, Theory, and the Rise of Christianity: A Response to Rodney Stark," *JECS* 6 (1998): 227–57; Elizabeth Ann Clark, "Holy Women, Holy Words: Early Christian Women, Social History, and the 'Linguistic Turn,'" *JECS* 6 (1998): 413–30; Clark, *History, Theory, Text: Historians and the Linguistic Turn* (Cambridge, MA: Harvard University Press, 2004). Note also the application of the theories of Pierre Bourdieu in Nicole Kelley's *Knowledge and Religious Authority in the Pseudo-Clementines: Situating the Recognitions in Fourth-Century Syria* (WUNT[2] 213; Tübingen: Mohr Siebeck, 2006).

[9] I here use the term "Christian apocrypha" to refer to the written products of ongoing reflection on the apostolic past by means of apostolic/subapostolic pseudepigraphy (e. g., books penned in the names of Paul, James, Peter, Thomas, the twelve apostles, Clement of Rome) and/or the fluid use of literary forms also found in the New Testament literature (e. g., gospels, acts, apocalypses); from a literary standpoint, such writings can thus be distinguished from the theological treatises, apologies, dialogues, heresiologies, homilies, etc., penned by Christian

have been pivotal, for instance, for fresh efforts to understand the continuities and discontinuities between apostolic and postapostolic times.[10] Such sources have also contributed to attempts to interrogate the elite, educated, literary, and male perspectives expressed by the Church Fathers.[11] Whereas doctrinal (especially Christological) concerns continue to predominate in Patristics, research on Christian apocrypha has brought new evidence and attention to social realities. Apocryphal acts and gospels, for instance, have proved to be rich sources for research on gender, sex, marriage, female leadership, childhood, and family.[12] Likewise, apocryphal apocalypses and martyrologies have opened a window onto a wealth of eschatological, cosmological, demonological, astrological, "magical," and mystical speculations largely absent from the writings of Church Fathers (and often ignored where present).[13] Whereas past scholarship tended to frame the Christian encounter with Graeco-Roman culture in terms of the

---

authors in their own names. On the category of "Christian apocrypha," see Éric Junod, "La littérature apocryphe chrétienne constitue-t-elle un objet d'études?," *Revue des études anciennes* 93 (1991): 397–414; Junod, "Apocryphes du Nouveau Testament: Une appellation erronée et une collection artificielle," *Apoc* 3 (1992): 17–46; Pierluigi Piovanelli, "Qu'est-ce qu'un 'écrit apocryphe chrétien' et comment ça marche? Quelque suggestions pour une herméneutique apocryphe," in *Pierre Geoltrain ou comment "faire l'histoire des religions?" Le chantier des origines, les méthodes du doute et la conversion contemporaine entre les disciplines*, ed. Simon Claude Mimouni and Isabelle Ullern-Weité (Turnhout: Brepolis, 2006), 173–87; Stephen Shoemaker, "Early Christian Apocryphal Literature," in *Oxford Handbook of Early Christian Studies*, ed. David Hunter and Susan Ashbrook Harvey (Oxford: Oxford University Press, 2008), 521–48. On the history of this terminology, see my discussion in Reed, "Afterlives." And see further now Andrew Gregory and Christopher Tuckett, eds., *The Oxford Handbook of Early Christian Apocrypha* (Oxford: Oxford University Press, 2015), esp. Tuckett's introductory comments on pp. 3–10; Piovanelli and Burke, *Rediscovering the Apocryphal Continent*, esp. Burke on "Entering the Mainstream: Twenty-Five Years of Research on the Christian Apocrypha" (pp. 19–48); Burke, ed., *Forbidden Texts on the Western Frontier: The Christian Apocrypha in North American Perspectives* (Eugene, OR: Cascade, 2015), especially the historiographical essays on North American trajectories by Jean-Michel Roessli ("North American Approaches to the Study of the Christian Apocrypha on the World Stage," pp. 19–51) and Brent Landau ("The 'Harvard School' of the Christian Apocrypha," pp. 58–77).

[10] Esp. Helmut Koester, "Apocryphal and Canonical Gospels," *HTR* 73 (1980): 105–30; François Bovon, "Canonical and Apocryphal Acts of Apostles," *JECS* 11 (2003): 165–94.

[11] The contrast is perhaps most poignantly drawn in Dennis Ronald MacDonald, *The Legend and the Apostle: The Battle for Paul in Story and Canon* (Philadelphia: Westminster, 1983).

[12] E. g., Virginia Burrus, *Chastity as Autonomy: Women in the Stories of the Apocryphal Acts* (New York: Edwin Mellen, 1987); Kate Cooper, *The Virgin and the Bride: Idealized Womanhood in Late Antiquity* (Cambridge, MA: Harvard University Press, 1996); Andrew S. Jacobs, "A Family Affair: Marriage, Class, and Ethics in the Apocryphal Acts of the Apostles," *JECS* 7 (1999): 105–38.

[13] This wealth is evident, e. g., in the cross-section of materials treated in Ra'anan S. Boustan and Annette Yoshiko Reed, eds., *Heavenly Realms and Earthly Realities in Late Antique Religions* (Cambridge: Cambridge University Press, 2004) by Jan N. Bremmer, ("Contextualizing Heaven in Third-Century North Africa," 159–73), Kirsti B. Copeland ("The Earthly Monastery and the Transformation of the Heavenly City in Late Antique Egypt," 142–58), and Fritz Graf ("The Bridge and the Ladder: Narrow Passages in Late Antique Visions," 19–33).

dangers of persecution, the rejection of polytheism, and the cautious embrace of philosophy, research on Christian apocrypha has exposed the complex cultural interactions evident in the adoption and subversion of popular "pagan" literary tropes, including the erotic narrative, the romance of recognitions, and even the epic.[14] Furthermore, inasmuch as work in Christian apocrypha often entails engagement with sources in Syriac, Coptic, Armenian, Arabic, etc., scholars in this subfield have helped to correct the traditional privileging of Greek- and Latin-speaking cultural spheres, stressing the regional and cultural diversity of Christianity within and beyond the Roman Empire.

Nevertheless, a different situation prevails with respect to the place of Judaism and "Jewish-Christianity" in Christian identity. On this topic, research on Christian apocrypha is still largely pursued within the confines of the framework and concerns defined by Patristic heresiologies and historiographies. A handful of apocrypha have been labeled "Jewish-Christian."[15] Yet the meaning and significance of this identification are still often interpreted in terms of Eusebius's account of the progressive decline of the Jerusalem church of James and Peter[16] and Epiphanius' description of Ebionites and Nazarenes as marginalized "heretical" sects with little influence on the church at large.[17] Most analyses of "Jewish-Christian" apocrypha fit these sources into the framework of a tradition-

---

[14] These connections were established already by Rosa Söder, *Die apokryphen Apostelgeschichten und die romanhafte Literatur der Antike* (Stuttgart, 1932). The significance of the redeployment of "pagan" novelistic tropes in apocryphal acts, however, has been an issue of renewed concern. See, e. g., Cooper, *Virgin and the Bride*; David Konstan, "Acts of Love: A Narrative Pattern in the Apocryphal Acts," *JECS* 6 (1998): 15–36; Virginia Burrus, "Mimicking Virgins: Colonial Ambivalence and the Ancient Romance," *Arethusa* 38 (2005): 49–88; Christine M. Thomas, *The Acts of Peter, Gospel Literature, and the Ancient Novel: Rewriting the Past* (Oxford: Oxford University Press, 2003). Epic echoes have been noted by Dennis Ronald MacDonald (e. g., *Christianizing Homer: The Odyssey, Plato, and the Acts of Andrew* [Oxford: Oxford University Press, 1994]). The plentiful literature on the Pseudo-Clementines as novel is surveyed and assessed in F. Stanley Jones, *Pseudoclementina*, 114–37.

[15] Most frequently: the Pseudo-Clementines and their hypothetical sources. Notable too are the *Apocalypse of Peter*, *Protevangelium of James*, *Gospel of the Hebrews*, *Gospel of the Nazarenes*, *Gospel of the Ebionites*, and *Gospel of Nicodemus*. One might argue also for the heuristic inclusion of the *Didascalia apostolorum* and/or *Apostolic Constitutions* on the grounds of their apostolic/subapostolic pseudepigraphy and their status as relatively overlooked sources in research on Patristics.

[16] So too Alan F. Segal, "Jewish Christianity," in Attridge and Hata, *Eusebius, Judaism, and Christianity*, 326. Note esp. *Hist. eccl.* 3.5.3 on the so-called "flight to Pella" – a tradition whose historicity has been questioned by Gerd Lüdemann, "The Successors of Pre-70 Jerusalem Christianity: A Critical Evaluation of the Pella Tradition," in *Jewish and Christian Self-Definition*, vol. 1: *The Shaping of Christianity in the Second and Third Centuries*, ed. E. P. Sanders (Philadelphia: Fortress, 1980), 161–73, J. Verheyden, "The Flight of Christians to Pella," *Ephemerides theologicae lovanienses* 66 (1990): 368–84; Johannes Munck, "Jewish Christianity in Post-Apostolic Times," *NTS* 6 (1959): 103–4.

[17] Esp. *Pan.* 29.1.1–9; 30.1.1–33, and discussion in F. Stanley Jones, *An Ancient Jewish Christian Source on the History of Christianity: Pseudo-Clementine Recognitions 1.27–71* (Atlanta: Scholars Press, 1995), 35–37.

al scholarly narrative about the first four centuries of Christian history that sees the process of Christianity's triumph in/over the Roman Empire as concurrent with the process of its separation from Judaism and the demise of "Jewish-Christianity."[18]

This article explores the possibility that "Jewish-Christian" apocrypha may have more to tell us about Jewish/Christian relations and the evolving place of Jews and Judaism in early and late antique Christian identity – that is, if we choose to listen to what these sources tell us about the diversity of Christian approaches to Jews, Judaism, Torah observance, ritual purity, and the chosenness of Israel, resisting the temptation to dismiss these voices as marginal and/or to assimilate them to perspectives espoused or described in Patristic literature.[19] As in other areas of research on early and late antique Christianity (e. g., gender, es-

---

[18] For an examination of the ways in which these traditional scholarly narratives have shaped research on the Pseudo-Clementines, see Chapter One in this volume. It is interesting to note the lack of attention to other Christian apocrypha in recent research on "Jewish-Christianity." This tendency is evidenced in two otherwise spectacular volumes on the topic: Simon Claude Mimouni and F. Stanley Jones, eds., *Le Judéo-Christianisme dans tous ses états* (Paris: Cerf, 2001); and Peter J. Tomson and Doris Lambers-Petry *The Image of the Judaeo-Christians in Ancient Jewish and Christian Literature* (WUNT 158; Tübingen: Mohr Siebeck, 2003). Of the twenty-two articles in *Le Judéo-Christianisme*, only four deal in any concerted fashion with Christian apocrypha; three discuss the Pseudo-Clementines (P. Geoltrain, "Le roman Pseudo-Clémentin depuis les recherches d'Oscar Cullmann," 31–40; C. Gianotto, "Alcune riflessioni a proposito di Recognitiones 1,27–71: La storia della salvezza," 213–30; Bernard Pouderon, "Aux origines du Roman clementin: Prototype pai'en, refonte judeo-hellenistique, remaniement chretien," 231–56) while the fourth considers some apocrypha when discussing "Jewish-Christianity" in Antioch (Clayton N. Jefford, "Reflexion on the Rôle of Jewish Christianity in Second-Century Antioche," 47–67). Of the sixteen in *Image of the Judaeo-Christians*, only two focus on apocrypha (Doris Lambers-Petry, "Verwandte Jesu als Referenzpersonen für das Judenchristentum," 32–52, in the context of literature associate with James; Richard Bauckham, "The Origin of the Ebionites," 162–81, in the context of a survey of our evidence for Ebionites). Notably, despite an overall focus on the New Testament and Church Fathers, these volumes do succeed in extending the range of sources brought to bear on "Jewish-Christianity" in other directions, including archaeological evidence (B. Pixner, "Nazorean on Mount Zion," in Mimouni and Jones, *Judéo-Christianisme*, 289 316; Zeev Safrai, "The House of Leontis 'Kaloubas' – a Judaeao-Christian?," in Tomson and Lambers-Petry, *Image of the Judaeo-Christians*, 245–66) and Rabbinic sources (Burton L. Visotzky, "Jewish-Christianity in Rabbinic Documents: An Examination of Leviticus Rabbah," in Mimouni and Jones, *Judéo-Christianisme*, 335–49; S. Verhelst, "Trois remarques sur la Pesiqta de-rav Kahana et le christianisme," in Mimouni and Jones, *Judéo-Christianisme*, 367–82; Gideon Bohak, "Magical Means for Handling *Minim* in Rabbinic Literature," in Tomson and Lambers-Petry, *Image of the Judaeo-Christians*, 267–79; William Horbury, "Toledot Yeshu," in Tomson and Lambers-Petry, *Image of the Judaeo-Christians*, 280–86). One finds a similar pattern in Oskar Skarsaune and Reidar Hvalvik, eds. *Jewish Believers in Jesus: The Early Centuries* (Peabody, MA: Hendrickson, 2007).

[19] See further Chapter Six in this volume; for attempts to sketch the other side of this picture, asking what "Jewish-Christian" literature may tell us about the Jewish history of the same period, see especially Chapters Nine and Ten as well. Note also Luigi Cirillo, "L'Apocalypse d'Elkhasaï: Son role et son importance pour l'histoire du Judaïsme," *Apocrypha* 1 (1990): 167–79. For a sense of how such materials relate to the representation of Jews and Judaism within Christian apocrypha more broadly, see now the very useful survey by Petri Luomanen of

chatology, ritual practice, oral tradition, literary production), research on the history of Jewish/Christian relations may benefit from more attention to apocryphal literature. "Jewish-Christian" apocrypha, in particular, may help to expose some shortcomings and oversights in common scholarly accounts of Jewish/Christian relations, both old and new, that treat Patristic representations of Christianity and Judaism as if representative of *all* Christians and Jews.[20]

In what follows, I will explore some of these potentialities by surveying some recent studies on specific "Jewish-Christian" apocrypha and bringing them into dialogue with discussions of Jewish/Christian relations from the fields of Patristics and Rabbinics alike. I will ask what a history of Jewish/Christian relations might look like if written from the perspective of sources like the *Apocalypse of Peter*, the *Protevangelium of James*, the *Didascalia apostolorum*, Pseudo-Clementine literature, the Ethiopian *Book of the Cock*, and the *Gospel of Nicodemus*. In this, my aim is not to impose any single definition of "Jewish-Christianity" on all of these diverse sources.[21] Rather, I uses this rubric as a heuristic focus for considering their significance for Jewish/Christian relations, and I thus reflect on the specific (and different) reasons that some scholars have seen fit to treat specific sources as "Jewish-Christian" rather than either "Christian" or "Jewish."[22] In the process, I hope to show how the vexed category of "Jewish-

---

"Judaism and Anti-Judaism in Early Christian Apocrypha," in Gregory and Tuckett, *The Oxford Handbook of Early Christian Apocrypha*, 319–42.

[20] For an eloquent argument for the importance of integrating these perspectives into our accounts of "mainstream" religious history, see John G. Gager, "Jews, Christians, and the Dangerous Ones in Between," in *Interpretation in Religion*, ed. S. Biderman and B. Scharfstein (Philosophy and Religion 2; Leiden: Brill, 1992), 249–57. On the distortions caused by privileging Patristic representations of religious difference, see also Ra'anan S. Boustan and Annette Yoshiko Reed, "Blood and Atonement in the Pseudo-Clementines and *The Story of the Ten Martyrs*: The Problem of Selectivity in the Study of Judaism and Christianity," *Hen* 30 (2008): 111–42.

[21] The most invaluable discussion of attempts at definition remains J. Carleton Paget, "Jewish Christianity," in *The Cambridge History of Judaism*, vol. 3: *The Early Roman Period*, ed. William Horbury, W. D. Davies, and John Sturdy (Cambridge: Cambridge University Press, 1999), 733–42. See discussion further below as well as in Appendix B.

[22] In other words, I here apply the adjective "Jewish-Christian" to those texts and figures that do not fit modern ideas about what constitutes "Jewish" identity, modern ideas about what constitutes "Christian" identity, and common modern assumptions about the two as mutually exclusive. This definition, like the term "Jewish-Christianity," is a modern invention. It is, however, a pointedly self-conscious one, aimed at interrogating some of the other modern concepts and categories that we take for granted. There are good arguments, of course, for limiting ourselves only to ancient categories ("Ebionite," "Nazarene," "Judaizer). Yet, if we choose to limit our understanding of the fluidity and hybridity of self-definition only to cases where an ancient witness sees and comments on someone else's identity (e. g., deeming someone else too "Jewish" to be "Christian" [Ignatius, *Magn.* 10] or too "Jewish" and "Christian" to be either [Jerome, *Epist.* 112.13]), we risk predetermining the conclusion that all fluidity and hybridity is heterodox, and we risk limiting our perspective on the diversity of biblically-based modes of self-definition to the perspectives of specific "orthodox" observers (especially those observers, like heresiologists, who happen to be most eager to categorize others). It is important, too, to

Christianity," freshly conceived, might serve as a useful tool for further scholarly exploration of the construction and negotiation of biblically based religious identities in different geographical and cultural spheres in Late Antiquity. To the degree that the label "Jewish-Christian" had functioned in modern scholarship to cordon off certain texts as irrelevant *both* for the history of Judaism *and* for the history of Christianity, it is certainly unhelpful and misleading.[23] Yet to the degree that it can serve to remind us that these histories are intertwined, it may aid us in recovering a richer range of premodern perspectives on identity and difference, and to work towards more integrative perspectives on Christianity and Judaism alike.

"Jewish-Christian" Apocrypha from the Second and Third Centuries

One of the most notable applications of research on "Jewish-Christianity" to the study of Christian apocrypha is Richard Bauckham's work on the *Apocalypse of Peter*.[24] Bauckham points to the need for this and other apocrypha to be "rescued as significant evidence of the early development of Christianity."[25] In his read-

---

recall that "Jewish" and "Christian" identities are themselves taking form in this period, such that different premodern observers hold different views; Epiphanius, for instance, cites materials related to Ps.-Clem., *Rec.* 1 as part of his treatment of the Ebionites as a "heretical" sect too close to Judaism, but Rufinus sees fit to translate the *Recognitions*, even though he himself does not hesitate to accuse Jerome of Judaizing! In light of such complexities of perception, representation, and identity polemics, the search for more firsthand evidence proves all the more important. In my view, this situation warrants the application of an etic category like "Jewish-Christianity" for heuristic aims (as opposed to essentialist or reductionism purposes). That there are some Jesus-followers in Late Antiquity who are being condemned by others for beliefs and practices perceived to be too close to Judaism seems to hint at the existence of a broader continuum of identities and perspectives than is usually allowed. Although much of this continuum may be lost to us, it strikes me as worthwhile to search all of our available sources for potentially relevant material.

[23] For a powerful critique of the "heresiographical" sense of the term and its modern as well as ancient consequences, see Daniel Boyarin, "Rethinking Jewish Christianity: An Argument for Dismantling a Dubious Category (To Which is Appended a Correction of My *Border Lines*)," *JQR* 99 (2009): 7–36. That there are other options, both in the history of the category itself and in the current study of what it has typically encompassed, has been made clear now by F. Stanley Jones, ed., *The Rediscovery of Jewish Christianity: From Toland to Baur* (Atlanta: Society of Biblical Literature, 2012).

[24] Richard Bauckham, "The *Apocalypse of Peter*: A Jewish Christian Apocalypse from the Time of Bar Kokhba," *Apoc* 5 (1994): 7–111; Bauckham, "Jews and Jewish Christians in the Land of Israel at the Time of the Bar Kochba War, with Special Reference to the *Apocalypse of Peter*," in *Tolerance and Intolerance in Early Judaism and Christianity*, ed. Graham N. Stanton and Guy G. Strousma (Cambridge: Cambridge University Press, 1998), 228–38.

[25] Bauckham, "Apocalypse of Peter," 7.

ing, *Apocalypse of Peter* emerges as a "rare example of an extant work deriving from a Palestinian Jewish-Christianity" of the second century.[26]

Bauckham highlights its concerns about false messiahs and its preoccupation with martyrdom (e. g., 1:4–5; 2:7–12; 9:1–4; 16:5). Specifically, he points to its intriguing allusions to many martyrs from the "house of Israel" (2:4, 7), among whom are believers and nonbelievers.[27] He reads these allusions with reference to the Bar Kokhba revolt (132–135 CE), both in light of the probable messianic claims of Shimon bar Kosiba and in light of his followers' violence against those Jews who did not support the revolt.[28] Correlating our evidence for this situation with Justin Martyr's claims that Christians were the victims of Jewish persecution during the revolt (*1 Apol.* 31.6), Bauckham suggests that *Apoc. Pet.* was penned as a response to such persecution by ethnically Jewish followers of Jesus.[29] In Bauckham's view, the Bar Kokhba revolt posed a special challenge to Christ-believing Jews: by virtue of their belief in Jesus as messiah, they numbered among those unwilling to accept bar Kosiba and, as a result, were viewed as traitors by those Jews who rallied to his cause of freeing Israel from Roman domination.

In support of the Jewish ethnicity of the author(s) of *Apocalypse of Peter*, Bauckham cites its hopes for the salvation of Israel and its use of Jewish apocalyptic traditions.[30] Seen from this standpoint, he suggests, *Apocalypse of Peter* is an important bridge between (pre-/non-Christian) Jewish apocalypses and (non-Jewish) Christian apocalypses: emerging from a "Jewish-Christian" community that cultivated Jewish apocalyptic traditions as well as beliefs in Jesus' status as the messiah, this apocalypse helps to show some of the process

---

[26] Bauckham, "Apocalypse of Peter," 8, see also 24–25.

[27] Richard Bauckham, "The Two Fig Tree Parables in the *Apocalypse of Peter*," *JBL* 104 (1985): 279. If Bauckham is correct about its understanding of martyrdom as a shared experience by Jewish and Christian/"Jewish-Christian" Bar Kokhba-resisters, the *Apocalypse of Peter* is an especially important addition to our evidence for the dialogue between Jewish and Christian narratives about martyrdom, speaking further to martyrology's place as a shared discourse and competitive domain among Jews and Christians in Late Antiquity. See Daniel Boyarin, "Martyrdom and the Making of Christianity and Judaism," *JECS* 6 (1998): 577–627; Galit Hasan-Rokem, *Web of Life: Folklore and Midrash in Rabbinic Literature* (trans. Batya Stein; Contraversions; Stanford: Stanford University Press, 2000), 114–25; Raʿanan S. Boustan, *From Martyr to Mystic: Rabbinic Martyrology and the Making of Merkavah Mysticism* (TSAJ 112; Tübingen: Mohr Siebeck, 2005), 99–198.

[28] Bauckham, "Apocalypse of Peter," 26–43.

[29] Bauckham, "Apocalypse of Peter," 37.

[30] Bauckham, "Two Fig Tree Parables," esp. 282–83. Central to Bauckham's reading are the versions of the parables of the budding fig tree and the barren fig tree in (Ethiopic) *Apoc. Pet.* 2. In the first parable, Christians are likened to shoots that sprout from Israel and bear fruit through their conversion and/or martyrdom; the second parable suggests that the tree will be uprooted and replaced if it does not sprout – yet in this context, Bauckham argues, the imagery expresses hope for this sprouting. One could go even further, in fact, reading *Apoc. Pet.*'s redeployment of these parables as an assertion of the special role of "Jewish-Christians" in the salvation of Israel.

by which Jewish apocalyptic traditions came to be adopted and transformed in Christian circles.[31]

James Davila has questioned Bauckham's hypothesis on the basis of the relatively scant internal evidence for Jewish self-definition in *Apocalypse of Peter*.[32] Similarly, I do not share Bauckham's confidence that the evidence supports an identification of *Apocalypse of Peter* with Christians of Jewish *ethnicity*.[33] It is possible, for instance, that "the house of Israel" could be here conceived as including Jews as well as Gentiles who are – in their own eyes at least – counted within the bounds of the chosen nation by virtue of their Christ-devotion and/or by virtue of their sharing in the suffering of persecution.[34]

---

[31] Bauckham, "Apocalypse of Peter," 8, 16–19.

[32] He notes, for instance, that references to halakhic infractions are missing from the lists of sins damned; James Davila, *The Provenance of the Pseudepigrapha: Jewish, Christian, or Other?* (JSJSup 105; Leiden: Brill, 2005), 44. See also Davila's impressive summary of our evidence for fluidity and hybridity of ancient identities; his summary makes clear the problems in assuming that our texts emerge from a religious landscape characterized only by those who are clearly Jewish, Christian, or "pagan" (*Provenance of the Pseudepigrapha*, 23–63).

[33] Much of this element of his argument rests on a problematic reading of our evidence for the *birkat ha-minim*. Bauckham reads *Apoc. Pet.*'s assertion of the place of Christians in the book of life as a response. To support this assertion, Bauckham depends heavily on the traditional reading of the *birkat ha-minim* in New Testament scholarship as a curse against "heretics" instituted in synagogues by second-century Rabbis seeking to "exclude Jewish Christians from the religious community of Israel" ("Apocalypse of Peter," 90; see further 87–91). The emergence of the *birkat ha-minim* in the second century, however, is hardly certain; indeed, the interpretation on which Bauckham depends has been critiqued on many grounds – not least because of the problems with assuming that Rabbis held sway over synagogues and had such power to exclude, already in the mid-second century (cf. Lee I. Levine, *Ancient Synagogue: The First Thousand Years* [New Haven: Yale University Press, 2000], 440–70). This reading depends on the assumption that the Talmudic attestations to this tradition (*y. Berakhot* 4.3; *b. Berakhot* 28b–29a) accurately reflect second-century realities and that this tradition is what Justin means when he writes of Jews cursing Christians in *Dial.* 16; 96 (cf. Reuven Kimelman, "Birkat Ha-Minim and the Lack of Evidence for an Anti-Christian Prayer," in *Jewish and Christian Self-Definition*, vol. 2: *Aspects of Judaism in the Greco Roman Period*, ed. E. P. Sanders, Albert I. Baumgarten, and Alan Mendelson [Philadelphia: Fortress, 1981], 226–44). Notably, Bauckham tries to nuance the traditional reading to acknowledge recent insights into the gradual establishment of Rabbinic power and influence over other Jews ("Apocalypse of Peter," 88). Nevertheless, his argument hinges on some degree of Rabbinic dominance in the time of the Bar Kokhba revolt. His proposed connections, moreover, are often vague: he sees a reference to the *birkat ha-minim*, for instance, in *Apoc. Pet.*'s condemnation of "those who blasphemed the way of righteousness" (i.e., 7:2 as rendered by Bauckham).

For reassessments of the relevant Rabbinic evidence, see now Yaakov Y. Teppler, *Birkat HaMinim: Jews and Christians in Conflict in the Ancient World*, trans. Susan Weingarten (TSAJ 120; Tübingen: Mohr Siebeck, 2007); Daniel Boyarin, "Once Again the *Birkat Hamminim* Revisited," in *La croisée des chemins revisitée: Quand l'Église et la Synagogue se sont-elles distinguées?*, ed. Simon Claude Mimouni and Bernard Pouderon (Patrimoines Judaïsme antique; Paris: Cerf, 2012), 91–106.

[34] Compare, e.g., Justin's expansion of the category of "Christian" to include pre-Christian figures who suffered for their faith (*1 Apol.* 46).

What is important, in my view, is not the ethnicity of the author(s) and audience but the fact of their self-identification with Jewish identity and their understanding of Christ devotion in continuity with Judaism (e. g., describing Christians as sprouts on the tree of Israel). Seen from this perspective, Bauckham's characterization of the Jewish apocalyptic matrix of *Apocalypse of Peter* fits well with David Frankfurter's suggestions about *Testaments of the Twelve Patriarchs*, *Ascension of Isaiah*, *5 Ezra*, and *6 Ezra*. Frankfurter proposes that these texts may reflect the literary activities of "continuous communities" that absorbed elements of Christ devotion as part of an evolving sectarian Jewish identity centered in prophetic, priestly, and scribal models.[35]

Scholars have long debated whether Old Testament pseudepigrapha like the *Testaments of the Twelve Patriarchs*, *Ascension of Isaiah*, *5 Ezra*, and *6 Ezra* are reworked Christian versions of Second Temple Jewish texts or works of Christian authorship that draw on earlier Jewish traditions.[36] Following the work of R. A. Kraft and M. de Jonge,[37] Frankfurter suggests that they may, instead, "reflect a type of Christ-devotion that is Jewish enough in frame of reference ... that calling it 'Christian' or 'Jewish' in a *mutually exclusive* sense will not suffice."[38]

With reference to the *Ascension of Isaiah*, *5 Ezra*, and *6 Ezra*, Frankfurter points to their interests in purity in particular. Although concerns with ritual purity are missing from *Apocalypse of Peter*, it does share with these texts a sharp concern for sexual purity. *Apocalypse of Peter* also shares with the *Testaments*

---

[35] David Frankfurter, "Beyond 'Jewish-Christianity': Continuing Religious Sub-cultures of the Second and Third Centuries," in Becker and Reed, *The Ways That Never Parted*, 134–35. On the *Testaments of the Twelve Patriarchs*, see also Marinus de Jonge, "The Future of Israel in the Testaments of the Twelve Patriarchs," *JSJ* 17 (1986): 196–211; Joel Marcus, "The *Testaments of the Twelve Patriarchs* and the *Didascalia Apostolorum*: A Common Jewish Christian Milieu?," *JTS* 6 (2010): 596–626. On *3 Baruch* and *5 Ezra*, see Martha Himmelfarb, "The Parting of the Ways Reconsidered: Diversity in Judaism and Jewish Christian Relations in the Roman Empire: 'A Jewish Perspective,'" in *Interwoven Destines: Jews and Christians through the Ages*, ed. Eugene J. Fisher (New York: Paulist, 1993), 55–57. Note also the case of the Odes of Solomon as recently reassessed in Michael Anthony Novak, "The *Odes of Solomon* as Apocalyptic Literature," *VC* 66 (2012): 527–50.

[36] See Davila, *Provenance*, for detailed discussion of the scholarly debates and the methodological problems and pitfalls involved in identifying such documents as well as Davila, "Did Christians Write Old Testament Pseudepigrapha That Appear to Be Jewish?," in Piovanelli and Burke, *Rediscovering the Apocryphal Continent*, 67–86.

[37] E. g., Robert A. Kraft, "The Multiform Jewish Heritage of Early Christianity," in *Christianity, Judaism and Other Greco-Roman Cults: Studies for Morton Smith at Sixty*, ed. Jacob Neusner (3 vols.; Leiden: Brill, 1975), 3:174–199; Kraft, "The Pseudepigrapha in Christianity," in *Tracing the Threads: Studies in the Vitality of Jewish Pseudepigrapha*, ed. John C. Reeves (Early Judaism and Its Literature Series 6; Atlanta: Scholars Press, 1994), 55–86; Kraft, "Setting the Stage and Framing Some Central Questions," *JSJ* 32 (2001): 371–95. Relevant works by Marinus de Jonge are many and include *Pseudepigrapha of the Old Testament as Part of Christian Literature: The Case of the Testaments of the Twelve Patriarchs and the Greek Life of Adam and Eve* (Studia in Veteris Testamenti pseudepigrapha 18; Leiden: Brill, 2003).

[38] Frankfurter, "Beyond Jewish Christianity," 137.

of the Twelve Patriarchs a common geographical origin (i. e., Roman Palestine) and the hope in the salvation of Israel as well as the close connection to the apocalyptic literature of Second Temple Judaism. Writing of the *Testaments of the Twelve Patriarchs, Ascension of Isaiah, 5 Ezra,* and *6 Ezra,* Frankfurter observes that "none of these texts rail against non-Christ-believing outsider-Jews but only against those who persecute them."[39] The same can be said of the *Apocalypse of Peter.*

In short, even if we do not accept a direct and limited association between "Jewish-Christianity" and Jewish ethnicity, we may be able to draw on the *Apocalypse of Peter* as supplementary evidence for "continuous communities" in second-century Palestine.[40] If the examples cited by Frankfurter show how some adopted an "allegiance to Christ … [as] a devotional orientation *within* a world of Torah observance and Jewish identity,"[41] The *Apocalypse of Peter* may provide an example of a combination of Christ-devotion and Jewish identity shaped by the experience of martyrdom, by beliefs in the Eschaton's immanence, and by assumptions about the centrality of Israel in eschatological events.

When we characterize the Christian response to the Bar Kokhba revolt solely from Patristic evidence, this event emerges as a key moment in the evolution of Christian anti-Judaism. Justin, for instance, sees the failure of the revolt as a sign of God's abandonment of Israel and as a punishment for the Jewish rejection of Jesus (e. g., *Dial.* 25–26; 103; *1 Apol.* 35; 38; 40). Writing in the wake of the revolt, he condemns Jews as a wicked people singled out by God for punishment and allied with demons (e. g., *Dial.* 11; 18–20; 23; 27; 43–46; 73; 92; 133). Accordingly, he discusses those Jews who accepted Christ only in passing and treats them as an exception to the general rule of Christ's abolition of Torah observance (*Dial.* 46–47).[42] By contrast, the author(s) of the *Apocalypse of Peter* acknowledge the shared Jewish and Christian experience of martyrdom. In the *Apocalypse of Peter*, Christ-belief and Jewish identity seem to be a natural connection, breached only by wicked persecutors misled by a false messiah.

In a 2004 article, Timothy Horner similarly seeks to establish the value of the *Protevangelium of James* for our understanding of the fluidity and interactions between biblically based religious identities in the second century CE.[43]

---

[39] Frankfurter, "Beyond Jewish Christianity," 140

[40] Frankfurter, "Beyond Jewish Christianity," 132.

[41] Frankfurter, "Beyond Jewish Christianity," 135.

[42] See further Jeffrey S. Siker, *Disinheriting the Jews: Abraham in Early Christian Controversy* (Louisville: Westminster/John Knox, 1991), 163–84; Judith Lieu, *Image and Reality: The Jews in the World of the Christians in the Second Century* (Edinburgh: T&T Clark, 1996), 177–82.

[43] Timothy J. Horner, "Jewish Aspects of the *Protevangelium of James*," *JECS* 12 (2004): 313–35; contrast M. Mach, "Are there Jewish Elements in the *Protevangelium of Jacobi?*" in *Proceedings of the World Congress of Jewish Studies* (Jerusalem: World Union of Jewish Studies, 1986), 215–22.

He suggests that traditional assumptions about the "Parting of the Ways" have foreclosed important lines of inquiry into this text's possible connections with Judaism. On the basis of its relative lack of resonance with Second Temple Jewish traditions, for instance, the *Protevangelium of James* has been deemed to lack significant Jewish features.[44] Drawing on a broader knowledge of early Judaism, rooted in more recent research on the early Rabbinic movement, Horner highlights its intriguing intersections with traditions preserved in the Mishnah. He thus rereads this source as "a document that uses Jewish imagery to address the concerns and criticisms that might have been important to people who understood Christianity within a predominantly Jewish matrix or those who were attempting to reinterpret the Jewish matrix in the light of Christian doctrine."[45]

Specifically, Horner situates the *Protevangelium of James'* concern to assert the purity and virginity of Mary with reference to Jewish critiques of traditions about Jesus' virgin birth (e. g., Origen, *Cels.* 1.32; *b. Sanhedrin* 67a).[46] He argues that Mary's purity and virginity are here defended in terms that prove most comprehensible when read alongside the ample materials about female purity preserved in the Mishnah – which shares *Protevangelium of James'* obsession with testing virginity as well as attesting a range of specific similar traditions.[47] Inasmuch as mishnaic traditions may help to explain otherwise unparalleled details in this text, he speculates that *"Prot. Jas.* would have been best understood – perhaps only fully understood – within a community that was familiar with concerns and images of contemporary Judaism."[48]

More recently, Horner's assessment of the *Protevangelium of James'* resonance with early Rabbinic traditions has been confirmed and extended by Lily Vuong.[49] On the basis of her inquiries into its representation of Mary, the Temple, and menstrual purity, Vuong argues for understanding *Prot. Jas.* as emerging from the same Syro-Palestinian milieu as the Mishnah, Tosefta, and *Didascalia apostolorum*, and as forming part of the dynamic continuum of Jewish, "Jewish-Christian," and Christian identities in contact and competition in Syria in particular.[50]

---

[44] Horner, "Jewish Aspects," 312–16.

[45] Horner, "Jewish Aspects," 314. Horner avoids the term "Jewish-Christian" because of its polemical associations and its specific association with Ebionites, typically thought to reject the virgin birth (Irenaeus, *Adv. haer.* 1.26.2; 3.21.1; 5.1.3). Instead, he locates the *Protevangelium of James* within what he calls "Christian Judaism" – "a term that is loosely defined as those Christians who maintained that Jesus was the prophetic Messiah but also saw no reason to reinterpret the Torah and its incumbent practices" ("Jewish Aspects," 333).

[46] Horner, "Jewish Aspects," 330.

[47] Horner, "Jewish Aspects," 318–29.

[48] Horner, "Jewish Aspects," 317

[49] Lily C. Vuong, *Gender and Purity in the Protevangelium of James* (WUNT² 358; Tübingen: Mohr Siebeck, 2013), esp. 68–69, 114–16, 152–53.

[50] Vuong, *Gender and Purity*, 193–239; Vuong, "'Let Us Bring Her Up to the Temple of the Lord': Exploring the Boundaries of Jewish and Christian Relations through the Presentation of

If so, this apocryphal gospel may shed light also on the ultimate background of Rabbinic traditions about Jesus' birth in a shared discourse about purity, virginity, and the mother of the messiah. Church Fathers since Justin attest Jewish/Christian debates over the interpretation of Isa 7:14 (e.g., Justin, *Dial.* 43.8; Origen, *Cels.* 1.43), and the classical Rabbinic literature preserves traditions about Jesus as the illegitimate *ben niddah* Yeshu ben Pandera (e.g., *b. Shabbat* 104b; *b. Sanhedrin* 67a).[51] Yet the evidence of the *Protevangelium of James* may show how debates over the virgin birth were more complex than a matter of exegetical polemics. If the *Protevangelium of James* does indeed evince some "Jewish-Christian" engagement with proto-Rabbinic purity *halakhah* in defense of Mary's virginity, then it may also help us to understand some of the broader background behind the surprising engagement with Christian ideas about Mary in later Jewish traditions about the mother of the messiah.[52]

Furthermore, for our present purposes, the *Protevangelium of James*' relative lack of engagement with Second Temple traditions proves no less significant than its possible engagement with proto-Rabbinic Judaism. Texts like the *Testaments of the Twelve Patriarchs*, *Ascension of Isaiah*, *5 Ezra*, *6 Ezra*, and *Apocalypse of Peter* have been deemed "Jewish-Christian" in the sense of standing in a radical continuity with Second Temple Jewish traditions that the usual language of "adoption" and "appropriation" does not suffice to explain. Yet, if Horner and Vuong are correct, the author(s) of the *Protevangelium of James* may

---

Mary in the *Protevangelium of James*," in *Infancy Gospels: Stories and Identities*, ed. Claire Clivaz et al. (WUNT 281; Tübingen: Mohr Siebeck, 2011), 418–32; Vuong, "Purity, Piety, and the Purpose(s) of the *Protevangelium of James*," in *"Non-Canonical" Religious Texts in Early Judaism and Early Christianity*, ed. James H. Charlesworth and Lee M. McDonald (London: T&T Clark, 2012), 205–21.

[51] Peter Schäfer, *Jesus in the Talmud* (Princeton: Princeton University Press, 2009).

[52] E.g., *y. Berakhot* 4.2; *Eikhah Rabbah* 1.16. On these traditions, see Hasan-Rokem, *Web of Life,* 152–60; Martha Himmelfarb, "The Mother of the Messiah in the Talmud Yerushalmi and Sefer Zerubbabel," in *The Talmud Yerushalmi and Graeco-Roman Culture III*, ed. Peter Schäfer (TSAJ 93; Tübingen: Mohr Siebeck, 2002), 369–89; Himmelfarb, "Sefer Zerubbabel," in *Rabbinic Fantasies: Imaginative Narratives from Classical Hebrew Literature*, ed. David Stern and Mark J. Mirsky (New Haven: Yale University Press, 1998), 67–90. On the broader place of Mary in Jewish/Christian interactions, see Stephen J. Shoemaker, "'Let Us Go and Burn Her Body': The Image of the Jews in the Early Dormition Traditions," *Church History* 68 (1999): 775–823; Peter Schäfer, *Mirror of His Beauty: Feminine Images of God from the Bible to the Early Kabbalah* (Princeton: Princeton University Press, 2002), 209–16; Schäfer, *Jesus in the Talmud* (Princeton: Princeton University Press, 2007). With regard to the similarities between Rabbinic traditions about the birth of the messiah and his mother (esp. *Eikhah Rabbah* 1.16) and New Testament infancy traditions (i.e., Matt 1–2; Luke 2), Rokem proposes that "These similarities, in details apparently lacking in any theological significance, suggest that these are neither polemics nor imitations but parallels typical of folk literature. Folk traditions were shared by those Jews who belonged to the majority and by others belonging to a minority group, who believed in Jesus as the Messiah" (*Web of Life*, 154). If Rokem is correct in reading these connections as reflections of a shared Jewish/Christian folklore in Syro-Palestine, then the *Protevangelium of James* may further enrich this picture.

accept and engage the halakhic discourse of the nascent Rabbinic movement in second-century Palestine and even attest its widening influence into some neighboring Syrian locales.

A similar engagement with early Rabbinic traditions can be found in the *Didascalia apostolorum*, a third-century Syrian work that arguably could be included in our category of "Jewish-Christian" apocrypha due to its apostolic pseudepigraphy. Charlotte Fonrobert has discussed the relevance of this text for forging a new understanding of "Jewish-Christianity" that reflects the full complexity of "Jewish" as well as "Christian" identity formation.[53] Building on the insights of Marcel Simon and Georg Strecker,[54] Fonrobert reads the *Didascalia* as attesting two kinds of "Jewish-Christianity." On the one hand, its authors use the narrative setting of the so-called Apostolic Council (Acts 15; *Did. apost.* 1; 24) to polemicize against those in their community who practice *kashrut*, menstrual purity, vegetarianism, asceticism, and regular ritual ablutions with water (*Did. apost.* 23–24).[55] The text shows a pointed concern to counter adherence to the "second legislation" (δευτέρωσις), a term which Fonrobert reads in terms of the emergent Oral Torah of early Rabbis. Interestingly, those critiqued for such practices clearly include Christians of Jewish lineage (*Did. apost.* 26) but do not seem to be limited to them.[56]

---

[53] Charlotte Elisheva Fonrobert, "The *Didascalia Apostolorum*: A Mishnah for the Disciples of Jesus," *JECS* 9 (2001): 483–509, esp. 484–87 on "Jewish-Christianity." The *Didascalia apostolorum* is also the focus of the sixth chapter of her book *Menstrual Purity: Rabbinic and Christian Reconstructions of Biblical Gender* (Contraversions; Stanford: Stanford University Press, 2000), the rest of which focuses on Rabbinic *halakhot* about menstrual purity. On the implications, see also Fonrobert, "Jewish Christians, Judaizers, and Christian Anti-Judaism," in *Late Ancient Christianity*, ed. Virginia Burrus and Rebecca Lyman (A People's History of Christianity 2; Minneapolis: Fortress, 2005), 234–55; Marcus, *"Testaments of the Twelve Patriarchs* and the *Didascalia Apostolorum."* See also Chapter Two in this volume.

[54] Marcel Simon, *Verus Israel: A Study of the Relations between Christians and Jews in the Roman Empire (AD 135–425)* (trans. H. McKeating; London: Littman Library of Jewish Civilization, 1986), esp. 88–90, 94, 310–18, 324–25; Georg Strecker, "Appendix 1: On the Problem of Jewish-Christianity," in Bauer, *Orthodoxy and Heresy*, 244–57.

[55] The occasion of the letter is that some are "observing holiness," "abstaining from flesh and from wine, and some from swine," and "keeping (something) of all the bonds which are in the second legislation" (*Did. apost.* 24); by means of the twelve apostles, the text encourages its readers to "keep from vain bonds; purifications, and sprinklings and baptisms, and distinction of meats" (*Did. apost.* 26). As a possible parallel for the practices not paralleled in biblical and Rabbinic *halakhot*, Fonrobert points to *t. Sotah* 15.11 (as paralleled and expanded in *b. Baba Batra* 60b), which counters Jews who refrained from meat and wine after the destruction of the Temple; "*Didascalia Apostolorum*," 491–502. For a different reading of the work's heresiology, see Charlotte Metheun, "Widows, Bishops, and the Struggle for Authority in the *Didascalia Apostolorum*," *Journal of Ecclesiastical History* 46 (1995): 204.

[56] Fonrobert resists the limitation of "Jewish-Christianity" to ethnically Jewish converts to Christianity. She thus eschews scholarly attempts to distinguish between "Jewish-Christians" and "Judaizing Christians" as the projection of modern concerns about ethnicity onto our ancient sources; "*Didascalia Apostolorum*," 499–501, cf. Strecker, "On the Problem of Jewish Christianity," 354.

On the other hand, Fonrobert highlights the authors' own knowledge about, and engagement with, third-century Jewish traditions. Discursive and hermeneutical parallels with traditions found in contemporaneous Rabbinic sources (especially Mishnah and Tosefta) suggest that their understanding of Christian identity has been significantly shaped by contacts with Jews of their time.[57] The enemies and interlocutors of the authors seem to see piety in terms of halakhic observance and thus mirror some of the most salient concerns of the early Rabbinic movement. But the authors also share much with their Jewish contemporaries. Not only do they stress orthopraxy over orthodoxy, but their concern for Scripture and authority seems to be articulated in the same "discursive space" that shaped Rabbinic midrash. To express their message, they employ many of the same hermeneutical assumptions and techniques. In a manner even more marked than the *Protevangelium of James*, the *Didascalia apostolorum* attests Christian engagement with distinctively post-70 varieties of Judaism but also evinces the spread of distinctively Rabbinic ideas from Roman Palestine into Syria.

The different articulations of Christian/"Jewish-Christian" identities in the sources surveyed so far also may shed new light on the most celebrated "Jewish-Christian" apocrypha from the second and third centuries – namely, the hypothetical sources of the Pseudo-Clementines.[58] Portions of *Rec.* 1, for instance, have long been associated with "Jewish-Christianity" due to their resonance with Epiphanius's description of the Ebionites in *Pan.* 30. Most cited in this regard are anti-Pauline traditions, polemics against animal sacrifice, and the account of the martyrdom of James, the last of which bears similarities to the nonextant Ebionite *Ascents of James* described in *Pan.* 30.16.6–9.[59]

Questioning the centrality of Epiphanius in the modern search for the Pseudo-Clementines' sources, F. Stanley Jones has opened the way for a new understanding of the scope and character of this source as well as for further attention to the self-definition and concerns internal to it. Proceeding instead from an analysis of internal criteria, he suggests that *Rec.* 1.27–71 preserves a "Jewish-Christian" source written in Palestine around 200 CE.[60] In a related article, he shows how its depictions of Paul, Peter, James, and apostolic history are articu-

---

[57] Fonrobert, "*Didascalia Apostolorum*," 501–8.

[58] For a thorough-going reading of the Pseudo-Clementines as reflecting the beliefs of the Ebionites more specifically, see Hans Joachim Schoeps, *Theologie und Geschichte des Judenchristentums* (Tübingen: Mohr Siebeck, 1949); and Schoeps, *Jewish Christianity: Factional Disputes in the Early Church* (trans. D. Hare; Philadelphia: Fortress, 1969; revised English version of *Judenchristentums* [Bern: Francke, 1964]).

[59] Portions of *Rec.* 1 have been identified with this text by Bousset, Schoeps, Strecker, Lüdemann, and Van Voorst; for a summary of these approaches, see Jones, *Ancient Jewish Christian Source*, 4–33.

[60] Jones, *Ancient Jewish Christian Source*, 157–68.

lated in direct contrast to Luke-Acts.[61] In effect, this source offers an alternative account of Christianity as emerging as a movement within Judaism. Jesus is here the prophet who comes after Moses to abolish the temporary measure of Temple sacrifice and to institute baptism in its place (*Rec.* 1.36.2; 1.39.2; 1.40.4–41.1; 1.59.1–3). Moreover, Jesus is the messiah awaited by the Jews and sent to save them, and Gentiles only fill the numbers left by those Jews who reject him – partly due, in fact, to the pernicious influence of Paul (*Rec.* 1.42, 50, 69–70).

The "Jewish-Christian" traditions in *Rec.* 1.27–71 have been much discussed and need not be reiterated here.[62] For our purposes, it will suffice to note their differences with other "Jewish-Christian" apocrypha. In contrast to the sources examined above, for instance, we might note what seem to be self-conscious attempts to present the followers of Jesus as part of Judaism: Peter asserts his Jewish identity (*Rec.* 1.32.1), Hebrew is celebrated as the divinely given original language of humankind (*Rec.* 1.30.5), and positive reference is made to circumcision as the "proof and sign of purity" (*Rec.* 1.33.5). Furthermore, followers of Jesus are depicted in discussion with other sects of Jews (especially Pharisees, Sadducees, and followers of John the Baptist; *Rec.* 1.60), and there is an explicit assertion that the only difference between followers of Jesus and other Jews is their belief in Jesus as messiah (*Rec.* 1.43.2; 1.50.3).

In addition, the Pharisees are here depicted as the group that stands closest to the Jesus movement; R. Gamaliel is even described as a secret sympathizer (*Rec.* 1.65.2–68.2). This surprisingly positive approach to the Pharisees also may point, as Albert Baumgarten has suggested, to a surprisingly sympathetic attitude towards Rabbinic Jews. Pharisees are here said to possess "the word of truth received from Moses' tradition" (1.54); they may be critiqued for hiding this key, as in Matt 23:13, but the assertion of their possession of extrascriptural Mosaic tradition nevertheless suggests the author(s)' surprising acceptance of

---

[61] F. Stanley Jones, *Pseudoclementina*, 207–29. Whether or not the Pseudo-Clementine tradition stands in direct continuity with the Jerusalem church of Peter and James, it remains significant, in my view, that its authors see themselves as heir to this tradition and imagine themselves as preserving this heritage against challenges by Pauline Christians; cf. Munck, "Jewish Christianity."

[62] See esp. Georg Strecker, *Das Judenchristentum in den Pseudoklementinen* (TU 70[2]; Berlin: Akademie-Verlag, 1981), 221–54; Jones, *Ancient Jewish Christian Source,* 157–68. One matter of debate is whether its authors see a need for Gentile followers of Jesus to undergo circumcision. Strecker tentatively posits a positive answer with appeal to *Rec.* 1.33.5 (*Judenchristentum*, 251). Jones, however, identifies *Rec.* 1.33.5 as part of the *Grundschrift*'s later additions to this source (*Ancient Jewish Christian Source,* 160); in his view, "the very notion of calling the nations to complete the number shown to Abraham (*Rec.* 1.42; compare *Rec.* 1.63.2; 1.64.2) contradicts the view that these Gentiles should first have to convert to Judaism (e.g., submission to circumcision) before entering Christianity" (*Ancient Jewish Christian Source,* 164). I would tend to side with Strecker, not least because the assertion of the commonality between Jesus' followers and other Jews in *Rec.* 1.43.2 and 1.50.3 implies a perceived commonality of practice. Perhaps more intriguing, however, is the text's own lack of explicit concern with the question of whether Gentile followers of Jesus should be circumcised.

emergent Rabbinic claims about the Oral Torah.[63] Like *Protevangelium of James* and the *Didascalia apostolorum*, this source may reflect some engagement with the traditions and concerns of the nascent Rabbinic movement. Whereas the *Protevangelium of James* appears to use such traditions towards polemic aims and whereas the *Didascalia apostolorum* counters them with Christianized counterparts, it seems to accept the Rabbinic claim to Mosaic authority and to attempt to integrate this claim into its own understanding of Jesus' teachings.

For our mapping of "Jewish-Christian apocrypha," some mention must also be made of the Pseudo-Clementine *Grundschrift* or Basic Source (i. e., the hypothetical third-century source posited to account for the ample parallels between the *Homilies* and *Recognitions*).[64] It is impossible to know for certain the precise contents of the *Grundschrift*; although its significance for the history of "Jewish-Christianity" is widely acknowledged, the reconstruction of the precise nature of its relevance thus proves tricky. Nevertheless, we can note readily some of the more strikingly "Jewish-Christian" features of the material paralleled in the *Homilies* and *Recognitions*. Like *Apocalypse of Peter* and the *Testaments of the Twelve Patriarchs*, for instance, this material depicts the fate of the Jews in more complex, irenic, and hopeful terms than other third-century Christian texts (cf. Tertullian, *Adv. Jud.* 3, 6, 8, 12–3). Also notable in this regard are its prescriptions for proper ritual practice, which encompasses dietary restrictions, ritual ablutions with water, and menstrual purity (*Rec.* 2.71–72; 6.9–11; 7.29, 34; 8.68; *Hom.* 7.8; 11.28–30; 13.4, 9, 19). In short, it seems to promote many of the same practices that the *Didascalia apostolorum* denounces. Inasmuch as these prescriptions seem to be tailored for Gentile followers of Jesus, we may be able to situate its pointed concerns for the impurities caused by contact with blood,

---

[63] Albert I. Baumgarten, "Literary Evidence for Jewish Christianity in the Galilee," in *The Galilee in Late Antiquity*, ed. Lee I. Levine (New York: Jewish Theological Seminary of America, 1992), 42–43. Notably, the source in *Rec.* 1.27–71 is contemporaneous with the redaction of the Mishnah (ca. 200 CE.), which contains only early echoes of what would later become the Rabbinic doctrine of the Oral Torah (see P. Schäfer, "Das Dogma von der mündlichen Torah im rabbinischen Judentum," in Schäfer, *Studien zur Geschichte und Theologie des rabbinischen Judentums* [Leiden: Brill, 1978], 153–97). It is thus striking that its depiction of the Mosaic tradition of the Pharisees/Rabbis seem to correspond to the Rabbinic claims voiced in *m. Avot* 1–5, which stresses the unbroken chain of trustworthy transmission of teachings from Moses to the Rabbis. By contrast, the *Homilies* appear to reflect knowledge of the doctrine of the Oral Torah in its more developed form (see below).

[64] Most studies have considered the parallel material relevant to "Jewish-Christianity" in terms of a hypothetical source of the *Grundschrift*, namely the *Kerygmata Petrou*; esp. Strecker, *Judenchristentum*. I am less than confident in our ability to reconstruct a nonextant source of the nonextant *Grundschrift*, esp. as internal literary evidence is here hardly univalent (as attested, e. g., by nearly a century of scholarly debates). I concur with Jones about the need for research on the Pseudo-Clementines' sources to turn its focus on the *Grundschrift* itself. For his tentative outline of its scope and contents, see "Eros and Astrology," 53–61.

semen, and idols with reference to halakhic discussions of Gentile impurity in early Rabbinic sources.[65]

In a broader sense, then, we may be able to locate the *Grundschrift* in a continuum of discussions about ritual purity that includes the early Rabbinic traditions about female and Gentile impurity in the Mishnah and Tosefta, the redeployment of related proto-Rabbinic traditions in the *Protevangelium of James*, and the *Didascalia apostolorum*'s Christian critique of such traditions from within a Jewish cultural matrix. Strikingly, the *Grundschrift* falls closer to the Rabbinic movement than earlier "Jewish-Christian" sources. Whether this confluence reflects the increased consolidation of the Rabbinic movement in the mid-third century and the spread of its influence and/or a concurrent shift away from Second Temple models of authority in geographically and culturally proximate "Jewish-Christian" circles, it suggests that some "Jewish-Christian" identities were being articulated in interaction with evolving Rabbinic Jewish identities.[66]

If so, it proves all the more striking that what we can reconstruct of the Pseudo-Clementine *Grundschrift* powerfully counters Marcionism – as Jones has richly demonstrated. In his view: "when taken together with the *Didascalia* and other late second and third century source such as Hippolytus' information on the Apamaean Elchasaite Alcibiades, Julius Africanus, Hegesippus, and the source of *Recognitions* 1.27–71, the Circuits [i. e., *Grundschrift*] should allow the field to rewrite the history of later Jewish-Christianity, this time on a secure basis."[67] To do so, however, is not just to posit a static survival from Christianity's first-century Jewish roots; rather, it is to recover a dynamic movement that seems to have been mobilized "into defensive and creative activity" by the encroachment of Marcionism and its "denial of the creator god, of the goodness of creation, and accordingly of the goodness of marriage and childbearing."[68] Even as Jones stresses that "the diversity among the Jewish-Christians, at all periods, should not be underestimated,"[69] he thus points to the possibility that much of what we know as "Jewish-Christianity" in third-century Syria, in particular, took form in response to the "direct and aggressive assault on its understanding of [the church's] Jewish heritage … from Marcionite Christianity."[70]

---

[65] On the relevant Rabbinic discussions, see Christine Hayes, *Gentile Impurities and Jewish Identities: Intermarriage and Conversion from the Bible to the Talmud* (Oxford: Oxford University Press, 2002), 107–92; and on their echoes in the Pseudo-Clementines, see Boustan and Reed, "Blood and Atonement" as well as Chapter Two in this volume.

[66] For attempts to correlate "Jewish-Christian" sources with what we know about the gradual consolidation and spread of Rabbinic power in Palestine and beyond, see Chapter Nine in this volume.

[67] F. Stanley Jones, *Pseudoclementina Elchasaiticaque inter Judaeochristiana: Collected Studies* (Orientalia Lovaniensia Analecta 203; Leuven: Peeters, 2012), 146.

[68] Jones, *Pseudoclementina*, 206.

[69] Jones, *Pseudoclementina*, 455.

[70] Jones, *Pseudoclementina*, 205.

"Jewish-Christian" Apocrypha from the
Fourth and Fifth Centuries

In studies of the Pseudo-Clementine literature, the significance of "Jewish-Christianity" has typically been limited to the very early stages in the redactional formation of the *Homilies* and *Recognitions*.[71] Elsewhere, I have questioned the degree to which this tendency is predicated on an outmoded understanding of early Jewish/Christian relations as defined by a single and simple "Parting of the Ways" between Judaism and Christianity.[72] Focusing on the fourth-century form of the *Homilies,* I have attempted to situate this version of the novel within its late antique Jewish as well as late antique Christian (and "pagan") contexts. It is clear that the *Homilies* contains more Jewish and "Jewish-Christian" elements than the *Recognitions* and that it reworks their shared material in a manner more irenic towards Judaism; like the *Testaments of the Twelve Patriarchs*, for instance, it outlines a two-path soteriology that allows for Jewish salvation through Moses and Gentile salvation through Jesus (*Hom.* 8.5–7; cf. *Rec.* 4.5).[73] Together with its connections with Rabbinic traditions, this positive representation of Judaism raises the possibility that the *Homilies* attest the survival – and, indeed, flourishing – of "Jewish-Christian" forms of belief and practice well into the fourth century.

If we look beyond the *Homilies'* preservation of earlier "Jewish-Christian" traditions to investigate the redactional choices that shaped its final form, two significant features emerge. First is the resonance with midrashic and halakhic traditions found in fourth- and fifth-century Rabbinic sources from Palestine. The *Homilies*, for instance, focuses more concertedly on issues of ritual purity than those sources discussed above, and it does so in a manner that resonates even more sharply with the Rabbinic discourse about Gentile impurity.[74] Knowledge of the Rabbinic doctrine of Oral Torah is even more expansive than in earlier sources, consistent with the articulation of this Rabbinic doctrine during this period (e. g., *y. Megillot* 4.1; *y. Pe'ah* 2.6; *b. Shabbat* 13a). Moreover, its account of the disputes between Peter and Simon Magus echo Rabbinic tales about disputes between Sages and *minim* ("heretics") in both form and content;[75] central to both is the defense of the singularity and goodness of God against the beliefs

---

[71] For the history of research, see Strecker, *Judenchristentum*, 1–34; F. Stanley Jones, "The Pseudo-Clementines: A History of Research," *Second Century* 2 (1982): 84–96, esp. 86.

[72] I.e., as discussed throughout the present volume, especially in the Introduction and Chapters One, Two, Six, and the Epilogue.

[73] See further Chapter Six in this volume.

[74] See Boustan and Reed, "Blood and Atonement" as well as Chapter Two in this volume.

[75] See Chapter Five in this volume. On the Rabbinic subgenre of dispute tales, see Richard Kalmin, "Christians and Heretics in Rabbinic Literature of Late Antiquity," *HTR* 87 (1994): 155–69.

of *minim* and the musings of philosophers.[76] Strikingly, even the *Homilies'* adoption, subversion, and rejection of elements from "pagan" culture – such as rhetoric, *paideia*, and the Graeco-Roman novel – find some parallels in Rabbinic sources redacted around the same time.[77]

Second is the representation of the relationship between Jews and followers of Jesus.[78] As noted above, some earlier "Jewish-Christian" apocrypha already seem cognizant of Rabbinic claims to possess and preserve an oral tradition going back to Moses. This connection is even more marked in the *Homilies*: the doctrine of the Oral Torah is surprisingly central to its epistemology and salvation history. By virtue of its distinctive approach to the idea of Jesus as True Prophet (see *Hom.* 1.19; 2.5–12; 3.11–28)[79] and its unique doctrine of the Law of Syzygies (*Hom.* 2.15–18; 3.59; cf. *Rec.* 4.59, 61), for instance, the *Homilies* presents all of human history as shaped by the activity of a series of prophets (e.g., Moses, Jesus) who are sent by God to proclaim the same message of truth and who are countered by a series of false prophets sent to contest them (e.g., Aaron, John the Baptist). In depicting the faithful transmission of prophetic knowledge from Jesus to Peter and his followers, the *Homilies* appeals to the faithful transmission of Moses' teaching by the Pharisees (*Hom.* 3.18–19). For this, oral tradition is central; the Written Torah alone does not suffice, since falsehoods were added to it during the course of its writing and written transmission.[80] Moses, however, "gave the Law with the explanations to certain chosen men, some seventy in number" (*Hom.* 2.38; cf. Num 11:16), and his prophetic knowledge remains among the Pharisees who "sit in Moses' seat [καθέδρα]" (*Hom.* 3.18; cf. Matt 23:2). Hence, according to the *Homilies*,

---

[76] See Chapter Five below, esp. on the parallels with *Bereshit Rabbah* 1.7, 8.8–9.

[77] See, e.g., Martin S. Jaffee, "The Oral-Cultural Context of the Talmud Yerushalmi: Greco-Roman Rhetorical *Paideia*, Discipleship, and the Concept of the Oral Torah," in *The Talmud Yerushalmi and Graeco-Roman Culture I*, ed. Peter Schäfer (TSAJ 71; Tübingen: Mohr Siebeck, 1998), 27–62; and Catherine Heszer, "Interfaces between Rabbinic Literature and Graeco-Roman Philosophy," in Schäfer, *Talmud Yerushalmi and Graeco-Roman Culture I*, 161–87; David Stern, "The Captive Woman: Hellenization, Greco-Roman Erotic Narrative, and Rabbinic Literature," *PT* 19 (1998): 91–127; Joshua Levinson, "The Tragedy of Romance: A Case of Literary Exile," *HTR* 89 (1996): 227–44.

[78] See Chapter Nine below for a more detailed analysis of its representation of Pharisees, in particular, in comparison with earlier sources.

[79] See Strecker, *Judenchristentum*, 145–53; L. Cerfaux, "Le vrai prophète des Clémentines," *RSR* 18 (1928): 143–63; Han Jan Willem Drijvers, "Adam and the True Prophet in the Pseudo-Clementines," in *Loyalitätskonflikte in der Religionsgeschichte: Festschrift für Carsten Colpe*, ed. Christoph Elsas and Hans G. Kippenberg (Würzburg: Königshausen & Neumann, 1990), 314–23; Charles A. Gieschen, "The Seven Pillars of the World: Ideal Figure Lists in the True Prophet Christology of the Pseudo-Clementines," *JSP* 12 (1994): 47–82.

[80] I.e., the doctrine of the false pericopes, on which see Strecker, *Judenchristentum*, 166–86. On possible Rabbinic awareness of this idea, see Schoeps, *Theologie und Geschichte des Judenchristentums*, 176–79, esp. on *Sifre Devarim* 26 (cf. *Vayiqra Rabbah* 31.4; *Devarim Rabbah* 2.6).

Christians can look to Jews as a model for the maintenance of monotheism and other true beliefs and practices (*Hom.* 4.13; 7.4; 9.16; 11.28; 16.14). Inasmuch as Moses was sent as a teacher for the Jews, Moses' prophetic knowledge is kept among them, whereas Jesus was sent to spread the same message to the Gentiles (*Hom.* 3.19; 8.6–7). Just as Moses' teachings are kept by the Pharisees who sit on his seat (καθέδρα; *Hom.* 11.29), so Jesus' teachings are faithfully kept by Peter, who passes his knowledge and authority onto the bishops who sit on his seat (καθέδρα; *Hom.* 3.70).[81]

As we have seen, there are some precedents in earlier "Jewish-Christian" apocrypha for the *Homilies'* attempts to articulate a Christian identity that retains the chosenness of Israel and the salvation of the Jews. Here, however, the argument is much more developed and plays a more central role in the defense of authentic apostolic teaching against "heretics" and "pagans." Apostolic succession is here outlined in a manner that not only appeals to the Rabbinic doctrine of the Oral Torah but also allows for the Pharisaic/Rabbinic succession from Moses (cf. *m. Avot* 1–5; *y. Ḥagigah* 1.7; *y. Megillot* 4.1) as a parallel line for the transmission of true prophetic teaching.[82]

Just as the third-century author(s) of *Rec.* 1.27–71 seem to counter the image of apostolic history in Luke-Acts, so the fourth-century Syrian redactors of the *Homilies* may respond to the heresiologies and historiographies of emergent Christian "orthodoxy" in the Roman Empire. Most striking are the parallels with Eusebius.[83] Penning his *Historia ecclesiastica* in nearby Palestine around the same time that the *Homilies* were being redacted in Syria,[84] Eusebius also drew on a variety of Hellenistic Jewish and earlier Christian sources to defend his particular understanding of apostolic succession. Whereas Eusebius presents the rise of Christianity as counterpoint to the decline of Judaism (*Hist. eccl.* 3.1.2), the *Homilies* offers a very different image of Christianity's origins and spread: its authors/redactors posit a radical continuity with Judaism while sharply critiquing Greek philosophy and *paideia*. Whereas Eusebius stresses the dispersal of the original "Jewish-Christians" (*Hist. eccl.* 3.5.3) and dismisses postapostolic "Jewish-Christianity" as a heterodox phenomenon (3.27.1–6), the authors/redactors of the *Homilies* claim to preserve the true teachings of James and Peter.

---

[81] See further Chapter Six below.

[82] On the shared prehistory of Christian and Jewish succession lists, see Amram Tropper, "Tractate *Avot* and Early Christian Succession Lists," in Becker and Reed, *The Ways That Never Parted,* 159–88, which also contains a helpful summary of scholarly opinions about their possible connections.

[83] For further discussion of such parallels, see Chapter Six below.

[84] The first edition of books I–VII of the *Historia ecclesiastica* is typically dated to 303 CE and the *Homilies* to 300–320 CE. Eusebius himself alludes to the transmission of texts from Edessa to Caesarea (*Hist. eccl.* 1.13). That the *Historia ecclesiastica* was soon translated into Syriac is suggested by the fact that it survives in a manuscript from 461/462 CE.

It may not be coincidental, in my view, that so much of our secondhand evidence for "Jewish-Christianity" comes from the fourth and fifth centuries.[85] Scholars have tended to mine the descriptions of Ebionites and Nazarenes by Eusebius, Epiphanius, Jerome, and others for hints about possibly continuities with apostolic traditions; this evidence for "Jewish-Christianity" has been culled for possible hints about social realities in the second and third centuries. It is widely assumed, for instance, that the comments about the Ebionites by Epiphanius pertain to the singular and same group discussed by Irenaeus. Especially insofar as we have no firsthand evidence for groups calling themselves "Ebionites" and inasmuch as our earliest references to Nazarenes come from the fourth century (Epiphanius, *Pan.* 29.1.1), it is worth considering whether Epiphanius and others are using the traditional heresiological rubric of "Ebionism" to encompass a range of different groups who combined Jewish identity and Christ devotion in ways that jarred with their own understanding of "Christianity."[86] If we limit the production and transmission of Pseudo-Clementine traditions to a single, purportedly marginalized sect like the Ebionites, moreover, we would be hard-pressed to explain our ample evidence for the broad circulation of the Pseudo-Clementine novels in a variety of forms and languages for many centuries thereafter.

If we follow the traditional model of the "Parting of the Ways," the growth of evidence for "Jewish-Christianity" in the fourth and fifth centuries seems counterintuitive if not paradoxical. Here too, however, the evidence of "Jewish-Christian apocrypha" proves useful in supplementing the picture of the period that we have from Patristic sources. Recently, for instance, Rémi Gounelle has proposed reading the late fourth-century *Gospel of Nicodemus* as a late antique "Jewish-Christian" apocryphon, citing its positive representation of Jews as well as its approach to the Jewish scriptures; the latter, in particular, departs from dominant patterns in early Christian exegesis but bears some parallels in Rabbinic midrash.[87] For Gounelle, such features raise the possibility of its origin in a community of ethnically Jewish believers in Jesus. Whatever the ethnic background of its authors, however, Phillip Fackler has argued that its treatment of Jews and Israel points to its promotion of a vision of the Christian past that differs strikingly from the anti-Jewish approaches that were coming to shape the emergent imperial Christianity of the Roman Empire at the time.[88] In Fackler's view, the *Gospel of Nicodemus* may help us to "recover other strate-

---

[85] This is clear, e. g., from even a skim of the sources collected in A. F. J. Klijn and G. J. Reinink, *Patristic Evidence for Jewish-Christian Sects* (NTSup 36; Leiden: Brill, 1973).

[86] Klijn and Reinink, *Patristic Evidence*, 43; Daniel Boyarin, *Border Lines: The Partition of Judeo-Christianity* (Divinations; Philadelphia: University of Pennsylvania Press, 2004), 207–8.

[87] Rémi Gounelle, "Un nouvel évangile judéo-chrétien? Les *Actes de Pilate*," in *The Apocryphal Gospels within the Context of Early Christian Theology*, ed. Jens Schröter (Leuven: Peeters, 2013), 364–71.

[88] Phillip Fackler, "*Adversus Adversus Iudaeos*? Countering Christian Anti-Jewish Polemics in the *Gospel of Nicodemus*," *JECS* 23 (2015): 413–44.

gies of distinction or different conceptions of identity between and among late antique Jews and Christians than those proposed by 'separatists'" like Church Fathers and Rabbis.[89]

Pierluigi Piovanelli has shown something similar for the Ethiopian *Book of the Cock*.[90] He proposes that this Ethiopian apocryphon preserves a "Jewish-Christian" source in its account of Saul/Paul's role in the arrest of Jesus. He suggests, more specifically, an Ebionite provenance, and he proposes that the anti-Jewish traditions within the text may reflect "inner controversies" between Jews and "Jewish-Christians" over Jesus' Passion.[91] Whereas anti-Pauline elements appear to have been downplayed during the course of the redaction of the Pseudo-Clementines, we here find an expanded polemic against Paul, concurrent with the expression of less positive views towards (non-Christian) Jews.

Most significantly, for our purposes, Piovanelli further points to the need to situate the *Book of the Cock*, Patristic quotations from "Jewish-Christian" gospels, and heresiological statements about Ebionites and Nazarenes in the context of the fourth-century Christianization of Roman Palestine – and the same might be said for the Pseudo-Clementine *Homilies* and the *Gospel of Nicodemus* as well.[92] In Piovanelli's view, "the irruption into the region of a new wave of nonnative pilgrims, clergymen, and monks … broke the delicate balance existing between different local communities" in Syro-Palestine.[93] As a result, some forms of "Jewish-Christianity" native to the region may have been absorbed by the nascent orthodoxies, both Christian and Rabbinic, which were in the process of solidifying power at the time. The encounter with a variety of local Syro-Palestinian groups that approached Christ devotion from a Jewish cultural matrix, however, seems to have left its traces on emergent Christian "orthodoxy" – and perhaps also on Rabbinic Judaism: "Jewish-Christian communities were able to transmit a part of their religious heritage to the Great Church and to the equally great synagogue that were reabsorbing them."[94]

---

[89] Fackler, "*Adversus Adversus Iudaeos*." A similar argument has been made for the Pseudo-Clementines by Dominique Côté, "Le problème de l'identité religieuse dans Syrie du IVe siècle: Le cas des *Pseudo-Clémentines* et de l'*Adversus Judaeos* de saint Jean Chrysostome," in Mimouni and Pouderon, *La croisée des chemins revisitée*, 339–70.

[90] Pierluigi Piovanelli, "The *Book of the Cock* and the Rediscovery of Ancient Jewish-Christian Traditions in Fifth-Century Palestine," in Henderson and Oegama, *The Changing Face of Judaism*, 308–22; Piovanelli, "Exploring the Ethiopic *Book of the Cock*, an Apocryphal Passion Gospel from Late Antiquity," *HTR* 96 (2003): 427–54.

[91] Piovenelli, "*Book of the Cock*," 312; Piovenelli, "Exploring the Ethiopic *Book of the Cock*," 445–46. If so, this source would be temporally and culturally proximate with Epiphanius (b. 310 in Palestine).

[92] Piovanelli, "*Book of the Cock*," 308. See also Boyarin, *Border Lines*, 202–14; Andrew S. Jacobs, *Remains of the Jews: Holy Land and Christian Empire in Late Antiquity* (Divinations; Stanford: Stanford University Press, 2004).

[93] Piovanelli, "*Book of the Cock*," 318.

[94] Piovanelli, "*Book of the Cock*," 319.

In turn, Piovanelli's insights push us towards a new perspective on the importance of still other apocrypha, such as the Pseudo-Clementine *Recognitions,* for our understanding of the history of "Jewish-Christianity." Comparison with the *Homilies* suggests this version of the Pseudo-Clementine novel was shaped by more "orthodox" perspectives. Nevertheless, by virtue of Rufinus's Latin translation, the *Recognitions* became a vehicle for the widespread circulation of much "Jewish-Christian" material. Although less "Jewish-Christian" than the *Homilies*, it includes *Rec.* 1.27–71 as well as some of the materials about ritual purity and Torah observance that seem to have been in the *Grundschrift.* Also significant in this regard is the *Apostolic Constitutions*, a collection which similarly circulated under the name of Clement and which is marked by the integration of earlier Hellenistic Jewish and "Jewish-Christian" materials.[95]

With the Christianization of the Roman Empire came imperially backed efforts to standardize Christian belief and worship, thereby intensifying efforts to collect, select, and translate earlier sources as well as catalyzing fresh reflection on the apostolic past and its meaning for the imperial church. If this push toward standardization did indeed lead to the increased marginalization or absorption of Syro-Palestinian "Jewish-Christian" groups, it also resulted in the broader circulation of writings voicing earlier "Jewish-Christian" approaches to Judaism and Christian praxis; although forged in the interactions between Jews and followers of Jesus in specific local settings, elements of these approaches remain embedded in documents such as the Pseudo-Clementine *Recognitions, Apostolic Constitutions*, and Patristic commentaries that quote "Jewish-Christian" gospels. Preserved within apocrypha like the Pseudo-Clementine *Homilies* and the *Gospel of Nicodemus*, moreover, we also find evidence for the contestation of the *contra Iudaeos* tradition that eventually came to dominate the imperial church.[96] Notably, moreover, the canonizing efforts of Athanasius, Eusebius, and others do not seem to have affected the popularity of many of the earlier "Jewish-Christian" apocrypha surveyed above – particularly outside the Roman Empire and on its margins, where a diversity of approaches to Christian and Jewish identities continued to flourish.[97]

---

[95] E.g., *Didascalia apostolorum* and so-called Hellenistic synagogual hymns. On the latter, see David A. Fiensy, *Prayers Alleged to Be Jewish: An Examination of the Constitutiones Apostolorum* (BJS 65; Chico: Scholars Press, 1985); E.G. Chazon, "A 'Prayer Alleged to be Jewish' in the *Apostolic Constitutions*," in *Things Revealed: Studies in Early Jewish and Christian Literature in Honor of Michael E. Stone*, ed. E.G. Chazon, D. Satran, and R.A. Clements (JSJSup 89; Leiden: Brill, 2004), 261–77.

[96] Not least because this process was slower than often suspected; see, e.g., Paula Fredriksen, "Roman Christianity and the Post-Roman West: The Social Correlates of the *Contra Iudaeos* Tradition," in *Jews, Christians, and the Roman Empire: The Poetics of Power in Late Antiquity*, ed. Natalie B. Dohrmann and Annette Yoshiko Reed (Philadelphia: University of Pennsylvania, 2013), 249–66.

[97] See Klijn, "Study of Jewish-Christianity"; Becker, "Beyond the Spatial and Temporal Lines"; and Shlomo Pines, *The Jewish Christians of the Early Centuries of Christianity Accord-*

Revisiting the Problem of "Jewish-Christianity"

Although the notion of "Jewish-Christianity" originated in research on the New Testament and Christian Origins,[98] a number of scholars have deemed the term irrelevant for describing the religious landscape of the first century. With more attention to the Jesus movement's Jewish context has come less certainty about the heurism of any simple contrast between "Gentile Christianity" and "Jewish-Christianity"; indeed, as Helmut Koester has stressed, "everyone in the first generation of Christianity was Jewish-Christian" in some sense or another.[99] Likewise, one might ask whether such a simple and clear-cut contrast applies to the second and third centuries – or even the fourth and fifth.

For the second century and following, the label "Jewish-Christian" has been used in various senses, mostly tied to the modern desire to discover what unique beliefs, practices, and outlooks may have been held by Christ-followers of Jewish ethnicity. Some senses of the term follow from the older use of this label in New Testament research à la Ferdinand Christian Baur; for instance, the term "Jewish-Christian" is often applied to [1] the direct heirs to the Jerusalem church of James and Peter and/or to [2] ethnically Jewish Christ-followers who "retained" those elements of Torah observance (e. g., circumcision, *kashrut*) attested but deemed unnecessary in the New Testament, especially in the Pauline epistles

---

ing to a New Source (Jerusalem: Israel Academy of Sciences and Humanities, 1965); Patricia Crone, "Islam, Judeo-Christianity and Byzantine Iconoclasm," *Jerusalem Studies in Arabic and Islam* 2 (1980): 87–94; John G. Gager, "Did Jewish-Christians See the Rise of Islam?," in Becker and Reed, *The Ways That Never Parted*, 361–72. On the ongoing production, transmission, and use of Christian apocrypha, see, e. g., Alain Desreumaux, "Remarques sur le rôle des apocryphes dans la théologie des Églises syriaques: l'exemple de testimonia christologiques inédits," *Apocrypha* 8 (1999): 165–77; Hans J. W. Drijvers, "Apocryphal Literature in the Cultural Milieu of Osrhoëne," *Apocrypha* 1 (1990): 231–47; Catherine Paupert, "Présence des apocryphes dans la littérature monastique occidentale ancienne," *Apocrypha* 4 (1995): 113–23; Martin McNamara, *The Apocrypha in the Irish Church* (Dublin: Dublin Institute for Advanced Studies, 1975); Máire Herbert and Martin McNamara, *Irish Biblical Apocrypha: Selected Texts in Translation* (Edinburgh: T&T Clark, 1989); Irena Backus, "Renaissance Attitudes to New Testament Apocryphal Writings: Jacques Lefèvre d'Étaples and His Epigones," *Renaissance Quarterly* 51 (1998): 1169–98; Backus, "Christoph Scheurl and His Anthology of 'New Testament Apocrypha' (1506, 1513, 1515)," *Apocrypha* 9 (2000): 133–56; Backus, "Praetorius' Anthology of New Testament Apocrypha (1595)," *Apocrypha* 12 (2001): 211–36; Francis Schmidt, "John Toland, critique déiste de la littérature apocryphe," *Apocrypha* 1 (1990): 119–45; Justin A. Champion, "Apocrypha, Canon and Criticism from Samuel Fisher to John Toland 1660–1718," in *Judaeo-Christian Intellectual Culture in the Seventeenth Century*, ed. A. P. Coudert et al. (Boston: Klewer, 1999), 91–117.

[98] See Simon Claude Mimouni, "Le Judéo-Christianisme ancien dans l'historiographie du XIXème et du XXème siècle," *REJ* 151 (1992): 419–28.

[99] Koester, "ΓΝΩΜΑΙ ΔΙΑΦΟΡΟΙ," 380. These senses are charted in Raymond E. Brown, "Not Jewish Christianity and Gentile Christianity but Types of Jewish/Gentile Christianity," *CBQ* 45 (1983): 74–79. Simon Claude Mimouni and others thus reserve the label "Jewish-Christian" for groups after 135 CE (see, e. g., *Le Judéo-christianisme ancien: Essais historiques* [Paris: Cerf, 1998]).

and Book of Acts.[100] Tacit, in many such cases, is the treatment of "Jewish-Christianity" as a fossilized relic of Christianity's Second Temple Jewish origins. In a sense, then, these modern scholarly approaches echo the treatment of Christians of Jewish lineage by Justin Martyr (*Dial.* 46–47): Justin accepts the combination of Christian belief with Jewish practice as an authentic expression of Christianity, but he also limits its significance. For Justin and most Church Fathers after him, the Jewish rejection of Jesus was central to an understanding of salvation history as culminating with Christianity's emergence as a (Gentile) world religion. To this narrative, the existence of Christians of Jewish lineage is a footnote at best and, at worst, a challenge. So too for modern scholars like Adolf von Harnack, who have trumpeted the significance of Gentile conversion to Christianity while downplaying Jewish adherence to Christianity as a limited phenomenon with little relevance for "mainstream" church history.[101]

Other modern definitions of "Jewish-Christianity" draw more heavily from later heresiological comments about Ebionites and Nazarenes. Thus, in some scholarly accounts, the features that are deemed as characteristically "Jewish-Christian" also include [3] the rejection of supersessionist approaches to Judaism, particularly as emblematized by the figure of Paul, [4] the articulation of a low Christology (e.g., the acceptance of Jesus as prophet but not messiah), [5] the privileging of the Gospel of Matthew, [6] antisacrificial polemics, and/or [7] ritual practices such as vegetarianism and ritual purification through water. Often, these various categories are presumed to be overlapping, due to the assumption that Torah observance, low Christology, etc., naturally follow only from Jewish ethnicity.[102] In effect, then, these approaches follow Epiphanius in conflating Jewish ethnicity with Jewish practice, reading "Jewishness" as a mark of deviance from a purported norm of Christian belief, and reifying "Jewish-Christianity" as a form of "heresy."

It is perhaps not surprising, then, that the very heurism of the category of "Jewish-Christianity" has come into question. After all, even as recent research has stressed that "Jewish" and "Christian" identities were not yet so clear-cut in Late Antiquity,[103] the category of "Jewish-Christianity" continues to be com-

---

[100] Other New Testament texts may well presume other halakhic perspectives, including interests in ritual purity. On Revelation, see David Frankfurter, "Jews or Not? Reconstructing the 'Other' in Rev 2:9 and 3:9," *HTR* 94 (2001): 403–27.

[101] Adolf von Harnack, for instance, accepted that "Jewish-Christianity" flourished in both apostolic and postapostolic times but saw this stream of tradition as having no influence whatsoever on the "Great Church" (*Lehrbuch der Dogmengeschichte* [repr. ed.; Darmstadt: Wissenschaftliche Buchgesellschaft, 1965], 317). The persistence of such views is discussed by A. F. J. Klijn, "The Study of Jewish-Christianity," *NTS* 20 (1974): 419–31, esp. 421–25.

[102] Of course, Paul himself stands as a clear challenge to this idea. For an incisive discussion of the problems with such assumptions, see Fonrobert, "*Didascalia Apostolorum*," 499–502.

[103] This is perhaps most eloquently put by Fonrobert, who asserts, "Our understanding of the formation of Jewish and Christian collective identities as separate identities depends on developing an intelligible way of discussing the phenomenon called 'Jewish Christianity,' one that

monly defined in terms that depend on outmoded views about Jewish identity and ethnicity, on the one hand, and Christian identity and "orthodoxy," on the other.[104] Just as research on late antique Judaism has shown that the former remained fluid and contested even in the first centuries of the Common Era,[105] so research on late antique Christianity has suggested that "orthodoxy" was in the process of being constructed even in the fourth and fifth centuries. Concurrent with questions about whether and when (and where and if) Christianity "parted ways" from Judaism in Late Antiquity,[106] some scholars have thus abandoned the term "Jewish-Christianity" altogether, questioning the traditional limitation of fluidity and hybridity to a single movement and critiquing the underlying assumption that "Judaism" and "Christianity" were, already, in this early period, firm identities separated by a single hybrid or "heretical" middle ground.[107]

At least for the moment, however, I would suggest there is some utility in retaining the category as heuristic – especially for unsettling entrenched scholarly assumptions about the mutual exclusivity of "Jewish" and "Christian" identities in Late Antiquity. Used in this sense, the adjective "Jewish-Christian" can be applied to sources [8] which exhibit more and different "Jewish" features than modern scholars typically associate with early and late antique Christianity, [9] which were shaped, in meaningful ways, by direct contact with post-Christian Judaism (especially Rabbinic Judaism), and/or [10] which self-consciously adopt a Jewish identity and/or self-consciously seek to recover elements of Christianity's Jewish heritage that other sectors of the church rejected.

This approach can integrate many of the features outlined above, and it does not preclude the reconstruction of specific groups that might lie behind certain texts or clusters of texts. Nevertheless, it attempts to avoid the imposition of any single image of "Jewish-Christianity" on all of our sources as well as the problematic equation of Jewish ethnicity with specific proclivities or limitations. To my view, a flexible definition of this sort has the benefit of opening our

---

is not marred by Christian theological prejudices, nor by unexamined assumptions about either 'Jewish' identity formation or its 'Christian' counterpart" (*"Didascalia Apostolorum,"* 484).

[104] See, e. g., Skarsaune and Hvalvik, eds., *Jewish Believers in Jesus: The Early Centuries* (Peabody, MA: Hendrickson, 2007) and the review by Adam H. Becker in *Biblical Theology Bulletin* 39 (2009): 45–47, as well as comments in Boyarin, "Rethinking Jewish Christianity."

[105] Shaye J. D. Cohen, *The Beginnings of Jewishness: Boundaries, Varieties, Uncertainties* (Berkeley: University of California Press, 1999).

[106] For a summary of the traditional scholarly account and emergent alternatives, see Adam H. Becker and Annette Yoshiko Reed, "Introduction: Traditional Approaches and New Directions," in Becker and Reed, *The Ways That Never Parted*, 1–34.

[107] E. g., Boyarin, "Rethinking Jewish Christianity"; Joan Taylor, "The Phenomenon of Early Jewish-Christianity: Reality or Scholarly Invention?" *VC* 44 (1990): 313–34; Frankfurter, "Beyond 'Jewish-Christianity,'" 131–44. See also the critiques of past research on "Jewish Christianity" in Klijn, "Study of Jewish-Christianity"; and Robert A. Kraft, "In Search of 'Jewish Christianity' and Its 'Theology': Problems of Definition and Methodology," *Recherches de Sciences Religieuse* 60 (1972): 81–96.

understanding of "Jewish-Christianity" to include more firsthand sources for fluidities and hybridities among biblically-based religious identities interacting in different ways in different locales.[108]

Past research on "Jewish-Christianity" depended heavily on Patristic sources largely because of perceived necessity. Equipped with a narrow understanding of "Jewish-Christianity" as a single phenomenon – the middle ground between two supposedly clear-cut entities – scholars sought "Jewish-Christianity" only in those sources that closely corresponded to New Testament traditions about Jewish members of the Jesus movement and/or to Patristic reports about Ebionites and Nazarenes. As a result, firsthand evidence for "Jewish-Christianity" was largely limited to the Pseudo-Clementine tradition and tended to be read in terms of an understanding of the history of Jewish/Christian relations based on the Church Fathers and classical Rabbinic literature.[109] Newly possible and newly pressing, however, is the task of recovering a broader base of firsthand evidence for studying the relationships between "Jewish" and "Christian" identities in Late Antiquity and beyond.

I hope that the survey above has shown some of the potential value of approaching apocrypha from this perspective and some of the benefits of bringing these neglected sources to bear on the scholarly conversation about Christian and Jewish self-definition. To the texts surveyed above might readily be added others, such as the Pseudo-Clementine epistles, the *Gospel of the Hebrews*, the *Gospel of the Nazarenes*, the *Gospel of the Ebionites*, and the Christian/Christianized forms of Old Testament pseudepigrapha such as the *Testament of Abraham* and the *Testament of Job*.[110]

In what ways, then, might this understudied evidence for "Jewish-Christianity" shed new light on the history of Jewish/Christian relations? Although any firm conclusions must await further investigation, I would like to conclude with some reflections on what more integrated research on "Jewish-Christian apocrypha" might bring to research about the history of Jewish/Christian relations.

Foremost is a focus on purity and practice.[111] Treatments of early Jewish/Christian relations based largely in Patristic materials often replicate the focus on

---

[108] The inclusion of a broader range of sources also may help to attenuate the traditional tendency to insist upon the limited regional scope of "Jewish-Christianity"; see Klijn, "Study of Jewish-Christianity," 421–25.

[109] Esp. Eusebius; see Chapter Six below.

[110] On the possibility that some of the latter might preserve evidence of a continuum of post-70 Jewish diversity that might have included some Christians, see Annette Yoshiko Reed, "Old Testament Pseudepigrapha and post-70 Judaism," in *Les Judaïsmes dans tous leurs états aux Ier–IIIe siècles*, ed. Simon Claude Mimouni, Bernard Pouderon, and Claire Clivas (Turnhout: Brepols, 2015), 117–48.

[111] So rarely have questions about ritual purity been asked of Patristic sources that one wonders whether this apparently "Jewish-Christian" feature is actually just an understudied aspect of Christian culture more broadly. Hayes charts a bit of this terrain in *Gentile Impurities*, 92–105, but there is much more that needs to be done in this area. A model in this respect is

doctrine in the writings of the Church Fathers. Whereas past scholarship focused too myopically on elements such as Christology, recent scholarship may stand at some risk of becoming too entranced with the power of elite rhetoric and writing to shape social realities. Discursive acts of definition and differentiation by literate elites surely contributed to the articulation of "Judaism" and "Christianity" as communal identities.[112] When we focus on such literary and discursive acts as determinative for religious self-definition, however, we may risk reinforcing, in a new way, the traditional privileging of Patristic and Rabbinic voices.[113] We risk, moreover, foreclosing the arduous and methodologically challenging – yet, in my view, pressing – task of trying to reconstruct, bit by bit, even small slivers of the daily and mundane negotiations of identity boundaries and shared cultural spaces "on the ground."

Second is a recognition of geographical diversity. The privileging of Patristic voices has encouraged a myopic focus on the Roman Empire that attention to apocrypha may help to correct – with notable consequences for the history of Jewish/Christian relations in particular. Above, we surveyed mainly sources from Syria and Palestine.[114] It is intriguing that West Syrian sources seem to be so rich in evidence for contact with early Palestinian Rabbinic traditions.[115] Further attention could be given to Egypt, Ethiopia, Persia, and Asia Minor too.

Lastly, the evidence of "Jewish-Christian" apocrypha also permits us to locate the rise of Christian anti-Judaism in a more diverse religious landscape that included other voices – from the second and third centuries, and even the fourth

---

Vuong, *Gender and Purity*, which situates the *Protevangelium of James* in triangulation with a variety of Jewish and Christian sources on purity and proper practice.

[112] Boyarin, *Border Lines*; Boyarin, "Justin Martyr Invents Judaism," *Church History* 70 (2001): 427–61; Boyarin, "Semantic Differences; or, 'Judaism'/'Christianity,'" in Becker and Reed, *The Ways That Never Parted*, 65–86.

[113] To Elizabeth Clark's call for the study of late antique Christianity to be reconceived as a "new intellectual history, grounded in issues of material production and ideology" (*History, Theory, Text*, 159), for instance, Virginia Burrus similarly responds by voicing her concern "with what might not be excluded by 'intellectual history' – namely, a fairly traditional version of Patristics focused primarily (if not exclusively) on the close study of the writings of the so-called Fathers, even if it is a version now newly and critically tuned to issues of power" ("Elizabeth Clark's *History, Theory, Text*: A (Somewhat) Confessional Reading," *CH* 74 [2005]: 814).

[114] See further Annette Yoshiko Reed and Lily C. Vuong, "Purity, *Paideia*, and the Partitioning of Christian and Jewish Identities in Roman Syria," in *Partings: How Judaism and Christianity Became Two*, ed. Hershel Shanks (Washington, DC: Biblical Archaeological Society, 2013).

[115] East Syrian Christian sources similarly attest contact, conflict, and competition with Babylonian Rabbinic traditions. See Naomi Koltun-Fromm, "A Jewish-Christian Conversation in Fourth-Century Persian Mesopotamia," *JJS* 47 (1996): 45–63; Adam H. Becker, "Bringing the Heavenly Academy Down to Earth: Approaches to the Imagery of Divine Pedagogy in the East-Syrian Tradition," in *Heavenly Realms and Earthly Realities in Late Antique Religions*, ed. Ra'anan S. Boustan and Annette Yoshiko Reed (Cambridge: Cambridge University Press, 2004), 174–94; Becker, "Anti-Judaism and Care for the Poor in Aphrahat's Demonstration 20," *JECS* 10 (2002): 305–27.

and fifth – who stressed the continuity and/or complementarity of Judaism and Christianity.[116] Patristic authors since Justin may speak with relative unanimity about the church replacing Israel as the chosen people of God, but other sources preserve other perspectives. Whereas Justin reads the persecution of Christians by Jews at the time of the Bar Kokhba revolt as a sign of the alliance between demons and the Jews, the author of *Apocalypse of Peter* refrains, even in the midst of such persecution, from damning all Jews together with these persecutors. The source in *Rec.* 1.27–71 denigrates Paul while celebrating R. Gamaliel as a secret Christian. And, around the same time that Eusebius is rereading all of Christian history in terms of his view of the Christianization of the Roman Empire as an emblem of Christianity's supersession of Judaism and "paganism," the authors/ redactors of the *Homilies* were similarly drawing on earlier Hellenistic Jewish and "Jewish-Christian" sources to articulate an alternative account of salvation history, wherein truth and salvation are possessed by Jew and Christian alike. That the *Book of the Cock* contains both anti-Pauline and anti-Jewish perspectives, interwoven together in its redacted form, also serves a poignant embodiment of the diversity of earlier opinions – as well as a pointed reminder that the voices of early "Jewish-Christians" did remain, embedded within a number of popular apocrypha and read widely in multiple languages, even where and when supersessionist perspectives on Judaism became generally accepted as an integral part of Christian identity.

---

[116] See Chapters Two, Five, and Six below as well as Côté, "Le problème de l'identité religieuse"; Fackler, "*Adversus Adversus Iudaeos.*"

Chapter Four

Hellenism and Judaism
in "Jewish-Christian" Perspective*

For scholars interested in the construction and negotiation of religious identities, the Pseudo-Clementines have long provided a rich mine. Since the very advent of modern discussion of "Jewish-Christianity," the *Homilies* and *Recognitions* have served as a locus for discussions of the problem of the interpenetration of "Christian" and "Jewish" identities in history, theory, and practice.[1] Their parallels with Patristic statements about lost Petrine and Jacobite writings have inspired speculation about their possible continuities with ancient articulations of Christian identity cultivated within the Jerusalem Church as well as their possible connections with later sects like the Ebionites.[2] Likewise, their prescriptions for Gentile Torah observance have inspired speculation about intersections with Judaism.[3] Their portrait of Simon Magus has been analyzed in relation to

---

* This chapter originally appeared in 2008 as "From Judaism and Hellenism to Christianity and Paganism: Cultural Identities and Religious Polemics in the Pseudo-Clementine *Homilies*" in *Nouvelles intrigues Pseudo-clémentines/Plots in the Pseudo-Clementine Romance*, ed. Frédéric Amsler et al. (Publications de l'Institut romand des sciences bibliques 6; Lausanne: Zèbre, 2008), 351–61; It is reprinted here with permission from Zèbre. This version has been substantially revised and expanded, especially in light of two important studies that appeared after its publication: James Carleton Paget, "Pseudo-Clementine *Homilies* 4–6: Rare Evidence of a Jewish Literary Source from the Second Century CE?," in Carleton Paget, *Jews, Christians, and Jewish Christians in Antiquity* (WUNT 251; Tübingen: Mohr Siebeck, 2010), 427–92; and Dominique Côté, "Rhetoric and Jewish-Christianity: The Case of the Grammarian Apion in the Pseudo-Clementine *Homilies*," in *Rediscovering the Apocryphal Continent: New Perspectives on Early Christian and Late Antique Apocryphal Texts and Traditions*, ed. Pierluigi Piovanelli and Tony Burke (WUNT 349; Tübingen: Mohr Siebeck, 2015), 369–89. Special thanks to James Carleton Paget for comments, challenges, and suggestions.

[1] Esp. Georg Strecker, *Das Judenchristentum in den Pseudoklementinen* (TU 70; 2nd ed.; Berlin: Akademie-Verlag, 1981). See further Chapter One and Appendix B in this volume.

[2] E. g., Heracleon *apud* Origen, *Comm. John,* 3.17; Clement of Alexandria, *Strom.* 1.29.182; 6.5.39; 15.128; Eusebius, *Hist. eccl.* 3.38.5; Epiphanius, *Pan.* 30.15–16. On Ebionites, see e. g. Hans Joachim Schoeps, *Theologie und Geschichte des Judenchristentums* (Tübingen: Mohr Siebeck, 1949).

[3] E. g., *Hom.* 2.19, 38; 3.18–19; 7.4–8; 11.28–30; J. Bergman, "Les éléments juifs dans les Pseudo-Clémentines," *REJ* 46 (1903): 89–98; A. Marmorstein, "Judaism and Christianity in the Middle of the Third Century," *HUCA* 10 (1935): 223–63; Albert I. Baumgarten, "Literary Evidence for Jewish Christianity in the Galilee," in *The Galilee in Late Antiquity*, ed. Lee I. Levine (New York: Jewish Theological Seminary of America, 1992), 39–50. See also Chapters Two and Nine in this volume.

anti-Pauline as well as anti-Marcionite polemics.[4] In addition, their intersections with so-called "Gnosticism" have been explored, especially in relation to distinctive ideas therein such as the True Prophet, Rule of Syzygy, and the doctrine of false pericopes.[5]

When the fourth-century Syrian provenance of the *Homilies* and *Recognitions* was determined at the turn of the twentieth century, some scholars tentatively broached questions about their dynamics of self-definition in a late antique context, looking to the Christological debates of the Nicene age and speculating about intersections with Arianism, in the case of the *Homilies*,[6] and possible Eunomian influences, in the case of the *Recognitions*.[7] For the most part, however, issues of self-definition in the Pseudo-Clementines have been investigated as part of the source-critical enterprise that has dominated research on these texts for the past century.[8] Questions about religious affiliations and identities have been oriented towards recovering possible sources that lie before and behind their fourth-century forms. Answers have been aimed at isolating and identifying those closest to the apostolic age.

It is only in recent years that research on the Pseudo-Clementines has begun to shift away from the reconstruction of hypothetical sources behind the putative *Grundschrift* and back to the surviving forms of the Pseudo-Clementine *Recognitions*,[9] *Homilies*,[10] and even the *Epistle of Peter to James* and *Con-*

---

[4] Gerd Lüdemann, *Opposition to Paul in Jewish Christianity* (trans. E. Boring; Minneapolis: Fortress, 1989), 185–90; Strecker, *Das Judenchristentum in den Pseudoklementinen*, 187; Terence V. Smith, *Petrine Controversies in Early Christianity: Attitudes towards Peter in Christian Writings of the First Two Centuries* (WUNT[2] 15; Tübingen: Mohr Siebeck, 1985), 11, 59–61; A. Salles, "Simon le magicien ou Marcion?," *VC* 12 (1958): 197–224. Cf. Dominique Côté, "La fonction littéraire de Simon le Magicien dans les Pseudo-Clémentines," *Laval Théologique et Philosophique* 57 (2001): 514–17.

[5] E.g., Gilles Quispel, "La lettre de Ptolémée à Flora," *VC* 2 (1948): 39–40.

[6] *Hom.* 16.15; 20.5, 7; Charles Bigg, "The Clementine Homilies," in *Studia biblica et ecclesiastica: Essays Chiefly in Biblical and Patristic Criticism*, vol. 2 (Oxford: Clarendon, 1890), 167, 191–92. See further Strecker, *Das Judenchristentum in den Pseudoklementinen*, 268; cf. Christopher Stead, *Divine Substance* (Oxford: Clarendon, 1977), 219–20.

[7] *Rec.* 3.2–11; John Chapman, "On the Date of the Clementines," *ZNW* 9 (1908): 21–27.

[8] For the history of research on these sources, see F. Stanley Jones, "The Pseudo-Clementines: A History of Research," *Second Century* 2 (1982): 8–33.

[9] See Chapter One above as well as Nicole Kelley, *Knowledge and Religious Authority in the Pseudo-Clementines: Situating the Recognitions in Fourth-Century Syria* (WUNT[2] 213; Tübingen: Mohr Siebeck, 2006); Kelley, "On Recycling Texts and Traditions: The Pseudo-Clementine *Recognitions* and Religious Life in Fourth-Century Syria," in *The Levant: Crossroads of Late Antiquity*, ed. Ellen Bradshaw Aitken and John M. Fosey (McGill University Monographs in Classical Archaeology and History 22; Leiden: Brill, 2013), 105–12; Kelley, "Pseudo-Clementine Polemics against Sacrifice: A Window onto Religious Life in the Fourth Century?," in Piovanelli and Burke, *Rediscovering the Apocryphal Continent*, 391–400.

[10] See Chapters One, Four, Five, and Six in this volume as well as Côté, "Rhetoric and Jewish-Christianity"; also Côté, "Le problème de l'identité religieuse dans la Syrie du IVe siècle: Le cas des Pseudo-Clémentines et de l'Adversus Judaeos de S. Jean Chrysostome," in

testation.[11] This shift in orientation has inspired a new appreciation of the Pseudo-Clementines as evidence for late antique Christian attempts to grapple with the perils and prestige of "pagan" culture. Where earlier research sought the lost heterodoxies behind the Pseudo-Clementines or chased elusive ancient "Jewish-Christian" documents, recent studies follow the preoccupation with "pagan" knowledge and culture in the texts themselves, attending both to their content and to their rhetoric. Studies by F. Stanley Jones, Mark Edwards, and Meinolf Vielberg, for instance, have explored the appropriation and subversion of the Graeco-Roman novel by the authors/redactors of the *Grundschrift*, *Recognitions*, and *Homilies*.[12] Seminal monographs by Dominique Côté and Nicole Kelley have further demonstrated their engagement – both positive and polemical – with "pagan" philosophical, ritual, theurgical, and astrological ideas current in Late Antiquity.[13] Likewise, Kate Cooper and Cornelia Horn have situated their novelistic narratives in relation to the social dynamics of "pagan" conversion and Christian families in Late Antiquity.[14] Setting aside both the question of sources and the older interest in the "Jewish-Christianity," such studies have situated the Pseudo-Clementines within a continuum of attempts to negotiate Christian identity in relation to Graeco-Roman culture in Late Antiquity.

In my view, the source-critical focus of past research on Pseudo-Clementines is rightly critiqued for its myopia, and much can be learned from analysis of their extant forms in relation to Christian *comparanda* from Late Antiquity.[15] Fresh attention to their negotiation of Christian identities in relation to "paganism," however, should not lead us to dismiss the place of Jews and Judaism in the

---

La croisée des chemins revisitée: Quand l'Église et la Synagogue se sont-elles distinguées?, ed. Simon Claude Mimouni and Bernard Pouderon (Paris: Cerf, 2012), 339–70.

[11] Kristine J. Ruffatto, "Moses Typology for Peter in the *Epistula Petri* and the *Contestatio*," *VC* 69 (2015): 345–67.

[12] F. Stanley Jones, *Pseudoclementina Elchasaiticaque inter Judaeochristiana: Collected Studies* (Leuven: Peeters, 2012), 114–206; Mark J. Edwards, "The Clementina: A Christian Response to the Pagan Novel," *Classical Quarterly* 42 (1992): 459–74; Meinolf Vielberg, *Klemens in den pseudoklementinischen Rekognitionen: Studien zur literarischen Form des spätantiken Romans* (Berlin: Akademie-Verlag, 2000); Williams Robins, "Romance and Renunciation at the Turn of the Fifth Century," *JECS* 8 (2000): 531–57.

[13] Kelley, *Knowledge and Religious Authority in the Pseudo-Clementines*; Dominique Côté, *Le thème de l'opposition entre Pierre et Simon dans les Pseudo-Clémentines* (Études Augustiniennes Série Antiquités 167; Paris: Études augustiniennes, 2001).

[14] Kate Cooper, "Matthidia's Wish: Division, Reunion, and the Early Christian Family in the Pseudo-Clementine *Recognitions*," in *Narrativity in Biblical and Related Texts/La narrativité dans la Bible et les textes apparentés*, ed. Geroge J. Brooke and Jean-Daniel Kaestli (Leuven: Peeters, 2000), 243–64; Cornelia B. Horn, "The Pseudo-Clementine *Homilies* and the Challenges of the Conversion of Families," in *The Pseudo-Clementines*, ed. Jan Bremmer (Leuven: Peeters, 2010), 170–91.

[15] See Chapter One in this volume, reprinting my 2003 article that argues this point. See also Nicole Kelley's comments in *Knowledge and Religious Authority in the Pseudo-Clementines*, esp. 25–27, as based on her 2003 dissertation on the *Recognitions*.

Pseudo-Clementine tradition. Their appropriation and representation of Jew-ishness may be no less telling, in fact, for understanding their fourth-century forms and seeking to situate them in their late antique Syrian contexts. Such a focus, moreover, may help us to work toward an approach to the *Homilies* and *Recognitions* that does not wholly reject the results of source-critical analysis but rather reverses the arrow of their application, setting aside the practice of excavating these texts for possible sources behind sources and focusing instead on the task of illumining the redactional and other literary practices that shaped the texts as we now have them.

In what follows, I experiment with such an approach through a focus on the Debate with Appion in *Homilies* 4–6. Most of the past scholarly discussion of this section of the *Homilies* has centered on its possible origins in an earlier source. Due to the partial parallel in *Rec.* 10.17–51 and Eusebius' passing men-tion of "dialogues of Peter and Apion" (*Hist. eccl.* 3.38.5), the possibility of such a source was raised early on, and speculation about its precise scope, date, and character has continued to be the main focus of scholarship on this section of the *Homilies* – with varying assessments, for instance, of the likelihood that such a source was used already by the authors/redactors of the *Grundschrift*,[16] as well as varying arguments for the possibility of its pre-Christian or non-Chris-tian Jewish provenance.[17] This position was countered by Georg Strecker, who pointed to resonances with the rest of the *Homilies* to make the case that this material originated as among the changes made by the authors/redactors of this version of the Pseudo-Clementine novel – a position that has been followed, most influentially, by F. Stanley Jones.[18]

In recent years, the discussion has moved forward in two different directions. Consistent with the trends noted above, Côté has suggested setting aside the question of sources and looking to the "literary purpose" of the representation

---

[16] F. Stanley Jones traces this idea already to Adolph Hilgenfeld, *Die clementinischen Recog-nitionen und Homilien nach ihrem Ursprung und Inhalt dargestellt* (Leipzig: J.G. Schreiber, 1848), while James Carleton Paget credits H. Waitz, *Die Pseudoklementinen. Homilien und Rekognitionem: Eine quellenkritische Untersuchung* (TU 10.4; Leipzig: Hinrichs, 1904); see further, Jones, "The Pseudo-Clementines," 27; Carleton Paget, *Jews, Christians, and Jewish Christians*, 427–28.

[17] For the view of this source as Jewish, see Werner Heintze, *Der Klemensroman und seine griechischen Quellen* (TU 40.2; Leipzig: Hinrichs, 1914), 48–50, 108–9, 112; Carl Schmidt, *Studien zu den Pseudo-Clementinen* (TU 46.1; Leipzig: Hinrichs, 1929), 160–239. Also Wil-liam A. Adler, "Apion's Encomium of Adultery: A Jewish Satire of Greek *Paideia* in the Pseudo-Clementine *Homilies*," *HUCA* 64 (1993): 28–30; Carleton Paget, *Jews, Christians, and Jewish Christians*, esp. 433–36, 451–59. For the argument that the entire novel goes back to a Jewish source – for which this section is the crux – see Bernard Pouderon, "Flavius Clemens et le Proto-Clément juif du Roman Pseudo-clémentin," *Apocrypha* 7 (1996): 63–79; Pouderon, "Aux origines du Roman Pseudo-clémentin," in *Le judéo-christianisme dans tous ses états*, ed. F. Stanley Jones and Simon Claude Mimouni (Paris: Cerf, 2001), 231–56.

[18] Strecker, *Das Judenchristentum in den Pseudoklementinen*, 79–87; Jones, *Pseudoclem-entina*, 37.

of Appion within the *Homilies* 4–6 as exemplary of a polemic against Greek *paideia* waged on the basis of rhetoric training and familiarity with philosophical trends in Late Antiquity.[19] The hypothesis of a Jewish source, however, has been newly revived by James Carleton Paget, who has carefully reassessed the relevant data and past research, making a compelling case for a second-century Jewish writing from Syria informing this section of the *Homilies*.[20]

Here, I would like to build on both findings in order to reconsider the ramifications of the Debate with Appion for the representation of Jews and Judaism within the *Homilies* – and especially in relation to what I shall suggest is a distinctively late antique repurposing of received binaries like "Greek"/"barbarian," "Greek"/"Jew," and "Hellenism"/"Judaism." This section of the *Homilies* features a sharp denunciation of Greek *paideia* that finds some precedent among earlier Christians, and – perhaps tellingly – particularly among Syrians such as Tatian.[21] The differences, however, remain notable. Rather than presenting Christianity as transcending ancestral customs or inaugurating a new *ethnos* or *genos*, the Debate with Appion depicts the Greek-educated Roman-born Clement as affirming his association with the apostle Peter as an act of abandoning his *patria* to take refuge with "the barbarian Jews." By virtue of the inclusion of this material in the *Homilies*, this version of the Pseudo-Clementine novel thus mounts an extended polemic against Greek education, mythology, philosophy, and ethics, repurposing older ideas about Hellenism and Judaism to promote its distinctive vision of an apostolic tradition in radical continuity with Judaism.

Greeks vs. "Barbarians" in *Homilies* 4–6

Whereas most of the *Homilies* recount the rivalry between Peter and Simon Magus,[22] the Debate with Appion in *Homilies* 4–6 depicts the conflict between Clement and the infamous Alexandrian anti-Semite Ap(p)ion. Whereas the novel is primarily concerned to distinguish the apostolic truth from the musings of "heretical" pretenders,[23] these chapters center on the contrast between Hellenism and Judaism. No reference is made to Jesus. The religion of Peter and Clement

---

[19] Côté, "Rhetoric and Jewish-Christianity," 371–72, taking the supposition of a source as "highly probable" but focusing on the function of *Homilies* 4–6 in the final form of the *Homilies*.

[20] Carleton Paget, *Jews, Christians, and Jewish Christians in Antiquity*, 427–92.

[21] Tatian, *Oratio ad Graecos* 2–3, 25–26. See further, e.g., Emily J. Hunt, *Christianity in the Second Century: The Case of Tatian* (London: Routledge, 2003), 144–75; Laura Nasrallah, "Mapping the World: Justin, Tatian, Lucian, and the Second Sophistic," *HTR* 98 (2005): 283–315. For the broader context, see also Nathanael J. Andrade, *Syrian Identity in the Greco-Roman World* (Cambridge: Cambridge University Press, 2013).

[22] Côté, *Le thème de l'opposition*.

[23] See Chapter Five below.

is described wholly in relation to the God, Law, monotheism, and piety of the Jews.[24]

The debates in these chapters are occasioned by Appion's shock that Clement – a Roman of good birth who is "equipped with all Greek learning" – could be "seduced by a certain barbarian called Peter to speak and act after the manner of the Jews" (4.7.2). Appion's accusation is familiar, echoing "pagan" polemics against both Jewish proselytes (e.g., Juvenal, *Sat.* 14.96–106; Tacitus, *Hist.* 5.5.2) and Gentile Christians (e.g., Origen, *Cels.* 5.25–41; Eusebius, *Praep. ev.* 1.2.1–4).[25] What is surprising, however, is Clement's answer. Denise Buell makes note of accusations of this sort that "lambasted Christians in ethnoracial terms" as those who "break with the past";[26] Christians are denounced by Celsus, for instance, as those who "have forsaken their *patria* and do not happen to be some one *ethnos* like the Jews" (Origen, *Cels.* 5.35). Origen marks the common answer to this accusation whereby Christians contest this framing of the past, "appealing to biblical narratives to argue for a historical period of human unity before there was a multiplicity of individual nations with their corresponding customs."[27] In this section of the *Homilies,* however, Clement seems happy to accept Appion's assessment of his attraction to monotheism as essentially a decision to abandon his Roman ancestral customs and Greek education to affiliate instead with the Jewish people.

In response to Appion's question of whether he acts "most impiously in forsaking the customs of his country and falling away to those of the barbarians" (4.7.3), Clement underlines the wickedness of the ancestral customs that he chose to abandon (4.8.1, 3, 6; cf. 4.11.1–2); these customs – Clement here argues – are inherently impious and thus rightly forsaken. When expounding upon the nature of this impiety, Clement takes specific aim at Greek *paideia,* asserting that "the whole learning of the Greeks is a most dreadful fabrication of a wicked demon" (4.12.1). The argument that follows has some precedent in Tatian's presentation of the Christian abandonment of Greek ancestral customs as warranted by the impiety of those customs (e.g., *Oratio ad Graecos* 28). An important difference in the *Homilies,* however, is the concurrent defense of Judaism. Clement does not just demonize Greek elite education; he also asserts, conversely, that "the doctrine of the 'barbarian Jews,' as you call them, is most pious, introducing One as the Father and Creator of all this world, by nature good and just" (4.13.3) and encouraging ethical action through promises of reward

---

[24] See esp. *Hom.* 4.7–8, 22, 24; 5.28.

[25] For the accusations against Jewish proselytes, see further Peter Schäfer, *Judeophobia: Attitudes toward the Jews in the Ancient World* (Cambridge, MA: Harvard University Press, 1997), 180–95.

[26] Denise Buell, *Why This New Race? Ethnic Reasoning in Early Christianity* (New York: Columbia University Press, 2005), 75.

[27] Buell, *Why this New Race,* 75.

and punishment (4.14.1–2).[28] In this, he voices a position more akin to Philo of Alexandria's description of Jewish proselytes (e.g., *Special Laws* 1.52–53).[29]

To support this assertion, Clement contrasts the good deeds that result from Jewish monotheism with the wicked deeds that result from the Greek belief in many gods who commit multifarious acts of impiety and impurity (*Hom.* 4.14.1–15.4, 17.1–2).[30] His argument echoes Hellenistic, early Jewish, and early Christian polemics against Greek mythology as offering a denigrated view of divinity that encourages human sinfulness.[31] Whereas earlier Christians such as Justin Martyr distinguished between the demonic inspiration of Greek religion and the glints of divine truth in Greek philosophy,[32] however, the *Homilies* here conflate the two, by means of its polemic against *paideia*. Clement here argues that elite "pagans" are the least pious of all precisely because of their education (4.17.1–20.3). They were weaned on Greek myths (4.19.1). Thanks to the rationalizations of allegory and philosophy, they live smug in the false belief that they can sin without consequence (4.20.1–2). Here too, the representation of Hellenism finds some precedent with Tatian. The concurrent treatment of Judaism, however, remains quite unprecedented among Christian sources, even as it recalls the discourse about Jewish and Greek wisdom in Greek Jewish writings from the *Epistle of Aristeas* to Philo.[33]

---

[28] This depiction of Judaism – as "barbarian" wisdom laudable for its embrace of monotheism, commitment to law and justice, and interest in inculcating ethics – resonates with Hellenistic Jewish traditions as well as with positive "pagan" statements about Jews and Judaism; see further John J. Collins, *Between Athens and Jerusalem: Jewish Identity in the Hellenistic Diaspora* (2nd ed.; Grand Rapids: Eerdmans, 2000), 6–15, 155–85; Guy G. Stroumsa, *Barbarian Philosophy: The Religious Revolution of Early Christianity* (WUNT 112; Tübingen: Mohr Siebeck, 1999), 60–72.

[29] Cf. Philo, *Life of Moses* 2.18–20, 44; Justin, *1 Apology* 21; Clement of Alexandria, *Protrepticus* 10.89.2.

[30] The emphasis on Jewish monotheism and ethics in contrast with the empty sophistry, licentiousness, and lasciviousness of Greek philosophers has precedents in the writings of Philo, on which see Maren Niehoff, *Philo on Jewish Identity and Culture* (TSAJ 86; Tübingen: Mohr Siebeck, 2001), 137–50. In contrast to *Homilies* 4–6, however, Philo distinguishes between the errors of the Egyptians, whom he treats as paradigmatic of polytheism, and the errors of the Greeks, whom he treats as philosophers. Niehoff notes, for instance, how "the Egyptians are denied Greek identity and culture" – a tendency which, in her view, may explain his otherwise surprising lack of engagement with Greek-educated Egyptians like Apion (p. 158). On Egyptianness in the *Homilies* see now Jan Bremmer, "Apion and Anoubion in the *Homilies*," in Bremmer, *Pseudo-Clementines*, 72–91.

[31] Richard P.C. Hanson, *Studies in Christian Antiquity* (Edinburgh: T&T Clark, 1985), 157–63.

[32] On Justin, see Oskar Skarsaune, "Judaism and Hellenism in Justin Martyr, Elucidated from His Portrait of Socrates," in *Geschichte – Tradition – Reflexion: Festschrift für Martin Hengel zum 70. Geburtstag*, vol. 3: *Frühes Christentum*, ed. Hubert Cancik, Hermann Lichtenberger, and Peter Schäfer (Tübingen: Mohr Siebeck, 1996), 585–611. Contrast also Clement of Alexandria's notion that philosophy was revealed to humankind by fallen angel(s) and, hence, contains sparks of divine wisdom (esp. *Strom.* 1.16–17; 5.1.10.2).

[33] Compare, e.g., *Epistle of Aristeas* 137–38, where those responsible for the myths and

In the narrative world of *Homilies* 4–6, Appion is impressed by Clement's pedigree, but it is precisely because of it that Clement knows the special dangers of *paideia* for demonic deception and defilement. The negative view of Greekness is striking, and through the mouth of Clement, it is made increasingly explicit throughout the fourth *Homily*, as in the following passage:

Lessons about their gods are much worse than ignorance – as we have shown from the case of those dwelling in the country, who sin less through their not having been instructed by Greeks. Truly, such fables of theirs and spectacles and books ought to be shunned – if it were possible, even their cities …. And what is worst, whoever is most instructed among them, is so much the more turned away from the judgment according to nature! (*Hom.* 4.19.2–20.2)

In response to Appion's accusations, Clement denounces Greek *paideia* and philosophy as inextricable from "pagan" polytheism and its impious mythology.[34] It is as a result, moreover, that Clement felt it necessary to take "refuge with the holy God and the Law of the Jews" (*Hom.* 4.22.2).

The fifth *Homily* serves as a narrative demonstration of the points that Clement makes in the fourth *Homily* – with Appion himself presented as an exemplar of the elite man drained of his morals by Greek *paideia* and corrupted by the models of the Greek myths that he claims merely to allegorize. There, Clement recalls a trick that he had played on Appion in his youth. By feigning love for a married women, Clement convinced Appion to write a letter justifying the practice of adultery with appeal to Greek mythology and philosophy.[35] As a result, he exposed Appion's immorality as well as his irrational hatred of Jews (5.2.4, 5.27.1–29.1). The sixth *Homily* extends the theme of the impiety of *paideia* by describing a second debate between Clement and Appion, wherein Clement exposes the impiety underlying "pagan" philosophical attempts to allegorize Greek myths (esp. 6.17.1–23.4).[36]

Throughout these chapters, as Côté has shown, "both Clement and Apion are presented as true *pepaideumenoi*," albeit with a contrast: "Clement, through his

errors of polytheism are precisely those who consider themselves "the wisest of the Greeks." On the parallels with Philo, see Adler, "Apion's Encomium of Adultery," 47–48; Carleton Paget, *Jews, Christians, and Jewish Christians*, 471–73. Carleton Paget notes, however, how Philo is notably much less "polarized" and hostile in this regard.

[34] I.e., it is due to this deliberate and consistent conflation that I here describe what is denounced as "Hellenism," even though the Greek equivalent to that abstract categorical term is not used in the text *per se*.

[35] See Adler, "Apion's Encomium of Adultery," on the appropriation and subversion of rhetorical models from Greek *paideia* in the fifth *Homily*.

[36] Cf. Tatian, *Oratio ad Graecos* 21; Athenagoras, *Legatio Pro Christianis* 22. As Karl Evan Shuve has shown, this suspicion of allegory can be understood as one position within a continuum of late antique Christian debates about proper exegesis, often mapped onto contrasts of Alexandria and Antioch; see "The Doctrine of the False Pericopes and Other Late Antique Approaches to the Problem of Scripture's Unity," in Amsler et al., *Plots in the Pseudo-Clementine Romance*, 437–45.

quest for truth, represents the limitations of *paideia*, whereas Apion, through his encomium of adultery, illustrates the immortality of the Greek culture."[37] The representation of Clement, moreover, may well mirror the self-positioning of those responsible for these chapters, which utilize "rhetorical skill as a polemical tool in order to show the vanity of Greek culture and more precisely its rhetorical component."[38] Building on insights from William Adler and others, Côté notes how the debates between Clement and Appion take up well-known forms and topics used in rhetorical training – as clear from Appion's letter in *Hom.* 5.10, but also from the focus of Clement's arguments on topics such as custom (cf. Dio Chrysostom, *Or.* 76), whether one must always obey one's parents (cf. Aulus Gellius, *Noct. att.* 2.7.1.), whether laws are set to warn against deeds that are naturally wrong, and whether and why country life is preferable to urban life (cf. Quintillian, *Inst.* 2.4.24; Dio Chrysostom, *Or.* 7).[39]

Seen from this perspective, it proves all the more striking that the Roman Clement is used in *Homilies* 4–6 to invert the valence of Hellenism's own self-defining contrast between "Greek" and "barbarian." The inversion recalls Josephus' arguments against "the Greeks" in the first book of *Against Apion*, even as it is also paralleled in the early Christian trope of Christianity as "barbarian philosophy"; perhaps the closest Christian parallel, again, can be found in the writings of the second-century Syrian Christian Tatian (e.g., *Oratio ad Graecos* 31, 35, 42). What is striking about the Debate with Appion, however, is that it articulates this inversion through rhetorical forms that would be familiar to educated Roman elites. It does so, moreover, not just to denigrate "the Greeks," but specifically to celebrate "the Jews" as those truly exemplary of the piety sought by lovers of truth.

Hellenism in Josephus, Tatian, and *Homilies* 4–6

Comparison with Josephus and Tatian is here instructive. In Josephus' *Against Apion*, for instance, the mocking of Greeks as inferior to those whom they deride as "barbarians" leads to a further inversion whereby the Jews – those whom Greeks dismiss as "the weakest of barbarians" (2.15) – are actually the most pious of all. Against Apion's contention that the Jews are the only *ethnos* that has never produced "any wonderful men amongst us, not any inventers of arts, nor any eminent for wisdom" (2.12), Josephus elevates Moses and argues that "the

---

[37] Côté, "Rhetoric and Jewish-Christianity," 388. See also Carleton Paget, *Jews, Christians, and Jewish Christians*, 462–63.

[38] Côté, "Rhetoric and Jewish-Christianity," 388.

[39] Adler, "Apion's Encomium of Adultery"; Côté, "Rhetoric and Jewish-Christianity," 381–82, 385–87.

laws we have given us are disposed after the best manner for the advancement of piety" (2.15).

Tatian similarly mocks the Greeks as inferior to "barbarians" (e. g., "Which of your institutions has not been derived from the barbarians?… What noble thing have you produced by your pursuit of philosophy?"; *Oratio ad Graecos* 1–2). Much like his teacher Justin, Tatian describes his own quest for truth as including consideration of Greek philosophy and culminating in his encounter with Jewish scriptures (i. e., "certain barbaric writings, too old to be compared with the opinions of the Greeks, and too divine to be compared with their errors") and their superior monotheism and ethics (e. g., "I was led to put faith in these [writings] by the unpretending east of the language, the inartificial character of the writers, the foreknowledge displayed of future events, the excellent quality of the precepts, and the declaration of the government of the universe as centered in One being"; 29). Tatian does not, however, align himself with the Jews. He emphasizes the greater antiquity and piety of Moses in relation to Homer and other Greeks, but he does so to laud Moses as "the founder of all barbarian wisdom" (31).

Both Josephus and Tatian appropriate the Graeco-Roman binary "Greek"/"barbarian" and invert its valuation with reference to both antiquity and ethics. Where Josephus uses this inversion as the basis to defend the Jews and their Law as the most pious, however, Tatian uses it to develop his teacher Justin's contrast between the *Logos*-based true philosophy of the Christians and the demon-inspired myth and ritual of the Greeks.[40] This contrast enables Tatian to globalize Greekness into a model of error, and in the process, he draws upon older Graeco-Roman and Jewish binaries of cultural difference without inserting any explicit language of "Christian" and "Christianity." When Tatian speaks of what "we" believe, however, he goes beyond an emphasis on monotheism and ethics to retell the history of the cosmos in terms of the activity of the *Logos* and to emphasize that "we announce that God was born in the form of a man" (21). Although he aligns himself with "barbarians" against "Greeks," moreover, it is not specifically in relation to the Jews but rather as "a disciple of the barbarian philosophy … born in the land of the Assyrians" (42).

Tatian provides an important precedent for globalizing the category of Hellenism, specifically by extending Justin's notion of demon-inspired Greek mythology and ritual practice to include philosophy and by doing so with appeal to the allegorical interpretation of Greek myths by those educated in Greek *paideia*. In *Homilies* 4–6, the contrast of divinely infused rationality and demonically inspired irrationality similarly undergirds the inversion of the valuation of "Greek"

---

[40] On this trope in Justin, see my discussion in "The Trickery of the Fallen Angels and the Demonic Mimesis of the Divine: Aetiology and Polemics in the Writings of Justin Martyr," *JECS* 12 (2004): 141–71.

vs. "barbarian." Here, however, the very purpose of this inversion is celebrate Judaism. As Carleton Paget notes, the "negative presentation of things Greek, of the world of Greek *paideia*, acts as a counterfoil to the strongly positive presentation of Judaism ... which in positing a divine monarch who rewards the righteous and punishes the wicked, creates a properly moral framework against which to live one's life" and is thus promoted as "the polar opposite to this Greek world" of immoral myths and morally bankrupt philosophers.[41]

In its concern for Judaism, the approach to mapping identities in *Homilies* 4–6 falls closer to how Josephus similarly counters Hellenism in conversation with Ap(p)ion.[42] In comparison, however, the binary "Greek"/"Jew" is far more globalized. Whereas Josephus counters Apion in part by exposing him as an Egyptian and questioning his claim to Greekness (2.3), Clement makes no such claim in *Homilies* 4–6; the Debate with Appion frames Hellenism as a matter of education rather than ethnicity, and it is for this reason that the Egyptian Appion can serve as its exemplar; Appion here functions – as Côté has shown – as "an idealized or caricatured defender of the *paideia*."[43] Clement's denunciation of *paideia*, philosophy, polytheism, "pagan" mythology, and allegory are thus framed in terms of an essential contrast of a unified transethnic "Hellenism" with a unified transethnic "Judaism" – that is, a set of doctrines about the unity of God associated with the Law and people of the Jews.[44] The combative character of this conflict is underlined not just by the demonization of *paideia* but also by the special interest in unmasking Appion's "unreasonable hatred for the Jews" (5.29) as a mark of the immorality, hatred of piety, and irrationality here depicted as the dirty truth behind Hellenism's cultured veneer.[45]

---

[41] Carleton Paget, *Jews, Christians, and Jewish Christians*, 463–65.

[42] Côté ("Rhetoric and Jewish-Christianity," 375) similarly stresses that like Josephus "the author of *Hom.* 4–6 intended to establish the superiority of Judaism over Greek culture."

[43] Côté, "Rhetoric and Jewish-Christianity," 379.

[44] I do not mean to suggest that the *Homilies* here has a concept of "Judaism" as "a religion" in any modern sense of the term; I here use the abstract noun, rather, to underline that the authors/redactors of the *Homilies*, no less than Patristic authors, are engaged in totalizing and globalizing categorizing that abstractifies, theorizes, and organizes local and historical patterns of similarity and difference.

[45] Côté posits that "the Pseudo-Clementine writers knew exactly who Apion was, but, for polemical reasons, chose to focus on the grammarian and his Greek culture, instead of the historian and his hostility to Judaism" ("Rhetoric and Jewish-Christianity," 379). I agree that Hellenism is the major theme here, but I read the treatment of Apion's anti-Judaism as closely connected to this theme in *Homilies* 4–6, even if elsewhere treated as distinct. It is notable, in my view, that Clement's story about Apion in the fifth *Homily* does not end with the establishment of his impiety but culminates in the revelation of anti-Judaism as his true motive. From Apion's philosophical profile – as Cote notes – we would think him an "unlikely disciple of Simon Magus" (372); it is his anti-Judaism, however, that is here used to explain their affiliation, thereby linking Hellenism with "heresy" as well. See further Chapter Five in this volume.

Judaism in the Debate with Appion and the *Homilies*

The pro-Jewish features of the Debate with Appion have been central to past attempts to posit an originally Jewish source behind it. Past studies have tended to emphasize the lack of reference to Jesus in this section and to posit that what is here depicted sounds more like conversion to Judaism than conversion to Christianity (e.g., *Hom.* 4.7–8, 22, 24; 5.28).[46] In *Hom.* 5.28, for instance, Clement recalls how "although I examined many doctrines of philosophers, I inclined to none of them, except only [the doctrines] of the Jews: a certain merchant of theirs sojourned here in Rome, selling linen clothes, and a fortunate meeting set simply before me the doctrine of the unity of God" (cf. 1.3.1–4.7). A contrast is often drawn with Clement's account in the first *Homily* of how he heard the reports and preachings in Rome about Jesus, prompting his travels to Judaea (1.6.2–7.8).

It is far from clear, however, whether it is helpful to retroject our modern sense of "conversion" as a clear-cut and one-time movement from one "religion" to another. Whether or not divergences in the accounts of Clement's youth may hint at the origins of this material in another source, it remains that the implication in the redacted form of the *Homilies* is that Clement had a boyhood encounter with a Jewish merchant that prepared him for his later receptivity to the message about the True Prophet, as he encountered progressively, first through an anonymous preacher in Rome, then through Barnabas in Alexandria, and finally by meeting Peter in Judaea and traveling with him. Nor it is odd that his boyhood encounter was left unmentioned at the outset; the novel, after all, is peppered throughout with flashbacks that dramatically reveal how events in the past have set the stage for developments in the present, pointing to the invisible hand of Providence at play in seemingly chance occurrences in the personal lives of Clement and his family. This movement between past and present is among of the main literary features of the *Homilies*.

Within the narrative world of the novel, as we now have it, even the lack of mention of the True Prophet in *Homilies* 4–6 here makes sense:[47] consistent with its concern for knowledge, truth, and appearance, the *Homilies* is consistent in marking the difference between private teachings and the truths therein revealed, such as about the True Prophet, Rule of Syzygy, and doctrine of the false pericopes in *Homilies* 2–3, and what is said to persuade in public, such as in Peter's public sermons and debates with Simon. Peter's initial teachings of Clement in the second *Homily*, in fact, outline all of these ideas in the narrative setting of private teaching, but also feature Peter making explicit what "we do

---

[46] See the helpful summary in Carleton Paget, *Jews, Christians, and Jewish Christians*, 431–35.

[47] Cf. Carleton Paget, *Jews, Christians, and Jewish Christians*, 447.

not wish to speak in public" and warning Clement accordingly about the limits of public debate (2.39).

Furthermore, the depiction of affiliation with Jews as coterminous with the teachings of Jesus is consistent with the representation of identity and difference within the *Homilies* itself. Elsewhere, Jewish proselytes are prominently included in the circles surrounding Peter, without noting any need for a second "conversion" (i.e., first from "paganism" to "Judaism," then from "Judaism" to "Christianity"). Justa, for instance, is explicitly called a Jewish proselyte and said to have been persuaded to leave "the nations/Gentiles" to join the Jewish people by none other than Jesus himself (2.19; 13.7). Even Clement's initial account about the reports he heard about Jesus while in Rome emphasize "his preaching the kingdom of the invisible God to the Jews" and prompt Clement to wish to travel to Judaea (1.6).

It is often noted that the term "Christian" is nowhere used in *Homilies* 4–6. But it is not used in the rest of the *Homilies* either. The terms "Jew," however, is frequent and positive, most often contrasted with "Greek" and "Gentile" alike. Here and elsewhere, moreover, the demons who inspire Greek religion and culture are contrasted with the "God of the Jews" proclaimed by the True Prophet Jesus and worshipped by Peter and his followers.

Yet a case for a Jewish source – as Carleton Paget has shown – can be made on the basis of other criteria. There are notable literary seams, for instance, that mark *Homilies* 4–6 as an "intrusion in the narrative" and suggest possible dependence on a source that was used only partially.[48] This section appeals heavily to "pagan" thinkers and traditions, in contrast to the focus on arguments from Scripture elsewhere in the *Homilies*. Partly as a result, it is full of *hapax legomena*. Even in cases when *Homilies* 4–6 raises similar to points to the rest of the *Homilies*, such as the importance of monotheism, this section does so with distinctive terminology.[49]

In my view, then, it is possible to follow Strecker's insights about the fit of these chapters with the rest of the *Homilies*,[50] while also maintaining the likelihood of its dependence here on a separate source. I am persuaded by Carleton Paget's suggestion that "what has been written about the 'Judaising' tendencies of the Homilist may do no more than explain why he was able to include the source he did rather than proving that he wrote it."[51] Also persuasive, in my view, is his argument for its Jewish authorship, on the basis of similarities with Josephus, Philo, and other Greek Jewish writings in its defense of Judaism against Hellenism, and his argument for its Syrian provenance, on the basis of

---

[48] Carleton Paget, *Jews, Christians, and Jewish Christians*, 460, 451–52.

[49] Carleton Paget, *Jews, Christians, and Jewish Christians*, 448.

[50] Strecker, *Das Judenchristentum in den Pseudoklementinen*, 79–87.

[51] Carleton Paget, *Jews, Christians, and Jewish Christians*, 446.

similarities with Tatian, Lucian, and others in its pointed defense of "barbarian" wisdom against Greek *paideia*.[52]

The possibility of such a source has notable ramifications for our understanding of post-70 Judaism. Here, however, my concern is not to reconstruct or situate such a source, but rather to ask what we might learn about the fourth-century form and late antique contexts of the *Homilies* by considering how and why such material has been integrated. Côté makes a parallel point with respect to the representation of Hellenism in *Homilies* 4–6: "while it is possible that the Basic Writer used Jewish material from the first or the second century," he notes, "since the final editing of the *Homilies* and *Recognitions* took place in the fourth century, we still have to ask the question of why Jew or Christians of that period needed to address the issue of Greek rhetoric."[53] Côté points to the prominence of Neoplatonism in late antique Syria, in particular, and also further suggests:

The polemic against Neoplatonism could be a key to a proper understanding of the Apion section and all the Clementine material related to the *paideia*. Let us have in mind, for instance, the orphic theogony of Hieronymus and Hellanicus and the Rhapsodic orphic version, and the fact that our most important witness of the orphic theologies are "Neoplatonists of the fifth and sixth century, who always are inclined to make Orpheus a member of their school."[54]

Côté's findings confirm and contribute to the recent discussions of the Pseudo-Clementines that we noted at the outset, which have been recovering the value of this literature for our understanding of Christian self-definition in relation to "paganism" and Hellenism in Late Antiquity. In what follows, I would like to ask whether the inclusion of the Debate with Appion material might also tell us something about the representation of Jews and Judaism in the fourth-century form and late antique contexts of the *Homilies*. At first sight, such a question might seem counterintuitive, contravening the conventional narrative about the formation of Christian identity whereby an early concern with self-definition in relation to Judaism in the first and second centuries is assumed to have given way, thereafter, to a concern with self-definition in relation to "paganism," especially at the advent of the Christianitzation of the Roman Empire. At the very least, as Carleton Paget notes, "it is certainly intriguing to note that the Homilist could pen some of the sentiments that he did and copy the section running from *Hom.* 4–6 at a time when others such as John Chrysostom were penning altogether more hostile comments on the Jews," and as such, "the existence of the

---

[52] Carleton Paget, *Jews, Christians, and Jewish Christians*, 466–77.

[53] Côté, "Rhetoric and Jewish Christianity," 388

[54] Côté, "Rhetoric and Jewish Christianity," 389, building on and quoting J. van Amersfoort, "Traces of an Alexandrian Orphic Theogony in the Pseudo-Clementines," in *Studies in Gnosticism and Hellenistic Religions Presented to Gilles Quispel on the Occasion of His 65th Birthday*, ed. Raymond van den Broek and Maarten Jozef Vermaseren (Leiden: Brill, 1981), 13–30, quote at 19.

Homilies, and in particular *Hom.* 4–6, raises important questions about a number of issues to do with developing ideas of Christian identity in the post-Constantinian world."[55]

For answering such questions, a focus on redaction may prove useful. If *Homilies* 4–6 does indeed go back to a Hellenistic Jewish source, its authors/redactors participate in a broader trend – that is: the redeployment of Hellenistic Jewish historiography and apologetics to address the challenges facing late antique Christians in a "pagan" culture, in particular. On the level of textual practice, the integration of *Homilies* 4–6 extends the early Christian collection and recontextualization of earlier Jewish materials; the *Homilies* thus stands in a long tradition of integrating received Jewish materials – often with very minor redaction – into new literary structures, as exemplified by the *Testaments of the Twelve Patriarchs* and other so-called "pseudepigrapha."[56] Such practices, however, also informed the reconceptualization of Christian identity in the fourth century in particular. In the wake of the Edict of Milan, Church Fathers such as Eusebius were actively collecting, integrating, and recontextualizing the writings of Hellenistic Jews such as Artapanus, Eupolemus, Philo, and Josephus – calling Judaism, in effect, as a witness in the debate against "paganism."[57] In what follows, then, I would like to look to whether and how similar aims and practices may have informed the integration of *Homilies* 4–6, first by comparing it to the partial parallel in *Recognitions* 10 and then by considering the meanings made by its particular placement within the *Homilies*.

---

[55] Carleton Paget, *Jews, Christians, and Jewish Christians*, 427–88.

[56] I would thus suggest that some of what might seem like contradictions or repetitions in content in the *Homilies* (e.g., in the different accounts of Clement's "conversion") reflects this particular mode of textual practice, which stands in a continuum with different types of ancient anthologizing but which especially recalls the use of different speakers and settings of direct speech in Jewish "pseudepigrapha" to frame and integrate materials that might otherwise look like doublets or repeated traditions. Much has been written about the Pseudo-Clementines and the Greek novel, but in this regard, the use of sources may resonate more with the enduring place of the practices of redaction and collection in Jewish literary production as well, on which see, e.g., David Stern, ed., *The Anthology in Jewish Literature* (Oxford: Oxford University Press, 2004). I thank James Carleton Paget for pushing me on this point.

[57] As exemplified, e.g., by Eusebius' *Praeparatio evangelium*. On his use of materials from Josephus' writings there and elsewhere, see Gohei Hata, "Eusebius and Josephus: The Way Eusebius Misused and Abused Josephus," *Patristica: Proceedings of the Colloquia of the Japanese Society for Patristic Studies* sup. 1 (2001): 49–66; Sabrina Inowlocki, "Eusebius of Caesarea's 'Interpretatio Christiana' of Philo's *De vita contemplativa*," *HTR* 97 (2004): 305–28; David DeVore, "Eusebius' Un-Josephan History: Two Portraits of Philo of Alexandria and the Sources of Ecclesiastical Historiography," *Studia Patristica* 66 (2013): 161–80.

Homilies 4–6 and *Rec.* 10.17–51

As noted above, some of the material from the Debate with Appion is paralleled in the tenth book of the *Recognitions*, albeit in a selective fashion with striking differences from the version in the *Homilies*.[58] The parallels raise the possibility that the Debate with Appion material may have been included in some form in the *Grundschrift* or was otherwise familiar to the authors/redactors of both the *Homilies* and *Recognitions*.[59] Here, however, my aim is not to revisit the much discussed question of the relationship between *Homilies* 4–6, *Rec.* 10.17–51, the *Grundschrift*, and the possible sources behind it. Rather, I am interested in what the comparison with *Rec.* 10.17–51 might tell us about the acts of redaction that shaped the *Homilies*. Can we learn anything about the *Homilies'* fourth-century authors/redactors by considering their choices with respect to this material? Is the Debate with Appion only integrated superficially, as a digression in the larger narrative? Or might it play a more significant role in the *Homilies'* unique take on the Pseudo-Clementine novel? To answer such questions, comparison with the *Recognitions* proves useful.

Even if we cannot know for certain how much of the material in *Homilies* 4–6 and *Rec.* 10.17–51 was taken directly from an early source, it is clear that the authors/redactors of the *Homilies* and *Recognitions* actively reworked this material and did so in quite different directions. One notable difference, for instance, is the connection between *paideia* and impurity, which appears in *Homilies* 4–6 but does not feature at all in *Rec.* 10.17–51; the demonological connections are there downplayed as well.[60] So too with Clement's affiliation with Jewishness. Within *Homilies* 4–6, as we have seen, Peter is described as a Jewish teacher of Clement, with no mention of his association with Jesus or his belief in any messiah. The parallel material in *Rec.* 10.17–51, by contrast, contains explicit references to Christ as the Son of God (10.47) and True Prophet (10.51) as well as to the Gospel (10.45).

---

[58] See *Hom.* 4.11.1–2 (cf. *Rec.* 10.39.4); 4.12 (cf. *Rec.* 10.50); 4.16 (cf. *Rec.* 10.20); 4.17 (cf. *Rec.* 10.35); 4.22.1 (cf. *Rec.* 10.41.11); 4.24.4 (cf. *Rec.* 10.33.2); 4.25.1–2 (cf. *Rec.* 10.35); 5.6 (cf. *Rec.* 10.23.1–3); 5.12.3–4 (cf. *Rec.* 10.20.4–5); 5.13.2–14.2 (= *Rec.* 10.22.2–8); 5.16.3–17.5 (≈ *Rec.* 10.26.2–4); 5.22.1 (cf. *Rec.* 10.28.3); 5.22.3 (cf. *Rec.* 10.27.1); 5.22.4 (cf. *Rec.* 10.23.1–3); 5.23.1–4 (≈ *Rec.* 10.24); 6.2.2–7 (≈ *Rec.* 10.17–20); 6.3.1–10.3 (cf. *Rec.* 10.30–34); 6.14.1–15.4 (cf. *Rec.* 10.41.1–9); 6.17.1–18. (cf. *Rec.* 10. 35–38); 6.22.1–2 (≈ *Rec.* 10.25.1–2); 6.23.2–3 (≈ *Rec.* 10.36.3–5).

[59] It is possible, as Carleton Paget notes, that "the Homilist, in spite of having knowledge of G [i.e., the *Grundschrift*], has decided to make independent use of a source already used by G and to reproduce it in a more original form" (*Jews, Christians, and Jewish Christians*, 461).

[60] In *Rec.* 10.17–51, the language of defilement is used only in a sexual sense (e.g., in descriptions of Jupiter defiling goddesses and human women; 10.21–23). Passing references to demons occur at 10.27, 48; there, however, demons are identified with "pagan" deities, and no effort is made to draw any direct connection between demons and philosophy.

The very themes in *Homilies* 4–6 that are absent in the partial parallel in the *Recognitions*, however, are richly resonant with the broader literary and theological context of the *Homilies*. Within *Homilies* 4–6, for instance, the effects of Greek *paideia* are described in terms that evoke the concern for ritual purity elsewhere in the *Homilies* (e. g. 7.4.2–5, 8.1–2; 11.28.1–30.3). *Paideia* here implants impieties that impede righteousness. And, much like ritual defilements in the Levitical laws of the Torah, these impieties are communicable.[61] According to Clement, this is why people who live in cities are more sinful than their rural counterparts (4.18.1): "those who are full of evil learning infect – even with their breath – those who associate with them" (4.18.3).[62] This repurposing of medical imagery, moreover, resonates with the depiction throughout the *Homilies* of demonic influence and indwelling as a causal factor in both polytheistic worship and bodily disease, to which pious Jews remain immune (9.16; 11.15–16).

Elsewhere in the *Homilies*, the contrast between piety and impiety is mapped onto the contrast between ritual purity and physical defilement; their respective results are health and sickness, corresponding to their respective origins in the divine and the demonic. Interestingly, this pattern is particularly evident in the material directly following the Debate with Appion in the *Homilies*. In the speeches of the seventh *Homily* and in the Tripolis cycle of sermons in *Homilies* 8–11, Peter argues that polytheism and idolatry defile both soul and body (e. g. 7.3.1–4; 9.9.1–4).[63] Illness first came into the world with the shedding of defiling blood into the air by the ancient Giants (8.17.1–2). When their bodies were destroyed by the purifying waters of the Flood, their spirits lived on to become the demons who strive, even to this day, to enslave humankind (8.18.1–20.4). People who consume sacrificial meat are thus inviting demons to corrupt their souls and defile their bodies (e. g. 7.3.4; 8.19.1–20.4; 9.9.2). In the Debate with Appion, much the same is said of Greek *paidiea*: it has demonic origins, it conveys impurity, and it encourages impiety. In both, moreover, the language of ritual pollution overlaps with the rhetoric of disease: just as the antediluvian shedding of blood once defiled the air with illnesses that only baptism can heal, so the air is similarly defiled by the very breath of educated Greeks (4.18.3).

---

[61] On the redeployment of medical models in the Pseudo-Clementines, see now Giovanni Battista Bazzana, "Healing the World: Medical and Social Practice in the Pseudo-Clementine Novel," in Piovanelli and Burke, *Rediscovering the Apocryphal Continent*, 351–68.

[62] Compare, e. g., *Hom.* 8.17.1, in which similar terms are used to describe the results of the antediluvian activities of the carnivorous and cannibalistic Giants, whose spirits later became the very demons who masquerade as "pagan" deities – "By the shedding of much blood, the pure air was defiled with impure vapor and sickened those who breathed it, rending them liable to diseases."

[63] On the latter, see now Bazzana, "Healing the World."

The same pattern holds in the case of the place of Jews and Jewishness in *Homilies* 4–6 and the partial parallel in the tenth book of the *Recognitions*.[64] The latter includes the polemic against Hellenism, but Judaism is nowhere in sight. In *Homilies* 4–6, however, Clement's critique of Greek philosophy, mythology, and education is framed as a defense of Jews and Judaism.[65] For this, the *Homilies* may be ultimately indebted to a Jewish source.[66] Yet it is no less significant that the concern for Jews and Judaism is also present and important in the fourth-century redacted form of the *Homilies*.

This concern is also consistent with the rest of the *Homilies*, which displays more interest in Jews and Judaism than the *Recognitions*, as well as more traces of contacts with the Jews of their time.[67] As I have shown elsewhere, the *Homilies'* authors/redactors present apostolic succession as parallel to the transmission of truth from Moses to the Jews.[68] Rather than focusing on differences between Jews and Christians, the *Homilies* depict them as united in the same goals: consistent with the longstanding battle of prophetic truth against false prophecy, both seek to promote piety and to uproot the truth of monotheism in a world filled with demons, impurity, "heretical" lies, and polytheistic error.[69] Part of the effect of integrating the Debate with Appion, then, is to develop the *Homilies'* distinctive dichotomy of true prophecy and false prophecy (e. g., the Rule of Syzygy) to include the more familiar binary contrast of Hellenism and Judaism.

Côté has shown how the argument from *paideia* against *paideia* in the Debate with Appion is consistent with "the strong influence *paideia* and rhetoric have

---

[64] One might also cite differences in their approaches to philosophy. In the Debate with Appion, the errors of Greek mythology are conflated with the errors of Greek philosophy. Not only do Greek myths foster impious deeds, but the most educated are the most wicked, and it is precisely the philosophers who belittle anyone who calls for piety. In the tenth book of the *Recognitions*, we find many of the same arguments about Greek mythology inspiring impious deeds. There, however, they are couched in a broader context wherein philosophy can also contribute to the cause of truth: Greek philosophy may be condemned for its empty sophistry and moral relativism, but at the same time aspects of philosophical authority are co-opted to enhance the intellectual and social prestige of Peter and his followers (see Kelley, *Knowledge and Religious Authority in the Pseudo-Clementines*, 36–81). The denunciation of Greek learning in the Debate with Appion is consistent with the more suspicious attitude towards philosophy in the *Homilies* as a whole.

[65] I.e., not only does Clement defend the piety and rationality of Judaism against those Greeks who dismiss it as merely "barbarian" (4.7–8), but he defends the Jews against those who hate them, by suggesting that the true roots of anti-Judaism lie not in any rational argument against Jewish doctrines, but rather in ethnic loyalties (e. g., Simon's Samaritan origins; 5.2.4) and the fervor of unrestrained lust (e. g., Appion's anger at the chastity of Jewish women and female proselytes to Judaism; 5.27).

[66] Carleton Paget, *Jews, Christians, and Jewish Christians*, 427–88.

[67] See Chapter One above. On possible awareness of late antique Jewish traditions, see further Chapters Five and Nine below as well as Baumgarten, "Literary Evidence for Jewish Christianity in the Galilee."

[68] See further Chapter Six in this volume.

[69] E. g., *Hom.* 3.3, 18–19, 47, 51; 8.5–7; 11.7–16; 16.14; also *Epistle of Peter to James* 1.2–5.

exerted on the Pseudo-Clementines" more broadly.[70] The concern for Hellenism here resonates, for example, not just with the choice to adoption and subvert the literary forms of the Greek novel but also with the emphasis on philosophy throughout this novel; the debate about philosophy between Clement and Appion, for instance, mirrors the uniquely philosophical character of the conflict between Peter and Simon in the Pseudo-Clementine tradition – which is "not, as in the apocryphal *Acts of Peter*, a fight with signs and miracles, but a pure battle of words and arguments."[71]

In the process, the assertion of Appion's alliance with Simon serves to concretize the connections between Hellenism and "heresy," on the one hand, and Judaism and Christianity, on the other.[72] In the Debate with Appion, as we have seen, the positive valuation of the identity label "Jew" is articulated in binary contrast to a negative sense of "Greek," even to the degree that anti-Judaism becomes a marker of Hellenism's true irrationality. Perhaps most notable, in this regard, is the *Homilies'* presentation of the tale of Clement's boyhood trickery of Appion. Although the content of the tale focuses on the impieties inspired by Greek mythology, it is here presented as Clement's attempt to expose Appion's anti-Judaism (5.2–3). Furthermore, the association of Hellenism with anti-Judaism occasions the revelation of a connection to the broader plot: Appion's anti-Judaism is presented as the true reason for his unholy alliance with the "heretic" and false prophet Simon Magus.[73]

The ramifications ripple well beyond this one section, not least because of the lack of any explicit labeling of Clement or other followers of Jesus as "Christians." In this, the *Homilies* differs notably from the *Recognitions*. As a result,

---

[70] Côté, "Rhetoric and Jewish Christianity," 379.

[71] Côté, "Rhetoric and Jewish Christianity," 379.

[72] The parallels with *Hom.* 4–6 are especially clear in Peter's comments in *Hom.* 3.3.2–4.2: "To those from amongst the Gentiles who were about being persuaded with respect to the earthly images that they are no gods, he [i. e., Simon] has contrived to bring in opinions of many other gods in order that, even if they cease from their mania for polytheism, they may be deceived to speak otherwise and even worse than they now do, against the sole government of God .... With us [i. e., the Jews], indeed, who have had handed down from our forefathers the worship of the God who made all things and also the mystery of the books that are able to deceive, he will not prevail. But with those from amongst the Gentiles – who have the polytheistic proclivity bred in them and who know not the falsehoods of the Scriptures – he will prevail much. Not only he – but if any other shall recount to those from among the Gentiles any vain, dreamlike, richly set out story against God, he will be believed, because from their childhood their minds are accustomed to take in things spoken against God."

[73] *Hom.* 5.2.4: "But I was aware that the man exceedingly hated the Jews, and also that he had written many books against them, and that he had formed a friendship with this Simon – not through desire of learning but because he knew that he was a Samaritan and a hater of the Jews – and that he had come forth in opposition to the Jews; therefore he had formed an alliance with him so that he might learn something from him against the Jews." Notable is the implication that Simon hates the Jews simply because he himself is a Samaritan; in effect, the dichotomy between "orthodoxy" and "heresy" is here framed in Jewish terms. See further discussion in Chapter Five.

moreover, the positive force of Jewishness within *Homilies* 4–6 also ripples throughout the work as a whole: the most prominent identity label for a prophetically aligned individual is "Jew" – both within this section and throughout the rest of the *Homilies* as well.

This similarity need not be an invention of the authors/redactors of the *Homilies* to be significant for understanding its aims and meaning. Indeed, one finds no dearth of examples of the late antique Christian repurposing of earlier Jewish materials – ranging from the Christian reception and collection of Jewish "pseudepigrapha" to the compilation of excerpts from these and other Jewish sources to witness the antiquity of the Christianized biblical past in late antique chronographical and related writings. Indeed, we owe the survival of many Greek Jewish sources, in particular, precisely to such Christian scribal and anthological efforts in Late Antiquity. Such comparanda demonstrate the ease with which scribal practices of anthologizing, reframing, and revision could be put to work to reframe Jewish materials in Christian terms – whether as preface or prediction of Christ and/or as prehistory or superseded past to the Church. By the fourth century, in particular, strategies of this sort were common and well established. Yet, as much as the rest of the *Homilies* speaks to the rhetorical training and ample literary skills of its authors/redactors, we find no Christianizing editorial efforts of this sort. If the Debate with Appion goes back to a Jewish source, its integration in the *Homilies* seems marked by a choice to retain the marks of its Jewishness. And this choice has notable consequences for the representation of identities, not just in the section about the Debate with Appion, but in the rest of the *Homilies* as well.

Homilies 4–6 and the Redaction of the *Homilies*

To understand the methods and aims of the *Homilies*' redactional integration of the Debate with Appion material, it is also useful to consider its location within the *Homilies*' distinctive arrangement of the Pseudo-Clementine novel.[74] In its present location, the Debate with Appion serves an important function, related to the relationship between Judaism and the religion of the True Prophet Jesus as preached by Peter. The first three *Homilies* introduce the contrast between apostolic truth and its many pretenders and enemies. It is here that the Rule of Syzygy is first revealed as a teaching transmitted in private from Peter to Clement and other followers, whereby all of human history is explained in starkly dichotomous terms, as an ongoing battle between true and false prophets (e.g., *Hom.*

---

[74] Among those who posit a Jewish source used already by the *Grundschrift*, most hold that the *Recognitions* preserve the original location of this material, near the novel's denouement; e.g., Heintze, *Der Klemensroman und seine griechischen Quellen*, 19; Adler, "Apion's Encomium of Adultery," 29.

2.15–18; 3.23–27). It is telling, in my view, that the Debate with Appion has been placed directly following this discussion. In effect, the *Homilies* here explore the battle between false and true prophets with reference to the traditional binary of "Greek"/"barbarian," through the mouth of Appion, and with reference to the traditional binary of "Greek"/"Jew," through the mouth of Clement, thereby articulating its idiosyncratic ideas about the Rule of Syzygy with reference to more traditional taxonomic contrasts.

Likewise, on the other side, the Debate with Appion material is framed by the seventh *Homily*, which expands upon the twinning of truth and falsehood with special reference to purity and ritual practice. The Tripolis sermons in *Hom.* 8–11 explore both sides of the dichotomy of true and false prophecy in terms of salvation history. The continuity between Judaism and true Christianity – embodied by Clement's defense of Judaism no less than Peter's self-proclaimed Jewishness – is here explained in terms of the equality and identity of Moses and Jesus (esp. 8.5–7; cf. *Rec.* 4.5).[75] Furthermore, the continuity between Hellenism and "heresy" – suggested by the reference to Appion's alliance with Simon in the fifth *Homily* – is here expanded with appeal to a genealogy of error that spans the whole of "pagan" religion and culture (e. g. 8.11–20; 9.2–18; 10.7–25; 11.12–15).

By virtue of the integration of the Debate with Appion material, then, the binary contrast between Hellenism and Judaism can be brought to bear on the *Homilies'* interpretation of human experience through the Rule of Syzygy. The battle between the two is revealed to be part of the perennial battle between true prophecy, which proclaims the one God, and false prophecy, which masquerades as its mirror image to promote impiety, idolatry, and polytheism.[76] Côté has shown how the rivalry between Simon and Peter is depicted as an instantiation of this broader dichotomy, explored along the lines of "orthodoxy" and "heresy."[77] When read in context of the rest of the *Homilies*, the debate between Clement and Appion becomes an exemplar of the same conflict between true and false prophecy, now transposed onto a different defining dichotomy, namely: Judaism and Hellenism. In the process, a path is thus laid for the affirmation of the con-

---

[75] See my discussion of this passage in Chapter One above.

[76] Clement's role in this battle may be foreshadowed in the first *Homily*. In the *Homilies'* version of the novel's beginning, Clement abandons his philosophical education and his Roman home to chase after news of "a certain man in Judaea ... preaching to the Jews the kingdom of the invisible God" (1.4). His voyage to Judaea is here interrupted by an unplanned detour in Alexandria (1.8), which is unparalleled in the *Recognitions*. In the *Homilies*, this detour occasions Clement's intervention in a public debate between philosophers and the Jewish Jesus follower Barnabas (1.9–12) – thereby introducing the contrast between Alexandria and Judaea as geographical foci for competing claims to truth and presaging Clement's own debate with the Alexandrian Appion.

[77] Côté, *Le thème de l'opposition*.

tinuity and common ground between Judaism and the true apostolic religion, as expressions of prophetic truth against prophetic falsehood.

There is reason to think that these dynamics reflect deliberate efforts at articulating identity by revisiting and reinterpreting received binaries ("barbarian"/"Greek," "Judaism"/"Hellenism," "orthodoxy"/"heresy"). Not only is this schema striking in its subversion of the binary of "Judaism"/"Christianity" that was becoming more prominent as a Christian matrix for mapping identity in Late Antiquity, but the text explicitly takes on the task of redefining the meaning of "Jew" and "Greek." In *Hom.* 11.16.2–4, which is unparalleled in the *Recognitions*, "Jew" and "Greek" are redescribed in a manner unconnected to ethnicity or lineage. The term "Jew" – the apostle Peter there explains to Clement – is rightly used of *anyone* who is pious and follows the Law given to them (i.e., teachings of Moses and/or Jesus). "Greek," by contrast, can refer to *anyone* who is impious. In effect, then, all followers of Peter (including Romans like Clement) are here redefined as "Jews" even if they are Gentiles by birth and lineage. Conversely, the followers of Simon Magus – and all "heretics" after them – are, in the final estimation, merely "Greeks."

Within *Homilies* 4–6, as we have seen, Appion gives voice to a negative interpretation of Jews and Judaism through the lens of the common Graeco-Roman binary of "Greek"/"barbarian," only to have Clement reverse the valuation so as to laud the piety and wisdom of the "barbarian Jews" as superior to the *paideia* of polluted and impious Greeks. Here, this negative sense of Greekness is further developed through teachings attributed to Peter, which reflect upon the common Hellenistic Jewish binary of "Jew"/"Greek": the positivity of the label "Jew" is presumed, while the negativity of the label "Greek" is emphasized through the conflation of Hellenism and "heresy." And, in the process, the battle between Judaism and Hellenism is presented as a perennial fight between truth and falsehood, which speaks to the struggle of the pious against the impious in all times and places.

In Late Antiquity, the authors/redactors of the *Homilies* are hardly alone in connecting Hellenism and "heresy"; this connection was a commonplace in Christian heresiology.[78] What is notable about the iteration in the *Homilies*, however, is its use of this connection to map a complementary connection between Judaism and true apostolic Christianity, precisely by virtue of its inclusion of

---

[78] E.g., Irenaeus, *Adv. haer.* 2.14.1–6; Tertullian, *Praescr.* 7; Hippolytus, *Haer.* 1 proem. 8–9; Epiphanius, *Pan.* 5–8; Alain Le Boulleuc, *La notion d'hérésie dans la literature grecque, IIe–IIIe siècle* (2 vols.; Paris: Études augustiniennes, 1985), 2:312–13; Gérard Valleé, *A Study in Anti-Gnostic Polemics: Irenaeus, Hippolytus, and Epiphanius* (Studies in Christianity and Judaism 1; Waterloo: Wilfrid Laurier University Press, 1981), 48–51, 80–82. In stark contrast with the *Homilies*, Epiphanius posits Judaism as a "mother-heresy" as well; see further Averil Cameron, "Jews and Heretics – A Category Error?," in Becker and Reed, *The Ways That Never Parted*, 356–59. For further comparison of Epiphanius with the *Homilies* see Chapter Five below.

earlier Jewish materials. The Debate with Appion material is pivotal to the *Homilies'* efforts to present Christians and Jews as a united front in the fight against the demons and doctrinal error that are emblematized by "pagan" culture. To do so, the *Homilies* evoke an idealized image of an apostolic past in continuity with Judaism, in stark contrast to the triumphalism and supersessionism of late antique Christians such as Eusebius. Just as Jesus and Moses are said to express the same message, so non-Christian Jews like the Pharisees, Jewish apostles like Peter, and Gentile Christians like Clement are all united – against Greek astrologers, Alexandrian philosophers, and Samaritan "heretics" – in their belief in the One God.

Remapping "Hellenism" and "Judaism" in Late Antiquity

Scholars have tended to read the Pseudo-Clementines through the lens of modern assumptions about the early history of the differentiation of "Christianity" from "Judaism."[79] Part of what proves so fascinating about this novel, however, is the degree to which its own mapping of identities resists such categories. It might be tempting to imagine their "Jewish-Christian" features as the survival of older fluidities "on the ground" that resist the elite literary discourses of Patristic difference making. Whether or not this is the case, however, the *Homilies* has been clearly shaped by the efforts of its authors/authors to define difference in their own terms – much like those Patristic authors who contributed to the construction of those categories that we now take for granted as "Christianity," "Judaism," and "religion." They do so, however, along different lines. As we have seen, their efforts to classify religious difference pivot on the repurposing the pre-Christian Jewish binary of Hellenism/Judaism,[80] especially by virtue of their integration of the Debate with Appion. Yet this choice does not seem to be merely a retention of older models; within the redacted form of the *Homilies*, it functions in part to resist emergent efforts to construct "Christian" as categorically contrastive with "Jew." If anything, in the *Homilies*, the category of "Judaism" is not contrasted with "Christianity" but rather expanded to include it: the two are a prophetic pair, presented as parallel linages of the same divine truth and, hence, as a united front against the polluting false prophecy of polytheism, philosophy, *paideia*, "heresy," and Hellenism.[81]

For this, I suggest that the inclusion of *Homilies* 4–6 is determinative. To the degree that this section's differences with the rest of the *Homilies* point to its

---

[79] See Chapter One above.

[80] For other examples of the late antique resonances and repurposing of this particular binary, see now Douglas Boin, "Hellenistic 'Judaism' and the Social Origins of the 'Pagan-Christian' Debate," *JECS* 22 (2014): 167–96.

[81] See further Chapters Five and Six in this volume.

possible origins in a Jewish source, its integration dovetails with the broader fourth-century Christian trend of repurposing excerpts of earlier Greek Jewish writings.[82] The similarities with the rest of the *Homilies*, however, point to an approach and attitude toward Jewishness that differ strikingly, for instance, with the approach and attitude that inform the culling and quotation of Jewish sources within the Christian chronographical tradition,[83] or Eusebius' extensive integration of excerpts from Greek Jewish authors like Artapanus, Demetrius, Eupolemus, Ezekiel the tragedian, Josephus, and Philo in the his *Praeparatio evangelica* and elsewhere.[84] Within *Homilies* 4–6, Jesus is nowhere mentioned, and Clement's piety is framed wholly in terms of his affiliation with "the barbarian Jews." Even while integrating such materials into a novel that celebrates the True Prophet Jesus and his apostle Peter, the authors/redactors make no effort to revise this Jewishness, nor to mark Jewish monotheism as prologue to a Christian present. Here as elsewhere in the *Homilies*, the label "Christian" is strikingly absent, even as the label "Jew" is used in a consistently positive sense, aligned with prophetic and apostolic truth.

By contrast, compiling earlier Jewish sources roughly around the same time (i.e., ca. 320s CE), Eusebius begins his *Praeparatio evangelica* by proclaiming his aim to "show the nature of Christianity" and by asking: "Are we Greeks or barbarians?" (*Praep. ev.* 1.1–2).[85] For Eusebius, this older binary is useful to adduce when introducing his anthological compilation of "pagan" and Jewish excerpts precisely to establish Christian difference from both: "we agree neither with the opinions of the Greeks nor with the customs of the barbarians" (1.2). If the authors/redactors of the *Homilies* do indeed integrate a Jewish source, they

---

[82] This trend has been most studied in relation to Philo and Josephus. See, e.g., Inowlocki, "Eusebius of Caesarea's 'Interpretatio Christiana,'" 305–28; Michael Hardwick, *Josephus as an Historical Source in Patristic Literature Through Eusebius* (Atlanta: Scholars Press, 1989); Ken Olson, "A Eusebian Reading of the *Testimonium Flavianum*," in *Eusebius of Caesarea: Tradition and Innovations*, ed. Aaron Johnson and Jeremy Schott (Hellenic Studies Series 60; Washington DC: Center for Hellenic Studies, 2013), 97–114.

[83] See further William A. Adler, *Time Immemorial: Archaic History and Its Sources in Christian Chronography from Julius Africanus to George Syncellus* (Dumbarton Oaks Studies 26; Washington, DC: Dumbarton Oaks, 1989).

[84] See further Arthur J. Droge, *Homer or Moses? Early Christian Interpretations of the History of Culture* (HUT 26; Tübingen: Mohr Siebeck, 1989), 168–93; Aaron P. Johnson, "Identity, Descent, and Polemic: Ethnic Argumentation in Eusebius' *Praeparatio evangelica*," *JECS* 12 (2004): 23–56; Sabrina Inowlocki, *Eusebius and the Jewish Authors: His Citation Technique in an Apologetic Context* (Ancient Judaism and early Christianity 64; Leiden: Brill, 2006); Inowlocki, "Eusebius' Construction of a Christian Culture in an Apologetic Context: Reading the *Praeparatio Evangelica* as a Library," in *Reconsidering Eusebius*, ed. Sabrina Inowlocki and Claudio Zamagni (VCSup 107; Leiden: Brill, 2011), 199–224. See also Carl R. Holladay, ed., *Fragments from Hellenistic Jewish Authors*, 4 vols. (Chico, CA: Scholars Press, 1983–1996).

[85] On this trope in Eusebius, see further Eduard Iricinschi, "Good Hebrew, Bad Hebrew: Christians as *Triton Genos* in Eusebius' Apologetic Writings," in Inowlocki and Zamagni, *Reconsidering Eusebius*, 69–86.

do so to communicate quite a different answer to much the same question: here, Christians are indeed "barbarians" – and, more specifically, "Jews."

Among the results is to destabilize any presumption of "Christianity" as categorically contrastive with "Judaism." Through the integration of what appears to be a non-Christian Jewish source or set of received traditions, pre-Christian Jewish tropes and taxonomies are here repurposed to paint a new picture of the true apostolic religion as an effort to recruit "pagans" to join the pious and monotheistic Jews in their longstanding battle against the demon-inspired philosophy and *paideia* of the Greeks. By virtue of the inclusion of the Debate with Appion, the *Homilies* thus depict Judaism's perennial conflict with Hellenism as continued by all authentically apostolic Christians – including even Gentile Christians like the Greek-educated Roman Clement. From a modern perspective, this position might seem pleasantly irenic. In its late antique context, however, it would have been quite sharply polemic. The *Homilies* associate Greek *paideia* with demons, impiety, impurity, and "heresy" as well as anti-Judaism. In the process, they dismiss a great many of their fellow Christians as merely "Greeks."

Chapter Five

Heresy, *Minut*, and the "Jewish-Christian" Novel*

In the history of scholarship on the Pseudo-Clementine *Homilies* and *Recognitions*, heresiological sources have played a central role. The *Homilies* and *Recognitions* offer two different versions of a novel about Clement of Rome, which recounts his conversion, his travels with the apostle Peter, their debates with Simon Magus and his followers, and the providential reunion of Clement's long-lost family. In their redacted forms, the *Homilies* and *Recognitions* both date to the fourth century.[1] For most of the twentieth century, however, scholars paid little attention to their literary forms and late antique contexts.[2] Instead, research on these texts was mainly source-critical in orientation, aimed at reconstructing their third-century shared source and at recovering the first-century traditions and second-century writings that may have been used by this source.[3]

* This chapter originally appeared in 2008 as "Heresiology and the (Jewish)Christian Novel: Narrativized Polemics in the Pseudo-Clementines," in *Heresy and Identity in Late Antiquity*, ed. E. Iricinschi and H. Zellentin (TSAJ 119; Tübingen: Mohr Siebeck, 2008), 273–98; it is reprinted here with permission from Mohr Siebeck. An earlier form was presented at Princeton University at the 2005 colloquium on "Making Selves and Marking Others: Heresy and Self-Definition in Late Antiquity." I am grateful to the conference organizers and attendees for their helpful comments, and thanks also to Gérard Vallée, Karl Shuve, Christopher Cubitt, Peter Petite, and Susan Wendel for further feedback. Grants from the National Endowment for the Humanities and the Social Science and Humanities Research Council of Canada provided support for research and writing this article. This version has been substantially revised, updated, and expanded, especially to integrate new research on heresiology and to expand the discussion of Rabbis and Samaritans, especially in conversation with Matthew Chalmers.

[1] The *Homilies* are commonly dated ca. 300–320 CE. This version of the Pseudo-Clementine romance of recognitions is extant in the original Greek and probably of Syrian provenance. It is in manuscripts of this version that we find prefaced the *Epistle of Peter to James*, *Contestation*, and the *Epistle of Clement to James*. The *Recognitions* is commonly dated ca. 360–380 CE. Although originally written in Greek, this version is now extant in full only in Rufinus' Latin translation (ca. 407 CE).

[2] Esp. Ferdinand Christian Baur, "Die Christuspartei in der korinthischen Gemeide, der Gegensatz des petrinischen und paulischen Christentums in der alten Kirche, der Apostel Petrus in Rom," *Tübinger Zeitschrift für Theologie* 4 (1831): 61–206. Notably, Baur had assumed a second-century date for these texts. Their fourth-century dates were established later in the nineteenth century; see C. Biggs, "The Clementine *Homilies*," in *Studia biblica et ecclesiastica* (Oxford: Clarendon, 1890), 2:191–92, 368–69; H. Waitz, *Die Pseudoklementinen: Homilien und Rekognitionem: Eine quellen-kritische Untersuchung* (TU 10.4; Leipzig: Hinrichs, 1904), esp. 372.

[3] Since the *Homilies* and *Recognitions* share so much material as well as the same basic novelistic structure (albeit with different arrangements, distinctive material in each, and redactional

For this, source critics found tantalizing clues in the heresiological literature of Late Antiquity. Most significant in this regard is Epiphanius' *Panarion*. In his comments on the so-called "heresy" of the Ebionites, Epiphanius describes a book which, like the Pseudo-Clementines, concerns the acts and teachings of the apostle Peter and is attributed to Clement of Rome (*Pan.* 30.15).[4] Later in the same passage (*Pan.* 30.16), he refers to another book used by the Ebionites, which concerns the apostle James and which bears some similarities to one specific portion of the Pseudo-Clementine *Recognitions*.[5]

Both for Baur and for later scholars like Hans Joachim Schoeps, the connection between the Pseudo-Clementines and the Ebionites seemed obvious.[6] The Pseudo-Clementines were seen to preserve traces of a "Jewish-Christianity"

---

variations that affect the emphasis and overall message of each) scholars speculate about their dependence on a single shared source. This hypothetical source, commonly called the *Grundschrift* or "Basic Source," is typically dated to the third century and situated in Syria. In light of the reference to ten books sent to James in *Rec.* 3.75, some scholars have speculated about a *Kerygmata Petrou* that may have been one of its sources (even as others dismiss the reference as merely a literary fiction); small portions of a possibly related text called *Kerygma Petrou* are quoted, e. g., by Heracleon (*apud* Origen, *Comm. John* 3.17) and Clement of Alexandria (*Strom.* 1.29.182; 6.5.39; 15.128). For other hypothetical sources of the *Grundschrift*, see below. For the history of scholarship on these sources, see F. Stanley Jones, "The Pseudo-Clementines: A History of Research," *Second Century* 2 (1982): 14–33; Pierre Geoltrain, "Le Roman Pseudo-Clémentin depuis les recherches d'Oscar Cullman," in *Le Judéo-christianisme dans tous ses états*, ed. Simon Claude Mimouni and F. Stanley Jones (Patrimoines; Paris: Cerf, 2001), 31–38; and for critique of past source-critical research, see, e. g., Jürgen Wehnert, "Literarkritik und Sprachanalyse: Kritische Anmerkungen zum gegenwärtigen Stand der Pseudoklementinen-Forschung," *ZNW* 74 (1983): 268–301; see also Chapter One in the present volume.

[4] I.e., *Periodoi Petrou*, described by Epiphanius as a Clementine pseudepigrapha about Peter that was used by Ebionites. This too is sometimes thought to be a source of the Pseudo-Clementine *Grundschrift* – although F. Stanley Jones has suggested that this is the title under which the *Grundschrift* itself circulated; see, most recently, his handy introduction to this source in F. Stanley Jones, trans., *The Syriac Pseudo-Clementines: An Early Version of the First Christian Novel* (Apocryphes 14; Turnhout: Brepols, 2014), 15–27.

[5] I.e., *Anabathmoi Jakobou*, which may have some relationship to *Rec.* 1.27–72, a portion of the *Recognitions* that also happens to be unparalleled in the *Homilies* and distinctive from the rest of the *Recognitions* in its language and viewpoints. See further F. Stanley Jones, *An Ancient Jewish Christian Source on the History of Christianity: Pseudo-Clementine Recognitions 1.27–71* (Texts and Translations 37, Christian Apocrypha Series 2; Atlanta: Scholars Press, 1995); Jones, *Pseudoclementina Elchasaiticaque inter Judaeochristiana: Collected Studies* (Orientalia Lovaniensia Analecta 203; Leuven: Peeters, 2012), 291–305; Robert E. Van Voorst, *The Ascents of James: History and Theology of a Jewish-Christian Community* (SBL Dissertation Series 112; Atlanta: Scholars Press, 1989).

[6] See esp. Hans Joachim Schoeps, *Theologie und Geschichte des Judenchristentums* (Tübingen: Mohr, 1949); Schoeps, *Jewish Christianity: Factional Disputes in the Early Church* (trans. D. Hare; Philadelphia: Fortress, 1969). Other scholars have been much less optimistic about our ability to reconstruct both the Ebionites and their relationship with the Pseudo-Clementines; see, e. g., Jones, *Pseudoclementina*, 513–14. For a summary of recent research, see now James Carleton Paget, *Jews, Christians, and Jewish Christians in Antiquity* (WUNT 251; Tübingen: Mohr Siebeck, 2010), 325–82.

widespread in apostolic times.[7] Accordingly, Epiphanius' comments were thought to attest an inevitable development: after Christianity's "Parting of the Ways" with Judaism, those who preserved and developed such traditions would – it was reasoned – surely have become a deviant minority, expelled as Judaizing "heretics" from a now dominant "Gentile-Christian" church.[8]

As a result of such views, scholars have tended to treat both the Pseudo-Clementines and the Ebionites as relics of an earlier age, more significant for our knowledge of Christian Origins than for our understanding of Christianity and Judaism in Late Antiquity.[9] This approach, however, has been shown to have its limits. Proceeding from these assumptions, for instance, it has proved difficult to pinpoint the relationship between the Ebionites, their nonextant books, the witness of Epiphanius, and the extant forms of the Pseudo-Clementines. Even after over a century of methodical investigation into their connections, source-critical research on the *Homilies* and *Recognitions* remains largely mired in debates over a variety of hypothetical sources of the *Grundschrift* and their possible filiations.[10]

Elsewhere, I have suggested that this seemingly counterintuitive focus on hypothetical sources of the *Grundschrift* reflects the continued influence of Baur as well as the continued sway of the model of the so-called "Parting of the Ways."[11] Behind the scholarly neglect of the extant forms of the Pseudo-Clementines (and even the *Grundschrift* itself), we may also find some tacit acceptance of Epiphanius' judgment of the Ebionites as petty "heretics." Just as the source-critical enterprise has necessitated a large degree of trust in the accuracy of Epiphanius' summaries and quotations, so too have studies of the Pseudo-Clementines tended to treat him as a trustworthy ethnographer of error, taking his comments largely at face value. F. Stanley Jones, for instance, has shown how source criticism of these texts has been hampered by a preference for the external evidence of heresiologists over internal evidence from the *Homilies* and *Recognitions* themselves.[12] Likewise, their association with Epiphanius' marginalized Ebionites may have contributed to the dearth of past research on their fourth-century forms and their late antique contexts.

---

[7] Schoeps, *Theologie und Geschichte des Judenchristentums*, 355–60, 457–79.

[8] Schoeps, *Jewish Christianity*, 12–13, 18–37.

[9] See esp. Chapter One in this volume.

[10] So too Jones, "Pseudo-Clementines," 14–33; Geoltrain, "Le Roman Pseudo-Clémentin," esp. 36; Dominique Côté, *Le thème de l'opposition entre Pierre et Simon dans les Pseudo-Clémentines* (Études Augustiniennes Série Antiquités 167; Paris: Institut d'Études Augustiniennes, 2001), 7–19; Nicole Kelley, *Knowledge and Religious Authority in the Pseudo-Clementines: Situating the Recognitions in Fourth-Century Syria* (WUNT[2] 213; Tübingen: Mohr Siebeck, 2006).

[11] See Chapter One in this volume.

[12] Jones, *Ancient Jewish Christian Source*, 35–37.

In what follows, I hope to help fill this lacuna by means of another approach to the same issues, questions, and connections. Instead of treating the Pseudo-Clementines as "heresy," I will attempt to read them as part of the late antique discourse of heresiology.[13] Epiphanius, then, will here serve us a very different purpose. Rather than appealing to him for evidence about the Ebionites (who may or may not have had a hand in producing this or related literature, even if they read or copied it), I will treat his *Panarion* as a prime example of late antique Christian heresiology. Accordingly, my focus will fall less on its content and more on its rhetoric and the assumptions that inform them.[14] This and other heresiological writings from Late Antiquity will serve as heuristic points of comparison and contrast with the Pseudo-Clementines – which, I will suggest, achieve many of the same aims, albeit within a narrativized framework. The choice of narrative for this purpose clearly reflects the Pseudo-Clementine appropriation and subversion of the genre and conventions of the ancient Greek novel.[15] I shall suggest, however, that its articulation in the *Homilies* might be better understood also with Rabbinic comparanda, both in relation to the place of Samaritans in Rabbinic heresiology and to the subgenre of Rabbinic disputation tales. Comparison with the *Panarion* will thus be coupled with comparison with contemporaneous *Bereshit Rabbah*, which shares – with both – a sharp concern for the denigration of philosophy as well as an interest in countering ideas about the multiplicity of the divine among those whom it deems *minim*/"heretics."

This experiment in reading the Pseudo-Clementines as heresiology forms part of my broader attempt to shed light on their fourth-century authors and redactors. It is often assumed that these texts were produced and read only on the margins of Christianity, by the Ebionites and groups like them. Whether or

---

[13] For a different approach to the same task, see now Jones, *Pseudoclementina*, 152–71, 516–31.

[14] Here, I am especially indebted to Averil Cameron's insightful essay, "How to Read Heresiology," *Journal of Medieval and Early Modern Studies* 33 (2003): 471–92. Happily, two new studies have now taken up the much-needed task of reconsidering Epiphanius as a writer and thinker in his own right, rather than merely mining his works: Young Kim, *Epiphanius of Cyprus: Imagining an Orthodox World* (Ann Arbor: University of Michigan Press, 2015); Andrew S. Jacobs, *Epiphanius of Cyprus: A Cultural Biography of Late Antiquity* (Berkeley: University of California Press, 2016).

[15] On the Pseudo-Clementines as novel, see Ben Edwin Perry, *Ancient Romances: A Literary-Historical Account of their Origins* (Sather Classical Lectures 37; Berkeley: University of California Press, 1967), 285–93; Tomas Hägg, *The Novel in Antiquity* (Berkeley: University of California Press, 1983), 154–65; Mark J. Edwards "The Clementina: A Christian Response to the Pagan Novel," *Classical Quarterly* 42 (1992): 459–74; William Robins, "Romance and Renunciation at the Turn of the Fifth Century," *JECS* 8 (2000): 531–57; Kate Cooper, "Matthidia's Wish: Division, Reunion, and the Early Christian Family in the Pseudo-Clementine *Recognitions*," in *Narrativity in Biblical and Related Texts/La narrativité dans la Bible et les textes apparentés*, ed. Geroge J. Brooke and Jean-Daniel Kaestli (Bibliotheca Ephemeridum Theologicarum Lovaniensium 149; Leuven: Peeters, 2000), 243–64; also Jones, *Pseudoclementina*, 114–37.

not we choose to accept the accuracy of Epiphanius' report about the Ebionite use of similar writings, however, we must also acknowledge the ample evidence for the *Nachleben* of these novels far beyond the allegedly isolated milieu of an Ebionite readership. The Pseudo-Clementines may not fit well with modern notions of "Christianity" in Late Antiquity as already long "parted" and mutually exclusive from "Judaism," and it might be tempting thus to presume their marginality in premodern times. Yet manuscript and other data for their late antique and medieval afterlives suggest otherwise. By the early fifth century, forms of the Pseudo-Clementine novel had been translated from their original Greek into both Latin and Syriac.[16] In addition, as F. Stanley Jones has recently noted, "the Pseudo-Clementine novel had an enormous impact on subsequent literature, with the Faust-sage representing only one branch of its influence," which also includes epitomes in Greek, Latin, Syriac, Ethiopic, Arabic, Georgian, and Armenian as well as "vernacular versions of the story in Icelandic, Old Swedish, Middle High German, Early South English, and Anglo-Norman."[17] Accordingly, these data push us also to look more closely at the texts themselves and to reassess their place within the religious landscape of Late Antiquity.[18]

If polemics can, in fact, provide the scholar with a cache of telling clues about religious self-definition and the social realities that shape it, then attention to the polemics (and the rhetorics of polemic) within the Pseudo-Clementines may help us to situate their authors/redactors within Late Antiquity. In contrast to an imposed dichotomy between so-called "Jewish-Christianity" and so-called "Gentile-Christianity," such an approach may help us to recover a richer sense of the interactions, reactions, and influences connecting the constellation of interconnected late antique traditions – Christian, Jewish, and "pagan" – with which the final forms of these novels seem to be both conversant and conversing.

Towards this goal, this inquiry will focus on the *Homilies*, the version of the novel in which such dynamics are most evident and explicit. I will begin by

---

[16] For Rufinus' Latin version, see Bernhard Rehm, *Die Pseudoklementinen*, vol. 2: *Rekognitionen in Rufins Übersetzung* (GCS 51; Berlin: Akademie-Verlag, 1965). The Syriac version includes *Rec.* 1–4.1 and *Hom.* 10–12.24; 13–14.12 and is preserved in a manuscript from 411 CE; see Wilhelm Frankenberg, *Die syrischen Clementinen mit griechischen Paralleltext* (TU 48.3; Leipzig: Hinrichs, 1937); Jones, *The Syriac Pseudo-Clementines*; Jones, *Pseudoclementina*, 322–41.

[17] Jones, *The Syriac Pseudo-Clementines*, 37. See further, e.g., Albert R. M. Dressel, *Clementinorum Epitomae Duae* (Leipzig: Hinrichs, 1859); Franz Paschke, *Die beiden griechischen Klementinen-Epitomen und ihre Anhänge* (TU 90; Berlin: Akademie-Verlag, 1966); Charles Renoux, "Fragments arméniens des *Recognitiones* du Pseudo-Clément," *Oriens Christianus* 62 (1978): 103–13; Margaret Dunlop Gibson, "Apocrypha Sinaitica," *Studia Sinaitica* 5 (1896): 15–54.

[18] As James Carleton Paget puts it in his review of Jones's *Pseudoclementina*: "The fact that Rufinus felt the need to translate [the *Recognitions*] into Latin, and that translations of either work exist in Syriac, Armenian, and Arabic, might point to some degree of popularity at a time when John Chrysostom was fulminating against Judaizing Christians in Antioch" (*Marginalia Review of Books*, 19 May 2013, http://marginalia.lareviewofbooks.org/).

exploring some of its rhetorical and ideological continuities with fourth-century Christian heresiology, looking especially to Epiphanius' *Panarion* as a point of comparison. Then I will consider the place of Hellenism and Samaritanism within the *Homilies'* heresiology, pointing to distinctively late antique Christian parallels for its treatment of Hellenism as well as distinctively late antique Jewish parallels for its treatment of Samaritanism. Finally, I will look to discursive continuities and cultural commonalities with other late antique examples of narrativized polemics, particularly in Rabbinic disputation tales featuring *minim*. In the process, I hope to demonstrate the value of bringing late antique Christian *and* late antique Jewish materials to bear on our interpretation of the *Homilies*, in the hopes of opening a new window onto its redacted form and the fourth-century authors/redactors responsible for it.[19]

The *Homilies* as Heresiology

Central to the *Homilies* in its present form is the rivalry between Peter and Simon Magus.[20] Much of the dramatic action in the novel is motivated by Peter's attempt to draw Simon into public disputation. During the course of the novel, both travel from city to city, spreading their respective beliefs to crowds of curious Gentiles. Not only does the novel claim to record the public debates between apostle and arch-heretic, but its authors/redactors put in the mouth of Peter sermons and statements that serve to situate Simon within a genealogy of error that stretches back to the very beginning of human history. In the process, as we shall see, the *Homilies* theorize the place of "heresy" in the cosmic plan of a singular and good God.

The *Homilies'* dramatization of disputation and totalizing approach to religious error fit well within the context of fourth-century Christianity.[21] This context, moreover, may help us to understand its characterization of Simon Magus.

---

[19] For "pagan" comparanda, see above on the Greek novel as well as Dominique Côté, "Une critique de la mythologie grecque d'après l'Homélie Pseudo-clémentine IV," *Apocrypha* 11 (2000): 37–57; Côté, "Les procédés rhétoriques dans les Pseudo-Clémentines: L'éloge de l'adultère du grammairien Apion," in *Nouvelles intrigues Pseudo-clémentines/Plots in the Pseudo-Clementine Romance*, ed. Frédéric Amsler et al. (Publications de l'Institut romand des sciences bibliques 6; Lausanne: Zébre, 2008), 189–210; Côté, "Rhetoric and Jewish-Christianity: The Case of the Grammarian Apion in the Pseudo-Clementine *Homilies*," in *Rediscovering the Apocryphal Continent: New Perspectives on Early Christian and Late Antique Apocryphal Texts and Traditions*, ed. Pierluigi Piovanelli and Tony Burke (WUNT 349; Tübingen: Mohr Siebeck, 2015), 369–89; Nicole Kelley, "Pseudo-Clementine Polemics against Sacrifice: A Window onto Religious Life in the Fourth Century?," in Piovanelli and Burke, *Rediscovering the Apocryphal Continent*, 391–400.

[20] For a comprehensive consideration of this theme, see Côté, *Thème de l'opposition.*

[21] See esp. Richard Lim, *Public Disputation, Power, and Social Order in Late Antiquity* (Berkeley: University of California Press, 1994).

Past research on the Pseudo-Clementine depiction of Simon has focused almost wholly on the question of his identity, reading this character as a cipher for some enemy of "Jewish-Christianity."[22] In light of the anti-Paulinism evident in a portion of the *Recognitions* and in an epistle now affixed to the *Homilies*, some scholars have suggested that the arch-heretic Simon here represents the apostle Paul, who is seen as an enemy of Peter by virtue of his supposed role in authoring "Gentile-Christianity."[23] Others have suggested that the character is used to represent Paul's most infamously anti-Jewish interpreter, namely Marcion.[24]

In his 2001 monograph on the disputes between Peter and Simon in the Pseudo-Clementines, however, Dominique Côté demonstrated that the anti-Pauline material in this literature is, in fact, rarely associated with Simon.[25] Likewise, as Mark Edwards also notes, the Pseudo-Clementine Simon does have many Marcionite traits, but Marcionism does not suffice to explain him.[26] Simon is here a conflate character. In him is combined some features from other traditions about Simon (such as his status as magician and his association with Samaria; see esp. *Hom.* 2.22–32; cf. Acts 8:9–24)[27] and some features associated with Marcion (such as his hatred of Jews and denial of the goodness of the Creator; esp. *Hom.* 5.2) but also a number of other features not easily explained

---

[22] Although many aspects of the Pseudo-Clementine characterization of Simon have parallels in other early Christian references to him (e. g., Acts 8:9–24; Justin, *1 Apol.* 26; Irenaeus, *Adv. haer.* 1.23), connections with the apostle Paul and/or Marcion have been cited most often, particularly by those who seek to highlight this literature's "Jewish-Christian" elements; both figures are associated with an antinomianism from which Jesus, Peter and the apostolic church are pointedly distanced. Consistent with the polemic against philosophy, others have seen him as a "pagan," or specifically Neoplatonist, enemy of Christianity, modeled on figures like Celsus (cf. Clement's debate with Appion in *Hom.* 4–6). See further A. Salles, "Simon le magicien ou Marcion?" *VC* 12 (1958): 197–224; Dominique Côté, "La fonction littéraire de Simon le Magicien dans les Pseudo-Clémentines," *Laval Théologique et Philosophique* 57 (2001): 513–23; Côté, *Thème de l'opposition*; Edwards, "Clementina," 462; Alberto Ferreiro, "Simon Magus: The Patristic-Medieval Traditions and Historiography," *Apocrypha* 7 (1996): 147–65.

[23] See esp. *Rec.* 1.70; *Epistle of Peter to James*; and discussion in Gerd Lüdemann, *Opposition to Paul in Jewish Christianity* (trans. E. Boring; Minneapolis: Fortress, 1989), 169–94. Also Georg Strecker, *Das Judenchristentum in den Pseudoklementinen* (TU 70; Berlin: Akademie-Verlag, 1958), 187; Terence V. Smith, *Petrine Controversies in Early Christianity: Attitudes towards Peter in Christian Writings of the First Two Centuries* (WUNT² 15; Tübingen: Mohr Siebeck, 1985), 11, 59–61.

[24] So Salles, "Simon le magicien ou Marcion." For critique, see Côté, "Fonction littéraire de Simon le Magicien," 514–17.

[25] Côté finds only one possible case, namely, Peter's statement to Simon in *Hom.* 17.14.2 ("You alleged that, on this account, you knew more satisfactorily the doctrines of Jesus than I do, because you heard His words through an apparition"), which some read as a reference to Gal 2:11; "Fonction littéraire de Simon le Magicien," 515–16.

[26] Côté, "Fonction littéraire de Simon le Magicien," 517–19; Edwards, "Clementina," 462.

[27] On the Pseudo-Clementine Simon's Samaritanism in the context of early Christian depictions of Samaritans, see Reinhard Pummer, *Early Christian Authors on Samaritans and Samaritanism* (TSAJ 92; Tübingen: Mohr Siebeck, 2002), 103–8, and on resonances with Rabbinic representations, see below.

through appeal to a single and simple enemy.[28] Côté thus concludes that Simon functions primarily as symbol in the Pseudo-Clementines, providing a literary foil for the characterization and exaltation of the apostle Peter.[29]

To Côté's conclusion, we might add that Simon's conflate characterization is also a narrative realization of a common heresiological trope: the view of Simon Magus as the very father of Christian "heresy." This understanding of Simon is made explicit in the sixteenth *Homily*:

Peter said to the assembled multitudes: "If Simon can do no other injury to us in regard to God, he at least prevents you from listening to the words that can purify the soul." On Peter saying this, much whispering arose amongst the crowds: "What necessity is there for permitting him to come in here, and utter his blasphemies against God?" Peter heard and said: "If only the word against God for the trial of humankind (τὸν κατὰ τοῦ θεοῦ πρὸς πειρασμὸν ἀνθρώπων λόγον) went no further than Simon! For there will be, as the lord said, false apostles, false prophets, heresies, desires for supremacy (ψευδαπόστολοι, ψευδεῖς προφῆται, αἱρέσεις, φιλαρχίαι; cf. Matt 24:24) – who, as I conjecture, finding their beginning in Simon, who blasphemes God, will work together in the assertion of the same opinions against God as those of Simon (τὸ τὰ αὐτὰ τῷ Σίμωνι κατὰ τοῦ θεοῦ λέγειν συνεργήσουσιν).[30] (*Hom.* 16.21)

Strikingly, the warning attributed to Jesus in Matt 24:24 ("For false messiahs and false prophets will appear and produce great signs and omens, to lead astray, if possible, even the elect") is here reframed to include "heresies," "false apostles," and "desires for supremacy."[31] In the process, the authority of Jesus and Peter is thus used to assert a radical continuity between Simon and all forms of postapostolic "heresy." Just as the first-century authors/redactors of the Gospel of Matthew use Jesus' prediction to speak to their own times, so the fourth-century authors/redactors of this Clementine pseudepigraphon use Peter's conjecture to assert that the errors of their own age are the same as those faced by the apostles.[32]

Even more relevant are Christian heresiological traditions that depict Simon as the beginning of a line of succession that proceeds in inverse parallel to apostolic succession from Peter. In his survey of traditions about Simon Magus from

---

[28] Côté, "Fonction littéraire de Simon le Magicien," 517–20; Côté, *Thème de l'opposition*, 191–96.

[29] Côté, "Fonction littéraire de Simon le Magicien," 510–22; Côté, *Thème de l'opposition*, 20–134.

[30] Translations of the *Homilies* here and below are revised from A. Roberts and J. Donaldson, ed., *Ante-Nicene Fathers*, vol. 8, *Fathers of the Third and Fourth Centuries* (repr. ed.; Grand Rapids: Eerdmans, 1951), 224–52, 324–30, with reference to the Greek text in B. Rehm, *Die Pseudoklementinen*, vol. 1, *Homilien* (GCS 42; Berlin: Akademie-Verlag, 1969).

[31] Notably, this is one of a number of sayings that the *Homilies* attribute to Jesus which find no direct counterpart in the New Testament; see further Leslie Lee Kline, *The Sayings of Jesus in the Pseudo-Clementine Homilies* (SBL Dissertation Series 14; Missoula: Scholars Press, 1975).

[32] On the apostolic past in the Pseudo-Clementines, see Chapter Six in this volume.

the Book of Acts to medieval literature, Alberto Ferreiro notes that this particular trope is characteristic of the fourth and fifth centuries.[33] This unified depiction of "heresy" represents a shift away from the earlier contrast, by authors like Irenaeus, between the unity of "orthodoxy" and the multiplicity of "heresies."[34] And, perhaps not surprisingly, the development of the trope of "heretical" succession appears to accompany an intensification of interest in apostolic succession, in general, and in the succession of bishops of Rome, in particular.[35]

The latter could not be more evident than in the *Homilies*. On one level, the entire narrative can be read as a defense of Clement of Rome's close connection to the apostle Peter.[36] This emphasis on proper succession is mirrored, in turn, by the depiction of Simon as both progenitor and paradigm of "heresy." The notion of "heretical" succession as a false counterpart and pretender to apostolic succession is communicated both by the narrative frame of the *Homilies* and by the sermons and speeches embedded within it.

Throughout the novel's narrative, Peter and Simon are paralleled in their twin activities of missionary travel, public preaching, and debate.[37] The Jewish Peter and the Samaritan Simon both seek to convert Gentiles away from "pagan" polytheism. In this, each has his own set of disciples. In both cases, these include three prominent Gentile travel companions, two of whom are paired (Aquila, Nicetas, and Clement for Peter; Appion, Annubion, and Athenodorus for Simon). This mirroring of opposites even extends to other elements of the plot, such as the tale of Clement's miraculous recovery of his long-lost family.[38] This, moreover, occurs in a series of recognition scenes in which masked iden-

---

[33] Ferreiro, "Simon Magus," 158–59. See also Ferreiro, "Sexual Depravity, Doctrinal Error, and Character Assassination: Jerome against the Priscillianists," *Studia Patristica* 28 (1993): 29–38; Ferreiro, "Jerome's Polemic against Priscillian in his *Letter* to Cetesiphon (133,4)," *Revue des Etudes Augustiniennes* 39 (1993): 309–32, on Jerome's concept of a female line of succession.

[34] E. g., Irenaeus, *Adv. haer.* 1.10–22; Alan Le Boulleuc, *La notion d'hérésie dans la literature grecque IIe–IIIe siècles* (2 vols.; Paris: Études augustiniennes, 1985), 1:233–34; Pheme Perkins, "Irenaeus and the Gnostics: Rhetoric and Composition in *Adversus Haereses* Book One," *VC* 30 (1976): 195–96; Annette Yoshiko Reed, "ΕΥΑΓΓΕΛΙΟΝ: Orality, Textuality, and the Christian Truth in Irenaeus' *Adversus haereses*," *VC* 56 (2002): 43–46.

[35] On the *successio haereticorum* in Hippolytus' *Elenchos* and Epiphanius' *Panarion*, see Gérard Vallée, *A Study in Anti-Gnostic Polemics: Irenaeus, Hippolytus, and Epiphanius* (Studies in Christianity and Judaism/Etudes sur le christianisme et le judaïsme 1; Waterloo: Wilfrid Laurier University Press, 1981), esp. 54–56, 70–72. As Vallée notes (55), this approach has its origins already with the Epistle of Jude and is already important in Irenaeus (*Adv. haer.* 1.23–28), even as it would only be developed in detail in the fourth century (71).

[36] See further now George E. Demacopoulos, *The Invention of Peter: Apostolic Discourse and Papal Authority in Late Antiquity* (Philadelphia: University of Pennsylvania Press, 2013), 21–25.

[37] Côté, *Thème de l'opposition*.

[38] See Edwards, "Clementina," 465, on the place of pairs and twins in the plot of the Pseudo-Clementine novels.

tities are revealed, thereby serving as a narrativized lesson in the pressing need to recognize truth in a world of misleading appearances.

The significance of this mirroring is made clear in the teachings attributed to Peter. Peter, for instance, often speaks of Simon as spreading a false gospel which, if not promptly countered, will inevitably be accepted as the true one: "heresy" is here deemed dangerous precisely because of the similarities that mask both its falsehood and the reality of its contrast with true "orthodoxy." And hence of Simon, Peter here laments:

> Though his deeds are those of one who hates, he is loved; and though he is an enemy, he is received as a friend; and though he is death, he is desired as a savior; and though he is fire, he is esteemed as light; and though he is a deceiver, he is believed as a speaker of truth. (*Hom.* 2.18)

Histories of "Heresy" in the *Homilies* and Epiphanius

In the *Homilies*, we thus find attempts at a systematic understanding of error that recall the tradition of Christian heresiology begun in the second century by Justin Martyr and Irenaeus and reflected, in its mature fourth-century form, by Epiphanius. For each, it does not suffice to counter individual "heresies." The concern is "heresy" itself, and its character and origins must be explained in a comprehensive and systematic manner. Following Irenaeus, Epiphanius' *Panarion* does so primarily through taxonomy, describing and categorizing each so-called "sect" and tracing their genealogies in meticulous detail.[39] As we have seen, the authors/redactors of the *Homilies* achieve the same goal largely through their conflate characterization of Simon Magus as the origins and embodiment of Christian "heresy" who, in effect, contains in potentiate all of the forms that lie in the future of the novel's pseudepigraphical author (i. e., Clement of Rome) and in the present of its late antique authors/redactors and readers.

Interestingly, both the *Panarion* and the *Homilies* go even further, rewriting even pre-Christian history in terms of Christian "heresy."[40] Both trace the evolution of religious error back to the very dawn of human existence, thus mapping religious difference onto the axis of time (*Pan.* 1–3; *Hom.* 8–10). The content of their summaries are strikingly similar as well.[41] In both, for instance, it is as-

---

[39] The overarching schema of Epiphanius' taxonomy is the principle that there are eighty total "heresies," as predicted by the reference to eighty concubines in Song of Songs 6:8–9. On this schema as well as his taxonomic and descriptive methods, see Vallée, *Study in Anti-Gnostic Polemics*, 65–74, 88–91. On the dynamics of Christian heresiology in relation to the organization of knowledge, see now Todd Berzon, *Classifying Christians: Ethnography, Heresiology, and the Limits of Knowledge in Late Antiquity* (Berkeley: University of California Press, 2016).

[40] On Epiphanius, see now Berzon, *Classifying Christians*, 130–50.

[41] See further Annette Yoshiko Reed, "Retelling Biblical Retellings: Epiphanius, the Pseudo-Clementines, and the Reception History of *Jubilees*," in *Tradition, Transmission, and Trans-*

serted that the first humans held no false belief or sectarian difference, such that their religion was, in effect, the same as each deems the true apostolic faith (*Pan.* 2.2.3–7; *Hom.* 8.10–11; 9.3). All false worship, including magic and astrology, began in the time of Nimrod who is sometimes called Zoroaster (*Pan.* 3.3.1–3; cf. 1.2; *Hom.* 9.4–8). Worship of gods originated with the deification of men (*Pan.* 3.9; *Hom.* 9.5) and found its most virulent form already in ancient Egypt (*Pan.* 3.11; *Hom.* 9.6; 10.16–18).[42]

To be sure, such similarities need not speak to any literary connections between the *Panarion* and the *Homilies*. Rather, the parallels between their accounts of error's evolution can be readily explained with reference to traditions about early human history in Jewish pseudepigrapha, Christian apology and chronography, and Hellenistic historiography.[43] What proves interesting, in my view, is that the two seem to draw on much the same mix of sources and/or traditions. Despite the notable differences in their choice of literary genres and in their conceptualization of what constitutes "orthodoxy," they seem to be shaped by much the same cultural context and to be familiar with much the same repertoire of received traditions – and, moreover, to redeploy a very similar selection of such received traditions for very similar aims.[44]

In integrating the genealogy of pre-Christian error into the history of Christian "heresy," moreover, both the *Panarion* and the *Homilies* depart from earlier heresiological tradition.[45] In each their own ways, they assert a radical continuity in religious deviance before and after the birth of Jesus. Blurring the lines between apology and heresiology, both label certain pre-/non-Christian traditions as

---

formation from Second Temple Literature through Judaism and Christianity in Late Antiquity, ed. Menahem Kister et al. (STDJ 113; Leiden: Brill, 2015), 306–21.

[42] Of course, there are differences too. The *Homilies'* account is distinguished by its emphasis on the role of demons in these developments and by its inclusion of a broader variety of non-Christian traditions, such as Persian fire-worship. In addition, it outlines the conflict between true and false worship, always and everywhere, as a practical contrast between health and disease – a trope that may have some connection with the common metaphor of "heresy" as poison to which "heresiology" is antidote (e. g., as evident in Epiphanius' choice of the title *Panarion* [medicine box] for his work, on which see Vallée, *Study in Anti-Gnostic Polemics*, 66–67), even as it moves well beyond it.

[43] E. g., *Jubilees*, Josephus, Justin Martyr, Julius Africanus. See further Reed, "Retelling Biblical Retellings"; William A. Adler, "The Origins of the Proto-Heresies: Fragments from a Chronicle in the First Book of Epiphanius's *Panarion*," *JTS* 41 (1990): 472–501.

[44] In other words: if Epiphanius knows of a source similar or related to the Pseudo-Clementine *Grundschrift*, it may be in part because he also knows many other sources that were also known and available to those who were reworking these materials, roughly at the same time, in neighboring Syria.

[45] The innovation of "firmly rejecting the claim that heresy began only in the apostolic age or with the Greek philosophers" is similarly emphasized, with reference to Epiphanius, by Berzon, *Classifying Christians*, 131.

"heresy."[46] What Todd Berzon notes of the power of this move for Epiphanius may apply for the *Homilies* as well:

Epiphanius articulates his vision of the world by creating a master narrative in which the history of the world and sectarian division become manifestations of a single intellectual genealogy of ethnogenic innovation. By beginning in the pre-Christian past (or the past that was not yet *manifestly* Christian), Epiphanius traces the history of heresy from Adam down to his own day ... In the process he subsumes the history of the world under a history of religion and religious deviation ... The past, then, is not some long-forgotten relic but a continued lived struggle between the truth of Christianity and the falsity of her protean opponents.[47]

For Epiphanius, the guiding principle for this move is the assertion that "in Christ Jesus there is neither Barbarian, Scythian, Greek, nor Jew" (*Pan.* 1.1.9; cf. Col 3:11; Gal 3:28) – a Pauline saying that he interprets in doubly historiographical and heresiological terms. He thus puts Barbarism, Scythianism, Hellenism, and Judaism at the historical roots of "heresy" (*Pan.* 1–20),[48] outlining their respective developments and tracing their links to later Christian sects (e. g., tracing the Ebionites to Judaism; *Pan.* 30). When this principle is put in practice in the *Panarion*, Hellenism and Judaism loom large (esp. 8.2.2), while Barbarianism and Scythianism become relegated primarily to primeval times. Interestingly, however, Samaritanism is here appended to the Pauline list, as a "heretical" offshoot of Judaism that bears its own branch of "heretical" progeny (*Pan.* 9–13). As a result, Epiphanius is able to present the very first Christian "heresy" – the Simonianism founded by the Samaritan Simon Magus – as a direct outgrowth of the most poisonous "heretical" product of an already "heretical" Judaism (*Pan.* 21).

The *Homilies* also treat pre-Christian traditions as "heresy," but they do so according to a different principle. This is the Rule of Syzygy (esp. 2.15–18; 3.59),[49] a concept both central and distinctive to the *Homilies*.[50] Consistent with

---

[46] For instance, both treat Greek philosophy as a natural extension of the early evolution of false worship that plays a role in the birth of "heresy." See *Pan.* 5–8 and discussion of *Homilies* below. On Epiphanius' conflation of Judaism and "heresy," see Averil Cameron, "Jews and Heretics – A Category Error?" in Becker and Reed, *The Ways that Never Parted*, 345–60.

[47] Berzon, *Classifying Christians*, 132.

[48] As Vallée notes, however, these traditions are deemed "heretical" inasmuch as they represent a departure or fragmentation of "the primeval truth ... transmitted orally, identical with the natural law which, in its turn, is identical with 'Christianity before Christianity' and ... became manifest with the advent of Christ"; Epiphanius deems Samaritanism, "gnostic" sects, and so on "heretical" in a more narrow sense as well; *Study in Anti-Gnostic Polemics*, 77–78.

[49] In light of the polemics against astrology in the Pseudo-Clementines (on which see Jones, *Pseudoclementina*, 114–37; Nicole Kelley, "Astrology in the Pseudo-Clementine *Recognitions*," *Journal of Ecclesiastical History* 59 [2008]: 607–29; Kelley, *Knowledge and Religious Authority in the Pseudo-Clementines*, 82–134), it may be significant that "syzygy" is a technical astronomical term (see, e. g., Ptolemy, *Almagest* 5.1, 10).

[50] Although the *Recognitions* includes brief reference to ten "pairs" (*Rec.* 4.59, 61: Cain and Abel, giants and Noah, Pharaoh and Abraham, Philistines and Isaac, Esau and Jacob, magicians

the *Homilies'* overarching concern with apostolic succession and the transmission of true knowledge, this rule serves to explain the place of "heresy" with primary reference to the transmission of prophetic truth.

The *Homilies* speak of Jesus as the "True Prophet," at times depicting him as the latest in a line of prophets and at times suggesting that he is an avatar of a single True Prophet who has been sent to earth on multiple occasions (esp. 1.19; 2.5–12; 3.11–28).[51] In either case, what is stressed is that Jesus proclaims the same message as his predecessors – among whom, most notably, numbers Moses. Likewise, its theory of the origins of error draws on a mirrored concept of succession and stresses the radical continuity between pre-Christian and Christian "heresy." Within the *Homilies'* salvation history, God-sent prophets never come alone. Rather, each is preceded by a false counterpart. To each prophet is paired a prophetic pretender, such that the history of salvation always runs parallel to the history of religious error. The result dovetails with a development that Gerard Vallée notes as characteristic of Christian heresiology in the fourth century: "the tradition of heresy now forms a counterpart to the history of salvation since the beginning of mankind."[52]

Within the *Homilies*, Peter's first explanation of the Rule of Syzygy (2.15–18) follows directly from a discourse on the True Prophet (2.5–14). The history of religious error is defined as a continuous line of false "female" prophecy, belonging this world, which runs alongside the continuous line of true "male" prophecy, which belongs to – and points towards – the World to Come (2.15; 3.23–27).[53] This dualistic system is attributed to the one true God,[54] who grants the means

---

and Moses, "the tempter" and Jesus, Simon and Peter, "all nations and he who shall be sent to sow the word among the nations," Antichrist and Christ), this concept is nowhere as developed as it is in the *Homilies* – let alone presented as a cosmic principle.

[51] For a general outline of the Pseudo-Clementine concept of the "True Prophet," see L. Cerfaux, "Le vrai prophète des Clémentines," *RSR* 18 (1928): 143–63. On the related yet distinctive depiction of the "True Prophet" in the *Recognitions* (which, e. g., seems to place more stress on Jesus' singularity), see Kelley, *Knowledge and Religious Authority in the Pseudo-Clementines*, 135–78.

[52] Vallée, *A Study in Anti-Gnostic Polemics*, 71.

[53] *Hom.* 2.15: "Since the present world is female, as a mother bringing forth the souls of her children, but the World to Come is male, as a father receiving his children from their mother, therefore into this world there come a succession of prophets, as being sons of the World to Come and having knowledge of men."

[54] Consistent with the extreme emphasis on monotheism throughout the *Homilies* (esp. 16–19; also 2.42–46; 3.30–59), the oneness of the God from which this dualism springs is explicitly asserted in *Hom.* 2.15: "Hence God, teaching men with respect to the truth of existing things, being Himself one, has distinguished all principles into pairs and opposites – He He Himself being one and sole God from the beginning, having made heaven and earth, day and night, light and fire, sun and moon, life and death. But humankind alone amongst these He made self-controlling, fit to be either righteous or unrighteous. To him also He has exchanged the image of Syzygies, placing before him small things first and great ones afterwards, such as the world and eternity."

to learn truth with one hand, but also gives error with the other, as a means of testing faith and teaching discernment.

The knowledge of this "prophetic rule" is thus depicted as epistemologically and soteriologically critical: "if men in God-fearing had understood this mystery, they would never have gone astray, but even now they would know that Simon, who now enthralls all men, is a fellow-worker of error and deceit" (*Hom.* 2.15). It is in private teachings to Clement and other close companions that Peter reveals the working of this rule:

Now, the doctrine of the prophetic rule (ὁ δὲ λόγος τοῦ προφητικοῦ κανόνος) is as follows: as in the beginning God, who is one, like a right hand and a left, made the heavens first and then the earth, so also he constituted all the syzygies (τὰς συζυγίας) in order ….

Therefore from Adam who was made after the image of God, there sprang first the unrighteous Cain and then the righteous Abel (see also *Hom.* 3.18–26; *Rec.* 3.61). Again, from him who amongst you is called Deucalion [i.e., Noah], two forms of spirits were sent forth, the impure and the pure, first the black raven and then the white dove. From Abraham also, the patriarchs of our nation sprang, two first: Ishmael first, then Isaac, who was blessed of God. And from Isaac himself, likewise, there were again two: Esau the profane, and Jacob the pious. So too, first in birth, as the firstborn in the world, was the high priest Aaron,[55] then the lawgiver Moses.

Similarly, the syzygy for Elijah, which was supposed to have come, has been willingly put off to another time, having determined to enjoy it conveniently hereafter. Therefore, also, he who was among those "born of woman" (Matt 11:11) came first [i.e., John the Baptist],[56] then he who was among the sons of men [i.e., Jesus] came second. (*Hom.* 2.16–17)

Peter then goes on explicitly to identify Simon and himself as one pair of rivals in this long doubled chain:

It is possible, following this order (τῇ τάξει), to perceive to which Simon belongs, who came before me to the nations/Gentiles (ὁ πρὸ ἐμοῦ εἰς τὰ ἔθνη πρῶτος ἐλθών), and to which I belong – I who have come after him and have come in on him as light on darkness, as knowledge on ignorance, as healing on disease. (*Hom.* 2.17)

Just as their rivalry is set against historical background, so it is also placed in eschatological context:

Thus, as the True Prophet has told us, a false Gospel must first come from some certain deceiver (πρῶτον ψευδὲς δεῖ ἐλθεῖν εὐαγγέλιον).[57] Then, likewise, after the removal of the

---

[55] The inclusion of Aaron in the evil line may be related to the polemic against sacrifice that pervades the Pseudo-Clementines. See, most recently, Nicole Kelley, "Pseudo-Clementine Polemics against Sacrifice: A Window onto Religious Life in the Fourth Century?," in Piovanelli and Burke, *Rediscovering the Apocryphal Continent*, 391–400.

[56] I.e., the syzygetical counterpart for Elijah is Jesus, following the common equation of Elijah with John the Baptist (Matt 11:14; 17:10–13; Luke 1:17). Notably, the *Homilies* hold a very negative view of John the Baptist, even depicting Simon Magus as one of his disciples (*Hom.* 2.23). Compare the depiction of John and his followers in *Rec.* 1.54.

[57] This statement is sometimes read as a veiled reference to Paul; see e.g., Lüdemann, *Opposition to Paul in Jewish Christianity*, 190.

Holy Place (μετὰ καθαίρεσιν τοῦ ἁγίου τόπου; i.e., the Temple), the true Gospel must be secretly sent abroad (εὐαγγέλιον ἀληθὲς κρύφα διαπεμφθῆναι) for the rectification of the heresies that shall be (εἰς ἐπανόρθωσιν τῶν ἐσομένων αἱρέσεων). After this, also, towards the End, the Antichrist must first come, and then our Jesus must be revealed to be indeed the Christ. After this, once the eternal light has sprung up, all the things of darkness must disappear. (*Hom.* 2.17)

That Simon and Peter are both sent to the Gentiles and compete for their souls is made further clear in *Hom.* 2.33–34. This passage uses Peter to describe his pairing with Simon in a manner consistent with the twofold salvation history outlined elsewhere in the *Homilies* (esp. 8–11), whereby Moses first came to the Jews and Jesus then to the Gentiles, each bearing the same prophetic message.[58] Peter begins with a restatement of the Rule of Syzygy:

You must perceive, brethren, the truth of the Rule of Syzygy (τῆς συζυγίας κανόνος), from which he who departs not cannot be misled. For since, as we have said, we see all things in pairs and opposites – and as the night is first and then the day; and first ignorance, then knowledge; first disease, then healing – so the things of error come first into our life, then truth supervenes, like the physician upon the disease. (*Hom.* 2.33)

He then explains its relevance first to the history of Israel, and then to the nations:

Therefore straightway, when our God-loved nation (τοῦ θεοφιλοῦς ἡμῶν ἔθνους; i.e., Israel) was about to be ransomed from the oppression of the Egyptians [i.e., during the Exodus], first diseases were produced by means of the rod turned into a serpent, which was given to Aaron, and then remedies were brought by the prayers of Moses.

Now also – when the Gentiles are about to be ransomed from religious service towards idols (καὶ νῦν δὲ τῶν ἐθνῶν μελλόντων ἀπὸ τῆς κατὰ τὰ εἴδωλα λυτροῦσθαι θρησκείας) – wickedness, which reigns over them, has by anticipation sent forth her ally like another serpent: this Simon whom you see, who works wonders (θαυμάσια) to astonish and deceive, not signs (σημεῖα) of healing to convert and save. (*Hom.* 2.33)

Likewise, in *Hom.* 3.59, the narrative setting of Peter's private teachings to his companions is used to make further explicit that the travels and public debates described in the novel should be understood in terms of Peter's participation in the continuing battle to counter polytheistic and "heretical" error with monotheistic and prophetic truth:

While I am going forth to the nations that say that there are many gods (εἰς τὰ ἔθνη τὰ πολλοὺς θεοὺς λέγοντα) – to teach and to preach that the God who made heaven and earth and all things that are in them is one (κηρύξαι καὶ διδάξαι ὅτι εἷς ἐστιν ὁ θεός, ὃς οὐρανὸν ἔκτισε καὶ γῆν καὶ τὰ ἐν αὐτοῖς πάντα), such that they are able to love Him and be saved – evil has anticipated me, and by the very Rule of Syzygy has sent Simon before me, in order that these men, even if they should cease from saying that there are many gods by disowning those that are called [gods] on earth, may think that there are many gods in

---

[58] For discussion of this salvation history and its importance for understanding of the "Jewish-Christianity" of the Pseudo-Clementines, see Chapter One in this volume.

heaven (ἐν οὐρανῷ πολλοὺς θεοὺς), so that, not feeling the excellence of the monarchy (τῆς μοναρχίας), they may perish with eternal punishment.

What is most dreadful, since true doctrine (ἀληθὴς λόγος) has incomparable power, is that he forestalls me with slanders and persuades them to this, not even at first to receive me, lest he who is the slanderer is convicted of being himself in reality a devil, and the true doctrine be received and believed. Therefore I must quickly catch him up, lest the false accusation, through gaining time, wholly get hold of all people! (*Hom.* 3.59; cf. *Rec.* 3.65)

As noted above, the Rule of Syzygy also serves as an epistemological function: it is emphasized that in the future (i.e., the novel's future = the reader's present) those who know the rule will be able to recognize Simon's successors for who and what they really are, even despite what they might appear to be (*Hom.* 16.21). This concern for the gap between reality and appearance is consistent with the epistemology expressed elsewhere in the *Homilies*, both by means of Clement's first-person accounts of his quest for truth (1.1–7) and by means of Peter's teachings about the True Prophet as the sole guarantor of truth (2.5–12). In each case, the message is the same: truth and falsehood appear similar and can each be made to sound persuasive, and the difference can only be identified by attention to their messengers and the lines of transmission in which they stand. The same message is also communicated through the narrative into which these teachings have been embedded. When read through the Rule of Syzygy, for instance, the combination of commonality and contrast in the characters of Peter and Simon makes perfect sense: the two appear similar *precisely because* they are paired opposites and syzygetical counterparts.[59]

In fact, much of the overarching narrative of the novel can also be read as a narrative embodiment and illustration of the Rule of Syzygy. Most striking in this regard is its conclusion, which finds Clement finally reunited with his long-lost family, only to have his father magically blighted with Simon's face (*Hom.* 20.12). Simon has wrought this magic in order to make a quick escape from his increasingly failed attempts to debate Peter (*Hom.* 20.14–16). The result, however, is a tragic splintering of the family that had been gradually yet progressively reunited concurrent with Clement's conversion and travels with Peter. The apostle, however, is readily able to recognize the true face of Clement's father even despite the magical power of Simon's spells (*Hom.* 20.12). Furthermore, in the end, the apostle even uses the tricks of "heresy" to spread the truth: he prompts Simon's doppelganger to proclaim publicly his errors in a surprising twist that serves to resolve the long series of debates firmly and finally in Peter's favor (*Hom.* 20.18–23).

Nevertheless, Peter's exposition of the Rule of Syzygy makes clear that this is only one in a series of battles between truth and error. In this sense, the rule represents the *Homilies'* distinctive articulation of the notion of twin lines of

---

[59] Côté, *Thème de l'opposition*, 29–32.

apostolic and "heretical" succession – a concern that fits with well within a fourth-century context marked by Christian efforts to delineate "orthodoxy" from "heresy" by means of public debates no less than treatises and councils. Epiphanius emphasizes the continuity between pre-Christian and Christian error, and in the process – as Berzon notes – he "conceptualizes the present age as an effort to reclaim humanity's dormant Adamic past."[60] The *Homilies* similarly frame apostolic truth as a return to the primordial. Here, however, this return is also presented in terms of a positive understanding of Jews and Judaism. Jesus is not the first teacher of truth, nor is Simon the first "heretic." Both are part of a sweeping pattern that begins in the primeval age and prominently features Moses and his Jewish heirs as a positive paradigms for the battle against "heresy" now fought also by Peter and other true followers of Jesus.

This treatment of Judaism marks the most striking point of difference between Epiphanius and the *Homilies*. Whereas Epiphanius treats Judaism as "heresy," the *Homilies* does quite the opposite: Judaism is here presented as paradigmatic of the prophetic truth that discerns and combats the false prophecy of "heretics" in every age. It is largely due to this difference that its authors/redactors draw the lines between "orthodoxy" and "heresy" in a manner quite distinct from what we find in Epiphanius and what we are accustomed to treating as representative of Christianity in Late Antiquity. To the degree that this distinctiveness might be deemed "Jewish-Christian," however, it also points us to the possibility that the heresiology of the *Homilies* was shaped by some familiarity or engagement with Judaism in Late Antiquity as well. To explore this possibility, it may be helpful first to look more closely at its representation of Hellenism and Samaritanism in relation to Judaism.

Hellenism and Samaritanism as "Heretical" Paradigms

As we have seen, the *Homilies* are similar to Epiphanius' *Panarion* in their expansion of the history of "heresy" to include pre-Christian traditions, in general, and in their treatment of Hellenism and Samaritanism, more specifically. With respect to the former, this similarity even includes a sharp denigration of Greek philosophy as a source of Christian truth.

As Dominique Côté has demonstrated, the *Homilies* mount an extended polemic against Greek philosophy and *paideia*.[61] Whereas polytheism is here presented as ignorance, philosophy – like "heresy" – is framed as error. Simon Magus, for instance, is here closely associated with Hellenism, in what appears

---

[60] Berzon, *Classifying Christians*, 132.
[61] See, most recently: Côté, "Rhetoric and Jewish-Christianity."

to be a Pseudo-Clementine innovation on the Simon Magus tradition.[62] Simon's followers, moreover, are a combination of philosophers and astrologers.[63]

The comparison with Epiphanius makes clear that the authors/redactors of the *Homilies* are hardly alone in rejecting philosophy even in a late antique age in which some Christians were taking more positive approaches to the challenge of negotiating Greek *paideia* and Christian piety. In *Pan.* 5–8, for instance, Epiphanius describes ancient Greek philosophical schools as "heresies," in an interesting twist on the original meaning of the Greek term *hairesis*. Although this connection has some precedent (e. g., Ireneaus, *Adv. haer.* 2.14), Epiphanius takes it far further, as Vallée has noted: "Not only is philosophy thereby rejected, but also all links between Christian thought and the ancient philosophical tradition."[64]

What Vallée notes of Epiphanius could be said of the *Homilies* as well. That the salvation of "pagans" requires the severing of links to Greek philosophy is here communicated, for example, through the novel's depiction of Clement. It is here stressed that Clement is a wellborn elite Roman with a proper Greek education (*Hom.* 1.3; 4.7). The novel begins with his realization of the empty sophistry of philosophy and its inability to address ultimate truths such as the fate of the soul (1.1–4). It is because of his resultant quest for truth that he discovers a different path, which leads him to Jewish monotheism (4.7–8, 22, 24; 5.28) and the True Prophet Jesus (1.6–22). Thereafter, Clement uses his education precisely to expose the vanity of Greek philosophy. In *Hom.* 1.9–12, Clement uses his rhetorical skills to intervene in a debate between Barnabas and a group of Alexandrian philosophers. Later, in *Homilies* 4–6, he takes on the Alexandrian grammarian Appion, demonizing Greek *paideia* and arguing against the Greek philosophical defense of "pagan" mythology. It is for this same reason, moreover, that the Jewish proselyte Justa is said to have ensured a proper Greek education for her adopted sons Aquila and Nicetas – that is, "in order that, disputing with the other nations, we might be able to convince them of their error," pursuing "an accurate study of the doctrine of the philosophers … in order that we might be better able to refute them" (13.7).

What is distinctive in the *Homilies* is the addition of anti-Judaism to the defining marks of religious error, in general, and to the "heresy" of Hellenism, more specifically. Throughout the novel, the denunciation of Hellenism is coupled with the defense of Judaism against anti-Judaism. When Clement argues

---

[62] Côté, *Thème de l'opposition*, 195–96. On the precedent in Hippolytus' association of Simon with Greek philosophy, see *Ref.* 6.7–20 and discussion in Jaap Mansfeld, *Heresiography in Context: Hippolytus' Elenchos as a Source for Greek Philosophy* (Philosophia Antiqua 56; Leiden: Brill, 1992), 172–77.

[63] E. g., Appion is an Alexandrian grammarian, Annubion an astrologer, and Athenodorus an Athenian Epicurean (*Hom.* 4.6).

[64] Vallée, *Study in Anti-Gnostic Polemics*, 81.

against Appion, for instance, he does so not just to expose the vanity of Greek philosophy but also to expose the irrational anti-Judaism behind the Egyptian grammarian's learned veneer.[65] It is this anti-Judaism, moreover, that is revealed to be the real reason for his association with the Samaritan Simon (*Hom.* 5.1–29). Hellenism and "heresy" are thus associated with anti-Judaism, no less than with Greek philosophy and *paideia*. Rather than present Judaism and Samaritanism as multiple buds on a single "heretical" branch, moreover, the two are contrasted in a manner exemplary of the ongoing battle between "orthodoxy" and "heresy" throughout human history.

This treatment of Judaism fits well within the *Homilies* as a whole, wherein the battle between "orthodoxy" and "heresy" is presented as an extension of the conflict between monotheism and polytheism, in general, and Judaism and Hellenism, in particular. In key passages, Peter describes Jesus, himself, and his followers as taking up the fight against polytheism first – and still – fought by Moses and the Jews (*Hom.* 2.33; 8.5–7; 11.7–16; 16.14). Just as God sought to free the Jews from polytheism by means of the Exodus from Egypt, working through Moses, so He now seeks to free Gentiles from the same error, working through Jesus. Following the Exodus, Aaron's idolatry and illness-inducing magic threatened the Jews' return to true monotheism but was ultimately thwarted by Moses' prayer and piety. Likewise, Simon's lies and magic now threaten Peter's efforts to gather the Gentiles to monotheistic piety and purity. Peter, however, assures his listeners that he, continuing the tradition of Jesus, will prevail (*Hom.* 2.33).

The result is an unusually positive assessment of the place of Judaism in Christian salvation history. Just as anti-Judaism here becomes a mark of "heresy," so Judaism is associated with the prophetic truth that fights against error in every age. This is consistent with the positive valuation of Judaism throughout this version of the Pseudo-Clementine novel: Jewish belief and practice are here cited as exemplary of the proper piety and worship to which Gentiles should also strive (*Hom.* 4.13; 7.4; 9.16; 11.28; 16.14). Nor is this role depicted as superseded with the coming of Jesus. Rather, Jews are held up in the *Homilies* as models for the proper belief and practice to which Gentile followers of Jesus should also strive.

Notably, this depiction of Jews and Judaism is also consistent with the positive prophetic component of the Rule of Syzygy discussed above. Central to the articulation of this rule is the positing of a series of past prophets proclaiming the same truth, including both Moses and Jesus. In the eighth *Homily*, the identity of their teachings is made explicit, even as it is emphasized that Moses was sent to the Jews and Jesus to the Gentiles. Accordingly, the *Homilies* depicts prophetic truth as transmitted through multiple parallel lines, including to a line of Jewish

---

[65] See the discussion of *Homilies* 4–6 in Chapter Four in this volume.

succession from the time of Moses to the Pharisees of Clement's time.[66] This Mosaic/Pharisaic line of succession is even adduced as a precedent for apostolic succession through Peter, which is here presented as its Gentile counterpart. And, perhaps most strikingly, neither line of succession is ever said to negate the other: Moses' teachings are faithfully kept by the Pharisees, who sit on his seat (11.29), just as Peter sits on the seat of Jesus, as will bishops after him (3.70).

Above, we noted how the Rule of Syzygy thus resonates with shifts in Christian heresiology in Late Antiquity, paralleling Epiphanius' expansion of the early Christian discourse about "heresy" to include the entire history of humankind. Perhaps no less notable, however, are the resonances with Rabbinic literature. The emphasis on the continuity of succession in the Jewish transmission of knowledge from Moses to the Pharisees departs strikingly from the early and late antique Christian denigration of the Pharisees.[67] Yet it results in a vision of the past that coheres strikingly with Rabbinic claims to authority, as Albert Baumgarten has observed.[68] To his observation, we might add that the presumed connection of Pharisees with Rabbis is predicated on a distinctively late antique development in Rabbinic representations of the past, absent from the Mishnah but prominent in the Talmud Bavli.[69] So too with the framing of the Mosaic knowledge that the Sages possess. In the *Homilies*, Peter teaches that "the Law of God was given by Moses, *without writing*, to seventy wise men, to be handed down, so that the government might be carried on by succession" (3.47) – seemingly reflecting some knowledge of distinctively Rabbinic ideas about the Oral Torah that developed in the third and fourth centuries.[70] Reminiscent of the

---

[66] On the theme of succession, see Chapter Six in this volume, and on the depiction of Pharisees, see Chapter Nine.

[67] Compare Matt 23:2, however, and see the more detailed discussion of Pharisees in Chapter Nine in this volume.

[68] Albert I. Baumgarten, "Literary Evidence for Jewish Christianity in the Galilee," in *The Galilee in Late Antiquity*, ed. Lee I. Levine (New York: JTSA, 1992), 42–43.

[69] Martin Jaffee, for instance, has shown that "the earliest rabbinic identification of Pharisees and Sages can be assigned to a source cited no earlier than fourth century CE Pumbedita (*b. Qiddushin* 66a), whereas a classical early portrayal of Pharisaic-Sadducean conflict (*m. Yadaim* 4:6–7) shows only that some elements of Pharisaic legal traditions were embraced by the Mishnaic editors. But neither the Tannaitic foundation of B. Qiddushin nor M. Yadaim 4:6–7 knows anything about the exclusively oral transmission of Pharisaic interpretative tradition"; *Torah in the Mouth: Writing and Oral Tradition in Palestinian Judaism, 200 BCE–400 CE* (Oxford: Oxford University Press, 2001), 57. "On the basis of rabbinic sources," he further stresses, "it is impossible to show that the Sages had a longstanding historical understanding of their own roots in ancient Pharisaic communities .... The absence of such memories in the Mishnah and Tosefta suggests that it was simply not a significant element in the larger rabbinic image of the past ... such connections begin to be cultivated in the Tannaitic and Amoraic traditions preserved in the Babylonian Talmud" (59–60).

[70] See esp. Jaffee, *Torah in the Mouth*, for the evidence that "the mature rabbinic conception of Torah in Mouth ... took shape among the Galilean Amoraim of the third and fourth centuries" (102). Notably, for our purposes, this connection remains significant whether or not Rabbinic succession from Moses is "the conceptual foundation upon which rabbinic Judaism rests,

teachings in *Sifre Devarim* that "two Torahs were given to Israel, one by mouth and one by script" (par. 351, *ad* Deut 33:10) and the further explication in Sifra that "the Torah was given with all its halakhot, details, and explanations through Moses on Mount Sinai" (Behuqotai, par. 8:12, *ad* Lev 26:46),[71] Peter here teaches that "the prophet Moses, by the order of God, gave (παραδεδωκότος) the Law with the explanations (σὺν ταῖς ἐπιλύσεσιν) to certain chosen men," distinguishing this succession of teachings from "the Written Law (γραφεὶς ὁ νόμος)" (*Hom.* 2.38).

Just as the *Homilies'* parallels with Christian heresiology dovetail with late antique innovations and expressions found in Epiphanius, so its parallels to Jewish traditions cluster in Late Antiquity as well. Following modern theological narratives about "Jewish-Christianity" as apostolic relic, one might expect to find parallels to the Pseudo-Clementines primarily in those biblical or Second Temple Jewish sources that constitute the Jewish cultural context for Christian Origins. The treatment of Moses, the Pharisees, and the Jewish people in the *Homilies*, however, dovetails instead with the distinctively post-70 elements of the Rabbinic tradition and especially with Rabbinic ideologies developed in the third and fourth centuries CE. Above, we noted how the *Homilies* seems shaped by much the same cultural milieu and reservoir of received traditions that shape the work of Epiphanius in fourth-century Roman Palestine. If such parallels point to the role of its fourth-century Syrian authors/redactors in shaping the distinctive heresiology of this version of the Pseudo-Clementine novel, so they also ground the plausibility of some familiarity or engagement with Rabbinic traditions cultivated in Roman Palestine around the same time.

If so, we might further ask: might the heresiology of the *Homilies* have any resonance with the Rabbinic discourse about *minut*? Below, I shall explore this possibility in relation to the narrativization of polemics in the *Homilies*, which – I shall suggest – may owe as much to the subgenre of Rabbinic disputation tales as to the genre of the Greek novel. First, however, I would like to touch upon its

---

and its ideological manifesto" – a long-standing scholarly truism recently contested by Adiel Schremer, "*Avot* Reconsidered: Rethinking Rabbinic Judaism," *JQR* 105 (2015): 287–311, quote at p. 310. Notably, Schremer's suggestion of inner-Jewish debate over such issues fits better with the sense that we get from the Pseudo-Clementines of a larger field of contestation over such issues of exegesis, revelation, and authority. Schremer argues that "the ideological claim that rabbinic halakhah is of Sinaitic origin and therefore has a divine status is defensive in its nature. It attempts to 'guard' rabbinic teaching from a polemical attack, which purports to debunk its authority by emphasizing its human origin" (p. 310); if this defensiveness is inner-Jewish in *Avot*, it may be similar but externally oriented in the *Homilies*, especially in light on its above-noted concern to counter "pagan," "heretical," and Samaritan anti-Judaism.

[71] For analysis of these two Rabbinic passages in their own contexts, see Jaffee, *Torah in the Mouth*, 91. Interestingly, for our purposes, Jaffee places the development of these ideas in interaction with, and reaction to, "the pedagogic assumptions of nonrabbinic, Greco-Roman predecessors and contemporaries" (p. 152).

treatment of Samaritanism.[72] Above, we have seen how the *Homilies'* treatment of Hellenism is akin to shifting ideas about its association with "heresy" among late antique Christians like Epiphanius and how the *Panarion*, in particular, also provides some precedent for the association of Samaritanism with pre-Christian "heresy." What is interesting about the latter, however, is that it also resonates with concurrent developments in Rabbinic heresiology, especially as found in the Tosefta and Talmud Yerushalmi.

The association of Samaritanism with Simon follows, in part, from New Testament and early Christian traditions. He is associated with the region of Samaria already in Acts 8, and in the second century Justin Martyr, who was himself raised as a "pagan" in Samaria, goes on to specify Gitta as Simon's hometown (*1 Apol.* 26). It is not until the Pseudo-Clementines, however, that Simon's association with the region of Samaria takes on a special heresiological importance in relation to what we would call Samaritanism. This association, moreover, is especially marked in the *Homilies*. Whereas the *Recognitions* variously associates Simon with Sadducees and Samaritans (*Rec.* 1.54, 2.7), Simon's Samaritanism is stable throughout the *Homilies*, and it is articulated in sharper contrast to the Jewish/Judaean affiliation of Jesus and Peter. In both the *Homilies* and *Recognitions*, Simon is first introduced in a manner that alludes to this contrast: Clement hears that "Peter, who was the most esteemed disciple of the man who had appeared in Judaea and who had done signs and wonders [i.e., Jesus], was going to have a verbal controversy next day with Simon, a Samaritan of Gitthi" (*Hom.* 1.15 ≈ *Rec.* 1.12). The *Homilies*, however, go beyond the implied evaluative geography. Not only does it add Simon's rejection of Jerusalem for Mount Gerizim to their shared material about his biography (*Hom.* 2.22; cf. *Hom.* 2.22–26 ≈ *Rec.* 2.7–15), but consistent with the association of "heresy" and anti-Judaism noted above, this version of the novel also describes Simon as "a Samaritan and a hater of the Jews," who teaches anti-Judaism to non-Jews like Appion (*Hom.* 5.2). It is precisely the *Homilies'* uniquely positive representation of Judaism, in other words, that seems to prompt its more negative depiction of Samaritanism. Here, Simon's association with Samaria is far from incidental but becomes a key element in his depiction as a false prophet and "heretic" standing in opposition to the Jewish apostle Peter.

Interestingly, this emphasis on the contrastive character of the relationship between Jews and Samaritans in the *Homilies* also finds some parallel in Rabbinic literature – and especially in late antique traditions. Lawrence Schiffman has pointed to a notable shift from Tannaitic treatments of Samaritans (Heb. *kutim*) as a group potentially within Israel or definitive of its edges, and toward

---

[72] The below discussion is indebted to Matthew Chalmers' in-progress dissertation research on the late antique representation of Samaritans.

Amoraic depictions of Samaritans as increasingly outside of Israel.[73] "While the Mishnah contrasted Samaritans with non-Jews," as Moshe Lavee similarly notes, "the Talmud contrasted them with Jews."[74] So too with the *Homilies*, which seems most akin to what Lavee terms as the "affiliation view" emergent in the Talmud Yerushalmi whereby the dispute over whether the Samaritan is "like a Jew/a non-Jew" is no longer a matter of classification for the sake of a limited legal context, as in the Tosefta, but becomes a generalization of identity within a binary system in which "a person should be either a Jew or a Gentile, and there is no place for marginal groups located in a kind of no man's land in between the social boundaries of these two groups."[75] So too within the Pseudo-Clementine tradition: whereas earlier materials preserved in the *Recognitions* depict Samaritans as Jewish sectarians in a sense akin to Sadducees (*Rec.* 1.54.4–5, 1.57.1), the *Homilies* draw a stark contrast and articulate a sharply binary system that pits the true prophetic messages shared by Judaism and Christianity, on the one side, against the false prophecy of Hellenism, "heresy," and Samaritanism, on the other.

In this sense, the Rabbinic emphasis on Samaritan alterity may help further to flesh out the discursive space that shaped the heresiology of the *Homilies*. And the converse may be true as well. Scholars, for instance, continue to debate the degree that the mishnaic neologism *minut* marks the emergence of a Rabbinic heresiology that can be likened to its much-discussed Christian counterparts in Justin and Irenaeus.[76] Perhaps more striking, however, are the parallels with the discourses of difference in the Pseudo-Clementine *Homilies*, whereby practices of classification go well beyond the bounds that we might see as defining "a religion," to span a global scope across space and time, and do so through sweepingly dichotomous lines, rather than intricately detailed differentiations of varieties of error in the writings of authors like Irenaeus and Epiphanius.

This move toward globalized binaries is clear from the case of Samaritans, who play an important role both within these Jewish and "Jewish-Christian" discourses of difference – initially functioning in taxonomically productive terms

---

[73] This shift is mapped in Lawrence H. Schiffman, "The Samaritans in Tannaitic Halakhah," *JQR* 75 (1985): 323–50; Schiffman, "The Samaritans in Amoraic Halakhah," in *Shoshannat Yaakov: Jewish and Iranian Studies in Honor of Yaakov Elman*, ed. Shai Secunda and Steven Fine (Brill Reference Library of Judaism 35; Leiden: Brill, 2012), 371–89.

[74] Moshe Lavee, "The Samaritan May be Included: Another Look at the Samaritan in Talmudic Literature," in *Samaritans: Past and Present*, ed. Menachem Mor and Friedrich V. Reiterer (Studia Samaritana 5; Berlin: de Gruyter, 2010), 147–74, quote at p. 150.

[75] Lavee, "The Samaritan may be included," 154–59, quote at p. 154.

[76] See esp. Alain Le Boulluec, *La notion d'hérésie dans la literature grecque IIe–IIIe siècles* (2 vols.; Paris: Études augustiniennes, 1985), 1:90; Daniel Boyarin, *Border Lines: The Partition of Judaeo-Christianity* (Divinations; Philadelphia: University of Pennsylvania Press, 2004); Boyarin, "Rethinking Jewish Christianity: An Argument for Dismantling a Dubious Category (to Which is Appended a Correction of My Border Lines)," *JQR* 99 (2009): 33–36; Naftali Cohn, "Heresiology in the Third-Century Mishnah," *HTR* 108 (2015): 508–29.

alongside other "Others" within Israel (e. g., Sadducees, *am ha-aretz*) and later assimilated into a binary classification system (i. e., Jews vs. Gentiles). And just as this dichotomous mode of classification is definitive of the *Homilies'* treatment of "pagan" traditions like Hellenism, so we might glimpse a parallel move in the Rabbinic trend, recently noted by Ishay Rosen-Zvi and Adi Ophir, towards "consolidating the binary division between the Jews and their 'others'" through "the stabilization of the Jew-goy distinction as a binary system" and "a systematic effort to eliminate various hybrid identities that existed in previous discourses and to locate them within one of these two categories."[77] At the very least, such parallels in these discourses of difference further point us to the potential value of expanding our late antique comparanda for the Pseudo-Clementines, not just to fourth-century Christian writings like the *Panarion*, but also to Rabbinic texts and traditions from around the same time.

Narrativized Polemics in the *Homilies* and Rabbinic Literature

Judaism is not the main concern of the authors/redactors, who seem preoccupied foremost with their polemics against "paganism" and "heresy." Nevertheless, as we have seen, the attitude towards Jews and Judaism in the *Homilies* is quite positive. Its authors/redactors present Christianity and Judaism as allies in the battle of truth against error. Together, the two make up the cause of "orthodoxy," which is defined primarily in terms of monotheism. On the other side are aligned Hellenism, "heresy," Samaritanism, and anti-Judaism. Far from functioning as a proto-"heresy," superseded past, or even a foil for self-definition, Judaism is here forerunner and ally of authentically apostolic Christianity. And, as we have seen, there are reasons to wonder whether this rather unique depiction relates to some awareness of Rabbinic or related Jews from the time of the *Homilies'* authors/redactors.[78]

We have seen how the treatment of religious error in the *Homilies* resonates with the content and concerns of late antique Christian heresiology as well as Rabbinic discourse of difference also distinctive to Late Antiquity. To extend the search for potentially profitable Jewish comparanda, I would like to turn now to consider the significance of the literary form of these materials in the *Homilies* – that is, its narrativization of heresiological and polemical tropes.

---

[77] Ishay Rosen-Zvi and Adi Ophir, "Paul and the Invention of the Gentiles," *JQR* 105 (2015): 1–41, esp. 3–13, quote at 1 and 12. I am less convinced by the Pauline portion of their argument. The example of Samaritans also suggests a slightly later shift than here argued.

[78] See Baumgarten, "Literary Evidence for Jewish Christianity"; A. Marmorstein, "Judaism and Christianity in the Middle of the Third Century," *HUCA* 10 (1935): 223–63; J. Bergman, "Les éléments juifs dans les Pseudo-Clémentines," *REJ* 46 (1903): 89–98. See further Chapter Nine in this volume.

The narrativity of this work is typically associated with its appropriation of the ancient Greek novel, and there are some early Christian precedents for the narrativization of polemics, particularly in the writings in the genre of dialogue.[79] I would like to suggest, however, that some formal parallels can be found also in Rabbinic literature. Most notable is the subgenre of disputation tales – that is: brief stories in which a Sage is approached in public by a "heretic" (*min*),[80] Samaritan, Gentile, philosopher, or Roman matron, who asks him a leading exegetical question. The questions typically concern cases where Scripture appears to say something that goes against Jewish/Rabbinic belief, and the Sage answers by refuting the exegesis, often (although not always) with another exegesis of the same passage.[81] Significantly, for our purposes, parallel examples cluster in Rabbinic texts that were redacted around the same time as the *Homilies* – and especially in *Bereshit Rabbah*, a midrashic compilation redacted in the early fifth century in Roman Palestine, concurrent with the compilation of the Talmud Yerushalmi. As with the *Homilies*, its redaction bears marks of a concern to answer and denigrate philosophical claims about the cosmos and Creation, in particular, and the midrashim therein include narratives recounting debates over biblical exegesis.[82]

Biblical exegesis is also central to the narrativized heresiology of the *Homilies*. In a manner reminiscent of Rabbinic tales of *minim*, the *Homilies* consistently depict Simon as arguing his points from Scripture. In *Hom.* 3.2, for instance, Peter is described as lamenting this very fact prior to their public debate in Caesarea:

Simon today is, as he arranged, prepared to come before everyone and to show from the Scriptures that He who made the heaven and the earth and all things in them is not the supreme God, but that there is another, unknown and supreme, as being in an unspeakable manner God of gods, and that he sent two gods, one of whom is he who made the world

---

[79] Interestingly, Christian narrativization of polemics seems especially marked in the *contra Iudaeos* tradition, consistent with the precedent set by Justin Martyr's *Dialogue with Trypho*.

[80] That some Rabbinic references to *minim* may refer to "Jewish-Christians" makes the parallels of form and content all the more striking, in my view, raising the possibility that influence may have been mediated, at least in part, by contacts in argumentative settings. On cases and places in which *minim* may refer to Christians, see R. Kalmin, "Christians and Heretics in Rabbinic Literature of Late Antiquity," *HTR* 87 (1994): 155–69.

[81] For more on this subgenre and Rabbinic traditions about *minim* more broadly, see Kalmin, "Christians and Heretics"; Naomi Janowitz, "Rabbis and their Opponents: The Construction of the 'Min' in Rabbinic Anecdotes," *JECS* 6 (1998): 449–62.

[82] Hans-Jürgen Becker, *Die grossen rabbinischen Sammelwerke Palastinas: Zur literarischen Genese von Talmud Yerushalmi und Midrash Bereshit Rabba* (TSAJ 70; Tübingen: Mohr Siebeck, 1999). On the antiphilosophical polemic that shaped its editorial arrangement of materials, see Peter Schäfer, "*Bereshit bara' 'elohim*: Zur Interpretation von Genesis 1,1 in der rabbinischen Literatur," *JSJ* 2 (1971): 161–66; Schäfer, "*Bereshit bara' 'elohim*: Bereshit Rabba, Parashah 1, Reconsidered," in *Empsychoi Logoi – Religious Innovations in Antiquity: Studies in Honor of Pieter Willem van der Horst*, ed. Alberdina Houtman, Albert de Jong, and Magda Misset-van de Weg (Leiden: Brill, 2008), 267–89.

(ὁ μὲν εἷς ἐστιν ὁ κόσμον κτίσας) and the other, he who gave the Law (ὁ δὲ ἕτερος ὁ τὸν νόμον δούς). These things he contrives to say so that he may dissipate the right faith (τὴν ὀρθὴν προεκλύσει πίστιν) of those who would worship the one and only God who made heaven and earth.

This characterization is later confirmed by Simon's own argument during this debate:

Why would you [i.e., Peter] lie, and deceive the unlearned multitude standing around you, persuading them that it is unlawful to think that there are gods and to call them so, when the Books that are current among the Jews (τῶν παρὰ Ἰουδαίοις δημοσίων βίβλων) say that there are many gods? Now I wish, in the presence of all, to discuss with you from these books the necessity of thinking that there are gods; first showing with respect to him whom you call God that he is not the supreme and omnipotent being inasmuch as he is without foreknowledge, imperfect, needy, not good, and underlying many and innumerable grievous passions. When this has been shown from the Scriptures, as I say, it follows that there is another [God], not written of (ἀπὸ τῶν γραφῶν), foreknowing, perfect, without want, good, removed froth all grievous passions. He whom you call the Creator (δημιουργόν) is subject to the opposite evils.

Therefore also Adam – the being made at first *after his likeness* – is created blind and is said not to have knowledge of good or evil and is found a transgressor and is driven out of Paradise and is punished with death. Similarly, He who made him, because He sees not in all places, says with reference to the overthrow of Sodom, *Come, and let us go down, and see whether they do according to their cry which comes to me; or if not, that I may know* (Gen 18:21). Thus He shows Himself to be ignorant. So too in His saying with respect to Adam, *Let us drive him out, lest he put forth his hand and touch the tree of life, and eat, and live forever* (Gen 3:22) – in saying *lest* He is ignorant; and in driving him out lest He should *eat and live forever*, He is also envious. Whereas it is written that *God repented that he had made humankind* (Gen 6:6), this implies both repentance and ignorance.[83] For this reflection is a view by which one, through ignorance, wishes to inquire into the result of the things that he wills, or it is the act of one repenting on account of the event not being according to his expectation. Whereas it is written *And the Lord smelled a scent of sweetness* (Gen 8:21), it is the part of one in need; and His being pleased with the fat of flesh is the part of one who is not good. His tempting, as it is written, *And God did tempt Abraham* (Gen 22:1) Is the part of one who is wicked and who is ignorant of the result of the experiment. (*Hom.* 3.38)

For the most part, the debates in the *Homilies* feature such lengthy discourses by Simon and Peter respectively. In some cases, however, we find briefer interchanges, in which the formal parallels with Rabbinic disputation tales are

---

[83] Cf. *Bereshit Rabbah* 27.4: "A certain Gentile asked R. Joshua b. Karhah: 'Do you not maintain that the Holy One, blessed be He, foresees the future?' 'Yes,' he replied. [The Gentile said:] 'But it is written, *And God repented that he had made humankind* (Gen 6:6)?' 'Has a son ever been born to you?' he inquired. 'Yes' was the answer. 'And what did you do?' 'I rejoiced and made all others rejoice,' he answered. 'Yet did you not know that he would eventually die?' 'Gladness at the time of gladness, and mourning at the time of mourning,' he [i.e., the Gentile] replied. 'So too with the Holy One, blessed be He' was his rejoinder."

especially clear. One particularly striking example can be found in the sixteenth *Homily*:

Simon said: "Since I see that you frequently speak of the God who created you, learn from me how you are impious even to him. For there are evidently two who created (οἱ πλάσαντες δύο φαίνονται), as Scripture says: *And God said, Let us make humankind in our image, after our likeness* (Gen 1:26). Now *Let us make* implies two or more – certainly not only one!"

Peter answered: "One is He who said to His Wisdom (εἷς ἐστιν ὁ τῇ αὐτοῦ σοφίᾳ εἰπών), *Let us make humankind*. But His Wisdom was that with which He Himself always rejoiced as with His own spirit (cf. Prov 8:30). It is united as soul to God, but it is extended by Him, as hand, fashioning the universe (cf. Prov 8:22–31).[84] On this account, also, one man was made and from him went forth also the female (cf. Gen 2:21–22)." (*Hom.* 16.11–12)

As in Rabbinic disputation tales, a "heretic" here cites an apparent inconsistency in Scripture, which must then be refuted, lest incorrect exegesis lead to incorrect beliefs.[85]

The topic of the contested beliefs is also notable. Particularly within *Bereshit Rabbah*, we find a number of disputation tales that assert the singularity and goodness of God as Creator. Just as the *Homilies'* depicts Simon as claiming "two who created," so the interpretation of Genesis 1:1 in *Bereshit Rabbah* 1.7 occasions fervent contestation of the idea that "two powers created the world":

Rabbi Isaac said … "No person can dispute and maintain that two powers gave the Torah or that two powers created the world [שתי רשויות בראו את העולם]. For 'And gods spoke [(pl.) וידברו אלהים]' is not written here, but *And God spoke* [(s.) וידבר אלהים; Exod 20:1]; 'In the beginning they created [(pl.) בראשית בראו]' is not written here, but *In the beginning He created* [(s.) בראשית ברא; Gen 1:1]."[86]

As is well known, classical Rabbinic literature is rife with references to those who "heretically" claim "two powers in heaven."[87] For our purposes, it also proves

---

[84] These same verses are cited in *Bereshit Rabbah* 1.1, with Wisdom interpreted as the Torah and said to have been consulted at Creation.

[85] As discussed below, the *Homilies* offers a solution to the problem of scriptural inconsistency that differs both from Rabbinic Jewish and from "orthodox" Christian approaches, namely the doctrine of false pericopes, as described by means of Peter's private conversations with Clement (*Hom.* 2.38–52; 3.4–6, 9–11, 17–21) as well as in his public debates with Simon (3.37–51; 16.9–14; 18.12–13, 18–22).

[86] Translations of *Bereshit Rabbah* are revised from the Soncino edition (H. Freedman, ed. and trans., *Midrash Rabba*, vol. 1, *Genesis* (London: Soncino, 1939) with reference to Julius Theodor and Chanoch Albeck, eds., *Midrasch Bereschit Rabbah mit kritischem Apparat und Kommentar* (3 vols.; repr. ed.; Jerusalem: Wahrmann 1965).

[87] The most extensive treatment of these traditions is still Alan F. Segal, *Two Powers in Heaven: Early Rabbinic Reports about Christianity and Gnosticism* (Leiden: Brill, 1979). On possible Rabbinic references to Simon Magus, see Hans Joachim Schoeps, "Simon Magus in der Haggada?" *HUCA* 21 (1948): 257–74. See also Burton Visotzky, "Goys 'Я'n't Us – Rabbinic Anti-Gentile Polemic in Yerushalmi Berachot 9:1," in Iricinschi and Zellentin, *Heresy and Identity in Late Antiquity*, 299–313.

significant that the Rabbinic subgenre of disputation tales, more specifically, is often used to contest dualistic and polytheistic interpretations of those passages in the Torah where God is described in terms that could suggest His plurality.

Perhaps most notable are the traditions collected in *Bereshit Rabbah* 8.8–9. *Bereshit Rabbah* 8.8 begins with a striking admission of the problems raised by the plural forms that Genesis uses to describe God:

R. Samuel b. Nahman said in the name of R. Yohanan: "When Moses was engaged in writing the Torah, he had to write the work of each day [i.e., of Creation]. When he came to the verse, *And God said, Let us make* (pl.) *humankind*, etc. (Gen. 1:27), he said: 'Sovereign of the Universe! Why do you furnish an excuse to *minim* [מה אתה נותן פתחון פה]?' 'Write!' He replied, 'Whoever wishes to err may err [הרוצה לטעות יטעה].'"

Using the subgenre of the disputation tale, *Bereshit Rabbah* 8.9 turns to address the specific problems raised by the Torah's use of *Elohim*, a Hebrew term for God that can be read as either singular or plural:

The *minim* asked R. Simlai: "How many gods [אלוהות] created the world?" "I and you must inquire of the first day," he replied, "as it is written, *For ask now of the first days*. 'Since the day *Elohim* created [(pl.) בראו] humankind' is not written here (i.e., in Deut 4:32), but *Elohim created* [(s.) ברא]."
   Then they asked him a second time: "Why is it written, *In the beginning Elohim* [s. or pl.] *created*?" "'In the beginning *Elohim* created [(pl.) בראו]' is not written here (i.e., in Gen 1:1)," he answered, "but *Elohim created* [(s.) ברא] *the heaven and the earth*."

The midrash then returns to Gen 1:27, addressing the issue of its use of plural verbal forms and pronominal suffixes when describing God:

R. Simlai said: "In every place [i.e., in the Torah] that you find a point supporting the *minim* [בכל מקום שאתה מוצא פתחון פה למינים], you find the refutation at its side [בצד אתה מוצא תשובה]!" They asked him again: "What is meant by *And Elohim said, Let us make* [(pl.) נעשה] *humankind in our image* [בצלמנו] *and our likeness* [בדמותנו]?" "Read what follows," he replied, "'And *Elohim* created [(pl.) ויבראו] humankind' is not written here (i.e., in Gen 1:27), but *And Elohim created* [(s.) ויברא]."

That this explanation does not suffice to explain the problem is made clear by the end of this unit, which features a shift from public to private discourse:

When they left, his disciples said to him [i.e., to R. Simlai]: "You dismissed them with a mere makeshift [קנה; lit. hollow reed]! But how will you answer us?" He said to them: "In the past Adam was created from dust, and Eve was created from Adam, but henceforth it shall be *In our image, after our likeness* (Gen 1:26): neither man without woman, nor woman without man, and neither of them without the Shekhinah."

Just as the Pseudo-Clementine Peter privately reveals teachings to his followers that might be misunderstood by the public,[88] R. Simlai is here depicted as offering to his disciples a more nuanced solution to the problem of plural forms

---

[88] E.g., the Rule of Syzygy and the doctrine of false pericopes, on which see above and below.

used of God in Genesis. This solution, moreover, recalls the admission of the complexity within the unity of the Godhead in Peter's appeal to Wisdom in *Hom.* 16.12; here, however, appeal is made to another feminine hypostasis of God, namely the Shekhinah.

What is striking about R. Simlai's answer to his disciples, however, is that the Sage never addresses the reason why Scripture contains misleading statements that need to be corrected by other statements beside them; he simply gives another exegesis. As in the tradition attributed to R. Samuel b. Nahman about Moses' complaint to God about the inclusion of the plural divine statement "Let us make humankind" in the Torah (*Bereshit Rabbah* 8.8), the inconsistency is fully admitted but never resolved.

The authors/redactors of the *Homilies* seem to face the same problem, but they offer a very different solution. Perhaps most striking is Peter's response to the litany of scriptural inconsistencies attributed to Simon in *Hom.* 3.38 (quoted above). At first, Peter defends the perfection of God and the characters of biblical heroes by citing additional biblical prooftexts, in a manner reminiscent of the arguments used by Sages in Rabbinic disputation tales:

Peter said: "You say that Adam was created blind, which was not so; for He would not have pointed out the Tree of the Knowledge of Good and Evil to a blind man and commanded him not to taste of it (Gen 2:17)." Then said Simon: "He meant that his mind was blind." Then Peter: "How could he be blind in respect of his mind, who, before tasting of the tree, in harmony with Him who made him, imposed appropriate names on all the animals? (Gen 2:20)"

Then Simon: "If Adam had foreknowledge, how did he not foreknow that the serpent would deceive his wife (Gen 3:1–5)?" Then Peter: "If Adam did not have foreknowledge, how did he give names to the sons of men as they were born with reference to their future doings, calling the first Cain, which is interpreted 'envy,' who through envy killed his brother Abel, which is interpreted 'grief'; for his parents grieved over him, the first slain? And if Adam, being the work of God, had foreknowledge, how much more so the God who created him?" (*Hom.* 3.42–43)

Peter then, however, denies outright any description of God as imperfect or ignorant:

And it is false, that which is written that *God reflected* (Gen 6:6), as if using reasoning on account of ignorance; and that the Lord tempted Abraham, that He might know if he would endure it; and that which is written *Let us go down …* (Gen 11:7). And, not to extend my discourse too far, but whatever sayings ascribe ignorance to Him, or anything else that is evil – being overturned by other sayings that affirm the contrary – are proved to be false! (*Hom.* 3.43)

At first, the implication of the falsehood of some portions of Scripture is tempered by a return to arguments based on other prooftexts:

Because He does indeed foreknow, He says to Abraham, *You shall assuredly know that your seed shall be sojourners in a land that is not their own …* (Gen 15:13). And what?

Does not Moses pre-intimate the sins of the people and predict their dispersion among the nations? If He gave foreknowledge to Moses, how can it be that He did not have it Himself?

Yet He has it! And if He has it, as we have also shown, it is an extravagant saying that He *reflected* (Gen 6:6) and that He *repented* (Gen 6:6) and that He *went down to see* (Gen 11:5) – and whatever else of this sort. (*Hom.* 3.43–44)

The resultant problem of scriptural inconsistency is then answered with a solution that is strongly reminiscent of R. Simlai's dictum whereby scriptural sayings that support "heresy" are always countered by other sayings close beside them (*Bereshit Rabbah* 8.9). Peter very similarly proclaims:

Thus the sayings accusatory of the God who made the heaven are both rendered void by the opposite sayings that are alongside of them and are refuted by Creation. (*Hom.* 3.46)

Unlike R. Simlai, however, Peter does not stop there. *Bereshit Rabbah* implies that its "heretics" readily accepted the Sage's dictum and that even his disciples were happy to settle for an alternative exegesis of the problematic passage. In the *Homilies*, however, Peter's battle with his own "heretic" prompts him to push his version of the dictum to its natural conclusion: he proposes that the seemingly "heretical" passages in Scripture are, in fact, not scriptural at all:

They were not written by a prophetic hand. Therefore also they appear opposite to the hand of God, who made all things. (*Hom.* 3.46)

This view reflects another idea distinctive to the *Homilies*, namely its theory that Scripture contains statements that imply God's multiplicity and imperfection only because false pericopes have been inserted therein.[89] This theory is complex in its own right, and its precise connections to other late antique traditions have yet to be adequately explored.[90] For our present purposes, it suffices to note that parallels in heresiology expose the *Homilies*' surprisingly close connections with Rabbinic tradition – even in the case of a doctrine that might seem at first sight to run completely contrary to Rabbinic ideology, namely the *Homilies*' denial of the perfection of Scripture. Not only does Peter explain this theory in an heresiological context that recalls Rabbinic disputation tales and voice a dictum that

---

[89] *Hom.* 2.38–52; 3.4–6, 9–11, 17–21, 37–51; 16.9–14; 18.12–13, 18–22.

[90] For this discussion of the doctrine of the false pericopes, I am indebted to my student Karl Shuve's work locating this doctrine within the context of late antique Jewish and Christian efforts to grapple with the problems raised by scriptural inconsistencies, esp. with regard to the character of God; Shuve, "The Pseudo-Clementine *Homilies* and the Antiochene Polemic Against Allegory" (MA thesis, McMaster University, 2007); Shuve, "The Doctrine of the False Pericopes and Other Late Antique Approaches to the Problem of Scripture's Unity," in Amsler et al., *Nouvelles intrigues Pseudo-clémentines*, 437–45. See also now Donald H. Carlson, *Jewish-Christian Interpretation of the Pentateuch in the Pseudo-Clementine Homilies* (Minneapolis: Fortress, 2013). On possible Rabbinic awareness of this idea, see Schoeps, *Theologie und Geschichte des Judenchristentums*, 176–79, esp. on *Sifre Devarim* 26 (cf. *Vayiqra Rabbah* 31.4; *Devarim Rabbah* 2.6).

recalls a Rabbinic sayings cited therein, but he goes on to explain the history of scriptural interpolation with appeal to the oral transmission of the Torah from Moses to the seventy elders (cf. Numbers 11) and on to their successors (*Hom.* 2.38; 3.47; cf. *m. Avot* 1.1).[91] In effect, the authors/redactors of the *Homilies* seem able to assert the imperfection of the Written Torah precisely because they accept the integrity of the Oral Torah.

Heresiology, Identity, and Polemics

Without further analysis, it is difficult to know the full import of these intriguing parallels. Some parallels in heresiological content and strategy, for instance, may reflect the character and argumentative tactics of specific enemies (e. g., Marcionites) shared by the Rabbis and the authors/redactors of the *Homilies*. Others may result from their common interest in defending the goodness of the Creator and in arguing for monotheism against dualism and polytheism. In my view, however, the formal parallels prove more telling, opening the possibility that similar heresiologies developed due to contacts between the authors/redactors of the *Homilies* and Rabbinic Jews.

At the same time, of course, the narrativization of heresiological tropes must be seen as a result of the authors/redactors' choice of the genre of the ancient Greek novel. Interestingly, it is particularly in the *Homilies* that we find fully exploited the polemical power latent in the adoption of a "pagan" literary form; for, as we have seen, the appropriation of the genre of the novel here serves an extended polemic against Hellenism as "heresy," as expressed both through the words of Peter and Clement and through the story itself. If the choice of genre reflects an intended readership of "pagans" and former "pagans," then the polemic proves all the more poignant. The literary form of the *Homilies*' polemic against Hellenism and "paganism" ironically exposes its authors/redactors' close connections with Graeco-Roman culture. A full understanding of these connections too must await further investigation. Nevertheless, it seems plausible that they reflect the cultural context and intended audience of our text – consistent with its characterization of Jesus as the teacher of Gentiles, its depiction of Peter as preaching for the conversion of "pagans," and its characterization of Clement as a Roman who found his Greek education insufficient to fill his spiritual needs.

---

[91] *Hom.* 2.38: "After the prophet Moses, by the order of God, gave (παραδεδωκότος) the Law with the explanations (σὺν ταῖς ἐπιλύσεσιν) to certain chosen men, some seventy in number (cf. Num 11:16), in order that they also might instruct such of the people as they chose, the Written Law (γραφεὶς ὁ νόμος) had added to it certain falsehoods against the God (ψευδῆ κατὰ τοῦ θεοῦ) who made the heaven and the earth and all things in them – the Wicked One having dared to work this for some righteous purpose." *Hom.* 3.47 is quoted above.

Consequently, the heresiology of the *Homilies* may speak to its place at a definitional interface between "Christianity," "Judaism," and "paganism" in Late Antiquity. Read from this perspective, the novel is an innovative redeployment of the discourse of Christian heresiology, the narrativization of which seems simultaneously to draw on the model of Rabbinic tales of disputations with *minim* – all framed and unified, moreover, by the overarching structure of the Graeco-Roman novel. The account of error thereby expressed differs radically from those found in the Christian heresiologies of those whom we now label "orthodox." This raises the intriguing possibility that the authors and redactors of the *Homilies* seek tacitly to counter, not only the "false apostles, false prophets, [and] heresies" predicted by Peter in *Hom.* 16.21, but also those Christians whose anti-Jewish and supersessionist views are, precisely in the fourth century, just in the process of being ratified by their "desires for supremacy."[92]

---

[92] On this possibility in relation to late antique Antioch, see Dominique Côté, "Le problème de l'identité religieuse dans la Syrie du IVe siècle: Le cas des Pseudo-Clémentines et de l'Adversus Judaeos de S. Jean Chrysostome," in *La croisée des chemins revisitée: Quand l'Église et la Synagogue se sont-elles distinguées?*, ed. Simon Claude Mimouni and Bernard Pouderon (Patrimoines Judaïsme antique; Paris: Cerf, 2012), 339–70.

Chapter Six

"Jewish-Christianity" as Counterhistory?*

With recent critiques of positivistic historicism and new concerns for cultural memory have come an acute sense of the past as always and already a product of practices of selection, collection, recollection, recontextualization, preservation, and omission.[1] In the centuries following the conquests of Alexander of Macedon, the ancient Greek past became a prime site for dialogue and contestation among the various cultures brought into contact by Hellenistic and Roman imperial rule.[2] Jews, and later Christians, numbered among those who defined themselves, both positively and negatively, in terms of their relationship to an idealized antiquity emblematized by Homer and Plato and enshrined in the rhetoric and education of late antique elites.[3]

For Jews and Christians, this "classical" past was often understood through the lens of another ancient era – a "biblical" past populated by ancient Israelite patriarchs, kings, priests, and prophets.[4] Jews and Christians appealed to bibli-

---

* This chapter was originally published in 2008 as "'Jewish Christianity' as Counter-history? The Apostolic Past in Eusebius' *Ecclesiastical History* and the Pseudo-Clementine *Homilies*," in *Antiquity in Antiquity: Jewish and Christian Pasts in the Greco-Roman World*, ed. Gregg Gardner and Kevin Osterloh (TSAJ 123; Tübingen: Mohr Siebeck, 2008), 173–216 – the proceedings of a 2006 Princeton University conference of the same name. This version has been revised and updated. It is reprinted here with permission from Mohr Siebeck. Research was supported by a grant from the Social Science and Humanities Research Council of Canada. Earlier versions and portions were presented at the University of Pennsylvania on February 12, 2007, and the University of California, Los Angeles, on April 20, 2007. Special thanks to Adam H. Becker, Ra'anan S. Boustan, Bob Kraft, Claudia Rapp, and Karl Evan Shuve for their questions and suggestions.

[1] On the past as "remembered present," see, e. g., Amos Funkenstein, *Perceptions on Jewish History* (Berkeley: University of California Press, 1993), 3–21.

[2] On the emergence of ideas about the classical past in Alexandrian scholarship, see, e. g., Rudolf Pfeiffer, *History of Classical Scholarship: From the Beginnings to the End of the Hellenistic Ages* (Oxford: Clarendon, 1968), 87–279.

[3] E. g., Erich Gruen, *Heritage and Hellenism: The Reinvention of Jewish Tradition* (Berkeley: University of California Press, 1998), esp. 246–91; Arthur J. Droge, *Homer or Moses? Early Christian Interpretations of the History of Culture* (HUT 26; Tübingen: Mohr Siebeck, 1988); Daniel Ridings, *The Attic Moses: The Dependency Theme in Some Early Christian Writers* (Göteborg: Almqvist & Wiksell, 1995); Averil Cameron, "Remaking the Past," in *Late Antiquity: A Guide to the Post-Classical World*, ed. Glen Warren Bowersock, Peter Brown, and Oleg Grabar (Cambridge, MA: Harvard University Press, 1999), 1–20.

[4] For the Jewish conceptualization of the biblical past, the Babylonian Exile and the return under Persian rule are widely viewed as critical precipitants. The process of remembrance, re-

cal history and heroes for diverse aims, ranging from apologetics and polemics to religious legitimization and ritual and communal etiology.[5] And, arguably, contact with parallel reflections on the classical past served to intensify the processes whereby the biblical past came to be conceptualized as both historical foundation and timeless paradigm for the present.[6]

Here, I am interested in how this shared biblical/Jewish past also helped to produce a third privileged realm in Christian cultural memory – namely, the "apostolic" past.[7] Already in the New Testament Book of Acts, the age of Peter, Paul, and the other apostles emerges as a locus for the historiographical articulation of Christian identity in relation to Judaism. Inasmuch as the apostles were credited with the faithful transmission and mediation of Jesus' message to later generations, these figures were readily redeployed by later authors as emblems of authority and authenticity in debates about theology, epistemology, and ritual practice.[8] Across the full range of our early Christian literature – including Patristic writings, so-called New Testament apocrypha, and Nag Hammadi literature – we find evidence of the explanatory and polemical power of the apostles as potently pivotal figures, perched between the life of Jesus and the institutionalization of the church. In texts ranging from Papias' *Logion Kyriakon Exegesis*

---

telling, and reflection seems to have been tightly tied to the practice of reading and writing, such that the intensive idealization of this past seems to have gone hand in hand with the elevation of certain texts to the status of "Scripture." For a summary of these developments and their ramifications, see James Kugel, *Traditions of the Bible: A Guide to the Bible As It Was at the Start of the Common Era* (Cambridge, MA: Harvard University Press, 1999), 2–6.

[5] Striking, in this regard, is the quantity of Second Temple Jewish literature that is composed in the name of an ancient biblical figure and/or that interprets or expands older scriptures (esp. Torah/Pentateuch); see further Annette Yoshiko Reed, "Pseudepigraphy, Authorship and the Reception of 'the Bible' in Late Antiquity," in *The Reception and Interpretation of the Bible in Late Antiquity*, ed. Lorenzo DiTommaso and Lucian Turcescu (The Bible in Ancient Christianity 6; Leiden: Brill, 2008), 467–90.

[6] As Glen Bowersock notes, "It can often happen that the partial appropriation of cultural motifs, images, and even ideas from another community or tradition deepens the understanding of one's own heritage"; "The Greek Moses: Confusion of Ethnic and Cultural Components in Later Roman and Early Byzantine Palestine," in *Religious and Ethnic Communities in Later Roman Palestine*, ed. Hayim Lapin (Bethesda: University Press of Maryland, 1998), 47.

[7] I.e., the first century CE. The term "apostle" is generally reserved for the twelve disciples whom Jesus chooses to be his apostles and spread his message in the Synoptic Gospels (Matt 10:2; Mark 3:14; Luke 6:13), together with Paul (e.g., Rom 1:1). For a recent discussion of the prehistory and development of the notion of the "apostle" as a link in the chain of tradition from Jesus to the church, see Theodore Korteweg, "Origin and Early History of the Apostolic Office," in *The Apostolic Age in Patristic Thought*, ed. A. Hilhorst (VCSup 70; Leiden: Brill, 2004), 1–10.

[8] This is perhaps most poignantly expressed by the proliferation of apostolic pseudepigrapha, ranging from letters penned in the name of Paul (e.g., Pastoral Epistles), gospels in the name of other apostles (e.g., Gospel of Philip, Gospel of Thomas), and ritual materials attributed to "the twelve" as a group (e.g., *Didache, Didascalia Apostolorum*). See Jean-Daniel. Kaestli, "Mémoire et pseudépigraphie dans le christianisme de l'âge post-apostolique," *Revue de théologie et de philosophie* 125 (1993): 41–63.

to the *Apocryphon of James*, the apostles are foci for the expression of anxieties attendant on the loss of the "living voice" of Jesus.[9] In apocryphal acts and Patristic heresiologies alike, stories about the apostles and their followers are used to explore the continuities and discontinuities between the life of Jesus and the norms of those communities that claimed to preserve his memory and message.[10] Appeals to apostles are prominent in arguments about the acceptable range of difference among those who claimed the name "Christian."[11] Likewise, in the first centuries of Christianity, discussions of their written, oral, and institutional legacy played a central role in debates about the nature, scope, and sources of religious authority.[12]

Interestingly, however, it is not until the fourth century that the idealization of apostles becomes explicitly articulated in terms of a periodization of history that elevates the apostolic age to a status akin to the biblical or classical past. Peter van Deun, for instance, points to Eusebius' *Ecclesiastical History* (2.14.3; 3.31.6) as the earliest known Christian text to apply the Greek adjective ἀποστολικός to a time period.[13] Eusebius here delineates the "apostolic period" (ἀποστολικῶν χρόνων) as encompassing the years from Christ's ascension to the reign of Trajan (3.31.6). Writing from a self-consciously postapostolic perspective, he describes this era as a bygone age of miracles and wonders (5.7.6) in which the light of truth shone so brightly that even "heresy" posed no real

---

[9] Papias expresses his preference for the "living voice" but nevertheless makes efforts to link written records of Jesus' life and sayings with apostles (Papias *apud* Eusebius, *Hist. eccl.* 3.29.4). Also poignant is the image, at the beginning of the *Apocryphon of James*, of the twelve disciples "all sitting together, recalling what the Saviour had said to each one of them, whether in secret or openly, and putting it into books" (*Apoc. James* 2.9–15 [Nag Hammadi codex I,2]). On orality, textuality, and the anxieties surrounding memory in early Christianity, see Werner H. Kelber, *The Oral and the Written Gospel: The Hermeneutics of Speaking and Writing in the Synoptic Tradition, Mark, Paul, and Q* (Philadelphia: Fortress, 1983); Pheme Perkins, "Spirit and Letter: Poking Holes in the Canon," *JR* 76 (1996): 307–27; Richard A. Horsley, Jonathan A. Draper, and John Miles Foley, eds., *Performing the Gospel: Orality, Memory, and Mark* (Minneapolis: Fortress, 2006).

[10] Note, e.g., the debates about women surrounding the apostle Paul; Dennis Ronald MacDonald, *The Legend and the Apostle: The Battle for Paul in Story and Canon* (Philadelphia: Westminster, 1983).

[11] The heresiological appeal to apostolic authority is perhaps most clear in the writings of Irenaeus. As is well known, he constructs "heresy" as the opposite of apostolic truth, depicting the apostles as guarantors of tradition and interpretation, and authenticating Christian writings through association with specific apostles (*Adv. haer.* 1.10.2; 3.1.1, 3.4.1–2; 4.33.8; 5.20.1–2; note also 3.1.1, 3.4.1; 4.33.8). See further Georg Günter Blum, *Tradition und Sukzession: Studien zum Normbegriff des Apostolischen von Paulus bis Irenäus* (Berlin: Lutherisches, 1963).

[12] Early examples include *1 Clem* 44.1–2.

[13] P. van Deun, "The Notion *Apostolikos*: A Terminological Survey," in Hilhorst, *Apostolic Age*, 49. After Eusebius, we increasingly find a notion of "apostolic times" as the age that saw the birth of the church (e.g., Epiphanius, *Pan.* 73.2.11). On later views of this age, see, e.g., B. Dehandschutter, "*Primum enim omnes docebant*: Awareness of Discontinuity in the Early Church: The Case of Ecclesiastical Office," in Hilhorst, *Apostolic Age*, 219–27.

threat (2.14.3). Eusebius also presents the apostolic age as determinative for all that came after: it was then, in his view, that Christianity spread throughout the known world (3.4.1), while Judaism fell to deserved decline (3.5.3).

Studies of Late Antiquity have richly explored the processes by which Christian reflection on classical and biblical pasts contributed to the delineation of a Christian collective identity as distinct from so-called "paganism." In what follows, I will ask how the construction and idealization of the apostolic past may have similarly served to articulate the place of Jews and Judaism in Christian self-definition. Towards this goal, I will examine two conflicting fourth-century representations of this period: the account of apostolic history in books 1–4 of Eusebius' *Ecclesiastical History* and the novelistic narrative about the apostolic past in the Pseudo-Clementine *Homilies*.

The contrast between them – I suggest – sheds light on the role of historiography in the articulation of collective identities in Late Antiquity and, moreover, may further our understanding of the fourth century as a formative age for the conceptualization of "Judaism" and "Christianity" as distinct entities with distinct histories. It may also help to expose some of the prehistory of our modern perspectives on the late antique past, as formed through selective acts of remembering and forgetting, forged in debates over identity and continuity, and indebted to the interplay between histories and counter-histories.

The Pseudo-Clementines and the History of the Apostolic Age

The Pseudo-Clementine *Homilies* and *Recognitions* are famous for presenting a picture of the apostolic age that differs radically from the image in the New Testament Book of Acts. For Luke, the story of the rise of Christianity is framed as the tale of the conversion of Gentiles and the spread of the gospel beyond Judaea.[14] By contrast, the *Homilies* and *Recognitions* offer a different vision: the Jerusalem church of Peter and James here remains central, and ethnic Jews continue to play a leading role in the church. Penned in the name of Clement of Rome, this pair of parallel novels tells of Clement's travels with the apostle Peter. Throughout these two accounts, Peter is depicted as the defender of the true teachings of Jesus, and the criterion for proper belief and practice is coherence with the Jerusalem church and its leader James.[15] Whereas Luke describes the

---

[14] I.e., as outlined in Acts 1:8, the narrative progression of Acts communicates its notion of the Christian community as spreading outwards from Jerusalem (2:1–8:3) to Judaea and Samaria (8:4–12:25), then throughout the eastern Mediterranean, and finally culminating at Rome (13:1–28:31); see Gregory E. Sterling, *Historiography and Self-Definition: Josephos, Luke-Acts, and Apologetic Historiography* (NTSup 64; Leiden: Brill, 1992), 348–49.

[15] Note, e. g., the instruction in *Hom.* 11.35 to "shun any apostle or teacher or prophet who does not first accurately compare his preaching with that of James, who was called the brother of my lord and to whom was entrusted to administer the church of the Hebrews in Jerusalem"

apostolic age as one of harmony between the apostles and downplays any conflict between Peter and Paul (cf. Galatians 2), the Pseudo-Clementines promote Peter and contain traces of anti-Pauline polemics.[16] Affixed to the *Homilies*, moreover, is a letter that purports to be written by Peter himself, wherein he bemoans the popularity of antinomian teachings among Jesus' Gentile followers and counters the misrepresentation of his own teachings as negating the need for Torah observance (cf. Acts 15).[17]

Could some elements in these accounts reflect historical reality? Might the Pseudo-Clementine literature preserve a lost Petrine perspective that was hostile to Paul, suppressed by Luke, and forgotten by the Gentile Christians who embraced Pauline and Lukan writings as normative? These are the questions that have, until recently, shaped research on the *Homilies* and *Recognitions*. For nearly a century, studies of these late antique texts have been primarily source critical. Scholars have approached the *Homilies* and *Recognitions* as mines for information about earlier eras, culling them for data about Christian Origins and using them to reconstruct first- and second-century forms of "Jewish-Christianity." Accordingly, the popularity of the Pseudo-Clementine literature has risen and fallen with scholarly judgments about their historical value as sources for early traditions about Peter, James, and the Jerusalem church.[18]

In recent years, however, attention has turned to the literary and rhetorical features of the Pseudo-Clementine literature. F. Stanley Jones, for instance, has proposed that the early source preserved in *Rec.* 1.27–71 (ca. 200 CE) is best read as a work of competitive historiography.[19] Jones demonstrates that *Rec.* 1.27–71 was dependant on Luke-Acts and was framed as a rival account of apostolic history. To Luke's image of the communal apostolic leadership of the primitive church, this source asserts James' preeminence (*Rec.* 1.43.3), depicting him as the bishop appointed by Jesus to lead the church.[20] James is the one credited with successfully spreading the message of Jesus to the Jewish people (*Rec.* 1.69.8;

(cf. *Rec.* 4.35). On James as bishop and as appointed leader of the early church, see *Rec.* 1.43, 66, 73, and the preface to the *Epistle of Clement to James*.

[16] G. Lüdemann, *Opposition to Paul in Jewish Christianity* (trans. E. Boring; Minneapolis: Fortress, 1989), 169–94.

[17] Esp. *Epistle of Peter to James* 2.3–4: "Some from among the Gentiles have rejected my legal preaching (νόμιμον … κήρυγμα), attaching themselves to certain lawless and trifling preaching (ἄνομόν … καὶ φλυαρώδη … διδασκαλίαν) of the man who is my enemy (τοῦ ἐχθροῦ ἀνθρώπου). Some have attempted these things while I am still alive, to transform my words by certain intricate interpretations towards the dissolution of the Law (εἰς τὴν τοῦ νόμου κατάλυσιν) – as though I myself were also of such a mind but did not freely proclaim it; God forbid!" Most scholars interpret Peter's "enemy" as Paul (cf. Galatians 2) and the one "transforming" Peter's message as Luke (cf. Acts 15). See further Chapter Eight in this volume.

[18] I discuss this tendency in the history of scholarship in more detail in Chapter One.

[19] F. Stanley Jones, *Pseudoclementina Elchasaiticaque inter Judaeochristiana: Collected Studies* (Orientalia Lovaniensia Analecta 203; Leuven: Peeters, 2012), 207–29.

[20] Jones, *Pseudoclementina*, 242.

cf. Acts 2:41; 4:4).[21] Furthermore, his success is here said to have been thwarted only because of "the enemy"; the Jewish people were persuaded by James' preaching, but their conversion was forestalled by his death, as precipitated by the pernicious efforts of Saul/Paul to undermine the Jerusalem church. Whereas Luke appeals to the Holy Spirit to authorize the mission to the Gentiles, *Rec.* 1.27–71 depicts the inclusion of the Gentiles as occasioned by the need to fill the number of the chosen left empty by the Jews.[22]

Elsewhere, Jones has similarly shed light on the literary and rhetorical features of the putative third-century source shared by the *Homilies* and *Recognitions* (i.e., the Pseudo-Clementine *Grundschrift*). Jones' reconstruction of the structure and aims of the *Grundschrift* highlights its points of resonance with debates about fate and astrology in late antique Syria.[23] Likewise, Mark Edwards, Dominique Côté, and others have investigated themes shared by both extant novels, exploring the strategic appropriation of "pagan" literary and philosophical tropes in the Pseudo-Clementine tradition.[24] Other recent studies have focused on the rhetoric of the redacted form of the *Recognitions*: Kate Cooper, William Robins, and Meinolf Vielberg have considered its adoption and subversion of the genre of the Greco-Roman novel,[25] while Nicole Kelley has investigated the dynamics of its discourse about knowledge, situating its concerns with authority and

---

[21] Jones, *Pseudoclementina*, 242.

[22] Jones, *Pseudoclementina*, 242–43. This contrast is emblematized by the differences between Acts 13:46 and *Rec.* 1.63.2, two parallel statements asserting that the mission to the Jews preceded the mission to the Gentiles. The statement in Acts 13:46 ("It was necessary that the word of God should be spoken first to you [i.e., Jews]. Since you reject it and judge yourselves to be unworthy of eternal life, we are now turning to the Gentiles!") is attributed to Paul and Barnabus; it occurs in the context of the rejection of Paul's preaching by a crowd of Jews (Acts 13:47) and is followed by Paul's appeal to Isa 49:6 as prophetic prooftext for the mission to the Gentiles (Acts 13:49). The parallel in *Rec.* 1.63.2 presents the same information with a different spin. The contrast is clearest with the Syriac version, in which Peter says: "Finally, I counseled them that before we should go to the nations to preach the knowledge of the God who is above all, they should reconcile their people to God by receiving Jesus" (trans. Jones). This is followed by polemics, not against the Jews as a people, but rather against the Temple and sacrificial cult.

[23] Jones, *Pseudoclementina*, 114–206.

[24] Mark J. Edwards, "The Clementina: A Christian response to the pagan novel," *Classical Quarterly* 42 (1992): 459–74; Dominique Côté, *Le thème de l'opposition entre Pierre et Simon dans les Pseudo-Clémentines* (Études Augustiniennes Série Antiquités 167; Paris: Institut d'Études Augustiniennes, 2001); Côté, "La fonction littéraire de Simon le Magicien dans les Pseudo-Clémentines," *Laval Théologique et Philosophique* 57 (2001): 513–23.

[25] William Robins, "Romance and Renunciation at the Turn of the Fifth Century," *JECS* 8 (2000): 531–57; Kate Cooper, "Matthidia's Wish: Division, Reunion, and the Early Christian Family in the Pseudo-Clementine *Recognitions*," in *Narrativity in Biblical and Related Texts/ La narrativité dans la Bible et les textes apparentés*, ed. George J. Brooke and Jean-Daniel Kaestli (Bibliotheca Ephemeridum Theologicarum Lovaniensium 149; Leuven: Peeters, 2000), 243–64; Meinolf Vielberg, *Klemens in den pseudoklementischen Rekognitionen: Studien zur literarischen Form des spätankiken Romans* (Berlin: Akademie-Verlag, 2000).

epistemology in the context of competing claims, both Christian and "pagan," in fourth-century Syria.[26]

In what follows, I will bring a similar perspective to bear on the *Homilies*, the oldest form of the Pseudo-Clementine novel to survive in full. The *Homilies* dates to the first half of the fourth century.[27] Like the hypothetical *Grundschrift* and later *Recognitions*, it probably took form in Syria.[28]

It is likely, in my view, that this text does indeed preserve earlier sources. Whatever the precise scope and character of these sources, however, the authors/redactors of the *Homilies* have clearly reworked their received material in ways that speak to their own time.[29] The language used to describe Jesus, for instance, betrays their engagement with Christological debates of the Nicene age.[30] Furthermore, the story of Clement is here framed as an extended defense of apostolic succession and an assertion of the antiquity and necessity of ecclesiastical offices.[31] Throughout this novel, tales about Peter's travels from city to city are punctuated by his ordination of bishops.[32] The *Homilies'* overarching

---

[26] Nicole Kelley, *Knowledge and Religious Authority in the Pseudo-Clementines: Situating the* Recognitions *in Fourth-Century Syria* (WUNT[2] 213; Tübingen: Mohr Siebeck, 2006); Kelley, "On Recycling Texts and Traditions: The Pseudo-Clementine Recognitions and Religious Life in Fourth-Century Syria," in *The Levant: Crossroads of Late Antiquity*, ed. Ellen Bradshaw Aitken and John M. Fosey (McGill University Monographs in Classical Archaeology and History 22; Leiden: Brill, 2013), 105–12; Kelley, "Pseudo-Clementine Polemics against Sacrifice: A Window onto Religious Life in the Fourth Century?," in Piovanelli and Burke, *Rediscovering the Apocryphal Continent*, 391–400.

[27] See further below.

[28] Its Syrian provenance was established by Gerhard Uhlhorn, *Die Homilien und Recognitionen des Clemens Romanus nach ihren Ursprung und Inhalt dargestellt* (Göttingen: Dieterische Buchhandlung, 1854), 381–429; Charles Biggs, "The Clementine *Homilies*," in *Studia biblica et ecclesiastica: Essays Chiefly in Biblical and Patristic Criticism*, vol. 2, ed. Samuel R. Driver, Thomas Killiam Cheyne, and W. Sanday, (Oxford: Clarendon, 1890): 191–92, 368–69. See, more recently, Jan N. Bremmer, "Pseudo-Clementines: Texts, Dates, Places, Authors and Magic," in *The Pseudo-Clementines*, ed. Bremmer (Leuven: Peeters, 2010), 1–23.

[29] On the value of situating the *Homilies* in its fourth-century context, see Chapters One, Four, Five, and Nine as well as Dominique Côté, "Rhetoric and Jewish-Christianity: The Case of the Grammarian Apion in the Pseudo-Clementine *Homilies*," in Piovanelli and Burke, *Rediscovering the Apocryphal Continent*, 369–89. See below for nineteenth-century research on the *Homilies*.

[30] Note the *Homilies'* statement – unparalleled in the *Recognitions* – that Christ the Son is "of the same substance (τῆς αὐτῆς οὐσίας)" as God the Father (16.16) and the use of the term ὁμοούσιος in *Hom.* 20.5, 7. These references were pivotal for Biggs' initial establishment of a date for the *Homilies* in the decades surrounding the Council of Nicaea ("Clementine *Homilies*," 167, 191–92). Biggs' suggestion of the *Homilies'* affinities with Arianism, however, have never been fully explored.

[31] Esp. *Ep. Clem.* 6–7, 12–18; *Hom.* 3.60–72.

[32] *Hom.* 3.60–73 (Zacchaeus in Caesarea; cf. Luke 19:5; *Hist. eccl.* 4.5.3); 7.5 (unnamed elder in Tyre); 7.8 (unnamed elder in Sidon); 7.12 (unnamed elder in Berytus); 11.36 (Maroones in Tripolis); 20.23 (unnamed elder in Laodicea). It is also notable that the *Epistle of Clement to Rome*, one of the two letters prefaced to the *Homilies*, tells of Clement's ordination by Peter in Rome (esp. 19).

narrative also functions to assert Clement's close relationship with Peter and, by extension, the connections between Rome and Jerusalem.[33] The novel's heresiological concerns, as embodied in its accounts of Peter's debates with Simon Magus (3.30–59; 16.1–21; 18.1–23; 19.24–20.10), similarly reflect its late antique context, as is perhaps most clear from its approach to the genealogy of error as an inverse parallel to apostolic succession.[34]

The *Homilies* has usually been dismissed as a record of a heterodox movement with no influence on the late antique church and/or treated as a relic of an apostolic "Jewish-Christianity" rendered irrelevant by the rise of "Gentile Christianity" and Christianity's "Parting of the Ways" with Judaism.[35] When we turn our attention to its final form and fourth-century context, however, this text may emerge as an important piece of evidence for the variety of voices in the late antique Christian discourse about "orthodoxy," Judaism, and the apostolic past.[36]

The *Homilies* and Eusebius' *Ecclesiastical History*

To recover the significance of the *Homilies* for our understanding of the fourth century, comparison with Eusebius' *Ecclesiastical History* proves helpful. Books 1–4 of the latter treat many of the same events, themes, and figures that make up the focus of the former: the life of Clement and his contacts with apostles (*Hist. eccl.* 3.4.9, 3.4.15), the activities of Simon Magus (2.1.11; 13.1–5), Peter's struggles against Simon (2.14.1–2.15.2), the Alexandrian Apion's slander against the Jews (2.5.3–4; cf. 3.38.5; *Hom.* 4–6), and – more broadly – the story of apostolic succession and the spread of Jesus' message beyond the bounds of Judaea.

---

[33] John Chapman, "On the Date of the Clementines," *ZNW* 9 (1908): 155.

[34] On the *Homilies* and late antique heresiology, see Chapter Five in this volume. On the trope of "heretical succession," see A. Ferreiro, "Sexual Depravity, Doctrinal Error, and Character Assassination in the Fourth Century: Jerome against the Priscillianists," *Studia Patristica* 28 (1993): 29–38.

[35] See further Chapter One above.

[36] The final form of the *Homilies* has not been a topic of focused inquiry since the nineteenth century. Especially notable – for our purposes – is the work of Gerhard Uhlhorn, who stressed the unity of the *Homilies* in its present form and the need to consider the aims of its redactors (*Homilien und Recognitionen*, esp. 153); note also Adolph Schliemann, *Die Clementinen nebst den verwandten Schriften und der Ebionitismus* (Hamburg: F. Berthes, 1844), 130–251; Adolph Hilgenfeld, *Die clementinischen Recognitionen und Homilien nach ihrem Ursprung und Inhalt dargetellt* (Leipzig: J. G. Schreiber, 1848). These studies, however, were penned prior to the establishment of its fourth-century date and thus seek to locate the text in the second century CE. Some interesting suggestions about the late antique context of the Pseudo-Clementines were made at the turn of the century, when its fourth-century date was established in Biggs, "Clementine *Homilies*," 157–93; John Chapman, "On the Date of the Clementines," *ZNW* 9 (1908): 147–59. Until recently, however, these suggestions have been largely ignored, consistent with the source-critical focus of almost all twentieth-century research on the Pseudo-Clementines.

Moreover, the two texts are temporally and geographically proximate. The first edition of the *Ecclesiastical History* (books 1–7) is typically dated between 290 and 312 CE,[37] a few decades before the compilation of the *Homilies*.[38] Whereas Eusebius penned his history in Caesarea, the *Homilies* was most likely compiled in Edessa or Antioch.[39] Eusebius himself attests the transmission of texts and traditions between these cities in the fourth century (*Hist. eccl.* 1.13).[40] The movement of material between Palestinian and Syrian locales is further evinced by the reception history of his *Ecclesiastical History*, which was translated into Syriac soon after its composition.[41]

To my knowledge, no study has explored the rhetorical and discursive parallels between these two texts. Rather, research on the Pseudo-Clementines has looked to the *Ecclesiastical History* mainly to test the historical accuracy of the description of figures and events in the *Homilies* and *Recognitions*.[42] In addition, scholars have appealed to Eusebius' references to Petrine and Clementine pseudepigrapha (3.3.2, 3.38.5) to support source-critical hypotheses concerning the ultimate origins of material now found in the *Homilies*.[43]

Due partly to the power of traditional metanarratives about "orthodoxy" and "heresy," on the one hand, and "Gentile Christianity" and "Jewish-Christianity," on the other, the *Homilies* and *Ecclesiastical History* have been studied in dif-

---

[37] Robert M. Grant, *Eusebius as Church Historian* (Oxford: Clarendon, 1980), 13–14; Andrew Louth, "The Date of Eusebius' *Historia ecclesiastica*," *JTS* 41 (1990): 111–23; Richard W. Burgess, "The Dates and Editions of Eusebius' *Chronici canones* and *Historia ecclesiastica*," *JTS* 48 (1997): 471–504.

[38] Since Biggs, scholars have concurred that the *Homilies* should be dated to the first half of the fourth century. A topic of continued debate, however, is whether it should be placed before or after the Council of Nicaea. C. Schmidt, O. Cullman, and G. Strecker, for instance, see the *Homilies* as pre-Nicene composition, while H. Waitz and B. Rehm place its composition shortly after 325 CE. See, e.g., Hans Waitz, *Die Pseudoklementinen: Homilien und Rekognitionen: Eine quellenkritische Untersuchung* (Leipzig: Hinrichs, 1904), 369; Georg Strecker, *Das Judenchristentum in den Pseudoklementinen* (TU 70; 2nd ed.; Berlin: Akademie-Verlag, 1981), 268; and the summary of the debate in Jones, "Pseudo-Clementines," 73–74.

[39] See above. Notably, Caesarea may have also played a part in the pseudepigraphical claims in the Pseudo-Clementine *Grundschrift*, albeit in a manner whose precise significance is now difficult to recover; cf. *Hom.* 1.20.2; *Rec.* 1.17.2.

[40] See, however, Sebastian Brock, "Eusebius and Syriac Christianity," in *Eusebius, Christianity, and Judaism*, ed. Harold W. Attridge and Gohei Hata (StPB 42; Leiden: Brill, 1992), 212–34.

[41] The Syriac translation survives in a manuscript from 461/462 CE (Leningrad, Public Library, Cod. Syr. 1, New Series). See William Wright and Norman McLean, *The Ecclesiastical History of Eusebius in Syriac* (Cambridge: Cambridge University Press, 1898).

[42] On one level, for instance, Hans Joachim Schoeps' *Theologie und Geschichte des Judenchristentums* (Tübingen: Mohr Siebeck, 1949) can be read as a comprehensive attempt to fit the evidence of the Pseudo-Clementine *Homilies* and *Recognitions* into the framework of Christian history laid out in Eusebius' *Ecclesiastical History*.

[43] In particular, Eusebius' statements in *Hist. eccl.* 3.38.5 have played an important role in scholarly debates about the sources of *Hom.* 4–6. For a summary of the various positions, see Jones, "Pseudo-Clementines," 27–31.

ferent specialist circles. Moreover, like the *Homilies*, the *Ecclesiastical History* has often been treated as a reservoir of data about earlier times and sources; scholars have too rarely considered its significance as a late antique narrative construction.[44]

In my view, however, there are good reasons to read the *Ecclesiastical History* and the *Homilies* in terms of a shared fourth-century discourse about the apostolic past. Not only are two texts contemporaneous, but they exhibit many of the same concerns. Both trace the paths of apostolic succession and assert ecclesiastical authority. They answer "pagan" critiques of Christianity and defend "orthodoxy" against "heresy." Moreover, they seek to map the place of Judaism in apostolic history and late antique Christian identity.

To address these concerns, Eusebius and the authors/redactors of the *Homilies* choose different literary genres.[45] It may be significant, however, that both engage in the large-scale appropriation and subversion of "pagan" literary forms: just as the *Homilies* is our earliest extant example of the Christian use of the genre of the Greco-Roman novel,[46] so Eusebius' *Ecclesiastical History* applies Hellenistic historiographical tropes to the whole of Christian history.[47]

---

[44] Elizabeth Clark, for instance, notes how the influence of Eusebius' *Ecclesiastical History* has rendered his own assumptions almost invisible. Although the accuracy of his details have often been questioned, not enough has been done to explore how his history "shores up claims for the dominance of the proto-orthodox Church, enhances its leaders' prestige, and justifies particular institutions and teachings"; *History, Theory, Text: Historians and the Linguistic Turn* (Cambridge, MA: Harvard University Press, 2004), 169. Important exceptions include Grant, *Eusebius as Church Historian*; Arthur J. Droge, "The Apologetic Dimensions of the *Ecclesiastical History*," in Attridge and Hata, *Eusebius, Christianity, and Judaism*, 492–509; Dale B. Martin, *Inventing Superstition: From Hippocrates to the Christians* (Cambridge, MA: Harvard University Press, 2004), 207–25.

[45] To a modern reader, their choice of different genres might seem to preclude their participation in a common discourse. This, however, may say more about the gap between premodern and modern notions of "history" than about literary production in Late Antiquity. That Eusebius and the authors/redactors of the *Homilies* express so many of the same concerns by means of these different genres may, in fact, confirm recent insights into the close connections between history and narrative in Greco-Roman culture. On these connections, see, e. g., Averil Cameron, ed., *History as Text: The Writing of Ancient History* (Chapel Hill: University of North Carolina Press, 1990), and on the novelistic background of both Greek and Jewish historiography, Arnaldo Momigliano, *The Classical Foundations of Modern Historiography* (Sather Classical Lectures 54; Berkeley: University of California Press, 1990), 15–16.

[46] Although novelistic tropes are evident in earlier Jewish and Christian literature (e. g., apocryphal acts), the Pseudo-Clementines are widely acknowledged to be the first full-fledged Christian novel still extant; Ben Edwin Perry, *Ancient Romances: A Literary-Historical Account of Their Origins* (Berkeley: University of California Press, 1967), 285–93; Tomas Hägg, *The Novel in Antiquity* (Berkeley: University of California Press, 1983), 154–65. On the Pseudo-Clementines' subversion of the genre, see the sources cited in n. 25 above.

[47] Cf. *Hist. eccl.* 1.1.3–5; Grant, *Eusebius as Church Historian*, 22–32. His debt to the histories of Hellenistic philosophical schools, in particular, is stressed by Momigliano, *Classical Foundations of Modern Historiography*, 140–41.

When we look beyond the issue of genre, we also see how the two texts are shaped by many of the same literary practices. Most notable is their integration, consolidation, and reworking of earlier source materials, including Hellenistic Jewish as well as early Christian writings.[48] To be sure, Eusebius signals his use of sources in a manner consistent with the conventions of the historical genre,[49] while the authors/redactors of the *Homilies* interweave them without notice.[50] Studies of Eusebius' use of sources, however, have shown how he – no less than the *Homilies* – reworks his received material in the service of his own aims.[51]

In addition, Eusebius and the authors/redactors of the *Homilies* may draw on much the same reservoir of sources, even as they hold different opinions about what constitutes authentic records of the apostolic past. Eusebius, for instance, is familiar with a variety of Petrine and Clementine pseudepigrapha (*Hist. eccl.* 3.3.2, 3.38.5), including a book that circulated in the name of Clement that records Peter's debates with Apion.[52] Although he cites these sources only to reject them, it is striking that he nevertheless felt compelled to mention them.

In turn, the *Homilies* contains hints of awareness of the Pauline epistles so central to Eusebius' understanding of "orthodoxy," even as its authors/redactors seek to purge the apostolic past of any traces of Paul's positive influence.[53] In other words, we find – in both texts – evidence for fourth-century efforts to consolidate certain images of the past by anthologizing, reworking, and reframing earlier sources. In each case, some sources are privileged, while others are subverted or silenced.

Like Eusebius, the authors/redactors of the *Homilies* seem to have drawn selectively on source materials to remodel the apostolic past in the image of their

---

[48] For a summary of research on the sources of the Pseudo-Clementines, see Jones, "Pseudo-Clementines," 8–33. On the possibility that *Hom.* 4–6 draws on a Hellenistic Jewish apology, for instance, see Werner Heintze, *Der Klemensroman und seine griechischen Quellen* (TU 40.2; Leipzig: Hinrichs, 1914), esp. 48–50, 108–9, 112; Carl Schmidt, *Studien zu den Pseudo-Clementinen* (TU 46.1; Leipzig: Hinrichs, 1929), 160–239; William A. Adler, "Apion's Encomium of Adultery: A Jewish Satire of Greek *paideia* in the Pseudo-Clementine *Homilies*," *HUCA* 64 (1993): 28–30; James Carleton Paget, *Jews, Christians, and Jewish Christians in Antiquity* (WUNT 251; Tübingen: Mohr Siebeck, 2010), 427–92.

[49] On Eusebius' sources, see, e.g., Grant, *Eusebius as Church Historian*, 17–19; Timothy D. Barnes, *Constantine and Eusebius* (Cambridge, MA: Harvard University Press, 1981), 130–31.

[50] See below on the possible motivations for this choice.

[51] E.g., Gohei Hata, "Eusebius and Josephus: The Way Eusebius Misused and Abused Josephus," *Patristica: Proceedings of the Colloquia of the Japanese Society for Patristic Studies*, sup. 1 (2001): 49–66; Sabrina Inowlocki, "Eusebius of Caesarea's *Interpretatio Christiana* of Philo's *De vita contemplativa*," *HTR* 97 (2004): 305–28.

[52] *Hist. eccl.* 3.38.5: "And certain men have lately brought forward other wordy and lengthy writings under his (i.e., Clement's) name, containing dialogues of Peter and Apion (Πέτρου δὴ καὶ Ἀπίωνος διαλόγους περιέχοντα)." Cf. Clement's debates with Apion in *Homiles* 4–6 and discussion below.

[53] See discussion below.

own particular vision of "orthodoxy." In my view, it may not be coincidental that they do so in the middle of the fourth century, concurrent with attempts – by Eusebius and others – to deny the continued place of Judaism in church history and Christian identity. For, as we shall see, they answer the denial of the vitality of "Jewish-Christianity" with a radical assertion. According to the *Homilies* Christianity's continuity with Judaism is not just inexorable, but the teachings of the two traditions are the same; the true apostolic religion is, in essence, the revelation of Judaism to the Gentiles.

Apostolic Succession and the Transmission of Truth

At the beginning of the *Ecclesiastical History*, Eusebius stresses his aim to narrate "the successions of the holy apostles" (τὰς τῶν ἱερῶν ἀποστόλων διαδοχὰς; 1.1.1).[54] As is well known, this aim lies at the heart of his history of the early church and shapes his focus on its teachers and leaders.[55]

Apostolic succession is similarly pivotal for the plot of the *Homilies*, which focuses on a single instantiation. The novel purports to record Clement of Rome's own account of how he came to Christianity, and it establishes his close relationship with the apostle Peter. In its descriptions of Peter's teachings, the theme of proper succession repeatedly arises. Peter presents himself as heir to Jesus, and he stresses that the truth that leads to salvation is known and verified through the lines of succession that run through the Jerusalem church (*Hom.* 2.6–12; 3.15, 19; 11.35). Jesus, as True Prophet, "alone knows the truth; if anyone else knows anything, he has received it from him or from his disciples" (2.12).[56]

The epistemological significance of succession is here matched by its importance for ensuring the legitimacy of leaders and institutions. Central to the *Homilies* are tales about Peter's journeys to preach in different cities, where he founds communities and appoints bishops (*Hom.* 3.72; 7.5, 8, 12; 11.36; 20.23). In the course of Peter's public preaching, he stresses the need for ecclesiastical offices that mirror and maintain proper succession: the sole rule of God over the cosmos is reflected in the bishop's monarchic rule over his community, which is

---

[54] English translations of Eusebius' *Ecclesiastical History* are revised from Geoffrey Arthur Williamson, trans., *Eusebius, The History of the Church from Christ to Constantine* (Baltimore: Penguin, 1965), with reference to Gustave Bardy, ed. and trans., *Eusèbe de Césarée, Histoire Ecclésiastique, Livres I–IV* (Sources chrétiennes 31; Paris: Cerf, 1952).

[55] Grant, *Eusebius as Church Historian*, 45–83.

[56] English translations of the *Homilies* are revised from Alexander Roberts and James Donaldson, eds., *Ante-Nicene Fathers*, vol. 8: *Fathers of the Third and Fourth Centuries* (repr. ed.; Grand Rapids: Eerdmans, 1951), 224–52, 324–30; with reference to Bernhard Rehm, *Die Pseudoklementinen*, vol 1: *Homilien* (Rev. ed.; GSC 42; Berlin: Akademie-Verlag, 1969); as well as Alain Le Boulluec et al., trans., "Roman Pseudo-clémentin: *Homélies*," in *Écrits apocryphes chrétiens II*, ed. Pierre Geoltrain and Jean-Daniel Kaestli (Paris: Gallimard, 2005), 1193–589. On the treatment of proper succession and the transmission of knowledge in the *Recognitions*, see Kelley, *Knowledge and Religious Authority in the Pseudo-Clementines*, 135–79.

legitimated through the succession from Jesus to Peter and which thus ensures the continued preservation and transmission of true teachings (3.60–71; also *Ep. Clem.* 2–6).

Whereas Eusebius treats the succession of bishops and Christian teachers as different lines that only sometimes converge,[57] the authors/redactors of the *Homilies* identify apostolic succession with the office of the bishop, and they present this line of succession as the sole conduit for the transmission of Christian truth. Just as the apostles are depicted as Jesus' true and trustworthy heirs, charged with preserving and spreading his teachings (*Hom.* 1.15; 7.11; 17.19), so proper succession vouchsafes the faithful transmission of these teachings and enables the institutional settings for their maintenance in belief and practice.

Primordial Truth, Jewish Succession, and Apostolic Teaching

In both the *Homilies* and the *Ecclesiastical History*, however, the importance of the era of the apostles goes well beyond the appeal to apostolic succession to authenticate teachings and to legitimize leaders and communities. This era is granted a special place in human history. In both texts, it is celebrated as a glorious age in which hidden truth shone forth upon the earth (e.g., *Hist. eccl.* 2.3.1–2; *Hom.* 1.18–19). In both, moreover, apostolic teaching opens the ways for the restoration of primordial religion (e.g., *Hist. eccl.* 1.2.18–19, 1.4.4, 1.4.15; *Hom.* 8.10; 10.6).

In the *Ecclesiastical History*, this assertion is explicitly framed as a response to "pagan" polemics against Christianity.[58] Lest anyone "imagine that his teaching is new and strange (νέαν … καὶ ξένην), framed by a man of recent date no different from other men" (1.4.1; also 1.2.1, 1.3.21, 1.4.15), Eusebius stresses Christ's status as Logos. Prior to the Incarnation, Christ played a part in creation (1.2.3–5, 8, 14–16) as well as appearing to Abraham, Moses, and other Hebrew patriarchs and prophets (1.2.6–21, 1.4.8). It was his revelation of the Torah to Moses that first enabled seeds of truth to spread to other nations (1.2.22–23). His role in spreading truth is also, according to Eusebius, evident in the predictions about his incarnation embedded in the writings of Moses and other Hebrew authors (e.g., 1.2.24–1.3.6), who thus serve as witnesses to the true antiquity of Christ and the Christian faith.

Not only did Christ play an important role in the cosmos before the birth of Jesus, but – Eusebius claims – there were Christians on the earth, long prior to the emergence of the group that now takes that name. Due to the Logos' activities among the Hebrews, some lived as Christians:

---

[57] Grant, *Eusebius as Church Historian*, 45–47.

[58] See further Droge, "Apologetic Dimensions of the Ecclesiastical History," 493–98. On the place of anti-"pagan" polemics in Eusebius' work more broadly, see Aryeh Kofsky, *Eusebius of Caesaria against Paganism* (Leiden: Brill, 2000).

With regard to all these men who have been witnessed as righteous, going back from Abraham himself to the first man, one would not be departing far from the truth in calling them Christians in practice if not in name (ἔργῳ Χριστιανούς, εἰ καὶ μὴ ὀνόματι). (*Hist. eccl.* 1.4.6)[59]

Eusebius stresses that Christianity is the same religion discovered in the age of Abraham, to whom Christ/Logos appeared in the guise of an angel (1.2.7; cf. Gen 18:1):

It is obviously necessary to regard the religion proclaimed in recent years to all nations through Christ's teaching as none other than the first, most ancient, and most primitive of all religions (πρώτην ... καὶ πάντων παλαιοτάτην τε καὶ ἀρχαιοτάτην θεοσεβείας), discovered by Abraham and his followers. (*Hist. eccl.* 1.4.10)

Consequently, he is able to argue that "the practice of religion as communicated to us by Christ's teaching is ... not new and strange (νέαν καὶ ξένην), but – if the truth be told – primary, unique, and true" (πρώτην ... καὶ μόνην καὶ ἀληθῆ; 1.4.15).

When describing the religion of Abraham, Eusebius takes care to clarify that the pious Hebrews of the distant past did not practice circumcision, kashrut, or Sabbath observance like later Jews (1.4.8, 11–13). The implications for the lack of continuity in the Jewish transmission of Abrahamic religion are developed in his references of the Mosaic Torah, which he describes as preserving true revelations of Christ/Logos in metaphors and mysteries (1.4.8). Eusebius' assertion of the continuity between Abraham and Christianity is thus predicated on the denial of any inherent connection between the patriarch and his Jewish heirs.[60]

The theme of discontinuity is also determinative in his descriptions of later forms of Judaism. In *Hist. eccl.* 1.10.3, Eusebius stresses the lack of continuity in the proper succession of the high priesthood under Roman rule, speculating about the resultant loss of knowledge about purity and ritual practice. Like-wise, in 3.10.4, he quotes Josephus' assertion that the "accurate succession of prophets" ceased at the time of Artaxerxes (cf. *Ag. Ap.* 1.8). As in his treatment of Christian history, succession is a key theme, and the question of continuity is pivotal. Here, however, the rhetoric of succession is used to convey rupture.

The issue of Jewish succession is also central to Eusebius' explanation of the precise timing of Jesus' earthly sojourn (*Hist. eccl.* 1.6.1–8).[61] He stresses that the proper succession of Jewish rulers continued unbroken from the days of Moses to the first century CE (1.6.2, 5–6). Citing LXX Gen 49:10, however, he

---

[59] This view of pre-Christian Christians builds, e.g., on Justin, *1 Apol.* 46.

[60] For the many precedents for this use of Abraham, see Jeffrey S. Siker, *Disinheriting the Jews: Abraham in Early Christian Controversy* (Louisville: Westminster/John Knox, 1991).

[61] Strikingly, διαδοχή and related terms occur five times in this single passage, and Eusebius here makes efforts to stress the continuity of royal and priestly succession between Moses and first-century Judaism – even during the Babylonian Exile, etc. – so as to be able to assert that the breaks in these lines occurred directly prior to the birth of Jesus.

proposes that the Incarnation occurred when the succession was finally broken (1.6.1–8); with the Idumaean Herod, "their rulers and leaders, who had ruled in regular succession from the time of Moses himself (ἐξ αὐτοῦ Μωυσέως κατὰ διαδοχὴν), came to an end" (1.6.4).

Consistent with Eusebius' stated aim of recording apostolic successions together with "the calamities that immediately after their conspiracy (ἐπιβουλῆς) against our Saviour overwhelmed the entire Jewish people" (1.1.2), books 1–4 of the *Ecclesiastical History* tell the story of Jesus and the apostles in counterpoint to the history of the Jews.[62] For this pattern, LXX Gen 49:10 serves to provide a prophetic explanation. In Eusebius' reading,[63] this verse becomes an ancient prediction of the time when the scepter would fall from Judah, thereby opening the way for the fulfillment of "the expectation of the nations" with the coming of Christ:

It was without question in his (i.e., Herod's) time that the advent of Christ occurred; and the expected salvation and calling of the Gentiles followed at once, in accordance with the prophecy (i.e., LXX Gen 49:10). As soon as the rulers and leaders of Judah – those from the Jewish people – came to an end, not surprisingly the high priesthood, which had passed in regular succession (ἐπὶ τοὺς ἔγγιστα διαδόχους), from generation to generation, was plunged into confusion. (*Hist. eccl.* 1.6.8)

Eusebius thus argues that a break in Jewish succession ushered in the birth of Jesus and the establishment of apostolic succession, just as the downfall of the Jewish nation accompanied the birth of a new nation, namely, the Christians (1.4.2).[64]

In the *Homilies*, the theme of succession similarly serves as a means to answer "pagan" critiques of Christianity. By means of speeches attributed to Peter, the text asserts that monotheistic piety is the natural state of humankind (*Hom.* 8.10; 10.6), to which polytheistic corruptions accrued, due to the weaknesses of humankind, the intervention of demons, and the teachings of false prophets (e.g., 1.18; 2.16–18; 3.23–25; 8.11–20; 9.2–18; 10.7–23). As in the *Ecclesiastical*

---

[62] See further *Hist. eccl.* 2.5.6–10; 3.5.2–7, 3.7.7–9, where calamities amongst the Jews are direct results of their mistreatment of Jesus and his apostles. For a discussion of the Christian precedents for this approach to Jewish history, see Grant, *Eusebius as Church Historian*, 97–113. On the extension of these views in his *Preparatio Evangelica* and *Demonstratio Evangelica*, see Aryeh Kofsky, "Eusebius of Caesaria and the Christian–Jewish Polemic," in *Contra Iudaeos: Ancient and Medieval Polemics between Christians and Jews*, ed. Ora Limor and Guy G. Stroumsa (Tübingen: Mohr Siebeck, 1996), 59–84. For a comprehensive survey of Eusebius' references to Jews and Judaism, see Jörg Ulrich, *Eusebius von Caesarea und die Juden: Studien zur Rolle der Juden in der Theologie des Eusebius von Caesarea* (Patristische Texte und Studien 49; Berlin: de Gruyter, 1999).

[63] There are precedents for this interpretation, e.g., in Irenaeus, *Adv. haer.* 4.10.2 and Origen, *Princ.* 4.1.3.

[64] The view of Christians as an *ethnos* is developed in more detail in his *Preparatio Evangelica*, on which see Aaron P. Johnson, "Identity, Descent, and Polemic: Ethnic Argumentation in Eusebius' *Praeparatio Evangelica*," *JECS* 12 (2004): 23–56.

History, Jesus' Incarnation is presented as ushering in a new era of illumination and salvation for the Gentiles, whereupon the apostles spread the truth of the most ancient religion to those long shackled by idolatry, polytheism, and impiety (e. g., *Hom.* 2.33; 3.19).

Where the texts differ, however, is in their presentation of Judaism. Like Eusebius, the authors/redactors of the *Homilies* stress that Jesus is not a new teacher: he is the ultimate source of all truth in every age. Instead of appealing to the doctrine of the Logos,[65] the *Homilies* presents Jesus as the True Prophet who "has changed his forms and his names from the beginning of the world and so reappeared again and again in the world" (*Hom.* 3.20).[66] He is identified with a series of prophets, including Adam and Moses, who were sent by God to preach the same message of monotheism (2.16–17; 3.17–21). In the *Homilies*, Jesus himself is thus placed in an ancient line of prophetic succession.[67]

Perhaps most notably, this understanding of succession enables the authors/redactors of the *Homilies* to assert the identity of Moses and Jesus. In *Hom.* 8.6–7, for instance, the two are presented as equal sources of the truth:

Jesus is concealed from the Hebrews who have taken Moses as their teacher (ἀπὸ μὲν Ἑβραίων τὸν Μωυσῆν διδάσκαλον εἰληφότων καλύπτεται ὁ Ἰησοῦς), just as Moses is hidden from those who have believed Jesus (ἀπὸ δὲ τῶν Ἰησοῦ πεπιστευκότων ὁ Μωυσῆς ἀποκρύπτεται). Since there is a single teaching by both (μιᾶς γὰρ δι' ἀμφοτέρων διδασκαλίας), God accepts one who has believed either of these. To believe a teacher is for the sake of doing the things spoken by God.

And our lord himself (i. e., Jesus) says that this is so: "I thank you, Father of heaven and earth, because you have concealed these things from the wise and prudent, and you have revealed them to sucking babes" (cf. Matt 11:25; Luke 10:21). Thus God Himself has concealed a teacher from some (i. e., Jews), who foreknew what they should do (τοῖς μὲν ἔκρυψεν διδάσκαλον ὡς προεγνωκόσιν ἃ δεῖ πράττειν), and He has revealed (him) to others (i. e., "pagans"), who are ignorant about what they should do (τοῖς δὲ ἀπεκάλυψεν ὡς ἀγνοοῦσιν ἃ χρὴ ποιεῖν). (*Hom.* 8.6.1–5)[68]

---

[65] This omission is consistent with the *Homilies*' polemic against Hellenistic philosophy, on which see below.

[66] See further L. Cerfaux, "Le vrai prophète des Clémentines," *RSR* 18 (1928): 143–63; Strecker, *Judenchristentum in den Pseudoklementinen*, 145–53; Han Jan Willem Drijvers, "Adam and the True Prophet in the Pseudo-Clementines," in *Loyalitätskonflikte in der Religionsgeschichte: Festschrift für Carsten Colpe*, ed. Christoph Elsas and Hans G. Kippenberg (Würzburg: Königshausen & Neumann, 1990), 314–23; Charles A. Gieschen, "The Seven Pillars of the World: Ideal Figure Lists in the True Prophet Christology of the Pseudo-Clementines," *JSP* 12 (1994): 47–82.

[67] Although the identification of Jesus as True Prophet serves primarily to stress his true antiquity and to strengthen the connection between Christianity and the Israelite/Jewish past, it is noted that Jesus is the last of the line and that he will be revealed in the end times as the *Christos* (*Hom.* 2.17). As such, the salvation of the Gentiles is depicted as a mark of the impending Eschaton.

[68] For a comparison with the parallel in *Rec.* 4.5, see Chapter One. God's justice in hiding Jesus from the Jews is addressed in *Hom.* 18.6–7. Inasmuch as the truth was long hidden from the Gentiles, it is deemed fair that the last avatar of the True Prophet is now hidden from the

In effect, Christianity is here granted an ancient pedigree by means of its equation with Judaism. Whereas Eusebius answers "pagan" critics of Christianity by constructing a Hebrew heritage from broken fragments of Jewish scripture and history, the *Homilies* depicts Jesus' teachings as essentially the revelation of Moses' teachings to the Gentiles.

Accordingly, in the *Homilies*, apostolic succession stands in a close relationship to succession amongst the Jews. Whereas Eusebius stresses the break in the succession of Jewish kings, priests, and prophets, the authors/redactors of the *Homilies* affirm the continued oral transmission of Moses' teachings among the Jews in a line that stretches from the seventy elders of Num 11:16 (*Hom.* 2.38; also *Ep. Pet.* 1.2) to the Pharisees of Jesus' time (*Hom.* 3.18–19; 11.29).[69] Just as the *Homilies* describes Moses and Jesus as two earthly manifestations of the True Prophet (2.16–17), sent by God to teach the same truths to different peoples (8.6–7), so its authors/redactors depict apostolic succession and Pharisaic succession as separate but equal lines for the transmission of true knowledge.

Interestingly, the authors/redactors of the *Homilies* establish the continuance of proper succession among the Jews with appeal to a saying of Jesus. Specifically, they repeatedly cite his assertion that the Pharisees sit in the "seat of Moses" (τῆς Μωϋσέως καθέδρας; cf. Matt 23:2; *Hom.* 3.18–19; 3.70; 11:29; also *Ep. Pet.* 1.2). In *Hom.* 3.18–19, for instance, Jesus' reference to the "seat of Moses" is used to explain how the transmission of Moses' teachings by Jews relates to the transmission of Jesus' teachings by apostles. Peter begins by affirming that the Pharisees, as Moses' heirs, possess the prophetic truth:

"Ask your father, and he will tell you; your elders, and they will declare to you" (Deut 32:7). It is necessary to seek this father (i. e., Adam = the True Prophet) and to make further search for these elders (i. e., the Jews)! But you have not sought out concerning the one to whose time belongs the kingdom and to whom belongs the seat of prophecy (τῆς προφητείας καθέδρα), even though he himself (i. e., Jesus = the True Prophet) points this out himself, saying: "The scribes and the Pharisees sit in the seat of Moses (τῆς καθέδρας Μωυσέως); all things that they say to you, hear them" (cf. Matt 23:2–3). "Hear them," he said, "as entrusted with the key of the kingdom (τὴν κλεῖδα τῆς βασιλείας), which is knowledge (cf. Luke 11:52),[70] which alone can open the gate of life, through which alone is the entrance to eternal life." (*Hom.* 3.18.1–3)

As in the traditions about the Pharisees in the Gospels of Matthew and Luke (Matt 23:2–3, 13; Luke 11:52), it is here affirmed that these Jews have the knowledge that leads to salvation – and that they have kept it to themselves. In Matthew and Luke, the Pharisees are sharply criticized on these grounds.

Jews (18.6). The text there affirms that the "way that leads to the kingdom" is still available to them, even though "things of the kingdom" are now hidden from them (18.7).

[69] These statements are unparalleled in the *Recognitions*.

[70] Note also Matt 16:19, where it is Peter who is said to have "the key of the kingdom of heaven" (τὰς κλεῖδας τῆς βασιλείας τῶν οὐρανῶν).

The authors/redactors of the *Homilies* offer a different interpretation of Jesus' words.[71] Jews are not blamed for keeping Mosaic wisdom from the Gentiles inasmuch as God's plan involves a division of prophetic labor. Consequently, it is the Pharisees' act of concealment that occasions the Incarnation:

"Truly," he says, "they possess the key, but those wishing to enter they do not suffer to do so" (cf. Matt 23:13). On this account, I say, he himself – rising from his seat (καθέδρας) like a father for his children, proclaiming the things which from the beginning were transmitted in secret to the worthy (τὰ ἀπὸ αἰῶνος ἐν κρυπτῷ ἀξίοις παραδιδόμενα κηρύσσων), extending mercy even to the Gentiles, and having compassion for the souls of all – neglected his own blood (ἰδίου αἵματος ἠμέλει). (*Hom.* 3.18.3–3.19.1)

The True Prophet, in other words, took on the form of Jesus precisely to reveal prophetic truths to Gentiles. Just as the *Homilies* here depict the "seat of prophecy" (ἡ τῆς προφητείας καθέδρα) as the source of salvific knowledge and describe the True Prophet as rising from this seat to come to earth, so the reader is assured that his teachings are still transmitted on earth through parallel lines of prophetic succession – with the Pharisees in the "seat of Moses" (τῆς καθέδρας Μωυσέως; 3.18–19, 70; 11:29) and Peter's bishops in the "seat of Christ" (τῆς Χριστοῦ καθέδρας; 3.60).

As in the *Ecclesiastical History* (1.6.1–8), Jewish succession is thus central to an explanation of the timing and motivation for the Incarnation. Whereas Eusebius focuses on Jewish kingship and asserts a first-century break in the continuity of Jewish royal and priestly lines of succession, the *Homilies* focuses on Jewish learning and affirm the continuity that links Moses to the Pharisees.

Accordingly, the authors/redactors of the Homilies use LXX Gen 49:10 in a manner quite different than did Eusebius. In both the *Ecclesiastical History* and the *Homilies*, this verse is interpreted as a Mosaic prediction of Jesus' Incarnation. Whereas Eusebius cites the verse to support his supersessionist approach to Jewish history (*Hist. eccl.* 1.6.1–8), the authors/redactors of the *Homilies* present it as a prooftext for Jesus' appointed status as the prophet who points Gentiles to the truths in the Jewish scriptures (*Hom.* 3.49).

---

[71] Elsewhere in the *Homilies*, Peter explains that when Jesus called Pharisees "hypocrites," he was referring only to some of them: "Our teacher, when dealing with certain of the Pharisees and scribes among us – who are separated yet as scribes know the matters of the Law more than others – still reproved them as hypocrites, because they cleansed only the things that appear to men …. He spoke the truth with respect to the hypocrites among them, not with respect to all of them (πρὸς τοὺς ὑποκριτὰς αὐτῶν, οὐ πρὸς πάντας). To some he said that obedience was to be rendered, because they were entrusted with the chair of Moses (cf. Matt 23:2). But, to the hypocrites, he said: 'Woe to you, scribes and Pharisees, hypocrites' (cf. Matt 23:13)" (*Hom.* 11.28–29). Cf. *Hom.* 3.70: "Therefore, honor the throne of Christ (θρόνον οὖν Χριστοῦ τιμήσετε); for you are commanded to honor the seat of Moses (ὅτι καὶ Μωυσέως καθέδραν τιμᾶν ἐκελεύσθητε), even if those who occupy it are accounted sinners (κἂν οἱ προκαθεζόμενοι ἁμαρτωλοὶ νομίζωνται)."

Not only do the *Homilies* allow for the Mosaic authority of the Pharisees, but they further propose that proper teaching and leadership are preserved among the Jewish people due to their maintenance of the succession from Moses. In *Hom.* 2.38, Peter asserts that Moses "gave (παραδεδωκότος) the Law with the explanations (σὺν ταῖς ἐπιλύσεσιν)" to the seventy elders.[72] This oral tradition is later linked to the continuance of proper leadership among the Jews:

The Law of God was given, through Moses, without writing (ἀγράφως) to seventy wise men (cf. Num 11:16), to be handed down (παραδίδοσθαι), so that the government might be carried on by succession (τῇ διαδοχῇ). (*Hom.* 3.47.1)

These assertions prove particularly intriguing in light of the authority claims being made by Rabbis in Palestine, around the same time that the *Homilies* was taking form in nearby Syria. Early Rabbis similarly used the rhetoric of succession to trace their authority to Moses (*m. Avot* 1–5).[73] And, by the fourth century, this assertion of continuity was being articulated in terms of claims to possess, not just the Written Torah, but also the Oral Torah revealed to Moses at Mt. Sinai.[74]

This confluence of ideas has led Al Baumgarten to suggest that the Pseudo-Clementine authors/redactors may have had contact with late antique Rabbis.[75] If so, then it proves all the more significant that the authors/redactors of the *Homilies* appear to accept the Mosaic authority of their Jewish contemporaries. Arguably, their own understanding of succession may even be shaped by an effort to accommodate Rabbinic authority claims into a Christian schema.[76]

---

[72] This assertion is significant inasmuch as the authors/redactors of the *Homilies* view the written scriptures as corrupted by interpolations; see *Hom.* 2.38–52; 3.4–6, 9–11, 17–21, 37–51; 16.9–14; 18.12–13, 18–22. See further Strecker, *Judenchristentum*, 166–86; Karl Evan Shuve, "The Doctrine of the False Pericopes and Other Late Antique Approaches to the Problem of Scripture's Unity," in *Plots in the Pseudo-Clementine Romance*, ed. Frédéric Amsler et al. (Publications de l'Institut romand des sciences bibliques 6; Lausanne: Zébre, 2008), 437–45.

[73] On the Rabbinic use of succession lists, see, e.g., Amram Tropper, "Tractate *Avot* and Early Christian Succession Lists," in *The Ways that Never Parted: Jews and Christians in Late Antiquity and the Early Middle Ages*, ed. Adam H. Becker and Annette Yoshiko Reed (TSAJ 95; Tübingen: Mohr Siebeck, 2003), 159–88; Michael Swartz, "Chains of Tradition from *Avot* to the 'Avodah Piyutim," in *Jews, Christians, and the Roman Empire: The Poetics of Power*, ed. Natalie B. Dohrmann and Annette Yoshiko Reed (Philadelphia: University of Pennsylvania Press, 2012), 189–208.

[74] E.g., *Sifre Devarim* 351; *y. Megillah* 4.1; *y. Pe'ah* 2.6; *Pesiqta Rabbati* 14b; *b. Shabbat* 13a; and discussion in Martin S. Jaffee, *Torah in the Mouth: Writing and Oral Tradition in Palestinian Judaism, 200 BCE–400 CE* (New York: Oxford University Press, 2001).

[75] The acceptance of Pharisaic claims to possess oral Mosaic traditions is one of several features that leads Baumgarten to suggest that they viewed "the Jewish past in much the same way as the Pharisees and/or their rabbinic heirs did"; "Literary Evidence for Jewish Christianity in the Galilee," in *The Galilee in Late Antiquity*, ed. Lee I. Levine (New York: Jewish Theological Seminary of America, 1992), 43. I discuss other Rabbinic parallels in Chapters Five and Nine.

[76] This is made explicit in *Ep. Pet.* 1–2, where proper Jewish succession is held up as a model for proper Christian succession: "I beg and beseech you not to communicate to any of the Gentiles the books of my preachings that I sent to you (τῶν ἐμῶν κηρυγμάτων ἃς ἔπεμψά σοι βίβλους) nor to anyone of our own tribe before trial. But if anyone has been proved and found

Whereas Eusebius seems to pattern his understanding of succession on the lineages of Hellenistic philosophical schools,[77] the *Homilies'* model of succession may be indebted instead to Rabbinic models.

At the very least, the views expressed in the *Homilies* represent a striking departure from the supersessionist ideas current in the Christianity of its time. Like Eusebius, the authors/redactors of the *Homilies* answer "pagan" critiques by arguing for an authentic Christian claim to continuity and connection with the biblical past. They, however, also affirm Jewish claims to continuity and connection with the same past. The result is a surprisingly harmonious picture of Judaism and Christianity, conceived in terms of supplementarity rather than supersession.

The Apostolic Mission

Despite their very different views of Jews and Judaism, the *Homilies* and *Ecclesiastical History* both characterize Christianity as a primarily Gentile phenomenon. Moreover, in both of these texts, this characterization has important ramifications for the scope and aims of the apostolic mission.

Eusebius describes the apostolic mission to the Jews in much the same manner as he portrays the Jewish people – as important for a delineated period of time but ultimately doomed to failure. When recounting the apostles' missionary activities prior to Saul/Paul, for instance, he notes that the apostles initially preached to Jews. He stresses, however, that they did so solely out of necessity (2.1.8; cf. Acts 11:19).

After describing Saul/Paul's commission by the risen Christ (2.1.14), however, Eusebius evokes a very different situation:

Thus, with the powerful cooperation of heaven, the whole world was suddenly lit by the sunshine of the saving Logos. At once, in accordance with the Holy Scriptures, the voice of its inspired evangelists and apostles went forth into all the earth, and their words to the ends of the world (cf. Ps 19:4). ... Those who, following ancestral tradition and ancient error, were shackled by the old sickness of idolatrous superstition (οἵ τε ἐκ προγόνων διαδοχῆς καὶ τῆς ἀνέκαθεν πλάνης παλαιᾷ νόσῳ δεισιδαιμονίας εἰδώλων τὰς ψυχὰς πεπεδημένοι) were freed, as it were – by the power of Christ and through the teachings

worthy, then to commit them to him, after the manner in which Moses delivered his books to the Seventy who succeeded to his chair (καθ' ἣν καὶ τοῖς ἑβδομήκοντα ὁ Μωυσῆς παρέδωκε τοῖς τὴν καθέδραν αὐτοῦ παρειληφόσιν).... For, his countrymen (i.e., the Jews) keep the same rule of monarchy and polity (τῆς μοναρχίας καὶ πολιτείας φυλάσσουσι κανόνα) everywhere, being unable in any way to think otherwise or to be led out of the way of the much-indicating scriptures. According to the rule (κανόνα) delivered to them, they endeavor to correct the discordances of the scriptures if anyone, not knowing the traditions (παραδόσεις), is confounded at the various utterances of the prophets. Therefore they charge no one to teach, unless he has first learned how the scriptures must be used. And thus they have amongst them one God, one Law, one hope."

[77] E. g., Momigliano, *Classical Foundations of Modern Historiography*, 140–41.

of his followers and the miracles they wrought – from cruel masters and found liberation from heavy chains. They turned their backs on demonic polytheism in all its forms (πάσης … δαιμονικῆς κατέπτυον πολυθεῖας) and acknowledged that there was one God only, the fashioner of all things. (*Hist. eccl.* 2.3.1–2)

Whereas Eusebius celebrates the worldwide spread of Christianity as the long-fated acceptance of Abraham's religion by the Gentiles who are the patriarch's true heirs (1.4.12; cf. Gen 18:18; Gal 3:15–29), the *Homilies* presents the apostolic mission as an attempt by Peter and other "Jewish-Christians" to convince "pagans" of truths already known to the Jews. Indeed, by the logic of *Hom.* 8.5–7, no Jewish mission is needed; Jews will be saved through the teachings of Moses, and the appointed task of Jesus and his apostles is solely to save "pagans."[78] Accordingly, the *Homilies* depicts Peter and the other apostles as proselytizing, not their fellow Jews, but only Gentiles like Clement.

The *Homilies* has been so celebrated by modern scholars as a source of "Jewish-Christian" traditions that it can be easy to forget that the text's own focus falls on "pagans."[79] Peter here preaches about the dangers of polytheism, idolatry, "magic," philosophy, and astrology (e.g., 1.7; 3.7–8; 7:20; 9.2–18; 10.7–24; 11.6–15; 14.4–5, 11; 15.5; 16.7), and Clement works to expose the impurity and impiety of Greek *paideia* (e.g., 1.11–12; 4.12–21; 6.12–25).[80] Moreover, consistent with the *Homilies'* twofold model of prophetic succession,

---

[78] We also find references elsewhere in the *Homilies* suggesting that Jews are already safe both from demonic influence (e.g., 9.20) and from temptations to polytheism and "heresy": "And with us, who have had handed down from our forefathers the worship of the God who made all things (καὶ ἡμῖν μὲν τοῖς ἐκ προγόνων παρειληφόσιν τὸν τὰ πάντα κτίσαντα σέβειν θεόν) as well as the mystery of the books which are able to deceive, he (i.e., Simon) will not prevail. But with those from among the Gentiles who have been brought up in the polytheistic manner (τοῖς δὲ ἀπὸ ἐθνῶν, τὴν πολύθεον ὑπόληψιν σύντροφον ἔχουσιν) and who do not know the falsehoods of the scriptures, he will prevail much" (3.4). Notably, this is one among several passages in which Peter is depicted as contrasting "us" with "Gentiles," thereby communicating his self-identification with the Jewish people.

[79] This focus is consistent with the prominence of Hellenism, flowering of Neoplatonism, and continued survival of "paganism" in fourth-century Syria, on which see, e.g., Glen Warren Bowersock, *Hellenism in Late Antiquity* (Ann Arbor: University of Michigan Press, 1990), 29–53; Han Jan Willem Drijvers, "The Persistence of Pagan Cults and Practices in Christian Syria," in Drijvers, *East of Antioch: Studies in Early Syriac Christianity* (Variorum Reprints; London: Variorum, 1984), XVI; Kelley, *Knowledge and Religious Authority in the Pseudo-Clementines*, 194–97.

[80] On Greek *paideia* in fourth-century Antioch, see, e.g., André Jean Festugière, *Antioche païenne et chrétienne: Libanius, Chrysostome et les moines de Syrie* (Paris: Boccard, 1959). Interestingly, Clement is credited in *Hom.* 4 with an opinion not unlike that expressed by Ephraim: "Blessed is the one who has never tasted the poison of the wisdom of the Greeks" (*De fide*, CSCO 154.7); see further Sebastian Brock, "From Antagonism to Assimilation: Syrian Attitudes towards Greek Learning," in *Syriac Perspectives on Late Antiquity* (Variorum Reprints; London: Variorum, 1984), V.19.

Jesus' followers are depicted as joining in the struggle against "paganism" long and still fought by the Jews.[81]

Peter, Paul, and Clement of Rome

Given the *Homilies'* focus on the Gentile mission, its omission of Paul is notable. The story of Christianity's spread is here told without any direct reference to the man elsewhere celebrated as "the apostle to the Gentiles" (Rom 11:13; Gal 2:2). When read in light of the extreme prominence of Paul in other fourth-century Christian writings,[82] the silence seems pointed.

Although the *Homilies* lacks the explicit anti-Pauline polemics found in other Pseudo-Clementine sources (e.g., *Rec.* 1.66–70; *Ep. Pet.* 2.3–7), the text may include an indirect jab at Paul's authority.[83] In the course of a debate about the nature of revelation (17.13–17), Simon Magus accuses Peter as follows:

> You claim that you have learned the things of your teacher exactly, because you have directly seen and heard him, but that it is impossible for another to learn the same thing by means of a dream or vision (ὁράματι ἢ ὀπτασίᾳ; cf. 2 Cor 12:1). (*Hom.* 17.13.1)

In his response, Peter makes his own position clear:

> Whoever trusts an apparition, vision, or dream is prone to error (ἡ δὲ ὀπτασία ἅμα τῷ ὀφθῆναι πίστιν παρέχει τῷ ὁρῶντι ὅτι θειότης ἐστίν). He does not know whom he is trusting; for it is possible it may be an evil spirit or a deceptive spirit, pretending in his speeches to be what it is not. (*Hom.* 17.14.3–4)

Peter, moreover, goes on to contest any authority rooted in visions and to defend his own apostleship. Interestingly, the words here placed in his mouth resonate both with Paul's defense of his apostleship and with his accusations of Peter (esp. Gal 1:11–2:21; 1 Cor 9:1–5; 15:7–9; 2 Cor 11:4–14):

---

[81] I explore these dynamics further in Chapter Four above.

[82] E.g., Margaret Mary Mitchell, *The Heavenly Trumpet: John Chrysostom and the Art of Pauline Interpretation* (HUT 40; Tübingen: Mohr Siebeck, 2000); Werner Erdt, *Marius Victorinus Afer, der erste lateinische Pauluskommentar: Studien zu seinen Pauluskommentaren im Zusammenhang der Wiederentdeckung des Paulus in der abendländischen Theologie des 4. Jahrhunderts* (Frankfurt am Main: Lang, 1980); Thomas F. Martin, "*Vox Pauli*: Augustine and the Claims to Speak for Paul, an Exploration of Rhetoric at the Service of Exegesis," *JECS* 8 (2000): 238–42; Andrew S. Jacobs, "A Jew's Jew: Paul and the Early Christian Problem of Jewish Origins," *JR* 86 (2006): 258–86. See also, more broadly, Maurice F. Wiles, *The Divine Apostle: The Interpretation of St. Paul's Epistles in the Early Church* (Cambridge: Cambridge University Press, 1967); William S. Babcock, ed., *Paul and the Legacies of Paul* (Dallas: Southern Methodist University Press, 1990).

[83] Although some have read the Pseudo-Clementine Simon as merely a cipher for Paul, I concur with Côté that this equation is too simplistic; see further "La fonction littéraire de Simon le Magicien dans les Pseudo-Clémentines," *Laval Théologique et Philosophique* 57 (2001): 514–16, 19.

If our Jesus appeared to you in a vision (δι' ὁράματος ὀφθείς), made himself known to you, and spoke to you, it was as one who is enraged with an adversary – and this is the reason why it was through visions and dreams (δι' ὁραμάτων καὶ ἐνυπνίων; cf. Acts 18:9) or through revelations that were from without (δι' ἀποκαλύψεων ἔξωθεν οὐσῶν; cf. Gal 1:16) that he spoke to you! Can anyone be rendered fit for instruction through apparitions (cf. Gal 1:11–12)? … How are we to believe you, when you tell us that he appeared to you? How is it that he appeared to you, when you entertain opinions contrary to his teaching?[84] If you were seen and taught by him and became his apostle, even for a single hour, then proclaim his utterances, interpret his teaching, love his apostles, and do not contend with me who accompanied with him (ἐμοὶ τῷ συγγενομένῳ αὐτῷ μὴ μάχου)! For you now stand in direct opposition to me (πρὸς … ἐναντίος ἀνθέστηκάς μοι) – who am a firm rock, the foundation of the church (cf. Matt 16:18)! … If you say that I am 'condemned' (καταγνωσθέντος; Gal 2:11), you bring an accusation against God, who revealed the Christ to me. (*Hom.* 17.19.1–6)

Ferdinand Christian Baur, Gerd Lüdemann, and others have proposed that this passage was meant to counter Paul's claim to be an apostle by virtue of his vision of the risen Christ (e. g., Gal 1:12; 1 Cor 15:8–10; also Acts 9:3–20).[85] If so, then the association with Simon may prove particularly significant, hinting at a view of Paul's heirs as truly "heretics."[86]

By contrast, Eusebius readily accepts Paul's claims. For him, in fact, it is a mark of Paul's preeminence that he became an apostle "'not of men neither through men, but by the revelation of Jesus Christ himself (δι' ἀποκαλύψεως δ' αὐτοῦ Ἰησοῦ Χριστοῦ) and of God the Father who raised him from the dead' (Gal 1:1) … being made worthy of the call by a vision and by a voice which was uttered in a revelation from heaven (δι' ὀπτασίας καὶ τῆς κατὰ τὴν ἀποκάλυψιν οὐρανίου φωνῆς ἀξιωθεὶς τῆς κλήσεως)" (*Hist. eccl.* 2.1.14).

---

[84] Lüdemann further suggests that the false gospel referenced in *Hom.* 2.17 is Paul's gospel (*Opposition to Paul in Jewish Christianity*, 185; so too Strecker, *Judenchristentum in den Pseudoklementinen*, 188–90).

[85] E. g., Ferdinand Christian Baur, "Die Christuspartei in der korinthischen Gemeide, der Gegensatz des petrinischen und paulischen Christentums in der alten Kirche, der Apostel Petrus in Rom," *Tübinger Zeitschrift für Theologie* 4 (1831): 116; Lüdemann, *Opposition to Paul in Jewish Christianity*, 185–88. Inasmuch as Baur followed nineteenth-century Pseudo-Clementine scholarship in dating the *Homilies* to the second century, this passage was central to his famous theory that the early church was split into Petrine and Pauline factions. For the history of research, see Lüdemann, *Opposition to Paul in Jewish Christianity*, 1–32, 303; Côté, "Fonction littéraire de Simon le Magicien," 515.

[86] Whether or not the tradition, in its present form, is anti-Pauline in any pointed sense, it functions in the *Homilies* as part of the overarching defense of an epistemology rooted in succession directly from Jesus' disciples – a point stressed by Kelley, *Knowledge and Religious Authority in the Pseudo-Clementines*, 135–38. Notably, the critique of knowledge gained from dreams and visions also resonates with debates about prophecy in the early fourth century; see Polymnia Athanassiadi, "Dreams, Theurgy and Freelance Divination: The Testimony of Iamblichus," *JRS* 83 (1993): 115–30. Here, as elsewhere, the authors/redactors of the *Homilies* may take full advantage of the polysemy that the novelistic genre permits, taking aim at multiple enemies.

In his account of apostolic history, moreover, Eusebius privileges the Pauline version of events, even to the detriment of Peter. In books 1–2 of the *Ecclesiastical History*, Eusebius follows the New Testament literature in granting Peter a central place in the earliest church and a leading role among the other apostles. When he turns to describe the worldwide spread of Christianity in book 3, however, it is Paul who looms large. As in Gal 2:7–10, Paul is credited with the mission to the Gentiles, while Peter's activities are almost solely limited to Jews.[87]

Book 3 opens with a summary account of the apostles' respective roles in spreading Christianity, articulated in explicit contrast to the purported decline of the Jews (3.1.1). Eusebius here celebrates the dispersion of Christ's apostles and disciples "throughout the known world" (ἐφ᾽ ἅπασαν ... τὴν οἰκουμένην): Thomas in Parthia, Andrew in Scythia, John in Asia (3.1.1). Following 1 Pet 1:1, he states that Peter preached to "the Jews of the Diaspora" (τοῖς [ἐκ] διασπορᾶς Ἰουδαίοις) in Pontus, Galatia, Bithynia, Cappadocia, and Asia (3.1.2).[88] The account, however, culminates with Paul. Following Rom 15:19, Eusebius credits the apostle with "preaching the Gospel of Christ from Jerusalem to Illyricum" (3.1.3).

Also telling are the parallel descriptions of Paul and Peter in *Hist. eccl.* 3.4.1–2. Here, Eusebius appeals again to Rom 15:19, together with the witness of Luke, to assert that Paul "preached to the Gentiles and laid the foundations of the churches from Jerusalem even unto Illyricum" (3.4.1). Peter, by contrast, is said to have "preached Christ and taught the doctrine of the new covenant to those of the circumcision (τοὺς ἐκ περιτομῆς)," and he is described as writing "to the Hebrews in the Diaspora (τοῖς ἐξ Ἑβραίων οὖσιν ἐν διασπορᾷ) in Pontus, Galatia, Cappadocia, Asia, and Bithynia" (3.4.2).[89] Although the activities of the two are paralleled, Paul is celebrated as the apostle responsible for Christianity's worldwide spread, while Peter is associated with the early mission to the Jews.[90]

In effect, Eusebius repeatedly elevates Paul as the one responsible for the worldwide spread of Christianity, which – in his presentation – is synonymous with its spread among Gentiles outside of Judaea. To this, Peter's preaching pales in significance; his mission is presented as a relic of the pre-Pauline pattern of preaching within Judaea and to Diaspora Jews (2.1.8).

Of course, Peter must be permitted some role in authorizing the succession of bishops in the church of Rome. Even in this role, however, Eusebius consistently

---

[87] The sole exception is *Hist. eccl.* 2.3.3, which follows Acts 10–11. Even there, however, Peter's activities remain geographically limited to Judaea.

[88] I.e., inasmuch as 1 Pet 1:1 is addressed to the "exiles of the dispersion" (παρεπιδήμοις διασπορᾶς) in these lands.

[89] Note also *Hist. eccl.* 2.7.1, where Peter is said to have met Philo of Alexandria when the two were in Rome.

[90] Contrast Irenaeus, *Adv. haer.* 3.1.1, where Matthew is associated with evangelizing Jews through his Gospel, while "Peter and Paul were preaching at Rome and laying the foundations of the church."

pairs him with Paul. Both Peter and Paul are associated with Rome by means of their martyrdoms (2.25.5, 8; 3.1.2–3). In *Hist. eccl.* 3.2.1, for instance, Eusebius presents Linus' rise to the Roman episcopacy as occurring after the martyrdoms of Paul and Peter. Rather than describing Linus as Peter's successor, however, Eusebius takes the opportunity to note his connection with Paul, associating the bishop with the figure of the same name in 2 Tim 4:21.[91] When he mentions Linus again in 3.4.9, it is in the context of a list of Paul's companions; even though Linus is here called Peter's successor, the connection with Paul remains primary. Accordingly, Eusebius refers to later bishops of Rome, not as the successors of Peter, but rather as those "who held the episcopate there after Paul and Peter" (3.11.2; also 4.1.1).[92]

Of special relevance, for our purposes, is Eusebius' approach to Clement of Rome.[93] The first reference to Clement in the *Ecclesiastical History* occurs in the context of his summary of early Christians associated with Paul (3.4.6–11). After discussing Luke, Crescens, and Linus, he adds that "Clement too, who became the third bishop of the church of the Romans, was Paul's co-laborer (συνεργὸς) and fellow combatant (συναθλητὴς), as he himself testifies" (3.4.9), identifying Clement with the man of the same name mentioned by Paul in Phil 4:3.[94] He repeats this claim in 3.15, when recounting the early succession of bishops at Rome. Whereas the *Homilies* purports to preserve Clement's first-person account of his travels with Peter, Eusebius aligns the famous Roman bishop solely with Paul.[95]

"Orthodoxy" and "Heresy"

We also find interesting points of contrast and comparison in their respective accounts of the rivalry between Peter and Simon Magus. This rivalry is central to the plot of the *Homilies*.[96] Throughout the novel, Peter's missionary travels are occasioned by the need to chase Simon. The apostle scurries from city to city along the eastern coastline of the Mediterranean, seeking to correct the errors spread by the "heretic" and to force him into public debates. Whereas Simon

---

[91] I.e. following Irenaeus, *Adv. haer.* 3.3.3.

[92] Cf. *Hist. eccl.* 3.36.2, where Ignatius is called the "chosen bishop of Antioch, second in succession to Peter." Note also the precedent of Irenaeus, who describes the Roman church as "founded and organized" by Peter and Paul (*Adv. haer.* 3.3.2). Eusebius seems to resolve the problem of the apparent conflict between Peter and Paul by identifying the "Cephas" of Gal 2:11 with someone other than Peter (*Hist. eccl.* 1.12.2); he does not explain Acts 15.

[93] Compare Irenaeus, *Adv. haer.* 3.3.3, in which Clement is associated with the apostles in general, rather than any specific apostle.

[94] In this identification, Eusebius likely follows Origen, *Comm. John* 1.29.

[95] Tertullian, by contrast, describes Clement as Peter's immediate successor as bishop of Rome (*De prae. haer.* 32).

[96] See further Côté, *Thème de l'opposition*, 22–59.

lures his listeners into idolatry and moral corruption, Peter preaches chastity, piety, and ritual purity (e. g., 3.2–4; 7.2–4, 8). Whereas Simon proclaims multiple divinities, Peter defends the unity and goodness of the One God who created the cosmos (e. g., 2.22; 3.38–40; 18.1–4).

In the *Homilies*, this rivalry is presented as part of a broader historical pattern, namely, the rule of syzygies. For every true prophet, we are here told that God sends a false one in advance: Cain came before Abel, Ishmael before Isaac, Esau before Jacob, Aaron before Moses, and John the Baptist before Jesus (2.16–17, 33; 7.2). Likewise for Simon and Peter:

> It is possible, following this order (τῇ τάξει), to perceive to which Simon belongs, who came before me to the Gentiles (ὁ πρὸ ἐμοῦ εἰς τὰ ἔθνη πρῶτος ἐλθών), and to which I belong – I who have come after him and have come in on him as light on darkness, as knowledge on ignorance, as healing on disease. (*Hom.* 2.17)

When Simon and Peter compete to persuade "pagans," they thus act as agents of true and false prophesy, taking up the perennial battle between the two. Just as Peter learns and transmits the truth, by virtue of his connection to the True Prophet Jesus, so Simon stands in a long line of error. According to the *Homilies*, "heresy" always precedes "orthodoxy."

By comparison, Eusebius' treatment of Simon and Peter is quite brief. Interestingly, however, it integrates many of the same elements found in the *Homilies*: Simon is the "author of all heresy," and his error is marked by the promotion of idolatry, sacrifice, and libations as well as by his own desire to be worshipped (*Hist. eccl.* 2.13.6; cf. *Hom.* 2.21). And, even as Eusebius stresses that "heresy" was not yet a real threat in the apostolic age (2.14.2), he nevertheless depicts the conflict between Simon and Peter as a battle between divine and demonic forces:

> At that time, the evil power (πονηρὰ δύναμις) which hates all that is good and plots against the salvation of humankind raised up Simon … to be a great opponent of great men, our Saviour's inspired apostles. Nevertheless, divine and celestial grace (ἡ θεία καὶ ὑπερουράνιος χάρις) worked with its ministers, by their advent and presence speedily extinguishing the flames of the evil one before they could spread. (*Hist. eccl.* 2.14.1–2)

As in the *Homilies*, Simon flees, and Peter gives chase:

> The sorcerer (γόης) of whom we have been speaking – having been struck as though his mind's eye by a divine miraculous flash of light when earlier, in Judaea, his evil machinations had been exposed by the apostle Peter – promptly undertook a very long journey overseas from East to West. (*Hist. eccl.* 2.14.4)

These similarities have led Robert Grant to propose that Eusebius here draws on an early version of the Pseudo-Clementine novel.[97] If he is correct, then the points of contrast with the *Homilies* prove all the more significant.

---

[97] Grant, *Eusebius as Church Historian*, 87. I.e., presumably the Pseudo-Clementine *Grundschrift*. Cf. Strecker, *Judenchristentum in den Pseudoklementinen*, 28, 84, 268.

In the *Ecclesiastical History*, the challenge posed by Simon is the impetus for Peter's journey to Rome, whereby he brings the wisdom of the East to the West and establishes Rome as a centre from which Christian truth then radiates (*Hist. eccl.* 2.14.5–6; cf. *Hom.* 1.16); Eusebius further claims that Peter's preaching in Rome is preserved in the Gospel of Mark (2.15.1).

In the *Homilies*, Simon's actions similarly motivate Peter's journeys, but Clement is the one who records his preachings (*Hom.* 1.1; also *Ep. Clem.* 19–20), and Rome proves less central. Clement hails from Rome, and his interest in Jesus is piqued when rumors reach Rome and when he sees an unnamed preacher proclaiming the message of eternal life (*Hom.* 1.6–7). To learn the truth, however, Clement must travel to its source in Judaea (1.7). The action of the novel is centered on the port cities of Palestine and Syria: Caesaria, Tyre, Sidon, Berytus, Byblos, Tripolis, Aradus, Laodicea. Consistent with the probable Syrian provenance of the *Homilies*, Peter's journeys are oriented towards – and culminate in – Antioch (11.36; 12.1, 24; 14.12; 16.1; 20.11, 13, 18, 20–21, 23). In the *Homilies*, this is the city where Peter bests Simon and where he has resolved "to remain some length of time" (12.24). Whereas Eusebius refracts the apostolic past through his belief in the centrality of Rome and the Roman Empire for Christian history, the *Homilies* privileges Syria.[98]

In addition, the *Homilies* and *Ecclesiastical History* offer very different assessments of "heresy," its appearance, and its power. Eusebius famously asserts that "orthodoxy" precedes "heresy." He depicts the former as the obvious truth, proclaimed in one voice by the apostles and all their true heirs; "heresies" are derivative, dividing, and ultimately impotent (esp. 4.7.13).[99]

By contrast, the *Homilies* depicts "heresy" as a dire challenge to "orthodoxy": not only does error precede truth, but the two are mirror images of one another.[100] Moreover, it can be difficult to determine the difference between them – not least because "heresy" is often the more popular of the two (*Hom.* 2.18).

Who, then, is here imagined as "heretical"? Consistent with the apostolic narrative setting of the *Homilies*, no reference is made to any specific postapostolic group. Rather, the nature of "heresy" is sketched solely by means of the conflate character of Simon.[101] In his speeches, he is credited with a number of Marcionite beliefs.[102] At the same time, however, he is also associated with

---

[98] Eusebius' dismissive approach to Syriac Christianity, both within and beyond the Roman Empire, is noted by Brock, "Eusebius and Syriac Christianity," 212.

[99] On the heresiologial comments in the *Ecclesiastical History*, together with their various sources, see, e. g., Grant, *Eusebius as Church Historian*, 84–96; Barnes, *Constantine and Eusebius*, 133–35.

[100] On the parallels between Peter and Simon, see Côté, *Thème de l'opposition*, 23–29.

[101] That the Pseudo-Clementine Simon is a conflate character, not to be identified with any single group or figure, has been convincingly established by Côté, "Fonction littéraire de Simon le Magicien," 513–23; see also Edwards, "Clementina," 462.

[102] A. Salles, "Simon le magicien ou Marcion?" *VC* 12 (1958): 197–224.

Samaritan anti-Judaism, Alexandrian philosophy, and Greco-Egyptian "magic" (e. g., 2.21–26; 5.2), and chief among his followers are an astrologer, an Alexandrian grammarian, and an Athenian Epicurean (e. g., 4.6). Consequently, as Côté has demonstrated, the *Homilies* departs from earlier traditions to stress Simon's link to Hellenism.[103] Within the *Homilies*, the figure of Simon may thus serve, not just to counter Marcionites, but also to establish the Gentile genealogy of "heresy" and to throw doubt on the "orthodoxy" of all Christians who draw on Hellenistic learning.[104]

"Jewish-Christianity"

For the authors/redactors of the *Homilies*, a term such as "Jewish-Christianity" would have likely seemed highly redundant. The *Homilies*, as we have seen, depicts the apostolic age as an extension of biblical and Jewish history, marked by the opening of a parallel line of salvation for the Gentiles. Perhaps not surprisingly, then, the terms "Christian" and "Christianity" are never used in the *Homilies*. The text speaks of Jews (and Pharisees in particular) as heirs to the teachings of the prophet Moses. Peter and Barnabus refer to their own Jewish ethnicity and self-identify with Jews and Israel (e. g., 1.13; 3.4; 9.20). Even when referring to Clement and other Gentile followers of Jesus, the text refrains from distinguishing them as "Christians." Most often, they are termed "God-fearers" (θεοσεβεῖς), the well-known label that we find elsewhere applied to Gentile sympathizers with Judaism.[105]

Moreover, in *Homilies* 11.16, the term "Jew" is redefined so as to include Jewish followers of Moses as well as Gentile followers of Jesus:

If anyone acts impiously, he is not pious. In the same way, if a foreigner keeps the Law, he is a Jew (ἐὰν ὁ ἀλλόφυλος τὸν νόμον πράξῃ, Ἰουδαῖός ἐστιν), while he who does not is a Greek (μὴ πράξας δὲ Ἕλλην). For the Jew, believing in God, keeps the Law (ὁ γὰρ Ἰουδαῖος πιστεύων θεῷ ποιεῖ τὸν νόμον). (*Hom.* 11.16)

The category of "Jew" here denotes anyone who follows the Law that God laid out for them. As a result, the category of "apostle" is not a subset or paradigm of "Christian"; rather, it serves to mark adherence to the true religion proclaimed by Moses and Jesus, in contrast to polytheistic and idolatrous "pagan" religions and the "heresies" that use Christ's name to promote false beliefs and impure practices.

---

[103] Côté, *Thème de l'opposition*, 195–96.

[104] See further Chapters Four and Five in this volume.

[105] E. g., Joyce Reynolds and Robert Tannebaum, *Jews and God-Fearers at Aphrodisias: Greek Inscriptions with Commentary* (Cambridge: Cambridge Philological Society, 1987), 48–66.

If Christianity and Judaism appear to be different, the reader of the *Homilies* is assured that this is only because God chose to hide the prophet of one from the followers of the other (8.6). Even as the *Homilies* thus acknowledges that most Jews and Christians are blind to Christianity's true nature as the divine disclosure of Judaism to other nations, it depicts those who understand as specially blessed. Through the mouth of the Jewish apostle Peter, the authors/redactors reveal that no one is richer in wisdom than the few who embrace both Moses and Jesus:

If anyone has been thought worthy to recognize by himself both (i. e., Moses and Jesus) as preaching one doctrine (καταξιωθείη τοὺς ἀμφοτέρους ἐπιγνῶναι ὡς μιᾶς διδασκαλίας ὑπ' αὐτῶν κεκηρυγμένης), that one has been counted rich in God, understanding both the old things as new in time and the new things as old. (*Hom.* 8.7; cf. *Rec.* 4.5)

Through Peter, they thus propose that there are two paths to salvation, and the two paths are actually one. Jews can be saved as Jews; Christians can be saved as Christians; and "Jewish-Christians" are the best of all.

By contrast, Eusebius promotes an image of Christianity as a new/old *ethnos* (e. g., 1.1.9) with a history and religion distinct from those of the Jews. To this effort, Jewish converts to Christianity would seem to pose a problem. Not only does their combination of Christian belief and Jewish ethnicity undermine his claims concerning the historical and spiritual disjunction between Judaism and Abrahamic/Christian religion, but the very fact of their belief in Jesus as messiah might speak against his theory that God brought the destruction of the Temple and other calamities to punish the Jews for rejecting Jesus and his apostles.[106]

Arguably, Eusebius solves such problems through his account of the Jerusalem church, on the one hand, and his description of the Ebionites, on the other. Both accounts echo his treatment of Judaism in poignant ways. And, in each case, issues of succession are emphasized.

We noted above how Eusebius stresses the discontinuity in Jewish history in multiple ways, extricating Abrahamic religion from Judaism and stressing the breaks in the lines of Jewish prophetic, royal, and priestly succession. Similarly, in his description of the Jerusalem church, there is a striking overdetermination in the assertion of discontinuity. When discussing the first Jewish revolt against Rome (3.5–8), Eusebius famously claims that the Christians of Jerusalem left the city for Pella prior to the Roman siege of 70 CE:

Furthermore, the people of the Jerusalem church (τοῦ λαοῦ τῆς ἐν Ἱεροσολύμοις ἐκκλησίας), by means of a prophesy given by revelation to acceptable persons there, were ordered to leave the city before the war began and settle in a town in Peraea called Pella. When those who believed in Christ from Jerusalem migrated (τῶν εἰς Χριστὸν πεπιστευκότων ἀπὸ τῆς Ἱερουσαλὴμ μετῳκισμένων), it was as if holy men had utterly

---

[106] That the problem of "Jewish-Christianity" was a "live" issue for Eusebius may be confirmed by several instances in which he seems to have changed his mind on related topics; see Grant, *Eusebius as Church Historian*, 15.

abandoned the royal metropolis of the Jews and the entire Jewish land, and the judgment of God (ἡ ἐκ θεοῦ δίκη) at last overtook them for their crimes against Christ and his apostles, completely blotting that wicked generation from among men. (*Hist. eccl.* 3.5.3)[107]

Following this passage, we might infer that there was no Christian presence in Jerusalem between the first Jewish War and the city's repopulation by Gentile Christians. Yet, when Eusebius later recounts the succession of bishops at Jerusalem (4.5.1–4), he lists its "Jewish-Christian" bishops up to the time of the Bar Kokhba revolt:

All are said to have been Hebrews (Ἑβραίους) in origin, who had received the knowledge of Christ legitimately (τὴν γνῶσιν τοῦ Χριστοῦ γνησίως καταδέξασθαι), with the result that those in a position to decide such matters judged them worthy of the episcopal office. For at that time their whole church consisted of Hebrew believers (ἐξ Ἑβραίων πιστῶν) who had continued from apostolic times (ἀπὸ τῶν ἀποστόλων) down to the later siege in which the Jews, after revolting a second time from the Romans, were overwhelmed in a full-scale war. (*Hist. eccl.* 4.5.2)

In contrast to *Hist. eccl.* 3.5.3, this passage assumes a Christian presence in Jerusalem after 70 CE. Here, Eusebius argues that it was the Bar Kokhba Revolt (4.6.1–3) that marked the break in the apostolic continuity of the Jerusalem church:

When in this way the city (i.e., Jerusalem) had been emptied of the Jewish nation (εἰς ἐρημίαν τοῦ Ἰουδαίων ἔθνους) and had suffered the total destruction of its ancient inhabitants (παντελῆ τε φθορὰν τῶν πάλαι οἰκητόρων), it was colonized by a different race (ἐλθούσης ἐξ ἀλλοφύλου τε γένους συνοικισθείσης) and the Roman city which subsequently arose changed its name and was called Aelia, in honor of the emperor Aelius Hadrian. And as the church there was now composed of Gentiles (τῆς αὐτόθι ἐκκλησίας ἐξ ἐθνῶν συγκροτηθείσης), the first one to assume the government of it, after the bishops of the circumcision (μετὰ τοὺς ἐκ περιτομῆς ἐπισκόπους), was Marcus. (*Hist. eccl.* 4.6.4).

To make this argument, Eusebius must posit that the lifespans of Jerusalem's first fifteen bishops were all extremely brief (4.5.1). Nevertheless, he stresses that the "Jewish-Christian" succession at Jerusalem was lost in 135 CE. From that point onwards – according to Eusebius – the bishops at Jerusalem were all Gentiles (see 5.12).

---

[107] The historicity of the tradition has been hotly debated. See, e.g., Johannes Munck, "Jewish Christianity in Post-Apostolic Times," *NTS* 6 (1959): 103–4; Marcel Simon, "La migration à Pella: Légende ou réalité?" *Recherches de science religieuse* 60 (1972): 37–54; Gerd Lüdemann, "The Successors of Pre-70 Jerusalem Christianity: A Critical Evaluation of the Pella Tradition," in *Jewish and Christian Self-Definition*, vol. 1: *The Shaping of Christianity in the Second and Third Centuries*, ed. E. P. Sanders (Philadelphia: Fortress, 1980), 161–73; Joseph Verheyden, "The Flight of Christians to Pella," *Ephemerides theologicae lovanienses* 66 (1990): 368–84; Jürgen Wehnert, "Die Auswanderung der Jerusalemer Christen nach Pella – historische Faktum oder theologische Konstruktion?" *Zeitschrift für Kirchengeschichte* 102 (1991): 321–55. For our present purposes, its accuracy proves less significant than its function in Eusebius' depiction of the fate of apostolic "Jewish-Christianity."

Whereas Eusebius' account of the flight to Pella served to extricate the fate of Jerusalem's Christians from the fate of the Jews, the list of Jerusalemite bishops conflates them: not only was the break in their succession caused by the purportedly deserved calamities upon the Jews, but it resulted in the replacement of Jews by Gentiles, simultaneously in the city of Jerusalem and within the Jerusalem church.[108] From a chronological perspective, the details of these two accounts of the Jerusalem church are contradictory. The two accounts, however, work together to make one point very clear: the Jerusalem church was marred by discontinuities, all caused by its geographical and ethnic associations with the Jews.

Furthermore, through his descriptions of the sect of the Ebionites (3.27; 5.8.10; 6.17), Eusebius effectively distinguishes the apostolic "Jewish-Christianity" of the Jerusalem church from all forms of "Jewish-Christianity" that came afterwards.[109] In second-hand sources like the heresiologies of Epiphanius and the sermons of John Chrysostom – as well as in firsthand sources like the *Homilies* – we find hints of continued efforts, by some late antique Christians, to combine Jewish and Christian identities in ways that differed from the combination that later came to be defined as "Christian."[110] For Eusebius, however, the Ebionites emblematize the "heretical" nature of all such efforts.

For Eusebius, "Jewish-Christianity" is numbered among the many and diverse "heretical" corruptions of the single and unchanging "orthodoxy" that was established already in the apostolic age – an "orthodoxy" that Eusebius defines with primary appeal to the apostle Paul and to the Gentile Christians who came after him. In Eusebius' schema, Ebionites are actually the heirs, not to the apos-

---

[108] The limitation of the influence of the Jerusalem church may also reflect Eusebius' general tendency, in his early writings, to downplay the sanctity of Jerusalem, associate it with Jewish failure, and deny it any central place in Christian thought – as no doubt spurred, at least in part, by the ecclesiastical rivalry between Jerusalem and Caesarea in his own time. See further Peter W. L. Walker, *Holy City, Holy Places? Christian Attitudes to Jerusalem and the Holy Land in the Fourth Century* (Oxford: Clarendon, 1990), 51–92.

[109] The continuity between the Jerusalem church and post-apostolic forms of "Jewish-Christianity" remains a topic of debate. For different assessments, see, e. g., Schoeps, *Theologie und Geschichte des Judenchristentums*; Johannes Munck, "Primitive Jewish Christianity and late Jewish Christianity: Continuation or Rupture?" in *Aspects du Judéo-Christianisme: Colloque de Strasbourg, 23–25 avril 1964* (Paris: Presses Universitaires de France, 1965), 77–94; Joan Taylor, "The Phenomenon of Early Jewish-Christianity: Reality or Scholarly Invention?" *VC* 44 (1990): 313–34.

[110] See Chapter One above as well as Robert Louis Wilken, *John Chrysostom and the Jews: Rhetoric and Reality in the Late Fourth Century* (Berkeley: University of California Press, 1983), 66–94; John G. Gager, "Jews, Christians, and the Dangerous Ones in Between," in *Interpretation in Religion*, ed. Schlomo Biderman and Ben-Ami Scharfstein (Philosophy and Religion 2; Leiden: Brill, 1992), 249–57. With regard to "Jewish-Christians," Stephen G. Wilson concludes that "the evidence seems to point neither to their rapid marginalization nor to their dominance after 70 CE, but rather to their survival as a significant minority"; *Related Strangers: Jews and Christians, 70–170 CE* (Minneapolis: Fortress, 1995), 158.

tolic "Jewish-Christianity" of the Jerusalem Church, but rather to the "heresy" of Simon Magus. Unlike the Jews and the Jerusalem church, the Ebionites are granted participation in an unbroken line of succession. This, however, is a line of error, which runs straight back to Simon by means of Menander (3.26–27).

As in the *Homilies*, Simon is thus placed in a genealogy of error that parallels and threatens the "orthodoxy" vouchsafed by apostolic succession. Whereas the *Homilies* uses this trope to associate "heresy" with Hellenism, Eusebius draws the lines of "heretical" succession so to include, amongst Simon's heirs, all Christ believers who reject Paul and observe the Torah (3.27).

History and Counterhistory

In modern historiography, it is Eusebius' image of the past that has prevailed. As Arthur Droge notes, the reception of the *Ecclesiastical History* has been largely marked by the embrace of his overall picture of Christian history:

From the publication of the *Ecclesiastical History* down to the modern era the history of early Christianity has been written and rewritten in the terms established by Eusebius. Not until the publication in 1934 of Walter Bauer's *Rechtgläubigkeit und Ketzerei im ältesten Christentum* was the Eusebian view of church history finally deconstructed and reconfigured. Though Eusebius' accuracy and veracity as a historian had been challenged by numerous scholars, from antiquity to the present, his description of the contours of early Christian history had generally been endorsed.[111]

Of course, modern scholars of early Christianity have had no choice but to depend on Eusebius. For a number of figures, events, and texts, he is our main or only source. Hence, it is perhaps not surprising that many of his opinions have become absorbed, naturalized, and internalized in the scholarly discourse about the development of Christianity. To this day, a number of his overarching categories and concerns are arguably embricated in the field of Patristics – embodied in its disciplinary boundaries and reinforced by the trajectories of training and research.[112]

---

[111] Droge, "Apologetic Dimensions of the Ecclesiastical History," 506. On the late antique, medieval, and early modern reception of the *Ecclesiastical History* – and especially the resurgence of its influence after the Protestant Reformation – see Momigliano, *Classical Foundations of Modern Historiography*, 141–52; Glenn F. Chesnut, "Eusebius, Augustine, Orosius, and the Late Patristic and Medieval Christian Historians," in Attridge and Hata, *Eusebius, Christianity, and Judaism*, 687–713; Irena Backus, "Calvin's Judgment of Eusebius of Caesarea: An Analysis," *Sixteenth Century Journal* 22 (1991): 419–37.

[112] Brock notes that "the all pervasive influence of Eusebius has meant that the existence of a third cultural tradition, represented by Syriac Christianity, has consistently been neglected or marginalized by church historians, both ancient and modern" ("Eusebius and Syriac Christianity," 212; so too Adam H. Becker, "Beyond the Spatial and Temporal Limes: Questioning the 'Parting of the Ways' Outside the Roman Empire," in Becker and Reed, *The Ways that Never Parted*, esp. 373–74). Arguably, Eusebius' depiction of Judaism has similarly helped to excuse

With regard to "heresy," "paganism," and Judaism, some efforts have been made to move beyond Eusebius' metanarratives. Just as Walter Bauer shed doubt on the Eusebian view of "heresy" as secondary and derivative,[113] so Marcel Simon challenged the portrayal of post-70 Judaism as a religion in decline.[114] The insights of the former have been debated and developed, particularly in the wake of the discoveries at Nag Hammadi,[115] while the insights of the latter are still being refined, not least because of increased interaction between specialists in Rabbinics and Patristics.[116] Likewise, the continued vitality – and, indeed, resurgence – of late antique "paganism" has been stressed by Peter Brown and others, concurrent with the emergence of Late Antiquity as a lively subfield of History.[117]

With respect to "Jewish-Christianity," however, Eusebian models still remain regnant. It is perhaps telling, for instance, that when Bauer deconstructed Eusebius' depiction of "orthodoxy" and "heresy," he neglected to consider those who saw Jewish practice as consonant with belief in Christ. Even in the revised edition of *Rechtgläubigkeit und Ketzerei im ältesten Christentum*, "Jewish-Christianity" earns only an Appendix.[118] Likewise, even when Simon mounted a concerted challenge to traditional views of Judaism's post-70 decline, he still dismissed "Jewish-Christians" as ossified relics of the apostolic past.[119]

---

generations of Patristics scholars from the need to study the literature and languages of late antique Judaism.

[113] Bauer's alternative account of "orthodoxy" and "heresy" is arguably founded on his interpretation of the *Ecclesiastical History* as an apologetic account with many deliberate omissions and misrepresentations; *Rechtgläubigkeit und Ketzerei im ältesten Christentum* (Tübingen: Mohr, 1934; rev. ed. by Georg Strecker, 1964), e.g. 135–49.

[114] Marcel Simon, *Verus Israel: A Study of the Relations between Christians and Jews in the Roman Empire (AD 135–425)*, trans. Henry McKeating (London: Littman Library of Jewish Civilization, 1986).

[115] See, e.g., Gerorg Strecker, "The Reception of the Book," rev. Robert A. Kraft, in Walter Bauer, *Orthodoxy and Heresy in Earliest Christianity*, ed. and trans. Robert A. Kraft and Gerhard A. Kroedel (2nd ed.; Philadelphia: Fortress, 1971), 286–316; Daniel J. Harrington, "The Reception of Walter Bauer's *Orthodoxy and Heresy in Earliest Christianity* during the Last Decade," *HTR* 73 (1980): 289–98; Karen L. King, *What is Gnosticism?* (Cambridge, MA: Harvard University Press, 2003), esp. 110–15.

[116] See, e.g., Albert I. Baumgarten, "Marcel Simon's *Verus Israel* as a Contribution to Jewish History," *HTR* 92 (1999): 465–78; and the essays collected in Limor and Stroumsa, *Contra Iudaeos*; and Becker and Reed, *The Ways that Never Parted*.

[117] See, e.g., Peter Brown, *The World of Late Antiquity, AD 150–750* (London: Thames & Hudson, 1971), 70–95; Garth Fowden, "Bishops and Temples in the Eastern Roman Empire 320–425," *JTS* 29 (1978): 53–78; Ramsey MacMullen, *Paganism in the Roman Empire* (New Haven: Yale University Press, 1981), esp. 62–72; Robin Lane Fox, *Pagans and Christians* (New York: Knopf, 1987); Pierre Chuvin, *A Chronicle of the Last Pagans* (trans. B.A. Archer; Cambridge, MA: Harvard University Press, 1990).

[118] I.e., Gerorg Strecker, "On the Problem of Jewish Christianity," in Bauer, *Orthodoxy and Heresy*, 241–85.

[119] Simon, *Verus Israel*, 238–44.

Although the bulk of our evidence for "Jewish-Christianity" comes from the late third, fourth, and fifth centuries, most scholars persist in characterizing its postapostolic fate as one of deterioration and/or irrelevance.[120] And, just as Eusebius frames the story of "Jewish-Christianity" as a tale of a first-century phenomenon that died with the rise of the Gentile church, so research on "Jewish-Christians" still remains the domain of specialists in the New Testament and Christian Origins. The phenomenon remains little discussed in research on Late Antiquity.

Somewhat surprisingly, postmodern studies have followed much the same path. In recent years, scholars have increasingly turned our attention to the rhetorical and discursive features of our late antique Christian literature. Inspired by poststructural approaches to language and postcolonialist approaches to power, they have read the writings of Eusebius and other Church Fathers not as unmediated descriptions of a fully-formed "Christianity" with an ancient and obvious "orthodoxy", but rather as part of the very process of constructing and promoting these categories and concepts.[121]

Such approaches have had exciting results, which have greatly enriched our understanding of Patristic literature, pushing us to read these texts with new attention to their gaps and silences as well as to the power struggles that their rhetorics can hide. At the same time, however, such approaches have sometimes served to reinscribe one of the most trenchant biases in the field of Patristics, namely, the privileging of retrospectively "orthodox" writings.[122] If earlier research had accepted Eusebius' own claim to be an objective archivist of the history of Christian "orthodoxy," more recent studies have tended to frame him as one of its architects – those who are ultimately responsible for creating, by means of their powerful rhetorics, "Christianity" as we know it. And, whereas earlier scholarship had naively accepted the negative assessment of "Jewish-Christianity" by Eusebius, Epiphanius, and others, such new approaches often relegate "Jewish-Christians" to the role of the suppressed, treating our evidence for "Jewish-Christianity" merely as an echo of the varied Christian voices that were silenced, excluded, and disenfranchised by literate elites in Late Antiquity.

---

[120] E. g., James Carleton Paget, "Jewish Christianity," in *The Cambridge History of Judaism*, vol. 3: *The Early Roman Period*, ed. William Horbury, W. D. Davies, and John Sturdy (Cambridge: Cambridge University Press, 1999), 750–52; Anthony J. Saldarini, "The Social World of Christian Jews and Jewish Christians," in Lapin, *Religious and Ethnic Communities*, 154.

[121] On this important recent shift in the field of Patristics, see Clark, *History, Theory, Text*; as well as the essays collected in Dale B. Martin and Patricia Cox Miller, eds., *The Cultural Turn in Late Ancient Studies: Gender, Asceticism, and Historiography* (Durham: Duke University Press, 2005).

[122] In this too, the influence of Eusebius is perhaps not irrelevant, inasmuch as his efforts contributed to the elevation of a select group of early Christian authors and philosophers (including, perhaps most strikingly, the much embattled Origen) to the status of "Church Fathers."

Daniel Boyarin, for instance, often cites the Pseudo-Clementines as evidence for the permeability between "Jewish" and "Christian" traditions "on the ground."[123] For him, however, this evidence forms part of the backdrop for the assertion that "Judaism" and "Christianity" were largely products of hegemonic discourse.[124] As a result, he disembodies second-hand statements about "Jewish-Christian" groups, like the Ebionites, from any connection to social reality.[125] Accepting that the religious landscape of Roman Palestine had long been devoid of any actual "Jewish-Christians," he reads these figures as a discursive embodiment of the fear of hybridity, produced – as if by thought experiment – by elite efforts to articulate a pure Christianity.[126]

In light of the current influence of Eusebius and the *Ecclesiastical History*, it may indeed be tempting to dismiss the *Homilies* as merely a remnant of the variety of lived forms of Christianity disenfranchised by elite discourses of self-definition. Yet, as we have seen, the authors/redactors of the *Homilies* are themselves engaged with the problem of how to construct "orthodoxy." They are hardly passive subjects of this discourse. Rather, they seek to engage as participants.

Moreover, the reception-history of the *Homilies* belies any effort to assert the isolation or marginality of their contribution. The *Homilies* was translated into Syriac soon after its composition.[127] In the East, it circulated in its original Greek as well as in multiple epitomes, which were translated into Arabic and other languages.[128] Quotations from the *Homilies* are also found in the writings

---

[123] E. g., Daniel Boyarin, *Dying for God: Martyrdom and the Making of Judaism and Christianity* (Stanford: Stanford University Press, 1999), 29–30; Boyarin, *Border Lines: The Partition of Judeo-Christianity* (Philadelphia: University of Pennsylvania Press, 2004), 43.

[124] Boyarin, *Border Lines*.

[125] I do not mean to suggest, of course, that we should take Patristic comments about "Ebionites" simply at face value. More plausibly, Eusebius and others apply the traditional heresiological rubric of "Ebionism" to a range of different groups in their own time, who combined elements of Jewish and Christian identity in ways that jarred with their own understandings of "Christianity"; see Albertus Frederik Johannes Klijn and Gerrit J. Reinink, *Patristic Evidences for Jewish-Christian Sects* (NTSup 36; Leiden: Brill, 1973) 43. Accordingly, the relationship between the Pseudo-Clementines and Ebionites is likely indirect.

[126] Boyarin, *Border Lines*, 207–9. For a similar critique of Boyarin's reading of our evidence for "Jewish Christianity," see Charlotte Elisheva Fonrobert, "Jewish Christians, Judaizers, and Anti-Judaism," in *Late Ancient Christianity*, ed. V. Burrus (A People's History of Christianity 2; Minneapolis: Fortress, 2005), 253–54.

[127] A Syriac translation of portions of the *Homilies* (≈ 10–14) survives, together with portions of the *Recognitions* (1–4), in a manuscript from 411 CE (British Museum add. 12150). For the text, see Wilhelm Frankenberg, *Die syrischen Clementinen mit griechischem Paralleltext: Eine Vorarbeit zu dem literargeschichtlichen Problem der Sammlung* (TU 48.3; Leipzig: Hinrichs, 1937); F. Stanley Jones, trans., *The Syriac Pseudo-Clementines: An Early Version of the First Christian Novel* (Apocryphes 14; Turnhout: Brepols, 2014).

[128] For editions, etc., see references in Jones, "Pseudo-Clementines," 6–7, 80–84.

of Byzantine chronographers.[129] In addition, the *Homilies* shaped views of the apostolic age in the West, in an indirect fashion, due to the reworking of the Pseudo-Clementine novel in the *Recognitions* and its Latin translation by Rufinus – the same translator responsible for redacting and translating Eusebius' *Ecclesiastical History*.[130] The *Recognitions* survives in over a hundred Latin manuscripts and seems to have been widely known in the European Christendom. If one wishes to question its status due to its listing among "apocrypha" within the so-called *Gelasian Decree*, moreover, one must contend with the place of "the *History* of Eusebius Pamphilii" on precisely the same list.

From the metanarratives of modern scholarship, we might expect the reception histories of the *Homilies* and *Ecclesiastical History* to have followed different paths. What is surprising, however, is how comparably little – at least in the early period – they seem to differ. Both texts found early audiences among Syrian Christians; both were used by chronographers in the Greek East; and both widely circulated in the Latin West in redacted forms, mediated by Rufinus.

It is not yet possible to reconcile all these pieces of evidence. Further analysis of the *Homilies* and *Ecclesiastical History* is needed to determine the precise meaning of the contrasts and connections noted above, and more work will need to be done if we wish to uncover the social realities that may have shaped the late antique creation and reception of these divergent perspectives on the apostolic past.

I suggest, however, that we might best begin by examining the most direct evidence for social practice found in these sources, namely, the evidence for the practice of writing. As noted above, the *Homilies* and *Ecclesiastical History* are significantly shaped by the practices of selecting, collecting, redacting, and reworking earlier sources. More specifically, the *Ecclesiastical History* is a "parade example" of counter-history – the process by which another group's history and sources are appropriated and reworked in the service of contrasting aims.[131] To tell the story of Judaism's demise, Eusebius quotes heavily from Josephus and Philo. Likewise, to tell the tale of the decline of "Jewish-Christianity," he draws heavily on Hegesippus, whose own account of the apostolic age appears to have

---

[129] As noted throughout Rehm, *Die Pseudoklementinen*, vol. 1: *Homilien*; e. g., 70, 72–73, 77, 85, 133, 277. See also William A. Adler, "Abraham's Refutation of Astrology: An Excerpt for Pseudo-Clement in the Chronicon of George the Monk," in *Things Revealed: Studies in Jewish and Christian Literature in Honor of Michael E. Stone*, ed. Esther G. Chazon, David Satran, and Ruth A. Clements (JSJSup 89; Leiden: Brill, 2004), 227–42.

[130] Rufinus' Latin translation of the *Recognitions* is dated to 406/407 CE; see Bernhard Rehm, *Die Pseudoklementinen*, vol. 2: *Rekognitionen in Rufinus Übersetzung* (GSC 51; Berlin: Akademie, 1969). On his translation of Eusebius' *Ecclesiastical History*, see Françoise Thelamon, *Païens et Chrétiens au IVᵉ siècle: L'apport de l'Histoire ecclésiastique de Rufin d'Aquilée* (Paris: Études augustiniennes, 1981).

[131] I use this category in the sense outlined in Amos Funkenstein, *Perceptions of Jewish History* (Berkeley: University of California Press, 1993), 36–49; Susannah Heschel, *Abraham Geiger and the Jewish Jesus* (Chicago: University of Chicago Press, 1998), esp. 14–16.

lionized James and the Jerusalem church; the possibility that Hegesippus himself may have been a "Jewish-Christian" makes Eusebius' appropriation of his writings all the more striking.[132] Moreover, Eusebius seems to know of some sources in the Pseudo-Clementine tradition and perhaps even makes use of them.[133]

Intriguing, in my view, is the possibility that the *Homilies* was compiled, at least in part, to counter this counter-history.[134] No less than Eusebius, the authors/redactors of the *Homilies* engage in the fourth-century discourse about "orthodoxy," using the apostolic past to promote models of authenticity and authority in the present. Here too, the practices of collection, redaction, and reinterpretation are central, and they serve a means of enshrining certain memories while negating others. In the service of their own vision of an authentically apostolic Christianity in radical continuity with Judaism, they invoke the sayings of Jesus, and they evoke the image, not only of the apostle Peter, but also of the Gentile bishop Clement. They allude to Paul in order to exclude him. Much like the *Ecclesiastical History*, the *Homilies* opens a window onto one picture of the late antique church, constructed by means of the preservation and reinterpretation of a carefully selected slice of its literary heritage and history. But, whereas Eusebius self-consciously pens a history cobbled from written documents derived from archives, the authors/redactors of the *Homilies* marshal their sources towards a different aim: they claim to preserve Clement's own firsthand account of his life and his eyewitness testimony to the mission and teachings of the apostle Peter.

If I am correct to interpret the contrasts between the two accounts in terms of active competition, we might further ask: is it possible to situate this discursive contestation in its social context? At present, of course, we can only speculate. It may be significant, however, that so many elements of Eusebius' understanding of Christianity are maligned as "heretically" Hellenistic by the *Homilies*. Eusebius, as a self-styled heir to Origen and Pamphilus, embraces allegorical interpretation and philosophical learning.[135] The *Homilies*, however, denounces all Greek *paideia* as "pagan" error, and its authors/redactors dismiss allegory and philosophy as merely a smoke screen for the polytheism and impi-

---

[132] For a recent discussion of Hegesippus' identity, see F. Stanley Jones, *Pseudoclementina*, 456–66. For our present purposes, the question of whether Hegisippus was a Jewish convert to Christianity proves less significant than the fact that Eusebius perceives and presents him as such because of his knowledge of Hebrew or Aramaic and because of his familiarity with "other matters as if taken from the Jewish unwritten tradition (ἐξ Ἰουδαϊκῆς ἀγράφου παραδόσεως)" (*Hist. eccl.* 4.22.9).

[133] See discussion above.

[134] I.e., whereas the early third-century source preserved in *Rec.* 1.27–71 may counter Luke-Acts (see above), the redacted form of the *Homilies* may counter late antique accounts that develop Luke-Acts. If so, then it proves particularly fitting that both Pseudo-Clementine novels so readily served – many centuries later – as a basis for F. C. Baur's modern counterhistory of apostolic times.

[135] Barnes, *Constantine and Eusebius*, 81–105.

ety to which "pagans" and "heretics" are demonically addicted (e. g., 2.22, 25; 4.12–20; 6.17–23).[136] Whereas Eusebius expands apostolic succession to include Alexandrian Christian philosophers and depicts the Egyptian city as an ancient center of Christian philosophical wisdom,[137] the *Homilies* presents Alexandria as a nexus of all things pernicious – including philosophy and allegory as well as sorcery, polytheism, astrology, "heresy," and anti-Judaism (*Hom.* 1.8–14; 2.22; 4–6 esp. 4.4).[138]

Such contrasts may point us to the possibility that the discursive contestation over the apostolic past in these two texts may speak to another struggle, coming in the wake of the importation of Alexandrian forms of Christianity into Syro-Palestine due to the influence of Origen, Pamphilus, and Eusebius in Caesaria. It is possible, for instance, that the literary activity that shaped the *Homilies* may represent the response of other forms of Christianity, perhaps native to the area.[139] If some Syrian and Palestinian Christians were claiming continuity with the Jerusalem church, it might help us to understand why Eusebius might make such efforts to disenfranchise "Jewish-Christianity" in the first place. In turn, if there were some Christians in the area who viewed themselves as heirs to the Jerusalem church of James and Peter, they might well be alarmed at the growing dominance of strikingly different views of Judaism, Hellenism, and Christianity.

Of course, further research is needed to determine the precise sociohistorical setting and literary aims of the *Homilies*. Nevertheless, it is my hope that the above inquiry has helped to expose the significance of this text for our understanding of the place of "Jewish-Christianity" in late antique Christian history and modern historiography.

When we consider the *Homilies* and our other evidence for "Jewish-Christianity" on their own terms – without trying to fit them into the historical narratives outlined by Eusebius and others – what emerges is a richer picture of ongoing debates about Judaism, often waged on the stage of the apostolic past. In many of our late antique sources, the age of the apostles is depicted as a pivot between Judaism and Christianity: it is presented as the era in which the truth

---

[136] Note esp. Clement's assertion in *Hom.* 4.12: "Therefore I say that the entire *paideia* of the Greeks is a most dreadful fabrication of a wicked demon (αὐτίκα γοῦν ἐγὼ τὴν πᾶσαν Ἑλλήνων παιδείαν κακοῦ δαίμονος χαλεπωτάτην ὑπόθεσιν εἶναι λέγω)." On the critique of *paideia* in the *Homilies*, see Chapter Four above; Adler, "Apion's Encomium of Adultery"; Dominique Côté, Rhetoric and Jewish-Christianity: The Case of the Grammarian Apion in the Pseudo-Clementine *Homilies*," in Piovanelli and Burke, *Rediscovering the Apocryphal Continent*, 369–89. On the polemic against allegory, see Shuve, "Doctrine of the False Pericopes."

[137] Grant, *Eusebius as Church Historian*, 46–47, 72–76.

[138] See also *Hom.* 6.23; 9.6; 10.16–18 on Egyptian religion as paradigmatic of false worship.

[139] I here build on Pierluigi Piovanelli's suggestion about the social and cultural context that shaped the anti-Pauline traditions in the Ethiopian *Book of the Cock*; see "The *Book of the Cock* and the Rediscovery of Ancient Jewish-Christian traditions in Fifth-Century Palestine," in *The Changing Face of Judaism, Christianity and Other Greco-Roman Religions in Antiquity*, ed. Ian H. Henderson and Gerbern S. Oegama (Gütersloh: Gütersloher, 2006), 308–22.

of the church's supersession of Judaism was actualized, as Christians multiplied and spread while Jews fell victim to war and destruction. This supersessionist narrative, however, was clearly not the only option. A very different version of events seems to have remained vital and viable, in the fourth century and beyond.

If Boyarin and others are correct to see the fourth century as a critical era for the setting of the boundaries between "Judaism" and "Christianity" in the Roman Empire,[140] then the *Homilies* also provides us with neglected evidence for the resistance that these efforts faced. Such resistance surely resonated in rich ways with the Syrian cultural context of the Pseudo-Clementine tradition.[141] The wide reception of the Pseudo-Clementine literature, however, cautions us against dismissing its message as relevant only for a certain locale.

The example of the *Homilies* might also serve to remind us – as modern historians – of the dangers of depending too heavily on retrospectively "orthodox" accounts. Eusebius makes efforts to extricate Judaism from Christian history, but his own use of sources hints at the enduring place of both Judaism and "Jewish-Christianity" in that history. Moreover, even in his own time, Eusebius' vision of the apostolic past appears to have been contested. In the *Homilies*, we may hear the answers of voices now forgotten, who resisted the efforts of those who sought to inscribe, in apostolic history, the decline of the Jews, the irrelevance of "Jewish-Christianity," and the parting of the church from its connections to a living Judaism.

---

[140] E. g., Boyarin, *Dying for God*, 18; Günter Stemberger, *Jews and Christians in the Holy Land: Palestine in the Fourth Century* (trans. R. Tuschling; Edinburgh: T&T Clark, 2000), 1–2.

[141] E. g., Reuven Kimelman, "Identifying Jews and Christians in Roman Syria-Palestine," in *Galilee through the Centuries: Confluence of Cultures*, ed. Eric M. Meyers (Winona Lake: Eisenbrauns, 1999), 301–33; Robert M. Grant, "Jewish Christianity at Antioch in the Second Century," in *Judéo-Christianisme: Recherches historiques et théologiques offertes en hommage au Cardinal Jean Daniélou* (Paris: Beauchesne, 1972), 93–108; Albertus Frederik Johannes Klijn, "The Study of Jewish Christianity," *NTS* 20 (1973–1974): 428–31; Strecker, *Judenchristentum in den Pseudoklementinen*, esp. 260; Strecker, "Problem of Jewish Christianity," 244–71; Charlotte Elisheva Fonrobert, "The *Didascalia Apostolorum*: A Mishnah for the Disciples of Jesus," *JECS* 9 (2001): 483–509; Wilken, *John Chrysostom and the Jews*; Han Jan Willem Drijvers, "Edessa und das jüdische Christentum," *VC* 24 (1970): 3–33; Drijvers, "Syrian Christianity and Judaism," in *The Jews Among Pagans and Christians in the Roman Empire*, ed. Judith Lieu, John North, and Tessa Rajak (London: Routledge, 1992), 124–46, esp. 142–43 on the fourth century; Kelley, *Knowledge and Religious Authority in the Pseudo-Clementines*, 197–200.

Part II

"Jewish-Christianity" in Jewish
History and Jewish Studies

Chapter Seven

Messianism between Judaism and Christianity*

By both ancient and modern accounts, the origins of Christianity form part of the history of Jewish messianism. Already in the first century CE, the New Testament literature attests the culling of prooftexts from Jewish scriptures to argue for Jesus' identity as the משיח (Gr. χριστός) long promised to the Jews.[1] Into Late Antiquity, and well beyond, Christian authors richly continued the practice, even while decrying Israel as superseded by the church or proclaiming the Torah as abrogated by the Gospel.[2] Likewise, within modern scholarship, the earliest movement surrounding Jesus is commonly characterized as a Jewish messianic sect.[3] Some scholars, in fact, thus reserve the term "Christianity" for

---

* This chapter was originally prepared and precirculated for the Tikvah Project on Jewish Thought's Working Group on Messianism at Princeton University from 2009 to 2011, and it was published in 2014 in the proceedings volume as "Messianism between Judaism and Christianity," in *Rethinking the Messianic Idea in Judaism*, ed. Michael L. Morgan and Steven Weitzman (Bloomington: Indiana University Press, 2014), 23–62. It is reprinted here with permission from Indiana University Press. I am grateful to Michael L. Morgan, our fellow Working Group members, and the Tikvah Project for a challenging and exciting intellectual experience. An earlier version was presented at Yale University on 6 October 2010. It benefited much from feedback from Leora Batnitzky, John Collins, Adela Yarbro Collins, John Gager, Martha Himmelfarb, Dale Martin, Benjamin Pollock, and Steve Weitzman. The present form owes much to ongoing discussions with David Stern and our cotaught graduate seminar on "Jewish and Christian Messianism" at the University of Pennsylvania in spring 2011.

[1] E. g., Martin Hengel, "Jesus der Messias Israels," in *Messiah and Christos: Studies on the Jewish Origin of Christianity Presented to David Flusser on the Occasion of His Seventy-Fifth Birthday*, ed. Ithamar Gruenwald, Shaul Shaked, and Gedaliahu G. Stroumsa (TSAJ 32; Tübingen: Mohr Siebeck, 1992), 155–76; Christopher Rowland, *Christian Origins: The Setting and Character of the Most Important Messianic Sect of Judaism* (2nd ed.; London: SPCK, 2002); David Flusser, "Jewish Messianism Reflected in the Early Church," in *Judaism of the Second Temple Period*, vol. 2: *The Jewish Sages and Their Literature* (trans. Azzan Yadin; Grand Rapids: Eerdmans, 2009), 258–88; James D. G. Dunn, *Christianity in the Making*, vol. 2: *Beginning from Jerusalem* (Grand Rapids: Eerdmans, 2009), 238–40.

[2] The "parade example" is Justin Martyr, on whom see further below.

[3] I.e., one of the many movements of the sort thought to have flourished in the first centuries of Roman rule (esp., 63 BCE to 135 CE). See, e. g., Wayne A. Meeks, *The Moral World of the First Christians* (Philadelphia: Westminster, 1987), 98–107; Christopher Rowland, *Christian Origins: The Setting and Character of the Most Important Messianic Sect of Judaism* (2nd ed.; London: S. P. C. K., 2002); David Flusser, "Jewish Messianism Reflected in the Early Church," in *Judaism of the Second Temple Period: The Jewish sages and their literature*, trans. Azzan Yadin (Grand Rapids: Eerdmans, 2009), 258–88; James Dunn, *Beginning from Jerusalem* (Grand Rapids: Eerdmans, 2009), 238–40.

a later age, when the movement reinvented itself as a distinct "religion."[4] For this move too, messianism has been deemed pivotal; "it is here" – as Gershom Scholem famously claimed at the beginning of *The Messianic Idea of Judaism* – "that the essential conflict between Judaism and Christianity has developed and continues to exist."[5]

Consequently, Christianity's origins in Jewish messianism have been richly discussed, not just in ancient Christian sources and modern scholarship about them, but also in studies of the phenomenology of Jewish messianism and assessments of Jesus' place in Jewish history. The present essay is an experiment in bringing these discussions into conversation with one another, around the question of the place of messianism in the production of Jewish/Christian difference. My aim is not to add to the rich corpus of studies that have sought to reconstruct early beliefs about Jesus against the background of Second Temple Judaism, nor to debate the determinative points of their divergence.[6] Rather, I shall ask how the relationship between Jewish and Christian messianism has been represented, both in antiquity and in modernity. Although I shall consider sources penned from Christian as well as Jewish perspectives, my inquiry is ultimately oriented towards the open question of what we might learn about Jewish messianism from Christianity, in general, and "Jewish-Christianity," in particular.

The notion that belief in Jesus as messiah is what differentiates Christians from Jews is now so widespread as to seem somewhat obvious. In what follows, I take this apparent obviousness as an invitation to look more closely. I shall reflect upon the prehistory, power, and limits of the trope of messianism as defining difference, examining some of the most influential articulations and subversions thereof. In the process, I hope to show how Christianity's origins in Jewish messianism has served as a potent site for reflection on religious identity – not just in the first century, but into Late Antiquity and well beyond.

---

[4] On these and related recent trends, see summary and references in Annette Yoshiko Reed and Adam H. Becker, "Introduction: Traditional Models and New Directions," in *The Ways that Never Parted: Jews and Christians in Late Antiquity and the Early Middle Ages* (TSAJ 95; Tübingen: Mohr Siebeck, 2003), 1–33.

[5] Or, more accurately, in Scholem's essay "Towards an Understanding of the Messianic Idea in Judaism," based on a 1959 German lecture ("Zum Verständnis der messianischen Idee im Judentum") and published in English translation as the opening essay in *The Messianic Idea in Judaism and Other Essays on Jewish Spirituality* (New York: Schocken, 1971), 1–36, quote at 1.

[6] Such discussions flowered particularly in the wake of the discovery of the Dead Sea Scrolls, on which see John J. Collins, *The Scepter and the Star: The Messiahs of the Dead Sea Scrolls and Other Ancient Literature* (New York: Doubleday, 1995). Also Gruenwald, Shaked, and Stroumsa, *Messiah and Christos*; James H. Charlesworth, ed., *The Messiah* (Minneapolis: Fortress, 1992); James H. Charlesworth, Hermann Lichtenberger, and Gerbern S. Oegema, eds., *Qumran-Messianism: Studies on the Messianic Expectations in the Dead Sea Scrolls* (Tübingen: Mohr Siebeck, 1998); Peter Schäfer and Mark Cohen, eds., *Toward the Millennium: Messianic Expectations from the Bible to Waco* (Studies in the History of Religions 77; Leiden: Brill, 1998); Magnus Zetterholm, ed., *The Messiah in Early Judaism and Christianity* (Minneapolis: Fortress, 2007).

In the process, I hope to shed light on the powerful but paradoxical place of Jewish messianism in Christian identity – *both* as an indelible mark of Christianity's Jewish origins *and* as the point of its purportedly defining distinction. Disagreements over messianic beliefs about Jesus are often cited as exemplary of Jewish/Christian difference and as the ultimate cause for the differentiation of these "religions." Often concurrent, however, is an acknowledgment of the commonalities on which this contestation is predicated (e. g., the very idea of a messiah, the historiography of messianic hope, the exegetical practice of deriving and defending messianic claims from Jewish scriptures). In ancient Christian sources and in modern scholarship about them, attention to messianism thus threatens to expose shared roots, entangled histories, and overlapping identities, even in the course of assertions of essential or inevitable difference.

Among modern Jewish thinkers, Scholem is hardly alone in pointing to messianism as that which splits Christianity from Judaism. Yet, as we shall see, there is a striking lack of firsthand evidence for ancient Jewish counterparts to such assertions; if anything, we glimpse Rabbinic resistance to Christian claims about the power of messianic and other beliefs to produce "religion" and difference. Ancient Christian sources often insist that Jews concur with Christians on everything about the messiah except his advent and identity, and modern scholars often take such claims at face value.[7]

Ancient Jewish sources model quite different approaches to mapping identity. That messianism and belief-based approaches to defining "Christian" are not mutually exclusive with lineage- and practice-based approaches to defining "Jew," moreover, was pointed out already in Late Antiquity, particularly within "Jewish-Christian" counterhistories of Christian origins.[8] Consideration of the full range of relevant sources from Late Antiquity thus leads us to question some common assumptions about messianic debates between ancient Jews and Christians, while also opening some new perspectives on Jesus' place among Judaism's multiple messiahs. A more integrative approach to the relevant late antique sources also highlights parallel dynamics at play in modern scholarship,

---

[7] To cite one recent example: William Horbury, *Messianism among Jews and Christians: Twelve Biblical and Historical Studies* (London: T&T Clark, 2003); see, however, the review by Wayne Meeks in *JQR* 95 (2005): 336–40.

[8] Here and below, I use the category of "counterhistory" in the sense outlined in Amos Funkenstein, *Perceptions of Jewish History* (Berkeley: University of California Press, 1993), 36–49; David Biale, *Gershom Scholem: Kabbalah and Counterhistory* (rev. ed.; Cambridge, MA: Harvard University Press, 1982); Biale, "Counter-history and Jewish Polemics against Christianity: The *Sefer Toldot Yeshu* and the *Sefer Zerubavel*," *JSS* 6 (1999): 130–45; Susannah Heschel, *Abraham Geiger and the Jewish Jesus* (Chicago: University of Chicago Press, 1998), 14–16; Michael Mack, *German Idealism and the Jew: The Inner Anti-Semitism of Philosophy and German Jewish Responses* (Chicago: University of Chicago Press, 2003), 12; cf. David Biale, "Historical Heresies and Modern Jewish Identity," *JSS* 8 (2002): 112–32, at 114–15.

illumining some of the process by which current notions about messianism and difference came to seem so natural.

Messianism and Difference

Scholem's quip about messianism as "essential conflict" has been much repeated in research on Christian origins and Jewish messianism. Scholars have hotly debated his assessment of the precise character of the conflict between Jewish and Christian messianism; few, however, have questioned his characterization of this conflict as "essential."[9] It remains axiomatic that beliefs about "the messiah" mark the boundary between "Christian" and "Jew."

This is perhaps not surprising: when Scholem made this assertion without argument in 1958, it was already a common trope among Jewish thinkers concerned with Christianity. In a lecture from 1928, for instance, Martin Buber describes eschatological expectation as a point of commonality between Christians and Jews that is simultaneously an unbridgeable divide:

> Your [Christian] expectation is directed towards a second coming, ours to a coming which has not been anticipated by a first …. Pre-messianically our destinies are divided. Now to the Christian the Jew is the incomprehensively obdurate man, who declines to see what has happened; and to the Jew the Christian is the incomprehensively daring man, who affirms in an unredeemed world that its redemption has been accomplished. This is a gulf which no human power can bridge.[10]

That Jewish/Christian difference in the present had its ultimate roots in a defining moment of messianic differentiation in the past was memorably articulated a decade later by Joseph Klausner. In the 1938 essay "The Jewish and the Christian Messiah," printed as an appendix to the third edition of *The Messianic Idea in Israel*, Klausner stresses that "at first, the only difference between Jews and

---

[9] Cf. William Scott Green, "Messiah in Judaism: Rethinking the Question," in *Judaisms and Their Messiahs at the Turn of the Christian Era*, ed. Jacob Neusner, William Scott Green, and Ernest Frerichs (Cambridge: Cambridge University Press, 1987), 1–13. For a range of positions, see Collins, *The Scepter and the Star*, 1–2; Jacob Taubes, "Scholem's Theses on Messianism Reconsidered," *Social Science Information* 21 4/5 (1982): 665–75, at 669–73; Moshe Idel, *Messianic Mystics* (New Haven: Yale University Press, 2000), esp. 19–20.

[10] Martin Buber, "The Faith of Judaism" (1928), repr. in Buber, *Israel and the World: Essays in a Time of Crisis* (New York: Schocken, 1948), 39–40. On the broader context, see David Novak, "The Quest for the Jewish Jesus," *Modern Judaism* 8 (1988): 119–38, at 125–30. Notably, Buber's views of Jesus himself are a good deal more complex than this characterization of "Jew" vs. "Christian" might suggest; see now Shaul Magid, "Defining Christianity and Judaism from the Perspective of Religious Anarchy: Martin Buber on Jesus and the Ba'al Shem Tov," *JJTP* 25 (2017): 36–58.

Christians was that the former believed that the Messiah was *still to come*, and the latter that the Messiah had *already come*."[11]

To this day, the maxims of Klausner and Scholem continue to set the tone for historical research on messianism, wherein comparisons of pre-Christian Judaism and the Jesus movement are often predicated on the claim of messianism's special significance as the present point of conflict between Christianity and Judaism or as the pivot on which the two first "parted ways." In the introduction to the 2007 volume *The Messiah in Early Judaism and Christianity*, for instance, Magnus Zetterholm can state without further explanation that "messianism scarcely constitutes a common ground for Jews and Christians and is certainly not the best starting point for Jewish/Christian relations. Rather, due to the unfortunate historical development of Jewish/Christian relations, 'the Messiah' has been the most important concept that distinguishes Christianity from Judaism."[12] One finds similar statements in contemporary Christian theological reflection on Judaism. Just as Buber's above-quoted statement was positively cited by the Protestant theologian Reinhold Niebuhr, so a similar emphasis on shared expectation and divided beliefs is also central to the characterization of Judaism in the current *Catechism of the Catholic Church*.[13] Even when the trope of messianic belief as defining difference is questioned or nuanced – whether in scholarship on the New Testament or in contemporary calls for interfaith dialogue – it remains widely cited as the presumed "common sense" about the origins, essence, and intractability of Jewish/Christian difference.[14]

---

[11] Joseph Klausner, *The Messianic Idea in Israel from Its Beginning to the Completion of the Mishnah* (Trans. William F. Stinespring; 3rd ed.; New York: Macmillan, 1955); Klausner, "The Jewish and the Christian Messiah" (1938), repr. in *Disputation and Dialogue: Readings in the Jewish-Christian Encounter*, ed. Frank E. Talmage (Jerusalem: Ktav, 1975), 59–70, at 65. Klausner (p. 70) goes on to enumerate their differences in a manner that presages Scholem's famous distinction between the two ("Toward an Understanding of the Messianic Idea," 1–2, 15–16), not with reference to Jesus, but rather with appeal to the public and private foci of their respective ideals of redemption.

[12] Zetterholm, *Messiah in Early Judaism and Christianity*, xxiv.

[13] For the former, see Reinhold Niebuhr, *Pious and Secular America* (New York: Scribner, 1958), 98, and for the latter, *Catechism of the Catholic Church* § 840; Mary C. Boys, "The Covenant in Contemporary Ecclesial Documents," in *Two Faiths, One Covenant?*, ed. Eugene B. Korn and John T. Pawlikowski (Lanham, MD: Rowman & Littlefield, 2005), 90–91. On popular diffusion of the trope, see also Harvey Cox, *Common Prayers: Faith, Family, and a Christian's Journey through the Jewish Year* (New York: Houghton Mifflin Harcourt, 2002), 125.

[14] So too Meir Soloveichik, "Redemption and the Power of Man," *Azure* 16 (2004) – with further examples. Within specialist scholarship on the historical Jesus, notably, the 1980s and 1990s saw important correctives to older ideas about a monolithic Jewish messianism, leading many to be more cautious of the tendency to use diverse Jewish sources to construct a single "Jewish Messiah," created for the sake of comparison with Jesus (e.g., Green, "Messiah in Judaism"; James H. Charlesworth, "From Messianology to Christology: Problems and Prospects," in Charlesworth, *Messiah*, 3–35). On the value and limits of these critiques, see Matthew Novenson, "Jewish Messiahs, the Pauline Christ, and the Gentile Question," *JBL* 128 (2009):

Important, for our purposes, is what the trope assumes and effaces. Perhaps most notably, it hinges on the assumption of a coherent Jewish set of beliefs about a singular, awaited messiah, as confirmed yet contradicted by claims about Jesus' fulfillment of the role. It effaces, thus, the irrelevance of messianic and other beliefs for most Jewish (especially halakhic) approaches to determining Jewish identity. As a result, the emphasis on the differentiating force of messianism and belief serves to naturalize not just modern views about the mutually exclusivity of "Jew" and "Christian," but also distinctively Christian perspectives on "religion," identity, and difference.

Precisely because the truth of the trope is not as self-evident as it first might seem, it may be instructive to unravel a bit of its genealogy. As we shall see, a number of ancient Christians assert that the belief that Israel's awaited messiah has already arrived is the only or main thing that separates Christians from Jews. Such assertions are prominent, as one might expect, among some of the early Christians most concerned with defining "Christianity" as distinct from "Judaism," such as Justin Martyr, Tertullian, and other Gentile Christian authors of the *contra Iudaeos* tradition. Interestingly, however, such views are also voiced within sources that use the Jewishness of Jesus and his apostles to promote a vision of Christianity centered on monotheism and Torah observance. The following statement, for instance, is attributed to the apostle Peter in the Pseudo-Clementine *Recognitions*, a fourth-century Christian work commonly thought to preserve "Jewish-Christian" traditions:

> The Jews have erred concerning the first coming of our Lord. But between them and us, there is disagreement about this matter alone. They themselves know and expect that the messiah is coming. They do not know that he has come already in humility, namely, as the one called Jesus." (*Rec.* 1.50.5–6)

When we look more closely, then, what appears to be a simple difference is revealed to be potently ambivalent: if divergent messianic beliefs are a point of differentiation between Christians and Jews, it is only because messianism marks Christianity's own origins as Judaism. Accordingly, so-called "Jewish-Christians" can argue for the essential *identity* of Judaism and Christianity on the exact same grounds that so-called Gentile Christians can argue for their essential *difference*.

For our understanding of Christianity's Jewish messianism, I suggest that this ambivalence proves telling. Divergent messianic beliefs are often cited as a point of distinction between Christianity and Judaism in ancient Christian literature as well as in modern scholarly, theological, and popular writings. At the same time, however, messianic expectations remain emblematic of the roots of Chris-

---

357–73, at 359–62; also Novenson, *Christ Among the Messiahs: Christ Language in Paul and Messiah Language in Ancient Judaism* (Oxford: Oxford University Press, 2012).

tian faith in Jewish history and, as such, retain the power to blur the boundaries between them, even long after their supposed "Parting of the Ways."

The dangerously doubled character of Christianity's Jewish messianism, for instance, lies at the heart of the one of the classic conundrums in modern scholarship on Christian origins: if the Jesus movement started out as a Jewish messianic sect, when and how did it cease to be such, and why is Christianity now a separate "religion"? An early and influential proposal was outlined by Ferdinand Christian Baur (1792–1860), one of the founding figures in the development of critical approaches to the New Testament. Significantly, for our purposes, it was by drawing upon the evidence of the Pseudo-Clementine *Recognitions* that he argued as follows:

The first disciples of Jesus adhered as nearly as possible to the Jewish religion and to the national worship. The only thing that distinguished them from the rest of the Jews was the conviction at which they had arrived, that the promised Messiah had appeared in Jesus of Nazareth. They saw nothing antagonistic to their national consciousness in this belief in Jesus as Messiah. Yet in this belief, simple and undeveloped as it was, a breach was introduced into their consciousness as Jews, which might seem insignificant at first, but could not fail to divide Judaism and Christianity further and further from each other.[15]

Here, the ambivalent power of Christianity's Jewish messianism is neutralized by the mapping of similarity and difference onto the axis of time: Baur invokes messianic beliefs about Jesus as a seemingly small yet crucial point of difference – the mustard seed for epochal religious change, a seed that grew to overshadow and obscure the ground from which it sprung. Interestingly, however, Baur's emphasis on the faithful Jewishness of Jesus' first followers (e. g., Peter, James) and the early vitality of "Jewish Christianity" helped to open the way for Jewish thinkers such as Abraham Geiger (1810–1874) and Heinrich Graetz (1817–1891) to reclaim Jesus as a Jewish figure, one as much a part of Jewish history as Christian theology.[16]

Already in the nineteenth century, messianism was cited as that which both links and divides the Jewish Jesus of history and the Christ of Christian faith. Yet there was also a sense that too much attention to such commonalities might threaten to subsume Christianity back into Judaism. David Friedrich Strauss (1808–1874), for instance, courted controversy with *Das Leben Jesu* in part because he depicted the New Testament as saying more about Jewish messianism than about Jesus:

---

[15] Quotations here and below are from the 1873 English translation of the second German edition: Ferdinand Christian Baur, *Paul, the Apostle of Jesus Christ* (trans. E. Zellar; 2nd ed.; London: Williams & Norgate, 1876), 1:42. In Baur's time, the Pseudo-Clementines were thought to date from the second century.

[16] On Geiger, see Heschel, *Abraham Geiger and the Jewish Jesus*. See below on Graetz as well as further discussion in Chapter Eleven in this volume.

The expectation of a Messiah had grown up amongst the Israelite people long before the time of Jesus, and just then had ripened to full maturity. And from its beginning this expectation was not indefinite, but determined, and characterized by many important particulars …. Thus many of the legends respecting him [i. e., Jesus] had not to be newly invented; they already existed in the popular hope of the Messiah, having been mostly derived with various modifications from the Old Testament, and had merely to be transferred to Jesus …. Such and such things must have happened to the Messiah; Jesus was the Messiah; therefore such and such things happened to him.[17]

Even among those who assumed an absolute distinction between Christianity and Judaism, inquiries into Christianity's origins in Jewish messianism could lead to unintentional blurrings of religious boundaries – opening the way, in turn, for unexpected crossings of Jewish and Christian historiographies. Such blurrings and crossings were a source of some anxiety among Christian scholars in the nineteenth and early twentieth centuries. Nevertheless, they proved pivotal for shaping present scholarship on Judaism and Christianity alike.

Particularly as scholars of ancient Judaism and Christianity now turn from positing an early "Parting of the Ways" to grappling with their intertwined histories, it might be useful to reflect on past efforts to make sense of messianism and Jewish/Christian difference. In what follows, I thus consider a range of representations and reflections of Christianity's ambivalent relationship to Jewish messianism. Special attention is paid to varying views of why this specific Jewish sect developed into a separate (demographically non-Jewish and often theologically anti-Jewish) "religion," as well as to discussions of messianism's power and danger as a force within Jewish history. My survey is highly selective, drawing sources from two periods: [1] the formative era for the self-definition of the two traditions as distinct, from the second to fourth centuries (especially in the Roman Empire), and [2] the formative era for the development of modern critical scholarship about them, in the nineteenth century (especially in Germany). Both eras have been deemed critical for the emergence of the categories of "Judaism" and "Christianity" as we now know them, and both have also been credited as crucibles in which was forged something of our current notion of "religion."[18] My hope, then, is that the juxtaposition of the two may help to open

---

[17] David Friedrich Strauss, *Das Leben Jesu kritisch bearbeitet* (2 vols.; Tübingen: Osiander, 1835–1836); quotation is from the English translation of the fourth German edition: *The Life of Jesus, Critically Examined* (2 vols.; trans. Marian Evans; New York: Blanchard, 1860), 1:65–66.

[18] On the second to fourth centuries as formative for the definition of "Christianity" and "Judaism" in terms of an emergent notion of "religion(s)," see Daniel Boyarin, *Border Lines: The Partition of Judaeo-Christianity* (Divinations; Philadelphia: University of Pennsylvania Press, 2004). On the nineteenth century, see Susannah Heschel, "Revolt of the Colonized: Abraham Geiger's *Wissenschaft des Judentums* as a Challenge to Christian Hegemony in the Academy," *New German Critique* 77 (1999): 61–62; cf. Leora Batnitzky, *How Judaism Became a Religion: An Introduction to Modern Jewish Thought* (Princeton: Princeton University Press, 2011).

a fresh perspective on the intertwined histories of Jews and Christians and on the discourses of identity and difference that cross and divide them.

Jewish Messianism and Christian Self-Definition

In current research on Christian Origins, Christianity's roots in Jewish messianism are rarely questioned.[19] What is debated, rather, is the degree of disjuncture in its subsequent development[20] and when, how, and why it came to emerge as a separate and largely non-Jewish "religion."[21]

Whether the determinative moment is placed with the teachings of Jesus or mission of Paul in the first century,[22] with the failure of the Bar Kokhba Revolt in the second century,[23] or with the Christianization of the Roman Empire beginning in the fourth century,[24] Jewish beliefs about messiahs are posited to have played a significant part – both positively and negatively. On the one hand, biblical exegesis, Jewish apocalypses and eschatology, and inner-Jewish debate seem to have been critical for the conceptualization of Jesus as "the Christ"

---

[19] Cf. N. T. Wright, *The New Testament and the People of God* (Minneapolis: Fortress, 1992), 341–45; Ron Cameron and Merrill P. Miller, eds., *Redescribing Christian Origins* (SBL Symposium Series 28; Leiden: Brill, 2004). With respect to the scope and definition of "messianism" in its ancient contexts, I here follow Collins, *The Scepter and the Star*; Peter Schäfer, "Diversity and Interaction: Messiahs in Early Judaism," in Schäfer and Cohen, *Toward the Millennium*, 15–17; Andrew Chester, *Messiah and Exaltation: Jewish Messianic and Visionary Traditions and New Testament Christology* (WUNT 207; Tübingen: Mohr Siebeck, 2007), 191–205. The suggestion by Charlesworth ("From Messianology to Christology," 9–13) that the study of messianism should be limited to sources where one finds the term "messiah" was an important corrective at the time, but it ultimately proved too reductive to capture the richness of the complex of messianic reading practices, eschatological speculations, liturgical practices, social structures, etc., in Judaism and Christianity.

[20] James D. G. Dunn, *Christianity in the Making*, vol. 1: *Jesus Remembered* (Grand Rapids: Eerdmans, 2003), 17–138; Dunn, *Beginning from Jerusalem*, 17–51.

[21] Becker and Reed, *The Ways That Never Parted*; Boyarin, *Border Lines*; Judith M. Lieu, *Christian Identity in the Jewish and Graeco-Roman World* (Oxford: Oxford University Press, 2004); Simon Claude Mimouni and Bernard Pouderon, eds., *La croisée des chemins revisitée: Quand l'Église et la Synagoguese sont-elles distinguées?* (Paris: Cerf, 2012).

[22] Gedaliah Alon, for instance, posits Paul and the triumph of Pauline Christianity as the "victory that transformed Christianity into a Gentile religion"; *The Jews in Their Land in the Talmudic Age, 70–640 CE* (trans. G. Levi; 2 vols.; Jerusalem: Magnes, 1980–1984), 296 – thus echoing Baur's model of apostolic history.

[23] Lawrence Schiffman, "At the Crossroads: Tannaitic Perspectives on the Jewish–Christian Schism," in *Jewish and Christian Self-Definition*, vol. 2: *Aspects of Judaism in the Graeco-Roman Period*, ed. E. P. Sanders, Albert I. Baumgarten, and Alan Mendelson (Philadelphia: Fortress, 1981), 115–56; James D. G. Dunn, *The Partings of the Ways: Between Christianity and Judaism and Their Significance for the Character of Christianity* (London: SCM, 1991), 238.

[24] Jacob Neusner, *Judaism and Christianity in the Age of Constantine: History, Messiah, Israel, and the Initial Confrontation* (Chicago: University of Chicago Press, 1987); Daniel Boyarin, *Dying for God: Martyrdom and the Making of Christianity and Judaism* (Stanford, CA: Stanford University Press, 1999).

by the first generations of his followers (and perhaps even, to some degree, by Jesus himself).[25] On the other hand, the resultant beliefs about Jesus – and the communities that cultivated them – were further shaped in response to the failure to persuade most of their fellow Jews. So too with the features that came to distinguish this particular Jewish messianic sect from its counterparts: the extension of soteriological claims and proselytizing efforts to non-Jews finds a likely motive in biblical and Second Temple Jewish beliefs about the ingathering of the nations in the messianic age, and it may have been spurred by puzzlement over the Jesus movement's lack of success convincing those most familiar with the Jewish scriptures.[26] The apostle Paul, for instance, laments that Jews "demand signs" and receive "Christ crucified" as a "stumbling block" (1 Cor 1:22–23); here, he presumably admits Jesus' lack of fit with acknowledged signs for Israel's messiah, due foremost to his death by crucifixion (cf. Deut 21:23; Gal 5:11; 6:12) and perhaps also to the failure to bring any discernible change to Jewish political circumstances under Roman imperial rule.[27]

By the time of the Gospels, decades later, the problem of "signs" has been addressed through the correlation of details in Jesus' life with prophesies from Jewish scriptures. One also sees reflected in the Gospels the collection of sayings concerning the "kingdom of God," together with the first fruits of reflection on the nature of the changes brought by the messiah's purported incarnation. The problems in positing Jesus' messianic identity, moreover, becomes dramatized in narratives about his discussions with disciples and other Jews. These narratives evoke the diverse range of ideas about messiahs (e. g., kingly, priestly, prophetic) familiar from other Second Temple Jewish sources, even as they might hint at his followers' lack of success in spreading the news to their fellow Jews that the messiah had already come and left, with seemingly little effect on earthly realities.

Whether or not the Jewish reception of the Jesus Movement's messianic claims played a major role in the initiation of proselytizing among non-Jews, "the Jewish rejection of Jesus" soon became a rallying cry for the Gentile Christian authors of the *contra Iudaeos* tradition – a tradition influential for the

---

[25] On Jesus, see Hengel, "Jesus der Messias Israels." On Paul, Novenson, "Jewish Messiahs, the Pauline Christ, and the Gentile Question" 357–73.

[26] E. g., Isa 2:1–4; 45:22–23; 49:5–6; 56:6–7; *1 En.* 90; Tob 14:5–7. Cf. Matt 10:5–15, 28:19; Rom 9–11. Novenson ("Jewish Messiahs, the Pauline Christ, and the Gentile Question," 373), has argued that Jewish messianism may hold the key to understanding Christianity's Gentile mission.

[27] Claudia Setzer notes that there is little evidence for early Jewish hostility over claims about Jesus as Messiah; *Jewish Responses to Early Christians: History and Polemics, 30–150 CE* (Philadelphia: Fortress, 1994), 10–12. She points, rather, to "the broader issue of a christological claim that God's Messiah is one who the law declares cursed due to his death on a cross" (10; cf. Deut 21:23; 1 Cor 1:22–23), together with perceived disloyalty to the Temple, abandonment of circumcision for proselytes, etc., by some – but not all – followers of Jesus (cf. Acts 4:2; 5:28; 6:11–14).

assertion of Christianity's distinction from, opposition to, and mutual exclusivity with Judaism (at first as literary rhetoric, but eventually as lived reality).[28] In one early example, *Dialogue with Trypho,* the second-century apologist Justin Martyr places objections to Christianity in the mouth of a Jewish refugee from the Bar Kokhba War.[29] In this imagined discussion, the identity of the messiah looms large, and it is presented, by both parties, as the root cause of their other differences. Trypho points to the abandonment of Torah observance, for instance, as a lamentable result of what he considers Justin's messianic mistake (*Dial.* 8). Justin counters by pointing to the failures of the two Jewish revolts against Rome (66–70 CE; 132–135 CE) as "proof" that it is Trypho and his fellow Jews who have erred. Drawing on prophetic denunciations of Israel in the Jewish scriptures and applying the hermeneutics of Deuteronomistic theodicy in isolation from the affirmation of Jewish chosenness, Justin reads the events of his time as divinely sent signs of Jewish sinfulness. By the Roman destruction of the Second Temple and the expulsion of Jews from Jerusalem, God is punishing them – Justin argues – for not recognizing Jesus as the messiah predicted by their own scriptures and prophets (*Dial.* 25.5; 26.1; 108.3). By Justin's logic, even Torah observance becomes preemptive preparatory punishment for what he sees as the one error that has determined the entire history and fate of Israel.[30]

Justin sets the main parameters for the *contra Iudaeos* tradition and Christian anti-Judaism. Yet one can glimpse something of the depth of his debt to Jewish messianism. In much of the *Dialogue with Trypho* (especially 30–57), Justin answers his invented interlocutor by culling prophesies from Jewish scriptures, among which are many of the classic Jewish prooftexts for the Davidic messiah. To this *tour de force* of messianic exegesis is joined the collection of biblical references and allusions to mediatory figures and phenomena that act on God's

---

[28] On the anti-Jewish rhetoric of the *contra Iudaeo*s tradition and its gradual impact on the social realities of Jewish/Christian difference, see Paula Fredriksen, "What Parting of the Ways? Jews and Gentiles in the Ancient Mediterranean City," in Becker and Reed, *The Ways That Never Parted,* 35–63; Ora Limor and Guy G. Stroumsa, eds., *Contra Iudaeos: Ancient and Medieval Polemics between Christians and Jews* (TSMJ 10; Tübingen: Mohr Siebeck, 1996).

[29] Justin, *Dial.* 1; 9.3. On the question of Bar Kokhba and messianism, see Peter Schäfer, "Bar Kokhba and the Rabbis," in *The Bar Kokhba War Reconsidered: New Perspectives on the Second Jewish Revolt against Rome,* ed. Peter Schäfer (TSAJ 100; Tübingen: Mohr Siebeck, 2003), esp. 15–17 on the title "Nasi." Schäfer stresses how the non-Rabbinic evidence for the Bar Kokhba Revolt "reveal[s] a Judaism that is not anachronistically archaic within a Rabbinic society in the process of consolidating itself; rather they allow us a glimpse of a Jewish society that is still much closer to the Maccabees, the Qumran community, and the Zealots than to the Rabbis" (22). Also useful, for our purposes, is his caution against overstressing the difference between "religious" and "political" Messiahs: "The distinction is here misguided and possibly even inspired the (later) Christian reinterpretation of the originally Jewish Jesus movement" (17). Cf. Dan Jaffé, "La figure messianique de Bar-Kokhba: Nouvelles perspectives," *Hen* 28 (2006): 103–23; Matthew V. Novenson, "Why Does R. Akiba Acclaim Bar Kokhba as Messiah?" *JSJ* 40 (2009): 551–72.

[30] Justin, *Dial.* 11; 18–20; 23; 43; 44; 46; 92. Also Justin, *1 Apol.* 32.4–6; 47–49; 53.2–3.

behalf (e. g., Wisdom; angel of YHWH), featuring many passages also familiar from Second Temple Jewish discussions of divine mediation.[31] Trypho is
depicted as engaged, interested, and impressed by this Torah-citing Gentile
philosopher, even if ultimately unconvinced by his interpretative acrobatics in
the service of a slain messiah.[32] Nevertheless, it is intriguing that the obdurately
Jewish Trypho is here made to acknowledge the points of agreement that make
such debate possible: "Be assured that all of our [i. e., Jewish] nation waits for
the messiah, and we admit that all the scriptures that you have quoted refer to
him" (Justin, *Dial.* 89). Justin denounces "the Jews" for sinfulness, hard-heartedness, and demonic alliances, and he critiques their teachers (Gr. διδάσκαλοι =
rabbis?) for incorrect exegesis.[33] Nevertheless, he still finds it important to claim,
with respect to the messiah, that they agree with Christians about *everything
except* his advent.

At first sight, this concern for continuity may seem puzzling. When situated
in its second-century context, however, it serves as a poignant reminder that,
for Justin's primary "pagan" audience, there was little distinguishing Jesus from
Shimon bar Koziba ("Bar Kokhba"), and for his Jewish contemporaries, there
was also little to suggest that the messianic age had already begun, despite so
many birth pangs of war and destruction.[34] From one perspective, then, one
can understand the *Dialogue of Trypho* as an expression of the hermeneutics of
messianic failure:[35] efforts are here made to argue that one claimed messiah, who
died before bringing his people redemption from foreign imperial oppression,
is revealed by Jewish scriptures as a true redeemer who shall return, in part by

---

[31] Justin, *Dial.* 55–61. On Justin's choice of prooftexts, Jewish parallels, possible "Jewish-
Christian" sources, etc., see Oskar Skarsaune, *Proof from Prophecy: A Study in Justin Martyr's
Proof Text Tradition: Text-Type, Provenance, Theological Profile* (NTSup 56; Leiden: Brill,
1987), 191–225, 288–89.

[32] Tessa Rajak, "Talking at Trypho: Christian Apologetic as Anti-Judaism in Justin's *Dialogue with Trypho the Jew,*" in *Apologetics in the Roman Empire: Pagans, Jews, and Christians,* ed. Mark Edwards, Martin Goodman, and Simon Price with Christopher Rowland (Oxford: Oxford University Press, 1999), 59–80.

[33] Justin, *Dial.* 90–142.

[34] That Christians were especially attuned to the messianic overtones of the movement surrounding Shimon bar Koziba is suggested by the fact – stressed by Schäfer ("Bar Kokhba and
the Rabbis," 17) – that "aside from Aqiva's play on words with 'Kokhba' and 'Kozeba' [i. e., in
y. Ta'anit 4.8; *Vayiqra Rabbah* 2.4] it is only the Christian sources that generally apply the name
'Bar Kokhba,' with its clearly Messianic overtones [i. e., in relation to Num 24:17]"; also Peter
Schäfer, *Der Bar Kokhba-Aufstand: Studien zum zweiten jüdischen Krieg gegen Rom* (TSAJ 1;
Tübingen: Mohr Siebeck, 1981), 51–52.

[35] Compare Taubes' comments about Jewish messianic examples of "when prophecy fails"
in "Scholem's Theses on Messianism Reconsidered," 669–70. Cf. Leon Festinger, Henry
W. Riecken, and Stanley Schachter, *When Prophecy Fails: A Social and Psychological Study
of a Modern Group That Predicted the Destruction of the World* (Minneapolis: University of
Minnesota Press, 1956); Simon Dein, "What Really Happens When Prophecy Fails: The Case
of Lubavitch," *Sociology of Religion* 62 (2001): 383–401.

suggesting that another claimed messiah brought catastrophe on his people in punishment for their lack of ability to recognize the first.

Justin's use of Jewish messianic traditions to condemn the Jews seems to be predicated on some degree of cultural proximity and an attendant anxiety of influence.[36] These traditions were no less helpful, however, for the defense of Christians against "pagan" misperception and Roman persecution, as becomes clear when we compare Tertullian's *Apology*. Writing in Latin in third-century North Africa, Tertullian makes an assertion that echoes the sentiment of Justin's Trypho. He states it, however, in even starker terms: "The Jews too, as those to whom the prophets spoke, were well aware that Christ was coming. Indeed, even now his advent is expected by them. Nor is there any other greater contention between them and us, than that they believe the advent has not yet occurred" (*Apol.* 21.15).[37] The context is Tertullian's defense of Christians against the "pagan" charge of foolish inconsistency for claiming antiquity due to their continuities with Judaism and their use of Jewish scriptures, while not accepting either the name or law of the Jews, and even admitting to having arisen in recent times. Messianism is cited by Tertullian as that which connects Jewish past and Christian present, and it is the assertion of Jewish agreement on everything except the messiah's advent that makes the connection plausible (cf. *Apol.* 16–20). Jewish messianism is pressed into the service of Christian apologetics, and its diversity is thereby reduced to the one difference that matters from the perspective of the early church: Jewish messianism is reimagined as Christology without Jesus. In the course of redressing "pagan" perceptions of Christians as choosing to be Jews without the benefits of Jewish antiquity or ancestral customs, Tertullian thus posits Judaism as Christianity deferred.[38]

But, we might ask, what are the implications of placing the pivot between Jewish and Christian identities on this particular point? Was the boundary imagined to be so thin that one might slip between religions, as easily as messianic rectitude might drift toward messianic error? Was the messianic age feared to be so ephemeral that its first advent might slip from mind? And, if so, what might this tell us about the character of Christian self-definition, on the one hand, and Jewish messianism, on the other?

Glimmers of such anxieties might be glimpsed in Tertullian's *Against Marcion*, wherein Jewish messianism serves simultaneously as that which authenticates

---

[36] Justin hailed from Samaria, and some of his exegetical traditions are paralleled in Rabbinic midrashim; see Marc Hirshman, *A Rivalry of Genius: Jewish and Christian Biblical Interpretation in Late Antiquity* (trans. Batya Stein; Albany: SUNY Press, 1996), 42–66.

[37] On this passage, see now Georges Tobias, "Die Rolle der Juden für Tertullians Darstellung der christlichen Gottesverehrung im Apologeticum, speziell in Apologeticum 21," *ZAC* 12 (2008): 236–49.

[38] On Tertullian's innovative use of the abstract *Iudaismus* as presaging later notions of Judaism as a "religion," see Steve Mason, "Jews, Judaeans, Judaizing, Judaism: Problems of Categorization in Ancient History," *JSJ* 38 (2007): 471–75.

proper Christology and as that which exemplifies Christological error. Marcion – it seems – pointed to Jewish rejection of Jesus as messiah as "proof" that Jesus was actually another messiah sent by another God, completely unrelated to Israel or the Jews. Tertullian describes and critiques this position as follows:

Marcion has laid down the position that the Christ who in the days of Tiberius was, by a previously unknown god, revealed for the salvation of all nations, is a different being from the one who was ordained by God the Creator for the restoration of the Jewish state and who is yet to come. Between these he interposes the separation of a great and absolute difference – as great as lies between what is just and what is good; as great as lies between the Law and the Gospel; as great, in short, as is the difference between Judaism and Christianity. (*Adv. Marc.* 4.6)[39]

Against Marcion, Tertullian takes pains to argue that Jesus is the Jewish messiah, sent as a Jew by the God of Israel to the people of Israel according to the predictions in Jewish scriptures.

Nevertheless, even as Tertullian stresses Jesus' Jewishness and the continuity of true Christianity with the Jewish scriptures, he does so by condemning Marcion's messianism as *too Jewish*:

Our heretics in their frenzy presumed to say that the messiah [i.e., Jesus] had come who had never been fore-announced. It followed, on their assumption, that the messiah who had always been predicted [i.e., in the Jewish scriptures] had not yet appeared. Thus they are obliged to make common cause with Jewish error and to construct their arguments with its assistance, on the pretense that the Jews were themselves quite certain that it was some other person who came. (*Adv. Marc.* 3.6)

To confirm the Jewishness of Christianity's messiah and messianism, in other words, Tertullian accuses the vehemently anti-Jewish Marcion of "Judaizing."[40] In this, we see some of the paradox of the doubled character of Christianity's relationship with Judaism, as emblematized by the messianism that is deemed both their common ground and their determinative difference.

These lines of argumentation were first developed at a time when Christians were marginal and persecuted in the Roman Empire. It is perhaps significant, however, that they crystallized with the empire's Christianization.[41] Most notably, the depiction of the rejection of Jesus as the defining feature of Jewish messianism – and, by extension, "Judaism" – was enshrined in ecclesiastical historiography by Eusebius of Caesarea. The fourth-century historian picked up and extended Justin's interpretation of first- and second-century events as signs of God's punishment of the Jews (*Hist. eccl.* 1.1.2; 2.5.6–10; 3.5.2–7, 7.7–9).

---

[39] It is perhaps telling that this and other statements by Tertullian are the earliest known uses of the Latin *Christianismus*.

[40] Tertullian's argument for Jesus as Jew is mounted largely on the blaming of Jews for his death – as becomes clear in the continuation of the above-quoted passage (*Adv. Marc.* 3.6).

[41] On this transformation, see Guy G. Stroumsa, "From Anti-Judaism to Antisemitism in Early Christianity?," in Limor and Stroumsa, *Contra Iudaeos*, 1–26.

In the hands of Eusebius, the failures of the two Jewish revolts against Rome (66–70 CE; 132–135 CE) and the success of Christians in the era of Constantine's Edict of Milan (313 CE) became evidence for Jewish messianic error and Christian messianic rectitude, respectively – in a manner deemed determinative for the diverging trajectories of the two traditions thereafter: Christianity's triumph is deemed concomitant with Judaism's decline.[42] For Justin, Jesus' failure to bring political dominion to the persecuted righteous perhaps resulted in a messiah with uncomfortably close affinities to the Zealots and Bar Kokhba. Eusebius, however, can claim belated triumphalism, due to an imperial success that resonated in new ways with the Davidic, monarchic, and militaristic themes so prominent in Second Temple Jewish messianism and its biblical sources.

Despite emergent notions of "Christianity" as the opposite of "Judaism," something of Christianity's Jewish messianic origins still persisted. These origins remained inscribed in its very name (Acts 11:26).[43] They were embedded in the scope of its canonical scriptures, as perennially a nexus for anxieties about Jewish origins, a potential source for Jewish influence, an inspiration for "Judaizing," and a temptation to exegetical exchange. Accordingly, it perhaps makes sense that messianism *qua* Christology would form the focus for the delineation of the center and boundaries of the imperial church as well.

Early inner-Jewish and anti-Jewish polemics surrounding claims about Jesus as Jewish messiah seem to have set much of the dynamics for the ecclesiastical determination of its orthodoxy and definition of "Others" during the Christianization of the Roman Empire in and after the fourth century CE. In the creation of imperial orthodoxy, messianic belief became a governing criterion even for what constituted a "Christian," as newly empowered ecclesiarchs set upon forging consensus through church councils and heresiography. In the concurrent construction and exclusion of "Others," Jews remained paradigmatic for a variety of intimate enemies, serving as a model for "heretics" ("Judaizing" and otherwise), whose distinctions were readily blurred in accusations of demonic inspiration to messianic error.[44]

---

[42] Robert M. Grant, *Eusebius as Church Historian* (Oxford: Clarendon, 1980), 97–113; Timothy D. Barnes, *Constantine and Eusebius* (Cambridge, MA: Harvard University Press, 1981), 101–4, 121, 135–36. On the extension of these views in *Preparatio evangelica* and *Demonstratio evangelica*, see Aryeh Kofsky, "Eusebius of Caesaria and the Christian-Jewish Polemic," in Limor and Stroumsa, *Contra Iudaeos*, 59–84. Cf. Jörg Ulrich, *Eusebius von Caesarea und die Juden: Studien zur Rolle der Juden in der Theologie des Eusebius von Caesarea* (Patristische Texte und Studien 49; Berlin: de Gruyter, 1999).

[43] I.e., as ultimately rooted in the rendering of Hebrew משיח as the Greek χριστός, as found already in the pre-Christian Jewish translations of biblical writings widely used by Jesus' followers and later Christians. See further Judith M. Lieu, *Neither Jew nor Greek? Constructing Early Christianity* (London: T&T Clark, 2005), 131–32, 192–93; Tim Hegedus, "Naming Christians in Antiquity," *SR* 33 (2004): 173–90.

[44] Averil Cameron, "Jews and Heretics – A Category Error?," in Becker and Reed, *The Ways That Never Parted*, 345–60.

Jewish Identities and "Jewish-Christian" Counterhistories

What is so striking about the dominant image of Jewish messianism in ancient Christian literature, however, is how little it corresponds to what else we know of the Judaism of its time. Despite the variety and fluidity of definitions of "Jew,"[45] one finds little sense that a choice of messiah would suffice to negate it.[46] Josephus, for instance, describes a number of charismatic leaders of Jewish renewal movements in the Roman period (including but not limited to Jesus), whose missions bear some messianic overtones; despite his own distaste for eschatological and revolutionary fervor, however, he makes no suggestion that these brigands, Zealots, and so on are not Jews.[47] Likewise, when seen from the perspective of Rabbinic halakhah – as Lawrence Schiffman has stressed – messianic belief is hardly determinative of Jewish or non-Jewish identity: a Jew who believes that Jesus is messiah remains a Jew.[48] And, indeed, the redactors of classical Rabbinic literature are surprisingly unembarrassed to associate R. Akiva with Bar Kokhba.[49]

---

[45] On antiquity, see Shaye J. D. Cohen, *The Beginnings of Jewishness: Boundaries, Varieties, Uncertainties* (Berkeley: University of California Press, 1999). On modernity, see Menachem Marc Kellner, *Must a Jew Believe Anything?* (London: Littman Library of Jewish Civilization, 2006).

[46] Against the old claim that the *birkat ha-minim* was instituted at the Council of Yavneh (*b. Berakhot* 28b–29a) as a measure against Christians and lies behind Christian traditions about the expulsion of Jesus' followers from first-century synagogues (John 9:22; 12:42; 16:2), see Reuven Kimelman, "*Birkat Ha-Minim* and the Lack of Evidence for an Anti-Christian Jewish Prayer in Late Antiquity," in Sanders, Baumgarten, and Mendelson, *Jewish and Christian Self-Definition*, 2:234–40. Also Peter Schäfer, "Die sogenannte Synode von Jabne," *Judaica* 31 (1975): 54–64, 116–24; Daniel Boyarin, "A Tale of Two Synods: Nicaea, Yavneh, and Rabbinic Ecclesiology," *Exemplaria* 12 (2000): 21–62; Boyarin, "Justin Martyr Invents Judaism," *CH* 70 (2001): 127–32. Against older tendencies to interpret all Rabbinic references to *minim* as concerning Christians, see Richard Kalmin, "Christians and Heretics in Rabbinic Literature of Late Antiquity," *HTR* 87 (1994): 155–69.

[47] Josephus, *Ant.* 17.271–84; 18.85–89; 20.47, 167–71; *War* 2.261–63, 433; 4.503; 6.300–309; 7.437–38; the case of Samaritans in *Ant.* 18.85–87 is a partial exception.

[48] Schiffman, "At the Crossroads"; Schiffman, *Who Was a Jew? Rabbinic and Halakhic Perspectives on the Jewish Christian Schism* (Hoboken, NJ: Ktav, 1985). Even in the delineation of "all Israel" in *m. Sanhedrin* 10.1, which includes some matters of doctrinal profession and eschatology, there is nothing pertaining to the Messiah.

[49] See *y. Ta'anit* 4.8; *Vayiqra Rabbah* 2.4. Nor does it seem that continued commitment to a slain Messiah suffices, in itself, to expel someone from the boundaries of Israel; in fact, later examples, like Sabbatai Zevi and the Lubavitcher Rebbe, suggest that the halakhic logic of Rabbinic Judaism does not necessitate that the death of a Messiah negates the Jewishness of those who continue to believe in him as such. See Joel Marcus, "The Once and Future Messiah in Early Christianity and Chabad," *NTS* 47 (2001): 381–401; Elliot R. Wolfson, *Open Secret: Postmessianic Messianism and the Mystical Revision of Menahem Mendel Schneerson* (New York: Columbia University Press, 2009); cf. David Berger, *The Rebbe, The Messiah, and the Scandal of Orthodox Indifference* (London: Littman Library of Jewish Civilization, 2001).

In sum, as Daniel Boyarin asserts:

There is no reason, *a priori*, for instance, why believing that Jesus was the messiah would be considered as beyond the pale of rabbinic Judaism, any more than Rabbi Akiva's belief in Bar Kokhba as messiah rendered him a heretic. Only the later success of Christianity determined, retroactively, that in its earlier relations with the Rabbis it was a separate religion. It took the historical processes of what we might call the long fourth century before the "parting of the ways" was achieved, and along that road, there was as much shared religious life and development as partition, as much consensus and dissensus. The religious histories intersect and intertwine.[50]

Accordingly, it is perhaps not surprising that we find so little in the way of ancient Jewish counterparts to the treatment of messianism and religious difference in the Christian sources noted above. Pseudepigraphical sources from the first century BCE/CE, such as the *Similitudes of Enoch*, *4 Ezra*, and *2 Baruch*, richly attest the Jewish cultivation of traditions about the messiah and the messianic age and include traditions that interpret and extend earlier apocalyptic materials (especially Dan 7) along much the same lines in the New Testament.[51] Josephus' accounts of the role of Zealots in the First Jewish Revolt (66–70 CE) hint at some of the sociohistorical contexts and consequences.[52] Nevertheless, pseudepigraphical sources are infamously elusive about the specific groups to which and against which they speak, and Josephus ducks any explicit discussion of messiahs, lest his Roman audience see rebellion as endemic to Jewish tradition. The earliest Rabbinic authors/redactors similarly evade specificity on the topic, collecting traditions open to multiple interpretations, rarely easily reduced either to a reaction against Christian claims or to a rationalistic rejection of messianic hope.

The assumption that messiahs and the messianic age lie in the future, rather than in the past or present, is tacit in most of these sources.[53] Yet one finds noth-

---

[50] Boyarin, *Dying for God*, 17–18.

[51] The similarities between *4 Ezra* (esp. 13) and Revelation are striking (as perhaps not surprising in light of their close dates), and the *Similitudes* famously includes the title "Son of Man," commonly used in the Gospels for Jesus (cf. esp. *1 En.* 46:1; 47:3; Matt 19:28; 25:31). See also 1QSa; 4Q246; 4Q369; *2 Bar.* 29–30; *5 Sib. Or.* 108–109, 414–33. As Collins (*The Scepter and the Star*, 168) shows, these first-century Jewish materials expose the problematic assumptions involved in traditional views of "high Christology" as a result of solely Hellenistic influence, in disjuncture from Jewish messianism. See further John J. Collin and Adela Yarbro Collins, *King and Messiah as Son of God: Divine, Human, and Angelic Messianic Figures in Biblical and Related Literature* (Grand Rapids: Eerdmans, 2008).

[52] John G. Gager, "Messiahs and Their Followers," in Schäfer and Cohen, *Toward the Millennium*, 37–46; Seth Schwartz, *Imperialism and Jewish Society, 200 BCE to 640 CE* (Princeton: Princeton University Press, 2001), 89–91.

[53] Not all. Note the equation of the "Son of Man" with the antediluvian Enoch in the *Similitudes*, as well as the identification of the Messiah with Hezekiah in one of the traditions preserved in *b. Sanhedrin* 99a. On the latter, compare *y. Sotah* 9.16; *y. Avodah Zarah* 3.1; *b. Berakhot* 28b; Justin, *Dial.* 48; and see the intriguing suggestions made by Mireille Hadas-Lebel, "Hezekiah as King Messiah: Traces of an Early Jewish-Christian Polemic in the Tannaitic

ing akin to the explicit emphasis on messianic belief as a boundary between religions. If anything, the early Rabbinic theorization of difference seems more akin to ritual theory than to comparative theology.[54] Even to the degree that Christianity would be retrospectively expelled from Judaism in the Rabbinic literature of Late Antiquity, it is largely by applying halakhic principles of partial communal exclusion to the figure of Jesus – whether by asserting his birth from Mary's adulterous tryst with a Roman soldier and his status as *mamzer* or by associating him with defiling deeds described as "abominations" in the Torah such as *zenut* and idolatry.[55]

It is only with caution, then, that we can speculate about the "other side" of the debates evoked by Justin and Tertullian to posit an ancient Jewish messianism that shares with Christians everything except faith in Jesus. Caution is especially warranted with respect to what we assume when framing our questions. Differentiation may well have been effected foremost by the manner in which messianism was even figured as a factor in identity. Conversely, the deepest commonalities may be those that are unstated within texts of both traditions (e. g., the subversion of Graeco-Roman ideas about world history, the countering of the totalizing claims of Hellenistic *paideia*, the absorption and inversion of elements of Roman imperial ideology, the parallel attempts to defuse messianism of its power to inspire imminent eschatological expectations while retaining its utopian horizon or harnessing its ethical force).

The evidence, moreover, speaks to a notable delay in Jewish "reactions" to the Christian appropriation of Jewish messianism: the Rabbinic literature of late antique Palestine contains some midrashic and other traditions that resonate with Christian claims and concerns.[56] But explicit level of engagement first finds literary expression outside the bounds of the Roman Empire, among the sages

---

Tradition," in *Jewish Studies at the Turn of the Twentieth Century: Proceedings of the 6th EAJS Congress, Toledo, July 1998*, ed. Judit Targarona Borrás and Angel Sáenz-Badillos (2 vols.; Leiden: Brill, 1999), 1:275–81.

[54] If there is a concern for boundary maintenance in the Mishnah, it arguably centers on the problem of daily life in an urban landscape pocked by sites of "pagan" worship, rather than on the problem of any messianists in their midst; Moshe Halbertal, "Coexisting with the Enemy: Jews and Pagans in the Mishnah," in *Tolerance and Intolerance in Early Judaism and Christianity*, ed. Graham N. Stanton and Guy G. Stroumsa (Cambridge: Cambridge University Press, 1998), 159–72.

[55] For the former, see *b. Shabbat* 104b; *b. Sanhedrin* 67a; cf. Origen, *Cels.* 1.28, 32; cf. Deut 23:3. For the latter, see *b. Berakhot* 17a–b; *b. Sanhedrin* 103a, 107b; cf. Lev 18:24–30; 19:31; 20:1–3. Compare, however, the case of Rabbi Eliezer in *b. Avodah Zarah* 16b–17a, which seems closest to reflecting something akin to the anxiety among Christian heresiologists.

[56] I.e., especially from the era of the Christianization of its local landscapes, but with some earlier precedents; Hirshman, *Rivalry of Genius*; Reuven Kimelman, "Rabbi Yohanan and Origen on the Song of Songs: A Third-Century Jewish-Christian Disputation," *HTR* 73 (1980): 567–95; Galit Hasan-Rokem, *Web of Life: Folklore and Midrash in Rabbinic Literature* (trans. Batya Stein; Contraversions; Stanford: Stanford University Press, 2000), 114–25, 152–60; Martha Himmelfarb, "The Mother of the Messiah in the Talmud Yerushalmi and Sefer Zerub-

of Sasanian Babylonia.[57] Extended Jewish counterhistories of Christianity (e. g., *Sefer Zerubavel, Toledot Yeshu*) appear to be an even later phenomenon.[58]

Interestingly, however, late antique efforts to bring Rabbinic perspectives to bear on Christianity's messiah and messianism might be glimpsed in "Jewish-Christian" sources from Syrian locales on Rome's shifting eastern border with the Sasanian Empire. In such sources, one finds evidence for reaction or resistance to the representation of Judaism by Justin and his heirs.[59] And some of these works also exhibit awareness and even acceptance of Rabbinic tradition – with serious consequences for their presentation of both Jesus' Judaism and Christianity's messianism.[60]

Foremost among them is the Pseudo-Clementine literature, a set of fourth-century texts (*Homilies, Recognitions, Epistle of Peter to James, Contestation, Epistle of Clement to Peter*) most famous for their possible preservation of early "Jewish-Christian" and anti-Pauline traditions associated with Peter, James, and the early Jerusalem church.[61] For our purposes, these texts prove significant for two main reasons: [1] they include discussions of beliefs about Jesus that depart from the *contra Iudaeos* tradition in a manner that further exposes the tensions in Christianity's Jewish messianism, and [2] precisely because of this, they were influential for the development of modern critical scholarship on the New Testament and apostolic age, helping to spark renewed recognition of the very origins of Christianity in Jewish messianism.

---

babel," in *The Talmud Yerushalmi and Graeco-Roman Culture III*, ed. Peter Schäfer (TSAJ 93; Tübingen: Mohr Siebeck, 2002), 369–89.

[57] Peter Schäfer, *Jesus in the Talmud* (Princeton: Princeton University Press, 2007).

[58] Martha Himmelfarb, "Sefer Zerubbabel," in *Rabbinic Fantasies: Imaginative Narratives from Classical Hebrew Literature*, ed. David Stern and Mark J. Mirsky (New Haven: Yale University Press, 1998), 67–90; Himmelfarb, *Jewish Messiahs in a Christian Empire* (Cambridge, MA: Harvard University Press, 2017); Biale, "Counter-history and Jewish Polemics," 130–45.

[59] See Chapter Six in this volume.

[60] Ps.-Clem. *Hom.* 2.19, 38; 3.18–19; 7.4–8; 11.28–30; J. Bergman, "Les éléments juifs dans les Pseudo-Clémentines," *REJ* 46 (1903): 89–98; A. Marmorstein, "Judaism and Christianity in the Middle of the Third Century," *HUCA* 10 (1935): 223–63; Albert I. Baumgarten, "Literary Evidence for Jewish Christianity in the Galilee," in *The Galilee in Late Antiquity*, ed. Lee I. Levine (New York: JTSA, 1992), 39–50. See further in this volume, especially Chapter Nine.

[61] The *Homilies* and the *Recognitions* are largely parallel novels written in Greek in the name of Clement of Rome; they are thought to draw from a common third-century source (i.e., the hypothetical Pseudo-Clementine *Grundschrift*). Much research on the Pseudo-Clementines has focused on reconstructing the second-century sources of the *Grundschrift*, with reference to lost texts mentioned by Patristic authors; its hypothetical sources include the *Kerygmata Petrou, Periodoi Petrou*, and *Anabathmoi Jakobou*. See F. Stanley Jones, "The Pseudo-Clementines: A History of Research," *Second Century* 2 (1982): 1–33, 63–96, as well as Chapter One in this volume. On "Jewish-Christian" elements in these works, see Hans Joachim Schoeps, *Theologie und Geschichte des Judenchristentums* (Tübingen: Mohr, 1949); Georg Strecker, *Das Judenchristentum in den Pseudoklementinen* (TU 70; 2nd ed.; Berlin: Akademie-Verlag, 1981). On possibly anti-Pauline traditions, see Gerd Lüdemann, *Opposition to Paul in Jewish Christianity* (trans. E. Boring; Minneapolis: Fortress, 1989), 185–90.

As we have seen, the first book of the Pseudo-Clementine *Recognitions* includes a line that stresses that the belief that the messiah had come is the only thing separating "us" and "them" (1.50.5–6, quoted above). Although similar at first sight to Tertullian's above-cited assertion in his *Apology*, it communicates quite another sense when read in context. The line forms part of the lead-up to the description of the martyrdom of James the brother of Jesus, wherein the apostle Peter is credited with a survey of the debates between different sects of first-century Jews.[62] He reports that most Sadducees, Samaritans, Pharisees, and scribes still await a messiah or eschatological prophet (1.50.5–6, 1.54). Others, however, believe that the messiah has already come. Among these are some who believe that John the Baptist is the messiah and has been "concealed" (1.54.8, 1.60.1–2), as well as some, such as Peter and James, who believe in Jesus as messiah. Yet even Jesus' followers are here made to admit that they can agree to disagree on such matters, as long as Jesus is not hated (1.60.6). A diversity of Jewish views about the messiah is thus evoked, and beliefs about Jesus are placed firmly in the realm of inner-Jewish debate; "Christian" here functions largely as a subset of "Jew."

That it is hate that differentiates is demonstrated by the text's accounts of the tragic events that follow, which are caused by the machinations of the high priest. Caiaphas, who is explicitly said to hate Jesus, conspires with Saul/Paul to persecute his followers (*Rec.* 1.61–62). At the very brink of the persuasion of many of the Jewish people over Jesus' status as Jewish messiah, Saul/Paul thus causes the death of James; even this, however, does not succeed in stopping the movement. It is implied that Saul/Paul therefore pretends to convert so as to use antinomian lies to destroy the movement from within (1.70–71).

The essential conflict is here placed, not between Jews and Christians, but between priestly and nonpriestly parties within Judaism – as replicated within Christianity by the conflict between Saul/Paul's antinomianism and what is proclaimed as the true apostolic religion of the Jerusalem church of James and Peter. This fits well with the understanding of Jesus' messianism in this portion of the Pseudo-Clementine *Recognitions*: Jesus is described as the messiah in the sense that he is the "prophet like Moses" predicted in the Torah and sent to abolish animal sacrifice in the Temple.[63] F. Stanley Jones has suggested that this portion of the Pseudo-Clementine *Recognitions* preserves an earlier source, which was composed to counter the narrative in the New Testament Book of Acts and which takes target particularly at Acts' depiction of the apostle Peter as agreeing with the antinomian Paul.[64] We will return below to consider how this

---

[62] E.g., Ps.-Clem. *Rec.* 1.53. Interestingly, sectarianism is here said to have spread only since the days of John the Baptist, and debate over the Messiah is said to have been sparked by the death of Jesus; inner-Jewish messianic debate is depicted as a first-century phenomenon.

[63] *Rec.* 1.36.2; 1.37; 1.39.1; 1.40.4–41.1; cf. Deut 18:15, 18.

[64] *Rec.* 1.27–71 (ca. 200 CE); cf. Acts 10; 15; Gal 2. See F. Stanley Jones, *Pseudoclementina*

material helped to shape Ferdinand Christian Baur's revisionist reconstruction of apostolic history. For now, it suffices to note that this "Jewish-Christian" version of events resonates with the dominant views of identity and difference reflected in early Rabbinic literature. Here too, debates about messianism remain firmly in the bounds of inner-Jewish discussion; a diversity of belief can be accepted, and the primary target for criticism is the priestly Jewish sect of the Sadducees.[65]

In another work in the same corpus, the Pseudo-Clementine *Homilies*, Christianity's Jewish messianism is reinterpreted in a manner even more resonant with Rabbinic perspectives. Here, assertions about Jesus as messiah are even configured so as to allow for Jewish salvation apart from any acknowledgment of him. Central for this move is a theory of concealment:

Jesus is concealed from the Hebrews who have taken Moses as their teacher and Moses is hidden from those who have believed Jesus. Since there is a single teaching [διδασκαλίας] by both, God accepts one who has believed either of these …. And our lord himself (i. e., Jesus) says that this is so: "I thank you, Father of heaven and earth, because you have concealed these things from the wise and prudent, and you have revealed them to sucking babes" (cf. Matt 11:25; Luke 10:21). Thus God Himself has concealed a teacher from some (i. e., Jews), who foreknew what they should do, and He has revealed [him] to others (i. e., Gentiles), who are ignorant about what they should do. Neither, therefore, are the Hebrews condemned on account of their ignorance of Jesus, by reason of Him who has concealed him, if, doing the things commanded by Moses, they do not hate him whom they do not know. Neither are those from among the Gentiles condemned, who know not Moses on account of Him who has concealed him, provided that these also, doing the things spoken by Jesus, do not hate him whom they do not know. (*Hom.* 8.6–7; cf. *Rec.* 4.5–6)

In the Pseudo-Clementine *Homilies*, Jesus' messianic significance is again understood in prophetic terms: he is the "prophet like Moses" – here in the sense of a teacher. Lest one assume that this necessitates a low Christology, his incarnation is also explained as one of a series of descents of the True Prophet from his heavenly throne.[66] Jesus is here proclaimed χριστός inasmuch as he is the last

Elchasaiticaque inter Judaeochristiana: Collected Studies (Orientalia Lovaniensia Analecta 203; Leuven: Peeters, 2012), 207–29; F. Stanley Jones, *An Ancient Jewish Christian Source on the History of Christianity: Pseudo-Clementine "Recognitions" 1.27–71* (Texts and Translations 37, Christian Apocrypha Series 2; Atlanta: Scholars, 1995).

[65] Baumgarten, "Literary Evidence," 42–43. The Christian arch-heretics Dositheus and Simon Magus are said to have been Sadducees in *Rec.* 1.54.3, thus evoking the treatment of Sadducees as a paradigmatic group of *minim* in early Rabbinic sources (esp. *m. Niddah* 4.2; also *Avot De-Rabbi Natan* A5); note also the polemics against those who deny resurrection, which resonate with depictions of Sadducees in both New Testament Gospels and early Rabbinic literature (e. g., *m. Sanhedrin* 10.1; *Bereshit Rabbah* 53.12). On the parallel redeployment of priestly and anti-priestly traditions in Jewish and Christian traditions, see Ithamar Gruenwald, "From Priesthood to Messianism," in Gruenwald, Shaked, and Stroumsa, *Messiah and Christos*, 75–93.

[66] Ps.-Clem. *Rec.* 2.16–17; 3.17–21. Jesus is here the True Prophet who "has changed his forms and his names from the beginning of the world and so reappeared again and again in the world" (*Hom.* 3.20). See Strecker, *Theologie und Geschichte des Judenchristentum*, 145–53;

of these prophets, the line of whom began with Adam and also included Moses. Because he is the last, he is the one who is sent to the nations, to usher in their eschatological transformation into Jews (3.16; cf. *1 En.* 90).

This seemingly strange Christology allows for an interesting solution to the problem of how Christianity's Jewish origins relate to Jewish/Christian difference. According to the Pseudo-Clementine *Homilies*, the appearance of difference between Jews and Christians is an illusion: just as Moses and Jesus are ultimately the same, and their teachings the same, so a pious Jew and a pious Christian are equivalent, even though they do not know it. Messianism is the end-time extension of Judaism to the Gentiles, and it is thus tied primarily to Christian self-definition; a pious Jew, by this logic, is in no need of Jesus. At the same time, however, that which might seem to be most uniquely "Christian" – that is, belief in Jesus as savior – is revealed to be a hidden mark of Christianity's true unity with Judaism.

For both Jews and Gentiles, moreover, it is not messianic or other beliefs that are deemed determinative in the Pseudo-Clementine *Homilies*, but rather monotheism and Torah observance. The former resonates with the text's extended polemics against Hellenistic *paideia* and Graeco-Roman polytheism, while the latter is consistent with the text's promotion of the observance of *kashrut* and ritual purity as required for Gentile believers in Jesus.[67] When explaining proper practice, for instance, the text even expands the category of "Jew" to include Torah-observant Gentiles: "If anyone acts impiously, he is not pious. Hence, if a foreigner keeps the Law, he is a Jew, but he who does not is a Greek. For the Jew, believing in God, keeps the Law. But he who does not keep the Law is manifestly a deserter through not believing God" (*Hom.* 11.16; cf. *Rec.* 5.34). Significantly, the contrast drawn here is not between "Jew" and "Christian," but rather between "Jew" and "Greek." The implication, as explored particularly in *Hom.* 4–6, is that the true heirs of Jesus and apostolic religion are aligned with Judaism in their monotheism, purity, and piety,[68] while "heretics" (here emblematized by Simon

---

L. Cerfaux, "Le vrai prophète des Clémentines," *RSR* 18 (1928): 143–63; Han Jan Willem Drijvers, "Adam and the True Prophet in the Pseudo-Clementines," in *Loyalitätskonflikte in der Religionsgeschichte: Festschrift für Carsten Colpe,* ed. Christoph Elsas and Hans G. Kippenberg (Würzburg: Königshausen & Neumann, 1990), 314–23; Charles A. Gieschen, "The Seven Pillars of the World: Ideal Figure Lists in the True Prophet Christology of the Pseudo-Clementines," *Journal for the Study of Pseudepigrapha* 12 (1994): 47–82.

[67] Pseudo-Clementine *Hom.* 7.8, e.g., instructs Gentiles "to abstain from the table of devils – that is, from food offered to idols – from dead carcasses, from animals that have been suffocated or caught by wild beasts, and from blood," and also "not to live any longer impurely; to wash after intercourse; that the women on their part should keep the law of purification [i.e., after menstruation]." Also *Epistle of Peter to James* 4.1–2; *Rec.* 2.71–72; 6.9–11; 7.29, 34; 8.68; *Hom.* 11.28–30; 13.4, 9, 19.

[68] Strikingly: particularly the Pharisees who sit on Moses' seat (cf. Matt 23:2) and who preserve and transmit the Oral Torah. See further Pseudo-Clementine *Hom.* 2.38; 3.18–19, 70; 11.29; *Epistle of Peter to James* 1.2.

Magus) are aligned with Hellenism in their polytheism, idolatry, and demonic pollution.[69] In the Pseudo-Clementine *Homilies*, messianic belief is denied the power of distinction. Rather, those who believe in Jesus as messiah are placed on both sides of what is asserted as the true dividing line: Torah observance versus Hellenistic *paideia*.

In the Pseudo-Clementine *Homilies*, we thus see the extension of older Hellenistic Jewish ideas about difference ("Greek" versus "Jew"), in contrast to the assertion of messianism as the major distinction ("Christian" versus "Jew") by Justin, Tertullian, and their heirs. That the text's targets are Hellenistic-educated Christians who follow the abrogation of the Torah associated with Paul is further suggested by the *Epistle of Peter to James*. In this pseudonymous letter, appended to the beginning of the *Homilies*, Peter claims that he has been misrepresented as antinomian:

Some from among the Gentiles have rejected my legal preaching, attaching themselves to certain lawless and trifling preaching of the man who is my enemy. Some have attempted these things while I am still alive, to transform my words by certain intricate interpretations toward the dissolution of the Law – as though I myself were also of such a mind but did not freely proclaim it; God forbid! (*Epistle of Peter to James* 2.3–4)

Peter's "enemy" seems to be Paul, while the one "transforming" his message seems to be Luke, the author of the Gospel of Luke and Book of Acts.[70] If so, it proves all the more striking that the letter points primarily to Jews as a model for Christian piety, community, and monotheism.[71]

Elsewhere, I have argued that much of the Pseudo-Clementine literature can be read as counterhistory, answering the *contra Iudaeos* tradition at a critical moment in its crystallization within the exegesis and historiography of the nascent imperial church: the *Epistle of James to Peter* and the first book of the Pseudo-Clementine *Recognitions* subvert the Gospel of Luke and Book of Acts. Likewise, the historiography of the Pseudo-Clementine *Homilies* is parallel and inverse to that of Eusebius.[72]

If the fourth-century compilation of these works was indeed shaped by such aims, however, it was a cry into the void.[73] The *contra Iudaeos* tradition shaped the dominant perspectives of post-Constantinian Christianity – despite the availability of other options – with long-standing consequences for Jewish history

---

[69] See Chapter Four in this volume.

[70] I.e., in relation to Galatians 2 versus Acts 10; 15.

[71] Especially *Epistle of Peter to James* 1–2. Note the positive appeals to Jews – and Pharisees in particular – as the true and trustworthy heirs of Moses throughout the *Homilies* (3.18.1–3; 3.70; cf. 11:28–29); see Chapter Nine in this volume.

[72] See Chapter Six in this volume.

[73] I borrow this phrase from Christian Wiese's *Challenging Colonial Discourse: Jewish Studies and Protestant Theology in Wilhelmine Germany* (trans. Barbara Harshav and Christian Wiese; Studies in European Judaism 10; Leiden: Brill, 2005) – for reasons that shall become clear below.

and for the trajectories of modern scholarship.[74] The Pseudo-Clementine literature circulated widely, and translations of portions thereof survive in multiple languages (e. g., Latin, Syriac, Arabic, Georgian, Armenian).[75] Yet these writings seem to have been valued by medieval Christian tradents for purposes other than their perspectives on Judaism.[76] In fact, the subversive potential of their counterhistories seems to have laid largely latent until modern times, when these writings resurfaced as a source for the critique of Christian theological perspectives on Jesus and Judaism – as predicated, moreover, on fresh attention to Christianity's origins in Jewish messianism.

Modern Counterhistories of Christianity and Jewish Messianism

Joseph Dan has speculated that "it is very probable that the anonymous author of the Hebrew or Aramaic original of the Jewish narratives on Jesus, the *Toledot Yeshu*, had access to sources similar to those used by the authors of the Pseudo-Clementine stories."[77] The possibility proves intriguing; for, indeed, parallels with Jewish mystical ideas in the Pseudo-Clementine *Homilies* have been widely noted at least since Graetz's 1846 *Gnostizismus und Judentums*.[78] Yet there is no clear evidence for the circulation of Pseudo-Clementine texts or traditions among late antique or medieval Jews, such that the implications of any apparent overlaps must remain uncertain (at least in the absence of further investigation). Throughout the Middle Ages, Pseudo-Clementine writings were certainly widely circulated among Christian readers, but they were read for reasons having little to do with the Jewishness of Jesus' apostles or the historical relationship of Christianity to non-Christian Judaism.[79]

This makes it all the more intriguing that the relevance of these "Jewish-Christian" sources for scholarship on Jewish and Christian history was first re-

---

[74] So already George Foot Moore, "Christian Writers on Judaism," *HTR* 14 (1921): 197–254.

[75] The *Recognitions*, e. g., survives in over one hundred manuscripts in Rufinus' Latin translation of 406 CE; Bernhard Rehm, *Die Pseudoklementinen*, vol. 2: *Rekognitionen in Rufinus Übersetzung* (GCS 51; Berlin: Akademie-Verlag, 1965), xvii–xcv, cix–cxi. See further Jones, "Pseudo-Clementines," 6–7, 80–84.

[76] Annette Yoshiko Reed, "The First Christian Novel: The Pseudo-Clementines and Their Early Reception," paper presented at *The Dark Ages Enlightened*, University of Pennsylvania Museum of Archaeology and Anthropology, 1 February 2008.

[77] Joseph Dan, "Armilus: The Jewish Antichrist," in Schäfer and Cohen, *Toward the Millennium*, 82 n. 23 – stressing, however, that "this intriguing subject has not yet been studied in any detail."

[78] Heinrich Graetz, *Gnostizismus und Judentums* (Krotoschin: Monasch, 1846), 110–15. By then, Augustus Neander's work (see below) was already well known, and August Friedrich Gfrörer had already called the Pseudo-Clementines a "Greek Zohar" (*Das Jahrhundert des Heils* [2 vols.; Stuttgart: Schweizerbart, 1838], 1:295–97). For the discussion from Neander to the present see Chapter Eleven.

[79] Reed, "First Christian Novel."

covered by a historian who was himself a Jewish convert to Christianity, namely, Augustus Neander (né David Mendel, 1789–1850). One cannot imagine a figure more qualified to make this recovery. A student of Friedrich Schleiermacher, Neander was the most prominent scholar of Christian history in Germany in his time, and some in fact even called him the "father of modern church history."[80] He made no secret of his Jewish ancestry and background, and he was well known among Jews of the time for his public denunciation of the charges of blood libel against Jews during the 1840 Damascus Affair.[81] Neander dealt with the Pseudo-Clementine *Homilies* in depth already in 1818, in an appendix to his *Genetische Entwickelung der vornehmsten gnostischen Systeme*[82] – a foundational work in the modern study of Gnosticism, as well as an important source for Christian historians like Baur and Jewish historians like Graetz.[83] In his early work on Judaism and "Gnosticism," Graetz cites Neander as the first to note Jewish parallels to these "Jewish-Christian" writings, and even Baur – often credited today as the scholar who inaugurated modern discussion of the Pseudo-Clementines – points to Neander as his inspiration in this regard.[84]

As noted above, the Pseudo-Clementines were a key source for Baur's critical rereading of canonical Christian accounts of apostolic history to reconstruct the first-century Jesus movement, as used together with the letters of Paul to shed

---

[80] So Philip Schaff, *History of the Apostolic Church* (trans. Edward D. Yeomans; New York: Scribner, 1853), 95; John McClintock and James Strong, *Cyclopaedia of Biblical, Theological, and Ecclesiastical Literature* (12 vols.; New York: Harper, 1876), 6:691, 887. On Neander's life, see Philip Schaff, *Saint Augustin, Melanchthon, Neander: Three Biographies* (London: Nisbet, 1886), 128–68; Deborah Hertz, *How Jews Became Germans* (New Haven: Yale University Press, 2007), 64–66, 182–83. On Neander, see also Chapter Eleven in this volume.

[81] It is in this capacity, for instance, that Neander makes an appearance in Graetz's *Geschichte der Juden: Von den ältesten Zeiten bis auf die Gegenwart* (11 vols.; Berlin: Beit & Co., 1853–1876); one wonders if Graetz knew of Neander even prior to using his work in his dissertation research. It is also in the context of the Damascus Affair that Neander is remembered at the beginning of the twentieth century in Isidore Singer, Cyrus Adler, et al., *Jewish Encyclopedia: A Descriptive Record of the History, Religion, Literature, and Customs of the Jewish People from the Earliest Times to the Present Day* (New York: Funk & Wagnalls, 1901–1906). See further Chapter Eleven.

[82] August Neander, *Genetische Entwickelung der vornehmsten gnostischen Systeme* (Berlin: Dümmler, 1818), 361–421. Today, Baur is often credited with bringing these sources to the attention of Christian historians, but Neander's role was widely acknowledged not just in his own time but at least until the beginning of the twentieth century; e. g., Fenton John Anthony Hort, *Notes Introductory to the Study of the Clementine Recognitions* (London: Macmillan, 1901), xiii.

[83] It is to this book, for instance, that Georg Wilhelm Friedrich Hegel owes his understanding of Gnosticism; Cyril O'Regan, *The Heterodox Hegel* (Albany: State University of New York Press, 1994), 135–36.

[84] Baur stresses this when countering claims concerning his indebtedness to Strauss; see *Kirchengeschichte des 19. Jahrhunderts* (Tübingen: Fues, 1862), 395, quoted after William Harrison De Puy et al., eds., *The Encyclopædia Britannica* (rev. ed.; 25 vols.; Chicago: Werner, 1893), 3:448.

doubt on the account in Acts.[85] What Acts sought to harmonize or suppress – Baur suggested – was a conflict between two parties in the first-century church: [1] the "Jewish Christianity" of Peter, James, and the Jerusalem church, which remained completely within the halakhic and nationalistic bounds of Judaism, and [2] Pauline Christianity, which was oriented toward Gentile converts, denying the need for Torah observance for salvation through Jesus and thus realizing Christianity's universalistic potential (or, more accurately: "that universal form of consciousness at which the development of mankind had arrived at the time when Christianity appeared").[86] For Baur and his heirs, the Pseudo-Clementines gave voice to the former.[87]

Baur sought to rewrite the history of Christianity in a manner freed from theological bounds, integrating political and religious elements, and oriented toward the universalistic horizon of Hegelian world history. Accordingly, he depicted the conflict between Petrine and Pauline parties in terms of a dialectic, the synthesis of which was early Christianity (which further developed in the subsequent struggle with Gnosticism, and so on). As noted above, Baur's work also played an important part in articulating the problem of the relationship between the Jewish Jesus of history and the non-Jewish faith of Christianity – a problem raised already by his colleagues in the Tübingen school and still debated in scholarship today.

At first sight, Baur's solution seems conventional. It was common at the time to assert that Jesus himself made a radical break from Judaism, rejecting his own Jewishness. Baur too placed the ultimate roots of Jewish/Christian difference in Jesus' unique "moral consciousness." Yet he posited that Jesus himself saw no need to break from Judaism, because he knew that "spirit" of his teaching would work itself out through history. Thus, Jesus – according to Baur – chose the paradigmatically nationalistic model of Jewish messianism as the vehicle for his message, precisely to test his people, so as to see whether they could see the true universalistic message hidden therein.[88] In Baur's schema, then, messianism became representative of both Judaism and particularism: it is what stood in the way of the origins of Christianity and universalism – the latter of which would

---

[85] I.e., as most famously laid out in Ferdinand Christian Baur, "Die Christuspartei in der korinthischen Gemeide, der Gegensatz des petrinischen and paulischen Christentums in der alten Kirche, der Apostel Petrus in Rom," *Tübinger Zeitschrift für Theologie* 4 (1831): 61–206.

[86] Ferdinand Christian Baur, *The Church History of the First Three Centuries* (trans. Allan Menzies; 3rd ed.; 2 vols.; London: Williams & Norgate, 1878), 1:5. On the broader context, see Heschel, *Abraham Geiger and the Jewish Jesus*, 106–18.

[87] So Ferdinand Christian Baur, "Über den Ursprung des Episcopats in der Christlichen Kirche," *Tübingen Zeitschrift für Theologie* 3 (1838): 14, etc.; see further Dunn, *Beginning from Jerusalem*, 32 n. 130, 73–74.

[88] Baur, *Church History*, 1:24–27. See further Matt Jackson-McCabe, introduction to *Jewish Christianity Reconsidered: Rethinking Ancient Groups and Texts*, ed. Matt Jackson-McCabe (Minneapolis: Fortress, 2007), 15–18.

be brought onto the stage of world history by Paul, the author of Christianity's "second beginning."[89] Baur did not, in other words, promote Christianity as the correct variety of Jewish messianism per se, since messianism was suspect. Rather, in his view, Christianity's Jewish messianic origins were the conditions of the formative struggle that allowed universalism to "break the bands" of nationalistic particularism.[90]

Baur's assertion that both Jesus and his first followers were *within* Judaism nevertheless proved alarming for many Christians of the time. Particularly if one accepts origins as determinative of essence, the danger arises that Christianity could be unmasked as simply Judaism or that the scholarly quest for the Jesus of history may lead to the discovery of a man who belongs more to the history of Jewish messianism than to the development of Christian dogma. Following Baur, Jesus' special "consciousness" and the differentiating power latent in the belief in him as messiah were all that stood in the way of proclaiming Paul the founder of Christianity. Baur practically said as much when he speculated that, without Paul, Christianity may have remained the "faith of a mere Jewish sect."[91]

One unintentional result of the work of Baur and the Tübingen school, then, was to open new avenues for Jewish thinkers to reclaim Jesus for Judaism and to integrate the apostolic age into the history of Jewish messianism. The potential implications for a defense of Judaism were not lost on German Jews of the time. It is striking, for instance, that both Geiger and Graetz – despite their many differences, mutual animosity, and opposing positions on religious reform – seem to have used the Tübingen school's findings in this fashion. Geiger's view of Jesus has been abundantly discussed, such that it will suffice to note that his treatment of early Christian history parallels much in the Pseudo-Clementines (whether directly or indirectly), even as it adopts and inverts the narrative of Christian origins posited by Baur and other liberal Protestant scholars of the time; in the course of arguing that Jesus was an ordinary Jew and dismissing Christianity as the invention of Paul, for instance, he adopts a positive association of Jesus with Pharisees, and he interprets controversies within the movement in terms of Judaism versus Hellenism.[92]

For our purposes, Graetz proves most relevant. Not only was his work seminal for mapping out the scope and trajectories of scholarship on the history of Jewish messianism, but he drew on Christian sources and scholarship to integrate

---

[89] Baur, *Church History*, 1:46.

[90] Baur, *Paul*, 3; Baur, *Church History*, 1:5–6.

[91] Baur, *Christian History*, 1:43.

[92] Heschel, *Abraham Geiger and the Jewish Jesus*, 64–65, 111–26; Michael Brenner, "Gnosis and History: Polemics of German-Jewish Identity from Graetz to Scholem," *New German Critique* 77 (1999): 45–50; Matthew Hoffman, *From Rebel to Rabbi: Reclaiming Jesus and the Making of Modern Jewish Culture* (Stanford: Stanford University Press, 2007), 34–51. Cf. Ken Koltun-Fromm, *Abraham Geiger's Liberal Judaism: Personal Meaning and Religious Authority* (Bloomington: Indiana University Press, 2006), 54–57.

Jesus and the early church into the full history of the Jews, particularly as told in his monumental eleven-volume *Geschichte der Juden*.[93] Furthermore, Graetz's understanding of Christianity is shaped by, and subordinated to, his recurrent concern with the power and dangers of Jewish messianism.[94] His understanding of messianism is outlined in his 1865 essay "The Stages in the Evolution of the Messianic Belief."[95] He begins by considering messianic traditions in the Hebrew Bible, which start with promises of restoration and vengeance. To this, he suggests an advance in the time of Hezekiah, whereby such promises were extended beyond Israel, even to the nation's enemies. For Graetz, this evidence serves to highlight the injustice of those who criticize ancient Israel and Judaism for "national particularism": "This great idea of universalism, of all nations belonging to God, of the brotherhood of all men, is the beautiful fruit of Judaism."[96]

Graetz goes on to posit that the messianic idea took a definite shape prior to the Babylonian exile, only after which uncertainty began to surround it. Persecution of the Jews by Antiochus IV in the mid-second century BCE inspired the fanciful apocalyptic visions of Daniel, and the tyranny of the rule of Herod in the first century CE sparked intensive messianic longing and biblical interpretation. Traditions about the messiah, multiplied and diversified by midrash, caused division. In turn, exegetical disputes led to a split between two types of messianism: the hope for a "political figure," who would free the people from the yoke of Rome, and the hope for an "inner redeemer."[97] Around each – according to Graetz – groups developed: the patriots, on one side, and the mystical Essenes, on the other.[98] In the first century, each had its own messiah: "Judah from Golan

---

[93] Heinrich Graetz, *Geschichte der Juden*; quotations and citations below are from the first American edition: *History of the Jews, from the Earliest Times to the Present Day* (ed. and trans. Bella Löwy (6 vols.; Philadelphia: JPS, 1891–1898).

[94] On the context as well as the controversies surrounding his views of both messianism and Christianity, see Michael A. Meyer, "Heinrich Graetz and Heinrich von Treitschke: A Comparison of their Historical Images of the Modern Jew," in Michael A. Meyer, *Judaism within Modernity: Essays on Jewish History and Religion* (Detroit: Wayne State University Press, 2001), 64–75; David N. Myers, *Resisting History: Historicism and Its Discontents in German-Jewish Thought* (Princeton: Princeton University Press, 2003), 35–67; Nils H. Roemer, *Jewish Scholarship and Culture in Nineteenth Century Germany: Between History and Faith* (Madison: University of Wisconsin Press, 2005), 56–58, 85–87; Israel Bartal, "Messianism and Nationalism: Liberal Optimism vs. Orthodox Anxiety," *Jewish History* 20 (2006): 5–17.

[95] Reprinted in Heinrich Graetz, *The Structure of Jewish History and Other Essays* (ed. and trans. Ismar Schorsch; New York: JTS, 1975), 151–72.

[96] Graetz, "Stages in the Evolution," 154–55, citing Isa 2:2–4; 19:24–25; Mic 4:1–3; Zech 9:1, 7; he also takes this opportunity to stress that humane laws of equality of all humankind can be found already in the Torah. The contrast with Baur's view of Jewish messianism as paradigmatic of nationalistic particularism is perhaps not coincidental.

[97] Graetz, "Stages in the Evolution," 160.

[98] Compare Graetz, *History of the Jews*, 2:29–30, which draws on Josephus to contrast the Essenes with the "more rationally minded Pharisees"; Graetz there depicts the Essenes as those who "united the highest and lowest aims – the endeavor to lead a pious life combined with the

representing political messianism, and John the Baptist (the Essene) representing inner messianism."[99] Graetz lauds Judah for his failed revolutionary efforts against Rome, whereby he "succeeded in inspiring nearly the whole nation to acts of heroism … and mounted a resounding, glorious martyrdom for its political independence and religious freedom."[100] John the Baptist, however, also fails and succeeds in a sense, inasmuch as he "paved the way for that great messianic phenomenon by which the messianic idea through a chain of a thousand miraculous events was brought to the nations of the earth, the non-Israelite world."[101]

Lest one imagine some mention of Jesus might come next, Graetz goes on to stress a proliferation of messianic claimants with no mention of the man from Nazareth. He cites Theudas, Simon of Cyprus, and the anonymous Egyptian (all mentioned by Josephus) as among those who "found some adherents and believers, but who died in disgrace without having accomplished anything"; Bar Kokhba, like Judah, is lauded for his heroic and patriotic efforts in leading a rebellion against Rome.[102] The ramifications are striking. That Graetz can survey the history of messianism with only oblique reference to Jesus functions to push Christianity to the margins of the development of Judaism's messianic spirit and its evolving contributions to the universal ideals of humankind.[103]

The next stage of development charted by Graetz is marked by the contrast between rationalism and mysticism, as contained already in Rabbinic tradition but exemplified by Maimonides and the Kabbalah.[104] Here, as elsewhere, Graetz does little to contain his hostility toward the latter.[105] Of the Zohar, for instance, he states that "it continues to this day to spread ruin among the Jews."[106] For this, Sabbatai Zevi proves exemplary, but even Spinoza is linked to the Kabbalah.

Despite telling the history of Jewish messianism as a story of a series of messianic failures fraught with political and heretical danger, Graetz concludes this

---

most vulgar superstitions," spurred by the aim of prophetic ecstasy, practicing asceticism in the hope for the restoration of prophetic visions, and living in expectation of the messianic age.

[99] Graetz, "Stages in the Evolution," 161.

[100] Graetz, "Stages in the Evolution," 161. This is consistent with Graetz's overarching efforts to assert the political element of Jewish peoplehood, resisting Judaism's reduction to spiritual or religious traditions; Alan L. Mittleman, *The Scepter Shall Not Depart from Judah: Perspectives on the Persistence of the Political in Judaism* (Lanham, MD: Lexington, 2000), 31–42.

[101] Graetz, "Stages in the Evolution," 161.

[102] Graetz, "Stages in the Evolution," 161–62.

[103] It is possible that this omission is a reaction to the controversies at the time surrounding his treatment of Christianity in his other works. On Graetz's inversion and subversion of the Christian historiography of his time – the polemical implications of which were quite clear to his Christian readers – see Mack, *German Idealism and the Jew*, 98–100.

[104] Graetz, "Stages," 163–69.

[105] On Graetz's views of mysticism, see Biale, *Gershom Scholem*, 22–23; Jonathan M. Elukin, "A New Essenism: Heinrich Graetz and Mysticism," *Journal for the History of Ideas* 59 (1998): 135–48.

[106] Graetz, "Stages in the Evolution," 168–69.

essay by stressing the vitality of the messianic vision into the future, returning to the prophetic ideals with which he began. This vision is framed in terms of Israel's exemplarity, both in religious creativity (for which even Saul/Paul is cited, alongside Isaiah, the Maccabees, and Rabbi Akiva) and in the capacity to endure suffering (i. e., toward this monotheistic people's "assigned mission" of serving as a "light to the nations").[107] By the end of the essay, it is clear why Graetz chose to begin by describing messianism as Pandora's Box, paired with the assertion that "the messianic idea, that constant hope for a better and more beautiful future, is the elixir of life which has granted the Jewish people its remarkable tenacity."[108]

This ambivalent image of messianism, at once Pandora's Box and elixir of life, is mirrored by the treatment of Christianity in Graetz's *Geschichte der Juden*: the birth of the religion is cited in relation to Israel's fate to be a "light to the nations,"[109] even as Christianity figures primarily as the main cause of Jewish suffering and persecution.[110] Furthermore, even though Jesus is there mentioned by name, Graetz undermines his uniqueness by describing the centuries around the Common Era as bustling with messianic claimants.[111] Jesus himself is said to have been a simple, pious man caught up in strange and extraordinary circumstances. His success is credited, not to any religious genius, but rather to the ready reception of his Essene teachings in the unlearned and superstitious Galilee and among the "lowest classes" neglected by other teachers.[112]

Graetz stresses, however, that Jesus "made no attack on Judaism itself; he had no idea of becoming the reformer of Jewish doctrine or the propounder of a new law." If there is any seed of Jewish/Christian difference with Jesus, it is only the danger of "heresy" that Graetz sees always lurking in Judaism's mystical messianisms. As an Essene, Jesus is aligned with what Graetz presents as messianism's dangerous apocalyptic and mystical stream; of this sect, for instance, he asserts that "through their indifference to all that concerned the State, as well as the affairs of daily life, they gradually led Judaism ... into the darkness and exaggerations of Mysticism."[113] Just as his description of Essenism thus foreshadows his treatment of later messiahs like Sabbatai Zevi, so it also alludes to the ultimate origins of Christianity's anti-Judaism in a mystical denial of worldly concerns: "Patriotism became more and more subordinate to the devotion that

---

[107] Graetz, "Stages in the Evolution," 170–71, quoting Isa 42:6.

[108] Graetz, "Stages in the Evolution," 151–52.

[109] I.e., he explains the success of Christianity as a result of its Judaism. Graetz, *History of the Jews*, 2:141–42, 385–87.

[110] Graetz, *History of the Jews*, 2:171–72.

[111] Graetz (*History of the Jews* 2:142) depicts messianic fervor as so heightened due to the political and religious malaise under Herod, in fact, that anyone of any distinction could claim to be a Messiah and gain followers!

[112] Graetz, *History of the Jews*, 2:148–57, 367.

[113] Graetz, *History of the Jews*, 2:28.

they felt towards their own sect, and thus by degrees they released themselves from the strong bands of nationality. There lay concealed in Essenism an antagonistic element to existing Judaism unsuspected by friends or foes."[114]

The appeal to Jesus' Essenism, however, has the force of denying Christianity's essence as a separate "religion." Even as Christianity's origins are placed at the moment when Jesus reveals his messianic secret, Graetz reminds his reader – in multiple asides – that Christianity is *actually* "Essenism, interwoven with foreign elements."[115] Negating the power of faith in Jesus as messiah to produce Jewish/Christian difference, he depicts Jesus as just one failed Jewish messiah among the many who arose under Roman oppression – and far from the last in the history of Judaism. Even as Christianity here serves as an exemplar of mysticism's potentially corrosive effects on the Jewish people, so the assertion of the post-Christian continuation of Essenism within Judaism (especially in Kabbalah), and the parallel between Jesus and Sabbatai Zevi,[116] relativizes Christian origins by subsuming them into a Jewish genealogy of error. In the process, Graetz casts upon Christianity the negative associations with Jewish messianism common in the German culture of his time.

Like Geiger, Graetz paints an image of the apostolic age that echoes elements from the Pseudo-Clementines, as mediated through Baur's theory of the two "parties" and its development in the Tübingen school.[117] Familiar with these sources from his early study of Judaism and Gnosticism, Graetz even quotes directly from them when describing Peter's connections to Judaism and antipathy toward Paul.[118] Just as Baur inverts the positive image of Peter, Judaism, and the Jerusalem church in the Pseudo-Clementines to construct his image of the particularistic "Jewish-Christian" party, so Graetz reappropriates Peter for Judaism and reworks Baur's image for positive aims.[119] Particularism becomes patriotism.

In addition, Graetz further emphasizes Baur's disjuncture between Jesus and Paul along the lines of the anti-Pauline polemics in the Pseudo-Clementines. Jesus and his other Jewish followers are placed firmly within Judaism; in fact, with respect to "Jewish-Christians," Graetz states that "the transition between Judaism and Christianity was not a striking one."[120] By contrast, Paul's apocalyptic fervor caused him to imagine that the eschatological suspension of Torah observance had begun; because of this error, he "conceived Christianity to be the

---

[114] Graetz, *History of the Jews*, 2:30.

[115] Graetz, *History of the Jews*, 2:142; also 2:171.

[116] For precedents, see Biale, "Historical Heresies," 115–23.

[117] Graetz, *History of the Jews*, 2:232–33, 368–70.

[118] *Epistle of Peter to James* 1–2 at Graetz, *History of the Jews*, 2:370–71.

[119] Graetz, *History of the Jews*, 2:372; in contrast to Paul's followers, "Jewish-Christians" are said to bear antipathy toward Rome.

[120] Graetz, *History of the Jews*, 2:373.

opposite of Judaism."[121] It was this – not belief in Jesus as messiah – that made Christianity a non-Jewish religion, according to Graetz. Consequently, Graetz places Christians on both sides of the boundary between Jew and Gentile, and he stresses the differences in their relations with the Jewish people, one harmonious and the other combative.

Nevertheless, one does find in Graetz's account of Christian origins some echo of Baur's assertion (quoted above) that belief in Jesus introduced a "breach," even among those of his followers who "adhered as nearly as possible to the Jewish religion and to the national worship" and had no intention of separating from it."[122] Initially, Graetz contrasts the "Jewish-Christian" belief in Jesus as "son of David" with the Pauline belief in Jesus as "son of God," lauding the former for its consistency with Jewish messianism. When forced to describe how the situation of initial harmony between Jews and "Jewish-Christians" finally came to an end, however, he appeals to messianic belief: "Jewish-Christians, also, did not remain content with the simple idea of Jesus as the messiah but gradually and unconsciously, like the heathen Christians, adorned him miraculous powers. The more the Jewish-Christian conception idealized Jesus, the more it became separated from Judaism, with which it still thought itself at one."[123] This belief, in turn, is linked to an abandonment of Torah observance, which is what – in Graetz's view – actually made "a total breach between Jews and Jewish-Christians inevitable."[124] Even in this, however, Christianity emblematizes a perennial danger *within* Jewish messianism. In the time of Jesus, as in the time of Sabbatai Zevi, Essenism makes porous the boundaries of the nation, corroding patriotism and raising the temptation of antinomianism.

The result is a powerful counterhistory, perhaps as radical in its reversals of Christian claims as Justin's second-century rereading of Jewish literature and history. Not only is Christianity pointedly denied the status of being the matrix for the origins of universalism and the framework for world history, but the separation of the Jesus of history from the Christ of faith in liberal Protestant scholarship is used to defuse the claimed power of belief in Jesus to produce religious difference and world-historical change. In Graetz's account, Christianity is reduced to its Jewish messianic origins, and the antipathy inspired by failed messiahs like Sabbatai Zevi is brought to bear on Jesus. Rather than a unique or world-changing phenomenon in its own right, it becomes – in the hands of Graetz – just another lesson in the dangers of Judaism's mystical messianisms,

---

[121] Graetz, *History of the Jews*, 2:231. Cf. *Vayiqra Rabbah* 13.3; *Midrash Tehillim* 146.4.

[122] Baur, *Paul*, 1:42.

[123] Graetz, *History of the Jews*, 2:373.

[124] Graetz, *History of the Jews*, 2:374; Graetz cites Matthew 23 in this regard, and he reads the Epistle to the Hebrews as the "letter of separation" sent from "Jewish-Christians" to Jews (2:374–76). Interestingly, he posits that it was also through Jewish-Christians that Gnostic, "semi-Christian" ideas entered Judaism (2:382–84).

and the backdrop for the Jewish people's continued struggles toward a truly messianic future. Like the Pseudo-Clementines before him, Graetz's counter-history draws on the doubled character of Christianity's origins in Jewish messianism, as a locus for the confirmation of commonality no less than the production of difference. Yet, in the process, his treatment of Jesus as one among many Jewish messianic claimants (not just in Jesus' own time but also after) does more than relativize Christian theological assertions; it sheds doubt on the idea that the acceptance or denial of the claims of a single messiah must have been seen from both sides as a "religion"-making moment.

Christianity and the Messiahs of Judaism

Scholars since George Foot Moore have noted how modern scholarship on ancient Judaism absorbed many of its categories, questions, and structure from the representations of Jews and Judaism in the Christian *contra Iudaeos* tradition.[125] In the case of modern understandings of messianism as defining difference, some traces might similarly remain, partly by virtue of the necessary dependence on Eusebius for the church's early history and on Justin for the reconstruction of the earliest Jewish/Christian debates. Up until very recently, for instance, studies of Christian origins routinely reconstructed Jewish messianism as the prehistory of the church, and diverse Jewish sources were often culled to create a single Jewish messianism in a manner oriented toward the comparison with the Jesus movement and Christianity, with little attention to post-Christian Jewish history and thought.[126] The ultimate failure of such efforts, however, has exposed the lack of any singular notion of "*the* messiah," even in pre-Christian Judaism. Particularly in the wake of the discovery of the Dead Sea Scrolls, the evidence mounts that messianic reflection was more akin to a fluid complex of traditions, cultivated both in exegetical reflection around a set of core biblical passages and in their application to specific figures and circumstances that sparked hope for divine deliverance.[127]

In light of this newer research, Strauss' proposal of reading the Gospels primarily as evidence for ancient Jewish messianism sounds far less strange then it seemed in the nineteenth century, and Graetz's placement of Jesus within the full history of Jewish messianism seems more pressing than perilous. Indeed,

---

[125] Especially Moore, "Christian Writers on Judaism."

[126] Green ("Messiah in Judaism," 4) went so far as to suggest that "the primacy of the messiah as a subject of academic study derives not from ancient Jewish preoccupation, but from early Christian word-choice, theology, and apologetics"; the Jewish Messiah – by his logic – is by definition a Christian construct. His position is meant as a critique of traditional New Testament scholarship on "Jewish background." But it proves puzzling in light of the full history of Judaism, which includes *many* non-/post-Christian messianic claimants.

[127] See Collins, *The Scepter and the Star*, and references there.

as we have seen, the effects of bringing the full history of Jewish messianism to bear on the case of Christianity can be illuminating. Such a perspective, for instance, helps us to notice some of what has been effaced by the common trope of messianism as defining difference, such as the place of messianism as a nexus for commonality, and the incommensurability of ancient Jewish and Christian approaches to defining identity and difference.

By means of conclusion, we might observe that something else has been effaced: when considered from this broader perspective, what is striking about the notion that Jews and Christians differ only in their beliefs about whether or not the messiah has come is its assumption of one messiah. That Jewish messianism, perhaps from its beginnings, allowed for a multiplicity of messiahs is suggested by the range of figures deemed "anointed" in biblical literature, as well as by the references to two messiahs found among the Dead Sea Scrolls and in later Rabbinic literature. It is this potential multiplicity, arguably, that also finds expression in the idea of the people Israel as messianic in a collective sense.

Similar beliefs might even be glimpsed before and behind Christianity – perhaps in the relationship between John the Baptist and Jesus, intriguing clues about which are preserved in the New Testament (e. g., Luke 3:15; also Matt 11:1; Luke 1:76; John 3:28, 31). It is unclear whether John the Baptist was hailed as a messiah during life and after death, as the Pseudo-Clementines suggest. Yet, at the very least, the anxiety surrounding John's status in relation to Jesus appears to have been an early focus for the development of messianic beliefs about Jesus as a singular messiah and as a pivotal figure for salvation history, rather than as simply another in a series of divinely anointed actors in end-time or epochal events.[128]

It is perhaps not coincidental, as we have seen, that this trope of multiple messiahs was so sharply articulated in the wake of the failure of the Bar Kokhba Revolt – a moment when Jesus might have seemed to Jews yet another failed messiah slain by Rome and have seemed to Romans yet more evidence for the tenacity of Jewish dreams of power. In the *contra Iudaeos* tradition, the similarities between the two figures were erased through the claim that Bar Kokhba's failure was punishment on the Jews for rejecting Jesus. The resultant contrast between (true, Christian) spiritual messiah and (false, Jewish) political messiah has had lasting consequences – even if we do not follow Scholem in positing the interiorization of messianic hope as characteristic of Christian messianism alone. The privileging of messianic belief as determinative for religious identity, for instance, may presage something of the disembedding of "religion" from the political in the post-Constantinian Christian culture of the Roman Empire.[129] The

---

[128] Oscar Cullman, *The Christology of the New Testament* (Philadelphia: Westminster/John Knox, 1959), 13–30.

[129] Much quoted in this regard is Schwartz's suggestion that the Christianization of Roman Palestine was accompanied by "the emergence of religion as a discrete category of human experience – religion's *disembedding*"; *Imperialism and Jewish Society*, 179.

reduction of Jewish messianism to the rejection of Jesus and the rereading of the entirety of Jewish history as shaped by this single choice reinforce this notion, while also contributing to the place of "Judaism" in the Christian imagination as the inverse mirror image of emergent "Christianity" and as the paradigm of religious error.[130]

It is interesting, then, that the authors/redactors of the Pseudo-Clementine literature resist the perspective of emergent imperial orthodoxy in part by multiplication: although Jesus here retains some singularity, it is only as the correct messiah of two (John versus Jesus) and as the last in a series of incarnations of the True Prophet, the primary exemplar for whom always remains Moses. Whereas Justin argues that the apparent commonalities between Christianity and Judaism conceal their essential opposition as true and false Israel, the Pseudo-Clementine *Homilies* depict the appearance of Jewish/Christian difference as hiding the true unity of their pious expressions. Concurrent, moreover, is a resistance of the reframing of Judaism as a "religion," as exemplified by the emphasis on Hellenism, rather than Christianity, as the opposite of Judaism. This too is given expression through multiplication: the Antichrist of the Pseudo-Clementine *Homilies* is not a Jew, but rather the exalted god-man proclaimed by the Hellenized heirs of Paul. Here, the birth of "heresy" is not patterned on the Jewish rejection of Jesus, but rather by the replication of Hellenism's original sin of polytheism in Paulinism.[131]

Multiplicity is also a hallmark of Graetz's discussions of messianism, which further point us to the range of possibilities within Jewish messianism, including but not limited to the acceptance or rejection of the belief in Jesus as messiah. Perhaps most striking is Graetz's assertion that even failed messiahs can have a positive effect for the Jewish people – albeit when they are political rather than spiritual. For Graetz, as we have seen, patriotism is what separates the heroic power of the political messiah from the danger of the (false, Essene, Christian) mystical messiah. This interpretation is consistent with his vision of the realization of Israel's messianic promise as ultimately a communal mission and achievement. Like the Pseudo-Clementines – and likely influenced by them – Graetz denies that belief in Jesus has the power to produce Jewish/Christian difference and resists casting Judaism as a "religion" akin to Christianity.[132] In fact, he effects the opposite, reducing Christianity to a tainted expression of Essenism.

---

[130] The messiah is multiplied here too, but only in the sense that Jesus is paired with a Jewish Antichrist.

[131] See Chapters Four and Five in this volume.

[132] Graetz's move can be read as an early reaction against what scholars in Religious Studies now acknowledge as the "enduring paradigm created with the solidification of Christianity as the prototype for religion in general ... as the frame of reference for what religion is" (Catherine Bell, "Paradigms Behind [and Before] the Modern Concept of Religion," *HT* 45 [2006]: 29–30; so also Jonathan Z. Smith, "Religion, Religions, Religious," in *Critical Terms for Religious Studies*, ed. Mark C. Taylor [Chicago: University of Chicago Press, 1998], 269–84; Talal Asad,

Lest one is tempted to imagine these counterhistories as wholly subversive and separate from the more familiar stories we are accustomed to treating as monolithically "mainstream," it is important to note those signs of cross-fertilization that point to a conversation. Graetz, for instance, may resist the reduction of Judaism to the "religious" in a manner reminiscent of what Boyarin suggests of early Rabbinic approaches to identity.[133] Yet Graetz's history and theory of messianism are shaped by a preoccupation with "heretics" not so dissimilar from those in the Christian discourses he critiques. For him too, improper messianism serves as a marker of "heresy." Just as the Jew of Christian heresiology models the "heretic," so the Christian here exemplifies inner-Jewish error and its dire dangers – most pressingly, for Graetz, Geiger, and other Jewish reformers of the time. And, of course, a century later, Scholem would answer Graetz with his own counterhistory, recovering the value of much of what Graetz dismissed as "Essene" in the course of reasserting messianism as a vital force in Jewish history. His account keeps much of the structure of that of Graetz but reverses its valence.[134] In the process, however, Scholem largely excised Christianity from Graetz's conceptualization of Jewish messianism – in part, through appeal to the traditionally Christian trope of the messiah as the defining point of difference between the two religions.

Not even Scholem, however, could succeed in subtracting Christianity from the history of Jewish messianism. After all, as Moshe Idel has shown, even their "essential conflict" attests their ongoing differentiation in development from shared roots:

The emergence of Christianity, a messianic religion drawing upon Jewish sources and attempting to reinterpret some of the messianic claims cherished by the Jews, problematized some of the earlier Jewish concepts, which were marginalized in order to make a clearer distinction between Judaism and Christianity. If early Christian views of the Messiah reflect Jewish strands, their separate developments should be treated together, as different options inherent in earlier sources but actualized in various, often antagonistic religious ambiances .... We may learn from the comparison between some Jewish and Christian forms of messianisms not only about the differences and tensions between them but also about common denominators, which stem from ancient Jewish views that were accepted by Christianity and eventually marginalized in subsequent Jewish texts though they recur in Ashkenazi Hasidim and Kabbalah.[135]

Genealogies of Religion: Discipline and Reasons of Power in Christianity and Islam [Baltimore: John Hopkins University Press, 1993], 28–29).

[133] Boyarin, *Border Lines*, 13, 202–4. For another example of the ways that messianism can unsettle notions of "religion" and "heresy," see Pawel Maciejko, *The Mixed Multitude: Jacob Frank and the Frankist Movement, 1755–1816* (Philadelphia: University of Pennsylvania Press, 2011), 41–62.

[134] Biale, *Gershom Scholem*, 71–93; Joseph Dan, "Scholem's View of Jewish Messianism," *Modern Judaism* 12 (1992): 117–28.

[135] Idel, *Messianic Mystics*, 24, 30.

As a result, as David Flusser notes, messianism remains the "parade example" of the importance of studying Judaism and Christianity in concert, in a manner that does not merely cull Jewish sources for "background" for Christianity, but also culls Christian sources for potential illumination of Judaism.[136] In certain cases, as Peter Schäfer has recently stressed, Jewish messianism may have been cultivated in reaction to Christian claims.[137] But if the histories of Jewish and Christian messianisms part, collide, and entwine, it is perhaps in ways that we have yet fully to recover – although always, it seems, in patterns more dynamic and complex than any simple contrast can capture. Consequently, it is perhaps not surprising that we glimpse something of their enduring entanglement even in the very discourse of messianic difference.

---

[136] Flusser, "Jewish Messianism," 258. Flusser's concern is with the New Testament, but – as we have seen – the same point can be extended to later materials.

[137] Peter Schäfer, *Die Geburt des Judentums aus dem Geist des Christentums: Fünf Vorlesungen* (Tübingen: Mohr Siebeck, 2010), 133–78.

Chapter Eight

Secrecy, Suppression, and the Jewishness of Christian Origins*

In a recent book bearing the title *The Lost Gospel*, Simcha Jacobovici and Barrie Wilson claim to have discovered "a document that was slated for the fire, but is now seeing the light of the day."[1] This document – they suggest – reveals "groundbreaking revelations about the life and times of Jesus of Nazareth" and "gives us a glimpse into a story untainted by later Roman theology."[2] What they adduce, however, is none other than the well-known Jewish pseudepigraphon *Joseph and Aseneth*. To build a case for the suppression of its true meaning, they make only the generalized claim that "in 312 CE … the Emperor Constantine became aligned with Pauline Christianity and the historical Jesus was eclipsed by Pauline theology," after which "only those Gospels that reflected this new theology were allowed to survive."[3]

Their hypothesis about *Joseph and Aseneth* is quite far-fetched, for reasons that Anthony La Donne deftly summarizes:

The *Lost Gospel* is based on a text that is not a gospel and was not lost. The authors attempt to explain that the manuscript was "lost" in the British Library, labeled British Library Manuscript Number 17,202. They give the impression that this document was all but neglected by modern interpreters as it collected dust in the archives. This is false, and they know it's false. They claim elsewhere that several copies of this story are "well preserved" in Christian monasteries, and that "Christians have read, treasured, translated, expanded, and preserved" this text. Even after admitting the fact, much of the first half of their book endeavors to promote *Joseph and Aseneth* as a grand conspiracy.[4]

As easy as it might be to dismiss this hypothesis, however, it is perhaps worth stopping to reflect upon the genealogy of the cultural context that makes it possible. Although extreme, the argument follows a familiar pattern in popular and scholarly discourse about noncanonical literature: "OT pseudepigrapha,"

---

* This chapter has not been published previously in any form. An earlier version was presented at Indiana University Bloomington, on 12 January 2017. Special thanks to Shaul Magid for the invitation and inspiration.

[1] Simcha Jacobovici and Barrie Wilson, *The Lost Gospel: Decoding the Ancient Text that Reveals Jesus' Marriage to Mary the Magdalene* (New York: Pegasus, 2014), 277.

[2] Jacobovici and Wilson, *Lost Gospel*, 277.

[3] Jacobovici and Wilson, *Lost Gospel*, 276–77.

[4] Anthony Le Donne, "Gronking Jesus," *Los Angeles Review of Books*, 6 March 2015.

"NT apocrypha," and related sources are habitually shrouded in the rhetoric of secrecy and suppression – and, whenever possible, connected to the period of Christian Origins.[5]

Today, the allure of concealment exposed and truth denuded resounds from popular novels like Dan Brown's *The Da Vinci Code* to the news coverage of papyrological discoveries like the *Gospel of Judas* or the *Gospel of Jesus' Wife*.[6] Even scholarly books about noncanonical texts are peddled under titles like *Lost Scriptures* or *Secret Scriptures Revealed*.[7] Specialists often lament this situation. But we might do well also to ask: what is it that naturalizes the assumption that the task of telling the origins of Christianity is best framed as if a hunt for lost texts and hidden truths? How has it come to seem so commonsensical that any noncanonical source (however well attested) might be deemed "lost" or "suppressed" and thereby suggested to be "untainted"? Why does the persuasive power of this trope resound so strongly in the popular imagination, especially but not only in North America? To what degree does this trope skew our present-day understanding of the Jewish and Christian past, and to what degree might attention to it help us to glimpse some neglected dynamics therein?

This chapter reflects upon these questions by focusing on what is perhaps the most ancient and influential complex of claims of this sort – namely, those surrounding the open secret of the Jewish origins of Christianity. To do so, I look to a much-cited but little-studied example of so-called "Jewish-Christian apocrypha":[8] the *Epistle of Peter to James*. This work was written in the third or fourth century CE, but it claims to preserve a first-century correspondence from the apostle Peter to James, another prominent disciple and apostle of Jesus as

---

[5] See further Annette Yoshiko Reed, "The Afterlives of New Testament Apocrypha," *JBL* 134 (2015): 401–25. Scott Fitzgerald Johnson similarly notes the "fashionable 'disjunctive' model of early Christian and late antique literature" as predicated on the notion that "a variety of literature available in the earliest Christian period ... was subsequently suppressed and destroyed under the authoritative regime of the Constantinian and post-Constantinian Christian empire"; "Apocrypha and the Literary Past in Late Antiquity," in *From Rome to Constantinople*, ed. H. Amirav and B. ter Haar Romeny (Leuven: Peeters, 2007), 47–66 at 50.

[6] E.g., Dan Brown, *The Da Vinci Code* (New York: Doubleday, 2003); "Ancient manuscript suggests new relationship between Jesus and Judas," *Associated Press*, 6 April 2006; John Noble Wilford and Laurie Goodstein, "Gospel of Judas Surfaces After 1,700 Years," *New York Times*, 6 April 2006, A1; Laurie Goodstein, "Document Is Genuine, but Is Its Story True?" *New York Times*, 7 April 2006, A20; Laurie Goodstein, "A Faded Piece of Papyrus Refers to Jesus' Wife," *New York Times*, 18 September 2012, National Desk, p. 1; James Bone, "Jesus 'Was Married,' Papyrus Scrap Reveals," *The Times* (London), 20 September 2012.

[7] Bart Ehrman, *Lost Scriptures: Books that Did Not Make It into the New Testament* (Oxford: Oxford University Press, 2003); Tony Burke, *Secret Scriptures Revealed: A New Introduction to the Christian Apocrypha* (Grand Rapids: Eerdmans, 2013). Notably, both books counter this tendency even as their titles evoke them.

[8] For my sense of this rubric, see Chapter Three above.

well as a fellow leader of the Jerusalem Church.[9] It forms part of the Pseudo-Clementine literature, a corpus of Greek writings from late antique Syria that purport to preserve the authentic teachings of Peter.[10] In the manuscripts, it features as the first among the materials prefaced to the *Homilies*, one of the two versions of a novel that claims to be penned by Clement of Rome and to recount what he learned through his travels to and with Peter. This *Epistle* is an early precedent for the trope of secrecy and suppression noted above: it includes an explicit claim to correct ideas that had been suppressed, and it also includes an explicit call to circulate writings secretly as a result. In both cases, it is Christianity's Jewishness that is ultimately at stake.

The *Epistle of Peter to James* opens and closes with an entreaty to transmit Peter's writings in a secret line, limited to worthy Jews. The letter begins, for instance, as follows:

Peter to James, lord and bishop (τῷ κυρίῳ καὶ ἐπισκόπῳ) of the holy church. Through the Father of All through Jesus Christ, always in peace. Knowing, my brother, how you are eager to contribute to the common advantage of us all, I urgently implore of you not to give a share of the books of my preaching that I sent to you (τῶν ἐμῶν κηρυγμάτων ἅς ἔπεμψά σοι βίβλους; cf. *Hom* 1.20; *Rec* 1.17) to anyone from among the Gentiles (μηδενὶ τῶν ἀπὸ τῶν ἐθνῶν), nor to one of our kinsmen before trial (μήτε ὁμοφύλῳ πρὸ πείρας). But if someone is found worthy after having been tested, then [I urgently implore of you]

---

[9] Below, I focus on mostly on the figure of Peter. With respect to its implications for the tradition surrounding James, see Gregory P. Fewster, "Ancient Book Culture and the Literacy of James: On the Production and Consumption of a Pseudepigraphal Letter," *ZAC* 20 (2016): 387–417. Fewster there considers the NT Epistle of James in "a trajectory with other early Christian documents, including the *Apocryphon of James*, the *Protevangelium of James*, and the *Epistula Petri*, that represent James as highly literate and capable to promote authoritative transmission of Jesus tradition" (390). The implications for our understanding of the *Epistle of Peter to James* are notable as well, not least with respect to how its pseudepigraphy "fits within a broader initiative within early Christianity to promote themselves and their early leaders as literate" (389) and thus "plays upon ancient social attitudes toward reading, affirming the literate status of their communities to outsiders and serving as a context within which the pseudepigraphal letter, along with its moral and social goals, could be valued and enacted" (390).

[10] One's dating of the *Epistle of Peter to James* largely depends on [1] whether one considers its original purpose as aimed to preface the nonextant shared *Grundschrift* of the Pseudo-Clementine *Homilies* and *Recognitions* (before 220 CE), or [2] whether one treats its current form as significantly shaped by its present placement among the prefatory materials to the *Homilies* (early fourth century); I am less convinced by efforts to reconstruct a nonextant source like the so-called *Kerygmata Petrou* behind the nonextant shared source of the versions that survive (for reasons I discuss in Chapter One of this volume) and am thus also less persuaded by attempts to situate this *Epistle* in the second century. That said, for our purposes here, what is most significant is that this *Epistle* remains – in any case – a late antique retrospective representation of the first-century past. On debates concerning the sources of the Pseudo-Clementines, F. Stanley Jones, "The Pseudo-Clementines: A History of Research," *Second Century* 2 (1982): 14–33; Jones, *An Ancient Jewish Christian Source on the History of Christianity: Pseudo-Clementine Recognitions 1.27–71* (Atlanta: Scholars Press, 1995), 20–36; Jones, *Pseudoclementina Elchasaiticaque inter Judaeochristiana: Collected Studies* (Orientalia Lovaniensia Analecta 203; Leuven: Peeters, 2012), 114–206.

to hand down (παραδοῦναι) to him according to the same manner in which Moses handed down (παρέδωκε) to the Seventy (cf. Num 11:16–25; *Hom* 2.38; 3.47) as those who
succeeded his chair (τὴν καθέδραν). (*Epistle of Peter to James* 1.1–2)

The allusion to the secret transmission of Peter's writings via James allows the
Epistle to authorize its own existence as an authentic letter from the first century
that only comes to light centuries later.[11] Secrecy, however, also serves purposes
beyond the literary conceit of pseudepigraphy – most significantly: to point to
Jewish followers of Jesus as those who truly possess and preserve the apostolic
tradition.

The importance of this coupling of apostolicity and Jewishness becomes clear
later in the *Epistle of Peter to James*, when Peter is made pseudonymously to
correct a popular misconception about his attitude toward the Torah/Law (Gr.
nomos):

For certain men from among the Gentiles have rejected the preaching by me concerning
the Torah/Law (τὸ δι' ἐμοῦ νόμιμον … κήρυγμα), accepting a certain lawless (ἄνομόν)
and foolish teaching of a man who is [my] enemy (τοῦ ἐχθροῦ ἀνθρώπου). And these
things certain men have attempted while I am still alive – that is, to transform my words
by certain intricate interpretations into the dissolution of the Torah/Law, as though I
also myself were thus disposed but would not preach [it] openly (μὴ ἐκ παρρησίας δὲ
κηρύσσοντος). Far from it! (*Epistle of Peter to James* 2.3–4)[12]

By linking secrecy to the specter of suppression, the *Epistle* is able to articulate
and authorize an esoteric image of Peter that differs from those in exoteric documents like the NT Book of Acts. Peter's true commitment to the Torah is here
emphasized in contrast to an antinomian "enemy" (often thought to be Paul) and
to "certain men" (often thought to include the author of the Book of Acts) who
are actively working to "transform" Peter's teachings to appear to be against the
very Jewish traditions that he is actually faithful in upholding.[13] The appeal to
secrecy and suppression serves to anticipate the question of why its late antique
readers might not already know of Peter's positivity toward the Torah and how

---

[11] On secrecy here as "literary conceit," see now Kelley Coblentz Bautch, "Concealment,
Pseudepigraphy and the Study of Esotericism in Antiquity," *Aries* 15 (2015): 1–9 at 6. The
authorizing strategy here, as Bart Ehrman notes, is thus essentially that of a "false author [who]
warns his ostensible reader to protect his writings against falsifications"; *Forgery and Coun-
terforgery: The Use of Literary Deceit in Early Christian Polemics* (Oxford: Oxford University
Press, 2012), 127.

[12] For the Greek text of this letter, see Bernhard Rehm, ed., *Die Pseudoklementinen*, vol. 1:
Homilien (GCS 42; rev. ed.; Berlin: Akademie-Verlag, 1969), 1–3. Here and below, translations
of the *Epistle of Peter to James* and *Homilies* are tentative but largely follow Alain Le Boulleuc
et al., trans., "Roman Pseudo-Clémentin: Homélies," in *Écrits apocryphes chrétiens*, vol. 2, ed.
Pierre Geoltrain and Jean-Daniel Kaestli (Paris: Gallimard, 2005), 1215–589.

[13] For a recent summary of the logic behind these identifications, see John G. Gager, *Who
Made Early Christianity? The Jewish Lives of the Apostle Paul* (New York: Columbia University Press, 2015), 101–5.

the opposite image of the apostle could come to circulate so widely.[14] What is evoked, in the process, is an alternative image of the apostolic age – not as a harmonious era of church unity, but rather as a period for which the suppressed truth only circulates now in secret documents.[15]

My aim, in what follows, is to use the *Epistle of Peter to James* as a lens onto shifting ideas about the power of secrecy, the fragility of textuality and memory, and the framing of Christianity's Jewishness as both hidden and public knowledge. To do so, I shall reconsider the above-quoted passages in the literary and historical context of the *Epistle* itself, understood on its own terms – as a third- or fourth-century text that reflects on the first-century past. In addition, however, I would like to make a case that the early modern "rediscovery" of this text may have helped to presage and shape some of the present-day preoccupation with the potential power of "NT apocrypha" as documents that are imagined to preserve hidden truths about the past *precisely because* of their alleged "loss" to purported programs of theological and/or textual suppression. After all, the *Epistle of Peter to James* is *not only* a text that talks explicitly about the transmission of texts in secret and the dangers of rupture in the preservation of teachings; it is *also* a text that was unknown to European Christendom during much of the Middle Ages, after which two manuscripts were recovered and printed at two key moments for early modern Western reflection on the Christian past and the problem of its forgotten and remembered Jewishness (i.e., Codex Parisinus Graecus 930 [P] and Codex Vaticanus Ottobonianus 443 [O]).

Rather than looking only to the *Epistle of Peter to James* in its own late antique context, then, this chapter will begin and end with key moments from its modern reception. I begin by progressing in reverse chronological order toward this era, moving back through two determinative historical moments for shaping the dominant lenses through which the *Epistle of Peter to James* is now studied. Here, I consider its impact on the nineteenth-century development of scholarly ideas about the Jewishness of Christian Origins, focusing on the German Protestant historian Ferdinand Christian Baur and his place in the development of modern historical-critical research on the apostolic age. Then I turn to the precedents in the early eighteenth century, focusing on the Irish philosopher John Toland and considering his ideas about "NT apocrypha," "Jewish-Christianity," esotericism, and censorship. Having traced some of the early modern genealogy of current scholarly treatment of the *Epistle*, I situate it in its literary and historical contexts in Late Antiquity. On the one hand, I suggest that early modern readings of the *Epistle of Peter to James* draw attention to some elements now

---

[14] Notably, the notion that Peter does not say openly what he really thinks is at the core of Paul's accusation against him at Gal 2:11–14 – what Paul there frames as hypocrisy, however, is here reframed as esotericism.

[15] On the construction and contestation of this harmonious image of the "apostolic age" in Late Antiquity, see Chapter Six in this volume.

neglected therein, particularly in relation to its concern with conspiracies of suppression and collusions of secrecy. On the other hand, I ask how this reception history may have skewed our current sense of its meaning and significance – not least because the thinkers who have most shaped scholarship upon it have read it from specifically Christian perspectives.

As we shall see, there are notable differences in the function of secrecy and suppression within the *Epistle of Peter to James* and for those modern Christian thinkers who have most shaped its current scholarly interpretation, perhaps particularly in relation to the place of Jewishness in the Christian past. Accordingly, I conclude with two key moments in the modern Jewish reception of this work and the complex of ideas about Peter and Paul associated with it: I look first to the representation of the apostolic age, "Jewish-Christians," and the *Epistle of Peter to James* in the enormously influential Jewish history of Heinrich Graetz in the nineteenth century. Then I consider the place of the Pseudo-Clementines and other "NT apocrypha" in the articulation of ancient Jewish and Christian history by Kaufmann Kohler in the twentieth century, especially as his ideas found wide diffusion within the 1907 *Jewish Encyclopedia*. What I shall propose, in the process, is that *both* the *Epistle* itself *and* our data for the reception of its modern "(re)discovery" may help us to understand some of the broader dynamics that inform current conspiracy theories about "apocrypha," censorship, and the Jewishly Christian past – pointing, in particular, to the culturally creative spaces that can be produced by the precariousness of textuality and memory, before and between Christianity and Judaism.

Ferdinand Christian Baur on Petrine "Jewish-Christianity," Lost and Rediscovered

Today, the Jewish "background" of Christianity has become an axiom of historical research on the New Testament. For this, Ferdinand Christian Baur is often cited as pivotal.[16] In the 1830s and following, Baur popularized the notion of a "primitive" and apostolic "Jewish-Christianity," which he associated with the apostles Peter and James, but which came to be displaced by the "Gentile

---

[16] From the perspective of history of New Testament Studies, as James D. G. Dunn notes, Baur "is the key figure in the quest of the historical church," not least due to his influential framing of the "programmatic question" of this quest as "how Christianity, instead of remaining a mere form of Judaism, although a progressive one, asserted itself as a separate independent principle, broke loose from it, and took its stand as a new enfranchised form of religious thought and life, essentially different from all the national particularities of Judaism"; *Beginning from Jerusalem* (Grand Rapids: Eerdmans, 2009), 31, quoting Ferdinand Christian Baur, *Paul: The Apostle of Jesus Christ* (London: Williams and Norgate, 1873), 1:3. See further now Martin Bauspieß, Christof Landmesser, and David Lincicum, eds., *Ferdinand Christian Baur und die Geschichte des frühen Christentums* (WUNT 333; Tübingen: Mohr Siebeck, 2014).

Christianity" associated with the apostle Paul – with the latter thus coming to predominate already within the New Testament.[17]

In rejecting the image of earliest church history as an era of harmony, Baur rooted his thesis in the privileging of those passages in the letters of Paul that describe conflicts with Peter and other leaders in the Jesus movement (esp. 1 Cor 1:12; Gal 2:11–14).[18] His argument for an ancient and hidden "Jewish-Christian" past, in particular, is buttressed by what he read as anti-Pauline statements in "NT apocrypha" associated with Peter – foremost the *Epistle of Peter to James* and related passages in the *Homilies*.[19] The very passages that we quoted above concerning secrecy and suppression thus functioned, for Baur, as a hermeneutical key for unlocking the hidden history of Christian origins: he approached these noncanonical sources as a resource for recovering the voices suppressed or silenced within the NT literature, thereby popularizing the culling of the Pseudo-Clementine corpus for remnants of anti-Pauline perspectives from the apostolic age.

In his seminal 1831 article "Die Christuspartei in der korinthischen Gemeide, der Gegensatz des petrinischen and paulischen Christentums," Baur proposed that "the Pauline letters to the Corinthians and Galatians on the one hand, and the Clementine *Homilies* on the other designate two extremes from which the polemics against the Apostle Paul in the most ancient church and the conflict be-

---

[17] First and most famously: Ferdinand Christian Baur, "Die Christuspartei in der korinthischen Gemeide, der Gegensatz des petrinischen and paulischen Christentums in der alten Kirche, der Apostel Petrus in Rom," *Tübinger Zeitschrift für Theologie* 4 (1831): 61–206. Baur is conventionally treated as "first to direct the attention of scholarship to Jewish Christianity as key for understanding the Christianity of the first two centuries" such that it has become a truism now that "the modern investigation of Jewish Christianity began with him"; Gerd Lüdemann, *Opposition to Paul in Jewish Christianity* (trans. E. Boring; Minneapolis: Fortress, 1989), 1. Baur, however, both had and acknowledged ample precedents; see further below and Chapter Eleven in this volume as well as David Lincicum, "F.C. Baur's Place in the Study of Jewish Christianity," in *Rediscovery of Jewish Christianity: From Toland to Baur*, ed. F. Stanley Jones (History of Biblical Studies 5; Atlanta: Society of Biblical Literature, 2012), 137–66.

[18] Dunn well describes the "lasting importance of Baur's initial insight: that substantial tensions and conflicts were a feature of earliest Christian development, as fierce as, if not more so, than the tensions and conflicts elsewhere in Second Temple Judaism. Baur sustains the myth of earliest Christian history as a clearly identifiable 'Christianity' (or 'Christian principle') breaking loose from 'Judaism.' But he banished for all time the 'myth of Christian beginnings' as an ideal period of church unity and unified expansion" (*Beginning from Jerusalem*, 35).

[19] Baur, "Christuspartei," 116–36; see further Lüdemann, *Opposition to Paul*, 2–3. Notably, Baur looked to Irenaeus (*Adv. haer.* 1.26), Eusebius (*Hist. eccl.* 3.27), and Epiphanius (*Pan.* 30) to reconstruct his ideas about Ebionites, and as a result, used the explicit anti-Paulinism associated with this sect in such secondhand reports as a lens through which to interpret possible allusions to Paul in the Pseudo-Clementine corpus and posit these allusions as preserving something of the hostility that Paul may have faced in his own lifetime; "Christuspartei," 114–15. In this context, the *Epistle of Peter to James* is important for containing the most unequivocally anti-Pauline statement in the Pseudo-Clementine corpus, thereby enabling Baur and others to read the representation of Simon Magus in the *Homilies*, in particular, in terms of Paul.

tween Pauline and Petrine Christianity played out."[20] Baur there introduced this contrast by pointing to the debate between Peter and Simon Magus in *Homilies* 17, which he reads as evidence for the denial of Paul's revelation-based apostleship by those followers of Jesus associated with Peter.[21] To read the polemics against Simon as a cipher for polemics against Paul, the *Epistle of Peter to James* proved critical. Baur adduced its reference to Peter's "enemy" (see above), and he read this reference as a direct counterpoint to Paul's report of a conflict with Peter in Galatians (esp. 2:11: "But when Cephas [i. e., Peter] came to Antioch, I opposed him to his face").[22] In Gal 2:11–14, Paul describes his conflict with Peter concerning the question of whether noncircumcised Gentiles could eat together with Jewish followers of Jesus, and he critiques Peter for sometimes following James in limiting commensality and community to other Jews. Of the *Epistle*, Baur proclaimed: "here, the situation is reversed!"[23]

The use of the *Epistle of Peter to James* as an intertext for Galatians 2 thus served to ground Baur's anti-Pauline interpretation of other passages in the Pseudo-Clementine corpus as well. In *Homilies* 2.17, for instance, Peter notes that Simon went to the Gentiles before him; for Baur, this lament can be read as an allusion more specifically to Paul's mission as "apostle to the Gentiles" and the spread of Pauline "Gentile Christianity."[24] So too for the "false apostles" mentioned in *Homilies* 11.35.[25]

Within Baur's 1831 article, references to the NT Book of Acts were largely limited to the footnotes.[26] Soon thereafter, his rereading of Paul's letters in counterpoint to the Pseudo-Clementines also served to ground a rereading of Acts, especially in his influential 1845 monograph on Paul.[27] Just as Baur privileged Pauline passages about conflicts within the Jesus movement, so he read Acts as

---

[20] Baur, "Christuspartei," 136.

[21] Baur, "Christuspartei," 116–20. This connection has been highly influential, even to the degree it often goes unquestioned; for a recent reassessment and critique, see Dominique Côté, "La fonction littéraire de Simon le Magicien dans les Pseudo-Clémentines," *Laval théologique et philosophique* 37 (2001): 514–17.

[22] Baur, "Christuspartei," 124–25. This position, too, is still widely followed in scholarship on the *Epistle of Peter to James*; see, e. g., Lüdemann, *Opposition to Paul*, 188–89 and further references there.

[23] Baur, "Christuspartei," 125. Notably, Baur later emphasizes that Pseudo-Clementine "Jewish-Christianity" is not completely identical to that in the age of Paul, even if still preserving the main elements thereof (*Paul*, 1.344).

[24] Baur, "Christuspartei," 125 – there citing Augustus Neander's more cautious speculation about this possibility already in *Genetische Entwicklung der vornehmsten gnostischen Systeme* (Berlin: Dümmler, 1818), 366.

[25] Baur, "Christuspartei," 126–27 n. 52; here too, the *Epistle of Peter to James* is adduced to counter the possible reading of Peter's opponents as non-/post-Pauline.

[26] Especially nn. 48 and 50.

[27] For a clear articulation of this triangulation, see, e. g., Baur, *Paul*, 1:84–89. Likewise, on p. 130 there, Baur reiterates his view that the *Epistle of Peter to James* refers to Gal 2:12, "only the affair is reversed." See further pp. 139, 144–45, 219–25.

a later attempt to overwrite such conflicts. When compared to Galatians and the *Epistle of Peter to James*, for instance, Acts 10 and 15 present a harmonious account of the relationship between Paul, Peter, and James; in Acts 15:13–20, James is made to voice the position of Paul that non-Jews can be included, even apart from the need for circumcision or full adherence to Jewish Law.[28] In the *Epistle of Peter to James*, Baur thus found support for his project of rereading Acts with a hermeneutics of suspicion. What this and other Pseudo-Clementine materials help to facilitate, in effect, is a reorientation of the traditional approach: Acts is no longer treated as a direct window onto the Christian past, nor as the main structuring narrative through which Pauline and other NT epistles should be interpreted, but rather as the historical product of choices of selectivity that preserve the perspective of one "party" by silencing another.

By virtue of such a reorientation, Baur and the Tübingen School could treat the tensions or contradictions *within* the New Testament literature as clues to its own hidden history, even as they looked *outside* of these Christian Scriptures to recover a broader sense of what shaped the origins of Christianity. This move is often cited as one of the founding moments in the development of historical-critical research on the New Testament. Baur and the Tübingen School are often credited as an important step in the emergence of secular scholarship on Christianity, not least for further enabling the separation of the "Jesus of history" from the "Christ of faith" – and the recovery of a Jewish Jesus in particular.[29]

Much has been written about how Baur thus helped to open the way for modern Jewish thinkers to reclaim Jesus for Jewish thought and history.[30] Below, I shall consider some of the consequences for modern Jewish approaches to Peter and Paul as well. Before doing so, however, it is necessary to look more closely at what Baur himself already assumes and to ask why.

Baur, for instance, took for granted that the *Epistle of Peter to James* was not actually written by Peter. Nevertheless, this assessment did not stop him from using this noncanonical text to reconstruct the background *behind* the New Testament – reading its pseudonymously Petrine words as preserving something of the "other side" of the story that Paul discusses in Galatians and also as revealing some of the perspectives allegedly suppressed by the harmonizing impulse of Acts. Already for Baur, in other words, we find naturalized the notion that

---

[28] Baur, *Paul*, 1.116–45. See further Lüdemann, *Opposition to Paul*, 5–6.

[29] Baur's thesis drew immediate critique, especially because of his late dating of NT writings to fit this schema. But see Dunn, *Beginning from Jerusalem*, 34–34 on how early responses to Baur by J. B. Lightfoot in English scholarship and Albrecht Ritschel in German scholarship rejected his dating but articulated modified positions and "provided an agenda which lasted through most of the twentieth century" for research on apostolic history within New Testament Studies (35). See also Lüdemann, *Opposition to Paul*, 7–32, on Baur's continued influence in setting the agenda for research on "Jewish-Christianity."

[30] See especially Susannah Heschel, *Abraham Geiger and the Jewish Jesus* (Chicago: University of Chicago Press, 1998).

there *are* hidden secrets about the Christian past, which NT literature silences or suppresses but which "NT apocrypha" can help to reveal and recover. And we also find the contention that the Jewishness of the origins of Christianity proves exemplary of what has been overwritten in and by Christian Scriptures. For the genealogy of these assumptions, one must look further back, not just to the Pseudo-Clementines themselves, but also to the early modern invention of the concept of "Jewish-Christianity" and the special place of the *Epistle* therein.

John Toland on Censored "Apocrypha" and the
Secret (Jewish) History of Christianity

Elsewhere, I have mapped out a number of the developments in the seventeenth and eighteenth centuries that contributed to the emergence of our current notion of "NT apocrypha" – whereby a heterogeneous group of gospels, epistles, acts, apocalypses, and other writings related to the apostolic past came to be collected and anthologized in the wake of the Protestant Reformation and the advent of printing, so as to become reified into a countercanon.[31] For our current purposes, it suffices to point to one key figure who contributed to this process with explicit appeal both to "Jewish-Christianity" and to the *Epistle of Peter to James* – namely, John Toland. More than a century before Baur, Toland posited "the distinction of Jewish and Gentile Christians."[32] Not only is Toland the earliest known author to use the term "Jewish-Christianity," and seemingly its very inventor,[33] but he did so to distinguish Peter's views from those of Paul, with explicit reference to the *Epistle of Peter to James*.

In his 1718 *Nazarenus*, Toland adduces this and other noncanonical literature as preserving what he deems "*The True and Original Plan Of Christianity*" and the revelation of a "*Christianity* [that was] no more than *Reformed Judaism*."[34] The implication – Toland suggests – is that Jesus himself remained completely committed to the Jewish Law, as did his Jewish followers after him:

I mean that the Jews, tho associating with the converted Gentiles, and acknowledging them for brethren, were still to observe their own Law thro-out all generations; and that the Gentiles, who became so farr Jews as to acknowledge ONE GOD, were not however to observe the Jewish Law: but that both of them were to be for ever united into one body

---

[31] Reed, "Afterlives." On the relation to the construction of "OT apocrypha" and "OT pseudepigrapha" as concepts and corpora, see also Reed, "The Modern Invention of Old Testament Pseudepigrapha," *JTS* 60 (2009): 403–36.

[32] John Toland, *Nazarenus, or Jewish, Gentile, and Mahometan Christianity* (London, 1718), 33.

[33] See Chapter Eleven in this volume, as well as the articles by Matti Myllykoski, Pierre Lurbe, Matt Jackson-McCabe, and F. Stanley Jones in Jones, ed., *Rediscovery of Jewish Christianity*, 3–104.

[34] Toland, *Nazarenus*, 33

or fellowship ... From this doctrine it follows (it's true!) that Jesus did not take away or cancel the Jewish Law in any sense whatsoever, Sacrifices only excepted; but neither does this affect any of the Gentile Christians now in the world.[35]

To explain how this Torah-observant Jewish Christianity became unknown, Toland adduces the above-quoted passage in the *Epistle of Peter to James* where Peter complains to James about the misrepresentation of his teachings. In a discussion flanked by a marginal note contrasting Acts 10 with Galatians 2, Toland renders *Ep. Pet.* 2.3 in both Greek and English, and he asserts it as proof for Paul's enmity to Peter:

Neither do I doubt but tis the Apostle to the Gentiles, that is aim'd at in an *Epistle of Peter to James*, prefixt by Cotelerius to the Clementines. The words of Peter (after entreating James not to communicate his Preachings to any Gentile, nor even to any Jew without previous examination) are there.[36]

Just as the *Epistle* describes Peter as imploring James to transmit the books of his teachings only to Jews so to protect his ideas from corruption, so Toland thus quoted this entreaty as part of his own claim to reveal the hidden Jewish history of Christian Origins.

In the citation of "Cotelerius," we can glimpse something of the catalyzing context. In 1672 Jean Baptiste Cotelier published a collection of what we now call "Apostolic Fathers" (*SS. Patrum qui temporibus apostolicis floruerunt opera*) that included the very first printing of the *Epistle of Peter to James, Contestation*, and *Homilies* (the last incomplete), rendering the texts as contained in Codex Parisinus Graecus 930 (P).[37] When Toland appeals to this *Epistle* to conjure an image of the Christian past as long "lost" yet newly possible to be recovered, he thus reflects a specific early modern moment in the West, during which more and more knowledge about Christian history was in fact coming to light, not least by virtue of new print technologies that enabled the widescale circulation of texts that had been previously been forgotten and/or accessible only in a few manuscripts, limited in number and often tucked away in monastic or other libraries.[38] It is partly as a result of this radical expansion of knowledge – and the intellectual ferment thereby inspired – that Toland could claim to be able to recover "lost" knowledge about the Christian past.[39]

---

[35] Toland, *Nazarenus*, 33

[36] Toland, *Nazarenus*, 23.

[37] Jean Baptiste Cotelier (Cotelerius), *S. S. patrum qui temporibus apostolicis floruerunt, Barnabae, Clementis, Hermae, Ignatii, Polycarpi opera edita et inedita, vera & supposititia* (Paris, 1672). In the 1699 Leipzig edition, the title was abbreviated by L.J. Ittig to *Bibliotheca Patrum Apostolicorum*, thus coining our current sense and corpus of "Apostolic Fathers"; David Lincicum, "The Paratextual Invention of the Term 'Apostolic Fathers,'" *JTS* 66 (2015): 139–48.

[38] I discuss this cultural moment and its consequences for the publication and dissemination of noncanonical Jewish and Christian literature in more detail in Reed, "Modern Invention."

[39] This romantic interest in recovering "lost" texts from the ancient Jewish and Christian past began already during the Renaissance, sparked in part by the Western European "redis-

Significantly for our purposes, Toland drew heavily upon the rhetoric of secrecy and suppression to do so: he was exuberant in giving voice to the contention that the various noncanonical texts that were increasingly coming to light in his time preserved a literary heritage of knowledge just as ancient and just as authentic (if not more so!) than the texts in the New Testament.[40] For this claim, moreover, Toland often pointed to the *Epistle of Peter to James* as a central prooftext. Of this "apocryphon," Toland further writes in *Nazarenus*, for instance:

This most remarkable and inconstably ancient piece, with others at least as ancient, which I cou'd cite were it needful, do manifestly show that this notion of Paul's having wholly metamorphos'd and perverted the true Christianity (as some of the Heretics have exprest it) and his being blam'd for so doing by the other Apostles, especially by James and Peter.[41]

Toland is here explicit in calling upon the *Epistle* both [1] as "lost" witness to a forgotten but ancient form of Christianity and [2] as a piece of proof for a purported process of inner-Christian censorship that began with Paul and already shaped the New Testament. No less important, however, is his somewhat ungrounded implication that this *Epistle* is one of numerous "apocrypha" that make this same point. In effect, Toland uses the secrecy and suppression within the *Epistle* to construct a notion of "NT apocrypha," more broadly, as if a recovered set of censored documents that are no less ancient or authentic than the NT literature.[42]

---

covery" and translation of Greek writings of Church Fathers preserved in Byzantium; see, e.g., C.L. Stinger, *Humanism and the Church Fathers: Ambrogio Traversari (1386–1439) and the Revival of Patristic Theology in the Early Italian Renaissance* (Albany: SUNY Press, 1977); W.P. Haaugaard, "Renaissance Patristic Scholarship and Theology in Sixteenth Century England," *Sixteenth Century Journal* 10 (1979): 37–60. The large-scale recovery and dissemination of writings related to apostles, however, awaited the era of British, French, and other colonial expansions, which facilitated further contacts with churches and monasteries in Africa, Eastern Europe, and the Middle East. The beginning of the eighteenth century, in particular, saw significant efforts to consolidate and organize the great mass of textual information about the past thereby discovered during and after the Renaissance and disseminated in scattered form and increased quantity after the advent of printing. I discuss this phenomenon in relation to J.A. Fabricius' 1713 *Codex pseudepigraphus Veteris Testamenti* in Reed, "Modern Invention"; see further references there. Interestingly, Fabricius' anthologies of "OT pseudepigrapha" and "NT apocrypha" are contemporaneous with Toland's writings and at points even refer to them.

[40] See further Justin A. Champion, "Apocrypha, Canon and Criticism from Samuel Fisher to John Toland, 1650–1718," in *Judaeo-Christian Intellectual Culture in the Seventeenth Century*, ed. A.P. Coudert et al. (Dordrecht: Kluwer, 1999), 91–117.

[41] Toland, *Nazarenus*, 24. Notably, part of the purpose of this argument is to use the *Epistle of Peter to James* to support his claims about the *Gospel of Barnabas* as "neither an original invention of the Mahometans [i.e., Muslims], nor any sign of the novelty of their Gospel."

[42] Notably, Toland does so just prior to collection of these materials by J.A. Fabricius in *Codex apocryphus Novi Testamenti* (Hamburg, 1703) – the volume typically credited with creating the concept of "NT Apocrypha." Fabricius collects diverse materials related to Jesus, Mary, and his apostles under this homogenized rubric, thereby contributing to the emergent concept of "NT Apocrypha" as a singular "countercanon." But Toland in some senses anticipates this

In making this argument, Toland's aim was not historical accuracy in quite the scholarly sense that Baur, for instance, would later appeal to the *Epistle of Peter to James*.[43] Rather, he adduced "Jewish-Christian" and other "NT apocrypha" to subvert the authority of church leaders of his own time. Toland was taking aim at the defense of the uniqueness of Scripture as the bulwark of a traditional notion of clerical authority in the culture wars of Enlightenment-era England.[44] At a time when the bounds of the Bible and Christian truth were policed by blasphemy laws and trials, his argument from and about "apocrypha" used such acts of suppression against themselves: if Scripture needed to be protected by such means – by his logic – it is perhaps not so special at all, but only defended as such by power-hungry clerics who must resort to censorship to monopolize their own power over the Christian past.

Notably, the anti-clerical weaponizing of "apocrypha" in *Nazarenus* extends Toland's project in some of his earlier publications. Already in 1699, he compiled an extensive "Catalogue of Books attributed in the Primitive Times to Jesus Christ, his Apostles and other eminent Persons."[45] Through this listing, Toland sought to relativize Christian Scripture by pointing to the sheer quantity of *other* sources related to Jesus and the apostles. There, for instance, Toland asserted that "there is not one single Book in the New Testament, which was not refus'd by som of the Ancients as unjustly fathr'd upon the Apostles."[46] In addition, he dramatically redescribed the closing of the Christian biblical canon as an act of censorship that continues what Paul had begun. It is not just that Paul "pervet'd" authentically ancient and apostolic "Jewish-Christianity" already in the first century; rather, Toland retells the tale of the Council of Nicaea, Constantine, and dawn of the Christianization of the Roman Empire in the fourth century as an extension of this erasure, claiming that "the prevailing Party [at Nicaea] did strictly order *all* those Books which offended them to be burnt, or otherwise supprest."[47]

---

move, not just through his 1699 "Catalogue of Books" but also through his practice of interpreting such so-called "apocrypha" in terms of one another, there and elsewhere.

[43] So F. Stanley Jones, "From Toland to Baur," in Jones, *Rediscovery of Jewish Christianity*, 123–36 at 124–25.

[44] See further Jonathan Sheehan, *The Enlightenment Bible* (Princeton: Princeton University Press, 2005), 39–44; Nicholas Keene, "A Two-Edged Sword: Biblical Criticism and the New Testament Canon in Early Modern England," in *Scripture and Scholarship in Early Modern England*, ed. A. Hessayon and N. Keene (Aldershot: Ashgate, 2006), 96–115.

[45] First published in John Toland, *Amyntor* (London, 1699), 20–41, and later expanded into *A Catalogue of Books … as Truly or Falsely ascrib'd to Jesus Christ, his Apostles, and other eminent persons* (London, 1726). See further Pierre Lurbe, "'Those Fabulous Dragons Teeth': Invented Beginnings, Lost Causes and New Beginnings in John Toland's *Amyntor* (1699)," *Études anglaises* 66 (2013): 134–46.

[46] Toland, *Amyntor*, 56.

[47] Toland, *Amyntor*, 92. Notably, Toland elsewhere depicts such suppression as part of a broader pattern seen throughout history and across cultures. In *Clidophorus*, he speculates as to how "some cunning persons thought they cou'd not better attain to Authority over the rest (which draws Riches after it of course) than by pretending to be masters of this same TRUTH.

To be sure, this claim about the fourth-century Christian burning of books does resonate with some of what we know about the Arian controversy.[48] Toland, however, radically expands this claim so as to conjure an image of book burning as a central component of the closing of the Christian biblical canon and the consolidation of imperialized ecclesiastical power under Constantine. One might wonder about the degree to which this move contributed to promoting, naturalizing, or popularizing the notion of noncanonical texts that we noted at the outset – i. e., as "document[s] … slated for the fire."[49] At the very least, it may have helped to foster the ease with which authors today can appeal, without any specific citation or documentation, to a pattern of Christian censorship that purportedly began with Paul and culminated when – as Jacobovici and Wilson put it – "the Emperor Constantine became aligned with Pauline Christianity and the historical Jesus was eclipsed by Pauline theology" and "only those Gospels that reflected this new theology were *allowed* to survive."[50]

If so, it proves especially poignant that this pattern resonates so richly with Toland's own career – which began with the burning of a book. In 1696, Toland published his first book, *Christianity not Mysterious,* which argued for rationality over biblical revelation and for which he was put on trial and ordered to be burnt at the stake.[51] By that time, he had fled Ireland, so in his absence, three copies of his book were ordered to be burned instead (a result that Toland

---

Next they gave out that they cou'd impart it to others, without putting them to any labor, or diverting them from any business. . . . Nor did these crafty Empires stop here. They knew the falsity of facts, and the fallacy of reasonings, might at one time or other be detected by men of penetration. Wherefore, as the Devil is God's ape, they boasted of a superior and supernatural knowledge, not subject to the rules of Criticism, nor a proper object of the Understanding. Nay, they went to a greater length, openly maintaining that it was lawful to ly for the public good, so that the common people (said they) being incapable of reflection, ought to be manag'd by guile, and to be deluded by agreable fables into obedience to their Governers" (*Clidophorus,* published as Part 2 of *Tetradymus* [Cornhill, 1720], 64). It was as a result of this pairing of religious teaching with greed for political and economic gain, Toland further argues, that secret transmission became necessary: "the Philosophers, therefore, and other well-wishers to mankind in most nations, were constrain'd by this holy tyranny to make use of a 'two-fold doctrine'; the one Popular, accomodat'd to the Prejudices of the vulgar, and to the reciev'd Customs or Religions: the other Philosophical, conformable to the nature of things, and consequently to TRUTH, which, with doors fast shut and under all other precautions, they communicated onely to friends of known probity, prudence, and capacity" (65–66).

[48] Dirk Rohrmann, *Christianity, Book-Burning, and Censorship in Late Antiquity* (Berlin: de Gruyter, 2016), 31–35.

[49] Jacobovici and Wilson, *Lost Gospel,* 276; italics mine.

[50] Jacobovici and Wilson, *Lost Gospel,* 277; italics mine.

[51] John Toland, *Christianity Not Mysterious, or, A Treatise Shewing That There Is Nothing in the Gospel Contrary to Reason, Nor above It and That No Christian Doctrine Can Be Properly Call'd a Mystery* (London, 1696). See further Justin A. I. Champion, *Republican Learning: John Toland and the Crisis of Christian Culture, 1696–1722* (Manchester: Manchester University Press, 2003), 70–71. Also Paul O'Higgins, "Blasphemy in Irish Law," *Modern Law Review* 23 (1960): 151–166 at 156–57; Geoff Kemp, "The 'End of Censorship' and the Politics of Toleration, from Locke to Sacheverell," *Parliamentary History* 31 (2012): 47–68.

merrily mocked as a process whereby "Popish Inquisitors … performed that Execution on a Book"). With the trial, moreover, came notoriety, propelling his public profile as a controversialist – and thus also the spread of his ideas about "apocrypha."[52] Even though Toland is perhaps best known today in relation to his importance for the development of Deism, he thus also has an important place in shaping popular notions of the Christian past as marked by suppressed Jewish and other truths that the discovery or decoding of "lost" books might suddenly reveal.

Secrecy and the Transmission of Torah and Truth in the *Epistle of Peter to James* and the *Homilies*

In the modern reception of the *Epistle of Peter to James*, we thus glimpse some critical moments in the popularization of the contemporary phenomenon that we noted at the outset, whereby noncanonical writings can be presumed, somewhat homogenously, to be potential sources of suppressed secrets about the Christian past. But how do these early modern readings compare to what we find in the *Epistle* itself? What purposes are served by secrecy and suppression within the *Epistle* and its own literary and historical contexts in Late Antiquity?

Since the turn of the twentieth century, specialist research on the Pseudo-Clementine corpus has been largely source critical, atomizing these fourth-century writings in the quest to discover possible first- or second-century materials embedded therein.[53] Partly as a result, its treatment of secrecy and suppression has attracted surprisingly little attention. If anything, source critics have taken the rhetoric somewhat at face value, reading the reference to Peter's secretly transmitted "books of my preachings" in *Ep. Pet.* 1.2 as an invitation to try to

---

[52] In his later writings, Toland makes quite clear how his own situation informed his interest in these and other past examples of secrecy and suppression. His 1720 *Clidophorus*, for instance, posits a perennial pattern whereby philosophers were forced to encode the true meanings of their words due to the dangers of suppression and censorship. Toland there consolidates medieval ideas about "exoteric and esoteric philosophy" and repurposes them as a call to free speech. He argues that truths that could be communicated among trusted friends and others in private were necessary to write with an eye to secret meanings to be unlocked only with a key, since surveillance and the threat of suppression "must of necessity produce shiftings, ambiguities, equivocations, and hypocrisy in all its shapes; which will not merely be call'd but actually esteem'd neccessarily cautious" (*Clidophorus*, 68). See further Champion, *Republican Learning*, 230–31; Annabel M. Patterson, *Censorship and Interpretation: The Conditions of Writing and Reading in Early Modern England* (Madison: University of Wisconsin Press, 1984), 24–26. Patterson notes how "Toland's theory of reading between the lines was a response to English political censorship at the end of the seventeenth century, and was clearly presented as only a temporary recourse. The goal is the open society" (25). On the contrast with the *Epistle of Peter to James*, see below.

[53] I discuss this pattern and its problems in detail in Chapter One in this volume; see further references there.

reconstruct a hypothetical text called the "*Kerygmata Petrou*" (lit. "Preachings of Peter"), which is posited as one of the nonextant sources behind the nonextant shared source that scholars reconstruct from the Pseudo-Clementine *Homilies* and *Recognitions*.[54]

On the one hand, attention to the eighteenth- and nineteenth-century reception of the *Epistle of Peter to James* helps to historicize the twentieth-century preoccupation with attempting to excavate the surviving forms of the Pseudo-Clementines for possible early materials embedded therein (even to the degree of seeking out "lost" sources of "lost" sources!). Indeed, seen from this perspective, the source-critical project of culling the fourth-century *Homilies* and *Recognitions* to reconstruct a putative second-century "*Kerygmata Petrou*" is yet another moment in the modern reception of this *Epistle*, providing yet another example of the rhetorical power of its claims to preserve suppressed secrets about the apostolic past.

On the other hand, the very prominence of these claims within its modern reception draws our attention to their overlooked significance for understanding the *Epistle of Peter to James* itself and also – I suggest – for understanding its function in its own literary and cultural context. Within the manuscript tradition, the *Epistle of Peter to James* is the first of three works prefaced to the *Homilies*. It is followed by the *Contestation*, which offers a brief narrative account of the *Epistle*'s positive reception by James, and by the *Epistle of Clement to James*, which claims to have been written after Peter's death. Whether or not the *Epistle of Peter to James* might have been originally penned as a preface to an earlier Petrine work that is now lost, or to an earlier nonextant form of the Pseudo-Clementine novel, it remains that its function in the form that comes down to us is to frame, authorize, and introduce the *Homilies*. When we focus on the place

---

[54] Despite being a document wholly reconstructed by modern source critics, the *Kerygmata Petrou* is commonly cited due to the inclusion in Wilhelm Schneemelcher's *New Testament Apocrypha* of a translation of a reconstruction thereof by Georg Strecker (i. e., *NTA* 2:531–41). Strecker elsewhere summarizes his reconstruction of the *Kerygmata Petrou* as based especially on the extraction of those materials from the *Homilies* and *Recognitions* that concern "[1] the 'true prophet,' how he passed through the world, and his relationship to the hostile female prophecy; also about [2] the exposition of the law by the 'true prophet' with material about the 'false pericopes'; connected with this are [3] anti-Pauline statements, which attempt to show Paul as an opponent of Peter and as one who was not approved by James, the representative of the true doctrine and bishop of Jerusalem; finally [4] material about baptism is given in which the strongly legalistic character of the work becomes evident"; "Problem of Jewish-Christianity," 258. Characteristic of the common logic behind the reconstruction of this early source is Helmut Koester's notion that "this hypothesis is the most plausible explanation for the appearance of large sections in the Pseudo-Clementines of which the Jewish-Christian character is totally obvious"; *Introduction to the New Testament* (Berlin: de Gruyter, 2011), 2:211 – i.e., presuming that any such Jewishness would necessarily be early and "retained" in a later document only by virtue of its inclusion of early source material. On this general pattern as an example of how the conventional model of the "Parting of the Ways" can skew modern scholarly readings of premodern sources, see Chapter One above.

of secrecy and suppression in the *Epistle of Peter to James*, we can see how it serves this function in a manner that goes well beyond the possible anti-Paulinism that has preoccupied modern readers since Toland and Baur. A reconsideration of these themes within this *Epistle* and in relation to the *Contestation* and *Homilies* – I suggest – shows how the *Epistle* functions both to emphasize the Jewishness of apostolic truth and to set up the distinctive treatment of Moses, the Torah, and Pharisees within the *Homilies*.[55]

Beginning at the very outset of this *Epistle* – as we have seen – the Jewishness of Peter and James is presented as a normative horizon for followers of Jesus. The letter begins with Peter's plea "not to give a share of the books of my preaching that I sent to you to anyone from among the Gentiles" (1.2). Far from dismissing "Judaism" as a superseded lineage of "Christianity," the *Epistle* figures Jewishness as emblem and guarantor of the trustworthy transmission of apostolic truth. This association of Jewish lineage and preservation of truth, moreover, is outlined in contrast to the threat of misinterpretation and suppression here associated with Gentiles. Not only does Peter ask for his writings to be given only to worthy Jews, but the necessity of this limited transmission is also presented as the danger of misinterpretation and the spread of misinformation by "certain men from among the Gentiles" (2.3).

In the rest of the *Epistle*, the focus falls on the assertion of continuity from Moses and on the elevation of Jewish succession from Moses as a model for the preservation of apostolic truth by followers of Jesus.[56] What is presented as the ideal to emulate is the Jewish transmission of the teachings of Moses via the seventy elders of Numbers 11, who are here twice described as "those who succeeded his chair" (τοῖς τὴν καθέδραν αὐτοῦ παρειληφόσιν; 1.2; 3.2). It is due to the transmission of knowledge in succession from Moses – the *Epistle* here claims – that the Jews of their own time have succeeded in preserving their commitment to "one God, one Law, one hope" (1.3). Peter asks for the exact same to be done for his books:

Consequently, in order that the same take place also among us, that the like, give the books of my preachings (τὰς βίβλους μου τῶν κηρυγμάτων) to the Seventy among our brothers, with the same mystery of instruction (μετὰ τοῦ ὁμοίου τῆς ἀγωγῆς μυστηρίου) so that

---

[55] I.e., whether because the *Epistle of Peter to James* was significantly redacted to fit its current function as part of a preface to the *Homilies* or because the *Homilies* so happens to integrate and preserve those key elements of the *Grundschrift* that resonate with the treatment of the theme of secrecy and knowledge in this *Epistle*. On the theme of secrecy in the *Homilies*, see now Kelley Coblentz Bautch, "Obscured by the Scriptures, Revealed by the Prophets: God in the Pseudo-Clementine *Homilies*," in *Histories of the Hidden God: Concealment and Revelation in Western Gnostic, Esoteric, and Mystical Traditions*, ed. April DeConick and Grant Adamson (Durham: Acumen, 2013), 120–36.

[56] On the depiction of Moses, see further Kristine J. Ruffatto, "Moses Typology for Peter in the *Epistula Petri* and the *Contestatio*," *VC* 69 (2015): 345–67.

they can furnish those whom they wish to furnish to take responsibility for a share of the teaching (διδασκαλίας). (*Epistle of Peter to James* 2.1)

In effect, then, Jewish teachers of Torah here model a solution to the problem of the misinterpretation of apostolic teachings: the *Epistle* points to Jews in their present as exemplary of how the transmission of truth in proper succession along a select line of trustworthy teachers can maintain monotheism, Mosaic truth, and community unity. It is only in this fashion that Peter's teaching, too, might be preserved against the division sown by antinomian and Gentile misinterpreters.[57]

Following Baur, scholarship has focused almost wholly on this *Epistle*'s possible anti-Paulinism. When one analyzes the *Epistle* on its own terms, however, one thus finds a different focus; as Kristine Ruffatto has noted, "the proper transmission of Mosaic tradition to the church is clearly the dominant theme."[58] Ruffatto makes a persuasive case that the main aim of the *Epistle* to assert that "only Peter is heir to the eternal law of Moses."[59] To this, I would add only one caveat: Peter may be presented as the heir among the apostles, but his role is not quite framed as singular.[60] Rather, Peter's place at the head of a chain of transmission of Moses' teachings, via Jesus, is paralleled by the separate transmission of these same teachings among Jewish teachers. Peter's role in the apostolic succession of Mosaic truth is never described as displacing, transcending, or superseding its Jewish tradents and transmission – and, if anything, it presumes this parallel line as a model for emulation *precisely because* of its successful continuance (esp. 1.3).

In paralleling Mosaic authority and Petrine writing, the *Epistle* also anticipates a more extensive argument made in the *Homilies*. There, Peter similarly appeals to the succession of proper Torah interpretation among the Jews, albeit with specific reference to the Pharisees as those who "sit on the chair of Moses" (τῆς Μωϋσέως καθέδρας; *Hom.* 3.18–19, 70; 11:29; cf. Matt 23:2; *Ep. Pet.* 1.2; 3.2). As I have shown elsewhere, this claim is made in a manner that resonates with distinctively Rabbinic claims to knowledge and authority.[61] In the *Homilies*, for instance, Peter reveals to Clement that what was passed down to Moses' Jewish

---

[57] In this, the *Epistle* lays the groundwork for an argument subsequently made in more detail in the *Homilies* – wherein "Judaism" is associated with the trustworthy prophetic teaching of monotheism across generations, in extended contrast to "Hellenism," which is there associated with the multiplication of opinions, philosophies, and deities (and hence with the threat of "heresy," especially among Gentiles). See Chapters Four and Five in this volume.

[58] Ruffatto, "Moses Typology," 349.

[59] Ruffatto, "Moses Typology," 347.

[60] I.e., Ruffatto concludes that "Peter alone is the guarantor of Moses' legacy; he is the authentic apostolic leader of Christians who remained committed to their Jewish heritage, such as the community behind the Pseudo-Clementines" ("Moses Typology," 347); I agree with her latter statement but would amend the former to include Jewish teachers as also "guarantors of Moses' legacy" through a separate and parallel line.

[61] See Chapter Nine in this volume.

successors was not the Written Torah *per se*, but rather "the Torah/Law with the explanations" (*Hom.* 2.38) as "given by Moses without writing" (3.47).[62] Consistent with the late antique association of Pharisees and Rabbis, moreover, the *Homilies* present them as a select line of Torah teachers who preserve the authentic teachings of Moses in a trustworthy chain of transmission to the present (cf. *m. Avot* 1–5).[63]

In the *Epistle of Peter to James*, a similar point is made, but the pedagogical ramifications come at the fore: Jews maintain their ethical monotheism – Peter there asserts – not as much because of their Scriptures as because of their teachers of Scripture, who belong to a lineage of knowledge transmission linked in a direct chain back to Moses.[64] It is these teachers, in fact, who are able to maintain unity of community and belief among the Jews even despite the "discordances of the Scriptures" and "polysemous voices of the prophets" (*Ep. Pet.* 1.4) This chain of teachers is what ultimately ensures that all of Moses' *homoethnoi* "observe the same rule of unity and way of life."[65] Whether or not it reflects any direct contact with the Rabbinic movement in particular, then, it remains that those responsible for the *Epistle* appear to know and accept similar claims by Jewish teachers of their time to stand in a chain of transmission from Moses and to serve as the custodians of the ancestral tradition of his Torah.[66] Like the *Homilies*, moreover, the *Epistle* echoes and mirrors these Jewish claims without displacing them.

Whatever the precise relationship to Rabbinic Judaism, attention to the representation of Jews and Pharisees in the *Homilies* thus helps to explain an other-

---

[62] E. g., *Sifre Devarim* 351; *y. Megillah* 4.1; *y. Pe'ah* 2.6; *Pesiqta Rabbati* 14b; *b. Shabbat* 13a; Martin S. Jaffee, *Torah in the Mouth: Writing and Oral Tradition in Palestinian Judaism, 200 BCE–400 CE* (New York: Oxford University Press, 2001).

[63] So Albert Baumgarten, "Literary Evidence for Jewish Christianity in the Galilee," in *The Galilee in Late Antiquity*, ed. Lee I. Levine (New York: Jewish Theological Seminary of America, 1992), 43.

[64] On the importance of transmission in the *Epistle of Peter to James* and *Contestation*, see Ruffatto, "Moses Typology"; she there notes, for instance, how "The verb παραδίδωμι is used nine times (*Ep. Pet.* 1.2 [bis]; 1.4; 3.1 [4x]; *Cont.* 2.2; 4.3); μεταδίδωμι eight times (*Ep. Pet.* 1.2; 2.1; 3.1; *Cont.* 1.1; 2.1 [bis]; 3.2; 5.3); δίδωμι five times (*Ep. Pet.* 2.1; *Cont.* 2.1 [bis]; 3.2; 4.1); ἀποδίδωμι twice (*Cont.* 3.2; 3.4); παραλαμβάνω twice (*Ep. Pet.* 2.2; *Cont.* 2.2); and ἐπιδίδωμι (*Cont.* 4.1), ἀναδίδωμι (*Cont.* 2.1) and μεταλαμβάνω (*Cont.* 4.3) each once" (349).

[65] Compare the rendering of this verse in Alain Le Boulluec et al., trans., "Homélies," in Geoltrain and Kaestli, *Écrits apocryphes chrétiens*, 2:1215–17 at 1216: "ils ne peuvent en aucune façon pense différemment ou se laisser distraire du droit chemin *par le multiples sens des Écritures*."

[66] The most famous example of such claims is *m. Avot* 1–5, but other late antique Jewish expressions of this same concern can be found also in Hekhalot literature, Jewish magical manuals, and piyutim. See now Michael Swartz, "Chains of Tradition from *Avot* to the *Avodah Piyutim*," in *Jews, Christians, and the Roman Empire*, ed. Natalie Dohrmann and Annette Yoshiko Reed (Philadelphia: University of Pennsylvania, 2013), 189–208. The examples discussed by Swartz are in competition with one another. If the Pseudo-Clementine examples can be read as part of the same discourse, they are distinguished by their presentation of their own chain as supplementary instead.

wise puzzling feature of the *Epistle of Peter to James*: its pseudonymous Peter places himself and James within a Jewish "we" – that is, a "we" who are among Moses' *homophuloi*, in contrast to Gentile *ethnoi*, and thus among those who continue to hold "one God, one Law, one hope." But Peter also describes a Jewish "they" who stand in succession from Moses and who preserve his teachings for the Jewish people – that is, "they" who provide the positive *exempla* that Peter asks James to emulate when transmitting "the books of my preachings."

Although puzzling at first sight, this doubled identity claim fits well with what is explained in more detail in the *Homilies*, where Peter reveals the divine secret that the teachings of Moses for the Jews are actually the same as the teachings of Jesus to the Gentiles. This point is made most clearly in a midrash on Matthew 11:25 that is framed as a private teaching of Peter to his disciples in the eighth *Homily*. Significantly, for our purposes, this midrash extends the *Epistle's* concern with the function of secrecy in the human transmission of knowledge, by pointing to the function of secrecy in the divine transmission of knowledge as well:

Jesus is concealed from the Hebrews who have taken Moses as their teacher, and Moses is hidden from those who have believed Jesus (ἀπὸ μὲν Ἑβραίων τὸν Μωυσῆν διδάσκαλον εἰληφότων καλύπτεται ὁ Ἰησοῦς, ἀπὸ δὲ τῶν Ἰησοῦ πεπιστευκότων ὁ Μωυσῆς ἀποκρύπτεται). For, since there is a single teaching by both, God accepts one who has believed either of these …. God Himself has concealed (ἔκρυψεν) a teacher [i. e., Jesus] from some who foreknew what they should do [i. e., Jews], and He has revealed (ἀπεκάλυψεν) to others, who are ignorant about what they should do [i. e., Gentiles].[67] Neither, therefore, are the Hebrews condemned on account of their ignorance of Jesus, by reason of Him who has concealed him, if, doing the things commanded by Moses, they do not hate him whom they do not know. Nor are those from among the Gentiles condemned, who know not Moses on account of Him who has concealed him, provided that they also, doing the things spoken by Jesus, do not hate him whom they do not know. (*Hom.* 8.6–7; cf. *Rec.* 4.5)

The teachings of Moses and Jesus are here asserted to provide two separate but equal paths to salvation – even if neither Jews nor Christians commonly know this to be the case. The narrative setting serves to present this truth as hidden: it is one of the secret teachings that Peter shares only with Clement and other select followers, in contrast to what he preaches in public. Peter's choice to withhold some information from the populace, moreover, is here paralleled with the very workings of divine occultation and revelation. The claim that there is a twofold path to salvation is here revealed together with the claim that God has hidden each of the two paths from those on the other, concealing the teacher of Jews from Gentiles and the converse.[68]

---

[67] Note the parallel in *b. Bava Batra* 12b: "From the day that the Temple was destroyed, prophecy was taken from the prophets and given to the foolish and the infants."

[68] Contrast the parallel in *Rec.* 4.5, which charts only *one* path to salvation, whereby all believers should follow *both* teachers: "But he who is of the Gentiles, and who has it of God to believe Moses, ought also to have it of his own purpose to love Jesus also. And again, the

In this particular passage, the focus falls on Jesus, with Peter stressing that it is only because of a divine plan that most Jews do not know his teachings. In effect, the appeal to divine secrecy serves to defang the common Christian anti-Jewish trope of the Jewish rejection of Jesus, even as the continuance of Jewish salvation through Moses and Torah is explicitly maintained. In the process, Peter can be celebrated as an apostle with special access to divine secrets, and Clement becomes elevated as a model of a follower who stands in this line and knows the whole of Peter's true teachings.

Neither the *Epistle of Peter to James* nor the *Homilies* ever use the term "Christian" to describe either Gentiles or Jews who follow Jesus – let alone any terms like "Gentile Christian" or "Jewish-Christian." To the degree that one might heuristically label these sources as "Jewish-Christian," moreover, it is certainly not in the sense meant by Baur. Rather, these sources articulate a doubled identity in a manner predicated on the claim that what might appear to be separated as "Christianity" and "Judaism" is actually identical.[69] Neither the *Homilies* nor the *Epistle of Peter to James* promote any aim of "converting" Jews to the belief in Jesus as messiah. What they promote, if anything, is the ideal of a Jewish leadership role in the Gentile *ecclesia*, as patterned after Moses and his successors. What is ultimately at stake, thus, is not the relationship between what we might call "Judaism" and "Christianity," but rather the preservation of a Jewish lineage of monotheistic teaching – in two parallel chains of tradition from Moses via the seventy elders and from Jesus via Peter and seventy followers. In effect, proximity to "Judaism" is presented as the main criterion by which readers of the *Epistles* and *Homilies* can distinguish between true and

---

Hebrew, who has it of God to believe Moses, ought to have it also of his own purpose to believe in Jesus; so that each of them, having in himself something of the divine gift, and something of his own exertion, may be perfect by both."

[69] Notably, this may be closer to Toland's sense of the term – at least in some passages in his writings. In light of Toland's interest in the Pseudo-Clementines, it is intriguing that he later cites the mutually hidden truth of the identical character of all "religions" as exemplary of the esoteric truth that needs to be hidden even into his own times. He begins the last section of *Clidophorus* by noting that "I have more than once hinted, that *the External and Internal Doctrine*, are as much now in use than ever, tho the distinction is not so openly and professed approv'd, as among the Ancients. This puts me in mind of what I was told by a near relation to the old Lord Shaftsbury. The latter conferring one day with Major Wildman about the many sects of Religion in the world, they came to the conclusion at last, that notwithstanding those infinite divisions caus'd by the interest of the Priests and the ignorance of the People, *All Wise Men are of the Same Religion:* whereupon a Lady in the room, who seem'd to mind her needle more than their discourse, demanded with some concern what that Religion was? To whom Lord Shaftesbursy reply'd, *Madam, wise men never tell.* And, indeed considering how dangerous it is made to tell the truth, tis difficult to know when any man declares his real sentiments of things" (*Clidophorus*, 94–95). Toland then goes on to expound on the necessity of secrecy in his own time but also to promote the ideal of a society in which secrecy would no longer be necessary: "*Let all men freely speak what they think, without being ever branded or punish'd but for wicked practices ... then you are sure to hear the whole truth, and till then very scantily, or obscurely, if at all*" (95–96).

false forms of "Christianity"; just as the *Homilies* presents true "Christianity" as the revelation of Moses' teachings by Jesus to the Gentiles, so the *Epistle* emphasizes that authentically apostolic truth can be discerned from the degree of its faithfulness to the Torah and Moses.

It is in the context of making the latter point that we find the much-quoted passage in the *Epistle of Peter to James* wherein Peter seems to blame Paul ("my enemy") for spreading an antinomian message and also to blame others (perhaps including the author of Acts) for twisting his words so that they seem to support a "dissolution of the Torah/Law." When read in its own context, it is clear that the main message is the necessity of properly trained teachers to preserve the proper interpretation of the Torah of Moses and teachings of Jesus alike. Controlled and limited circulation of books is depicted as potentially preserving the truth against the danger that what is "said" and "heard" can be misinterpreted. Yet the emphasis on *who* can possess the books points also to a poignant sense of the misinterpretation that can be fostered by writing no less than speech: when books circulate freely, written words can fall prey to the same threat of misinterpretation as the heard word.[70] Only when books are transmitted along proper lines of succession – and, hence, together with orally transmitted teachings about their interpretation – can they serve to protect true knowledge in a corrupt world. To circulate Peter's preachings "with the same mystery of instruction (μετὰ τοῦ ὁμοίου τῆς ἀγωγῆς μυστηρίου)" as the teachings of Moses, then, is to limit their transmission to a small and select line of Jewish and Jewish-taught tradents. Secrecy here is not so much an end in itself, but rather a strategy of conservation through restricted transmission. To the degree that the *Epistle of Peter to James* can be called "esoteric," then, it is not in the sense of "esotericism wherein the concealed is fundamentally impervious to language and thought"; what we find here, rather, is more similar to what Ra'anan Boustan describes as the "indigenous conception of secrecy in Hekhalot literature" whereby "what is centrally at stake ... is the precision with which their teachings are transmitted and put into practice."[71]

---

[70] On the broader context of this suspicion of writing, see Coblentz Bautch, "Obscured by the Scriptures," 125–26.

[71] Ra'anan Boustan, "Secrets without Mystery: Esotericism in Early Jewish Mysticism," *Aries* 15 (2015): 10–15 at 12–13. Boustan there counters readings of Hekhalot literature that assume "that secrecy must address mystery – an object characterized chiefly by its ineffability" – and "recapitulate the highly selective reception of Jewish traditions within European Christian culture, thereby perpetuating problematic trends within the modern study of religion" (11). To be sure, the continuum of Jewish approaches to secrecy includes some cases of esotericism linked to ineffability. As Elliot Wolfson has shown, for instance, "the view of secrecy promoted by kabbalists ... relates to the inability to communicate the secret, which is not to be explained primarily in terms of the unworthiness of a particular recipient but is rather associated with the inherent ineffability of the truth that must be kept secret"; *Open Secret: Postmessianic Messianism and the Mystical Revision of Menahem Mendel Schneerson* (New York: Columbia University Press, 2012), 33. Wolfson, however, also notes how even kabbalists often participate

The need for such strategies of conservation is clear from the statement subsequently attributed to Peter about the dangers of not following the model of Moses:

If it does not take place in this way, the word (λόγος) of truth will be divided among us into many opinions. And this I know, not being like a prophet, but seeing already the beginning of the same evil. (*Epistle of Peter to James* 2.2)

This prediction is typically cited as a sign of some self-consciousness about the belated and pseudonymous character of the letter. At the same time, however, it resonates with the representation of "heresy" in the *Homilies*, especially in relation to its interpretation of the predication attributed to Jesus in Matt 24:24. Peter there paraphrases this saying as warning of the spread of "false apostles, false prophets, heresies, desires for supremacy (ψευδαπόστολοι, ψευδεῖς προφῆται, αἱρέσεις, φιλαρχίαι)," and he explains that Jesus thus knew already of how "heretics," "finding their beginning in Simon, who blasphemes God, will work together in the assertion of the same opinions against God as those of Simon (τὸ τὰ αὐτὰ τῷ Σίμωνι κατὰ τοῦ θεοῦ λέγειν συνεργήσουσιν)" (*Hom.* 16.21). As elsewhere in the *Homilies*, divine knowledge on earth is depicted as threatened by demons, precariously preserved, and in continual need of guarding and protection from those false pretenders who claim to be – and appear to be – so much like true apostles.[72] Transmission of texts and teachings to a limited group, then, is here promoted for the sake of the aim of maintaining the truth of monotheism in an impure world that is infested with demons, swayed by "heretics," corrupted by power, and ultimately hostile to the truth.

In this too, the teachings of Jesus are presented as having been presaged by the Torah of Moses. Just as the *Epistle of Peter to James* focuses on the problem of the misinterpretation of Peter's teachings, so the *Homilies* grapple with the problem of the misinterpretation of Moses' teachings as well.[73] The negative exemplar there is Simon Magus and what is suppressed is monotheism. To his followers, Peter reveals that Simon attempts in public debates "to show from the Scriptures that He who made the heaven and the earth and all things in them is not the supreme God, but that there is another, unknown and supreme ... and that he sent two gods, one of whom is he who made the world (ὁ μὲν εἷς ἐστιν

---

in a discourse about secrecy which is more akin to what Boustan describes for the Hekhalot literature and which is arguably more widespread within Jewish tradition – that is, "the rhetoric of esotericism based on the presumption that secrets must be withheld from those not fit to receive them, an orientation hinted at in classical rabbinic thought and developed more systematically by medieval philosophical exegetes, especially Maimonides" (33).

[72] Mostly but not only through the *Homilies'* distinctive doctrine of the "Rule of Syzygy," which teaches that true prophets and teachers are always paired with false counterparts – see discussion in Chapter Six.

[73] On the *Homilies'* "theory of God's hiddenness or obscurity within the Hebrew Scriptures," see further Coblentz Bautch, "Obscured by the Scriptures," 122–24

ὁ κόσμον κτίσας) and the other, he who gave the Torah/Law (ὁ δὲ ἕτερος ὁ τὸν νόμον δούς)" (*Hom.* 3.2). Later, in their public debate, Simon even accuses Peter of deceptively suppressing the *polytheistic* truth about the Torah.[74] It is to combat the polytheism of such "heretical" claims that Peter privately reveals to Clement and his disciplines that misleading passages have been added to the Written Torah and that it is thus necessary to read Scripture in line with the teachings of the True Prophet concerning monotheism and the essential goodness of God, Israel, and the patriarchs of the Jewish people.[75]

It is in response to the problem of the polytheistic misinterpretation of the Torah, moreover, that *Homilies* outlines its distinctive epistemology, whereby the True Prophet "alone knows the truth [and] if anyone else knows anything, he has received it from him or from his disciples" (*Hom.* 2.12). Just as the teachings of Moses and Jesus are said to be the same, so the True Prophet is also equated with both Moses and Jesus (2.16–17). Furthermore, like God Himself, the True Prophet is associated with selective occlusion and disclosure. Peter, for instance, there explains to Clement what Jesus really meant when he said that Pharisees "possess the key, but those wishing to enter they do not suffer to do so" (*Hom.* 3.18–19; cf. Matt 23:13) by pointing to the limitation of Moses' teachings to the Jews prior to the arrival of Jesus. Consistent with its two-path soteriology, the *Homilies* outlines a twofold revelation in which the teachings of True Prophet came to humankind in successive stages: the True Prophet, as Moses, proclaimed teachings to be "transmitted in secret to the worthy (ἐν κρυπτῷ ἀξίοις παραδιδόμενα κηρύσσων)" – i. e., Israel – but later rose up again from his throne in heaven to return to earth, as Jesus, with the aim of "extending mercy even to the Gentiles" (3.18). What was reserved initially for Jews, then, is later held back from them, and for this reason Jesus is said to have "neglected his own blood (ἰδίου αἵματος ἠμέλει)," teaching Gentiles but not Jews even despite "having compassion for the souls of all" (3.19).

In the *Epistle of Peter to James*, the emphasis is less on the separate audiences of exoteric teaching and more on the preservation of a unity of truth through esoteric transmission. Whereas the *Homilies* explain why Jews might not understand Jesus, this *Epistle* counters Gentile notions of Peter as denying the

---

[74] E.g., Simon Magus to Peter in *Hom.* 3.38: "why would you lie (ψευδόμενος), and deceive the unlearned multitude standing around you, persuading them that it is unlawful to think that there are gods and to call them so, when the Books that are current among the Jews (τῶν παρὰ Ἰουδαίοις δημοσίων βίβλων) say that there are many gods?"

[75] See further *Hom.* 2.38–52; 3.4–6, 9–11, 17–21, 37–51; 16.9–14; 18.12–13, 18–22; Georg Strecker, *Das Judenchristentum in den Pseudoklementinen* (TU 70; 2nd ed.; Berlin: Akademie-Verlag, 1981), 166–86; Karl Evan Shuve, "The Doctrine of the False Pericopes and Other Late Antique Approaches to the Problem of Scripture's Unity," in *Plots in the Pseudo-Clementine Romance*, ed. Frédéric Amsler et al. (Publications de l'Institut romand des sciences bibliques 6; Lausanne: Zébre, 2008), 437–45; Donald H. Carlson, *Jewish-Christian Interpretation of the Pentateuch in the Pseudo-Clementine Homilies* (Minneapolis: Fortress, 2013).

eternity and continued validity of the Torah of Moses. In addition, the correction of antinomian misinterpretations of Peter occasions an emphasis on Jesus' commitment to the Torah as well. Those who pervert Peter's words also pervert Jesus' own teachings:

For such a thing is to act against the Law/Torah of God that was spoken through Moses and that was witnessed by our lord [i. e., Jesus] with regard to its eternal permanence (περὶ τῆς ἀιδίου αὐτοῦ διαμονῆς). Thus he said: "The heavens and the earth shall pass away, but not one iota or one dot shall pass away from the Law/Torah" (cf. Luke 16:17; Matt 5:18). And he has spoken thus "in order that all things might come to pass" (cf. Matt 24:34). But those who profess [to know] my mind – I do not know how! – undertake to explain my words, having heard statements from me, attempt to interpret what I said more prudently (οἱ δὲ οὐκ οἶδα πῶς τὸν ἐμὸν νοῦν ἐπαγγελλόμενοι, οὓς ἤκουσαν ἐξ ἐμοῦ λόγους, ἐμοῦ τοῦ εἰπόντος αὐτοὺς φρονιμώτερον ἐπιχειροῦσιν ἑρμηνεύειν), telling those whom they instruct that my meaning is that which I never considered (λέγοντες τοῖς ὑπ' αὐτῶν κατηχουμένοις τοῦτο εἶναι τὸ ἐμὸν φρόνημα, ὃ ἐγὼ οὐδὲ ἐνεθυμήθην). And if they dare to tell such lies against me while I am still alive, how much more so will those after me dare to do so (εἰ δὲ ἐμοῦ ἔτι περιόντος τοιαῦτα τολμῶσιν καταψεύδεσθαι, πόσῳ γε μᾶλλον μετ' ἐμὲ ποιεῖν οἱ μετ' ἐμὲ τολμήσουσιν;)? (*Epistle of Peter to James* 2.5–7)

Having affirmed the eternal value of the Torah and again emphasized than any antinomian picture of Peter is false, the end of the *Epistle* repeats the pleas from the beginning concerning the transmission of his writings:

In order, therefore, that such things not occur, I urgently implore, on account of this, not to give a share of the books of my preachings that I sent you (τῶν ἐμῶν κηρυγμάτων ἃς ἔπεμψά σοι βίβλους) to anyone either of the same tribe [i. e., Jews] nor of a foreign tribe before trial (μηδενὶ … μήτε ὁμοφύλῳ μήτε ἀλλοφύλῳ πρὸ πείρας). But if anyone tested is discovered worthy, then [I urgently implore you] to hand down to him according to the manner of Moses, according to which he handed down to the Seventy as those who succeeded his chair (καθ' ἣν τοῖς ἑβδομήκοντα παρέδωκεν τοῖς τὴν καθέδραν αὐτοῦ παρειληφόσιν) in order that they could thus guard the beliefs and hand down the rule of truth everywhere, interpreting everything according to our tradition (πρὸς τὴν παράδοσιν ἡμῶν). (*Epistle of Peter to James* 3.1–3)

Here, it is made further clear that Peter's writings can also be entrusted to men who might be non-Jews as well, as long as they are tested and deemed worthy and capable of "interpreting everything according to *our* tradition." And, again, it is stressed that the truth is kept safe by oral and written knowledge in a tradition (Gr. *paradosis*) transmitted along a single authorized line of succession from Jesus through Peter and James, just as also through a single authorized parallel line of succession from Moses through the Seventy Elders.

The theme of secrecy continues in the *Contestation* directly following, which recounts how James reacts to Peter's letter and follows this request. Here, further specifications are made: the books of Peter's teachings can only be entrusted to those who are circumcised, baptized or purified, and also trained and taught for six years. They must take them with them when they travel, and as they near death, they must either pass them along to a worthy son or deposit them with a bishop. What is claimed, thus, is that the texts that follow have not circulated in public but are nonetheless ancient and authentic – and, in fact, even more so than those words of Peter that have been circulating in public and thus open to misinterpretation. The implication, here too, is to vouchsafe that which follows as the true teachings of Peter and to explain why different images of Peter are current (e.g., perhaps especially in Acts). Whatever their precise origins, the *Epistle of Peter to James* and *Contestation* serve an important authorizing function both with respect to themselves and to the *Homilies* – namely: to explain how first-century Petrine teachings might seem to emerge anew in Late Antiquity.

As we have seen, however, the theorization of secrecy within the *Epistle of Peter to James* also serves to set up distinctive ideas within the *Homilies*, particularly in relation to its treatment of Jews and Judaism. In addition, it anticipates the narrative structure of the *Homilies,* wherein Peter's private instructions to Clement and other followers are often distinguished from his public preaching to crowds of "pagans" and his public debates with Simon Magus. Throughout the *Epistle, Contestation*, and *Homilies* alike, moreover, the aim remains the promotion of the unity of a monotheistic message, whereby Gentiles like Clement learn proper ritual practice and oneness of God from those in a Jewish line of transmission of Jesus' teachings like Peter and James. The theorization of knowledge transmission in the *Epistle of Peter to James* thus goes well beyond self-authorizing claims to speak also to broader concerns about the loss of knowledge about the past and the difficulties of preserving teachings intact, even with the aid of writing. If anything, textualization is marked as fraught with the danger of the suppression of the truth through the overwriting silencing wrought by "intricate interpretations." What is lionized, as in the Rabbinic literature of the time, is orality – not only the Oral Torah vouchsafed through the line that leads back to Moses, but the teachings of Jesus as vouchsafed by those Jews, like Peter, who followed him during his own lifetime.[76]

The image of the Jewishness of Christian Origins in the *Epistle of Peter to James* thus differs from the "Jewish-Christianity" that Baur later uses to reconstruct. Here, Jews are not saved through Jesus, but rather through continued fidelity to Moses. Accordingly, the Jewishness of Christianity is not maintained by one "party" of Jesus' followers dialectically struggling with another to enable one "religion" to spring forth anew: it is, rather, the revelation that there is really one single truth, accessible through two equal yet mutually hidden paths. To the degree that one finds conflict, it is between the true apostles and their followers (Peter, James, Clement) and those who claim to teach about Jesus but are ac-

---

[76] With respect to the *Homilies*, Coblentz Bautch notes how "orality trumps written texts" to such a degree that "the bias toward oral traditions extends naturally to the sayings of Jesus as well" as to the Torah of Moses; "Obscured by the Scriptures," 124.

tually heretically antinomian Hellenes (Simon Magus) – and in this mission to preserve monotheism, true apostles are on the same side as Pharisees and other Jews. In the process, moreover, the *Epistle of Peter to James* reframes Christian supersessionism as an act of radical suppression, an erasure of the truth that Jewish and Christian teachings are not just compatible but the same – and, in fact, allies in the perennial battle against the polytheism of "pagans" and "heretics." Just like knowledge of "oral explanations" can counter the misinterpretation of the Written Torah by "heretics" like Simon Magus who adduce Torah when preaching a multiplicity of gods, so the secret transmission of Peter's teaching is here said to have the power to counter the suppression of his commitment to the Torah against those antinomian enemies who seek to censor the truth of the essential Jewishness of the teachings of Jesus and Peter alike.

It is perhaps not surprising that Toland would find much to use in these texts. Even aside from the notions of secrecy and suppression noted above, the *Epistle of Peter to James, Contestation*, and *Homilies* advance a doubled notion of truth that is not dissimilar to his distinction of esoteric and exoteric philosophies, and they conjure a vision of the truth as endangered from power and corruption in a manner similar to what Toland evokes of censorship in his own time. But even Toland's appeals to the dangers about suppression – like those of Baur after him – are ultimately predicated in a trust in the power of books to preserve. Whereas Toland presumes new mechanics and materialities of textual reproduction that enable a work's survival even if multiple copies might be seized or burnt, this *Epistle* assumes a sense of the book more common prior to mechanical print – that is: as a more precarious object that might be passed in secret, lost, forgotten, or found, but also as an object that serves primarily as an aid to orality, memory, and teaching, rather than the sole or dominant locus of authority in its own right. This sense of the subordination of textuality to orality is largely lost in its early modern reception. In the course of this reception, however, it is perhaps precisely this sense of textual precariousness that the *Epistle* ultimately helps to bequeath to Toland and Baur (and perhaps to us as well) – that is: the allure of a "lost" text that suddenly resurfaces centuries later, bearing the promise of an esoteric and thus "untainted" source emerging anew to speak suppressed Jewish secrets from the Christian past.

From the Christian Reception of the *Epistle of Peter to James* to Its Modern Jewish Afterlives

The aims of the *Epistle to Peter of James* failed, in one sense, and succeeded, in another. In the fourth century and following, far more supersessionist and anti-Jewish visions of the Christian past would come to prevail, even further overwriting the Jewishness of Jesus and his apostles. It was the other version of the Pseudo-Clementine novel – the somewhat later and less pro-Jewish *Recognitions* – that became widely known in the Latin West, as did the other letter in the corpus, the *Epistle of Clement to Peter*. Both were translated into Latin by Rufinus, and the latter came to circulate separately (and eventually as part of the "false decretals") due to its utility for defending the Petrine lineage of the Papacy of nascent Roman Catholicism. The Pseudo-Clementine concern with succession, thus, was put largely to the defense of Roman supremacy. Largely as a result, the *Recognitions* and the *Epistle of Clement to Peter* were continually transmitted and widely read in European Christendom[77] – or, until their authorship became contested as part of the Protestant polemic against "Papal forgeries" during the Reformation and following.[78] To the degree that the *Recognitions* retains some "Jewish-Christian" elements similar to the *Homilies*, they seem to have gone largely unnoticed during its medieval and early modern reception.

The *Epistle of Peter to James* and the *Homilies*, by contrast, seem to have circulated largely outside the Roman Empire, within Byzantium and beyond. What I would like to suggest, however, is that their "(re)discovery" in the West played a major part in the early modern impact of the "Jewish-Christian" elements of the Pseudo-Clementine corpus. The very history of the material transmission of the manuscripts of the *Epistle of Peter to James* may have thus contributed to the work's own impact on both popular and scholarly ideas about the power of "lost" texts to reveal secrets about Christianity's Jewish past.

Modern interest in "Jewish-Christianity" developed precisely in the immediate wake of the printing of the two Greek manuscripts of the Pseudo-Clementine *Homilies* – both of which begin with the *Epistle of Peter to James*. The *Epistle*'s own rhetoric of secrecy and suppression, in turn, seems to have informed the sense of the importance of these printings as moments of "(re)discovery," One of the two known manuscripts, Codex Parisinus Graecus 930 (P), was first published by Cotelier in 1672. We have noted already how this first printed edition

---

[77] I.e., even despite the inclusion in the so-called *Gelasian Decree* (sixth century?) of "the Itinerary in the name of Peter the apostle, which is called the nine books of the holy Clement" (a list that, notably, also includes "the *History* of Eusebius Pamphilii ... the works of Tertullian ... the works of Lactantius ... the works of the other Clement, of Alexandria," and many other writings that are not considered to be "NT apocrypha" at all by our definition today). That the *Recognitions* was commonly known – and also served other purposes – is clear from its survival in over a hundred Latin manuscripts. Note also Aquinas' rather off-handed reference to its ideas about the soul in *Summa Theologiae* 117.4: "Further, in the *Itinerary of Clement* it is said in the narrative of Nicetas to Peter, that Simon Magus, by sorcery retained power over the soul of a child that he had slain, and that through this soul he worked magical wonders. But this could not have been without some corporeal change at least as to place. Therefore, the separate soul has the power to move bodies locally." Aquinas also adduces it as a source for Petrine teachings in his *Commentary on John* § 1761.

[78] On Calvin's knowledge and dismissal of the *Recognitions*, e. g., see Anthony Lane, *John Calvin: Student of the Fathers* (Edinburgh: T&T Clark, 1999), 75–76. Notably, such polemics remained common well into the seventeenth and eighteenth centuries.

was received – as we see from Toland – with the thrill of the possibility that long-lost "apocrypha" might reveal ancient secrets long suppressed, not least with respect to the concept that he thereupon invented as "Jewish-Christianity." So too with the other manuscript. In 1837, in the immediate wake of Baur's initial foray into the Pseudo-Clementines and "Jewish-Christianity," Albertus R. M. Dressel proclaimed his "discovery" of a second, complete manuscript, Codex Vaticanus Ottobonianus 443 (O). Interestingly, Dressel did so in a manner quite similar to the recent claims about *Joseph and Aseneth* as "Lost Gospel" that we noted at the outset – that is, "discovering" an already-known and catalogued but little-publicized manuscript while sitting in a library.[79]

Nevertheless, Dressel's rhetoric served to draw an enormous amount of attention to the text, which is often cited in NT manuals of the time as exemplary of the ways in which manuscript finds could open up entirely new vistas on the Christian past.[80] Part of the optimism about the possibility of new approaches to the New Testament in the age of Baur was precisely predicated this sense that new discoveries could completely upend what was known of the Jewish and Christian past at any moment. Accordingly, it is perhaps not surprising that Baur redeploys some of the rhetoric that we find already in Toland. Nor is it perhaps surprising that popular and scholarly discourse continues to do so today, especially in the wake of mid-twentieth-century discoveries like the Dead Sea Scrolls and Nag Hammadi Library.

Comparison with the reception of the *Recognitions*, however, also helps to highlight the degree to which the reception of the *Epistle of Peter to James* that we traced above is part of a distinctively *Christian* story about shifting ideas of secrecy and suppression. As noted above, the medieval reception of the *Recognitions* in Rufinus' Latin translation repurposed the emphasis on succession in

---

[79] Jones has now shown (*Pseudoclementina*, 9–10) how this manuscript seems to have been known already to Francisco Torres in the sixteenth century and used in his discussions of the *Apostolic Constitutions*. Nevertheless, it did not attract sustained attention until "discovered" and printed by Dressel in 1837. As such, its reception stands as yet another example of the importance of printing in fostering the impression of a modern era of "rediscovery" of supposedly "lost" manuscripts of ancient literature.

[80] One report from the late 1880s reflecting on "new discoveries" recounts the story of Dressel's "discovery" of this manuscript in the Vatican Library and notes the importance of this find for "the speculations of the Tübingen School concerning the early history of the Christian Church" ("Fifty Years of Documentary Discoveries on Church History," *Church Quarterly Review* 25 [1887]: 182–203 at 185–87, with reference to Gotthard Victor Lechler, *Urkundenfunde zur Geschichte des christlichen Altertums* [Leipzig: Alexander Edelmann, 1886]). The place of this "discovery" in the popular imagination is attested in textbooks of the time; Marvin R. Vincent's *Student's New Testament Handbook* (London: James Nisbet, 1893), for instance, includes a listing for Dressel as "Discoverer of the missing portion of the *Homilies* in 1837" (p. 32), and Paton James Gloag's *Introduction to the Synoptic Gospels* (Edinburgh: T&T Clark, 1895) cites Dressel's find as exemplary of how "within the last half century there have been several discoveries of remarkable manuscripts, which have had an important bearing upon various questions connected with biblical criticism" (x).

the Pseudo-Clementine novel to trumpet Peter and Clement for the apostolic succession of what became Roman Catholicism. For this reason, the Clementine authorship of the *Recognitions* was brought into question in the context of Protestant and other anti-Catholic polemics against Papal power. So too for the *Epistle of Clement to James*, especially by virtue of its circulation as part of the Pseudo-Isidorian decretals.[81]

The early modern unmasking of such subapostolic works as forgeries is itself an important element in the genealogy of current notions of Christian history as a story about the suppression of truths about the apostolic past. The Pseudo-Clementine *Recognitions* and *Epistle of Clement of James* have a part in this story – as part of the received heritage of "Apostolic Fathers" thereby rejected as Catholic propaganda. Yet, as we have seen, the early modern "(re)discovery" of the *Epistle of Peter to James* and *Homilies* enabled a different narrative, whereby Peter became associated instead with an authentic past that is uncorrupted by any ecclesiastical power. If anything, Toland's Pseudo-Clementine Peter is not just anti-Paul but also anti-Papal – the secret Peter whose ideas are said to have been perverted by Paul and whose writings are said to have been burned alongside other "apocrypha" at the Council of Nicaea.[82] And, as we have seen, it is precisely the claims in the *Epistle of Peter to James* that make this possible. In place of the common Protestant pairing of anti-Jewish and anti-Catholic polemic, moreover, Toland follows this *Epistle* in deploying Peter's Jewishness as an emblem of the antiquity and authenticity of the true Christianity that was suppressed through the course of Christian history.

---

[81] On the Pseudo-Isidorian decretals in their ninth-century context, see Constance Bouchard, *Rewriting Saints and Ancestors: Memory and Forgetting in France, 500–1200* (Philadelphia: University of Pennsylvania Press, 2014), 77–83. What Bouchard suggests for scholarship on the Middle Ages can be applied to scholarship on the Pseudo-Clementines and Late Antiquity as well: "the modern study of medieval documents long focused on 'what really happened' and thus ignored forged documents completely or at best relegated them to the spuria section of an edition. But if one examines memory as an active process, in which it was but a small step from thinking about the past, to reconceptualizing the lessons of the past, to reworking the past to how it should have been, then forgeries become an important element" (63).

[82] The circulation of such ideas about the Pseudo-Clementine *Recognitions* in the time of Toland is clear from the comments of Thomas Traherne in his *Roman forgeries; or, A true account of false records discovering the impostures and counterfeit antiquities of the Church of Rome* (London, 1673), 184–90, which includes a lengthy discussion of the *Epistle of Clement to James*, complete with quotations. He also comments there on the *Recognitions*: "Among his other Monuments (saith Binius) there are ten books of the circuits of Peter; which by some are called, *The Itinerary of Clement*, by others his *Recognitions*: Which since they are stuffed with Loathsome Fables, and the Fathers abstained from the use of them, as Gelasius also in a Roman Council rejected them for Apocryphal; all wise men will advisedly abstain from reading them. Forgeries are (you see) thick and threefold in the Church of Rome: but this of Clement's *Itinerary*, which Binius disswadeth all men from reading, even ten Books, *Cum insulsis fabulis reserti*, since they are stuft with loathsome Fables, I desire you to take special notice of; because this Confession of his will discover him to be either a false man, or a Fool. It is a delicate Snare" (188).

What, then, of its Jewish reception? For the medieval and early modern periods, evidence is lacking, but we do find interesting examples of the influence of the Pseudo-Clementines on modern Jewish thought, beginning in the nineteenth century in the wake of Baur's studies. For this, the clearest and most influential example is that of Heinrich Graetz, who actually quotes directly from the *Epistle of Peter to James* in his *Geschichte der Juden*. Consistent with his contention that "the development of Christianity, as an offspring of Judaism, so long, namely, as its adherents belonged to the Jewish communion, forms a part of Jewish history," Graetz includes not just Jesus in his Jewish history but also Peter, James, and later "Jewish-Christians" and Ebionites.

In introducing the topic, Graetz largely follows Baur's theory of two conflicting "parties":

The Paulinian doctrine of the superfluity of the Jewish law had thrown into the bosom of primitive Christianity the seed of discord, that split the adherents of Jesus into two great parties, which again branched off into smaller sects with peculiar views and rules of action. Sectarianism did not first arise in Christianity, as is commonly assumed, in the second century, but prevailed at its very inception as a necessary consequence of antagonistic fundamental doctrines. The two parties, which at the very beginning of this period stood directly opposed to each other, were the Jewish Christians, on the one side, the Gentile Christians on the other. The Jewish Christians, as the primitive congregation, being constituted of Jews, clung most closely to Judaism.[83]

In the process, Graetz's account follows a familiar pattern within the Jewish scholarship of his time in citing pro-Torah statements by Jesus. Rather than using such statements only to underline Jesus' own Jewishness, however, he also associates them with the tradition as continued by "Jewish-Christians" – citing, in particular, those sayings from the Gospel of Matthew that are used by the *Epistle of Peter to James* to make this very point:

They observed the Jewish law in all its parts, and pointed to the example of Jesus, who had lived in accordance with the Jewish law. They put into the mouth of the founder of their religion the words: "For verily, I say unto you, 'til heaven and earth pass, one jot or one tittle shall in no wise pass from the law, till all be fulfilled" [Matt 5:18]; again, "Think not, that I am come to destroy the law, or the prophets; I am not come to destroy, but fulfill" [Matt 5:17]. With a directly hostile sentiment against the law-despising Gentile Christians they insisted on the saying of Jesus, "Whosoever shall break one of these least commandments, and shall teach men so, he shall be called the least in the kingdom of heaven but whosoever shall do and teach them, the same shall be called great in the kingdom of heaven" [Matt 5:19].[84]

---

[83] Heinrich Graetz, *History of the Jews*, vol. 4: *From the Downfall of the Jewish State to the Conclusion of the Talmud*, trans. James K. Gutheim (New York: American Jewish Publication Society, 1873), 56.

[84] Graetz, *History of the Jews*, 4:56.

To this, Graetz also added some further information about Ebionites from heresiological literature – albeit reinterpreted in light of his own theory of Christianity's direct lineage from Essenism:

Even the devotion of the Jewish Christians to Jesus was not of the kind to alienate them from Judaism. They regarded him as a holy, morally great man, who had been begotten in a natural way by his parents, Joseph and Mary, from the lineage of David. They assumed, that this son of David had promoted the kingdom of heaven, by teaching men, to live in poverty and humility, to despise riches, and to love and assist each other as brothers, as children of God, and because he had fulfilled the whole law as none before had done. Their motto was the aphorism of Jesus, "Blessed are the poor, for theirs is the kingdom of heaven" [cf. Matt 5:3]. Like the Essenes, from whose midst Christianity has certainly sprung, they lived in a close order, had a common treasury, to which each member had to contribute his property: From this contempt of riches and predilection for poverty they bore the name Ebionites (Needy), which name, however, was interpreted by their Christian opponents into a nickname, as if they were poor in spirit, because they would not recognize Jesus as the only begotten Son of God.[85]

Elsewhere, Graetz depicts Essenism as a perennial force within Jewish history – given expression in Jewish mysticism no less than in some forms of Jewish messianism.[86] Accordingly, the implication here is that the true origins of Christianity forms part of a pattern of *Jewish* history and, moreover, is preserved precisely by those whom the church derided as "heretical" Ebionites.

If Essenism marks the continuity of "Jewish-Christianity" with the rest of Jewish history, for Graetz, so anti-Paulinism marks its increasing discontinuity from what becomes the rest of Christian history:

Paul, his disciples and the congregations founded by them upon the basis of rejecting the law, were bitterly hated by the Jewish Christians. They could not heap too much contumely and defamation on the apostle "of the prepuce," even long after his death, because he had spread errors and taught Christianity against the meaning and intention of its founder.[87]

The Christian account of Christian origins, thus, is here presented as the product of a double erasure – first of the Jewishness of the Essene Jesus by the Hellene Paul and then of the antiquity of "Jewish-Christianity" by later heresiologists. Of "Jewish-Christians," Graetz thus reports that "the Christians did not regard them as the primitive congregation, from which they had primarily sprung themselves with the obliteration of every Jewish trace, but as sectarians of a later date."[88]

---

[85] Graetz, *History of the Jews*, 4:57.

[86] See further Jonathan M. Elukin, "A New Essenism: Heinrich Graetz and Mysticism," *Journal for the History of Ideas* 59 (1998): 135–48, as well as my discussion in Chapters Seven and Ten in this volume.

[87] Graetz, *History of the Jews*, 4:57. On Graetz's views of Paul, see further Daniel R. Langton, "The Myth of the 'Traditional View of Paul' and the Role of the Apostle in Modern Jewish–Christian Polemics," *JSNT* 28 (2005): 69–104 at 77–79.

[88] Graetz, *History of the Jews*, 4:57.

In this, Graetz largely follows Baur. Yet he innovates from both Jewish and Christian scholarly precedents by virtue of his historical application of the Pseudo-Clementines. Elsewhere, I have discussed these dynamics in relation to Jewish messianism as well as Jewish mysticism.[89] Here, my interest is in the work that is done by the *Epistle of Peter to James* in articulating a distinctively Jewish variation of the above-noted narrative of the origins of Christianity as a suppressed history that can be recovered especially from "apocrypha." Graetz, after all, does not limit himself to quoting the New Testament, and neither does he focus only on Jesus when asserting the Jewishness from which Christianity originated. In his account, rather, the *Epistle of Peter to James* is framed and quoted as the voice of those "Jewish-Christians" that history would have otherwise silenced. Accordingly, it makes sense that he chooses to quote the much-repeated lines in which Peter laments the misrepresentation of his teachings by Gentiles followers of his "enemy." What is notable, however, is that Graetz chooses to expand this quote to include precisely the context that Toland and Baur omit – namely: the *Epistle*'s presentation of Judaism as a model to emulate for the transmission of apostolic truth.

Graetz describes "Jewish-Christians" as admiring of the Sages of Yavneh, and he does so in terms taken directly from the *Epistle of Peter to James*:

With a kind of admiration of the unity and unanimity which prevailed within the Jewish body, guided by the Jamnian Synhedrin, in contrast to the dissensions and divergences within the Christian congregation, a member of the Jewish Christian party wrote: "The widely scattered Jews observe, to this day, the same law concerning the unity of God and practices of life, and can by no means entertain a diverging opinion, or be induced to deviate from the settled meaning of the ambiguous words of Scripture. For it is by traditionary rules that they try to reconcile the ambiguous passages of Scripture. For this reason they permit no one to teach who has not first learned how to expound the Sacred Writings. Hence they have one God, one law, one hope ... If we do not adopt the same system, the one word of truth will be split into many opinions. I do not know this as a prophet, but because I have looked into the root of the evil. For some of the Gentiles had spurned my message, which agreed with the law, by following the lawless and farcical doctrine of an adversary (Paul)" [*Ep. Pet.* 1.3]. These words are attributed to the second chief apostle, Simon Kephas [i. e., Peter].[90]

For Graetz, it is this appeal to the unity of the Jewish people that allows the evidence for "Jewish-Christians" to speak to Jewish history, in general, and the story of the rise of the Rabbis, more specifically. In his hands, Baur's theory of the "two parties" is thus reread in terms of "dissensions and divergences" rampant in Christianity from its beginnings, and the *Epistle of Peter to James* further enables the contrast with Jewish unity under the leadership of the Sages at and after the so-called "Council of Yavneh/Jamnia." In the process, Paul is presented

---

[89] See Chapters Seven and Ten in this volume.
[90] Graetz, *History of the Jews*, 4:57.

as a caesura in Jewish history – the moment of rupture that eventually results in the emergence of a Christianity that forgets its roots in Judaism. What Graetz shares with the *Epistle* itself (and the Pseudo-Clementines more broadly) is thus a sense of supersessionism as essentially an act of suppression. It is in this sense that Graetz – and his distinctive use of the Pseudo-Clementines – also proves influential for what becomes a common modern Jewish notion of Christianity as the product of Paul's severing of its connections with Judaism.

It is perhaps telling, for instance, that the 1907 *Jewish Encyclopedia* entry on "Saul of Tarsus" can begin with the simple assertion of Paul as "the *actual* founder of the Christian Church as opposed to Judaism."[91] This encyclopedia synthesized the results of nineteenth-century German Jewish *Wissenschaft des Judentums* for a popular English-speaking audience in the United States, and its inclusion of a number of entries on early Christianity extend, in many ways, the basic pattern already set by Geiger and Graetz. Significantly, for our purposes, the main points of innovation and extension are precisely in relation to the historical value granted to "NT apocrypha."

The *Jewish Encyclopedia* entries on Christianity were authored almost wholly by Kauffman Kohler, who is best remembered today as an early leader of Reform Judaism in America.[92] Yet his scholarly work, here and elsewhere, was shaped by a concerted interest in culling "NT apocrypha" to recover the Jewishness of the Christian past. If Graetz's account of the apostolic age exemplifies the Jewish purposes to which Baur's theories about ancient Christianity could be put, then, Kohler shows how readily Toland's approach to "apocrypha" could be redeployed to recover Christian sources for ancient Judaism as well.

Kohler's entry on Peter, for instance, begins by summarily dismissing the historicity of the account in the NT Book of Acts.[93] Kohler even goes so far as

---

[91] Kauffman Kohler, "Saul of Tarsus," in *The Jewish Encyclopedia*, ed. Isidore Singer et al (12 vols.; New York: Funk & Wagnalls, 1907), 11:79; italics mine. On Kohler's views of Paul, see further Langston, "Myth of the Traditional View of Paul," 79–81.

[92] On Kohler's scholarship in relation to his life, see esp. Yaakov Ariel, "Christianity through Reform Eyes: Kaufmann Kohler's Scholarship on Christianity," *American Jewish History* 89 (2001): 181–91. Although sorely understudied, Kohler's ideas are significant due to their impact on popular and scholarly Jewish perceptions of Christianity through the *Jewish Encyclopedia*. Furthermore, Ariel observes that "Kohler stood at the centre of almost every development, as well as controversy, in American Jewish life between the 1870s and the end of his presidency of the Hebrew Union College in the early 1920s"; "*Wissenschaft des Judentums* Comes to America: Kaufmann Kohler's Scholarly Projects and Jewish-Christian Relations," in *Die Entdeckung des Christentums in der Wissenschaft des Judentums*, ed. Gorge K. Hasselhoff (Berlin: de Gruyter, 2010), 165–82 at 167. On Kohler in contrast to more recent reflection on Jesus and Christianity among American Jews, see Shaul Magid, *American Post-Judaism* (Bloomington: Indiana University Press, 2013), 131–56, esp. 147, 151, 308.

[93] Kauffman Kohler, "Simon Cephas," in *Jewish Encyclopedia*, 11:366–68 – there stating quite unequivocally that "the acts recorded of Peter (in Acts i. 15, ii. 14 et seq., iii. 1–11, iv. 8 et seq., v. 29 et seq., viii. 14 et seq., ix. 32, x. 1–xi. 18, xv. 4 et seq.) cannot claim historical character" (11:366).

to proclaim that "Little value can ... be attached to Gal. ii. 9 (a spurious epistle), where Peter is charged by Paul with hypocrisy."[94] Between his denigration of Acts and his dismissal of Galatians, however, Kohler includes a long section on Peter in the Pseudo-Clementines that asserts the apostle's Jewishness:

The representation of Peter found in the Clementine writings, especially in those parts based upon older sources (the "*Kerygma Petri*"?) ... is quite different from that given in the Acts. The speeches of Peter in Acts iii. 13–26 and elsewhere are animated by the same spirit of hostility to the Jews which pervades the Gospels; the Peter of the Clementines is, in speech and mode of living, a Jew. He departs from Judaism only in that he recognizes in the crucified Jesus the "Prophet" predicted by Moses (Deut. xviii. 15), and through whom sacrifice was abolished and baptism substituted therefore .... He lays all possible stress upon the Law, while the Prophets are secondary. On the other hand, he calls Paul "an enemy" of the Church .... But he is especially insistent on the prohibition against eating with the Gentiles, unless they be baptized, and on "abstaining from the table of devils," that is, from food offered to idols and from dead carcasses, from animals suffocated or torn by wild beasts, and from blood. He insists also upon washing after every pollution, and upon the observance of the Levitical purifications by both sexes .... In the original "Preaching of Peter," thirty, or sixty, or one hundred commandments for the Jewish converts are singled out (comp. *Ḥul.* 92a; *Midr. Teh. to Ps.* ii. 5; *Gen. R.* xcviii. 14). "Man is the true image of God" (not Christ only!); "The pure soul bears His likeness"; "therefore we must honor God's image by offering food to the hungry and clothing to the naked, caring for the sick, sheltering the stranger, visiting him who is in prison, and affording the "needy all the help we can" ("*Homilies,*" xi. 4, xvii. 7). Accordingly, Peter acts in regard to food, prayers, fasts, and ablutions exactly as does a pious Jew.[95]

The entry goes on to follow the Pseudo-Clementines for details on the life and travels of Peter while continuing to deny the antiquity of NT accounts of Peter (e. g., 1 and 2 Peter). In addition, Kohler stresses that the Pseudo-Clementine "passages show the close relation of this teaching, attributed to Peter, to that of the rabbinical schools."[96] Not only does he follow the *Epistle of Peter to James* in referring to Paul as an "enemy," but he similarly uses the *Jewishness* of early Christian documents as the measure of their antiquity and authenticity.

So too in his entry on "Saul of Tarsus." There, Kohler notes that "records containing the views and opinions of the opponents of Paul and Paulinism are no longer in existence."[97] Nevertheless, he takes for granted that "the history of the early Church has been colored by the writers of the second century, who were anxious to suppress or smooth over the controversies of the preceding period, as is shown in the Acts of the Apostles."[98] Following Baur, Graetz, et

---

[94] Kohler, "Simon Cephas," 11:367.

[95] Kohler, "Simon Cephas," 11:367.

[96] Kohler, "Simon Cephas," 11:367–68.

[97] Kohler, "Saul of Tarsus," 11:79.

[98] Kohler, "Saul of Tarsus," 11:79 – i. e., as in the position of Baur discussed above. Notably, Kohler was trained in Germany before moving to America and took much inspiration from Geiger in particular. Yaakov Ariel aptly describes the productive ambivalence of his relationship

al., Kohler discusses "Jewish-Christians" as anti-Pauline, citing both from the Pseudo-Clementines (in this case: *Rec.* 1.70–73) and from Patristic references to Ebionites.[99] Likewise, his familiarity with the Pseudo-Clementines is clear from his passing reference to how Paul was "different from Simon Magus … with whom he was at times maliciously identified by his opponents."[100] Ultimately, however, his own narrative of Christian origins echoes this very polemic: Kohler consistently laments the Hellenizing innovations of Paul, and he adduces the Pseudo-Clementines to propose that the earliest Christians did not share those Pauline beliefs that Kohler most condemns (e. g., Trinity, deification of Jesus).[101] Daniel Langston thus posits that Kohler, along with Graetz, "arguably should be credited with the formation and establishment of the traditional Jewish view of the apostle Paul itself," as marked by the "reclamation of Jesus as a Jew and a new interest in Paul as the proper (negative) representative of Christianity";[102] if so, it is notable that the Pseudo-Clementines play a part in the very partitioning of Christian history and literature that makes this possible.

What Kohler does for the Pseudo-Clementines, largely following Graetz, he also extends to a number of other "NT apocrypha." His contention that "apoc-

---

to German Protestant scholarship: "The acceptance of the Higher Criticism of the Bible had a deep meaning for Kohler's intellectual life and public agenda. Adopting what was in essence a German Protestant academic methodology, he had to contend with its Jewish unfriendly nature. He would find himself spending much of his intellectual efforts trying to correct what he considered to be a biased Christian interpretation, which treated Judaism with contempt. In that he was not different from a number of German Jewish *Wissenschaft des Judentums* scholars, who, while accepting in principle the methodologies of the German academic disciplines, wished to defend Judaism from what they considered uneven theories and to offer a Jewish correction to the Christian conclusions"; "*Wissenschaft des Judentums* Comes to America," 166.

[99] Kohler, "Saul of Tarsus," 11:80. Note also the entry on "Antinomianism" by Kohler and Ginzberg (1:630–32), where the Pseudo-Clementine *Recognitions* is quoted in relation to the problem of Paul's purported rejection of the Jewish Law: "If it be asked how came it that Paul, the former Jew, the strict Pharisee, arrived at a conception of the Law so offensive to the Jewish standpoint, the reply must be made that he learned the art of destroying the Law by the Law, or, as the author of the Clementine writings has it, *ex lege discere quod nesciebat lex* ('Recognitiones,' ii. 54), from his Pharisaic masters."

[100] Kohler, "Saul of Tarsus," 11:86.

[101] In his *Jewish Encyclopedia* entry on "Trinity" with Samuel Krauss (12:260–71), e.g., Kohler cites the *Homilies* as evidence for resistance to the development of ideas about the divinity of Jesus: "Although the Judæo-Christian sect of the Ebionites protested against this apotheosis of Jesus ('Clementine Homilies,' xvi. 15), the great mass of Gentile Christians accepted it." In his entry on "Christianity in Relation to Judaism" (4.49–59), Kohler similarly proclaims that "in vain did the early Christians protest against the deification of Jesus ('Clementine Homilies,' xvi. 15)" – perhaps tellingly, "Jewish-Christian" is here elided with "early Christian."

[102] Langton, "Myth of the Traditional View of Paul," 77, 80. Langton also adds Martin Buber to this list. His logic here is that "for those Jewish thinkers in the nineteenth and twentieth centuries who wished to define themselves against Christianity, Paul came to replace Jesus as a symbol of Christianity *per se*. For those concerned to defend themselves against Christian critique of Judaism, Jesus had become more useful as a good Jew rather than the preeminent symbol of the antithesis of Judaism; and Paul emerged as his unfortunate successor" (103).

rypha" preserve something of what is suppressed in the New Testament, for instance, is clear from his treatment of the *Acts of Paul and Thecla:* not only does he quote its physical description of Paul, but he describes it as "an apocryphal book which has been proved to be older and in some respects of greater historic value than the canonical Acts of the Apostles."[103] Even as he dismisses most of the Pauline Epistles (including Romans and Galatians!) as second-century creations, moreover, Kohler looks to the *Didache* and *Didascalia apostolorum* as Christian sources that preserve a more ancient Jewish tradition. It is this Jewish tradition that he suggests "made it possible for Paul and his associates to establish Christianity among the Gentiles" and also served as the basis for the best of its ideas; in his view, for instance, "it is exactly from such synagogue manuals for proselytes as the *Didache* and the *Didascalia* that the ethical teachings in the Epistles of Paul and of Peter were derived."[104]

Kohler, in effect, pushes the above-noted trope of secrecy and suppression to its logical conclusion: if Pseudo-Clementine and other "NT apocrypha" are really sources that preserve suppressed secrets from and about Christianity's Jewish past, then they are also sources for ancient Judaism. The overwritten Jewishness of Christianity, thus, opens opportunities for the scholar to reread some "NT apocrypha" with an eye to older Jewish materials integrated therein. It is by reasoning along these lines, in fact, that Kohler made his most significant and lasting contribution to scholarship on both Judaism and Christianity, famously discovering pre-Christian Jewish liturgical materials embedded in the fourth-century Christian *Apostolic Constitutions*.[105]

Less well-known today, but no less notable, was his attempt to use such "apocrypha" to try to reconstruct an ancient Jewish reform movement that he posited as influential on the development of both Rabbinic Judaism, via the Pharisees, and early Christianity, via the Essenes, John the Baptist, and Jesus.[106] Through this reconstruction, Kohler argues for the profound Jewishness of Jesus in a manner that is indebted to Geiger and Graetz but also highly original. Kohler, as Yaakov Ariel notes, "believed that Jesus was inspired by the Hasidim, whom Kohler defined as a virtuous and ascetic group that served as the avant-garde of the Pharisees," and as a result, "the pedigree of Christianity was good since it

---

[103] Kohler, "Saul of Tarsus," 11:79–80. See also Kaufman Kohler and Samuel Krauss, "Simon Magus," in *Jewish Encyclopedia*, 11:371–73.

[104] Kohler, "Saul of Tarsus," 11:81.

[105] Kauffman Kohler, "Über die Ursprünge und Grundformen der synagogalen Liturgie: eine Studie," *Monatsschrift für Geschichte und Wissenschaft des Judentums* 11 (1893): 489–97; Kohler, "The Origin and Composition of the Eighteen Benedictions with a Translation of the Corresponding Essene Prayers in the *Apostolic Constitutions*," *HUCA* 1 (1924): 387–425.

[106] I.e., following Graetz rather than Geiger. For a summary of this theory, see Kohler's entry on "The Essenes" in the *Jewish Encyclopedia* (5:224–32). The broader implications are expounded in a later synthetic book on the topic, published posthumously: Kohler, *The Origins of the Synagogue and the Church* (New York: Macmillian, 1929).

started as a righteous Jewish sect."[107] In effect, Kohler offered a new solution to the problem of whether Jesus was a Pharisee or an Essene by positing the Hasidim as a more ancient movement related to both.

This filiation, in turn, enabled his culling of "NT apocrypha," not just to recover *Christian* history, but also to recover *Jewish* history. The implications were hardly limited to the question of the precise place of Judaism in the origins of Christianity. The result – Ariel suggest – is the reconstruction of a pre-Christian Jewish movement that also recalls the Reform Judaism of his own time:

He credited the Hasidim for bringing about many of the meaningful, and in his view positive, developments in Judaism in the generations before and during Jesus' era. Among other things, he claimed that the Hasidim were the ones who invented the synagogue and turned it into the preferred gathering place in Jewish life. When Kohler writes on the Hasidim one can sense that he sees himself and his movement as following in the footsteps of what he considers the avant-garde of a developing Judaism, a movement that pioneered in adjusting Judaism to the changing times.[108]

For our present purposes, it suffices to note that Kohler also took a similar approach to the Pseudo-Clementines, taking seriously the texts' own claims to be "Christian" in a manner that is simultaneously and completely "Jewish."[109] The *Jewish Encyclopedia* thus dedicates an entire entry to the Pseudo-Clementines, which focuses mostly on the *Homilies* and emphasizes parallels in Jewish literature. Most such parallels concern the points of seeming contact and concern with Rabbinic tradition noted above. Some, however, extend Graetz's earlier explorations of possible connections with Jewish mysticism.[110] Perhaps most striking, however, is that this "Jewish-Christian" corpus is treated as so much as part of Judaism that references to this corpus occur even in entries not focused on Christianity, such as those on blood, dualism, *Sefer Yetzirah*, the Kabbalah, and Adam Kadmon; especially in Kohler's entries, moreover, this corpus is sometimes adduced simply as an example of Essenism or "Jewish *gnosis*" rather than "Jewish-Christianity" *per se*.[111] In effect, Kohler puts into practice what Toland outlines in theory as the power of "apocrypha" to preserve the Jewishness of

---

[107] Ariel, "Christianity through Reform Eyes," 183–84.

[108] Ariel, "Christianity through Reform Eyes," 183.

[109] Kauffman Kohler, "Clementina, or Pseudo-Clementine Literature," in *Jewish Encyclopedia*, 4:114–16. Contrast the treatment of Christian literary materials in the more recent *Encyclopedia Judaica*, which does not dedicate whole entries to these or other "NT apocrypha" but only to "Church Fathers" like Origen and Jerome.

[110] See Chapter Ten in this volume. In the *Jewish Encyclopedia*, the debt to Graetz's treatment of the Pseudo-Clementines is clearest in the entries on "Sefer Yetzirah" (12:602–6) and on "Cabala" (3:456–479), both of which Kohler coauthored with Loius Ginzberg.

[111] It is clear that Kohler's hand is here at work. The Pseudo-Clementines are cited as evidence for the Essenes, for instance, in the entry on "Dualism" that Kohler cowrites with Emil G. Hirsch (*Jewish Encyclopedia*, 5:5). But they are adduced more specifically as evidence for "Jewish-Christianity" in the entry on "Adam Kadmon" by Louis Ginzberg (1:181–83) and in entry on "Blood" by Marcus Jastrow and Hermann L. Strack (3:259–60).

the Christian past, and in the process, he also reads a number of "apocrypha" through the lens of the *Epistle of Peter to James* and *Homilies*, wherein authentically ancient apostolic tradition is actually a variety of Judaism.

Censorship between Cultural Amnesia and Cultural Creativity

In a recent monograph on memory and forgetting in medieval France, Constance Bouchard suggests that there is much to be learned from those documents commonly dismissed as "forgeries":

> The modern study of medieval documents long focused on "what really happened" and thus ignored forged documents completely or at best relegated them to the *spuria* section of an edition. But if one examines memory as an active process, in which it was but a small step from thinking about the past, to reconceptualizing the lessons of the past, to reworking the past to how it should have been, then forgeries become an important element.[112]

The example of the *Epistle of Peter to James* shows how such documents can also come to shape how questions are even asked about "what really happened" and which sources are used to answer them and how. Above, we have seen how the modern reception of this *Epistle* has contributed to the naturalization of an idea of "apocrypha" as potentially "untainted" sources that speak to a suppressed past – especially in relation to the Jewish past overwritten in and by the New Testament. The results may often skew historical scholarship, but at the same time, the phenomenon also remains important in its own right. Just as forgetting and overwriting are critical components of cultural memory, so acts of erasure (whether real or imagined) open up spaces for creative reencounters with the past.

If our current sense of "apocrypha" as repositories of "lost" or "suppressed" truths about the religious past thus has some precedent in Late Antiquity no less than early modernity, it is perhaps in the power of the rhetoric of secrecy and suppression to posit ruptures in the past that also open new spaces for reflection on what came prior. In the case of Toland and Baur, the pairing of secrecy and suppression in the *Epistle of Peter to James* facilitates an argument for "apocrypha" as valuable sources for Christian history, relativizing, supplementing, and subverting the New Testament. Together with the *Homilies*, this *Epistle* also inspires more concerted reflection on Christianity's Jewishness as well as the possibility of forms of Christianity that are not defined in contrast to Judaism. In the case of Graetz and Kohler, the Pseudo-Clementines enable the recovery of some of Christian literature and history as Jewish literature and history. What the seeming anti-Paulinism of the Pseudo-Clementines, in particular, allows for the partitioning of a period of Christianity's Jewish past, before Paul, as an

---

[112] Bouchard, *Rewriting Saints and Ancestors*, 63.

era readily (re)appropriated as part of the history of the Jews. The possibility of a distinctive "Jewish-Christianity" in continued competition with Paulinism, moreover, opens the door for some Christian sources to be culled for information about Judaism even after Paul – especially in the case of "apocrypha" that claim to have preserved in secret precisely what needed to be protected from suppression.

These dynamics in the modern reception of the Pseudo-Clementines, however, point to what is perhaps the most powerful function of the trope of secrecy and suppression within the *Epistle of Peter to James* itself – that is, to overwrite its own origins as a product of the third or fourth century, rather than the first. As we have seen, Toland totally takes for granted that the *Epistle of Peter to James* is a source that speaks to the first and second centuries – so much so, in fact, that he cites its supposed later "loss" as evidence for the burning and suppression of "apocrypha" in precisely the era in which it was actually composed. Baur, Graetz, and Kohler treat the Pseudo-Clementines as later and pseudonymous. Nonetheless, their use of these materials remain oriented to Jesus and the apostolic age. Even when this *Epistle* is presented as a forgery in the name of Peter, it is still treated as possibly preserving secret Jewish knowledge about the very origins of Christianity and, thus, as potentially subverting the images of the first-century past in Christian Scripture. And this characterization continues to shape scholarship on these and other "apocrypha" – both in the assumption that their significance lies in their relevance for Christian Origins and in the dominance of source-critical approaches that seek to extract possible earlier sources from within them.

When we consider the *Epistle of Peter to James* in its own context, however, we can see that its authors/redactors engage in much the same project as its modern readers – namely, revisiting the first century with an eye to the silences and tensions in the New Testament. At a precarious moment of historical and cultural change, perched at the precipice of the Christianization of the Roman Empire, the authors/redactors of this *Epistle* looked back to the age of the apostles, to ponder what might have been silenced or suppressed. In this, moreover, they were not alone: in the fourth century, in particular, a number of Christians were also selectively compiling, consolidating, and textualizing the received literary heritage of the apostolic past, and a number of Jews were doing the same for the tannaitic past as well. And, in each of these cases – as for Toland, Baur, Graetz, and Kohler – what appears to have been lost or forgotten is also precisely what opened up a new space for creative reengagement with the Jewishness of the Christian past.

Chapter Nine

When Did Rabbis Become Pharisees?*

When did Pharisees become Rabbis? Beginning already in the 1970s, Peter Schäfer returned to the primary data to interrogate the conventional wisdom concerning their connection.[1] At the time, it was still a truism that Pharisees became Rabbis, and Judaism became Rabbinic, soon after the fall of the Second Temple in 70 CE. The equation of the two had long contributed to the representation of the tannaim as already the leaders of Palestinian Jewry and to the resultant reading of the Mishnah as a mirror of "normative" Jewish practice.[2] Not only

---

* This chapter was originally published in 2013 as "When Did Rabbis Become Pharisees? Reflections on Christian Evidence for Post-70 Judaism," in *Envisioning Judaism: Essays in Honor of Peter Schäfer on the Occasion of his Seventieth Birthday*, ed. Raʿanan S. Boustan et al. (TSAJ 119; Tübingen: Mohr Siebeck, 2013), 2:859–96. As with so much else, it had its seed in a conversation with Peter Schäfer during my time as his research assistant at Princeton; I dearly miss our daily conversations during those idyllic years, and I am delighted for the opportunity to express a bit of my gratitude to Peter. Earlier versions were presented at the Katz Center for Advanced Judaic Studies at the University of Pennsylvania on 17 October 2007 and at Duke University on 8 March 2013. The present version reflects further research supported by my fellowship-year at the Katz Center. Part four of this essay also draws on work with Ingrid Heidelberger on the interpretation of the Gospel of Matthew in the Pseudo-Clementine literature, as supported by a Penn Undergraduate Research Mentorship summer grant. This version has been revised and updated. It is reprinted here with permission from Mohr Siebeck.

[1] Peter Schäfer, "Die sogenannte Synode von Jabne: Zur Trennung von Juden und Christen im ersten/zweiten Jahrhundert n. Chr.," *Judaica* 31 (1975): 54–64, 116–24; Schäfer, "Die Flucht Johanan b. Zakkai aus Jerusalem und die Gründung des 'Lehrhauses' in Jabne," *ANRW* 2.19.2 (1979): 43–101; Schäfer, *Der Bar Kokhba-Aufstand: Studien zum zweiten jüdischen Krieg gegen Rom* (TSAJ 1; Tübingen: Mohr Siebeck, 1981); Schäfer, "Der vorrabbinische Pharisaismus," in *Paulus und das antike Judentum*, ed. M. Hengel and U. Heckel (WUNT 58; Tübingen: Mohr Siebeck, 1991), 125–76. On the broader context within the fields of Rabbinics and Jewish history, see Seth Schwartz, "Historiography on the Jews in the 'Talmudic Period': 70–640 CE," in *The Oxford Handbook of Jewish Studies*, ed. Martin Goodman (Oxford: Oxford University Press, 2002), 79–114, and further bibliography there, with discussion of Schäfer at 104–6. See below for the context in New Testament Studies.

[2] For the classic articulation of Pharisaic dominance, see Louis Finkelstein, *The Pharisees: The Sociological Background of Their Faith* (2 vols.; Philadelphia: JPS, 1938); the relevant Rabbinic sources are collected in Jacob Neusner, *The Rabbinic Traditions about the Pharisees before 70* (3 vols.; Leiden: Brill, 1971), which concludes with a detailed bibliographical essay on earlier trends and studies (3:320–68). For a concise summary of the shift that concerns us here, engaging and extending Schäfer's work, see Catherine Hezser, *The Social Structure of the Rabbinic Movement in Roman Palestine* (TSAJ 66; Tübingen: Mohr Siebeck, 1997), 69. For further bibliography, together with more recent trajectories, see Daniel R. Schwartz, "Introduction: Was 70 CE a Watershed in Jewish History?" in *Was 70 CE a Watershed in Jewish*

did Schäfer help to expose the questionable historicity of modern narratives about Yavneh/Jamnia, but he pointed to the surprising paucity of early evidence for any simple connection between Pharisees and Rabbis. Both through his own publications and through his support of others, he contributed to bringing the relationship of "Pharisaism" and "Rabbinism" into the arena of data-driven debate.

In the late 1990s and early 2000s, one sees a new picture of late antique Judaism taking shape – perhaps especially in the pages of conference proceedings and book series edited by Schäfer.[3] In place of the view of the Rabbis as a unified group that took on the mantle of Jewish leadership in the immediate aftermath of the first Jewish Revolt, new accounts posited the slow spread of Rabbinic influence in the first four centuries of the Common Era – imagined less in terms of the leaders and academies of later times, and more in terms of networks of teachers and students with an initially limited sway on the practices and piety of the populace.[4] In place of the view of Pharisaic/Rabbinic authority as ratified, institutionalized, or officialized at a "synod" or "council," new questions were raised concerning the subtle and informal ways in which early Rabbis – like other subelites and purveyors of *paideia* in the Roman Empire, and like other holy men in Late Antiquity – amassed social prestige and cultural capital.[5] In the process, a number of once-common assumptions have been called into question, including the Roman imperial patronage of the tannaim, the utility of the Mishnah as a transparently descriptive account of normative Jewish practice, and the "official" closure of the biblical canon and

---

History? On Jews and Judaism before and after the Destruction of the Second Temple, ed. Daniel R. Schwartz and Zeev Weiss (Ancient Judaism and Early Christianity 78; Leiden: Brill, 2012), 1–19; note, however, that Schäfer and other German scholars are largely absent from his survey of the newer perspectives emerging since the 1970s (pp. 8–15), even despite the insightful treatment of German scholarship in the summary of earlier research (pp. 6–8).

[3] In addition to the various TSAJ and Princeton University Press publications cited above and below, see Peter Schäfer, ed., *The Talmud Yerushalmi and Graeco-Roman Culture I* (TSAJ 71; Tübingen: Mohr Siebeck, 1998); Schäfer and Catherine Heszer, ed., *The Talmud Yerushalmi and Graeco-Roman Culture II* (TSAJ 79; Tübingen: Mohr Siebeck, 2000); Schäfer, ed., *The Talmud Yerushalmi and Graeco-Roman Culture III* (TSAJ 93; Tübingen: Mohr Siebeck, 2002); Schäfer, ed., *The Bar Kokhba War Reconsidered: New Perspectives on the Second Jewish Revolt against Rome* (TSAJ 100; Tübingen: Mohr Siebeck, 2003).

[4] E. g., Hezser, *Social Structure of the Rabbinic Movement*; Hezser, "Social Fragmentation, Plurality of Opinion, and Nonobservance of Halacha: Rabbis and Community in Late Roman Palestine," *JSQ* 1 (1993–1994): 234–51; Hayim Lapin, "The Origins and Development of the Rabbinic Movement in the Land of Israel," in *Cambridge History of Judaism*, vol. 4: *The Late Roman-Rabbinic Period*, ed. Steven T. Katz (Cambridge: Cambridge University Press, 2006), 206–29.

[5] E. g., Shaye J. D. Cohen, "The Place of the Rabbi in the Jewish Society of the Second Century" (1992), repr. in Cohen, *The Significance of Yavneh and Other Essays in Jewish Hellenism* (TSAJ 136; Tübingen: Mohr Siebeck, 2010), 282–96; Seth Schwartz, *Imperialism and Jewish Society: 200 BCE to 640 CE* (Princeton: Princeton University Press, 2001), 101–214. For a synthesis, see now Hayim Lapin, *Rabbis as Romans: The Rabbinic Movement in Palestine, 100–400* (Oxford: Oxford University Press, 2012).

expulsion of Christians at Yavneh.[6] Among the results have been a waning of confidence in the possibility of reconstructing a single "Pharisaic-Rabbinic Judaism" by correlating Rabbinic traditions with references to Pharisees from Josephus and the New Testament,[7] and an intensification of debate about the degree of continuity in Palestinian Judaism after the failed rebellions of the first and second centuries CE.[8]

Such critical reappraisals have inspired renewed efforts to redescribe late antique Judaism in a manner that does justice not only to classical Rabbinic literature but also to other Jewish literary, archaeological, and documentary data, on the one hand, and to contextualizing and comparative evidence for Roman imperial and provincial cultures, on the other.[9] In what follows, I would like to explore some of the profits and pitfalls of bringing Christian literary evidence to bear on this enterprise as well. To do so, I trace representations of Pharisees from the Gospel of Matthew in the late first century to the Pseudo-Clementine *Homilies* in the early fourth century, with special attention to Matthew 23 and its history of interpretation. My question is the opposite of that with which we began; instead of asking when Pharisees became Rabbis, I am here interested in when Rabbis became Pharisees – or, rather, when Christian authors began to interpret the Pharisees of Jesus' time as equivalent to the Rabbis of their own.[10]

---

[6] See sources cited above, as well as Martin Jacobs, *Die Institution des jüdischen Patriarchen: Eine quellen- und traditionskritische Studie zur Geschichte der Juden in der Spätantike* (TSAJ 52; Tübingen: Mohr Siebeck, 1995); Daniel Boyarin, "A Tale of Two Synods: Nicaea, Yavneh, and the Early History of Orthodox Judaism," *Exemplaria* 12 (2000): 21–62; Boyarin, "Justin Martyr Invents Judaism," *CH* 70 (2001): 427–32.

[7] At least among historians of Judaism. See below, however, on New Testament scholarship.

[8] The most prominent case for disjuncture has been made by Seth Schwartz in *Imperialism and Jewish Society*, 103, 129, and passim; see also Schwartz, "Was there a 'Common Judaism' after the Destruction?" in Boustan et al., *Envisioning Judaism*, 1:1–21. Note also the reflections on the historiography of continuity versus rupture between the first Jewish revolt and the Bar Kokhba revolt in Peter Schäfer, "Bar Kokhba and the Rabbis," in *Bar Kokhba War Reconsidered*, 1–22. For more recent reflections – and reactions – see the essays in Schwartz and Weiss, *Was 70 CE a Watershed*; and section 2 of Lee I. Levine and Daniel R. Schwartz, eds., *Jewish Identities in Antiquity: Studies in Memory of Menahem Stern* (TSAJ 130; Tübingen: Mohr Siebeck, 2009).

[9] The most influential precedent remains the work of E. R. Goodenough; see esp. *Jewish Symbols in the Greco-Roman Period*, vol. 12: *Summary and Conclusions* (New York: Pantheon, 1965), 184–98 – the implications of which were only gradually explored. Examples from the 1980s relevant for our purposes include Shaye J. D. Cohen, "Epigraphical Rabbis" (1981), repr. in Cohen, *Significance of Yavneh*, 227–43; Peter Schäfer, *Synopse zur Hekhalot-Literatur* (TSAJ 2; Tübingen: Mohr, 1981); Schäfer, *Hekhalot-Studien* (TSAJ 19; Tübingen: Mohr, 1988). A recent burst of renewed efforts to characterize late antique Judaism on the basis of other types of data is evident, for instance, in recent volumes such as Zeev Weiss et al., eds., *"Follow the Wise": Studies in Jewish History and Culture in Honor of Lee I. Levine* (Winona Lake: Eisenbrauns, 2010); and Natalie B. Dohrmann and Annette Yoshiko Reed, eds., *Jews, Christians, and the Roman Empire: The Poetics of Power in Late Antiquity* (Philadelphia: University of Pennsylvania Press, 2013).

[10] I.e., the Rabbis of the Mishnah, etc. The title "rabbi" appears in Matt 23:7 in relation to

To what degree might the patterns in the Christian evidence correlate with what we know about the self-representation and status of the Sages whom we know from the Mishnah, Tosefta, and Talmudim, and what might these "outside" perspectives reveal about visibility of Rabbinic Jews as a distinct set of local legal/ritual experts in the Roman Near East?

At least since the 1960s,[11] specialist research on the New Testament has engaged the possibility that the Pharisees of the gospels might encode the Rabbis of the time of the gospel writers (i. e., late first century CE). In the spirit of the above-cited works by Schäfer – and his broader contribution to correcting the misapplication of late antique Jewish sources to the study of the New Testament[12] – sections one and two of this essay use Matthew 23 as a test case for assessing scholarly attempts to align New Testament references to Pharisees with early Rabbinic history. I focus on a line of research that has sought to explain Matthew's anti-Jewish polemics as responses to the purported triumph of the Pharisees and/or the Rabbinic institution of the *birkat ha-minim* allegedly at Yavneh/Jamnia – an approach that became popular around the same time that specialist research in Rabbinics was shedding doubt on the historicity of these very notions of Rabbinic self-definition and authority.[13] What I shall suggest is that this test case offers an apt locus for reflecting on the methodological challenges of correlating Christian and Jewish histories more generally.

That the potential value of Christian evidence for the historiography of Judaism is not exhausted by the New Testament, however, has been richly demonstrated by Schäfer as well, particularly in recent publications such as *Die Geburt des Judentums aus dem Geist des Christentums*.[14] In the third and fourth sections

---

Pharisees, but the questions remains whether its usage is yet specific to the movement that we now call "Rabbinic"; see further below.

[11] Most influentially: W. D. Davies, *The Setting of the Sermon on the Mount* (Cambridge: Cambridge University Press, 1964).

[12] E. g., Peter Schäfer, "New Testament and Hekhalot Literature: The Journey into Heaven in Paul and In Merkavah Mysticism," *JJS* 35 (1984): 19–35, as well as his above-cited "Die sogenannte Synode von Jabne" and "Der vorrabbinische Pharisaismus."

[13] For the classic formulation, see W. D. Davies and Dale C. Allison, *A Critical and Exegetical Commentary on the Gospel according to Matthew* (3 vols.; Edinburgh: T&T Clark, 1988–1997), 1:133–38. The continued influence of Davies' ideas about Matthew and Yavneh is noted and charted by Donald Senior, *The Gospel of Matthew* (Nashville: Abingdon, 2011), 75–84. On contemporary concerns of anti-Semitism as the broader context for such hypotheses, see Anthony J. Saldarini, "Reading Matthew without Anti-Semitism," in *The Gospel of Matthew in Current Study: Studies in Honor of William G. Thompson, S. J.*, ed. David Aune (Grand Rapids: Eerdmans, 2001), 166–84. I do not mean to imply that presentist concerns render these hypotheses invalid; for, indeed, current concerns can sometimes draw attention to understudied elements of ancient sources. What I do wonder, however, is whether such concerns have resulted in the survival of some historical reconstructions even after the scholarly questioning of the historicity of the core elements on which they were based. See further below.

[14] Esp. Peter Schäfer, *Die Geburt des Judentums aus dem Geist des Christentums: Fünf Vorlesungen* (Tübingen: Mohr Siebeck, 2010).

of this essay, I thus turn to evidence from the second, third, and fourth centuries CE, tracing some trajectories in early Christian interpretation of Matthew 23 and representation of Pharisees. In this, I take up a question raised by Shaye J. D. Cohen in his seminal 1984 article on "The Significance of Yavneh."[15] From his analysis of the relevant Rabbinic data, Cohen establishes that the earliest known Rabbis never self-identify as Pharisees, and he points to Patristic evidence that fits the same pattern – albeit stressing that a "thorough study of the fathers ... is needed to confirm this observation."[16] Here, I hope to contribute to this broader task.[17] Rather than limiting myself to "the fathers," I look also to anonymous and pseudonymous Christian sources, including subapostolic writings, church orders, and so-called "pseudepigrapha" and "apocrypha."[18]

Special attention will be given to sources from Roman Palestine and Syria commonly categorized as "Jewish-Christian" such as the *Didache*, *Didascalia apostolorum*, and Pseudo-Clementine *Homilies*. For the present purposes, it suffices to set aside the question of whether these works are "Jewish-Christian" in the sense of having been produced by ethnically Jewish followers of Jesus or by the direct heirs of the Jerusalem Church.[19] What makes them potentially useful as sources for supplementary data for Jewish history is their relative proximity to Rabbinic sources – not just in provenance, but sometimes also in form, content, and/or concern.[20] The second-century *Didache* and third-century *Didascalia apostolorum*, for instance, are practically oriented "church orders" that address some of the halakhic issues discussed in the Mishnah and Tosefta, sometimes using similar exegetical techniques.[21] Inasmuch as the *Didache* is

---

[15] Shaye J. D. Cohen, "The Significance of Yavneh" (1984), repr. in Cohen, *Significance of Yavneh*, 44–70; see also Cohen, "Were Pharisees and Rabbis the Leaders of Communal Prayer and Torah Study in Antiquity? The Evidence of the New Testament, Josephus, and Early Church Fathers" (1999), repr. in Cohen, *Significance of Yavneh*, 266–81. I here cite pagination from the reprinted versions of this and related essays, which Cohen has updated with bibliographical and other details germane to my argument here.

[16] Cohen, "Significance of Yavneh," 70. Still much needed, in particular, is a comprehensive treatment of reference to Pharisees in Origen's writings.

[17] See already Boyarin, "Justin Martyr Invents Judaism," 453–55, who extends Cohen's findings to discuss Justin Martyr in particular, while also pointing to the Pseudo-Clementines as a promising topic. The value of integrating Christian evidence for Rabbinization is similarly noted by Seth Schwartz, "Rabbinization in the Sixth Century," in Schäfer, *Talmud Yerushalmi and Graeco-Roman Culture III*, 58.

[18] On the tendency for the study of Jewish/Christian relations to compare only Patristic and Rabbinic sources, see above Chapter Three in this volume.

[19] The most useful discussion of the issue of definition remains James Carleton Paget, "Jewish Christianity," in *The Cambridge History of Judaism*, vol. 3: *The Early Roman Period*, ed. William Horbury, W. D. Davies, and John Sturdy (Cambridge: Cambridge University Press, 1999), 733–42; see also Chapter Three and Appendix B in this volume.

[20] I.e., "relative" in relation to Patristic sources.

[21] Charlotte Elisheva Fonrobert, "The *Didascalia Apostolorum*: A Mishnah for the Disciples of Jesus," *JECS* 9 (2001): 483–509; Jonathan A. Draper, "Pure Sacrifice in *Didache* 14 as Jewish Christian Exegesis," *Neotestamenica* 42 (2008): 223–52, esp. 225, on the need

used by the *Didascalia apostolorum*, and later integrated along with it into the fourth-century *Apostolic Constitutions*, they have been held up as the closest known Christian counterparts to the Mishnah, Tosefta, and Talmudim.[22] Just as the *Didascalia apostolorum* might exhibit some awareness of the Mishnah,[23] so the fourth-century authors/redactors of the Pseudo-Clementine *Homilies* seem familiar with Rabbinic claims to possess the Oral Torah given to Moses at Mt. Sinai.[24] Consequently, such sources offer an important complement to images of Judaism in Patristic literature.

It is notoriously difficult, of course, to derive historical information from Christian references to Judaism; such statements are copious but typically tell the historian much more about Christian exegesis, heresiology, and self-definition than about Jews *per se*.[25] What I would like to ask here is whether it might nevertheless be possible to glimpse some hints of changing social realities behind shifting patterns of conventionalized representation, precisely by drawing on the more critical approaches to Rabbinic literature and Jewish history mentioned above. If the Rabbinization of Palestinian Jewish society was, in fact, a phenomenon of the fourth to sixth centuries,[26] rather than the first, might we find any hints of this in Christian literature from nearby locales? Are there shifts in images of Jews or readings of the gospels that might mirror – however darkly –

---

to reread this and other Syro-Palestinian "church orders" in terms of halakhic exegesis, on analogy with Rabbinic literature by virtue of overlapping concerns and questions. Note also Joseph G. Mueller, "The Ancient Church Order Literature: Genre or Tradition?" *JECS* 15 (2007): 337–80, approaching the *Didache, Apostolic Tradition*, and *Didascalia apostolorum* as "a self-consciously apostolic tradition that presents such rules as flowing from halakhic and aggadic interpretation of the OT" (379).

[22] So, e.g., Eva M. Synek, "Die Apostolischen Konstitutionen – ein 'christlicher Talmud' aus dem 4.Jh.," *Biblica* 79 (1998): 27–56.

[23] So Fonrobert, *"Didascalia Apostolorum,"* 495.

[24] So Albert I. Baumgarten, "Literary Evidence for Jewish Christianity in the Galilee," in *The Galilee in Late Antiquity*, ed. L. Levine (New York: JTSA, 1992), 39–50.

[25] E.g., Judith M. Lieu, *Image and Reality: The Jews in the World of the Christians in the Second Century* (Edinburgh: T&T Clark, 1996); Ora Limor and Guy G. Stroumsa, eds., *Contra Iudaeos: Ancient and Medieval Polemics between Christians and Jews* (Leiden: Brill, 1996); Andrew S. Jacobs, "The Lion and the Lamb: Reconsidering Jewish–Christian Relations in Antiquity," in *The Ways That Never Parted: Jews and Christians in Late Antiquity and the Early Middle Ages*, ed. Adam H. Becker and Annette Yoshiko Reed (TSAJ 95; Tübingen: Mohr Siebeck, 2003), 95–118.

[26] Although my study here culminates with the fourth century, I do not mean to imply that Rabbinization was a *fait accompli* even then; it is in that era, rather, that one begins to find mounting evidence of different forms for the visibility and prominence of Rabbis in Jewish society, even to "outsiders." Note, e.g., Seth Schwartz's cautious formulation: "The evidence of the laws, inscriptions, archaeology, and Christian and Rabbinic texts may be taken together to argue that in the fourth century, the local Jewish religious community was beginning to become an important institutions ... [and] especially in Palestine, functionaries *some of whom had connections to the Rabbinic movement*, were starting to become important in Jewish religious life, though their influence was not yet paramount" ("Rabbinization in the Sixth Century," 65; italics mine).

the changing landscapes of Palestinian Judaism between the first and fourth centuries? What I shall suggest is that the equation of Pharisees with Rabbis that is not yet found in Matthew 23 may be discovered in the history of its interpretation in Late Antiquity – perhaps initially among Syrian "Jewish-Christians."

Matthew 23 in the "Shadow of Yavneh"

In specialist study of the New Testament, discussion of Pharisees and Rabbis has revolved around the Gospel of Matthew, a text traditionally understood as the most "Jewish" of the gospels. Matthew's Jesus, after all, locates his own teachings firmly in the tradition of the Sinaitic revelation, famously proclaiming that he comes not "to abolish the Law or the Prophets" but rather "to fulfill" them (5:17). Furthermore, even as he asserts his own status as Son of God, he appears to grant some authority to his Pharisaic and scribal interlocutors, referring to them as those who "sit on the seat of Moses" (23:2). Just as ancient readers speculated about Matthew's Hebrew original or Jewish origins and audience (e. g., Papias *apud* Eusebius, *Hist. eccl.* 3.39; Irenaeus, *Adv. haer.* 3.1.1; Eusebius, *Hist. eccl.* 3.24.5–6; 5.10.3; 6.25.4; John Chrysostom, *Hom. Matt.* 1.7; Jerome, *Vir. ill.* 3) and posited its popularity among the "Jewish-Christian" sect of the Ebionites (Irenaeus, *Adv. haer.* 1.26.2; 3.11; Epiphanius, *Pan.* 28.5.1; 30.3.7, 13.1–8, 14.1–5),[27] so modern scholars have consistently focused on this gospel when seeking parallels to Rabbinic history, midrash, and halakhah.[28]

For the identification of Matthew's Pharisees with Rabbis, the crux has been Matthew 23, which contains perhaps the most positive reference to Pharisees in the entire New Testament, alongside the most scathing critiques. In Matt 23:2, Jesus tells his disciples that "the scribes and Pharisees sit on the seat of Moses," and he instructs them to "do whatever they say and keep it" (cf. 15:1–14). What follows, however, is a series of increasingly venomous accusations. Matthew's Jesus calls them "hypocrites" (23:13, 15, 23, 25, 27, 29) who "do all their deeds only to be seen" – making "their phylacteries broad and their fringes long" (23:5), seeking out "the place of honor at banquets and the best seats in the assemblies" (23:6; cf. Luke 11:43),[29] and striving only "to be greeted with re-

---

[27] Interestingly, Epiphanius, *Pan.* 30.13.1–8, 14.1–5, takes pains to specify that these various "heretics" use a different version of Matthew, "falsified and distorted" to their own liking – thus defusing the implication in Irenaeus, *Adv. haer.* 3.11 that the use of only this gospel leads to "heresy."

[28] Recent examples include Lawrence M. Wills, "Scribal Methods in Matthew and *Mishnah Abot*," *CBQ* 63 (2001): 241–57; Herbert W. Basser, *Mind Behind the Gospels: A Commentary to Matthew 1–14* (Boston: Academic Studies Press, 2009); see further below. Contrast Lloyd Gaston, "The Messiah of Israel as Teacher of Gentiles," *Interpretation* 29 (1975): 24–40; Douglas R. A. Hare, "How Jewish is the Gospel of Matthew?" *CBQ* 63 (2000): 264–77.

[29] Compare Mark 12:38/Luke 20:45–47 on "scribes."

spect in the marketplaces and to have people call them *Rabbi*" (23:7; cf. 26:25, 49; Mark 9:5; 11:21; 14:45; John 1:38, 49; 3:2, 26; 4:31; 6:25; 9:2; 11:8).[30] In a series of "Woe" oracles upon "the scribes and Pharisees,"[31] he further asserts that they "lock people out of the kingdom of heaven" (23:13; cf. Luke 11:52 on νομικοί) and "tithe mint, dill, and cumin" to the neglect of "justice and mercy and faith" (Matt 23:23; cf. Luke 11:42), likening them to "blind guides" (Matt 23:16, 24; cf. 17, 19, 26; also 15:14). They clean only "the outside of the cup and of the plate" (23:25; cf. Luke 11:39) and are thus also "like whitewashed tombs," beautiful on the outside but rotting within (Matt 23:27). "You snakes, you brood of vipers! How can you escape being sentenced to hell?" (23:33), says the Matthean Jesus, before calling them murderers as well: he accuses the Pharisees of building and decorating the tombs of the prophets, even as their own hands drip with the blood of Israel's righteous, whom they flog in their assemblies and pursue from town to town (23:34; cf. Luke 11:47–51).

What accounts for the fervor with which Jesus and/or Matthew condemn the Pharisees? At least since the nineteenth century, it has been common to read these figures in terms of the claimed continuity of "Pharisaism" and "Rabbinism."[32] Among early New Testament scholars, Matthew's special association with Judaism was seen to make this gospel a trustworthy witness to its decline; Jesus' critiques of the Pharisees in Matthew 23 were often treated as accurate assessments of the Judaism which Jesus was said to have rejected and which Christianity was believed to have superseded.[33] Conversely, for Jewish historians beginning already with Abraham Geiger,[34] Jesus' saying about the "seat of Moses" in Matt 23:2–3 signaled his own acceptance of Pharisaic authority;

---

[30] On "rabbi" as an honorific title not necessarily linked to the figures we know as such from the Mishnah, etc., see discussion below.

[31] Compare Luke 11:37–54. John Kloppenborg posits "scribes and Pharisees" as "almost certainly Matthean," while Helmut Koester argues for its presence in Q, as changed by Luke to *nomikoi* (11:46, 52) and as expanded by Matthew with the addition of "hypocrites" (23:13, 23, etc.); see John S. Kloppenborg, *Formation of Q* (Philadelphia: Fortress, 1987), 142 n. 175; Helmut Koester, *Ancient Christian Gospels* (Harrisburg: Trinity, 1990), 163–64. Interestingly, for our purposes, Luke 11:45 suggests that the evangelist here reapplies familiar critiques of Pharisees to νομικοί instead.

[32] See further Roland Deines, *Die Pharisäer: Ihr Verständnis als Spiegel der christlichen und jüdischen Forschung seit Wellhausen und Graetz* (WUNT 101; Tübingen: Mohr Siebeck, 1997); Christian Wiese, *Challenging Colonial Discourse: Jewish Studies and Protestant Theology in Wilhelmine Germany* (Studies in European Judaism; Leiden: Brill, 2005). "The history of scholarship on the Pharisees" – as Neusner stresses – "cannot be divorced from the history of Judaism and Christianity in the nineteenth and twentieth centuries, from the sociology of the Jews in Europe and the USA, and from the interrelationships between the two religious traditions" (*Rabbinic Traditions about the Pharisees*, 3:322).

[33] Perhaps most famously: the use of Matthew 23 as direct evidence for Pharisees – and thus Judaism in general – in Adolf von Harnack, *Das Wesen des Christentums* (Leipzig: Hinrichs, 1900), 66.

[34] E. g., Abraham Geiger, *Judaism and Its History* (trans. M. Mayer; London: Trübner, 1866), 216.

this passage could therefore serve as a prooftext for the antiquity of the role of Pharisees and Rabbis as the leaders of the Jewish people. Accordingly, in the 1920s, George Foot Moore could pair his scathing critique of Christian scholars for basing their reconstruction of "late Judaism" on New Testament images of Pharisees with a call to look to the Mishnah and Talmud for information about Judaism in the age of Jesus.[35] Ernest von Dobschütz went so far as to suggest that the author of Matthew was a Rabbi himself.[36]

We find similar approaches in more recent scholarship as well, particularly in the wake of World War II, which prompted renewed efforts to grapple both with the problem of anti-Judaism in the New Testament and with Moore's diagnosis of the biases in Christian scholarship on Judaism.[37] One prominent line of research proposed reading Matthew as a direct response to the Pharisees' purported rise to dominance between 70 and 90 CE. By this logic, the powerful ambivalence towards Pharisees in Matthew 23 reflects a direct reaction to changes in late first-century Judaism – with Yavneh emblematizing a shift away from a diverse Second Temple Judaism that could encompass Jewish followers of Jesus (i.e., the Jewish "background" of Jesus, Matthew, et al.) and toward an "exclusivistic" Rabbinic Judaism from which even "Jewish-Christians" were expelled (i.e., the Judaism that Matthew and others condemn).[38] Most famously, W.D. Davies interpreted the Sermon of the Mount as a point-by-point answer to the consolidation of Pharisaic-Rabbinic Judaism at the "council" of Yavneh.[39] Benedict Viviano further proposed that the "seat of Moses" in Matt 23:2 is a reference to it; he was so confident of the connection, in fact, that he dated the gospel with this "council" as *terminus post quem*.[40]

A variety of other interpretations have been proposed in the great mass of articles (and several books) on Matthew 23 in the last fifty years.[41] Matthew's

---

[35] E.g., George Foot Moore, "Christian Writers on Judaism," *HTR* 14 (1921): 197–254; Moore, "The Rise of Normative Judaism: To the Reorganization at Jamnia," *HTR* 17 (1924): 307–73.

[36] Ernst von Dobschütz, "Matthäus Rabbi und Katechet," *ZNW* 27 (1928): 338–48. This suggestion is positively (if cautiously) cited by Davies and Allison, *Critical and Exegetical Commentary*, 3:699.

[37] On the broader context here, see Annette Yoshiko Reed and Adam H. Becker, "Introduction: Traditional Models and New Directions," in Becker and Reed, *The Ways That Never Parted*, esp. 9–16.

[38] I.e., with this purported expulsion sometimes correlated to Matt 23:34.

[39] Davies, *Setting of the Sermon on the Mount*, 90, 292, etc. It is an understatement to say that Davies placed much emphasis on the influence of Yavneh: "Much as the World Council of Churches is in the twentieth century air," he opined, "so was Jamnia in the air of the late first-century Jewish and Christian life" (p. 90).

[40] Benedict T. Viviano, "Social World and Community Leadership: The Case of Matthew 23:1–12, 34," *JSNT* 39 (1990): 11.

[41] For a concise summary of the relevant trends in Matthean scholarship, with further relevant references, see Donald Senior, "Between Two Worlds: Gentiles and Jewish Christians in Matthew's Gospel," *CBQ* 61 (1999): 1–23 at 1–5.

positive references to the Pharisees and the "seat of Moses" (23:2) have been variously interpreted as a symbol of the Rabbis' legal authority, a metaphor for a Pharisaic Sanhedrin or Rabbinic *bet din*, an allusion to Rabbinic ordination, or a special chair or place of honor set aside for Rabbis within synagogues.[42] Although far from universal or uniform, what these studies largely share is the appeal to the post-70 Rabbinic rise to power to blunt the force of Matthew's anti-Jewish polemics.

In Davies' influential commentary with Dale C. Allison, for instance, the age of Matthew is described as one in which "a highly self-conscious, deliberate and probably aggressive Pharisaism was asserting itself to reunite the people of Israel ... defining itself in opposition to others, including Christians" – the result of a process whereby "[i]n the aftermath of the revolt one religious group emerged dominant, the Pharisees" and "first under Johannan ben Zakkai and later under Gamaliel II ... undertook to preserve and reform the Judaism that survived the war with Rome."[43] This picture of late first-century Judaism is familiar from nineteenth- and early twentieth-century accounts of ancient Jewish history, which tend to stress 70 as a turning point and to trumpet Yavneh as a moment of Pharisaic triumph.[44] It is quite far, however, from Cohen's assessment that "Rabbinic materials preserve some relics of the ideology and organization which characterized pre-70 Pharisaism, but these sectarian relics are few and far from central in Rabbinic self-definition,"[45] or from Schäfer's programmatic statement that

man hat sich aufgrund unserer Quellenlage davor zu hüten, die Brücke zwischen Pharisäern und Rabbinen kurzschlüssig zu schlagen. Natürlich haben bei den Rabbinen pharisäische

---

[42] E. g., David E. Garland, *The Intention of Matthew 23* (NTSup 52; Leiden: Brill, 1979); Viviano, "Social World"; Viviano, "The Pharisees in Matthew 23," *Bible Today* 27 (1989): 338–44; Hans-Jürgen Becker, *Auf der Kathedra des Mose: Rabbinisch-theologisches Denken und antirabbinische Polemik in Matthäus 23,1–12* (Berlin: Institut Kirche und Judentum, 1990); Steve Mason, "Pharisaic Dominance before 70 CE and the Gospels' Hypocrisy Charge (Matt 23:2–3)," *HTR* 83 (1990): 363–81; Anthony J. Saldarini, "Delegitimation of Leaders in Matthew 23," *CBQ* 54 (1992): 659–80; Mark A. Powell, "Do and Keep What Moses Says (Matthew 23:2–7)," *JBL* 114 (1995): 419–35; Patrick J. Hartin, "The Woes against the Pharisees (Matthew 23,1–39): The Reception and Development of Q 11,39–52 within the Matthean Community," in *From Quest to Q*, ed. Jon M. Asgeirsson, Kristin de Troyer, and Martin W. Meyer (Leuven: Peeters, 2000), 265–83, esp. n. 22. Important related discussions include Amy-Jill Levine, *The Social and Ethical Dimensions of Matthean Salvation History* (Lewiston: Mellen, 1988); David C. Sim, *The Gospel of Matthew and Christian Judaism: The History and Social Setting of the Matthean Community* (Studies of the New Testament and Its World; Edinburgh: T&T Clark, 1998).

[43] Davies and Allison, *Critical and Exegetical Commentary*, 3:692–94. For a recent defense of this position, see Dale C. Allison, *Studies in Matthew: Interpretation Past and Present* (Grand Rapids: Baker, 2005), 210–16.

[44] See further Schwartz, "Introduction: Was 70 CE a Watershed in Jewish History?," 1–19, esp. 6–8.

[45] Cohen, "Significance of Yavneh," 58.

Elemente weitergewirkt, aber keineswegs nur solche. Die Forschung muß in verstärktem Maße fragen, welche anderen Elemente bei den Rabbinen weitergewirkt haben.[46]

For all the sophistication in the interpretation of New Testament literature in terms of sources, redaction, reinterpretation, and representation, one finds no sense that the "council" of Yavneh might have been "a product of the late myth-making discourse of the Talmuds," as has been argued by Daniel Boyarin,[47] nor any acknowledgement of how "[r]abbinic origins are obscured by the very stories that Rabbinic texts tell and the very traditions they preserved," as Hayim Lapin has stressed.[48]

In fact, the reading of Rabbis into Matthew rests upon the very traditions that Schäfer, Cohen, and others have shown to be historically questionable on the basis of the earliest Rabbinic sources.[49] That these theories were becoming popular at the same time as the reassessments noted above is thus striking. Both, after all, represent revisionary trends within their respective fields. As in the reassessments of Rabbinic evidence noted above, the rereading of Matthew by Davies and others is predicated on treating the gospel as a reflection of events at its own time, rather than merely a window onto the life of Jesus. That the same is not done for amoraic representations of Yavneh, Yohanan ben Zakkai, the *birkat ha-minim*, and the like – even despite the ostensible concern for issues of Jewish/Christian relations, as well as the frequent citation of Schäfer and Cohen[50] – stands as a poignant example of the potential pitfalls involved in the correlation of Jewish and Christian histories.

To be sure, some New Testament scholars have noticed that their assessments of the "council" of Yavneh differ from those common in the field of Rabbinics. The range of responses is instructive. Some, such as Davies and Allison, sidestep engagement with basic questions concerning the relevant Rabbinic traditions and their utility for reconstructing the history of the late first century; they maintain that "Matthew engaged the larger world of Jamnian Pharisaism" and answer critiques by positing "Jamnia" as "process" rather than "event," even while

---

[46] Schafer, "Der vorrabbinische Pharisaismus," 173; the latter occurs in the course of the discussion with Martin Hengel recorded at the end of the article (pp. 172–75).

[47] Boyarin, "A Tale of Two Synods," 28–30 – taking up an argument anticipated by Schäfer in his 1975 "Die sogenannte Synode."

[48] Lapin, *Rabbis as Romans*, 56. For a concise, accessible summary of what we do and do not know about the origins of the Rabbinic movement, see there pp. 45–56.

[49] So also Boyarin, "Justin Martyr," 428–33.

[50] For instance, Schäfer's "Die sogenannte Synode" and Cohen's "Significance" are cited even in the first volume of Davies and Allison's *Critical and Exegetical Commentary* (1:136 n. 104). Notably, they seem to interpret Schäfer's skepticism about Yavneh as "synod" as a matter of timing – as if merely a difference in opinion concerning *when* the Pharisees triumphed and expelled those whom they deemed "deviant" – rather than a reoriented perspective, reconsidering Rabbinic self-definition as not simply Pharisaic and pressing for renewed engagement with the tannaitic traditions themselves, read in distinction from retrospective amoraic, medieval, and modern perspectives.

speculating on the basis of modern examples about the "amazing rapidity of changes often impelled by cataclysmic events such as the revolt against Rome in AD 66 and the collapse of the Jewish state in AD 70."[51] Others, such as J. Andrew Overmann, have posited a Galilean provenance for this gospel in place of its traditional association with Antioch – thereby keeping the imagined social setting largely intact while limiting its scope to a local struggle;[52] this same move enables Anthony J. Saldarini, for instance, to maintain that Matthew's aim was "to promote his interpretation of Judaism over that of other Jewish leaders, especially those of emerging Rabbinic Judaism," while admitting that "[o]nly gradually did the Rabbinic movement create and impose its views on all Israel."[53]

Surprisingly few have taken the seemingly more straightforward path suggested by Anders Runesson, who sees the limited evidence for Rabbinic hegemony in the late first century as pointing to the possibility that Matthew's Pharisees are actually Pharisees.[54] Most seem wary to abandon the notion of Yavneh as a pivot point for purported Pharisaic triumph and Christian expulsion, in relation to which Matthew might be dated and located, and against which its anti-Judaism might be explained.[55] Consequently, the call for critical assessment of Rabbinic sources has gone largely unheeded among scholars of the New Testament, as has the demonstration of meaningful differences in Pharisaic and Rabbinic modes of self-definition. For all the debate concerning Matthew's positioning "inside" or "outside" of Judaism,[56] surprisingly little has been done to draw on critical perspectives in the study of Rabbinics to revisit what this "Judaism" entailed at the end of the first century.

---

[51] Davies and Allison, *Critical and Exegetical Commentary*, 3:699–700.

[52] The logic is laid out most explicitly in J. Andrew Overmann, *Church and Community in Crisis: The Gospel According to Matthew* (Valley Forge: Trinity, 1996), 16–19; although see already Overmann, *Matthew's Gospel and Formative Judaism: The Social World of the Matthean Community* (Minneapolis: Fortress, 1990).

[53] Anthony J. Saldarini, *Matthew's Christian-Jewish Community* (Chicago: University of Chicago Press, 1994), 7, 9, see also 13–18.

[54] Anders Runesson, "Behind the Gospel of Matthew: Radical Pharisees in Post-war Galilee?," *Currents in Theology and Mission* 37 (2010): 460–71, esp. 467–68. See also Runesson, "Rethinking Early Jewish–Christian Relations: Matthean Community History as Pharisaic Intragroup Conflict," *JBL* 127 (2008): 95–132.

[55] A poignant example of the implications for the study in Jewish/Christian relations is the section on the Gospel of Matthew in Stephen G. Wilson's *Related Strangers: Jews and Christians 70–170 CE* (Minneapolis: Fortress, 1995), 46–55. For this, Wilson chooses the dramatic title, "The Shadow of Yavneh." What follows, however, is a discussion of the problems with assuming Rabbinic dominance already in the first century. Insofar as Wilson refrains from the anachronistic approach of reading all of the Rabbinic literature as "background" to the gospels, he limits the search for parallels to tannaitic traditions. Of these, he is able to find few, and he thus ends up justifying the significance of Yavneh for Matthew mainly through a vague appeal to their shared interest in "law and ethics."

[56] I.e., whether polemics are *intra muros* or *extra muros*; for a survey of the full range of positions, see Graham N. Stanton, *A Gospel for a New People: Studies in Matthew* (Edinburgh: T&T Clark, 1993), 118–39.

Contextualizing Matthew 23: Rabbinic and Epigraphical Data

For our purposes, the problem of Matthew's Pharisees is instructive inasmuch as it points to some of the challenges involved in trying to write history from both Jewish and Christian sources. Perhaps foremost are the tendency to over-read connections and the temptation to conjure dramatic moments of historical change. Indeed, part of the reason that theories about Matthew and Yavneh prove so alluring is because of their promise to align the story of Christian Origins with the story of the rise of the Rabbis. Even noble scholarly efforts at comparison, however, can birth suggestions that strain the primary sources on both sides – particularly when one corpus of sources is pressed into the service of another.

Related is the challenge of perspective. Certain arguments can seem compelling when primary sources from one corpus are correlated to modern synthetic summaries about another – only to unravel when primary sources of different types are put into direct conversation, each on their own terms. For this, the illusion of a seamless fit of Matthean social setting and Rabbinic history is perhaps a "parade example"; it can be maintained only by ignoring [1] Rabbinic literature and critical scholarship on it, [2] related epigraphical evidence, and [3] the patterns of representation and interpretation in later Christian sources. Below, we shall delve into the third component in some detail. By means of contextualization, it may be useful to touch upon the first and second as well.

As noted above, a critical approach to the relevant Rabbinic sources – distinguishing tannaitic from amoraic materials – undermines the direct equation of Pharisees and tannaim presumed in much New Testament scholarship, as well as the trope of their Yavnean/Jamnian triumph to impose a new "exclusivism" upon their fellow Jews. As Cohen has demonstrated, "[t]he tannaim never explicitly call themselves 'Pharisees,' nor is any individual Rabbi ever called a Pharisee" in tannaitic traditions:

The tannaim use *perushim* with reference not only to the Pharisees of old but also to contemporary "separatists" or "ascetics," whose conduct can be either condemned or approved. Either way, these *perushim* have no connection with the Pharisees. In contrast to the tannaim who display little interest in establishing themselves as Pharisees, the amoraim, especially the amoraim of Babylonia, begin to see themselves more clearly as the descendants of the Pharisees. ... In sum: at no point in antiquity did the Rabbis clearly see themselves either as Pharisees or as the descendants of Pharisees. ... This changes somewhat in amoraic texts, but even here identification with the Pharisees is not all that frequent and *perushim* is still used as a term of abuse. The identification with the Pharisees is secure and central for the first time only in an early medieval text, the *scholia* to the Scroll of Fasting.[57]

---

[57] Cohen, "Significance of Yavneh," 56–57.

Against the view of "Rabbis as Pharisees triumphant who define 'orthodoxy,' expel Christians and other heretics, and purge the canon of 'dangerous' books," Cohen stresses that "there is no indication that the Rabbis of the Yavnean period were motivated by a Pharisaic self-consciousness or … an exclusivistic ethic."[58]

Whether we follow Cohen in speculating that "the Rabbis were latter-day Pharisees who had no desire to publicize the connection,"[59] or follow Catherine Hezser in emphasizing that not all early Rabbis were Pharisees,[60] or follow Lapin in wondering whether Rabbis "who as a movement had no significant 'genealogical' link with Pharisees, at a later period drew connections between themselves and Pharisees retrospectively in order to provide themselves a pedigree reaching back to the Second Temple period and beyond,"[61] the pattern remains striking. It is only in later sources that one begins to find evidence for the Rabbinic embrace of a distinctively Pharisaic past.[62] However tempting it might be to explain away the violence of Matthew's rhetoric by appealing to Rabbinic power, it remains unclear whether the Rabbis of Matthew's time ever possessed (or sought) such power. Even if they did, there is no reason to think that they did so in the name of "the Pharisees."

The term "Rabbi," of course, appears as a title desired by Pharisees already in Matt 23:8. On the basis of this verse, Davies and Allison argue for the formalization of "Rabbi" as a title among Pharisees at Yavneh and, in turn, use Matthew's knowledge of this detail to support their dating of the gospel around 90 CE.[63] Even David Sim – who is generally more cautious in this regard – uses a comparison with the ways that Jesus is addressed in other gospels to argue that "the scribes and Pharisees were beginning to appropriate the title ['Rabbi'] for themselves" in Matthew's time and that "the use of this title by those in [Matthew's] own community would tend to blur rather than reinforce the distinctions he wished to create between them and the teachers of the parent body."[64]

What might seem plausible from the literary evidence of the gospels, however, becomes far less obvious when we extend our purview to encompass other materials. In his classic survey of the use of "Rabbi" in ancient inscriptions, for instance, Cohen cautions:

---

[58] Cohen, "Significance of Yavneh," 44.

[59] Cohen, "Significance of Yavneh," 58. For a recent reassessment of the evidence linking Pharisees and Rabbis, see Lapin, *Rabbis as Romans*, 46–49.

[60] Hezser, *Social Structure of the Rabbinic Movement*, 69–77, building on the engagement with Cohen's findings in Schäfer, "Der vorrabbinische Pharisaismus," and stressing inner-Rabbinic as well as broader Jewish variety.

[61] Lapin, *Rabbis as Romans*, 48.

[62] Boyarin, "A Tale of Two Synods," 28–30. Also Boyarin, "Justin Martyr Invents Judaism," 427–37, exploring implications for understanding the New Testament and early Christian literature.

[63] Davies and Allison, *Critical and Exegetical Commentary*, 1:135.

[64] Sim, *Gospel of Matthew*, 123, and contrast his cautious articulation at 114–15.

The term "Rabbi" is ambiguous. It may be either a popular designation for anyone of high position, notably – but not exclusively – a teacher, or it may be a technical term for someone who has been "ordained" and has achieved status and power within that society which produced the Mishnah, the Talmudim, and related works … we have no reason to assume that every Jew so designated helped to write the literature and shape the Judaism we call Rabbinic.[65]

In his recent reassessment of the relevant epigraphical materials, Lapin reconsiders Cohen's analyses and integrates further examples. He concludes that Cohen's "suggestion that the Rabbinic use of Rabbi as a title (i.e., designating someone Rabbi X) continues Second Temple-period practice is not supported by the epigraphical evidence" since "the great bulk of the inscriptions appears to date from the fourth century and later."[66] If anything, however, the reassessment reinforces Cohen's overarching point;[67] Lapin reveals "limited epigraphical evidence that does imply a connection with the Rabbinic movement," but it is "later than the classical period explicitly covered by Palestinian Rabbinic texts and points to incipient 'Rabbinization' in the fourth through the sixth centuries."[68]

Furthermore, as Lapin notes, the theory of the exclusive appropriation of the title "Rabbi" by first-century Pharisees cannot be hung solely on the hook of the purposed response in Matt 23:8:

[I]n its present form and context the Gospel of Matthew clearly understands the address *Rabbi* to be appropriate to a teacher, and to be claimed by Pharisees. Precisely because the passage is polemical, the association with Pharisees has to have enough to it to stick, but it cannot be taken as evidence that the form of address was exclusively "owned" by Pharisees. In any case, this passage and the Gospels more generally fail to give positive evidence of when, whether, and which men were known with the title Rabbi X.[69]

Here again, when we situate the New Testament evidence in broader perspective, the reading of Matthew as an answer to Yavneh becomes far less plausible.

Whether or not the distinction between Pharisee and Rabbi is "gratuitous" for late antique Palestine – as Fergus Millar has recently suggested[70] – it thus remains relevant for countering the retrojection of late antique realities onto earlier periods. For example, Jesus is addressed as "Rabbi" in both Mark and John (Mark 9:5; 11:21; 14:45; John 1:38, 49; 3:2, 26; 4:31; 6:25; 9:2; 11:8; cf. Matt 26:25, 49), and the term is explained in the latter as meaning "teacher"

---

[65] Cohen, "Epigraphical Rabbis," 235.

[66] Hayim Lapin, "Epigraphical Rabbis: A Reconsideration," *JQR* 101 (2011): 311–46 at 313.

[67] Esp. Cohen, "Epigraphical Rabbis," 241–42.

[68] Lapin, "Epigraphical Rabbis," 313. The pattern, in other words, makes the matter of Matthew 23 trickier but – as we shall see – fits better with what we shall find in the Pseudo-Clementines below.

[69] Lapin, "Epigraphical Rabbis," 318; see also Lapin, *Rabbis as Romans*, 48.

[70] Fergus Millar, "Inscriptions, Synagogues and Rabbis in Late Antique Palestine," *JSJ* 42 (2011): 253–77.

(John 1:38). The distinctions drawn by Cohen and Lapin help us to understand this pattern of attestation as less likely the product of diachronic development (e. g., from Mark's generalized Jewish usage, to Matthew's reaction to its alleged Pharisaic appropriation at Yavneh) than a reflection of the term's relative flexibility throughout the first century and beyond.

Contextualizing evidence of this sort also helps us to avoid a tautological argument, whereby the assumption of a connection guides the selection and interpretation of the very evidence that is used to support it. To read Matthew's Pharisees as the sages of Yavneh, for instance, one must also downplay certain elements in the gospel's description of them, such as their zeal to win converts (Matt 23:15), their veneration of the tombs of prophets (23:29), their demonological concerns (9:34; cf. Mark 3:21–22, Luke 11:14–15), their frequent fasting (Matt 9:14/Mark 2:18/Luke 5:33), and their pointed interest in heavenly signs (Matt 16:1/Mark 8:11, cf. Luke 12:54–56) – elements typically treated as contrary to Rabbinic ideology.[71] If we no longer presume the hegemony of the Rabbis already in the age of the gospels, however, we can also abandon the older assumption that Matthew must be *either* read as an answer to Rabbinic Judaism *or* situated completely "outside" of the Judaism of its time.

When we remove Matthew from the imagined shadow of Rabbinic hegemony, moreover, we notice that the text itself does not depict the Pharisees as all that powerful. Matthew's Pharisees are described, after all, not as having the honor and respect of the populace, but rather as seeking and striving after them (Matt 23:5–6), and as struggling mightily to gain converts to their cause (22:15). They desire to plot Jesus' demise (12:14; 22:15), but all they can do is engage him in exegetical and halakhic debates (15:1–14; 19:3; 22:16–22; 22:35–46). It may be telling, for instance, that Pharisees are given no active role in Matthew's account of the Passion, despite their earlier efforts (21:44–46); it is only the priests and elders who are able to assert any influence in relation to Jesus' arrest. After chapter 23, in fact, Pharisees disappear from Matthew's account until after Jesus' death, when they come to Pilate with the priests to ask about his tomb (27:62).

We have noted a tendency to reconstruct the "social setting" of Matthew through the lens of certain modern views of the Jewish past, according to which no Rabbis existed before 70 or Yavneh, and no Pharisees existed thereafter. In the case of Matthew 23, the result may be a false dichotomy. When discussing the positive reference to Pharisees as sitting "in the seat of Moses," for instance, scholars have tended to operate under the assumption that there are only two choices: one can *either* attribute the saying to one of Matthew's sources – wheth-

---

[71] In addition, some of the oft-cited parallels between Matthew's Pharisees and later Rabbis include features that likely applied to almost all other Jews at the time, such as Sabbath observance (Matt 12:2/Mark 2:24/Luke 6:2); in the case of handwashing (Matt 15:1–2), the Marcan parallel even specifies that the practice was common among Jews in general (Mark 7:3–4).

er Jesus himself, Q, or a "Jewish-Christian" source – in which case it is a statement about Pharisees, *or* one can attribute it to those responsible for Matthew, in which case the Pharisees must encode Rabbis. But perhaps, as Runesson suggests, Matthew's Pharisees may be Pharisees. It is not implausible, after all, that some might have chosen to retain the name after 70 or even 90;[72] indeed, as Martin Goodman has recently stressed, this is certainly the most straightforward way to understand the relevant statements by Josephus.[73]

Seen in broader perspective, the anti-Pharisaic polemics in Matthew seem more likely to reflect a situation of localized competition between two relatively powerless groups with overlapping audiences and aims. By virtue of its scripturalization as a privileged record of the Christian past, Matthew's depiction of this competition came to shape the way some later readers framed the relationship of "Judaism" and "Christianity" writ large. It would be misleading, however, to project these categories back into the first century. We might better imagine Matthew and his opponents as active agents in a shared intellectual field, performing Torah expertise and piety to garner authority in the eyes of their local populace in the wake of the Jewish war, concurrent with the collapse of the social and political structures that had buttressed older priestly and sectarian models of religious authority. To the degree that Matthew 23 provides evidence for the social and religious landscape of its time, it is as part of an array of scattered clues – together with the writings of Josephus, the earliest traditions in the Mishnah, and works like *4–6 Ezra* and *2–3 Baruch* – to a late first-century Judaism that remained decentralized, shifting, and locally variegated.

---

[72] If so, this might help to shed light on the broader context behind early attempts by Rabbis seemingly to distance themselves from the sectarian label – on which see further below. The continued use of the name "Pharisee" by some Jews may also shed light on the scattered references to ascetic and separatist *perushim* (e.g., *m. Sotah* 3.4; *m. Ḥagigah* 2.7; *t. Berakhot* 3.25; *t. Sotah* 15.11; *t. Shabbat* 1.15; *y. Sotah* 3.4/19a). Similarly, Epiphanius' surprisingly detailed description of Pharisaic ascetics in *Pan.* 15 is suggestive. In the middle of the second century, moreover, Justin Martyr includes Pharisees in a list of the Jewish sects of his own times (*Dial.* 80) – even despite his apparent awareness of some contemporary Jewish teachings; see further below.

[73] Martin Goodman, "Religious Variety and the Temple in the Late Second Temple Period and Its Aftermath," *JJS* 60 (2009): 202–13 at 212: "That Pharisees, Sadducees and Essenes were still the main philosophies of Judaism in the nineties CE was of course explicitly asserted by Josephus in the *Antiquities* and in his *Vita*, and there is no reason whatsoever to read his account of the present state of Judaism as an historical report on Jewish philosophies which had ceased to exist." On evidence for the post-70 survival of other Second Temple sects, at least in some form, see also his earlier essay on "Sadducees and Essenes after 70 CE," in *Crossing the Boundaries: Essays in Biblical Interpretation in Honour of Michael D. Goulder*, ed. Stanley E. Porter, Paul M. Joyce, and Daniel E. Orton (Leiden: Brill, 1994), 347–56. Goodman's analyses provide good models for how such inner-Jewish variegation can be effectively illumined without reifying inner-Jewish difference into separate "Judaisms," dichotomous contrasts, or the like.

Early Christian Perspectives on Matthew 23 and Pharisees

The identification of Matthew's Pharisees with Yavnean sages has served as a lynchpin not only for modern attempts to correlate apostolic and tannaitic history, but also for the notion that contacts between Christianity and Rabbinic Judaism were limited to this shared first-century past, soon after which the two "parted ways." Yet, far from discouraging the correlation of Christian and Rabbinic Jewish histories, the problems with this theory point us to the necessity of looking to post-New Testament Christian sources. Above, we noted how fresh analyses of Rabbinic and epigraphical data have cast doubt on traditional chronologies of religious change: a number of the developments traditionally associated with the immediate wake of the destruction of the Temple in 70 CE have been shown to be the results of slower processes, seemingly coalescing in the fourth century and following. In what follows, we turn to the *Nachleben* of Matthew to see if similar patterns might be discovered, asking whether and when early Christian reflections on Pharisees reveal any awareness of Rabbis or incipient Rabbinization.

If the tannaim were widely known to be the heirs of the Pharisees at the end of the first century, one would expect to find continuity in the polemics against Jews by second- and third-century Christians, in general, and Matthew's heirs, in particular. Especially if tannaim took on the mantle of Jewish leadership from Pharisees, one would also expect the arsenal of anti-Pharisaic statements in the gospels to be used against Jews. As noted above, however, Cohen's preliminary survey of Patristic evidence has revealed a different pattern:

The fathers of the second, third, and fourth centuries do not identify contemporary Judaism with Pharisaism. Tertullian, Cyprian, the *Dialogue of Timothy and Aquila*, and Aphrahat attempt to refute Judaism, but they either do not mention the Pharisees at all or mention them only in New Testament quotations. Even Origen, who lived in Palestine and knew a great deal about Judaism, does not refer to contemporary *didaskaloi* and *sophoi* as Pharisees. … All of this is somewhat surprising since the New Testament accords the Pharisees such a prominent role and provides so many anti-Pharisee polemics which would have been very useful to anti-Jewish writers. Obviously these fathers did not know of the connection between the Pharisees and the Rabbis. … Sometime in the fourth century this begins to change. Jerome refers to contemporary Rabbis as Pharisees and explicitly identifies the *deuteroseis* of Barachibas with the *traditiones* of the Pharisees … In any case, the patristic testimony concerning the Pharisees is remarkably parallel to the Rabbinic: in the second century little or no connection is made between the Rabbis and the Pharisees, but in the fourth the connection starts to become clear.[74]

In this section and the next, I look to the history of interpretation of Matthew 23 to determine whether Cohen's assessment can be confirmed across a broader range of Christian sources. The result – as we shall see – is largely positive.

---

[74] Cohen, "Significance of Yavneh," 68–70.

Perhaps most significantly, the pattern persists even among those of Matthew's heirs with the most cultural and geographical proximity to Rabbinic Judaism.

The early second-century *Didache*, for instance, is widely acknowledged as standing in the closest relationship with the Gospel of Matthew; the two may have even been produced within the same community.[75] There, however, Pharisees disappear. When discussing proper practices for fasting and prayer, *Didache* 8 contrasts the true apostolic religion with the practices of "hypocrites" in a manner that recalls the rejection of Pharisaic fasting practices in Matthew (6:16–18; 9:14–15). Yet, in the *Didache*, the theme of hypocrisy takes on a different valence; it is reconceived as a danger within the community (e. g., 2; 4; 5) as well as a feature of some of its closest – now unnamed – opponents. Allusions to Matthew 23 are absent as well.

In second-century interpretation of Matthew 23, references to Pharisees are similarly absent. Even the allusion to Matt 23:31–32 in *Barn.* 5:11, for instance, omits explicit reference to them.[76] The same pattern is found in works like *5 Ezra* and the *Apocalypse of Peter*, which may preserve second-century expressions of Matthean Christianity.[77] In *5 Ezra* 1:30–33, allusions to Matt 23:34–38 are interwoven into a divine revelation to Ezra, thereby retrojecting the notion that the slaying of God's prophets was among the sins that lead to Israel's supersession; specific reference to Pharisees, however, has been omitted.[78] If Graham

---

[75] On this work, in general, see Jonathan A. Draper, ed., *The Didache in Modern Research* (Arbeiten zur Geschichte des Antiken Judentums und des Urchristentums 37; Leiden: Brill, 1996); and for discussion of the connection with Matthew, see Huub Maria van de Sandt, ed., *Matthew and the Didache: Two Documents from the Same Jewish-Christian Milieu?* (Minneapolis: Fortress, 2005); Huub Maria van de Sandt and Jürgen K. Zangenberg, eds., *Matthew, James, and Didache: Three Related Documents in Their Jewish and Christian Setting* (SBLSymS 45; Atlanta: SBL, 2008).

[76] See Édouard Massaux, *The Influence of the Gospel of Saint Matthew on Christian Literature* (3 vols.; Macon: Mercer University Press, 1991), 1:69. Apart from this *Epistle of Barnabas* reference and those in Justin's *Dialogue* (on which see below), Massaux finds only a handful of other cases of possible pre-Irenaean references to Matthew 23, most of which are somewhat vague allusions – i. e., *Barn.* 19:3 (cf. Matt 23:12; *Did.* 1:2), *1 Clem.* 48:6 (Matt 23:11), Ignatius, *Phil.* 6.1 (cf. Matt 23:27), *Odes Sol.* 7:16–17 (cf. Matt 23:39), *Prot. Jas.* 23:3 (cf. Matt 23:35), Heracleon fragment 46 (Matt 23:15, 28), and P.Oxy. 840 (Matt 23:25, 33). See Massaux, *Influence of the Gospel of Saint Matthew*, 1:31, 71–72, 93–94; 2:77–78, 231, 259–60, 273–74. It is worth stressing that explicit references to Pharisees are absent in these cases as well; whatever we make of any individual example, the overall pattern thus remains interesting.

[77] So Graham N. Stanton, "5 Ezra and Matthean Christianity in the Second Century" (1977), repr. in Stanton, *Gospel for a New People*, 256–77.

[78] To be sure, the narrative setting of the work is during Ezra's time as "a captive in the country of the Medes in the reign of Artaxerxes, king of the Persians" (*5 Ezra* 1:3); that said, the style of *ex eventu* prediction here allows for some signaling of specificity if the authors/redactors so wished. On *5 Ezra* and other "pseudepigraphical" evidence for early identities combining elements later distinguished as "Jewish" and "Christian," see Martha Himmelfarb, "The Parting of the Ways Reconsidered: Diversity in Judaism and Jewish/Christian Relations in the Roman Empire," in *Interwoven Destines: Jews and Christians Through the Ages*, ed. Eugene J. Fisher (New York: Paulist, 1993), 55–57; David Frankfurter, "Beyond 'Jewish Christianity':

Stanton is correct to read the *Apocalypse of Peter* as similarly attesting the second-century continuation of Matthean Christianity with further reflection on changes within Judaism in the wake of the failure of the Bar Kokhba Revolt,[79] it is striking that Pharisees are absent there too. Indeed, even when *Apocalypse of Peter* alludes to the "blind guides" of Matthew 23, it is with reference to the "priests and the people" instead of Pharisees (72.10–13).

The evidence of these second-century anonymous and pseudonymous works suggests that the patterns that Cohen finds in "the fathers" may reflect more than the heresiological discourse of an elite line of Christian philosophers and ecclesiarchs. As Cohen notes, for instance, Justin Martyr seems to understand the Pharisees as a different group from those whom he terms the *didaskaloi* of his *Dialogue*'s Jewish interlocutor Trypho.[80] Justin includes Pharisees in the list of Jewish sects that he cites when explaining inner-Christian difference to Trypho (*Dial.* 80); he assumes, however, that a Jew like Trypho would not consider these sects to be worthy of the name "Jew."[81]

Twice in the *Dialogue* (i.e., 17.4; 137.2), Justin may allude to Matthew 23 when describing the Pharisaic rejection of Jesus, but the references remain in the realm of the religious difference of a past age.[82] Likewise, in the one case where he applies the anti-Pharisaic statements of Matthew 23 to the Jewish *didaskaloi* of his own time (Matt 23:23–24, 27, in *Dial.* 112.4–5), he strikingly omits any reference to Pharisees, even as he points to those who wish to be called "Rabbi, Rabbi!"

At first sight, we might seem to find a partial exception in *Dial.* 17.4, where Justin accuses Jews of spreading pernicious lies about Jesus in reaction to his condemnation of Pharisees as "hypocrites," in a manner reminiscent of Matt 23:34. In Justin's reference to the condemnation to which this purported propa-

---

Continuing Religious Sub-cultures of the Second and Third Centuries and Their Documents," in Becker and Reed, *The Ways That Never Parted*, 131–44.

[79] Stanton, "5 Ezra," 272–77. See also Richard Bauckham, "The Apocalypse of Peter: A Jewish Christian Apocalypse from the Time of Bar Kokhba," *Apoc* 5 (1994): 7–111; Bauckham, "Jews and Jewish Christians in the Land of Israel at the Time of the Bar Kochba War, with Special Reference to the *Apocalypse of Peter*," in *Tolerance and Intolerance in Early Judaism and Christianity*, ed. G. N. Stanton and G. G. Stroumsa (Cambridge: Cambridge University Press, 1998), 228–38.

[80] See Cohen, "Significance of Yavneh," 51–52, 69–70 n. 16, 70. Compare, however, the "scribes" of *Dial.* 103.

[81] This important passage has been richly discussed. Especially relevant for our purposes are Cohen, "Significance of Yavneh," 51–52; and Boyarin, "Justin Martyr Invents Judaism," esp. 453–55.

[82] As Massaux notes, *Dial.* 17.4 seems to paraphrase or interweave Matt 23:13, 16, 23, 24, 27 with Luke 11:42, 52 – in contrast to *Dial.* 112.4–5 which clearly draws on Matt 23:6–7, 24. On the use of Matt 23:15 in *Dial.* 122.1, and the possible allusion to Matt 23:31, 37/Luke 11:48, 13:24 in *Dial.* 95.2, see Massaux, *Influence of the Gospel of Saint Matthew*, 3:51–52, 77–78, 88. Massaux does not treat *Dial.* 137.2 as an echo of Matthew 23. On its relevance for the representation of Pharisees, see Cohen, "Significance," 69 n. 70.

ganda responds, however, polemics against Pharisees paraphrased from Matthew 23 are folded into those against moneychangers and scribes paraphrased from Matt 11 and Luke 11. Furthermore, Justin's appeal to sayings of Jesus is here guided by his overarching aim of aligning Christian history with predictions from Isaiah ("And Isaiah cries justly: 'By reason of you, my name is blasphemed among the Gentiles' and 'Woe unto their soul, because they have devised an evil device against themselves saying: Let us bind the righteous, for he is distasteful to us'"; cf. LXX Isa 3:9–11; 52:5). We find something similar in *Dial.* 121–122: Justin makes an allusion to Matt 23:15 in relation to Jewish conversion, and Pharisees are absent. Yet his aim is not to address Jewish conversion in his present, but rather to argue that Isaiah's prediction of Israel as a "light to the nations" (Isa 49:6) and related prophetic statements refer to Christians rather than Jews.[83]

In other Patristic writings from the second and third centuries, the anti-Pharisaic statements in Matthew 23 are redeployed in a variety of ways – mostly having nothing to do with Jews. Irenaeus, for instance, quotes Jesus' statements about the "seat of Moses" in Matt 23:2–4 to argue against Marcion's claim that Jesus rejected the Torah (*adv. Haer.* 4.12.4).[84] Also common is the use of this and other portions of Matthew 23 in discussions of proper pedagogy, with Pharisees either unmentioned or treated as symbols of improper Christian teaching.[85] An allusion to Matt 23:2–4, thus, is used to warn against "those teachers 'who teach but do not do" in *Ad uirgines epistulae duae* 1.11, attributed to Clement of Rome, and Tertullian appeals to the same verses to critique Christian bishops who do not practice the chastity they preach in *Mon.* 7–8. Similarly, the admonitions in Matt 23:8–12 are cited apart from the context of Pharisees seeking to be called "rabbi" in Matt 23:7, for purposes ranging from the argument for Jesus' monotheism (Matt 32:9 in Irenaeus, *Adv. Haer.* 4.1.2), to instructions for proper Christian prayer (Matt 23:9 in Tertullian, *Or.* 2.2), to discussions of Hellenistic philosophy (Matt 23:10 in Clement, *Strom.* 4.7). Matthew's "scribes and Phari-

---

[83] I.e., it is not clear whether Justin here makes a similar move to Origen as discussed below, using Matthew 23 (here esp. vv. 23, 24, 27) as a source of negative *exempla* for methods of Christian biblical exegesis.

[84] Irenaeus' logic is that Jesus in Matt 23:2–4 accepted the authority of the Torah and the authenticity of its Jewish transmission, and only critiqued the Pharisees for not observing it; accordingly, the words of Jesus himself can be brought against the Marcionite contention that Jesus rejected both the Torah and the deity who gave it to Moses and the Jews. An interesting related case is Tertullian, *Marc.* 4.27.6, where Jesus' woes against Pharisees, despite his prohibition of cursing, are used to argue for the weakness of Marcionite reading practices, by which one would be forced to deem even Christ inconsistent or multiple. Given the anti-Marcionite context, Tertullian draws instead on the Lucan parallel to Matthew 23 (i.e., Luke 11:38, etc.), which itself already transforms one anti-Pharisaic statement into an emphasis on God's oneness (11:40); here too, Tertullian's concern is less with Pharisees or any Jews of his own time than with the argument against Marcionite dualism that Christ "expressly declared that to the same God belongs the cleansing of a man's external and internal nature."

[85] The latter is explicit, e.g., in Augustine, *Ep.* 208.4–5; see also *On Christian Doctrine* 4.27 – which similarly attests the continued use of Matthew 23 for these aims.

sees" can also serve as negative *exempla* for Christian exegetes: Origen presents the "Woes" of Matthew 23 as a warning to Christians who limit themselves to literal readings, stressing that one should "interpret the words 'Woe unto you Scribes and Pharisees, hypocrites' (Matt 23:13) as having been said to everyone that knows nothing but the letter!" (*Comm. Matt.* 10.14).

For all that these same authors also engage in anti-Jewish polemics, they do not apply the anti-Pharisaic polemics of Matthew 23 to the Jews of their own time.[86] Perhaps most surprising in this regard is the treatment of Matt 23:27, wherein Jesus likens the Pharisees to "whitewashed tombs." In modern times, in the hands of scholars like Adolf von Harnack, this verse would become exemplary of Jesus' denunciation of Rabbinism as dead legalism.[87] For Tertullian, however, Matt 23:27 speaks to the transformative character of resurrection (*Res. mort.* 19.4). For Clement of Alexandria, this verse helps to answer the question of how often Christians should take baths (*Paed.* 9.3).

From what I can tell thus far, the early history of interpretation of Matthew 23 confirms Cohen's assessment of Patristic references to Pharisees: the significance of the Pharisees in second- and third-century Christian literature is largely limited to their past status as Jesus' opponents, and they are treated as Jewish sectarians rather than Jewish leaders. To be sure, there are many possible reasons for the lack of correlation of Pharisees to Rabbis in second- and third-century Christian sources; it could reflect [1] Christian lack of knowledge or concern about Jews of their own time, and/or [2] the status of the tannaim as not prominent enough to be perceived by outsiders as a distinctive group with influence beyond certain locales, and/or [3] some sense, however passing, of a decline in those who embraced the name "Pharisee," and/or [4] some familiarity with the distinctive early Rabbinic discourse of difference that denigrates sectarianism/ *minut*. If the first seems more likely for those with less geographical and cultural proximity to Palestinian Judaism, such as Irenaeus and Tertullian, the second, third, and fourth are also possible in cases such as the *Didache*, *5 Ezra*, *Apocalypse of Peter*, and Justin Martyr.

For the possibility that Patristic representations of Pharisees reflect some knowledge of their Rabbinic counterparts, the evidence of Origen proves pivotal. Origen lived in Caesaria in the third century, studied with Jewish teachers, and is widely noted as the earliest Patristic author with extensive firsthand contact with Jews who exhibit characteristically Rabbinic features.[88] Cohen suggests that the wider pattern holds for him as well: Origen discusses both the Pharisaic

---

[86] A possible exception is Justin, *Dial.* 112.4–5, on which see above – although there too, what is at stake may be proper Christian interpretation of biblical prophets rather than polemics against Jews *per se*.

[87] Harnack, *Das Wesen des Christentums*, 66.

[88] Nicholas de Lange, *Origen and the Jews: Studies in Jewish–Christian Relations in Third-Century Palestine* (Cambridge: Cambridge University Press, 1976).

opponents of Jesus and the Jewish *didaskaloi* and *sophoi* of his own time, but he does not seem to equate them.[89]

Notably, the preface to Origen's *Commentary on the Song of Songs* does refer to their δευτέρωσις – a term which, as Hillel Newman stresses, "has no precedent in Greek as a term describing a form of tradition or instruction" but is a calque on "*Mishnah* … a parochial term stemming from Rabbinic circles."[90] The choice to adopt the term δευτέρωσις is a notable break from the earlier Christian discourse of Pharisaic and other postbiblical Jewish tradition. Read against the background the rich precedents provided by New Testament discussions of παράδοσις extending Matt 15:1–20/Mark 7:1–32, the adoption of this neologism represents a sudden and surprising "enlargement of the Christian vocabulary of Jewish tradition," which – William Horbury suggests – can be most plausibly situated among "contacts between gentile Christians, Christian Jews, and non-Christian Jews."[91]

Even if we question whether δευτέρωσις reflects Rufinus' translation rather than Origen's original articulation, a plausible case for the term's introduction from Rabbinic/proto-Rabbinic/Rabbinic-like circles into third-century Christianity can be made from the *Didascalia apostolorum*.[92] There too, we find evidence of increased knowledge of Rabbinic or related Jewish traditions, alongside a seeming reticence to read Rabbis as Pharisees and the adoption of the Greek neologism δευτέρωσις (cf. Syr. *tinyan nimosa*). The Syrian Christian community whom it addresses includes converts from "the former People" (i.e., Jews), and among the problems discussed is their continued observance of *kashrut*, menstrual separation, and other practices of ritual purity (*Did. Apost.* 23–24, 26).[93]

---

[89] Cohen, "Significance of Yavneh," 69 n. 66; cf. de Lange, *Origen and the Jews*, 34–35. Firm conclusions in this case must await a more systematic study working through the ample listings of quotations and allusions to Matthew 23 and other key New Testament passages about Pharisees in volume 3 of J. Allenbach et al., eds., *Biblia Patristica: Index des citations et allusions bibliques dans la littérature patristique* (5/7 vols.; Paris: CNRS, 1975–1982). For the present essay, I have worked through all of the other entries in *Biblia Patristica* for the possible use of Matthew 23 in second- and third-century sources, on the basis of the online Biblindex (http://www.biblindex.mom.fr/), together with the pre-Irenaean materials surveyed by Massaux's three volumes on Matthew's earliest reception (see n. 76 above), but the potentially relevant materials in Origen are plentiful and complex enough to require separate analysis.

[90] Hillel I. Newman, "The Normativity of Rabbinic Judaism: Obstacles on the Path to a New Consensus," in Levine and Schwartz, *Jewish Identities in Antiquity*, 169.

[91] William Horbury, "The New Testament and Rabbinic Study: An Historical Sketch," in *The New Testament and Rabbinic Literature*, ed. R. Bieringer et al. (JSJSup 136; Leiden: Brill, 2010), 3–6, quote from p. 6.

[92] See Cohen, "Significance of Yavneh," 52–53; although not mentioned in the original article, note the addition of a thoughtful discussion of one key passage in the 2010 reprint.

[93] See further Fonrobert, "*Didascalia Apostolorum*"; also Fonrobert, "Jewish Christians, Judaizers, and Anti-Judaism," in *Late Ancient Christianity*, ed. V. Burrus (A People's History of Christianity 2; Minneapolis: Fortress, 2005), 253–54. There is also a concern with those "abstaining from flesh and from wine" (*Did. apost.* 24), which Fonrobert ("*Didascalia Apostolorum*," 491–502) explains with reference to *t. Sotah* 15.11 and *b. Baba Batra* 60b, which counter Jews who refrained from meat and wine after the destruction of the Temple. If she is

Although the *Didascalia apostolorum* includes an unusual density of direct allusions and references to Matthew 23 (e. g., Matt 23:34 in *Did. Apost.* 19; Matt 23:38 in *Did. Apost.* 23; Matt 23:18–22 in *Did. Apost.* 26), these passages are again cited without reference to Pharisees – even when materials from Matthew 23 are brought to bear on concerns about menstrual purity practices with intriguing parallels in contemporaneous Rabbinic discussions.[94]

The *Didascalia apostolorum* claims to have been written by the twelve apostles after the so-called "Apostolic Council" (cf. Acts 15). Yet, despite the narrative setting in the apostolic past, there is no attempt to link the leaders or teachers of "the former People" with Pharisees. Instead, throughout the text, Pharisees emblematize sectarianism. Their sectarianism is also imagined as a characteristic of the pre-Christian Jewish past – a reality that was passing away already in the age of the apostles. Jesus' warning in Matt 16:6 to "Beware of the leaven of the Pharisees and of the Sadducees" is thus interpreted not in terms of Rabbis or Jews at all; rather, it is presented together with the warning against entering "the cities of the Samaritans" in Matt 10:5 as Jesus' prediction of the dangers of Christian "heresies and schisms" (*Did. Apost.* 25) – a demonically-inspired danger that shifted from "the former People" (i. e., Jews) to "the People" (i. e., the church; *Did. Apost.* 23). In short, Pharisees and Jewish sectarianism are not portrayed either as a present reality among Jews or as a present threat to Christians, but rather as a negative *exemplum* from the Jewish past for the Christian present. Both the representation of Pharisees and the image of Jewish difference in the *Didascalia apostolorum* thus recall their counterparts in Rabbinic literature – albeit here redeployed for different aims.

The similarity may not be coincidental. Charlotte Elisheva Fonrobert has suggested that the *Didascalia apostolorum* can be read as a Christian "counter-Mishnah." Not only does it counter those in its own community who are "observing holiness," "abstaining ... from swine" (*Did. Apost.* 24), and practicing "purifications, and sprinklings and baptisms, and distinction of meats" (*Did. Apost.* 26), but it does so by delegitimizing the Jewish δευτέρωσις – here identified with the commandments given to Israel after the episode of the Golden Calf. In Fonrobert's estimation, the critiques of this δευτέρωσις are most plau-

---

correct, hints of knowledge of distinctively Rabbinic traditions in Roman Syria are paired with evidence for continued variety in the forms of Judaism from which some Syrian Christians originated and to which some remained faithful.

[94] Charlotte Elisheva Fonrobert, *Menstrual Purity: Rabbinic and Christian Reconstructions of Biblical Gender* (Stanford: Stanford University Press, 2000), 160–210; as well as my discussion in Annette Yoshiko Reed, "Parting Ways over Blood and Water? Beyond 'Judaism' and 'Christianity' in the Roman Near East" [2012], reprinted in revised form as Chapter Two in this volume. The other references to Pharisees in the *Didascalia apostolorum* occur in quotes or paraphrases on New Testament passages – Matt 5:20 in *Did. apost.* 9; Mark 2:16–17/Matt 9:11–12/Luke 5:30–31 in *Did. apost.* 10; Acts 15:5 in *Did. apost.* 24.

sibly understood as having been "triggered by the author(s)' knowledge of the consolidation of the mishnaic traditions into a canonical text."[95]

From the fourth to sixth centuries, the term δευτέρωσις comes into common parlance in the post-Constantinian church – used by writers like Eusebius and Jerome, and in Roman legal codes (esp. Justinian, *Novella* 146), seemingly in relation to the halakhic teachings of the Rabbis.[96] Fonrobert argues, however, that the *Didascalia apostolorum* offers the earliest known Christian attestation of the use of the term.[97] If she is correct, then we may here see a case in which awareness of Rabbinic Jews by Syrian "Jewish-Christians" preceded (and possibly informed) the representation of the Rabbinic movement by other Christians – or, in other words, that the expansion of Christian awareness about Rabbinic Judaism, in the fourth and fifth centuries, was not merely a result of occasional conversations between individual learned Christians and individual learned Jews in the wake of the intensification of Christian pilgrimage to the Holy Land; rather, it might also reflect the growing prestige of Rabbis and Rabbi-like figures and/or the growing prominence of Rabbinic and related ideas among local communities of Jews known to "Jewish-Christians" in the Roman Near East.

In the final section of this essay, I would like to make a similar argument with regard to the Christian equation of Pharisees and Rabbis. Whereas Cohen places the origins of this development with Jerome, I suggest that we may see the connection made already by the Syrian Christians responsible for the Pseudo-Clementine *Homilies*. What is notable – I suggest – is that this move entails the introduction of a new interpretation of Matthew 23, which connects Pharisees to the Jewish present, salvages their reputation, and reinterprets their authority on the "seat of Moses" in terms of knowledge about the oral exposition of the Torah.[98]

---

[95] Fonrobert, "*Didascalia Apostolorum*," 496. For a different reading of its heresiology, see Charlotte Metheun, "Widows, Bishops, and the Struggle for Authority in the *Didascalia Apostolorum*," *Journal of Ecclesiastical History* 46 (1995): 204.

[96] For more and less maximalist readings of the connections, compare Marcel Simon, *Verus Israel: A Study of the Relations between Christians and Jews in the Roman Empire AD 135–425* (London: Littman Library of Jewish Civilization, 1986), 89; Hillel I. Newman, "Jerome and the Jews" [Hebrew] (PhD dissertation, Hebrew University of Jerusalem, 1997), 42–51 and passim; Schwartz, "Rabbinization in the Sixth Century," 55–69.

[97] Fonrobert, "*Didascalia Apostolorum*," 495–98. Cf. Azzan Yadin-Israel, "*Qabbalah*, Deuterōsis, and *Semantic* Incommensurability: A Preliminary Study," in Boustan et al., *Envisioning Judaism*, 2:917–40.

[98] It should be noted that the most famous relevant reference from Jerome – the correlation of Pharisaic traditions with δευτέρωσις in *Ep.* 121.10 – is in part an interpretation of Matt 15; Epiphanius, *Pan.* 33.9, similarly discusses δευτέρωσις in relation to Matt 15:5. As Horbury stresses ("New Testament and Rabbinic Study," esp. 6–10), even new information about Jews was consistently mediated through reflection on the New Testament, albeit in shifting ways reflecting shifting circumstances and concerns.

"Jewish-Christian" Re-readings of Matthew's Pharisees

The Pseudo-Clementine *Homilies* is one of two forms of a novel claiming to preserve a firsthand account of Clement of Rome's conversion to Christianity and travels with the apostle Peter. In contrast to the other version, the *Recognitions*, it survives in Greek and appears to be pre-Nicene (ca. 300–320 CE?).[99] Both works hail from Roman Syria, and the *Homilies* in particular seem to have taken form among Syrian Christians similar to those against which the *Didascalia apostolurum* argues. In the *Didascalia apostolorum*, for instance, the narrative setting of the "Apostolic Council" of Acts 15 is used to lend apostolic authority to a teaching that washing for menstrual purity undoes baptism (*Did. Apost.* 26). By contrast, the *Homilies* puts words in the mouth of Peter himself requiring menstrual purity of even Gentile converts (*Hom.* 7.8; 11.30; cf. *Rec.* 6.11), while also "correcting" Acts' portrayal of Peter by having him also maintain *kashrut* and insist that true Christians cannot eat with those who are impure.[100]

---

[99] I here set aside source-critical issues, because most of the themes discussed below happen to be distinctive to the *Homilies*. It is worth noting, however, that the overarching differences between the *Homilies* and *Recognitions* are starkly evident in their divergent treatment of Matthew 23. The citations of Matthew 23 and other references to Pharisees in the earliest strata of the Pseudo-Clementines (ca. 200 CE?) – *Rec.* 1.27–72 (e. g., Matt 21:13 in *Rec.* 1.54.7; also *Rec.* 1.59 on Moses and Jesus) – present the Pharisees as sectarians, thereby fitting well with the pattern noted above (Baumgarten, "Literary Evidence," 42; see also Chapter One in this volume). The rest of the *Recognitions* treats Pharisees in strongly negative terms, drawing on Matthew in a manner nearly opposite to the *Homilies*. The positive statements about Pharisees in Matt 23:2–3 that are cited multiple times in the *Homilies* (3.18.2; 3.51.1; 3.20.2; 11.29.1), for instance, are never mentioned in the *Recognitions*, while the negative statements about Pharisees in Matt 23:5–6 are referenced in *Recognitions* (2.46.5) but never in the *Homilies*. Likewise, the positive twist on Matt 23:13 in *Hom.* 3.18.2 (cf. 18.15.7; 18.16.2) contrasts with the negative valence of *Rec.* 2.30.1. Note also *Rec.* 2.46, where the positive element of Matt 23:13 is used against Marcionite beliefs, but immediately countered by the critiques in Matt 23:5–6 – the opposite pattern as in *Hom.* 3.18, but similar to Peter's countering of Marcionite beliefs placed in the mouth of Simon Magus in *Hom.* 18.15–16. For an accessible account of the source-critical issues, see F. Stanley Jones, "The Pseudo-Clementines: A History of Research," *Second Century* 2 (1982): 84–96; Jones, *An Ancient Jewish Christian Source on the History of Christianity: Pseudo-Clementine Recognitions 1.27–71* (Texts and Translations 37, Christian Apocrypha Series 2; Atlanta: Scholars Press, 1995); Jones, *Pseudoclementina Elchasaiticaque inter Judaeochristiana: Collected Studies* (Orientalia Lovaniensia Analecta 203; Leuven: Peeters, 2012), 114–37.

[100] For the practices incumbent on the Gentile convert in both the *Didascalia apostolorum* and Rabbinic literature, see Ps.-Clem. *Hom.* 7.4, 8; 11.28–30; 13:4, 9, 19; cf. *Rec.* 2.71–72; 6.9–11; 7.29, 34; 8.68; for more detailed discussion, see Chapter Two in this volume. Note that the countering of Acts is made explicit in the Petrine letter that circulated at the beginning of the *Homilies*: "Some from among the Gentiles have rejected my legal preaching (νόμιμον … κήρυγμα), attaching themselves to certain lawless and trifling preaching (ἄνομόν … καὶ φλυαρώδη … διδασκαλίαν) of the man who is my enemy (τοῦ ἐχθροῦ ἀνθρώπου). Some have attempted these things while I am still alive, to transform my words by certain intricate interpretations towards the dissolution of the Law (εἰς τὴν τοῦ νόμου κατάλυσιν) – as though I myself were also of such a mind but did not freely proclaim it; God forbid!" (*Ep. Pet.* 2.3–4).

Significantly, for our purposes, the Pharisees of Matthew 23 play an important part in the *Homilies*' articulation and defense of the authentic apostolic religion promoted by Peter.[101]

Within the Pseudo-Clementine *Homilies*, there are three references to Pharisees. All occur in speeches attributed to Peter, and two of the three quote and interpret Matthew 23, which is also referenced six other times.[102] The first occurs in the context of the articulation of the text's main doctrines in *Hom* 3.1–28, framed as Peter's private words to his followers prior to a public debate with the "heretic" Simon Magus.[103] Here, Peter reveals to Clement and others that Simon's true aim is to try to "show from the Scriptures that he who made the heaven and the earth, and all things in them, is not the Supreme God, but that there is another, unknown and supreme … and that he sent two gods, one of whom is he who made the world and the other he who gave the Law" (3.2).[104] The portrayal of Simon with Marcionite features is underlined by the assertion that Simon "comes to do battle with us, armed with the false chapters of the Scriptures" (3.3) – that is, pentateuchal passages that seem to imply divine multiplicity or to undermine God's perfection. Peter stresses that Simon's argument is not meant for "us" Jews "who have had handed down from our forefathers the worship of the God who made all things," but rather for "those from amongst the Gentiles who have the polytheistic fancy bred in them and who know not the falsehoods of the Scriptures" (3.3) and who are easily lured by "any vain, dreamlike, richly set out story against God" (3.4). Even as Clement is assured that the criteria of divine unity and perfection suffice to determine which interpretations of the Torah are true, he is warned that both sides can produce seemingly persuasive pentateuchal prooftexts.[105]

To this admission of the Torah's flexibility in the hands of demonically devious exegetes, Peter proclaims the stability of prophetic truth, not least by revealing the unity of the True Prophet, who is at once Adam, Moses, and Jesus

---

[101] See further Chapter Six in this volume.

[102] I.e., Matt 23:2–3 in Ps.-Clem. *Hom.* 3.18.2; 3.51.1; 3.20.2; 11.29.1; Matt 23:13 in *Hom.* 3.18.2; 18.15.7; 18.16.2; cf. *Rec.* 1.54.7; 2.30.1; 2.46.3; Matt 23:25–28 in *Hom.* 11.28.4–29.2; cf. *Rec.* 6.11.2–3. Interestingly, the positive statements about Pharisees in Matt 23:2–3 are cited multiple times in the Homilies but never mentioned in the Pseudo-Clementine *Recognitions*, while the negative statements about them in Matt 23:5–6 are referenced in *Rec.* 2.46.5 but never in the *Homilies*; note also Matt 23:9 in *Rec.* 8.8.2.

[103] On the figure of Simon here, see esp. D. Côté, *Le thème de l'opposition entre Pierre et Simon dans les Pseudo-Clémentines* (Études Augustiniennes Série Antiquités 167; Paris: Études augustiniennes, 2001); Côté, "La fonction littéraire de Simon le Magicien dans les *Pseudo-Clémentines*," *Laval Théologique et Philosophique* 57 (2001): 513–23.

[104] On the Pseudo-Clementines' anti-Marcionite concerns, see F. Stanley Jones, *Pseudoclementina*, 152–71, 516–31.

[105] E.g., Ps.-Clem. *Hom.* 3.10: "Simon, who is going to discuss in public with us tomorrow, is bold against the monarchy of God … he is going to offer many scriptural proofs, but we also can easily show many passages from them that he who made the world alone is God, and that there is none other besides him."

(Ps.-Clem. *Hom.* 3.17–20; also 2.16–17). The first of the text's four citations of Matt 23:2–3 (3.18.2; also 3.51.1; 3.20.2; 11.29.1) serves to explain the purpose of the True Prophet's incarnation as Jesus. In *Hom.* 3.18–19, Peter adduces Deut 32:7: "Ask your father, and he will tell you; your elders, and they will declare to you." Having established that the "father" is the True Prophet, he brings Matt 23:2 as an intertext to establish the identity of "the elders" as "the scribes and Pharisees." That these "elders" also "declare" prophetic truths is, after all, suggested by Jesus' assertion that "the scribes and the Pharisees sit in the seat of Moses," that one must listen to them in "all things that they say to you," and that the they are "entrusted with the key of the kingdom," which "is knowledge, which alone can open the gate of life, through which alone is the entrance to eternal life." As in Matthew, the positive statement is qualified: Peter cites Matt 23:13 to assert that Pharisees "possess the key but those wishing to enter they do not suffer to do so" (*Hom.* 3.18.2; cf. 18.15.7, 16.2; *Rec.* 1.54.7; 2.30.1; 2.46.3). Rather than occasioning any critique of Jews or Pharisees, however, their limitation of knowledge and salvation is here adduced as part of the explanation of Jesus' role in salvation history: he was sent to the Gentiles to bring the knowledge and salvation already available to the Jews (3.19). Just as the Pharisees sit in the "seat of Moses" (τῆς καθέδρας Μωυσέως), so Jesus is said to have risen from the "seat of prophecy" (τῆς προφητείας καθέδρα) to come to earth for the sake of the nations.[106]

This two-path soteriology is explained in more detail in Pseudo-Clementine *Hom.* 8.5–7. There, Moses and Jesus are explicitly asserted to be two teachers of the same truth – Moses for the Jews and Jesus for the Gentiles.[107] In place of the accusations of Pharisaic blindness in Matthew 23 we find a redeployment of the rhetoric of divine concealment in Matt 11:25. Peter here reveals that "Jesus has been concealed from the Hebrews who have taken Moses as their teacher" but also that "Moses is hidden from those who have believed Jesus" (*Hom.* 8.6), thereby linking the former to Jesus' saying in Matt 11:25/Luke 10:21 that "I thank you, Father of heaven and earth, because you have concealed these things from the wise and prudent, and you have revealed them to sucking babes." This double concealment is tied, in turn, to a divine purpose: each group is meant to seek salvation by following the teachings of the specific prophet whom God has sent to them. Among the implications, however, is that Moses' Jewish heirs must not be blamed for not accepting Jesus, provided that they "do not hate him whom they do not know" (8.7).

Accordingly, throughout the Pseudo-Clementine *Homilies*, the Jewish apostle Peter is depicted as teaching Gentiles about monotheism, ritual purity, and other

---

[106] On this passage in relation to the theme of succession, see Chapter Six above.

[107] For analysis of this passage and comparison with the parallel in *Rec.* 4.5, see Chapter One in this volume.

truths depicted as also preserved among the Jews – and Pharisees in particular.[108] Yet the Pharisaic preservation of Mosaic teachings is not only set up as a parallel earthly lineage for divine and prophetic knowledge; it is also presented as a paradigm for the trustworthy transmission of truth in an impure world. Just as the *Homilies* points to the oral transmission of prophetic knowledge in the Pharisaic/Jewish line of succession that parallels the Petrine/apostolic, so it also depicts the "seat of Moses" (τῆς καθέδρας Μωυσέως; 3.18–19; 3.70; 11.29) as parallel and precedent for the "seat of Christ" (τῆς Χριστοῦ καθέδρας; 3.60). The presentation of Pharisees is inextricably integrated into the *Homilies*' overarching concern with questions of trustworthy transmission and its distinctive vision of apostolic succession as paralleling, rather than superseding, its Jewish counterpart.[109]

It is in the context of discussing transmission and succession that we find the most striking parallels with characteristically Rabbinic ideas. In Ps.-Clem. *Hom.* 2.38, for instance, Peter explains how Moses "gave (παραδεδωκότος) the Law with the explanations (σὺν ταῖς ἐπιλύσεσιν), in order that they also might instruct such of the people as they chose." The nature of these "explanations" is made clear in *Hom.* 3.47, which further specifies that alongside the Written Torah, "the Law of God was given through Moses without writing (ἀγράφως) to seventy wise men (cf. Num 11:16), to be handed down (παραδίδοσθαι), so that the government might be carried on by succession (τῇ διαδοχῇ)." Baumgarten is correct – I think – to see some connection to the Rabbinic doctrine of the Oral Torah.[110] Not only do the authors/redactors of the *Homilies* draw the same type of doubled distinction as do the Rabbis, but they describe the explications of the Torah as having been revealed at Mt. Sinai. The oral interpretative tradition is associated both with oral transmission and with an unbroken line of succession from Moses (cf. *m. Avot* 1–5).

For Baumgarten, these traditions point to a surprising convergence: the Pseudo-Clementine authors/redactors seem to have seen "the Jewish past in much the same way as the Pharisees and/or their Rabbinic heirs did."[111] From our analysis above, I would suggest that the convergence is even more striking than Baumgarten suggests. After all, the authors/redactors of the *Homilies* do not merely reproduce Pharisaic traditions, whether from the gospels or elsewhere. Rather, their representation of "the Law of God … given, through Moses" resonates most strongly with Rabbinic traditions that were being richly developed in the third and fourth centuries, when the Oral Torah began to rival the Written

---

[108] E. g., Ps.-Clem. *Hom.* 2.33; 8.5–7; 11.7–6; 16.14; see Chapter Four above.

[109] See further Chapter Six in this volume.

[110] Baumgarten, "Literary Evidence for Jewish Christianity," esp. 42–43.

[111] Baumgarten, "Literary Evidence for Jewish Christianity," 43.

Torah in revelatory status.[112] What they accept, in other words, is not merely the Pharisaic παράδοσις; the claim and its formulation are more distinctly Rabbinic. As a result, the *Homilies* reshape the authority of Matthew's Pharisees (esp. 23:2–3) in a manner that matches contemporaneous Rabbinic traditions. If our above analysis building on Cohen is correct, the *Homilies* offer an otherwise unprecedented interpretation of Matthew 23, with reference to the Jews of their own time: they read Moses and his Torah in terms of Rabbinic ideas, but also affirm its proper succession in a line continuous with the Pharisees who occupy his "seat."[113]

Perhaps most surprisingly, the authors/redactors of the Pseudo-Clementine *Homilies* appear to accept such claims – even to the point of using them to support their own anti-Marcionite twist on the elevation of the Oral over the Written. As we have seen, they present the former as the only way to interpret the latter properly. In addition, it is on the basis of the preeminence of Oral Torah that they argue for the propensity of non-Jews to be mislead by polytheistic or dualistic readings of passages like Gen 1:26, 3:22, 11:7, or 18:21 (*Hom.* 3.38; 3.42–46; 16.11–12);[114] anyone who stands outside of the line of transmission of proper Torah interpretation by teachers of proper succession is at special risk of falling prey to "heresy." According to the *Homilies*, this is ultimately the problem that Jesus sent his apostles to rectify, but it remains an active battle, not least due to the pairing of evil exegesis and anti-Judaism by the Samaritan Simon (e.g., 2.17, 33; 3.59; 5.1–29).

That the authors/redactors of the Pseudo-Clementine *Homilies* read the Pharisees in positive terms is suggested not just by their emphasis on Matt 23:2–3 and their alignment of Pharisees with apostles, but also by their somewhat defensive approach to Matthew's polemics against them. In one passage (*Hom.* 3.70), they seem to use the Matthean charge of Pharisaic hypocrisy to their advantage: the assertion that Jesus' followers should always honor the bishop who sits on the "throne of Christ" is underlined by the argument that they were instructed to honor "the seat of Moses" even when those sitting upon it were accounted as sinners.[115] Later, however, they use Peter to exonerate the Pharisees *as a group*

---

[112] E.g., *Sifre Devarim* 351; *y. Megilluh* 4.1; *y. Pe'ah* 2.6; *Pesikta Rabbati* 14b; *b. Shabbat* 13a; and discussion in Martin S. Jaffee, *Torah in the Mouth: Writing and Oral Tradition in Palestinian Judaism, 200 BCE–400 CE* (Oxford: Oxford University Press, 2001).

[113] Some association of the Oral Torah with scribes and Pharisees may also be tacit in Ps.-Clem. *Hom.* 3.50–51. There, Peter first points to the error of the Sadducees as rooted in their dependence on Written Torah alone; when establishing the divine origins of the true Torah, however, he cites Jesus' act of sending his disciples to "the scribes and *didaskaloi* ... who really know the true things of the Law."

[114] On parallels with contemporaneous Rabbinic disputations with *minim* concerning some of the same verses, see *Bereshit Rabbah* 1.7 and 8.8–9 as well as my discussion in Chapter Five above.

[115] Ps.-Clem. *Hom.* 3.70: "Therefore, honor the throne of Christ (θρόνον οὖν Χριστοῦ τιμήσετε); for you are commanded to honor the seat of Moses (ὅτι καὶ Μωυσέως καθέδραν

from the charge of hypocrisy. During a discussion of the practices incumbent on Gentile followers of Jesus (*Hom.* 11.28–30), Peter paraphrases the critique of the Pharisees attributed to Jesus in Matt 23:25–26 with respect to their concern for external cleanliness. Yet the critique is raised for the sake of qualification.[116] The apostle admits that "our teacher, when dealing with certain of the Pharisees and scribes among us – who are separated yet as scribes know the matters of the Law more than others – still reproved them as hypocrites, because they cleansed only the things that appear to men" (*Hom.* 11.28). He takes care to clarify, however, that this statement must not be understood as a condemnation of every Pharisee: Jesus "spoke the truth with respect to those hypocrites among them – not with respect to all of them (πρὸς τοὺς ὑποκριτὰς αὐτῶν οὐ πρὸς πάντας)."[117] This clarification, in turn, occasions the reiteration of Pharisaic authority by means of yet another quotation of Matt 23:2: "To some he said that obedience was to be rendered, because they were entrusted with the seat of Moses" (*Hom.* 11.29). Subsequently, further consideration of the faults of the hypocrites found among the Pharisees is used as the basis for arguing that Gentile converts must strive after purity both in their souls and in their bodies. This argument, in turn, occasions Peter's instruction to Gentile converts, not just to keep away from impure foods, but also to practice menstrual separation and wash after intercourse and seminal emissions.

Although the precise notion of Gentile impurity differs from those outlined in the Mishnah, Tosefta, and Talmud Yerushalmi, it is intriguing that the authors/redactors of the Pseudo-Clementine *Homilies* attribute ritual impurity to Gentiles at all – an idea that Christine Hayes suggests is a Rabbinic innovation.[118] Furthermore, just as Rabbinic halakhot about Gentile impurities tend to involve arguments by analogy either to the *zav* or to idols, so the *Homilies'* instructions for Gentile purity focus on genital emissions and idol worship as the two sources of pollution for Gentiles.[119] That the *Homilies* prescribe ritual purity practices with direct reference to the Pharisees, then, may be neither coincidental, nor merely a matter of Matthean exegesis; especially when read alongside the text's references to Moses' reception and transmission of the Law of God ἀγράφως,

---

τιμᾶν ἐκελεύσθητε), even if those who occupy it are accounted sinners (κἂν οἱ προκαθεζόμενοι ἁμαρτωλοὶ νομίζωνται)."

[116] I.e., in contrast to the parallel in Ps.-Clem. *Rec.* 6.11, which may reflect more of the thrust of the *Grundschrift* in this case.

[117] Notably, this reading of Matthew 23 as condemning only the hypocrites among the Pharisees, and not Pharisees in general, resonates with the treatment of Pharisees in *b. Sotah* 22b: "King Yannai said to his wife: "Do not fear the Pharisees, nor those who are not Pharisees, but the hypocrites (lit. tainted men) who conduct themselves as good Pharisees externally, and would like to receive the reward of Phineas, though their sins are those of Zimri."

[118] Christine Hayes, *Gentile Impurities and Jewish Identities: Intermarriage and Conversion from the Bible to the Talmud* (Oxford: Oxford University Press, 2002), 107. For the contrast with the *Didascalia apostolorum*, see Chapter Two in this volume.

[119] Hayes, *Gentile Impurities*, 122–31; also Chapter Two above.

the framing and content of its teachings about Gentile ritual purity may signal some awareness of distinctively Rabbinic traditions.

If I am correct to suggest that the authors/redactors of the Pseudo-Clementine *Homilies* reread Matthew's Pharisees as Rabbis, they present these figures as possessing the oral traditions revealed to Moses on Sinai, as entrusted with the knowledge through which Jews can be saved, and as paradigms of monotheism and ritual purity. Within the *Homilies*, Pharisees occupy a "seat of Moses" that is paralleled to the "throne of Christ" occupied by bishops with authentic apostolic/Petrine teaching – both of which, moreover, draw authority from the same heavenly "seat of prophecy" to connect past and present. Here, Pharisees are no longer a relic of Judaism's sectarian past; they have been revivified with a Rabbinic spirit.

Within this early fourth-century text, we may thus glimpse what scholars have sought in vain to find in the first century with Matthew – namely, evidence for the perceived prominence and prestige of Rabbis, concurrent with their association with the Pharisees of Jesus' time. If so, the depiction of the Pharisees in the Pseudo-Clementine *Homilies* may offer an interesting perspective on the beginnings of Rabbinization – glimpsed, as if sideways, through the eyes of surprisingly sympathetic Syrian outsiders. It may prove significant, for instance, that the *Homilies* make no reference to the Pharisees' leadership roles in synagogues, even despite the precedent of Matt 23:6.[120] What they seem to know and accept – and may even emulate – is the Rabbis' self-proclaimed status as arbiters of correct Torah interpretation and as the earthly guardians of true teachings passed in unbroken succession from Moses. If the authors/redactors of the *Homilies* do liken themselves to these sages, they do so with appeal to their intellectual prestige and exegetical prowess. This is perhaps fitting, since it seems unlikely that the *Homilies* were penned by Christians in positions of ecclesiastical or political power. What they claim to possess, rather, are the true teachings of Jesus passed in unbroken succession from Peter.

This claim makes much sense when we recall that the Pseudo-Clementine *Homilies* is not primarily concerned to discuss Jews and Christians, but rather to counter competing visions of apostolic belief and practice.[121] Peter's enemies in the *Homilies* are lead by the Samaritan Simon Magus, and they derive their wisdom from Alexandria and Athens (e. g., *Hom.* 2.21–26; 4.6; 5.2); they are depicted as philosophers, magicians, and grammarians who seek both to persuade

---

[120] Compare Schwartz's conclusions with respect even to the later evidence from Jerome: "That Jerome ... can use Rabbinizing language to describe Jewish religious experts may inform us that Rabbis and Rabbi-types were becoming important in Jewish religious life by the middle and later fourth century, especially in Palestine"; he stresses, however, that "Jerome ... testifies to something less than the canonization of the mishnah and the diffusion and authority of its interpreters among the Jews of Palestine" ("Rabbinization in the Sixth Century," 65).

[121] See further Chapter Six above, for the ways that this account of apostolic history counters those of Acts and Eusebius in particular.

the Syrian populace and to sway the hearts of prominent Romans like Clement and his father. Whereas Peter's Samaritan, Egyptian, and Greek enemies are unified in their appeal to Greek *paideia* (esp. *Hom.* 4–6),[122] Peter himself is aligned with the Pharisees, who proclaim the Torah, monotheism, and prophetic truth in place of polytheism and Hellenistic philosophy.[123]

Elsewhere, I have suggested that demonization of Alexandria in the Pseudo-Clementine *Homilies* may have been framed in response to the importation of Alexandrian forms of Christianity into Roman Palestine and Syria, due to the activities of Origen, Pamphilus, and Eusebius in Caesaria.[124] To be sure, the prominence of Greek *paideia* is similarly bemoaned by Ephrem.[125] When we examine the depiction of Simon Magus in the *Homilies*, however, we may see hints of a more specific concern with the flowering of Syrian Neoplatonism in its theurgical articulations, particularly in Apamea under Iamblichus. Like Iamblichus, the authors/redactors of *Homilies* respond to Roman imperial realities by creatively reconfiguring "Greek" and "barbarian" identities – albeit in this case, by appealing to the antiquity and authenticity of the Jews, rather than Egyptians. Rabbis, in other words, may have fit well with the ideal of "barbarian wisdom" and/or role of native informant that these Syrian Christians wished to claim for themselves – or, at least, to deploy against those whom they deemed too "Greek" to be Jesus' true heirs.

Within the narrative world of the Pseudo-Clementine *Homilies*, moreover, Greek, Egyptian, Samaritan, and Christian intellectuals all argue under a Roman gaze; throughout the *Homilies*, for instance, it is ultimately for the sake of Clement and his father – both from the family of Caesar (e.g., *Hom.* 12.18; 14.6) – that debates are waged between apostles, philosophers, and "heretics." It is only the Pharisees who stand apart. In this, we may find perhaps the most intriguing contrast between the Pharisees of the Gospel of Matthew in the first century and the Pharisees of the *Homilies* in the fourth. Matthew's Pharisees "cross land and sea" to make a convert (Matt 23:15). By contrast, the Pharisees of the *Homilies* are disengaged from the debates into which Peter, Barnabas, and other Jewish apostles of Jesus are pressed to participate. If the debates of the *Homilies* do evoke the tensions between different native subelites in Roman Syria vying for patronage and prestige, it may be significant that its Rabbinized Pharisees embody a different approach to the negotiation of local and imperial identities. They do not strive to persuade the populace, nor do they couch their

---

[122] On the innovation of Simon's link to Hellenism here, see Côté, *Le thème de l'opposition*, 195–96.

[123] See further Chapters Four and Six in this volume.

[124] See further Chapter Six in this volume.

[125] "Blessed is the one who has never tasted the poison of the wisdom of the Greeks" (Ephrem, *De fide*, CSCO 154.7); see Sebastian Brock, "From Antagonism to Assimilation: Syrian Attitudes towards Greek Learning," in Brock, *Syriac Perspectives on Late Antiquity* (Variorum Reprints; London: Variorum, 1984), V.19.

"barbarian wisdom" in Greek *paideia*. Whatever authority they bear, they gain by upholding, transmitting, and embodying the teachings of Moses among the Jews.

"Jewish-Christian" Evidence for Jewish History?

Modern narratives about ancient Judaism often retroject all meaningful change onto a small set of dramatic moments – foremost the destruction of the Temple in 70 CE, but also its imagined aftermath in a decisive "council" of Yavneh around 90 CE or some clear-cut "Parting of the Ways" with Christianity, then or thereafter. The assumption that the late first century was the pivotal age in the post-Temple transformation of Judaism, Christianity, and Jewish/Christian relations is often built into the very structure of modern scholarly inquiries; it is to this time that scholars have traditionally looked when seeking formative shifts in Christianity and Rabbinic Judaism, the dynamics of their interaction, and their self-definition as distinct. Attention to the tannaitic and New Testament traditions themselves, however, frustrates any tidy narrative about early competition, polemics, or expulsion. Yet, as we have seen, the correlations that cannot yet be found in the surviving first-century data begin to intensify in the third and especially fourth century and following.

Contrary to what the modern model of "Parting" leads us to expect, it is only later that Christian references to Jews and Judaism begin to dovetail with what we know about Rabbis from Rabbinic, epigraphical, and other evidence.[126] Among the overlaps, moreover, is the emergence of a shared image of the past in Rabbinic, "Jewish-Christian," and Patristic sources from Late Antiquity – part of the ultimate origins, perhaps, of the modern notion of the formative first century, retrojectively reimagined as a transformative age when tannaim and apostles established post-Temple identities and institutions with rapid decisiveness, unquestioned authority, and lasting success.

As noted at the outset, much has been done by Schäfer, Cohen, and others to expose the amoraic reimagining of the Pharisaic and Yavnean past, and its effects on modern scholarly treatments of tannaitic and New Testament traditions alike. To this, our analysis has offered supplementary evidence for the process by which New Testament images of the first-century past came to be reread in terms of Rabbis – also beginning in the fourth century, precisely when some sages were starting to embrace elements of a distinctively Pharisaic heritage, and when epigraphic, archaeological, and other data point to their increasing prominence in Palestinian Jewish society. Consequently, if the test case of Matthew's Pharisees points to the perils of reading Rabbis into the New Testament, it also

---

[126] Schwartz, "Rabbinization in the Sixth Century," 65.

speaks to the necessity of correlating broader patterns across centuries, using different types of data – both Christian and Jewish, both literary and nonliterary.

In place of the older quest for discrete pieces of "proof" for unidirectional arrows of "influence" or "dependence," such an approach entails collaborative efforts towards the slower task of mapping a scatter chart of overlaps and tracing the subtle effects of shared discourses and contested spaces. This approach – which Schäfer programmatically articulated for Rabbinic Judaism and Graeco-Roman culture[127] – is slower but also more substantial, not least because it engages specialists in different subfields. Analyzed in this manner, Christian sources can be profitably brought to bear upon renewed efforts to "test" or revise Rabbinocentric accounts of late antique Judaism from the evidence of inscriptions, iconography, archaeology, Hekhalot literature, and *piyyutim*. Indeed, as we have seen, this trend has already borne interesting results, as historians interested in Rabbinization have brought new questions to bear on Patristic sources. Against the temptation of reading a text from one tradition as a straightforward "reaction" to another, however, our treatment of Matthew 23 and its *Nachleben* has highlighted the inner-Christian dynamics of exegesis, heresiology, polemics, and memory that mediate even those representations that seem most plausibly to reflect direct contact with Jews.

What I would like to add, by means of conclusion, is a call to look to a broader range of Christian sources as well. Like the interpretation of the New Testament through the Mishnah, the engagement of Rabbinics with Patristics has the allure of correlating materials which have been influential in shaping images of "Judaism" and "Christianity" from Late Antiquity and the Middle Ages, and which remain authoritative within some communities today. This focus may lead us to miss other sources that prove no less useful for reconstructing the intertwined histories of Jews and Christians. In addition, a broader range of Christian sources allows for a more nuanced assessment of the local, exegetical, and other factors that shape the patterns of representation even within the writings of more familiar texts and authors. In the process, we may gather further clues concerning the points of crossing in Jewish and Christian traditions – not just in the late antique landscapes of the Christianized Holy Land, but also on the increasingly common terrain of a newly reimagined past.

---

[127] Peter Schäfer, "Introduction," in Schäfer, *Talmud Yerushalmi and Graeco-Roman Culture I*, 14–15; see also Schäfer, *Mirror of His Beauty: Feminine Images of God from the Bible to the Early Kabbalah* (Princeton: Princeton University Press, 2002), 229–34.

Chapter Ten

Rethinking "Jewish-Christian" Evidence
for Jewish Mysticism*

In a much-cited passage from his 1946 *Major Trends in Jewish Mysticism*, Gershom Scholem speculates about a formative phase of *"merkabah* mysticism" in "the anonymous conventicles of the old apocalyptics" of the Second Temple period.[1] The suggestion is offered in the course of his argument for contextualizing Hekhalot literature as continuous with the esoteric discourses to which allusion is made in *m. Ḥagigah* 2.1, *t. Ḥagigah* 2.3–4, and related Rabbinic traditions.[2] Scholem explicitly states his aim not to delve into Second Temple materials, and *Major Trends* includes no sustained analysis of works like *1 Enoch*, even as he here alludes to them as "undoubtedly containing elements of Jewish mystical religion" and as possibly linked to later Hekhalot literature by "subterranean but effective, and occasionally traceable, connections."[3] Nevertheless, his passing nod to "the old apocalyptics" remains among the most referenced parts of Scholem's corpus, inspiring decades of investigation into the "mysticism" of early Enochic pseudepigrapha, the Dead Sea Scrolls, and the New Testament.

---

* This chapter originally appeared in 2013 as "Rethinking (Jewish-)Christian Evidence for Jewish Mysticism," in *Hekhalot Literature in Context: From Byzantium to Babylonia*, ed. Ra'anan S. Boustan, Martha Himmelfarb, and Peter Schäfer (TSAJ 153; Tübingen: Mohr Siebeck, 2013), 349–77. An earlier version was presented at a 2010 conference of the same name at Princeton University; I am grateful to Ra'anan S. Boustan, Peter Schäfer, Martha Himmelfarb, Dominique Côté, and Todd Krulak for feedback and suggestions. It is reprinted here, with some revisions and updates, with permission from Mohr Siebeck.

[1] Gershom Scholem, *Major Trends in Jewish Mysticism* (repr. ed.; New York: Schocken, 1995), 43. It is the boldest form of the argument – quoted here – that is most often cited and repeated, sometimes with the force of Scholem's authority seemingly obviating the need for primary source or other support. On the more tenuous tone and delicate argumentation in some of his later writings, see below.

[2] I.e., recast here in terms of three phases in the evolution of a single movement, with a focus on arguing for continuity between the "Merkabah mysticism of late and post-Talmudic times" and what Scholem reconstructs as the "Merkabah speculation of the Mishnaic teachers"; Scholem, *Major Trends in Jewish Mysticism*, 43. For detailed engagement with the main argument, see David J. Halperin, *The Faces of the Chariot: Early Jewish Responses to Ezekiel's Vision* (TSAJ 16; Tübingen: Mohr Siebeck, 1988); Peter Schäfer, *Hekhalot-Studien* (TSAJ 19; Tübingen: Mohr Siebeck, 1988); Schäfer, *Hidden and Manifest God: Some Major Themes in Early Jewish Mysticism* (trans. A. Pomerance; Albany: SUNY Press, 1992); Schäfer, *The Origins of Jewish Mysticism* (Tübingen: Mohr Siebeck, 2009).

[3] Scholem, *Major Trends in Jewish Mysticism*, 40–43; cf. Schäfer, *Origins of Jewish Mysticism*, 9–17.

One line of research – initiated by Ithmar Gruenwald and taken up most recently by Rachel Elior and Andrei Orlov – claims to find confirmation of Scholem's suggested connections in the recurrence of motifs (e. g., heavenly ascent, elevation of Enoch) from apocalyptic and other Second Temple sources (esp. *1 Enoch*) in later Hekhalot writings (esp. *3 Enoch*), albeit to the exclusion of the Rabbinic sages so central to Scholem's own argument.[4] Following this logic, moreover, shared motifs suffice to establish "*merkabah* mysticism" as a "religious movement of distinctive character" already in the age of Jesus and Paul.[5] Whereas Scholem sought pre-Christian roots for Hekhalot traditions in part to "disprove the old prejudice according to which all the productive religious energies of early apocalyptic were absorbed by and into Christianity,"[6] scholars such as Christopher Morray-Jones cite his suggestions as license to mine Hekhalot writings for "background" to the New Testament and Christian origins.[7]

The historicity of such connections is taken for granted within some sectors of specialist research on the New Testament.[8] Among specialists in Hekhalot literature and late antique Judaism, by contrast, the notion of a single mystical tradition running through Second Temple, New Testament, and Hekhalot literatures has met with much skepticism.[9] Peter Schäfer, Martha Himmelfarb, and

---

[4] Ithamar Gruenwald, *Apocalyptic and Merkavah Mysticism* (Leiden: Brill, 1980); Rachel Elior, *The Three Temples: On the Emergence of Jewish Mysticism* (Oxford: Littman Library of Jewish Civilization, 2004); Andrei A. Orlov, *The Enoch-Metatron Tradition* (TSAJ 107; Tübingen: Mohr Siebeck, 2005). Notably, much of this research does not go much beyond Scholem in evidentiary terms; Gruenwald, for instance, stresses in relation to *1 En.* 14 that "it is quite difficult to show the direct historical connection between Jewish apocalyptic and the Hekhalot literature" even if "the literary connections are almost self-evident," but he cites as his main example of the latter "the fact that the ancient Jewish mystical tradition is mainly focused on the vision of the divine Merkavah" (p. 45).

[5] Perhaps most influentially for New Testament Studies: Alan F. Segal, *Paul the Convert: The Apostolate and Apostasy of Saul the Pharisee* (New Haven: Yale University Press, 1992), 34–71. See below for further studies, as well as for Scholem's treatment of Paul.

[6] Scholem, *Major Trends in Jewish Mysticism*, 43.

[7] See his contributions to Christopher Rowland and Christopher R.A. Morray-Jones, *The Mystery of God: Early Jewish Mysticism and the New Testament* (Compendia rerum Iudaicarum ad Novum Testamentum 12; Leiden: Brill 2009), which also collects and synthesizes the ample bibliography on the topic in specialist research on the New Testament.

[8] See sources cited below, as well as James M. Scott, "Heavenly Ascent in Jewish and Pagan Traditions," in *Dictionary of New Testament Background*, ed. Craig A. Evans and Stanley E. Porter, Jr. (Downers Grove, IL: InterVarsity, 2000), 447–51; Jon C. Laansma, "Mysticism," in Evans and Porter, *Dictionary of New Testament Background*, 725–37. Note, however, the critique of Bruce Chilton, *Rabbi Jesus: An Intimate Biography* (New York: Doubleday, 2000), in Charles L. Quarles, "Jesus as Merkabah Mystic," *Journal for the Study of the Historical Jesus* 3 (2005): 5–22. On the counterparts to these discussions in scholarship on medieval Jewish mysticism, see further below.

[9] The most prominent exception to this pattern is the work of Philip S. Alexander; see, e. g., "From Son of Adam to Second God: Transformations of the Biblical Enoch," in *Biblical Figures Outside the Bible*, ed. Michael E. Stone and Theodore A. Bergren (Harrisburg: Trinity, 1998), 87–122; Alexander, "What Happened to the Jewish Priesthood After 70?" in *A Wander-*

Ra'anan Boustan, for instance, have critiqued the decontextualized comparison of motifs extracted from far-flung corpora, and Schäfer, in particular, has persistently questioned the sleight of hand whereby later Jewish sources have been made to serve as "background" for earlier Christian ones.[10] Nevertheless, Scholem's speculations continue to set the terms for the discussion: the relevance of Christian evidence to the historiography of Jewish mysticism has been largely reduced to the question of the continuity between Hekhalot literature and Second Temple Judaism.[11]

Reflecting on parallel debates about Jewish mysticism and *gnosis*, Guy Stroumsa has cautioned against the temptation to grapple only with Scholem and the debates in his wake.[12] This practice has tended to exacerbate disagreement, polarizing positions perhaps less dichotomous than they might appear. A broader purview – Stroumsa proposes – may help to establish some grounding from which, more pragmatically, to move ahead. In what follows, I would like to suggest something similar with respect to the profits and perils of bringing Christian sources to bear on the history of Jewish mysticism. Here too, fresh attention to older scholarly perspectives might help us to historicize our own approaches, exposing some of the assumptions embedded in the ways that we frame our categories and questions, select our texts and intertexts, and interpret them. Older perspectives might also remind us of sources now ripe for reconsideration.

In the first part of this essay, I reflect on the place of Christian evidence in modern reconstructions of the origins and history of Jewish mysticism, both before and after Scholem. In the second and third parts, I turn to consider the same issues with a focus on the Pseudo-Clementine *Homilies*, a "Jewish-Christian" work from fourth-century Syria, which was richly discussed in relation to Jewish mysticism by Heinrich Graetz and Shlomo Pines but dismissed by Scholem as a "hodge-podge" relevant only for its preservation of several fossilized frag-

---

ing Galilean: Essays in Honour of Seán Freyne, ed. Zuleika Rodgers, Margaret Daly-Denton, and Anne Fitzpatrick McKinley (JSJSup 132; Leiden: Brill, 2009), 3–34.

[10] See sources cited above, as well as Peter Schäfer, "New Testament and Hekhalot Literature: The Journey into Heaven in Paul and in Merkavah Mysticism," *JJS* 35 (1984): 19–35; Martha Himmelfarb, "Heavenly Ascent and the Relationship of the Apocalypses and the Hekhalot Literature," *HUCA* 59 (1988): 73–100; Himmelfarb, "Merkavah Mysticism since Scholem: Rachel Elior's *The Three Temples*," in *Wege mystischer Gotteserfahrung: Judentum, Christentum, und Islam*, ed. Peter Schäfer (Schriften des Historischen Kollegs Kolloquien 65; Munich: Oldenbourg, 2006), 19–36; Ra'anan S. Boustan, "The Study of Heikhalot Literature: Between Mystical Experience and Textual Artifact," *Currents in Biblical Research* 6 (2007): 130–60; Boustan, "Rabbinization and the Making of Early Jewish Mysticism," *JQR* 101 (2011): 482–502.

[11] On this relationship and the possibility of new paths for exploring it, see my reflections in "Categorization, Collection, and the Construction of Continuity: *1 Enoch* and *3 Enoch* in and beyond Apocalypticism and Mysticism," *MTSR* 29 (2017): 268–311.

[12] Guy G. Stroumsa, "Gnosis and Judaism in Nineteenth-Century Christian Thought," *JJTP* 2 (1992): 45–62. Indeed, as Stroumsa reminds us, "'discoveries' often reflect our ignorance, benign or malign, of history and of the history of research" (p. 46).

ments of archaic *gnosis*.[13] Whether or not the *Homilies* can be used to illumine the context of the Hekhalot literature *per se*, I shall suggest that it provides an interesting lens through which to reflect on challenges in the historiography of Jewish mysticism, particularly with respect to late antique sources and contexts.

Christianity in the Historiography of Jewish Mysticism

Already with Giovanni Pico della Mirandola (1463–1494), one finds attested the contention that mystical streams of Judaism are the ones that flow closest to Christianity. Setting much of the tone for Christian scholarship on Jewish mysticism in early modernity (and, to some degree, to this day), Pico famously claimed mysticism as Judaism's inner soul and secret history – the continuous oral and written transmission of pre-Christian teachings that so happens to mirror and presage Christianity.[14] Not only did he connect the Kabbalah with the seventy secret books said to be reserved for the wise in *4 Ezra* 14:45–47, but he posited the secret history of Judaism as "a religion not so much Mosaic as Christian ... the mystery of the Trinity, the Incarnation of the Word, the divinity of the Messiah."[15]

That such images could have consequences became dramatically clear during the Reformation and Counter-Reformation, when the campaign to censor and burn the Talmud was paired with the promotion of the printing of the *Zohar*. Influential for both was a Jewish convert to Catholicism, Sixtus of Sienna, whose assessments of the Talmud and Kabbalah found wide circulation in one of the earliest reference books on extrabiblical sources for the Christian study of the Bible.[16] Through his *Bibliotheca sancta*, first published in 1566, as well as through his involvement in discussions surrounding the printing of Hebrew texts, Sixtus did much to delineate the scope of Jewish parallels studied by Christian scholars

---

[13] Gershom Scholem, *On the Kabbalah and Its Symbolism* (trans. R. Manheim; repr. ed.; New York: Schocken, 1996), 172; Scholem, *Origins of the Kabbalah* (trans. A. Arkush; repr. ed.; Princeton: Princeton University Press, 1990), 141. On this pattern in research on the Pseudo-Clementines more broadly, see Chapter One in this volume.

[14] See further, e.g., Bernard McGinn, "Cabalists and Christians: Reflections on Cabala in Medieval and Renaissance Thought," in *Jewish Christians and Christian Jews, from the Renaissance to the Enlightenment*, ed. Richard H. Popkin and Gordon M. Weiner (Dordrecht: Kluwer, 1994), 11–34; Moshe Idel, *Kabbalah in Italy, 1280–1510* (New Haven: Yale University Press, 2011), 227–35.

[15] Giovanni Pico della Mirandola, *On the Dignity of Man* (trans. C. G. Wallis; repr. ed.; Indianapolis: Hackett, 1998), 29–30.

[16] I.e., Sixtus of Siena, *Bibliotheca sancta ex præcipuis Catholicæ Ecclesiæ auctoribus collecta* (Venice, 1566), 110ff, 125ff, for the defense of the Kabbalah and condemnation of the Talmud respectively. I discuss some of the broader context in relation to the reception of early Jewish apocalypses and other Second Temple texts and traditions in Annette Yoshiko Reed, "The Modern Invention of Old Testament Pseudepigrapha," *JTS* 60 (2009): 403–36; see esp. 418–19 on Sixtus.

and brought to bear on the study of the New Testament.[17] His much-repeated list of alleged slanders against Christianity in the Talmud helped to shape the Christian image of Rabbinic literature as emblematizing the Judaism that could be deemed the abject opposite of the Christian West – not least through his arguments for its burning or censorship.[18] Likewise, his placement of the Kabbalah, positively alongside what is now called "Old Testament Pseudepigrapha," may have been influential in the pairing of the two corpora as privileged sources for the esoteric, spiritual, experiential, hidden Judaism at Christianity's true origins. In contrast to the Talmud, he lauded the Kabbalah as "a more secret exposition of divine Law, received by Moses from the mouth of God, and by the fathers from the mouth of Moses in continuous succession, received not written, but orally," further fostering the notion of mystical materials as attesting the secret, proto-Christian history of Judaism, allegedly suppressed by talmudic Sages,[19]

If distant echoes of these ideas can still be heard today, it is perhaps partly due to their integration into nineteenth-century German research on Christian Origins by Jews and Christians alike. In the writings of Graetz, for instance, one finds the image of Jewish mysticism as the dark *syzygy* of Rabbinic rationalism and Jewish nationalism, as exemplified by the Essenism that he places equally at the roots of Christianity and the Kabbalah.[20] This notion was developed already in his 1846 *Gnosticismus und Judentum* and widely diffused among Jewish intellectuals through his seminal *History of the Jews*. In this, however, Graetz owed much to Augustus Neander (né David Mendel, 1789–1850), a Jewish convert to Christianity who had explored similar ideas already in his influential 1818 monograph on *gnosis*.[21] By the 1830s, in fact, Ferdinand Christian Baur

---

[17] On the place of this work in the history of biblical scholarship as well as the debates of the Counter-Reformation, see Irena Backus, *Historical Method and Confessional Identity in the Era of the Reformation (1378–1615)* (Studies in Medieval and Reformation Thought 94; Leiden: Brill, 2003), 212–18.

[18] See further Kenneth R. Stow, "The Burning of the Talmud in 1553, in Light of Sixteenth-Century Catholic Attitudes toward the Talmud," *Bibliothèque d'Humanisme et Renaissance* 34 (1972): 435–59, esp. 456–57; Amnon Raz-Krakotzkin, *The Censor, the Editor, and the Text: The Catholic Church and the Shaping of the Jewish Canon in the Sixteenth Century* (trans. Jackie Feldman; Philadelphia: University of Pennsylvania Press, 2007), 123–24.

[19] Sixtus, *Bibliotheca sancta*, 110v, with translation from Stow, "Burning of the Talmud," 457. On the very same page, in fact, Sixtus posits the Kabbalah as a missionary tool that enables Christians to "stab Jews with their own weapon."

[20] Heinrich Graetz, *Gnosticismus und Judentum* (Krotoschin: Monasch, 1846); Graetz, *History of the Jews, from the Earliest Times to the Present Day* (6 vols.; trans. B. Lowy; Philadelphia: JPS, 1891–1898), 2:28, 142, 148–57, 171, 367. See also Jonathan M. Elukin, "A New Essenism: Heinrich Graetz and Mysticism," *Journal for the History of Ideas* 59 (1998): 135–48.

[21] August Neander, *Genetische Entwickelung der vornehmsten gnostischen Systeme* (Berlin: Dümmler, 1818), 361–421; cf. Graetz, *Gnosticismus und Judentum*, 4–5 and *passim*. Here and below, I use the term "*gnosis*" to refer to the complex of related ancient traditions discussed under that rubric by nineteenth-century German historians such as Neander and Baur, as well as the philosophers in conversation with them, such as Georg Wilhelm Friedrich Hegel. This understanding of "*gnosis*" must thus be distinguished from more specific notions of "Gnosticism,"

had built upon Neander's work for his famous use of the Pseudo-Clementines as a source for "Jewish-Christianity,"[22] and August Friedrich Gfrörer could take for granted that the Pseudo-Clementines might be termed a "Greek *Zohar*."[23] As with Scholem's subsequent romantic reversal of the rationalism of Graetz's account, so Graetz may have ironically reinscribed something of the structure of the dominant Christian narratives that he sought to counter and subvert.[24]

Given this tangled lineage, it is perhaps not surprising that the search for Christian parallels for Jewish mysticism might remain methodologically perilous to this day, even in historical research where the possibility of parallels serves mainly pragmatic aims. Furthermore, even with far more evidence at hand than available to Neander, Graetz, or Scholem, the present-day scholar who seeks to reconstruct a history of Jewish mysticism is still faced with frustratingly large gaps between those data that might seem best to attest it. The Second Temple Jewish apocalypses that tell of ancient heroes snatched up by God into heaven are separated by many centuries – as well as notable differences of genre, aim, and perspective – from the ritually achieved "descents to the *merkabah*" described in the Hekhalot literature in relation to rabbis like R. Akiva and R. Ishmael.[25] In turn, the medieval manuscripts in which the latter are preserved stand at some remove from the strictures and cautionary tales about the exposition of *ma'aseh merkabah* in the Rabbinic literature of Late Antiquity – those sources that might seem, at first sight, to hold all the main clues as to whether traditions now known, in full, only in medieval forms may or may not stand in direct lineage with those attested, nearly a millennium prior, in pre-Christian works like the *Book of the Watchers* or *Songs of Sabbath Sacrifice*.[26] Reconstructing the

---

first developed in relation to the notices about Sethians, Valentinians, et al., in the writings of Irenaeus, Epiphanius, and other Christian heresiologists, and now reconsidered in the light of the Nag Hammadi literature. See discussion below.

[22] Ferdinand Christian Baur, "Die Christuspartei in der korinthischen Gemeide, der Gegensatz des petrinischen and paulischen Christentums in der alten Kirche, der Apostel Petrus in Rom," *Tübinger Zeitschrift für Theologie* 5 (1831): 61–206. Baur is quite explicit about his debt to Neander in this regard in *Kirchengeschichte des 19. Jahrhunderts* (Tübingen: Fues, 1862), 395.

[23] August Friedrich Gfrörer, *Das Jahrhundert des Heils* (2 vols.; Stuttgart: Schweizerbart, 1838), 1:295–97.

[24] See further David Biale, *Gershom Scholem: Kabbalah and Counterhistory* (2nd ed.; Cambridge, MA: Harvard University Press, 1982); Michael Brenner, "Gnosis and History: Polemics of German-Jewish Identity from Graetz to Scholem," *New German Critique* 77 (1999): 45–60.

[25] Martha Himmelfarb, *Ascent to Heaven in Jewish and Christian Apocalypses* (Oxford: Oxford University Press, 1993); Annelies Kuyt, *The "Descent" to the Chariot: Towards a Description of the Terminology, Place, Function, and Nature of the Yeridah in Hekhalot Literature* (TSAJ 45; Tübingen: Mohr Siebeck, 1995).

[26] Boustan, "Study of Heikhalot Literature"; David J. Halperin, *The Merkabah in Rabbinic Literature* (New Haven: Yale University Press, 1980); Peter Schäfer, "Research on Hekhalot Literature: Where Do We Stand Now?" in *Rashi 1040–1990: Hommage à Ephraïm E. Urbach*, ed. G. Sed-Rajna (Paris: Cerf, 1993), 229–35. On the gap of time and geography separating all

relationships among the relevant traditions from solely inner-Jewish evidence, moreover, entails efforts to divine patterns of connection between traditions shaped by anonymous or pseudonymous authors and redactors. As perhaps to be expected, the results have been varied and contested.[27]

As a result, the possibility of Christian parallels can be especially tantalizing. Named authors with clear geographical associations and datable writings are almost as common in the Christian literatures of Late Antiquity as they are rare in their Jewish counterparts. To find even a single uncontested point of connection, then, could serve like a peg, pinning date and place to theories that might otherwise seem relegated to the realm of unfalsifiable hypotheses. And, accordingly, "proof" of this sort has been sought even by those historians of mysticism who might seem most content to make recourse to secrecy, esoteric channels of transmission, or "subterranean streams" to connect materials of far-flung date and provenance.

Over a decade after the statements cited at the outset, for instance, even Scholem himself seemed more circumspect about asserting the obviousness of a connection between Second Temple Judaism and Hekhalot literature. With respect to the claims made for the Dead Sea Scrolls in this regard, for instance, his 1960 *Jewish Gnosticism, Merkabah Mysticism, and Talmudic Tradition* sounded a note of skepticism:

It has been maintained that "a pre-Christian Judaism of Gnostic character … which hitherto could be inferred only from later sources is now attested to by this newly discovered Dead Sea Scrolls." It is said too that this Jewish Gnosis is still deeply rooted … in later Jewish apocalyptic. Although such a hypothesis is psychologically and historically quite plausible, *I must admit that I have come to view these statements with much skepticism.* As a careful reader of these texts, I have not been able to detect those special terms and shades of meaning ….. It has even been said that the scrolls are essentially mystical documents and that the experiences spoken of in the Scroll of Hymns are genuinely mystical experiences. If so, we would then possess the first documents of Jewish mysticism preserved in Hebrew, and it would only be fair to look for the continuation of the tradition in later Jewish developments. *But whether this point … will prove true is highly debatable.*[28]

To ground his argument against Graetz for the antiquity of the Jewish traditions attested in the Hekhalot literature, Scholem thus turned instead to Christian evidence.

---

of these from the Kabbalah as first attested in the *Bahir*, see Scholem, *Origins of the Kabbalah*, 3–48; Schäfer, *Mirror of His Beauty* (Princeton: Princeton University Press, 2002).

[27] E. g., Philip S. Alexander, "3 Enoch and the Talmud," *JSJ* 18 (1987): 40–68; Christopher R.A. Morray-Jones, "Hekhalot Literature and the Talmudic Tradition: Alexander's Three Test Cases," *JSJ* 22 (1991): 1–39.

[28] Gershom Scholem, *Jewish Gnosticism, Merkabah Mysticism, and Talmudic Tradition* (New York: JTSA, 1960), 3–4; italics mine. See now Michael D. Swartz, "The Dead Sea Scrolls and Later Jewish Magic and Mysticism," *DSD* 8 (2001): 182–93.

Scholem, of course, notes that "ecstatic journeys are well-known in Jewish literature from the days of the early apocalypticists to those of the Hekhaloth," but refrains from arguing for a direct connection of the two based solely on the common motif.[29] In Paul's allusion to "a man … caught up into the third heaven … into Paradise" in 2 Cor 12:2–4, however, he finds first-century evidence to pin down the connection: "Paul's testimony is a link between these older Jewish texts and the Gnosis of the Tannaitic Merkabah mystics."[30] Similarly, Scholem posits a further clue to the antiquity of the discourse of *Shi'ur ha-Qomah* in Origen of Alexandria's statement that only mature Jews are permitted to study the beginning of Genesis, the beginning and end of Ezekiel, and Song of Songs (see preface to *Hom. Cant.* [PL 13.63]).[31] Speculating that mystical reflection on the body of God might lurk behind the seeming Jewish discomfort with the Songs of Songs noted secondhand by Origen, he emphasizes the implications for dating: "If it is thus true that Origen's statement and our fragments of *Shiur Komah* explain each other, there can no longer be any valid reason to assign a late date to the sources from which these fragments derive."[32] In each case, what is at stake for Scholem in identifying a Christian parallel is the possibility of an early (and ideally pre-Christian) dating – in the case of Paul, to establish the antiquity of what he sees as the core of the Hekhalot literature in heavenly ascent, and in the case of Origen, to establish an ancient Jewish lineage for the anthropomorphic reflection of the divine that might connect the Hekhalot literature to the Kabbalah.[33]

---

[29] Scholem, *Jewish Gnosticism*, 18; cf. Himmelfarb, "Heavenly Ascent."

[30] Scholem, *Jewish Gnosticism*, 18.

[31] Scholem, *Jewish Gnosticism*, 36–42; cf. Halperin, *Faces of the Chariot*, 322–58; Schäfer, *Origins of Jewish Mysticism*, 183–84, 306–15. Compare also Scholem's rearticulation of the same argument in *On the Mystical Shape of the Godhead: Basic Concepts in the Kabbalah* (trans. J. Neugroschel; New York: Schocken, 1991), 29–33, with reference to *2 Enoch*, Justin Martyr, the Pseudo-Clementines, and Mandean traditions.

[32] Scholem, *Jewish Gnosticism*, 40. Other examples include his discussion of the *Apocalypse of Zephaniah*, where he notes that "even if we should assume that we are dealing here with an early Christian apocalypse, the quotation [about "Palaces"] would still prove how much common ground existed between the ideas and terminology used in such early Christian texts and the Hekhalot literature" – emphatically stressing that "it stands to reason that this common ground was *Jewish*" (p. 19; italics mine). He makes a similar argument (p. 41), albeit more telegraphically, about the Pseudo-Clementine literature, as noted below. Compare his appeal to Revelation and the *Apocalypse of Abraham* on p. 23.

[33] Pushing the antiquity of the Hekhalot literature even further back than was posited in *Major Trends in Jewish Mysticism* (i. e., before the fourth and fifth centuries) is Scholem's main aim here, as he stresses repeatedly; *Jewish Gnosticism*, 8, 23. See Scholem, *On the Mystical Shape*, 30, for a sharp articulation of what's at stake in relation to Graetz's image of *Shi'ur Qomah* traditions as having developed in interaction with Islamic anthropomorphism. For Scholem, the antiquity of Jewish anthropomorphism is also key to arguing both for the central position of mysticism within Rabbinic Judaism and the possibility that Jewish monotheistic reflection on God's forms preceded the dualism of non-Jewish *gnosis*, rather than arising in reaction to it

Above, we noted one of the epiphenomenal results of this line of discussion, namely, the embrace of Hekhalot literature by some New Testament specialists as yet another mine to cull for "background" to Jesus and the New Testament.[34] This is perhaps not surprising: it has long been commonplace in scholarship on the New Testament to approach the entirety of Judaism (and, indeed, much of the Mediterranean world) as "background" for the drama of Christian origins; such practices go back at least as early as Sixtus of Sienna, and their pursuit continues unabated today. What proves more puzzling, to my mind, is the persistence of the counterpart in research on Jewish mysticism, whereby Christian parallels are not just selectively plucked but also filtered through the unexamined assumption that any Jewish counterpart must be earlier in date.[35] Since Scholem, entire debates about how best to date and situate the ascent practices that he placed at the very heart of the Hekhalot literature have thus turned on the interpretation of two infamously slippery verses in 2 Corinthians, with Paul either helping or hindering the plausibility of the presumption that unbroken lines of development connect this literature to the *Book of the Watchers* (esp. *1 En.* 14) and other early texts from Second Temple times.[36]

Scholem's pattern of argumentation has been perhaps as influential as his ideas: for others too, Christian parallels offer the possibility of datable moments

(p. 34–35); cf. Scholem, *Origins of the Kabbalah*, 18–24; Guy G. Stroumsa, "Forms of God: Some Notes on Metatron and Christ," *HTR* 76 (1983): 269–88 at 287–88.

[34] See below, as well as Morton Smith, "Two Ascended to Heaven – Jesus and the Author of 4Q491," in *Jesus and the Dead Sea Scrolls*, ed. James H. Charlesworth (New York: Doubleday, 1992), 290–301; James M. Scott, "The Triumph of God in 2 Cor 2.14: Additional Evidence of Merkabah Mysticism in Paul," *NTS* 42 (1996): 260–81; James R. Davila, "The Hodayot Hymnist and the Four Who Entered Paradise," *RevQ* 17 (1996): 457–78; Davila, "The Hekhalot Literature and the Ancient Jewish Apocalypses," in *Paradise Now: Essays on Early Jewish and Christian Mysticism*, ed. April D. DeConick (SBL Symposium Series 11; Atlanta: SBL, 2006), 105–25; Timo Eskola, *Messiah and the Throne: Jewish Merkabah Mysticism and Early Christian Exaltation Discourse* (WUNT 142; Tübingen: Mohr Siebeck, 2001).

[35] This tendency is perhaps enabled by a tendency to approach parallels of materials deemed "mystical" or "esoteric" as bearing a different burden of proof or logic of connection than those otherwise common in historical research; see further Annette Yoshiko Reed, *Fallen Angels and the History of Judaism and Christianity: The Reception of Enochic Literature* (Cambridge: Cambridge University Press, 2005), 247, 269–70.

[36] Compare, e. g., Schäfer, "New Testament and Hekhalot Literature," esp. 19–20; Segal, *Paul the Convert*, 34–71; Christopher R. A. Morray-Jones, "Paradise Revisited (2 Cor 12:1–12): The Jewish Mystical Background of Paul's Apostolate, Part 1: The Jewish Sources," *HTR* 86 (1993): 177–217; Morray-Jones, "Paradise Revisited (2 Cor 12:1–12): The Jewish Mystical Background of Paul's Apostolate, Part 2: *Paul's* Heavenly Ascent and Its Significance," *HTR* 86 (1993): 265–92; James D. Tabor, *Things Unutterable: Paul's Ascent to Paradise in its Graeco-Roman, Judaic, and Early Christian Contexts* (Lanham, MD: University Press of America, 1986); Johannes A. Loubser, "Paul and the Politics of Apocalyptic Mysticism: An Exploration of 2 Cor 11:30–12:10," *Neotestamentica* 34 (2000): 191–206; Paula Gooder, *Only the Third Heaven? 2 Corinthians 12.1–10 and Heavenly Ascent* (London: T&T Clark, 2006); M. David Litwa, "Paul's Mosaic Ascent: An Interpretation of 2 Corinthians 12.7–9," *NTS* 57 (2011): 238–57.

in the history of Jewish mysticism but also opportunities to backdate the Jewish portion of the pair – whether extant or hypothetical.[37] Even otherwise unassailable historians have argued along these lines, for example, to posit traditions about the elevation of Enoch as Metatron in the late Hekhalot macroform *3 Enoch* as necessarily predating or "influencing" the similar images of Jesus as angel and Christ in New Testament, early Christian, and so-called "gnostic" sources – even despite the fact that the relevant materials concerning Jesus are attested many centuries prior to *3 Enoch*.[38] Likewise, Pauline ideas such as that of a primal ἄνθρωπος, or the metonym of messiah and first man, have been cited as proof for the pre-Christian antiquity of Jewish mystical traditions first attested in medieval forms in distinctively Christian cultural contexts.[39]

The problems with such approaches have been often noted most extensively by Schäfer. Not only has he stressed that "comparison of isolated motifs … can always only be provisional," but he has interrogated the place of Christian parallels in the historiography of the Hekhalot literature as well as the Kabbalah.[40] Despite such interventions, however, notions of the "*merkabah* mysticism" of Jesus, Paul, and John of Patmos continue to be accepted in some scholarly cir-

---

[37] I.e., the pattern of argumentation in Scholem, *Jewish Gnosticism*, 18–19, 41–42, etc., whereby a Christian text with a late Jewish parallel or hypothetical Jewish source can be cited as evidence to prove the existence of a putatively ancient Jewish motif or idea – sometimes by the logic, moreover, that any Jewish influence on Christianity must be placed before the purported "parting" of the two religions.

[38] Stroumsa, "Forms of God," esp. 281–84; Moshe Idel, "Enoch is Metatron," *Immanuel* 24–25 (1990): 222–23; Jarl E. Fossum, *The Image of the Invisible God* (Göttingen: Vandenhoeck & Ruprecht, 1995). Compare, however, Daniel Boyarin, "Beyond Judaisms: Metatron and the Divine Polymorphy of Ancient Judaism," *JSJ* 41 (2010): 323–65.

[39] Idel ("Enoch is Metatron," 223), for instance, reflects upon the striking absence of traditions about the elevated Adam in the Hekhalot literature in light of its prominence in the Kabbalah, and he makes note of the prominence of Adamic themes in Christianity as well as the fact that "the Kabbalah that developed the concept of the Supernal Adam flourished precisely in Christian regions" while in "areas under Islamic influence, by contrast, nothing of the kind came to the surface during the hundreds of years preceding the growth of the Kabbalah in Europe." Even while admitting that "any suggestion that originally Jewish conceptions were suppressed for centuries in Jewish sources has inherent difficulties," Idel nevertheless concludes that "it is likely to be more convenient than the alternative" (p. 223). From the standpoint of the Jewish materials, it may make sense to admit that "it is possible, certainly, that the author of the *Zohar* was familiar with some Book of Adam … and in this manner a possibly Christian conception … entered the Jewish source," while also positing that "no less plausible, however, is the possibility of a survival of an apparently pre-Christian conception" (p. 230). My point here, rather, is that such logic can become problematic when it becomes a principle through which seemingly parallel Christian sources are read.

[40] Schäfer, "New Testament and Hekhalot Literature," 34; Schäfer, *Mirror of His Beauty*; Schäfer, *Die Geburt des Judentums aus dem Geist des Christentums* (Tübingen: Mohr Siebeck, 2010). See also Annette Yoshiko Reed, "From Asael and Šemiḥazah to Uzzah, Azzah, and Azael: *3 Enoch* 5 (§§ 7–8) and Jewish Reception-History of *1 Enoch*," *JSQ* 8 (2001): 105–36; Reed, *Fallen Angels and the History of Judaism and Christianity*, 233–72 – with respect to the *Book of the Watchers*, *3 Enoch*, and the possibility of Jewish "back-borrowing" from Byzantine Christian chronographical materials.

cles – typically among those with primary training in either pre-Rabbinic or later medieval periods. These ideas have been pursued, moreover, increasingly in isolation from newer lines of specialist research on the Hekhalot literature, which have been turning away from questions of "origins" and towards questions of context – and, hence, to the investigation of late antique Jewish *comparanda*.

Recent research has pointed to the value of looking to liturgical, magical, and other late antique Jewish sources to contextualize Hekhalot literature, as well as the importance of paying heed to medieval manuscripts and trajectories.[41] In what follows, I shall suggest that we may wish to attend to a broader range of Christian materials too, including late antique "Jewish-Christian" materials understood on their own terms and in their own settings. The allure of antiquity has facilitated the focus on the New Testament and has helped to naturalize the mining of later sources for earlier Jewish traditions, but much may be missed when the utility of Christian parallels is reduced to the validation of the place of mysticism in Christianity's Jewish "background."

"Jewish-Christian" Evidence for Jewish Mysticism?

Interestingly, the use of Christian parallels to posit pre-Christian traditions of Jewish mysticism has been dominant mainly in the wake of Scholem and his re-reading of the apostle Paul as *yored ha-merkabah*. In earlier research, more emphasis fell on late antique parallels, including "Jewish-Christian" sources placed in varying degrees of conflict and contact with the broad-based Neoplatonizing and related intellectual trends that scholars of an earlier age called "*gnosis*."[42]

Graetz, for instance, may have been infamously skeptical about the antiquity of the Hekhalot literature, but he posited an early connection between Jewish mysticism, non-Jewish *gnosis*, and "Jewish-Christianity" already in *Gnosticismus und Judentum*.[43] Following Neander, Baur, and others, he accepted the sec-

---

[41] See essays and bibliography in Boustan, Himmelfarb, and Schäfer, eds., *Hekhalot Literature in Context*.

[42] See further Stroumsa, "Gnosis and Judaism"; Arnaldo Momigliano, "Prologue in Germany (Unpublished, 1979)," in *Nono contributo alla storia degli studi classici e del mondo antico*, ed. Riccardo Di Donato (Rome: Edizioni Storia e Letteratura, 1992), 543–62.

[43] Note that Scholem (*On the Kabbalah*, 172) credits Graetz as the first to note a possible connection between *Sefer Yetzirah* and the Pseudo-Clementines. Graetz does so while arguing against the direct connection of *Sefer Yetzirah* with Marcosians posited in Johann Franz Buddeus, *Introductio ad historiam philosophiae Ebraeorum* (Halle, 1702), which he critiques for not distinguishing between different stages in the development of Kabbalah; see Graetz, *Gnosticismus und Judentum*, 109–10. Graetz points to the Pseudo-Clementine *Homilies* as a closer parallel, building on Neander's understanding of those works as second-century "Jewish-Christian" writings that polemicize against *gnosis* while simultaneously absorbing or appropriating some ideas: "Wohl aber hat der Geist des *Buches Iezira* mit dem Ideengange eines halb gnostischen Buches vieles gemein, von dem es jedoch in der Form himmelweit verschieden ist. Ich meine

ond-century date for the Pseudo-Clementine *Homilies*. He consequently brought them to bear on his allegorical reading of the Rabbinic tale of the four who entered *pardes* (*t. Ḥagigah* 2.3–4) as a parable about the Jewish encounter with *gnosis*.[44] Most striking, however, are the parallels he notes with *Sefer Yetzirah* – a work which Graetz, at the time, approached as a second-century work as well; these include the idea of spatial "extensions," the emanation of primal elements from the spirit of God, and the theory of opposites.[45] From such parallels, he posited the early synthesis of a Jewish *gnosis* due to the transmission of traditions into Rabbinic Judaism by "Jewish-Christians."[46] This *gnosis* – he went on to suggest – was embraced by no less a figure than Rabbi Akiba so as to be effectively battled on its own ground, in a manner both presaging and preparing for later inner-Jewish struggles over the Kabbalah.[47]

In his later work, Graetz abandoned an early dating for *Sefer Yetzirah*, and at the end of the nineteenth century, the Pseudo-Clementine *Homilies* were shown to be creations of the early fourth century CE, rather than the second.[48] In addition, the discovery of the Nag Hammadi literature in the middle of the twentieth century rendered irrelevant much of the debate about *gnosis* that made the theories of Neander and Graetz so timely in their own age.[49] That something valuable might nevertheless remain in their insights, however, was suggested in a 1989 article by Shlomo Pines.[50]

---

hier die *Clementinen* oder *Pseudoklementinen*, einem halb gnostischen halb antignostischen Buche aus dem zweiten Jahrhundert, welches nach der kritischen Untersuchung Neanders einen Nazaräer zum Verfasser haben soll, und daher bald gnostische Voraussetzungen hat, bald nieder gegen den radicalen Gnosticismus polemisirt" (p. 110). See also p. 23 n. 19, where he cites *Hom* 11.6 as a parallel to *b. Avodah Zarah* 47, and p. 41, where he quotes a speech it attributes to Simon Magus to expound the "gnostic" perspective on the Demiurge. In his section on "Die jüdischen Gnostiker" (p. 55), the Pseudo-Clementines serve as an example of what he means by this category (i. e., as encompassing even those not necessarily Jews by birth, and hence applying to Valentinius as well; see further Stroumsa, "Gnosis and Judaism," 49). I am not certain whether the different chapter numbering reflects printing mistakes or his use of an edition not known to me: he cites *Hom.* 11.6 as 9.6, for instance, and *Hom.* 18.1 as 17.

[44] Graetz, *Gnosticismus und Judentum*, 102–3.

[45] Graetz, *Gnosticismus und Judentum*, 109–15.

[46] This position, notably, is maintained even after he abandons an early dating for *Sefer Yetzirah*; see, e. g., Graetz, *History of the Jews*, 2:380–81.

[47] See further Brenner, "Gnosis and History," 48–50.

[48] Charles Biggs, "The Clementine *Homilies*," in *Studia biblica et ecclesiastica: Essays Chiefly in Biblical and Patristic Criticism*, vol. 2 (Oxford: Clarendon, 1890), 191–92, 368–69; Hans Waitz, *Die Pseudoklementinen: Homilien und Rekognitionem: Eine quellen-kritische Untersuchung* (TU 10.4; Leipzig: Hinrichs, 1904), 372; John Chapman, "On the Date of the Clementines," *ZNW* 9 (1908): 147–59.

[49] Philip S. Alexander, "Comparing Merkavah Mysticism and Gnosticism: An Essay in Method," *JJS* 35 (1984): 1–18. For the twentieth-century trajectories, see now Karen L. King, *What is Gnosticism?* (Cambridge, MA: Harvard University Press, 2005).

[50] Shlomo Pines, "Points of Similarity between the Exposition of the Doctrine of the *Sefirot* in the *Sefer Yeẓira* and a Text of the Pseudo-Clementine *Homilies*: The Implications of this Resemblance," *Proceedings of the Israel Academy of Sciences and Humanities* 7 (1989): 63–142.

Like Graetz, Pines focused on *Hom.* 17.7–12, where God is described first in surprisingly anthropomorphic terms (esp. 17.7) and then in relation to his "extensions" into space (17.9–10). Earlier works by Scholem, notably, had pointed in passing to the former as signaling some "connection with Jewish Gnostic fragments extant in the Hebrew and Aramaic texts of the *Shi'ur Komah*."[51] Yet for Pines, the latter proves most significant due to the possible parallel with *Sefer Yetzirah*. In the mouth of the apostle Peter is here placed an understanding of God's six spatially-situated yet infinite "extensions" (Gr. ἐκτάσεις) which – Pines argues – belong to the prehistory of the doctrine of the ten *sefirot*.[52]

For Pines, the connections prove interesting precisely because they are so puzzling, resonating with "pagan," Jewish, and Christian traditions alike. Rather

---

To be sure, Pines does not frame his own inquiry in terms of any such recovery of older scholarly perspectives. He makes only a passing reference to Graetz, signaling in a footnote (p. 79 n. 154) that he is preceded in connecting *Sefer Yetzirah* with the Pseudo-Clementines only by Graetz and in Abraham Epstein's brief statements dependant on Graetz in "Recherches sur le Sefer Yeçira," *REJ* 29 (1894): 73.

[51] Scholem makes this suggestion in *On the Mystical Shape of the Godhead* (p. 30) in the course of his argument for the antiquity of *Shi'ur Qomah* traditions, pointing to its reference to the divine body as "incomparably more luminous than the spirit with which we perceive it," together with the emphasis on God's "beauty" (cf. Heb. יופי), in *Hom.* 17.7–8. In his *Jewish Gnosticism*, a passing reference to the Pseudo-Clementine description of God as having bodily form in *Hom.* 3.7 and 17.7–8 is further used to posit that "it may therefore be surmised that the Gnostic Markos took the variant of the *Shiur Komah* that he used for his doctrine of the 'Body of Truth' from sources of a strictly *Jewish* character" (p. 41; italics mine). For attempts to ground this suggestion in Pauline sources, see Stroumsa, "Forms of God," 280–84, 287–88; Charles Mopsik, "La datation du Chi'our Qomah d'après un texte neotestamentaire," *RSR* 2 (1994): 131–44. By contrast, Schäfer (*Origins of Jewish Mysticism*, 313) dismisses the entire line of argument, stressing that the sources cited "discuss the well-known problem of anthropomorphism … and have nothing to do with the *Shi'ur Qomah* in a technical sense." For consideration and critique of the variations of Scholem's argument offered by Jarl Fossum (e. g., "Jewish-Christian Christology and Jewish Mysticism," *VC* 37 [1983]: 260–87) and others, see now Dominique Côté, "La forme de Dieu dans les *Homélies Pseudo-clémentines* et la notion de Shiur Qomah," in *"Soyez des changeurs avisés": Controverses exégétiques dans la literature apocryphe chrétienne*, ed. Gabriella Aragione and Rémi Gounelle (Cahiers de Biblia Patristica 12; Strasbourg: Université de Strasbourg, 2012), 69–94.

For our present purposes, it is notable that Scholem's references to the Pseudo-Clementines never go beyond the level of stray suggestions tossed out as possibilities, fleetingly raised in the course of broader arguments, quickly dropped, and left undefended, or alternately raised for the sake of highlighting its derivative or irrelevant character (*On the Mystical Shape*, 214; Scholem, *On the Kabbalah*, 172). Inasmuch as the Pseudo-Clementines was so central for Graetz's mounting of the opposite argument about the ultimate priority of non-Jewish/dualism versus Jewish/monotheistic *gnosis*, one wonders whether Scholem is ultimately unwilling to commit to making an argument rooted in these works; the very hybrid character that makes them such a rich reservoir for motifs, moreover, may also undermines their utility for a vision of Jewish mysticism as a unified (and uniformly Jewish) tradition with roots in ancient *gnosis* and clear-cut phases of development thereafter. What is a central source for Graetz's understanding of Jewish *gnosis*, in any case, becomes for Scholem merely a footnote to the history of Jewish *gnosis*/mysticism.

[52] Pines, "Points of Similarity," 79–87.

than limiting himself to Jewish parallels, Pines shows how the ἐκτάσεις of the Pseudo-Clementine *Homilies* make sense in relation to Stoic philosophy and terminology, as well as to the cosmological ideas of the third-century Christian philosopher Bardaisan of Edessa. When pushed to speculate on the directionality of possible "influence," he cautiously posits that the ferment of ideas in the late antique Syrian milieu, as reflected by the Pseudo-Clementines and Bardaisan alike, might have served as one crucible for ideas in *Sefer Yetzirah*.[53]

For our purposes, Pines' suggestions are especially important to note, inasmuch as his article is sometimes cited to suggest the opposite. Moshe Idel, for instance, references Pines in support of his appeal to the "second-century Pseudo-Clementine *Homilies*" as a source for relevant motifs for Jewish mystical ideas and for noting how the "Pseudo-Clementinian *Homilies* and *Recognitions* preserved important Jewish traditions, some of which have parallels in medieval Jewish esotericism."[54] Pines, thus, is referenced seemingly in support of a second-century dating not accepted since the age of Graetz, as well as for the extension of Scholem's approach to these and other Christian sources. When discussing the prehistory of the *golem*, Idel similarly cites Pines and follows Scholem – in that case, pointing to the demiurgic theurgy attributed to Simon Magus in the Pseudo-Clementine *Homilies* (2.32, 34; 4.4) and *Recognitions* (2.9, 3.57), wherein the arch-heretic is described as having created a human boy out of air.[55] Despite the fourth-century date of the Pseudo-Clementines, and Pines' detailed arguments in relation to *Sefer Yetzirah* in a late antique context,[56] Idel treats these "Jewish-Christian" materials only as vessels for a few lost sparks of "a hypothetical archaic Jewish tradition."[57] The other possibility – that traditions could have traveled into Jewish mysticism from "Jewish-Christian" circles and/

------

[53] But note already Graetz, *Gnosticismus und Judentum*, 116 – who does not argue for direct "influence" connecting the Pseudo-Clementines with *Sefer Yetzirah*, but rather suggests that: "Diese Nachweisungen werden wohl den Schluß über alle Zweifel sichern, daß die Abfassungszeit des *Buches Iezira* in eine Zeit fallen muß, wo die eben entwickelten Ideen und Methoden im Schwange waren, wo die gnostischen Vorstellungsweisen, welche doch unstreitig in den angeführten Parallelen erkennbar genug durchblicken, geläusig und verständlich waren."

[54] Moshe Idel, "Sabbath: On Concepts of Time in Jewish Mysticism," in *Sabbath: Idea, History, Reality*, ed. Gerald L. Blidstein (Goldstein-Goren Library of Jewish Thought 1; Beer Sheva: Ben Gurion University of the Negev Press, 2004), 57–94 at 59 and n. 4.

[55] Scholem, *On the Kabbalah*, 172; Moshe Idel, *Golem: Jewish Magical and Mystical Traditions on the Artificial Anthropoid* (Albany: SUNY Press, 1990), 5–8.

[56] For a ninth-century date and Islamic cultural context for *Sefer Yetzirah*, see now Steven M. Wasserstrom, "*Sefer Yeṣira* and Early Islam: A Reappraisal," *JJTP* 3 (1993): 1–30; Wasserstrom, "Further Thoughts on the Origins of *Sefer yeṣirah*," *Aleph* 2 (2002): 201–21. An early date is maintained by Yehuda Liebes, *Torat ha-yesirah shel Sefer yeṣirah* (Jerusalem: Schocken, 2000) on grounds similar to those posited already by Graetz. See, however, Y. Tzvi Langermann's critique of Liebes in "On the Beginnings of Hebrew Scientific Literature and on Studying History through *Maqbilot* (Parallels)," *Aleph* 2 (2002): 169–89 at pp. 176–89. His methodological reflections on the assessment of parallels is relevant here as well.

[57] Idel, *Golem*, 6.

or commonly emerged from the intellectual ferment of late antique Syria – is closed off.[58]

Much like Pines himself, however, I would suggest that it is precisely this seemingly hybrid character that might make this source potentially so relevant for tracing the transmission and transformation of ideas. As a Greek novel compiled in fourth-century Syria by Christians who seem to have self-identified as Jews, the *Homilies* exhibit deep antipathy but also deep familiarity with Hellenistic *paideia*, in keeping with what seems to have been the bilingual Greek and Syriac milieu in which they took form, possibly in Edessa.[59] Moreover, they signal both awareness and acceptance of the Rabbinic traditions of their own time – as demonstrated by Al Baumgarten with respect to traditions about the Pharisees and Oral Torah, as well as argued by myself and others in relation to tales about disputations with *minim*, the halakhic discourse about menstrual purity, and the midrashic defense of biblical monotheism against the denigration of the Demiurge.[60] Indeed, as David Aaron and Alon Goshen-Gottstein have shown, the Pseudo-Clementines' anthropomorphic imagery of God – which Scholem and Idel treat as "mystical" – also makes sense when read in the context of the ethics of the Mishnah (e. g., *m. Sanhedrin* 4.5) and the exegetical logics of various Rabbinic midrashim (e. g., *Qohelet Rabbah* 8.2).[61]

---

[58] Contrast, however, Elliot Wolfson's reading of the anthropomorphism of this passage in synchronic terms, drawing out the philosophical issues at play both in the Pseudo-Clementine *Homilies* and in later kabbalistic writings in *Through a Speculum That Shines* (Princeton: Princeton University Press, 1997), esp. 139. Note also his thoughts on the possibility of "Jewish-Christian" materials informing later Jewish mystical traditions through multiple possible channels in *Along the Path: Studies in Kabbalistic Myth, Symbolism, and Hermeneutics* (Albany: SUNY Press, 1995), 67–69. See also 191–92 n. 16 there for bibliography pointing to potential avenues for extending Pines' insights about the fertile Syrian milieu.

[59] See esp. *Homilies* 4–6, and discussion in William Adler, "Apion's Enconomium of Adultery: A Jewish Satire of Greek Paideia in the Pseudo-Clementine *Homilies*," *HUCA* 64 (1993): 15–49; Dominique Côté, "Une critique de la mythologie grecque d'après l'Homélie Pseudo-clémentine IV," *Apocrypha* 11 (2000): 37–57; Côté, "Les procédés rhétoriques dans les Pseudo-Clémentines: L'éloge de l'adultère du grammairien Apion," in *Nouvelles intrigues Pseudo-clémentines: Plots in the Pseudo-Clementine Romance*, ed. Frédéric Amsler et al. (Publications de l'Institut romand des sciences bibliques 6; Lausanne: Zébre, 2008), 189–210; Côté, "Rhetoric and Jewish-Christianity: The Case of the Grammarian Apion in the Pseudo-Clementine *Homilies*," in *Rediscovering the Apocryphal Continent: New Perspectives on Early Christian and Late Antique Apocryphal Texts and Traditions*, ed. Pierluigi Piovanelli and Tony Burke (WUNT 349; Tübingen: Mohr Siebeck, 2015), 369–89; James Carleton Paget, *Jews, Christians and Jewish Christians in Antiquity* (WUNT 251; Tübingen: Mohr Siebeck, 2010), 427–92. Also Chapter Four in this volume.

[60] See, e.g., *Hom.* 2.19, 38; 3.18–19; 7.4–8; 11.28–30; Albert I. Baumgarten, "Literary Evidence for Jewish Christianity in the Galilee," in *The Galilee in Late Antiquity*, ed. Lee I. Levine (New York: JTSA, 1992), 39–50; cf. J. Bergman, "Les éléments juifs dans les Pseudo-Clémentines," *REJ* 46 (1903): 89–98; A. Marmorstein, "Judaism and Christianity in the Middle of the Third Century," *HUCA* 10 (1935): 223–63. See further Chapter Five in this volume.

[61] Alon Goshen-Gottstein, "The Body as Image of God in Rabbinic Literature," *HTR* 87 (1994): 171–95; David H. Aaron, "Shedding Light on God's Body in Rabbinic Midrashim:

Early scholars from Sixtus to Graetz accepted the Pseudo-Clementines' own claims to preserve the teachings of Peter, James, and the Jerusalem Church, considering them as "Jewish-Christian" in part by virtue of their temporal proximity to the Jewish origins of Christianity. If more recent scholars of Christianity have been puzzled to find such an interest and acceptance of Judaism among what we now know to be fourth-century texts, it is perhaps because they frustrate the assumption that any contacts between Christian and Jewish traditions are only a matter of the Second Temple Jewish "background" of Christianity.[62] Yet, in the Pseudo-Clementine *Homilies*, one finds an even more positive image of Judaism, and closer self-affiliation with non-Christian Jews, than anywhere in the New Testament – including the view of Judaism as an equal and independent path to salvation, the requirement of *kashrut* and ritual purity of Gentile followers of Jesus, the privileging of Jewish genealogy and practice, and hints of awareness and acceptance of distinctively Rabbinic authority claims.[63] It is perhaps telling, moreover, that those Gentiles who piously follow Jesus are never called "Christians," but rather "God-fearers." Indeed, if we follow the text's own self-presentation, it is even possible to reread it as part of a broader and shifting set of "para-Rabbinic" traditions that – like and alongside the Hekhalot literature – attest the spreading prestige of Rabbinic authority in Late Antiquity, even while appealing to this authority for their own aims.[64]

Rereading Ps.-Clem. *Hom.* 17.7

Most of the arguments cited above, particularly since Scholem, have been mounted with reference to the same small set of Christian intertexts, with selected lines and passages often quoted and repeated without concern for their setting, function, or context.[65] Despite differences of opinion, moreover, studies in this area have largely shared the assumption that one investigates connections across "religions" on the level of motifs, such that analysis begins with the atomization of sources into comparable units and is aimed at what lies before and behind the extant texts. To be sure, Scholem and others have shown how

---

Reflections on the Theory of a Luminous Adam," *HTR* 90 (1997): 299–314, and esp. pp. 310–11 on the common "haggadic matrix" with *Qohelet Rabbah* 8.2. Aaron's methodological insights resonate with the sources and scholarship under consideration here as well.

[62] On this pattern, see Chapter One in this volume.

[63] See Chapter Six in this volume.

[64] At least in its present forms, on which see now Ra'anan S. Boustan, "The Emergence of Pseudonymous Attribution in Hekhalot Literature," *JSQ* 14 (2007): 18–38.

[65] An important exception is Wolfson, *Through a Speculum That Shines* – see esp. p. 139 on the Pseudo-Clementines – which pursues a comparative treatment by highlighting philosophical issues and argumentation, understood synchronically, rather than reduced to a diachronic line of development.

the extraction and filiation of motifs can be used to construct compelling narratives about the evolution of Jewish mysticism, with gaps in the Jewish literary record filled through the culling of Christian sources for the relics of purportedly pre-Christian Jewish ideas. The assumptions underlying this method, however, remain questionable and may well undermine the results. What I would like to suggest, in what follows, is that the possibility of Christian "parallels" for Jewish mysticism may be more effectively explored in engagement with the literary, rhetorical, and cultural contexts of the sources themselves – in this case, the Pseudo-Clementine *Homilies*.

When we reread the Pseudo-Clementines and related sources in their own terms, for instance, it may be significant that they resist the clear-cut categorization of "religions" (i. e., "Christian" as distinct from and postdating "Jewish") on which an atomizing approach is predicated. Scholem himself signals the stubborn hybridity of the Pseudo-Clementines in the course of dismissing them as a "strange Jewish-Christian-Hellenistic hodge-podge."[66] More heuristic, however, is the approach laid out recently by Elliot Wolfson in a study of the *Gospel of Truth*. Taking seriously the text's self-presentation, he stresses that its author and circle "likely did not identify themselves exclusively as Jews or as Christians but as individuals graced with a wisdom that allowed them to exist concurrently as both Jews and Christians," further emphasizing that "from this perspective even the notion of syncretism is not precise since there is no evidence for two distinct and clearly demarcated phenomena that need to be combined."[67] Much the same can be said of the fourth-century Syrian authors/redactors of the Pseudo-Clementine *Homilies*: to the degree that categories like "Judaism" and "Christianity" would even make sense to them, the two are presented as parallel proclamations of the same truths, both charged with the preservation of the purity of monotheism in a world defiled by idolatry, polytheism, and Hellenism.[68]

With respect to the *Gospel of Truth*, Wolfson notes how the common categorization of "religions" proves misleading when applied to certain texts, and he further suggests experimenting with alternative approaches by reengaging older scholarship:

It is obviously too simplistic to identify in a one-to-one correspondence Jewish-Christianity and Gnosticism, but it is reasonable to revive the locution of Wilhelm Bousset and to speak of a "Jewish-Christian *gnosis*." In line with more current research, however, I would

---

[66] Scholem, *On the Kabbalah*, 141.

[67] Elliot R. Wolfson, "Inscribed in the Book of the Living: *Gospel of Truth* and Jewish Christology," *JSJ* 38 (2007): 234–71 at 236–37.

[68] On the persistence of other modes of categorization in the Roman Near East into the fourth century, even despite the adoption of Ignatius' neologisms in westward locales, see Chapter Three in this volume. On the argument against those who denounce Judaism and embrace Hellenism, and especially those who do so in the name of Jesus, see e. g., *Hom.* 1.9–12; 4–6, esp. 5.1–29; 8.6–7.

argue that this expression denotes a hybridity that, at once, reinforces and destabilizes the hyphen that separates and connects the two foci of identity construction, Judaism and Christianity.[69]

Similarly, in the case of the Pseudo-Clementine *Homilies*, renewed attention to older treatments of *gnosis* may be useful to ponder in relation to Neander and Graetz – and perhaps foremost for a sense of what has been effaced by twentieth-century trends, both by virtue of the reconceptualization of *"gnosis"* after the discoveries at Nag Hammadi and by virtue of the reconceptualization of "mysticism" in the wake of Scholem. Indeed, Scholem himself bemoaned the reduction of older notions of *gnosis* into a "Gnosticism" narrowly defined by Valentinian, Sethian, and other writings discovered at Nag Hammadi.[70] Yet we might similarly attend to the epiphenomenal effects of his own telling of the history of Jewish mysticism, not just as "one of the Jewish branches of Gnosticism," but also as a "religious movement of distinctive character" located firmly within Judaism.[71] In the process of establishing its authenticity as purely Jewish, *contra* Graetz, he also contributed to narrowing the discussion about its relationship to non-Jewish traditions – with the relationship of "Christian" to "Jewish" largely reduced to a calculus of the priority of origins, framed within a linear succession of discrete "phases." Lost in the process is attention to the possibility of the continued interaction between traditions, as well as the need to contextualize discussion of Jewish and Christian sources in a broader continuum that includes contemporaneous "pagan" traditions in their various distinctive local forms and expressions.[72]

Pines has pointed to the transcreedal intellectual ferment in the late antique Syrian milieu in which the Pseudo-Clementines took form. This is also the context emphasized, more recently, in specialist research on the Pseudo-Clementine *Homilies* and *Recognitions*, which has turned away from the source-critical inquiries of twentieth-century scholarship on these texts to recover a sense of the fourth-century settings of their formation.[73] Returning to the insights of John Chapman, for instance, Dominique Côté and others have demonstrated how the Pseudo-Clementines have been shaped by both polemic and proximity with

---

[69] Wolfson, "Inscribed in the Book of the Living," 237.

[70] Scholem, *Origins of the Kabbalah*, 21 n. 24.

[71] Scholem, *Origins of the Kabbalah*, 21; Scholem, *Major Trends in Jewish Mysticism*, 43.

[72] Following Neander, for instance, Graetz approached *gnosis* as an essentially transcreedal phenomenon in both social and intellectual terms, and hence a channel for Jewish ideas to flow into non-Jewish traditions as well as the converse; Graetz, *Gnosticismus und Judentum*, 4–5, 55–61; Graetz, *History of the Jews*, 2:374–82.

[73] See Chapter One in the volume as well as Nicole Kelley, *Knowledge and Religious Authority in the Pseudo-Clementines* (WUNT[2] 213; Tübingen: Mohr Siebeck, 2006), esp. 182–204; Dominique Côté, "Le problème de l'identité religieuse dans la Syrie du IVe siècle: Le cas des Pseudo-Clémentines et de l'Adversus Judaeos de S. Jean Chrysostome," in Mimouni and Pouderon, *La croisée des chemins revisitée*, 339–70.

Neoplatonic and other "pagan" philosophical traditions that flourished in late antique Syria.[74]

If the *Homilies'* references to Pharisees as trustworthy tradents of ethical monotheism and oral "explanations of the Law" in unbroken succession from Moses (e. g., *Hom.* 2.38; 3.18–19; 11.29; also *Ep. Pet.* 1–2) encode late antique rabbis, for instance, their function is to articulate Christianity as an ancient prophetic truth like Judaism, waging a common battle against idolatry, polytheism, Greek philosophy, and Egyptian religion (e. g., 2.16–17; 3.17–25; 8.11–20; 9.2–18; 10.7–23).[75] Likewise, those against whom its authors/redactors speak – as embodied by Simon Magus, Appion, and other enemies of Peter and Clement – seem to include not just Marcionites in Edessa and other Hellenized Christian interpreters of Paul, but also contemporary Syrian Neoplatonists like Porphyry and Iamblichus.[76] Simon, for instance, is described repeatedly as having "made statues walk" (e. g., 2.32), recalling legends associated with Iamblichus in particular. Likewise, the description of Simon's creation of a boy from air recalls the tale of Iamblichus' creation of two boys from water,[77] no less than the talmudic tale of Rava's creation of a boy from earth (*b. Sanhedrin* 65b) and the later Jewish traditions concerning the *golem* discussed by Scholem and Idel. Even as the Pseudo-Clementine authors/redactors voice different ideas about divinity, materiality, sacrifice, and prophecy than their "pagan" Syrian contemporaries, they share a set of common questions, concerns, and terminology – as often explored, moreover, with self-conscious appeals to ancient forms of "barbarian" wisdom claimed to lie before and beyond the knowledge of Greeks and Romans.[78]

---

[74] See above, as well as Dominique Côté, *Le thème de l'opposition entre Pierre et Simon dans les Pseudo-Clémentines* (Études Augustiniennes Série Antiquités 167; Paris: Études augustiniennes, 2001), esp. 109–33; Kelley, *Knowledge and Religious Authority*, esp. 36–81, 194–96, 200–4; Kelley, "Pseudo-Clementine Polemics against Sacrifice: A Window onto Religious Life in the Fourth Century?," in *Christian Apocryphal Texts for the New Millennium: Achievements, Prospects, and Challenges*, ed. Pierluigi Piovanelli (Leiden: Brill, 2015), 391–400; Ra'anan S. Boustan and Annette Yoshiko Reed, "Blood and Atonement in the Pseudo-Clementines and *The Story of the Ten Martyrs*: The Problem of Selection in the Study of Ancient Judaism and Christianity," *Hen* 30 (2008): 333–64 at 348–49; Claire Clivaz, "Madness, Philosophical or Mystical Experience? A Puzzling Text: Pseudo-Clementine *Recognitiones* II 61–69," *ZAC* 13 (2009): 475–93. See also Chapman, "On the Date of the Clementines," esp. 158.

[75] See Chapters Six and Nine in this volume.

[76] That a multiplicity of enemies are addressed through the conflate figure of Simon has been persuasively demonstrated by Dominique Côté, "La fonction littéraire de Simon le Magicien dans les Pseudo-Clémentines," *Laval Théologique et Philosophique* 37 (2001): 513–23; cf. A. Salles, "Simon le magicien ou Marcion?," *VC* 12 (1958): 197–224.

[77] Iamblichus creates boys from water by calling them up from two springs by invoking its Eros and Anteros, from which they embraced him as a father; for discussion of the relevant passage from Eunapius, *Lives of the Philosophers*, see Gregory Shaw, *Theurgy and the Soul: The Neoplatonism of Iamblichus* (University Park: Penn State Press, 1971), 125–26.

[78] In this respect, recent research on the Pseudo-Clementines confirms the basic contours, if not the precise details, of the insights of Neander and Graetz, who characterized them as

In a recent article, Côté brings this late antique philosophical context to bear on the interpretation of *Hom.* 17.6–12.[79] His focus falls on the famous passage about God's human form:

Knowing therefore that we knew all that was spoken by him and that we could supply proofs [ἀποδείξεως], he sent us to the ignorant nations [ἔθνη] to baptize them for remission of sins, and he commanded us to teach them, first the initial and greatest commandment, to fear the Lord God and to serve only Him.[80] He spoke of the fear that God whose angels they are who are "the angels of the least of the believers amongst us, who stand in heaven continually contemplating the face [πρόσωπον] of the Father" (Matt 18:10).[81] For He has a form [μορφὴν] primarily and solely for the sake of beauty [κάλλος], not for utility.[82] He does not have eyes so that He may see with them; for He sees on every side because, in His body, He is incomparably brighter than the seeing spirit [βλεπτικοῦ πνεύματος] within us, and He is more splendid than all, so that compared with Him even the light of the sun would be reckoned as darkness. Nor does He have ears for the sake of hearing. He hears, perceives, moves, acts, makes – from every side. Rather, He has the most beautiful form for the sake of humankind, in order that the "pure in heart" (Matt 5.8) can see Him, so that they may rejoice for what they have suffered.[83] He has stamped humankind with the greatest seal [σφραγῖδι] – as it were – with His own form, in order that he may be ruler and lord of all, and that all shall be subject to him.[84] Hence, one who discerns that He is the All [τὸ πᾶν] and that humankind is His image [εἰκόνα] – for He is Himself invisible, but His image, humankind, is visible – honors His visible image, which is humankind. Whatever one does to a person, whether good or bad, is regarded as having

---

expressions of anti-*gnosis* simultaneously exemplary of Jewish *gnosis* (Neander, *Genetische Entwickelung*, 361–421; Graetz, *Gnosticismus und Judentum*, esp. 55, 110).

[79] Côté, "La forme de Dieu."

[80] I.e., as Peter is depicted as having done for Clement in *Hom.* 3.7, on which see below.

[81] For a reading of this passage as part of the *Nacheleben* of Matt 18:10, see now Bogdan G. Bucur, "Matt. 18:10 in Early Christology and Pneumatology: A Contribution to the Study of Matthean Wirkungsgeschichte," *NovT* 49 (2007): 209–31.

[82] Compare the characterization of Adam's heel as "outshining the globe of the sun" in *Vayiqra Rabbah* 20.2, and see discussion in Goshen-Gottstein, "Body as Image of God," 179–83, especially in reference to beauty and luminosity. Scholem, as noted above, suggests that κάλλος here is equivalent to the use of יופי in *Shi'ur Qomah*; *On the Mystical Shape*, 30.

[83] Compare the statement in *Chaldean Oracles*, fragment 142, that "it is for your sake that bodies are attached to our self-revealed manifestations," on which see further Sarah Iles Johnston, "*Fiat Lux, Fiat Ritus*: Divine Light and the Late Antique Defense of Ritual," in *The Presence of Light: Divine Radiance and Religious Experience*, ed. Matthew T. Kapstein (Chicago: University of Chicago Press, 2004), 15.

[84] There is an intriguing parallel in *m. Sanhedrin* 4.5, which gives four reasons why Adam was created alone, the last of which is "to portray the grandeur of the Holy One, blessed be He; for a person mints many coins with a single seal, and they are all alike one another. But the King of kings of kings ... minted all human beings with that seal of his with which he made the first person, yet not one of them is alike. Therefore everyone is obliged to maintain: 'On my account, the world was created.'" Among the other reasons, notably, is "so that the *minim* should not say that there are many domains in heaven." See Alexander Altman, "*Homo Imago Dei* in Jewish and Christian Theology," *JR* 48 (1968): 241–42 for a comparison of the seal imagery in this mishnah with Philo's use of σφραγίς, and note that our Pseudo-Clementine example falls closer to the former.

been done to Him.[85] Therefore the judgment which proceeds from Him shall go forth, giving to everyone according to their merits; for He avenges His own form [μορφὴν]. (*Hom.* 17.7)[86]

Against Scholem, Morray-Jones, and Jarl Fossum, Côté stresses that it is misleading to cull anthropomorphic motifs from this passage to posit a direct relation to Jewish mysticism, since many of the apparent similarities can be explained with reference to the fourth-century Syrian setting of the Pseudo-Clementines, as well as the specific literary context of the passage in question, which is articulated in the style of philosophical dialogue and in counterpoint to "pagan" tropes placed in the mouth of Simon.[87]

Côté deftly explains the context, and what is at stake, as follows:

Le contexte peut se résumer ainsi. Dans le cadre d'une discussion sur la nature de Dieu, qui est censée avoir lieu à Laodicée et qui met aux prises le magicien Simon et l'apôtre Pierre, Simon défend la thèse dithéiste d'un dieu suprême, immatériel et inaccessible, le dieu bon et inconnu de Jésus, qu'il ne faut pas confondre avec le dieu juste et vengeur, connu des hommes depuis Adam, le démiurge, le dieu créateur de la Bible, alors que Pierre défend la thèse monarchiste de l'unité absolue du Dieu créateur, qui n'est nul autre que le dieu de Jésus, le Dieu qui conformément aux enseignements de Jésus lui-même possède bel et bien une forme. Selon le rapport que Zachée fait à son maître avant le débat, l'argumentation de Simon porte plus particulièrement sur la forme de Dieu, un enseignement de Pierre plus pernicieux que l'idolâtrie, sur la contradiction entre les paroles de Jésus et la doctrine de Pierre, et, troisièmement, sur la supériorité de la vision sur l'évidence. Pierre engage donc le débat en commençant par démontrer que son enseignement s'accorde avec les paroles de Jésus. Il rappelle ainsi que le Dieu qu'il faut adorer exclusivement, selon le commandement de Jésus, c'est le Père, "dont les anges, ceux des plus petits d'entre les croyants parmi nous, qui se tiennent dans le ciel, contemplent sans cesse la face." Or, si le Père a une face, c'est qu'il a une forme, un corps et tous ses membres. Dans la logique du passage, la précision est importante puisque c'est sur le modèle de cette forme que Dieu a créé l'Homme: "Car il a modelé l'homme sur sa propre forme, comme avec le plus grand sceau, afin qu'il fût le chef et le seigneur de toutes choses et que tout fût à son service." Le Dieu unique de Pierre n'a donc rien d'un être abstrait et inaccessible, comme l'Être

---

[85] Much the same argument is found in Rabbinic sources, e.g., *Mekhilta de R. Ishmael Bahodesh* 11; *b. Moʿed Qatan* 15b; see also the statements attributed to Ben Azzai in *Sifra* Lev 19:17 and *t. Yebamot* 8.7, as well as the discussion in Goshen-Gottstein, "Body as Image of God," 187–91. Notably, the Pseudo-Clementine *Homilies* denies Adam any sinfulness whatsoever, and it thus not faced with the problem that Goshen-Gottstein there discusses with respect to whether Adam's sin affected the bearing of the divine image or light by him and his offspring.

[86] Translations here and below follow Pines, "Points of Similarity"; and Alain Le Boulluec et al., "Roman Pseudo-clémentin: Homélies," in *Écrits apocryphes chrétiens II*, ed. Pierre Geoltrain and Jean-Daniel Kaestli (Paris: Gallimard, 2005), 1193–589, with some changes in consultation with the Greek text in Bernhard Rehm, *Die Pseudoklementinen*, vol. 1: *Homilien* (GCS 42; Berlin: Akademie-Verlag, 1969), as well as the suggestions of Bucur, "Matt. 18:10 in Early Christology and Pneumatology," 216.

[87] Côté, "La forme de Dieu." Côté mostly engages with the line of New Testament research discussed above, and he thus critiques Scholem, Morray-Jones, and Fossum in particular.

suprême de Simon, des gnostiques et des platoniciens. C'est le Dieu créateur, législateur, le dieu dont la forme lumineuse est assise sur un trône et adorée par les anges.[88]

He does not deny the possibility that some ideas reflected in the Pseudo-Clementines might be related in some way to those that later arise in Jewish mystical literature.[89] What he here stresses, rather, is the myopia of considering the passage on anthropomorphism only in terms of Jewish and Christian parallels – as if simply a question of the possible "Jewish-Christian" preservation of a characteristically "Jewish" anthropomorphism.[90] If the "pagan" evidence points to a more complex continuum of positions on all sides, it also highlights the need to take seriously the literary setting of this passage as part of a debate about the character of the divine, articulated in terms informed by Neoplatonic, Stoic, and other Hellenistic philosophical traditions.

Côté points to the neglect of an important point in the references to this work by Scholem and others: to take the comments on the anthropomorphic form of God in *Hom.* 17.7 as the basis for arguing for an early dating for *Shi'ur Qomah* traditions, one must ignore the comments attributed to Peter just a few verses later. There, visionary experience is associated with Peter's enemy, the arch-heretic Simon Magus, who complains of Peter's denial thereof:

You (i.e., Peter) claim that you have learned the things of your teacher (i.e., Jesus) exactly, because you have directly seen and heard him, but that it is impossible for another to learn the same thing by means of a dream or vision (ὁράματι ἢ ὀπτασίᾳ; cf. 2 Cor 12:1). (*Hom.* 17.13.1)

In fact, the above-quoted passage, attributed to Peter, is part of a debate that culminates with the apostle's strident denial of visionary experience as a basis

---

[88] Côté, "La forme de Dieu."

[89] In his words: "Il faut préciser que nous ne cherchons pas ici à démontrer que la notion de corps de Dieu dans les *Homélies* doit uniquement se comprendre en rapport avec la philosophie grecque …. Il note tout simplement au passage l'influence de la pensée grecque dans l'élaboration d'une notion tout à fait juive, *sans être exclusivement juive*, la notion de corps divin, dans les milieux judéo-chrétiens du IVe siècle en Syrie" (italics mine; Côté, "La forme de Dieu").

[90] This contrast between the form of the Jewish God and the formless of the Platonic *qua* Christian God is asserted already by Justin Martyr (*Dial.* 114), and has been taken as a maxim by many modern scholars, even when exceptions are enumerated (cf. Goshen-Gottstein, "Body as Image of God," 176). It is not entirely clear, however, whether the reality was ever quite so simple in this regard, not least because the question of divine form was also an argument among "pagan" intellectuals and a topic of inner-Christian debate at the time. See further, e.g., Hubert Cancik and Hildegard Cancik-Lindmaier, "The Truth of Images: Cicero and Varro on Image Worship," in *Representation in Religion: Studies in Honour of Moshe Barasch*, ed. Jan Assman and Albert I. Baumgarten (Studies in the History of Religions 89; Leiden: Brill, 2001), 43–62; Carl W. Griffin and David L. Paulsen, "Augustine and the Corporeality of God," *HTR* 95 (2002): 97–118. See also Stroumsa, "Forms of God," which notes the possible "pre-Platonic Orphic" origins of Greek views of the divine macranthropos (p. 269) but considers anthropomorphism in Hermetic and "gnostic" materials as attesting "traces of early Jewish conceptions" (p. 273).

for knowledge about the divine.[91] Peter first answers Simon by pointing to the problem of demonic deception:

> Whoever trusts an apparition, vision, or dream is prone to error (ὁ δὲ ὀπτασίᾳ πιστεύων ἢ ὁράματι καὶ ἐνυπνίῳ ἐπισφαλής ἐστιν). He does not know whom he is trusting; for it is possible it may be an evil spirit or a deceptive spirit, pretending in his speeches to be what it is not. (*Hom.* 17.14.3–4)

At the debate's denouement, however, this point is extended into a categorical stress on the limits of revelation in relation to knowledge and authority:

> If our Jesus appeared to you (i. e., Simon) in a vision (δι' ὁράματος ὀφθείς), made himself known to you, and spoke to you, it was as one who is enraged with an adversary – and this is the reason why it was through visions and dreams (δι' ὁραμάτων καὶ ἐνυπνίων; cf. Acts 18:9) or through revelations that were from without (δι' ἀποκαλύψεων ἔξωθεν οὐσῶν; cf. Gal 1:16) that he spoke to you! Can anyone be rendered fit for instruction through apparitions (cf. Gal 1:11–12)? ... How are we to believe you, when you tell us that he appeared to you? How is it that he appeared to you, when you entertain opinions contrary to his teaching? If you were seen and taught by him and became his apostle, even for a single hour, then proclaim his utterances, interpret his teaching, love his apostles, and do not contend with me who accompanied with him (ἐμοὶ τῷ συγγενομένῳ αὐτῷ μὴ μάχου)! For you now stand in direct opposition to me (πρὸς ... ἐναντίος ἀνθέστηκάς μοι) – who am a firm rock, the foundation of the church (cf. Matt 16:18)! ... If you say that I am 'condemned' (καταγνωσθέντος; Gal 2:11), you bring an accusation against God, who revealed the Messiah to me. (*Hom.* 17.19.1–6)

The denial of authority from visionary experience, notably, is also echoed in the orientation towards other heavenly realities throughout the work. The *Homilies*, for instance, include references to a heavenly throne, called variously καθέδρα and θρόνος, which is depicted as the seat from which the True Prophet descends first as Adam and Moses, and later as the Messiah (2.16–17; 3.17–21). Yet it is a heavenly throne without a heavenly Temple, described in a work that denies the Temple even within the Torah. In keeping with the emphasis on this-worldly lines of succession over otherworldly visions or travels, moreover, its earthly counterparts are the "chair of Moses" that symbolizes the trustworthy transmission of oral teachings from Moses to the Pharisees (3.18–19, 70; 11.29) and the "seat of Christ" that emblematizes the parallel transmission of the same teachings from Jesus and Peter to Clement and other bishops (3.60–71).[92]

That the denial of visionary experience seems to take aim particularly at the claims associated with Paul in 2 Cor 14 (cf. Gal 1:12; 1 Cor 15:8–10; Acts 9:3–20)[93] further highlights the methodological perils of culling motifs

---

[91] Or at least when claimed apart from proper lineage or succession; see further Nicole Kelley, *Knowledge and Religious Authority in the Pseudo-Clementines: Situating the* Recognitions *in Fourth-Century Syria* (WUNT² 213; Tübingen: Mohr Siebeck, 2006), 135–38.

[92] See Chapter Six in this volume.

[93] I.e., whether meant directly as an anti-Pauline polemic and/or indirectly as a means of challenging the Paulinism of Marcion or others. This passage was read as a veiled anti-Pauline

from Christian sources to cobble a pre-Christian Jewish lineage for later Jewish mystical ideas and practices. Such tensions also bring us back to reconsider the early insights of Neander and Graetz; even if they were naïve to treat the Pseudo-Clementines as a window onto second-century debates, their positing of various transreligious syntheses wrought in the course of inner-/interreligious debates reminds us of the complexity of the sources and their settings, countering the more recent tendency to assume self-isolated Jewish, Christian, and "pagan" trajectories connected only by shared "origins" or scattered points of "influence."

Extending Côté's argument with these broader points in mind, then, we might do well to look to the place of *Hom.* 17.7 within the argument of the work as a whole. After all, the problem of true and false form, and true and false vision, recurs throughout the novel – not just in the speeches attributed to Peter and others, but also within the narrative itself. With further analysis, in fact, we see how Peter's statements in *Hom.* 17.7 about the divine μορφή (i.e., form), the human εἶδος (i.e., image), and the σφραγίς (i.e., stamp) of the former on the latter stand at the climax of an argument introduced early in the work and interwoven throughout it. A sense of this overarching argument, moreover, illumines its connections *both* to the Rabbinic traditions with which its authors/redactors appear to claim common ground *and* to the "pagan" philosophical traditions that they thereby critique.

The *Homilies* is framed as a novel, purporting to preserve the first-person account of Clement of Rome's journey from "paganism" to true religion. The action is set into play by the young Clement's dissatisfaction with philosophy as a way to discern "what is the righteous thing that is pleasing to God" and "whether the soul is immortal or mortal" (*Hom.* 1.4; see further 1.1–13, 17). Such questioning leads Clement to leave his native Rome to travel to Judaea, following rumors of a man "preaching to the Jews the kingdom of the invisible God and saying that whoever reforms his manner of living should enjoy it" (1.6). Clement thus comes to meet Peter, and it is in the context of the apostle's very first teachings to him (3.1–28) that we also find the text's first reference to the divine μορφή:

Impiety against Him [i.e., God], in the matter of *theosebeia*, is to die saying there is another god, whether superior or inferior, or saying in any way that there is one besides Him who really is. For the One, who truly is, is He whose form the body of man bears [οὖ τὴν μορφὴν τὸ ἀνθρώπου βαστάζει σῶμα], for whose sake the heaven and all the

---

polemic by Ferdinand Christian Baur (e. g., "Die Christuspartei in der korinthischen Gemeide," 116); on this position and its history, see further Gerd Lüdemann, *Opposition to Paul in Jewish Christianity* (trans. E. Boring; Minneapolis: Fortress, 1989), 1–32, 185–88. See, however, Côté, "La fonction littéraire de Simon le Magicien," 514–16, 519. As I have stressed elsewhere, moreover, the critique of knowledge gained from dreams and visions here resonates with debates about prophecy in the early fourth century, on which see Polymnia Athanassiadi, "Dreams, Theurgy and Freelance Divination: The Testimony of Iamblichus," *JRS* 83 (1993): 115–30.

stars – though in their essence superior – submit to serve him who is in essence inferior, on account of the form of the Almighty [διὰ τὴν τοῦ κρείττονος μορφήν]. (*Hom.* 3.7)

Here, as throughout the *Homilies*, the ultimate point is the singularity of God. The recognition of humankind as sharing God's shape is cited in service of the argument for monotheism and as a proof for its ethical horizon.

Later, the same language of form and likeness is used to expound the negative counterpart of the monotheism that is here depicted as the Jewish truth revealed by Jesus to the Gentiles. In four public sermons attributed to Peter during his sojourn at Tripolis (*Homilies* 8–11), he preaches to crowds of "pagans" on the topic of the genealogy of error and the path to salvation. To convince them to abandon polytheism and purify themselves to serve the God of Israel, Peter here reveals the true history and workings of idolatry. Ancient people – he contends – "erected statues of the dead in their own forms," but with the passing of generations, their mortal status was forgotten, and they were adored as gods (9.4). Demons then took advantage of the situation:

They draw to their own will those who partake of their table [i.e., through sacrifice to idols], being mixed up with their understanding by means of food and drink, metamorphizing in dreams according to the likenesses of the wooden images [μεταμορφοῦντες ἑαυτοὺς κατ' ὄναρ κατὰ τὰς τῶν ξοάνων ἰδέας], that they may increase error. For the wooden image is neither a living creature, nor does it have a divine spirit. The demon that appeared abused the form [ὁ δὲ ὀφθεὶς δαίμων τῇ μορφῇ ἀπεχρήσατο]. How many, likewise, have been seen by others in dreams. When they have met one another when awake and compared them with what they saw in their dream, they have not accorded. The dream is not a manifestation but is either the production of a demon or of the soul, giving likenesses to present fears and desires; the soul, being struck with fear, conceives likenesses in dreams. (*Hom.* 9.15.1–4)

In the third sermon at Tripolis, this argument is developed with specific reference to the place of animal imagery in Egyptian worship – here presented as exemplary of the problems in the polytheistic approach to divine form that plague even the Greeks (10.17). In the fourth and final sermon of the cycle, the contrast between Jewish and non-Jewish approaches is finally made explicit:

You are the image of the invisible God [θεοῦ τοῦ ἀοράτου ἐστὲ εἰκών]. Therefore, do not let those who would be pious say that idols are images of God and therefore that it is right to worship them [ὅθεν οἱ εὐσεβεῖν βουλόμενοι μὴ τὰ εἴδωλα λεγέτωσαν θεοῦ εἰκόνα εἶναι καὶ διὰ τοῦτο δεῖν αὐτὰ σέβειν]! For the image of God is humankind [εἰκὼν γὰρ θεοῦ ὁ ἄνθρωπος]. He who wishes to be pious towards God does good to man, because the body of man bears the image of God (cf. Gen 9:6). All do not yet bear His likeness, but the pure mind of the good soul does. As we know that man was made after the image and after the likeness of God (cf. Gen 1:26), however, we tell you to be pious towards him, so that the favor may be accounted as done to God, whose image he is. Therefore it behooves you to give honor to the image of God – which is humankind – in this way: food to the hungry, drink to the thirsty, clothing to the naked, care to the sick, shelter to the stranger, and visiting him who is in prison, to help him as you can .... Can it therefore be said that for the sake of piety towards God, you worship every form, while in all things you injure man who is really the image of God, committing murder, adultery, stealing, and dishonoring him in many other respects? ... Being seduced by some malignant reptile to malice, by the suggestion of polytheistic doctrine, you are impious towards the real image – which is humankind – and think that you are pious towards senseless things. (*Hom.* 11.4–5)

Here, Peter's argument against polytheism is framed in terms familiar from the interpretation of Gen 1:26.[94] Whereas Pauline and other Christian interpreters read this verse in terms of Christ, the Pseudo-Clementine understanding of "image" falls closer to the appeal to this verse in Rabbinic traditions both to call for ethical action (e. g., *m. Sanhedrin* 4.5) and to contrast Jewish worship with idolatry (e. g., *Vayiqra Rabbah* 34.3).[95]

In *Hom.* 17.7, this argument is largely reiterated in the context of a debate with Simon – and, hence, with sayings of Jesus as prooftexts (esp. Matt 18:10) and in a manner that answers Simon's denial of high divinity to the Demiurge. That Simon believes that the God who created the cosmos was not the same as the Supreme God witnessed by Jesus was revealed already in Peter's first private teachings of Clement (e. g., 3.2) and in Simon's first statements against Peter (e. g., 3.38). In the culminating debate at Laodicea (*Hom.* 16–19), the two face off over the question of divine unity and goodness, with secret doctrines now revealed by both parties. In the course of these debates, Simon's misreading of the Jewish scriptures (esp. Gen 1:26) to "mold from them the forms of many gods" and Peter's proper interpretation whereby "the form of Him who truly exists, comes to knowledge of the true type from our own shape" since "the soul within us is clothed with His image for immortality" (16.10, see further 16.11–12); the latter, moreover, is presented as the σφραγίς that promises afterlife judgment and ensures the immortality of the souls of the righteous (16.19). That the contrast is not between an anthropomorphic "Jewish" God and an invisible "Christian" god, moreover, is clear from Simon's critiques of Peter in *Hom.* 17.3, which center on the debate between worship with statues and worship without them. In effect, Simon's own words unmask his position as a "heretical" attempt to use the words of Jesus to uphold the old polytheism.

The famous passage in the seventeenth *Homily*, quoted above, is part of Peter's answer to Simon's charge. The passage picks up on the themes raised

---

[94] The Greek term εἰκών is used in LXX Gen 1:26 to render Hebrew צלם. On the Jewish and Christian interpretation of these terms, see Altman, "*Homo Imago Dei*," 235–59. Note also the importance of Gen 1:26 in the argument between Simon (who points to God's statement "Let us make humankind" to posit divine multiplicity) and Peter (who stresses the creation of humankind in the "image of God" to stress divine unity) according to the Pseudo-Clementine *Homilies* (e. g., 3.38, 16.11–12). For a comparison with *Bereshit Rabbah* 8.8–9, see Chapter Five above.

[95] The Pauline identification of Christ as God's "image" (2 Cor 4:4; Col 1:15; 3:10; Eph 4:24) and "form" (Phil 2:6) set the tone for most Patristic literature (e. g., Altman, "*Homo Imago Dei*," 244–47). Contrast the identification of all humankind with this "image" in *m. Sanhedrin* 4.5, etc., on which see above.

throughout the work to underline God's singularity and the proper worship of him, not through statues, but through ethical action towards other people. Just as the teachings and speeches attributed to Peter revolve around the human recognition of God's true nature as the One God long known to the Jews and now revealed by Jesus to the Gentiles, so the same themes are echoed in the narrative. Interspersed with the sermons and debates is the tale of Clement's rediscovery of his long-lost family (esp. *Hom.* 12–15). His recognition of the truths preached by Peter are thus paired with his recognition of his twin brothers, who are already Christians, and their discovery of their mother, who soon converts as well. Furthermore, the final debate between Simon and Peter is framed as a battle to persuade Clement's own father Faustus.

That Peter stands on the side of truth against appearance, moreover, is reinforced by the novel's narrative conclusion (*Hom.* 20). After Peter wins the battle of words, Simon intervenes with magic, exchanging faces with Faustus. Peter alone recognizes the true forms behind the appearances, unmasking the ruse and using it to his favor. The narrative arc of the novel thus parallels and underlines the distinction made in *Hom.* 17 between the epistemological positions of Simon and Peter: Simon may argue persuasively for the power of sight to shape the soul, both in the case of statues and visions, but Peter remains the paradigm of the ability to see truth beyond appearance due to his status in a line of succession of prophetic truths.

Particularly since Scholem, scholars have tended to read *Hom.* 17.7 in terms of a contrast posited by Justin Martyr (*Dial.* 114; cf. Ps 8:4) between "Jewish" anthropomorphism and "Christian" embrace of the invisible god of Platonism. Attention to the literary and argumentative context of the *Homilies*, however, suggests a different concern. The argument resonates less with any Jewish/Christian differentiation than with the discussion of the efficacy and function of sight, statues, visions, and dreams, current among "pagan" intellectuals in late antique Syria.[96] Even as the assertion of humankind as εἰκών of God clearly draws on LXX Gen 1:26, for instance, it also resonates with the technical Neoplatonist sense of the latter as denoting a "stepping stone pointing to the original that gives the viewer access to a hidden or absent reality."[97] For Porphyry, as Todd Krulak has recently shown, this sense could be used in relation to those who "impressed the invisible onto visible forms" through the creation of statues

---

[96] For some interesting "pagan" intertexts, e.g., see Athanassiadi, "Dreams, Theurgy and Freelance Divination"; Johnston, "*Fiat Lux, Fiat Ritus*"; Todd C. Krulak, "Invisible Things on Visible Forms: Pedagogy and Anagogy in Porphyry's Περί ἀγαλμάτων," *Journal of Late Antiquity* 4 (2011): 343–64.

[97] Deborah T. Steiner, *Images in Mind: Statues in Archaic and Classical Greek Literature and Thought* (Princeton: Princeton University Press 2001), 5. I.e., in contrast to εἴδωλα and φαντάσματα, on which see further pp. 63–70. See also Jan N. Bremmer, "Iconoclast, Iconoclastic, and Iconoclasm: Notes Towards a Genealogy," *Church History and Religious Culture* 88 (2008): 1–17, esp. 2–4.

of gods.[98] In the Pseudo-Clementine *Homilies*, the participation of the divine in the material world is similarly at stake. Consistent with the overarching aim to argue against idolatry and polytheism, however, the efficacy of statues is undermined through the emphasis on what is argued to be truly the visible form of the invisible divine that is stamped in material form – namely, humankind. Perhaps not coincidentally, the logic is the same as we find in Rabbinic traditions such as *Vayiqra Rabbah* 34.3, where Jewish belief in humankind as God's image is contrasted with "pagan" use of statues in worship.[99]

The triangulation is poignantly persistent. The imagery of light in *Hom.* 17.6–12 resonates with Iamblichus' theorization of divine engagement with the material world (e.g., *De myst.* 1.9; 2.3–4), no less than with Jewish traditions about prelapsasian Adam. Similarly, the language of stamping calls upon the reciprocal logic of Stoic optic theory to evoke the engagement of divinity into materiality,[100] even as it simultaneously echoes the imagery of stamp and coin in *m. Sanhedrin* 4.5. Such connections surely need further investigation, but it is clear that much is missed when motifs from this passage are examined in isolation from the rest of the *Homilies* and its late antique Syrian context, as if fossilized fragments of pre-Christian Jewish mysticism fortuitously preserved in muddied soil. To do so is to not only to skew the meaning of the passage, but also to miss an opportunity to shed light upon one distinctively late antique local context, in which "pagan," Jewish, and Christian intellectuals seem to have been engaged in intensive reflection on form and vision, sight and light, materiality and divinity.

From Parallels to Contexts

Passing references to Pseudo-Clementine parallels can be found scattered in discussions of a surprisingly broad range of times and topics pertaining to Jewish mysticism – including reflections on divine form, light, time, and space, as well as the demiurgic theory of the *golem*, traditions surrounding Adam, and

---

[98] Krulak, "Invisible Things on Visible Forms."

[99] In *Vayiqra Rabbah* 34.3, Hillel is credited with comparing "pagan" treatment of idols falsely thought to be images of God with the Jewish treatment of humankind as the true image of God – albeit in this case with respect to washing.

[100] I.e., wherein the imagery of the stamp is central for expressing the reciprocity of sight and light. That Iamblichus similarly redeploys this language and theory to describe the mediation between materiality and divinity makes the association here all the more intriguing; see further Johnston, "*Fiat Lux, Fiat Ritus*," 18 and references there. On other Stoic echoes in this passage, particularly with respect to space, see Pines, "Points of Similarity," 73–76. See also Knut Kleve, "On the Beauty of God: A Discussion between Epicureans, Stoics, and Sceptics," *Symbolae Osloenses* 13 (1978): 69–83.

the doctrine of the transmigration of the soul of the messiah.[101] When treated in isolation, one or another motif might appear to attest this or that posited "phase." Despite containing a puzzling concentration of motifs also found in later Jewish mystical corpora, however, the Pseudo-Clementines simply do not fit into one or another modern narrative about the history of Jewish mysticism. This "Jewish-Christian" literature may preserve fourth-century Syrian "snapshots" of some strands of ideas in the course of development. Yet it also presents a poignant example of what is lost when the literary and argumentative strands of sources are unraveled for the harvesting of parallels.

If the Pseudo-Clementines can indeed be culled for some "Jewish-Christian" evidence for early Jewish mysticism, then, their significance may be as much historiographical as historical. If multiple ideas later important for Jewish mystical traditions might be found in these fourth-century Syrian writings, it is clearly not yet as components combined and configured into the characteristic patterns of thought and practice that we might label – looking in retrospect at their expressions in literary corpora – as "Hekhalot," "Kabbalah," or so forth. One can explain some traditions therein in terms of materials absorbed from Jewish traditions of its time, Rabbinic and otherwise. Other connections may well be less direct, reflecting the development of similar traditions from similar sources, or against similar enemies, or in a similar milieu.

This is frustrating but perhaps also telling. Indeed, Neander may have been correct to notice that the Pseudo-Clementine *Homilies* is an unusually synthetic work. It weaves together strands from traditions that we now tend to try to distinguish as "Jewish," "Christian," "gnostic," or "pagan," as if these categories were always and everywhere so clear-cut. Likewise, Graetz may not have been off-base to suggest that "Jewish-Christians" of the sort responsible for the Pseudo-Clementines might have sometimes served as channels for the transmission of Hellenistic, Christian, and other traditions into Judaism. It is intriguing, too, to ponder whether Late Antiquity knew any "Jewish-Christians" akin to Sixtus in the sixteenth-century Italy or Neander in the nineteenth-century Germany – those who wielded some special status, even despite some social peripherality, due to their double positioning as "native informants." Pines may have been on to something, as well, when he pointed to the geographical location of the Pseudo-Clementines as perhaps the most important element to notice. In the case of Syrian "Jewish-Christians" operating in a bilingual Greek and Syriac milieu, one wonders whether their writings are so perplexingly rich in parallels with other corpora because of their setting at the shifting borders of two Empires, along the roads connecting Rome and Persia, and hence also Palestine and Babylonia.

---

[101] E. g., Graetz, *Gnosticismus und Judentum*, 109–15; Scholem, *Jewish Gnosticism*, 41; Scholem, *On the Mystical Shape*, 29–33, 214; Scholem, *On the Kabbalah*, 172; Pines, "Points of Similarity"; Idel, "Sabbath," 59; Idel, *Golem*, 5–8; Wolfson, *Through a Speculum*, 139.

It remains to be see whether fresh attention to these and other sources traditionally studied under the rubric of "Jewish-Christianity" might illumine something of the late antique transmission and transformation of traditions that eventually found expression in the coalescence of certain distinctive combinations within the Hekhalot literature and other forms of Jewish mystical writings. Precisely because many of these sources prove so puzzling, they may also serve as a heuristic "check" on the temptation to hang sweeping theories on the hooks of far-flung parallels, or to generalize the development of Jewish mysticism in terms of clear-cut phases, sweeping trajectories, or broad-based dichotomies. Likewise, the shifting place of such puzzling sources in modern research should perhaps give us pause when tempted by the triumphalism of the scholarly construction of new metanarratives about "mysticism" in each generation, recalling something of the older insights that newer narratives efface and elide.

Chapter Eleven

The Modern Jewish Rediscovery
of "Jewish-Christianity"*

Among the most momentous developments in recent research on "Jewish-Christianity/Christian Judaism" has been the emergence of a more accurate genealogy of modern scholarship on the topic. In the wake of World War II and the Holocaust, the intensified interest in the place of Judaism in Christian self-definition helped to spark fresh concern for "Jewish-Christianity." Particularly in North American research, however, the topic was initially revisited with a rather limited sense of the prior scholarly discussion, crediting Ferdinand Christian Baur for the recovery of "Jewish-Christianity" as a vital force in apostolic history.[1] To be sure, cautious scholars signaled that Baur had precedents.[2] Nevertheless, it became habitual to bracket off the history of research as

---

* This chapter has not been published previously in any form. Portions thereof were presented as "Jewish-Christianity in Christian and Jewish Historiography: The Case of Augustus Neander," at the 2013 Annual Meeting of the Society of Biblical Literature, Jewish-Christianity/Christian Judaism Section; "Jewish-Christianity between Ancient Identity and Modern Scholarship," at the Katz Center for Advanced Judaic Studies, 13 October 2014; "Jesus' Jewish Apostles and the History of the Jews: Memory, Mysticism, and the Modern Invention of 'Jewish-Christianity,'" at New York University, 10 March 2016. Research for this chapter was supported by a year-long fellowship from the Katz Center as part of the 2014–2015 theme year on "New Perspectives on the Origins, Context, and Diffusion of the Academic Study of Judaism."

[1] I.e., especially with reference to Baur's famous use of the Pseudo-Clementines to reconstruct the perspectives of a "Jewish-Christian" Petrine party that dominated the movement prior to its supposed suppression or supersession by Paulinism, beginning in "Die Christuspartei in der korinthischen Gemeide, der Gegensatz des petrinischen und paulischen Christentums in der alten Kirche, der Apostel Petrus in Rom," *Tübinger Zeitschrift für Theologie* 4 (1831): 61–206.

[2] "It is traditional in accounts of the history of the study of Jewish Christianity to being with the work of F. C. Baur," as James Carleton Paget notes, citing as representative examples Gustav Hoennicke in 1900s, Albertus Frederik Johannes Klijn in the 1970s, and Gerd Lüdemann in the 1980s; Carleton Paget further observes how Baur "set the tone for much of the subsequent debate about Jewish Christianity precisely because in it he attributed to the phenomenon such a significant role in the formation of second-century Christianity, and it was to his opinions that scholars reacted (and continue to react) either positively or negatively"; see "The Definition of the Terms Jewish Christian and Jewish Christianity in the History of Research," in *Jewish Believers in Jesus: The Early Centuries*, ed. Oskar Skarsaune and Reidar Hvalvik, (Peabody, MA: Hendrickson, 2007), 23–24. This pattern is also noted and charted in Matt Jackson-McCabe, "The Invention of Jewish Christianity in John Toland's *Nazarenus*," in *The Rediscovery of Jewish Christianity: From Toland to Baur*, ed. F. Stanley Jones (History of Biblical Studies 5; Atlanta: Society of Biblical Literature, 2012), 68; David Lincicum, "F.C. Baur's Place in the Study of Jewish Christianity," in Jones, *The Rediscovery of Jewish Christianity*, 139.

beginning with Baur. This is the origin myth of modern scholarship on "Jewish-Christianity" that predominated throughout the twentieth century, particularly in English-language literature, gaining an aura of conventionalism through repetition in countless surveys prefacing dissertations, books, and articles. It is only in the past decade that scholars have begun to contest this conventionalized habit and systematically work to correct its conceptual effects.

Most prominent, in this regard, have been the collaborative efforts of the Society of Biblical Literature "Jewish-Christianity/Christian Judaism" section, which has revisited the genealogy of the modern concept and category of "Jewish-Christianity" precisely by focusing attention on developments before Baur.[3] Some of the fascinating results have now been handily collected in accessible form in the 2012 volume, edited by F. Stanley Jones, on *The Rediscovery of Jewish Christianity: From Toland to Baur*. By recovering the role of John Toland (1670–1722), this volume radically reorients our sense of the early history of modern reflection on "Jewish-Christianity," expanding the cultural contexts of its cultivation, beyond the German Protestant settings of nineteenth-century New Testament scholarship, back into the debates between rationalist radicals and religious traditionalists in early Enlightenment England. Not only does Toland's 1718 *Nazarenus* mark the first known published use of the term "Jewish-Christianity" in English,[4] but – as Matt Jackson-McCabe there notes – Toland was the first "to re-describe a group long known as Nazarenes in terms of 'Jewish Christianity.'"[5] Toland, moreover, further speculated that the Torah-observant Christianity of the Ebionites and Nazareans was the religion of Jesus himself – or, in his words: *"The True and Original Plan of Christianity."*[6]

---

[3] See the brief pre-Baur survey in Carleton Paget, "Definition of the Terms," 24–30, who similarly stresses that we "would do better to begin at a much earlier point" than 1831 when tracing the history of research (p. 23). See already David Patrick, "Two English Forerunners of the Tubingen School: Thomas Morgan and John Toland," *Theological Review* 14 (1877): 593–601; Hella Lemke, *Judenchristentum zwischen Ausgrenzung und Integration: Zur Geschichte eines exegetischen Begriffes* (Hamburger Theologische Studien 25; Munster: LIT, 2001), 105–70, on the precedents for German Protestant treatment of the topic in English Deism in particular.

[4] Jackson-McCabe, "Invention of Jewish Christianity," 81–82. That said, one finds various attestations of terminology of "Jewish-Christians" and "Christian Jews" for over a century prior, as Matti Myllykoski has shown ("'Christian Jews' and 'Jewish Christians': The Jewish Origins of Christianity in English Literature from Elizabeth I to Toland's *Nazarenus*," in Jones, *Rediscovery of Jewish Christianity*, 4).

[5] Jackson-McCabe, "Invention of Jewish Christianity," 69. He also notes that Toland was the first to pair this rubric "with its inevitable mate *Gentile Christianity*." On the latter, see now Terence L. Donaldson, "'Gentile Christianity' as a Category in the Study of Christian Origins," *HTR* 106 (2013): 433–58.

[6] John Toland, *Nazarenus, or Jewish, Gentile, and Mahometan Christianity* (London, 1718), 33; Myllykoski, "Christian Jews," 35–36; Jackson-McCabe, "Invention of Jewish Christianity," 77–79; Pierre Lurbe, "John Toland's *Nazarenus* and the Original Plan of Christianity," in Jones, *Rediscovery of Jewish Christianity*, 56–58. Jackson-McCabe, "Invention of Jewish Christianity," 69.

In the foreword to Jones' 2012 volume, Lawrence Welborn notes how attention to Toland thus "makes possible a startling 'alternative history' of the critical study of Christian Origins."[7] What I would like to suggest, in what follows, is that it might do quite a bit more than that, opening up new horizons, approaches, and questions. This is not least because Jones' volume models the benefits of approaching the history of modern research, not just to trace a thin teleological line to our own present, but also to historicize scholarly practice and assumptions, particularly with reference to those voices from the past that more presentist perspectives habitually efface. This volume is thus an important addition to a growing corpus of recent studies by prominent historians of ancient Judaism and Christianity, such as Guy Stroumsa and Elizabeth Clark, who have sought to recover more integrative perspectives on the genealogies and formative settings of their modern study.[8] Like those studies, moreover, it has the potential to open a space for further conversation with early modernists like David Ruderman, Susannah Heschel, and Christian Weise, who have analyzed evolving practices of scholarship on the ancient past in relation to those specific European contexts most formative for the making of our current ideas about Judaism, Christianity, and "religion."[9]

My aim, in what follows, is to explore some of this potential, by bringing the new historiography of "Jewish-Christianity" into conversation with these and other reflections on the modern cultural histories of scholarship on ancient Jews and Judaism. Whereas past inquiries into the modern discourse about "Jewish-Christianity" have focused on Christian scholars and settings, however, I here attend to the questions of when, how, and why early research on "Jewish-Christianity" intersected with *Wissenschaft des Judentums* and other formative scholarship on Jews and Judaism pursued from the perspective of Jewish Studies.

Ruderman, Heschel, Wiese, and others have demonstrated the surprising degree to which the work of early modern Jewish and Christian scholars could cross-fertilize one another, even in settings where their scholarly practice remained institutionally distinct – and especially in relation to debates about Jesus, Judaism, and Christian Origins. Did any similar interaction mark early

---

[7] L.L. Welborn, "Series Editor's Foreword," in Jones, *Rediscovery of Jewish Christianity*, vii.

[8] Guy G. Stroumsa, *A New Science: The Discovery of Religion in the Age of Reason* (Cambridge, MA: Harvard University Press, 2010); Elizabeth Ann Clark, *Founding the Fathers: Early Church History and Protestant Professors in Nineteenth-Century America* (Philadelphia: University of Pennsylvania Press, 2011).

[9] E.g., David Rudermann, *Connecting the Covenants: Judaism and the Search for Christian Identity in Eighteenth-Century England* (Philadelphia: University of Pennsylvania Press, 2007); Susannah Heschel, *Abraham Geiger and the Jewish Jesus* (Chicago: University of Chicago Press, 1998); Christian Weise, *Challenging Colonial Discourse: Jewish Studies and Protestant Theology in Wilhelmine Germany* (Studies in European Judaism; Leiden: Brill, 2005).

scholarship on "Jewish-Christianity"? In reflecting upon this question, I am less interested in determining priority (i.e., who said what first) and more concerned to chart networks of connection and diffusion (i.e., how ideas spread, by what channels, to whom, and by which specific works they were popularized and mediated into different intellectual circles). My main concern, rather, is how and when the modern discussion of "Jewish-Christianity" came to be received as having anything to do with Jews and Judaism.

When and how are "Jewish-Christians" understood as part of the history of Jews and Judaism, framed in its own terms, rather than as part of Christian treatments of Jews and Judaism as preface or backdrop to Christian Origins? To answer this question, I here focus on the reception of those writings most closely linked to the modern study of "Jewish-Christianity," namely, the Pseudo-Clementine literature. After noting some of the elements of this literature that helped to inspire the modern invention of the category of "Jewish-Christianity," I turn to consider the place of the Pseudo-Clementines and "Jewish-Christians" in Heinrich Graetz's enormously influential history of the Jewish people. Then, I investigate Graetz's sources for his description of "Jewish-Christians," high-lighting the influence of Augustus Neander, a preeminent nineteenth-century German church historian who was himself a Jewish convert to Christianity. Neander – I shall suggest – may be more significant than typically credited for the path "from Toland to Baur." But his example is perhaps even more significant in reminding us that there were other paths too – from Neander to Graetz, from Graetz to Gershom Scholem, from Scholem to Shlomo Pines to Elliot Wolfson, and beyond.

The Pseudo-Clementines, John Toland, and the
Modern Invention of "Jewish-Christianity"

The Pseudo-Clementine literature consists of two novels, both written in Greek, which purport to record the story of the conversion of Clement of Rome, his travels with the apostle Peter, and Peter's debates with the arch-heretic Simon Magus. These two works, the *Homilies* and the *Recognitions,* date from the fourth century, but they are framed as the first-century writings of Clement him-self, claiming to preserve his eyewitness testimony to the true preachings and practices of Peter. Together with two epistles and related material prefaced to the *Homilies*, they promote an account of apostolic history that directly contradicts the New Testament Book of Acts.[10]

---

[10] See further F. Stanley Jones, *Pseudoclementina Elchasaiticaque inter Judaeochristiana: Collected Studies* (Orientalia Lovaniensia Analecta 203; Leuven: Peeters, 2012), 207–29; A.L.A. Hogeterp, "Judaism and Hellenism in the Pseudo-Clementine Homilies and the Ca-

Within both the Pseudo-Clementine *Homilies* and *Recognitions*, Peter is depicted as proclaiming the need for even baptized Gentiles to strive toward Torah observance by adopting purity practices, such as menstrual separation, as well as some dietary restrictions on meat (e. g., *Hom.* 7.8.1–3). The *Homilies* goes even further. There, Pharisees are painted in positive terms as heirs to Moses, and the transmission of the Torah is depicted as vouchsafed by the transmission of traditions about its interpretation without writing from Moses to his successors, thus guarding against the heretical misinterpretation of its written forms through an unbroken lineage of knowledge (e. g., *Hom.* 3.47). Not only is the Jewish transmission of the Torah from Moses thus elevated as a model for the proper transmission of prophetic truths from Jesus via Peter, but the *Homilies* further reveals that the teachings of Jesus are actually identical with those of Moses (e. g., *Hom.* 8.6–7): Jesus is lauded as the "True Prophet" who was sent to the earth so that the Law and monotheism long known to the chosen people Israel might be revealed to the other nations as well.

Inasmuch as the *Homilies* use Peter to reveal the identity of the teachings of Moses and Jesus, the result is a schema with two separate lines in the succession of truth, preserved by Pharisees and apostles respectively, and allowing for separate paths of Jewish and Gentile salvation.[11] Even as Peter here celebrates those Jewish apostles and proselytes who know and teach both, he stresses that it suffices for salvation if Jews and Gentiles each follow their own path – that is, provided that Gentile Christians do not hate non-Christian Jews, nor the converse. The *Homilies* thus depart rather radically from the antinomian and anti-Jewish tropes common in late antique Christian literature. And, in the process, its authors/redactors remake the memory of the Jewish past in a manner more akin to Rabbinic traditions of their own time.[12] Among the results is a striking elevation of postbiblical Judaism as a model of unity and piety for Gentile followers of Jesus – who, notably, are here not even called "Christians" but rather "God-fearers," a common term for Gentile sympathizers with the Jewish people.

From the standpoint of the history of antiquity, the Pseudo-Clementine corpus is thus significant as a rare reservoir of firsthand evidence for the conceptualization of Christianity as complementary with Judaism – a position otherwise known to us primarily from hostile secondhand reports by heresiologists like Irenaeus and Epiphanius concerning the Ebionites and the Nazoraeans.[13] Inasmuch as the Pseudo-Clementines hail from the fourth century, this corpus provides rare glimpses of inner-Christian resistance to the anti-Judaism of Justin Martyr and

---

nonical Acts of the Apostles," in Jan N. Bremmer, *The Pseudo-Clementines* (Studies on Early Christian Apocrypha 10; Leuven: Peeters, 2010), 59–71.

[11] See Chapters One and Six above for detailed discussion of the key passages.

[12] See esp. Chapter Nine in this volume.

[13] See Albertus Frederik Johannes Klijn and Gerrit J. Reinink, *Patristic Evidence for Jewish-Christian Sects* (NTSup 36; Leiden: Brill, 1973), 95–281.

his heirs, as well as attesting the continued creative contestation of the memory of the apostolic past long after the texts of the New Testament – and even at the very cusp of the Christianization of the Roman Empire.[14]

I would like to suggest that the Pseudo-Clementines may bear some significance from the standpoint of the history of modernity as well – not least because they served as the direct inspiration for much of the modern reflection on "Jewish-Christianity" noted at the outset. Throughout the Middle Ages, the Pseudo-Clementines circulated in multiple versions, manuscripts, and languages. But they were prized for reasons other than their approach to Judaism. In Late Antiquity and the Middle Ages, their call for Christians not to hate Jews dissipated like a "cry into the void." The very elements that lay latent in their medieval reception, however, eventually became the hallmark of their modern reception – which (in turn) formed the core and catalyst for the modern scholarly construction of the very category of "Jewish-Christianity."

In part, this pattern in the reception of the Pseudo-Clementines may reflect the widespread popularity of the Latin translation of the *Recognitions* by Rufinus. This version – which does not survive in Greek but is extant in over a hundred manuscripts in Latin – contains fewer explicitly pro-Jewish features than the *Homilies*, at least in Rufinus' translation, and it lacks the *Epistle of Peter to James*. It is at the very least intriguing that European interest in the "Jewish-Christian" elements of the Pseudo-Clementine tradition seems to have awaited the rediscovery and print dissemination of the two known Greek manuscripts of the Pseudo-Clementine *Homilies* – both of which begin with the above-quoted epistle.[15] Popular and scholarly curiosity about the Pseudo-Clementines was sparked first in the wake of the printing of Codex Parisinus Graecus 930 (P) in the late seventeenth century, and again in the wake of the "discovery" and printing of Codex Vaticanus Ottobonianus 443 (O) in the early nineteenth century, and in both cases, this curiosity was one key catalyst for discussions of "Jewish-

---

[14] See Chapter Six in this volume.

[15] I.e., the tenth-century Codex Parisinus Graecus 930 (P) and the sixteenth-century Codex Vaticanus Ottobonianus 443 (O). Portions of the *Homilies* also survive in Syriac translation in manuscripts from 411 CE (British Library Additional 12,150) and 587 CE (British Library Additional 14,609). See now F. Stanley Jones, trans., *The Syriac Pseudo-Clementines: An Early Version of the First Christian Novel* (Apocryphes 14; Turnhout: Brepols, 2014), 38–44, 251–338. The *Recognitions*, by contrast, were well known across Europe and debated apart from the discourse of rediscovery that surrounding the *Homilies*. For some representative examples of the early modern discussion surrounding the *Recognitions*, see Irena Backus, "Renaissance Attitudes to New Testament Apocryphal Writings: Jacques Lefèvre d'Étaples and His Epigones," *Renaissance Quarterly* 51 (1998): 1169–98; Backus, "Calvin and the Greek Fathers," in *Continuity and Change: The Harvest of Late Medieval and Reformation History*, ed. Robert James Bast, Andrew Colin Gow, and Heiko Augustinus Oberman (Leiden: Brill, 2000), 253–78 at 265–66, 271; Backus, *Historical Method and Confessional Identity in the Era of the Reformation (1378–1615)* (Studies in Medieval and Reformation Thought 94; Leiden: Brill, 2003), 206–7, 228.

Christianity." As with other manuscript publications of the time, these were met with a sense of excitement about the potential of "lost" texts hidden away in distant monasteries and dusty libraries to reveal suppressed or forgotten truths from and about the Christian past.[16]

In the early eighteenth century, this sense of "rediscovery" was poignantly expressed – and powerfully weaponized – by Toland, an English Deist controversialist who adduced a number of newly published "apostolic apocrypha" as ammunition for his attacks upon the canon and authority of the Church.[17] Toland's *Nazarenus* dramatizes this sense of rediscovery particularly with the *Gospel of Barnabas*, but he also marks it explicitly for the *Epistle of Peter to James*. He there mentions the epistle as "prefixt by Cotelerius to the Clementines" – that is, referencing Jean Baptiste Cotelier's 1672 collection of "Apostolic Fathers," wherein is found the very first printed edition of the *Homilies*, together with the *Epistle of Peter to James* and the other prefatory materials, as rendered from Codex Parisinius Graecus 930 and printed in Greek with parallel Latin translation.[18] When Toland uses these Pseudo-Clementine materials to conjure a hidden Christian past – as supposedly suppressed by late antique ecclesiarchs like Eusebius, Epiphanius, Athanasius, and the ecumenical councils enabled by the Christianization of the Roman Empire – he thus reflects something of a sense of the newly modern sharing of religious knowledge that had been hidden in the past.[19]

At the time, scholars, printers, and bibliographers were indeed recovering and disseminating more and more knowledge about ancient Christianity, not least by virtue of new print technologies that enabled the wide dissemination of texts

---

[16] See further Chapter Eight in this volume.

[17] On the broader context, see Justin A. Champion, "Apocrypha, Canon, and Criticism from Samuel Fisher to John Toland, 1650–1718," in *Judaeo-Christian Intellectual Culture in the Seventeenth Century*, ed. Allison P. Coudert et al. (Dordrecht: Kluwer, 1999), 91–117; Champion, *Republican Learning: John Toland and the Crisis of Christian Culture, 1696–1722* (Manchester: Manchester University Press, 2003).

[18] Jean Baptiste Cotelier, *SS. Patrum qui Temporibus Apostolicis floruerunt, Barnabae, Clementis, Hermae, Ignatii, Polycarpi opera edita et inedita, vera, et suppositicia; una cum Clementis, Ignatii, Polycarpi actis atque martyriis* (Paris: Petri Le Petit, 1672), 529–746.

[19] In a discussion flanked by a marginal note contrasting Acts 10 with Galatians 2, Toland renders some text from the *Epistle of Peter to James* in both Greek and English, and he stresses that "Neither do I doubt but tis the Apostle to the Gentiles [i.e., Paul], that is aim'd at in an *Epistle of Peter to James*, prefixt by Cotelerius to the Clementines. The words of Peter (after entreating James not to communicate his Preachings to any Gentile, nor even to any Jew without previous examination) are there" (*Nazarenus*, 23). Toland quotes at length then further notes: "This most remarkable and inconstably ancient piece, with others as least as ancient, which I cou'd cite were it needful, do manifestly shot; that this notion of Paul's having wholly metamorphos'd and perverted the true Christianity (as some of the Heretics have exprest it) and his being blam'd for so doing by the other Apostles, especially by James and Peter, is neither an original invention of the Mahometans, nor any sign of the novelty of their Gospel [i.e., *Gospel of Barnabas*]" (p. 24).

that had been previously been accessible only in a few manuscripts, limited in number and access. Toland drew on this reservoir of newly disseminated knowledge for his polemical aims, asserting that texts like the Pseudo-Clementines and *Gospel of Barnabas* actually preserve "THE TRUE AND ORIGINAL PLAN OF CHRISTIANITY."[20] What was suppressed by the bishops of the Council of Nicaea – Toland claimed – was none other than the secret truth that "CHRISTIANITY [was] no more than REFORMED JUDAISM."

It is in this context that Toland coined the term "Jewish-Christianity" and popularized the notion that "apocryphal" writings like the *Gospel of Barnabas*, *Epistle of Peter to James*, and Pseudo-Clementine *Homilies* attest the true Jewishness of Christianity, suppressed by later ecclesiarchs. And this coinage, as Jones has shown, marks the beginning of modern discussion of "Jewish-Christianity": Toland's own aims and approach were quite far from what we might call critical scholarship, but "it is in the attempts to refute Toland's studies that the opponents are drawn into extensive historical argumentation [and] this discussion marks the beginning of the modern academic debate" about "Jewish-Christianity."[21]

The debate intensified in the nineteenth century, when scholars began to analyze the Pseudo-Clementines in much more detail, whereupon their recovery as historical sources served as one of the central catalysts for the articulation of modern critical approaches to the New Testament and apostolic history alike. As noted at the outset, the German Protestant scholar Ferdinand Christian Baur is typically credited for this development. Baur and the Tübingen School used the Pseudo-Clementines to relativize and interrogate their canonical counterparts, rereading the Book of Acts in particular "against the grain" with an eye to what was harmonized, glossed over, suppressed, and omitted therein. By reading the Pseudo-Clementines as the "other side" to the story preserved in the New Testament, moreover, Baur went beyond the widespread emphasis on Jesus as Jew to posit the essential Jewishness even of the earliest Church and its theology.[22]

---

[20] Toland, *Nazarenus*, 33 (capitalization in original!) – on which see further Myllykoski, "Christian Jews," 35–36; Lurbe, "John Toland's *Nazarenus*," 56–58; Jackson-McCabe, "Invention of Jewish Christianity," 77–79. Notably, Toland's own aims destabilize Daniel Boyarin's argument for consistently heresiological character of the modern category "Jewish-Christianity" ("Rethinking Jewish Christianity: An Argument for Dismantling a Dubious Category [To Which is Appended a Correction of My *Border Lines*]," *JQR* 99 [2009]: 7–36.) Far from the product of a "heresiology" that evokes a hybrid in the course of constructing pure identities through contrast, "Jewish-Christianity" provided a means for Toland to turn the Protestant prioritization of origins against itself, revealing the originary Jewishness of Christianity and, thus, unsettling the authority of those ecclesiarchs who claimed to be the sole possessors of Christian truth.

[21] F. Stanley Jones, "From Toland to Baur," in Jones, *Rediscovery of Jewish Christianity*, 123–36 at 124–25. I.e., Toland's own purpose and positioning may not have been critical or historical, but he nevertheless shaped scholarship as we know it.

[22] So, e. g., Ferdinand Christian Baur, *The Church History of the First Three Centuries*, trans. Allan Menzies (2 vols.; 3rd ed.; London: Williams & Norgate, 1878), 1:43. If not for Paul, in fact, Christianity would have remained (in his words) the "faith of a mere Jewish sect."

By mapping the Pseudo-Clementines' dichotomous Rule of Syzygy, and their accounts of Peter's conflict with Simon Magus, onto a Hegelian dialectic, Baur articulated his signature theory of the division of the primitive church into two conflicting "parties."[23] The non-canonical Pseudo-Clementines – by his reading – preserved the more ancient "Jewish-Christianity" of Peter, James, and the Jerusalem Church, while the canonical texts of the New Testament were shaped by the "Gentile- Christianity" associated with Paul, which would come to supplant and suppress its more primitive rival – resulting in the emergence of Christianity as a non-Jewish (and even anti-Jewish) religion.

Much has been written about Baur, in this regard, and increasingly also about Toland as well. My question here, however, is how, when, and why our ancient sources for "Jewish-Christianity" came to be received by modern readers as having anything to do with Jews and Judaism. Toland was engaged in intellectual interchange with John Selden (1584–1654), a Christian legal scholar known for his interest in the Talmud.[24] It would be going too far, however, to treat *either* Selden's Christian Hebraism or Toland's "Jewish-Christianity" as an engagement with Judaism *per se*.[25] In both cases, Judaism remains a construct at play in what Jackson-McCabe describes as the "competition among Christian intellectuals to authorize rival mythological and ethical constructions of 'true Christianity' in the midst of the English Enlightenment."[26] So too – I would suggest – with Baur and the Tübingen School in nineteenth-century Germany; for them too, Judaism was not so much a living tradition to be engaged in dialogue as it was a passive and past subject for Christian analysis – a topic to be studied for the sake of inner-Christian debates about Christian theology and historiography, especially in relation to the exegesis and exposition of the New Testament.

Today, "Jewish-Christianity" has again attracted fresh scholarly attention, alongside the Pseudo-Clementines – albeit in new intellectual contexts and institutional settings, shaped now by the collaborative participation of Jewish, Christian, and other scholars of the New Testament and Judaism alike. It is in this context that scholars such as Charlotte Elisheva Fonrobert and Burton Visotzky have lamented the longstanding tendency whereby "Jewish-Christianity" has

---

[23] Most famously in Baur, "Die Christuspartei in der korinthischen Gemeide."

[24] Toland, *Nazarenus*, 30; on which see further Myllykoski, "Christian Jews," 35.

[25] Jackson-McCabe, "Invention of Jewish Christianity," 87–89. Nor is it based in any notion of Judaism notably different from his time. To my knowledge, Toland himself did not look to any Rabbinic sources either to understand or to contextualize his notion of "Jewish-Christianity." It thus remains striking – as Pierre Lurbe notes – that Toland pairs "his focus on the Jewish roots of Christianity'" with a seemingly "daring stance against supersessionism" ("John Toland's *Nazarenus*," 65).

[26] Jackson-McCabe, "Invention of Jewish Christianity," 81. Inasmuch as Toland "composed *Nazarenus* not merely as an account of *early* Christianity but as an account of *true* Christianity," the modern invention of "Jewish-Christianity" was a "byproduct of Toland's attempts to lay claim to the mythic source of Christian authority – Jesus and the apostles – for his own Enlightenment ethos of rationality, universal humanity, and tolerance" (p. 70).

been studied almost wholly as a part of Christian history.[27] My question here, however, is a different one, oriented instead to its modern reception. As much as scholars might work today to correct the longstanding limitation of "Jewish-Christianity" to a topic of Christian history, we might also do well to ask: was this always the case?

If one reads the summaries of the history of research that introduce current studies of the New Testament and early Jewish/Christian relations, one would certainly think that "Jewish-Christianity" has always been centered in the study of Christianity, in general, and the New Testament, in particular. Throughout the twentieth century and to this day, such summaries consistently credit Baur with founding the modern study of "Jewish-Christianity," and they trace a thin line from nineteenth-century German Protestant theology, to the birth of modern critical research on the New Testament, to the increased scholarly concern after the Holocaust and World War II for understanding Christianity's origins from with Judaism. In the last twenty years, scholars have intensively revisited the modern genealogy of the very concept and category of "Jewish-Christianity," concurrent with the rise of interest in early Jewish/Christian relations.[28] Even among those who look before Baur to highlight figures like Toland, however, it still remains conventional to trace a teleology of scholarly progress wherein Judaism remains figured as a *passive* subject of Christian misunderstanding or understanding (i. e., with the latter associated with the past, and the former with the present or future). Some recent iterations may point to the interventions today by Jewish and other scholars of Rabbinic Judaism, such as Daniel Boyarin. Yet, even in such cases, we find a striking neglect of earlier Jewish scholars or precedents – even in the early twentieth century, let alone the nineteenth.

The curiousness of this conventional omission will be obvious to scholars familiar with *Wissenschaft des Judentums*. After all, a very rich and extensive discussion of "Jewish-Christians" can be found already in its most prominent, widely diffused, and enduringly popular historiographical product – namely, Graetz's eleven-volume *Geschichte der Juden*.[29] This work was first published

---

[27] Charlotte Elisheva Fonrobert, "The *Didascalia Apostolorum*: A Mishnah for the Disciples of Jesus," *JECS* 9 (2001): 483–509; Burton Visotzky, "Prolegomenon to the Study of Jewish-Christianities in Rabbinic Literature," in *Fathers of the World: Essays in Rabbinic and Patristic Literatures* (WUNT 80; Tübingen: Mohr Siebeck, 1995), 129–49.

[28] See Appendix B in this volume.

[29] Heinrich Graetz, *Geschichte der Juden: Von den ältesten Zeiten bis auf die Gegenwart* (11 vols.; Berlin: Beit, 1853–1876). In his bibliographical essay on Graetz for *Oxford Bibliographies Online*, Amos Bitzan gives the following handy summary of its complex publication history: "Graetz began his history with Volume 4, which covered the time period from 'the fall of the Jewish state to the completion of the Talmud,' published in 1853. He then published Volume 3, which ranged from 'the death of Judah Maccabee to the fall of the Jewish state,' in 1856. Owing to hesitation on the part of his publisher, Graetz did not include an important chapter on the origins of Christianity in this first edition of Volume 3; it was added in the second edition of the work, published in 1863. After the publication of Volume 3 (first edition),

between 1853 and 1876, and it was widely republished and translated thereafter. In what follows, I would like look more closely at Graetz's treatment of "Jewish-Christianity," exploring his place in the modern reception of the Pseudo-Clementines as well as his precedent for the use of sources by and about "Jewish-Christians" as evidence *both* for interpreting Jewish sources *and* for writing the history of the Jewish people.

Heinrich Graetz and the Jewishness of "Jewish-Christians"

Much has been written about Graetz's depictions of Jesus and the origins of Christianity within the controversial third volume of his *Geschichte der Juden* – which was first published in 1856, without this chapter, but which was eventually published in full, with the chapter reintegrated, in the second edition of 1863. In that infamous chapter, Jesus is associated with the Jewish sect of the Essenes, and – as Jonathan Elukin, Peter Schäfer, and others have shown – Christianity is thereby relativized as one of multiple expressions of an inner-Jewish stream of esotericism with a long Jewish history both before and after Jesus himself.[30]

Graetz published Volumes 5–11 sequentially, concluding the Geschichte der Juden with Volume 11 on the modern period (1760–1848), in 1870 …. Volume 1 was published in 1874 and covered 'the history of the Israelites from its ancient origins (1500) to the death of King Solomon (977 in the pre-Christian era).' Part 1 of Volume 2 was published in 1875, ranging from 'the death of King Solomon (ca. 977 in the pre-Christian era) to the Babylonian exile (586).' Part 2 of Volume 2 followed in 1876, ending with the death of Judah Maccabee"; Bitzan, "Heinrich Graetz," in *Oxford Bibliographies Online, Jewish Studies*, ed. David Biale (New York: Oxford University Press, 2012), DOI: 10.1093/OBO/9780199840731-0047.

   German quotes from volume four below are from the 1908 edition of *Geschichte der Juden: Vom Untergange des jüdischen Staates bis zum Abschluss des Talmud*, and English translation reflects the first English translation of the fourth volume, which was undertaken by Rabbi James K. Gutheim and issued as a stand-alone book by the American Jewish Publication Society in 1873. Compare the later combination of the third and fourth volumes as part 2 of the English translation of Graetz's entire history, first published by the Jewish Publication Society of America in 1893 (trans. P. Bloch). Although the latter is more widely used today, my focus here is on the place of Christianity in the fourth volume, as distinct from the later articulations and controversies surrounding the treatment of Jesus and Christian Origins in the third volume.

[30] So, e. g., in Graetz, *Geschichte der Juden*, 4:70: "Das junge Christentum war als Glückskind in die Welt getreten. Es war schon ein glücklicher Wurf, daß eben dieser feuereifrige, unruhige, leidenschaftliche Saulus von Tarsus aus einem Verächter nicht nur Anhänger, sondern auch Hauptbegründer geworden war. Denn er hatte ihm erst die rechte Bahn geöffnet, 'in die Fülle der Heiden einzugehen'; ohne ihn hätte sich die Jesus lehre als Bekenntnis einer unfertigen, halbessäischen, aus unwissenden Jüngern und zweideutigen Jüngerinnen bestehenden Sekte schwerlich lange behaupten können." See further Heinrich Graetz, *Gnosticismus und Judentum* (Krotoschin: Monasch, 1846); Graetz, *History of the Jews: From the Earliest Times to the Present Day*, ed. and trans. B. Löwy (6 vols.; Philadelphia: JPS, 1891–1898), 2:28, 142, 148–57, 171, 367; Jonathan M. Elukin, "A New Essenism: Heinrich Graetz and Mysticism," *Journal for the History of Ideas* 59 (1998): 135–48; Peter Schäfer, "'Adversus cabbalam' oder Heinrich Graetz und die jüdische Mystik," in *Reuchlin und seine Erben: Forscher, Denker,*

A focus on the Pseudo-Clementines and "Jewish-Christianity," however, leads us to the less studied topic of his treatment of Christianity within the fourth volume of *Geschichte der Juden*, which covers the "Talmudic Age" and which was the first of the series to be published (i.e., appearing in 1853). At the end of chapter four of that volume, Graetz explains his rationale for even including Christianity within a history of the Jewish people. Significantly, for our purposes, he does so by appealing foremost to "Jewish-Christians." "The development of Christianity, as an offspring of Judaism ... forms a part of Jewish history" – Graetz there argues – for precisely as long "as its adherents belonged to the Jewish communion."[31] This rationale resonates with his later choice to include the origins of Christianity so prominently in volume three. In the immediate context of volume four, however, it serves to introduce the fascinating fifth chapter. There, Graetz covers the topic of "Jewish-Christian" sects like the Ebionites, alongside Jewish "gnostics" and proselytes, and he treats each of these groups with a focus on their relevance for the history of the Jewish people, in general, and their value for understanding the age of the Tannaim, more specifically.

In the case of Christianity, then, it is only "Jewish-Christianity" that here makes its postapostolic forms even apt for inclusion in a history of the Jewish people. It is to make this point, thus, that Graetz recounts the early split of the "parties" of Peter and James from that of Paul. The "Jewish-Christianity" of the former is still a part of the history of the Jews long after the death of Jesus and into the Talmudic age, while the "Gentile-Christianity" of the latter becomes marked as always and already separate. Just as Paul is an "enemy of Judaism," so the "religion" he founds is the "opposite of Judaism" – never really a part thereof.

Conversely, Graetz points the early participation of "Jewish-Christians" in Jewish peoplehood. Like their Jewish compatriots, but unlike their Gentile-Christian counterparts, for instance, Ebionites are here said to foster a deep hatred of the Roman Empire and thus to partake of Jewish patriotism. Graetz further depicts the Ebionites as modeling their own piety on that of the Tannaim. Interestingly, for our purposes, he does so by quoting from the *Epistle of Peter to James,* interpreting it through the lens of Talmudic traditions about Yavneh, and equating the character of Simon Magus in the Pseudo-Clementines with Paul:

With a kind of admiration of the unity and unanimity which prevailed within the Jewish body, guided by the Jamnian Synhedrin, in contrast to the dissensions and divergences within the Christian congregation, a member of the Jewish Christian party wrote: "The

---

Ideologen und Spinner, ed. Peter Schäfer and Irina Wandrey (Ostfildern: Thorbecke, 2005), 189–210.

[31] Graetz, *History of the Jews*, 4:54; cf. Graetz, *Geschichte der Juden*, 4:68: "Die Entwickelung des Christentums, als eines Sprosses des Judentums, an dessen Wurzeln es sich genährt hatte, bildet namentlich solange seine Anhänger noch zum jüdischen Verbande gehörten, einen Teil der jüdischen Geschichte."

widely scattered Jews observe, to this day, the same law concerning the unity of God and practices of life, and can by no means entertain a diverging opinion, or be induced to deviate from the settled meaning of the ambiguous words of Scripture. For it is by traditionary rules that they try to reconcile the ambiguous passages of Scripture. For this reason they permit no one to teach who has not first learned how to expound the Sacred Writings. Hence they have one God, one law, one hope. ... If we do not adopt the same system, the one word of truth will be split into many opinions. I do not know this as a prophet, but because I have looked into the root of the evil. For some of the Gentiles had spurned my message, which agreed with the law, by following the lawless and farcical doctrine of an adversary (Paul)." These words are attributed to the second chief apostle, Simon Kephas (Peter). But the Jewish Christians not only characterized Paul's messages and teachings, of which he boasted so much, as lawless and farcical, but even gave him a nickname that should brand him and his whole faction. They called him Simon Magus, a semi-Jewish (Samaritan) magician, who had enchanted the world by his words.[32]

Graetz evokes this poignant period of harmony, however, in part to explain how it eventually came to an end. Equating the Ebionites of Christian heresiology with the *minim* mentioned in Rabbinic literature, he suggests that "Jewish-Christians" were increasingly hated by both sides – particularly as the Jewishness of their "Jewish-Christian" faith came to be corrupted by the "heathen" and Hellenizing elements of ascendant Paulinism:

The Paulinian doctrine gained ground apace and was able to maintain itself as the true and sole, as the Catholic (universal), Christianity. It was, therefore, natural that all these sects, Ebionite, Nazarenes, Masboteans, by degrees were partly absorbed by the continually growing communion of Gentile Christians, partly lingered on in small numbers and a dejected state, an object of contempt for Jews and Christians. The Jews also hated them under the name of Minim, in which term they comprised all sects that had sprung from Judaism, but had renounced it either as a whole or in part.[33]

This is what leads to their denunciation through the institution of the *birkat ha-minim*, in his estimation, and thus also to the moment when the history of Christianity finally separates from the history of the Jews.

Graetz frames this separation as tragic for the Jews, inasmuch as Paul's invention of Christianity as the "opposite of Judaism" would thus prevail, inspiring centuries upon centuries of the Church's persecution of Jews. But he also describes this separation as tragic for the Christians – a loss of their own true origins in a poignantly formative moment of forgetting. "Jewish-Christians," he writes, "observed the Jewish law in all its parts, and pointed to the example of Jesus, who had lived in accordance with the Jewish law."[34] Theirs was the more ancient and authentic form of Christianity – formed prior to the antinomian innovations of Paul and fiercely contesting them thereafter. Yet it was Paul's Gentile

---

[32] Graetz, *History of the Jews*, 4:58; cf. Graetz, *Geschichte der Juden*, 4:76–77, there citing "*Clementis homiliae*, ed. Dressel. Anfang."

[33] Graetz, *History of the Jews*, 4:66; cf. Graetz, *Geschichte der Juden*, 4:85.

[34] Graetz, *History of the Jews*, 4:56; cf. Graetz, *Geschichte der Juden*, 4:74–76.

Church that succeeded in promoting itself as "universal" (i. e., "Catholic") such that in the end "Christians did not regard [the "Jewish-Christians"] as the primitive congregation, from which they had primarily sprung themselves with the obliteration of every Jewish trace, but as sectarians of a later date."[35]

At first sight, Graetz may seem simply to reiterate the theory made famous by Baur. Not only did Graetz's volume appear well after Baur's seminal 1831 article on the two conflicting apostolic "parties," but his notes point the reader to the extension thereof by Adolf Hilgenfeld (to whose redactional hypothesis about the Gospel of Matthew Graetz also later alludes).[36] When Graetz introduces the topic of "Jewish-Christianity," moreover, he does so in terms that align his own narrative with the interventions of Baur and the Tübingen School, stressing that

Sectarianism did not first arise within Christianity, as is commonly assumed, in the second century, but prevailed at its very inception as a necessary consequence of antagonistic fundamental doctrines ... [with] two parties, which ... stood directly opposed to each other, ... the Jewish Christians, on the one side, the Gentile Christians on the other.[37]

A closer look, however, exposes some notable differences in both contextualization and articulation, revealing Graetz's own engagement with the topic as much more than a reaction or even redeployment of Baur. First is the matter of sources. Graetz, for instance, draws directly on the Pseudo-Clementine *Homilies* and its appended *Epistles*, wherein Jews and Judaism are elevated as models for Christian practice. That Graetz consults the work directly, moreover, is clear from his use of the edition of Albertus R. M. Dressel – newly published at the time and integrating the "rediscovery" in 1837 of the second Greek manuscript (i. e., Codex Vaticanus Ottobonianus 443 [O]).[38]

Like Baur, Graetz appeals to the contrast between Peter and Simon Magus, and he reads parts of the *Homilies'* representation of the latter as a cipher for Paul. In his *Geschichte*, however, the material about Simon Magus in the Pseudo-Clementines is also used for another purpose. When Graetz turns to discuss "gnostics," directly after "Jewish-Christians," he draws upon this work as a source of secondhand evidence for the types of anti-Jewish *Gnosis* that he depicts as posing a challenge for the Tannaim. When discussing "gnostics," for instance, Graetz explains how "the writings of their Jewish-Christian opponents" are alone in preserving their systems of thought in their entirety, and he then goes on to paraphrase the beliefs attributed to Simon Magus in the Pseudo-Clementine *Homilies* when describing the essence of the *Gnosis* against which

---

[35] Graetz, *History of the Jews*, 4:66; cf. Graetz, *Geschichte der Juden*, 4:85.

[36] Esp. Graetz, *Geschichte der Juden*, 4:74–75.

[37] Graetz, *History of the Jews*, 4:56.

[38] Albertus R. M. Dressel, *Clementis Romani quae feruntur Homilae viginti nunc prinum integrae* (Göttingen: Sumptibus Librariae Dieterichianae, 1853) – which, notably, is dedicated to none other than Augustus Neander!

Rabbis like Akiba were battling in the second century as well.[39] Consequently, Graetz departs from Baur's characterization of the Pseudo-Clementines as examples of "Christian *Gnosis*," reading them as *anti*-gnostic in their aims and closer to Judaism.[40] Within Graetz's history, the anti-gnostic "Jewish-Christians" of the Pseudo-Clementines therefore form part of a continuum defined on one end by Jewish anti-gnostics like Rabbi Akiba, in the middle by Jewish "gnostics" like Aher and purportedly Valentinius, and on the other extreme by anti-Jewish "gnostics" like Marcion.[41]

From this distinctive schema – as well as the fitting of figures therein – it is clear his treatment of "Jewish-Christianity," the Pseudo-Clementines, and *Gnosis* owes significant debts also to the work of an earlier thinker – namely, Augustus Neander. Not only was Neander a German Jewish convert to Christianity and the most prominent Church Historian of his time, but he authored a foundational 1818 book on *Gnosis*, which was the first systematic study of the phenomenon and which attempted to categorize all known "gnostic" groups and figure as *either* Jewish *or* anti-Jewish.[42]

In the relevant section of his *Geschichte*, Graetz does not cite Neander by name, but he does point the reader to his own dissertation-based book, published in 1846, on the very topic of *Gnosis* and Judaism.[43] It is there that Graetz engages Neander's ideas in more explicit terms. At the outset, for instance, he lauds Neander as the first to bring order to the chaos of evidence for *Gnosis*. Not only does he follow Neander in categorizing varieties of *Gnosis* as either Jewish or anti-Jewish, but he draws on Neander's use of the Pseudo-Clementines *both* to illumine the early "Jewish-Christianity" of Ebionites and Nazoreans *and* to shed light on their anti-Jewish gnostic opponents.[44] It is this framework,

---

[39] Graetz, *History of the Jews*, 4:67.

[40] Thus stressing the importance of this "Jewish-Christian" evidence for *Gnosis*, e. g., also in Graetz, *Geschichte der Juden*, 4:86: "Die Gnostiker oder richtiger Theosophen, zwischen Judentum, Christentum und Heidentum schwebend, wie sie aus diesen drei Kreisen Vorstellungen und Gedankenformungen aufnahmen, gingen auch aus den Anhängern der drei Religionen hervor. Von ihrem Lehrbegriffe sind bisher nur unzusammenhängende Bruchstücke, einzelne Fäden aus einem fremdartigen Gewebe, bekannt geworden, welche lediglich durch die Schriften ihrer christlich-jüdischen Gegner erhalten sind."

[41] Graetz also follows Neander in identifying some of the "gnostics" known from Irenaeus, et al., as Jews; e. g., in his list of known names in *Geschichte der Juden*, 4:87: "Die berühmtesten Namen der Gnostiker waren Saturnin, Basilides und Valentinus, *wohl Juden der Abstammung nach*; ferner des letztern Schüler Markos und Bardesanes, *ersterer ein Jude*, letzterer ein Christ aus der Euphratgegend; dann Kerinth, Kerdon mit seinem sophistischen Schüler Marcion, endlich Karpokrates, der fleischliche Kommunist und Tatian, der Urheber strenger Enthaltsamkeit, der Vorläufer der Mönche."

[42] August Neander, *Genetische Entwickelung der vornehmsten gnostischen Systeme* (Berlin: Dümmler, 1818).

[43] Graetz, *Gnosticismus und Judenthum*.

[44] Neander, *Genetische Entwickelung*, 361–421; Graetz, *Gnosticismus und Judenthum*, esp. 4, 37, 57, 59.

in turn, that enables Graetz also to draw from the secondhand heresiological reports by Church Fathers like Irenaeus, reading them through the lens of the Pseudo-Clementine polemics against Simon Magus, in order also to illuminate Rabbinic and other Jewish sources – ranging from *Sefer Yetzirah*, to the mishnaic strictures on study of *ma'aseh bereshit* and the *merkavah*, to the famous story in the Tosefta about the four who entered *pardes*.[45]

Graetz makes explicit reference to Neander, in fact, when adducing the Pseudo-Clementine *Homilies* as an anti-gnostic "Jewish-Christian" work of the second century. For Graetz, the "Jewish-Christianity" of this text is what enables its use as evidence for a project of Jewish intellectual history, and he underlines its connections to post-Christian Judaism by developing Neander's notions of parallels with *Sefer Yetzirah*.[46] At the time, Graetz approached *Sefer Yetzirah* as a second-century work associated with none other than Rabbi Akiba.[47] From its parallels with the Pseudo-Clementines,[48] he thus posited the early synthesis of a Jewish *Gnosis* due to the transmission of traditions into Rabbinic Judaism in

---

[45] Graetz, *Gnosticismus und Judentum*, 102–3. Just as Neander creates a taxonomy of *Gnosis* through a focus on Judaism, so Graetz reads *t. Ḥagigah* 2.3–4 as a parable for the continuum of Judaism in the second century, ranging from the Jewish *Gnosis* of *minim* to its critique and rejection by the Rabbis.

[46] Shortly before Graetz's study, August Friedrich Gfrörer could thus take for granted that the Pseudo-Clementines might be termed a "Greek *Zohar*"; August Friedrich Gfrörer, *Das Jahrhundert des Heils* (2 vols.; Stuttgart: E. Schweizerbart, 1838), 1:295–97 – there crediting Neander as well.

[47] Note that Gershom Scholem (*On the Kabbalah and Its Symbolism*, trans. R. Manheim [repr. ed.; New York: Schocken, 1996], 172) credits Graetz as the first to note a possible connection between *Sefer Yetzirah* and the Pseudo-Clementines. Graetz does so while arguing against the direct connection of *Sefer Yetzirah* with Marcosians posited in Johann Franz Buddeus' *Introductio ad historiam philosophiae Ebraeorum* (Halle, 1702), which he critiques for not distinguishing between different stages in the development of Kabbalah; see *Gnosticismus und Judentum*, 109–10. Graetz points to the Pseudo-Clementine *Homilies* as a closer parallel, building on Neander's understanding of those works as second-century "Jewish-Christian" writings that polemicize against *Gnosis* while simultaneously absorbing or appropriating some ideas: "Wohl aber hat der Geist des *Buches Iezira* mit dem Ideengange eines halb gnostischen Buches vieles gemein, von dem es jedoch in der Form himmelweit verschieden ist. Ich meine hier die *Clementinen* oder *Pseudoklementinen*, einem halb gnostischen halb antignostischen Buche aus dem zweiten Jahrhundert, welches nach der kritischen Untersuchung Neanders einen Nazaräer zum Verfasser haben soll, und daher bald gnostische Voraussetzungen hat, bald nieder gegen den radicalen Gnosticismus polemisirt" (p. 110). See also p. 23 n. 19, where he cites *Hom* 11.6 as a parallel to *b. Avodah Zarah* 47, and p. 41, where he quotes a speech it attributes to Simon Magus to expound the "gnostic" perspective on the Demiurge. In his section on "Die jüdischen Gnostiker" (p. 55), the Pseudo-Clementines serve as an example of what he means by this category (i.e., as encompassing even those not necessarily Jews by birth, and hence applying to Valentinius as well; see further Guy G. Stroumsa, "*Gnosis* and Judaism in Nineteenth-Century Christian Thought," *JJTP* 2 [1992]: 45–62 at p. 49). I am not certain whether the different chapter numbering reflects printing mistakes or his use of an edition not known to me: he cites *Hom.* 11.6 as 9.6, for instance, and *Hom.* 18.1 as 17.

[48] Graetz, *Gnosticismus und Judentum*, 109–15. Such parallels include the idea of spatial "extensions," the emanation of primal elements from the spirit of God, and the theory of opposites

part through contact with "Jewish-Christians."[49] Rabbi Akiba – he went on to suggest – sought to understand anti-Jewish *Gnosis* so as to be able to battle it on its own ground, in a manner paralleling what Neander claims for the author of the Pseudo-Clementine *Homilies*.[50]

Michael Brenner has richly explored how Graetz's notion of *Gnosis* was shaped by his own self-positioning in nineteenth-century debates against Abraham Geiger and other German Jewish Reformers – as Graetz himself signals in his preface to his dissertation.[51] And, as David Biale and others have noted, Graetz's understanding of *Gnosis* would have a rich afterlife of its own, inaugurating a long debate about the origins of Jewish mysticism.[52] To these insights, I suggest that we might also add its role in ensuring the continued place of "Jewish-Christian" sources – and the Pseudo-Clementines in particular – within specialist research on Jewish mysticism, as comparanda commonly adduced to illumine texts like *Sefer Yetzirah* and the *Zohar*, even among those scholars who now eschew the older category of *Gnosis*.[53]

It is clear, in other words, that Graetz's treatment of the Pseudo-Clementines and "Jewish-Christianity" are much more than a response or reaction to the Christian scholarship of his time. Both its context and its consequences are far richer, providing important precedents for the use of "Jewish-Christian" and other Christian sources for understanding Rabbinic and other Jewish sources, while also speaking to contemporary inner-Jewish controversies. Within his *Geschichte*, moreover, "Jewish-Christians" form the pivot for a striking structural reorientation, whereby the story of the origins and early history of Christianity becomes subsumed as part of Jewish history – with Christian history thus subordinated to the history of the Jewish people, not least through the claim that "Jewish-Christians" preserve something of the originary Jewishness that the Church itself so tragically forgot.

Augustus Neander, *Gnosis*, and "Jewish-Christianity"

Graetz's emphasis on forgetting proves all the more poignant, inasmuch as his own place in this formative modern age of research on "Jewish-Christianity"

---

[49] This position, notably, is maintained even after he abandons an early dating for *Sefer Yetzirah*; see, e.g., Graetz, *History of the Jews*, 2:380–81.

[50] On the latter, see Michael Brenner, "Gnosis and History: Polemics of German-Jewish Identity from Graetz to Scholem," *New German Critique* 77 (1999): 45–60 at 48–50.

[51] Brenner, "Gnosis and History,"

[52] David Biale, *Gershom Scholem: Kabbalah and Counter-history* (2nd ed.; Cambridge, MA: Harvard University Press, 1982), 36–53; Peter Schäfer, "Ex Oriente Lux? Heinrich Graetz und Gershom Scholem über den Ursprung der Kabbala," in *Jahrbuch des Historischen Kollegs 2003* (Munich: Oldenbourg, 2004), 69–90; Brenner, "Gnosis and History," 46, 54–59.

[53] See Chapter Ten above.

would itself become forgotten – at least outside specialist scholarship on Jewish mysticism. Renewed attention to Graetz, moreover, leads us to notice yet another puzzling modern erasure – namely, the neglected place of the Jewish convert Neander in inaugurating the modern study of "Jewish-Christianity," *Gnosis,* and the Pseudo-Clementines alike.[54] In what follows, then, I would like to reflect briefly on Neander's context and contribution as well. It may be useful for our understanding of Graetz to recover his major precedent for bringing attention to the Jewish contexts and comparanda for the Pseudo-Clementines and *Gnosis* alike. But it may also tell us something about current scholarship on "Jewish-Christianity" that the contributions of both Graetz and Neander are now so consistently ignored – even by those contemporary historians of antiquity who now aim to recover the forgotten originary Jewishness of the Christian past.

Born David Mendel in 1789,[55] Neander was a relative of Moses Mendelsohn and studied Classics in his youth. His first publication was a Latin oration in 1805, arguing for civic rights for Jews in relation to state offices (*De Judaeis optima conditione in civitatem recipiendis*).[56] Despite sharing some such concerns with some of the founding figures of *Wissenschaft des Judentums,* Neander's path to a scholarly career would be quite a different one – with a rapid rise through the academic ranks enabled by his conversion to Christianity in 1806. Neander credited his conversion to the inspiration of Friedrich Schleiermacher, who would become a teacher and mentor to him, eventually helping him to procure a post in the University of Berlin.

Although largely forgotten today,[57] Neander was given a place, in his own time, among the ranks of Hegel and von Ranke. He was widely hailed as the

---

[54] To be sure, Neander was not the first to bring the Pseudo-Clementines to the conversation about "Jewish-Christianity"; already in the late eighteenth century, as Jones notes, "Semler pointed to the Pseudo-Clementines as evidence of the negative attitude that the Jewish Christians held towards Pauline Christians" – perhaps indebted to Toland ("From Toland to Baur," 129, and see p. 95 on Toland's use of the Pseudo-Clementines). Nevertheless, it remains that both Graetz and Daur stress their direct debt to Neander in this regard, and his analysis is certainly far more extensive and detailed.

[55] Philip Schaff, *History of the Apostolic Church,* trans. Edward D. Yeomans (New York: Scribner, 1853), 95; John McClintock and James Strong, *Cyclopaedia of Biblical, Theological, and Ecclesiastical Literature* (New York: Harper, 1876), 6:887, also 691. On Neander's life, see further Philip Schaff, *Saint Augustin, Melanchthon, Neander: Three Biographies* (London: J. Nisbet, 1886), 128–68; Deborah Hertz, *How Jews Became Germans* (New Haven: Yale University Press, 2007), 64–66, 182–83.

[56] Mark Fountain, *Historiography of August Neander* (New York: Peter Lang, 1995), 21. When later given the chance, however, Neander would not defend the rights of nonconverted Jews to teach in universities; see further Michael A. Meyer, "Judaism and Christianity," in *German-Jewish History in Modern Times,* vol. 2: *Emancipation and Acculturation, 1780–1871,* ed. Michael A. Meyer, Michael Brenner, and Mordechai Breuer (New York: Columbia University Press, 1997), 168–98 at 181–82 – there discussed in the context of the Damascus affair and reactions by Jewish converts.

[57] I.e., for Toland, Christianity's Jewish origins were among the arsenal of archaic truths that

"modern father of Church History," and Adolf von Harnack recounts how his popularity among his students was second only to that of his own teacher Schleiermacher.[58] Neander's many books were widely read throughout the nineteenth century, and in translation they would be formative for English-language research on Church History – particularly in North America, due to the influence of his student Philip Schaff.[59]

Even Baur is quite explicit in crediting Neander directly, as part of the inspiration for his famous theory of the "two parties" – and especially for providing the reading of the Pseudo-Clementines that made it possible:[60]

I had begun my critical inquiries long before Strauss, and set out from an entirely different point of view. My study of the two epistles to the Corinthians led me first to seize clearly the relation of the apostle Paul to the other apostles. I was convinced that in the letters of the apostle themselves there was enough from which to infer that this relation was something very different from that usually supposed – that, in short, instead of being a relation of harmony, it was one of sharp opposition, so much so that on the part of the Jewish Christians the authority of the apostle was held everywhere in dispute. A closer investigation of the Pseudo-Clementine *Homilies*, to whose significance in reference to the earliest period of Christian history Neander first drew attention, led me to a clearer understanding of this opposition.[61]

---

could be marshaled to undermine and unsettle the institutionalized Christianity of his own time. For Neander, the matter seems to have been more complex.

[58] Adolf von Harnack, "August Neander" [1889], in *Reden und Aufsätze* (Gieszen: Alfred Töpelmann, 1904), 1:195. See Fountain, *Historiography of August Neander*, 1–11, for assessments of David Friedrich Strauss, J.B. Lightfoot, Philip Schaff, and others of Neander's influence in his own time, in stark contrast to the lack of contemporary attention to him.

[59] Clark, *Founding the Fathers*, 79–83.

[60] In his study of Baur, Peter Hodgson points to Neander as "the historian with whom Baur is most continuously in dialogue in his own Church-historical studies"; *The Formation of Historical Theology: A Study of Ferdinand Christian Baur* (New York: Harper & Row, 1966), 159. Lincicum similarly notes how Neander is among the direct "proximate sources" for Baur's ideas of "Jewish-Christianity" in particular ("F.C. Baur's Place," 145–46, there with special reference to Baur, "Die Christuspartei in der korinthischen Gemeide"). Together with Karl August Credner and Johann Ernst Christian Schmidt, Neander is among the scholars most heavily cited in Baur's celebrated studies of the topic from the 1830s (i.e., those publications so often heralded as marking the very birth of the modern study of "Jewish-Christianity"). Or, more specifically, as Jones puts it: "Baur followed Credner in the view that the Ebionites shared a common root with the Essenes. ... Baur picked up the use of the Pseudo-Clementines in this context from both Credner and August Neander, who had not referred to any previous scholar when they did so. Baur furthermore adopted Neander's differentiation between the Nazoraeans and the Ebionites. The Ebionites were later than the Nazoraeans and arose after the war in the vicinity of Pella through admixture of Essene and doctrines and practice with the Christian faith" (Jones, "From Toland to Baur," 129–30). Even if Baur later came to a position closer to that of Toland – namely, that "Ebionites are the oldest Jewish Christians" – his position in these articles was influenced by Neander (130).

[61] Ferdinand Christian Baur, *Kirchengeschichte des neunzehnten Jahrhunderts*, ed. Eduard Zeller (Tübingen: Fues, 1862), 395, quoted after William Harrison De Puy, ed. *The Encyclopædia Britannica* (rev. American ed.; Chicago: Werner, 1893), 3:448.

The intellectual context for this interchange is nicely evoked by Arnaldo Momigliano:

In the early 1830's a remarkable upsurge of interest in Philo and in Alexandrian Judaism in general was noticeable in Germany. The purpose of this research was to ascertain whether Philo had influenced St. Paul and altogether contributed to the development of Christianity. ... This new research added to the importance of a relatively older book by one of Droysen's teachers: the *Genetische Entwickelung der vornehmsten gnostischen Systeme* by A. Neander, which had appeared in 1818. Neander had propounded a distinction between Jewish and anti-Jewish Gnostics and had indicated the relevance of Jewish Gnostics (among whom he included Philo) to the origins of Christianity. The topical interest of Neander's book was recognized by F. Chr. Baur who developed Neander's thesis in his book *Die christliche Gnosis* (1835) to the point of connecting Schleiermacher with anti-Jewish Gnosis and Hegel with Jewish or pro-Jewish Gnosis.[62]

Today, it is rather difficult to imagine the energy surrounding "the notion of *Gnosis*, which Neander and Baur had forcibly made a contemporary issue" in the nineteenth century[63] – let alone the dominance of taxonomies that order both past and present knowledge in relation to gradations of *Gnosis* and anti-*Gnosis*. The alternate dichotomy of "Hellenism" and "Judaism" propounded by Droysen has now come to be so naturalized that other such categories might strike us as counterintuitive – particularly in the wake in the discovery of the Nag Hammadi codices, which has shifted the taxonomic habits of historians of ancient religions towards ever more specific delineations of varieties of "gnostics" and, hence, further and further away from the older, more expansive rubric of *Gnosis* current in the nineteenth century.[64] At the time, however, its "topical relevance" was noticed by a number of German intellectuals, and no less a thinker than Hegel would base his own notion of *Gnosis* quite explicitly on Neander.[65]

---

[62] Arnoldo Momigliano, "J. G. Droysen between Greeks and Jews," *HT* 9 (1970): 147–48; cf. Neander, *Genetische Entwickelung*, 361–421. Today, Baur is often credited today with bringing these sources to the attention of Christian historians, but Neander's role was widely acknowledged not just in his own time but at least until the beginning of the twentieth century; Fenton John Anthony Hort, for instance, stresses that "seventy years ago a new spirit was breathed into the study of the inner life of Christian antiquity by Neander's historical writings. The peculiar interest of the Clementine literature could not escape the notice of one who followed with such warm and careful sympathy even the most seemingly eccentric movements of religious thought, and he made it the subject of an appendix to his essay on the principal 'Gnostic' systems. From that time the Clementine literature has received a large measure of attention, and has even been taken by one great school of criticism [i. e., the Tübingen school] as the principal key to the true history of the apostolic age. Yet the right understanding of it must in great measure depend on a knowledge of its own historical position, and this cannot be said to have been as yet securely ascertained" (*Notes Introductory to the Study of the Clementine Recognitions* [London: MacMillan, 1901], xiii).

[63] Momigliano, "J. G. Droysen between Greeks and Jews," 148.

[64] See Chapter Ten in this volume.

[65] See further Cyril O'Regan, *The Heterodox Hegel* (Albany: SUNY Press, 1994), 135–36.

For Neander, Baur, and Graetz alike, *Gnosis* denoted a stream of thought that did not include only those Valentinian and related sects and ideas condemned by heresiologists like Irenaeus, but also the whole fluid complex of late antique extensions and expressions of Neoplatonism, esotericism, Hermeticism, and theurgy. It was this notion that was flexible enough also to include a distinctively Jewish *Gnosis*, which Neander developed with reference to Philo, the Therapeutae, and the Essenes, while also signaling some connections with the Kabbalah. It was this same sense of Jewish *Gnosis*, in turn, which occasioned Neander's groundbreaking analysis of the Pseudo-Clementine *Homilies* as a "Jewish-Christian" source shaped by second-century Ebionite polemics against the anti-Jewish *Gnosis* of Marcion and others – as well as Graetz's redeployment thereof.

Baur's own extension of Neander's ideas would entail de-emphasis on questions concerning Judaism but also a rereading of the Pseudo-Clementines as an expression of a "fully conscious" form of "Christian *Gnosis*."[66] This rereading, in turn, shaped Christian scholarship on "Gnosticism" into the twentieth century. Yet, as we have seen, Neander's ideas about Jewish *Gnosis* would have a much richer afterlife in Jewish Studies, as would his use of the Pseudo-Clementines as a "Jewish-Christian" witness to it – both thanks to Graetz.

Even in Jewish Studies, however, Neander's influence would go largely uncredited. Neander, for instance, was the first modern scholar to outline a systematic notion of the Jewish origins of specific "gnostic" Christian sects – a position more recently trumpeted by Birger Pearson, who has credited Israel Friedlander for the original insight.[67] Guy Stroumsa, however, has noticed how Friedlander makes his argument in 1898 with the very same readings of the very same texts as did Neander in 1818,[68] and Stroumsa thus suggests that "it is hard to refrain from thinking that [Friedlander] found the idea in Neander's works, which remained widely read throughout the nineteenth century."[69] Yet the reminders of Momigliano and Stroumsa remain exceptions to the broader pattern whereby Neander's innovations become increasingly forgotten and thus attributed instead to later thinkers like Baur and Friedlander. Even modern historians, such as Brenner, who have traced the place of *Gnosis* in modern Jewish thought, have emphasized Baur's influence on both Graetz and Friedlander, while omitting Neander altogether.

My concern here is not merely to catalogue omissions. I am interested, rather, in what these omissions might tell us about modern Jewish scholarship in relation to its Christian counterparts, and the converse. For this, it is interesting to re-

---

[66] See further Jones, *Pseudoclementina*, 86–87.

[67] E. g., Stroumsa, "Gnosis and Judaism," 46, 52–54.

[68] Stroumsa, "Gnosis and Judaism," 52–53; for this – as Stroumsa has noticed – Friedlander himself "makes no mention of Neander (or of other scholars, for that matter)."

[69] Stroumsa, "Gnosis and Judaism," 52–53

flect also upon the reception of Neander's own Jewishness – both by Jews and by Christians, and both in his own time and after his death. At the time that Graetz wrote his dissertation, for instance, he would have been well aware of Neander's Jewishness, due to his involvement in the 1840 Damascus Affair as one of the Jewish converts to Christianity who spoke up to defend their fellow Jews against charges of blood libel. It is in this capacity, for instance, that Neander makes an appearance in volume eleven of Graetz's *Geschichte der Juden*,[70] and this is also much of the reason that he earns an entry in the *Jewish Encyclopedia*.[71]

Today, some historians of modern German Jewry point to Neander as a rare case of a conversion from conviction,[72] while others wonder whether to include

---

[70] Graetz, *Geschichte der Juden* vol. 11 (first ed. 1870; quoted here after 2nd ed. [1900], p. 481): "A French journal had challenged the baptised Jews to state upon oath and to the best of their knowledge, whether they had ever found among their former co-religionists or in Jewish writings, the slightest trace or precept concerning the abominable crime imputed to the unhappy people in Damascus [i.e., in 1840]. Several Jews who had been converted to Protestantism, and even held posts in the Church, asserted the innocence of the Jews of this crime – amongst others, Augustus Neander, known as the Church historian and a man of tender conscience."

[71] Note his entry in Isidore Singer, et al., *Jewish Encyclopedia: A Descriptive Record of the History, Religion, Literature, and Customs of the Jewish People from the Earliest Times to the Present Day* (New York: Funk and Wagnalls, 1901–1906), 9:198: "German Church historian; born at Göttingen Jan. 17, 1789; died at Berlin July 14, 1850. Prior to his baptism his name was 'David Mendel,' and on his mother's side he was related to Moses Mendelssohn. He attended the gymnasium at Hamburg, where he had for his associates Varnhagen von Ense and Adelbert von Chamisso. At the age of seventeen he embraced Christianity. After studying theology at Halle under Schleiermacher, and at Göttingen, he established himself as a privat-docent at Heidelberg in 1811, and in the following year was appointed assistant professor of theology. At this time he published his monograph, *Ueber den Kaiser Julianus und Sein Zeitalter*. In 1813 he was appointed professor of Church history in the newly established University of Berlin, and published his monograph on St. Bernard. This was followed by his essays on the Gnostics in 1818 and St. Chrysostom in 1822, in which latter year appeared his *Denkwürdigkeiten aus der Geschichte des Christenthums und des Christlichen Lebens*, a third edition of which was issued in 1845. In 1825 his great work, *Allgemeine Geschichte der Christlichen Religion und Kirche*, began to appear at Hamburg, the last volume of which, the eleventh, was not issued until 1852. An English translation by Torrey, in five volumes, was published at Boston in 1847–51. His *Gesch. der Pflanzung und Leitung der Christlichen Kirche Durch die Apostel* appeared in 1833; his *Leben Jesu* in 1837. These two works are practically introductions to his *Allgemeine Geschichte*. Two other works of his were published posthumously, *Wissenschaftliche Abhandlungen* (1851) and *Christliche Dogmengeschichte* (1857). Neander's works, most of which have been translated into English, have secured for him a lasting place among the greatest ecclesiastical historians. He has come to be regarded as the father of modern Church history. His *Leben Jesu* was written as an answer to the *Leben Jesu* of David Friedrich Strauss, which had been submitted to him by the government for his opinion as to its heretical character, and as to whether it should be prohibited. His answer to the government will be ever memorable: 'Scholarly works are to be fought with the weapons of science, not by the power of the state.' When the Jews of Damascus were being persecuted in 1846, and the old 'blood accusation' was revived, he publicly and vigorously denounced the 'medieval lie.'"

[72] E.g., Hertz, *How Jews Became Germans*, 182–83.

him, instead, as one of the more numerous examples of "career conversion"[73] – a common pattern at a time when German Christian missionizing efforts focused largely on Jews in Prussia, rather than peoples beyond, and when the options for ambitious Jews were limited and ever narrowing.[74] However one might speculate about his motives for converting as a young man, it is notable that Neander himself made no secret of his Jewish ancestry and background throughout his career.[75] During his own lifetime, in fact, this Jewishness seems to have enhanced his persona as a Church Historian and the reception of his scholarship by Christians. In much Christian literature of the time – both scholarly and popular – Neander is held up as an exemplar of the ideal Jewish convert.[76] Not only is his name commonly cited in missionary literature, but hagiographical accounts of his life are commonly prefaced to reviews of his books, and his learning and intellect are widely adduced in arguments for the truth of Christianity.[77] The tale

---

[73] E.g., Neander is included on a list of such conversions, contrasted to Zunz, et al., in Hermann Levin Goldschmidt, *The Legacy of German Jewry*, trans. David Suchoff (New York: Fordham University Press, 2007), 148–49.

[74] Notably, Neander converted prior to the 1812 Edict in Prussia which made Judaism a tolerated religion in Prussia but curtailed community rights and was ambiguous about access to prestigious posts, thus leading to a rise in conversions; Hertz, *How Jews became Germans*, 106–9 and Graph 1.

[75] Fountain, "Historiography of August Neander," 20: "For his part, Neander neither deprecated nor made much comment on his Jewish origins. He was sometimes cited as an exemplary figure by organizations involved in evangelistic missions to Jews, but was never himself a part of such an effort."

[76] Especially but not only after his death; see, e.g., John C. Moore, "The Synagogue and the Church," *British and Foreign Evangelical Review* 89 (1874): 441–55; Otto Krabbe, Review of *Neander's Werke*, *British Quarterly Review* 46 (1867): 305–50, reprinted in *The Living Age* 100 (1869): 131–54.

[77] Fountain, for instance, observes how "as a Jew, nurtured in the writings of Plato and finally converted to Christianity," Neander was frequently described by his Christian students, colleagues, and contemporaries "as one who personified the evolution of Christian thought" (*Historiography of August Neander*, 13). This is clearest in Philip Schaff's summary: "By birth and early training an Israelite ... full of childlike simplicity, and of longings for the Messianic salvation; in youth, an enthusiastic student of the Grecian philosophy, particularly of Plato, who became, for him, as for Origen and other church fathers, a scientific schoolmaster, to bring him to Christ he had, when in his seventeenth year he received holy baptism, passed through, in his own inward experience, so to speak, the whole historical course, by which the world had been prepared for Christianity; he had gained an experimental knowledge of the workings of Judaism and Heathenism in their direct tendency towards Christianity; and thus he had already broken his own way to the only proper position for contemplating the history of the church; a position, whence Jesus Christ is viewed as the object of the deepest yearnings of humanity, the centre of all history, and the only key to its mysterious sense. ... In theology, he was at first a pupil of the gifted Schleiermacher, under whose electrifying influence he came during his university studies at Halle, and at whose side he afterwards stood as colleague for many years in Berlin. He always thankfully acknowledged the great merits of this German Plato, who, in a time of general apostacy from the truth, rescued so many young men from the iron embrace of Rationalism .... But he himself took a more positive course, rejecting the pantheistic and fatalistic elements which had adhered to the system of his master from the study of Spinoza, and which, it must be confessed, bring it, in a measure, into direct opposition to the simple gospel and the old faith

of his conversion was often retold to such effect, and his example was even used to exegete the letters of Paul, to whom he was often compared – as an exemplar of the "new man" who simultaneously embodied the purportedly purified Judaism at the very heart of Christianity.[78]

To what degree did this double positioning shape Neander's own scholarly concerns and their reception? To be sure – as Susannah Heschel has stressed – Neander was no less negative towards Pharisees than other Christians of his time. Yet his descriptions of Philo, in particular, may point to his identification with a different type of Judaism. Likewise, it remains difficult not to imagine at least something of his own circumstances when reading his compelling descriptions of "Jewish-Christians," particularly within his later synthetic writings. When writing of the Pseudo-Clementine *Homilies*, in particular, Neander sympathetically evokes its vision of Christianity as a purified form of Judaism, and he also lauds the text for exhibiting (in his words) "the supra-nationalist element of Judaism ... presented in peculiar strength."[79] His descriptions of the motives and settings of its author are no less evocative:

When the Jews, Judaizing Christians, and Christians of pagan descent were standing in stern opposition to one another, when Judaism, attacked in various ways by the Gnostics, was placed in the most unfavorable light, the thought occurs to some individual of this particular Ebionite tendency to compose a work that might serve to reconcile these opposite views – a work of an apologetic and conciliatory tendency – a notable phenomenon in the ferment of that chaotic period, to which a new breath of life, setting everything in motion, had been communicated by Christianity, and in which the most heterogeneous elements could be fused together, what was really profound meeting and mingling with what was altogether fantastic.[80]

Whether or not such connections were deliberate on his part, it remains that in the "ferment" of his own "chaotic age," Neander's books did end up having some of the same effects – helping to bridge Christian and Jewish scholarship on the shared Jewish and Christian past, while also drawing the attention of his Christian contemporaries to the Jewishness of Christianity's own essence and origins.

The very Jewishness that enhanced his persona in life, however, also appears to have contributed to the increasing neglect of him and his scholarship after his

---

of the church"; Schaff, *History of the Apostolic Church with a General Introduction to Church History*, trans. Edward D. Yeomans (New York: Charles Scribner, 1854), 96–97

[78] In the course of his description of Paul, for instance, Philip Schaff notes that "Neander, a converted Jew, like Paul, was short, feeble, and strikingly odd in his whole appearance, but a rare humility, benignity, and heavenly aspiration beamed from his face beneath his dark and bushy eyebrows. So we may well imagine that the expression of Paul's countenance was highly intellectual and spiritual, and that he looked 'sometimes like a man and sometimes like an angel'"; *History of the Christian Church: Apostolic Christianity, AD 1–100* (3rd ed.; New York: Charles Scribner's Sons, 1889), 295.

[79] Johann August Wilhelm Neander, *General History of the Christian Religion and Church*, trans. Joseph Torrey (Boston: Crocker & Brewster, 1853), 1:353.

[80] Neander, *General History*, 1:353.

death in 1850. His student Schaff wrote about Neander in hagiographical terms and extended the earlier discourse about his embodiment of the pure Jewishness within Christianity, telling the story of his life alongside those of Augustine and Melanchthon.[81] Here too, his Jewishness looms large:

If there ever was a sincere and intelligent convert from Judaism to Christianity it is Neander. The new name which he assumed at his baptism in 1806, was Johann August Wilhelm Neander …. His chief name expressed at the same time the fact that he had become a new creature in Christ Jesus. He belongs to the line of converts which begins with Paul of Tarsus. His transition was less abrupt and radical than that of the former persecutor, but he resembles the Apostle of the Gentiles in purity of motive, strength of conviction, unselfish devotion to the religion of his choice, and zeal for the freedom in Christ from the bondage of legalism, as also in the weakness (if not the awkwardness) of his "bodily presence" (2 Cor. 10:10). He bore the heavenly treasure in an earthen vessel. When the King of Prussia once asked him, 'What is the best evidence of Christianity?' he is said to have replied, "The Jews, your Majesty." Thus was Neander fitted out for his life-work, to be the historian of Christianity. Moses and Plato were the tutors who led him to Christ and enabled him to view the Christian religion as the fulfilment of all the nobler aspirations of the Jewish and Gentile world, and as the final and perfect religion of mankind. Before him church history had been degraded by German Rationalism into a godless history of human errors and follies. Neander effected a revolution. He revealed in it a golden chain of manifestations of Christ's truth and love and a fulfilment of His promise to be with His disciples to the end of the world. … He sympathized with everything that is Christian, whether he found it in the Greek or Roman or Evangelical churches, or among persecuted heretics. … In the hands of Rationalists and Deists church history was a dreary desert. Neander changed it into a garden of God, full of flowers and fruits.[82]

Even already within the 1889 celebration speech for him delivered by Adolf von Harnack in Berlin, his Jewishness becomes presented, instead, as an obstacle to be overcome: a "shell" to be shed for a new birth and a paradox for his acceptance of Christ as savior.[83] So too would Harnack's model of Church History displace that of Neander, resulting in a shift in the early twentieth century, away from Neander's expansive vision of Christian history, its sources, and its Jewish roots, wherein even "heretical" ideas spoke to the historical development of the Church, toward Harnack's more narrow focus on the preservation of the correct doctrine of the "Great Church" – to which "Jewish-Christianity" was, in his view, just as utterly irrelevant as Judaism.[84]

---

[81] Schaff, *Saint Augustin, Melanchthon, Neander*, 128–65.

[82] Schaff, *Saint Augustin, Melanchthon, Neander*, 133.

[83] Harnack, "August Neander," 193–218. This trend seems to have preceded his death; Fountain (*Historiography of August Neander*, 20), for instance, notes how "in later years some of Neander's opponents engaged in anti-Semitism to disparage his scholarship."

[84] Against Baur, Harnack argues that the Church was shaped by "conflicts and compromises" but "not, however, by conflicts with Ebionitism, which was to all intents and purposes discarded as early as the first century," and he is thus quite explicit that "a history of Jewish Christianity and its doctrines does not therefore, strictly speaking, belong to the history of dogma"; *History of Dogma*, trans. Neil Buchanan (7 vols.; Gloucester, MA: Peter Smith, 1974), 1:293–94. He

Yet, as we have seen, even while the memory of Neander's own contributions were increasingly forgotten within Christian scholarship and its secular heirs, his ideas about "Jewish-Christianity" continued to shape Jewish scholarship on Christianity via Graetz. And, perhaps no less significantly, he influenced the very notion that Christianity, by virtue of its Jewish origins, Jewish apostles, and the influence of early "Jewish-Christians," *could* and *should* form part of a history of the Jews. Through the mediation of Graetz, moreover, Neander's ideas about the Pseudo-Clementines and Jewish *Gnosis* would also have a lively afterlife in Jewish Studies. Long after his work on *Gnosis* had been largely abandoned by specialists of early Christianity, his ideas about Jewish *Gnosis* have continued to live on within research on Jewish mysticism – fostered among towering figures in that field such as Scholem, Shlomo Pines, Moshe Idel, and Elliot Wolfson.[85] Among the results has been the enumeration of even further Jewish parallels with the Pseudo-Clementines.[86]

Remembering and Forgetting "Jewish-Christianity" and *Wissenschaft des Judentums*

What might we learn, then, from triangulating Graetz, Neander, and Baur? Are their interconnections on this topic atypical or representative for the lineages and networks of knowledge that shaped the modern concept and study of "Jewish-Christianity"? Although such questions await further inquiry, it is clear that the nineteenth-century discourse about "Jewish-Christianity" cannot be reduced to a matter of inner-Christian concerns, nor even to an appended dynamic of Jewish responses or reactions to them. Major figures in the discussion include Christians like Baur and Jews like Graetz, but both build upon the earlier intervention of a Jewish convert, Neander, who was also the most prominent Church Historian of his time. When we triangulate the three, we can glimpse something of a shared project of recovering the lost memory of the place of "Jewish-Christians" in the apostolic and tannaitic past (for different aims but with overlapping themes and sources), and we can trace the intertwining of threads thereof within nine-teenth-century German thought – prior to their separation, within early twen-tieth-century research, into self-contained and ever-smaller specialist circles within New Testament Studies and Jewish Studies respectively.

I would like to suggest, moreover, that the recovery of neglected insights from *Wissenschaft des Judentums* might also contribute to current scholarship on "Jewish-Christianity" and the intertwined histories of ancient Jews and Chris-

---

similarly asserts that "the Pseudo-Clementines contribute absolutely nothing to our knowledge of the origin of the Catholic Church and doctrine" (315).

[85] I survey this research in detail in Chapter Ten above.

[86] See Chapter Ten above.

tians. The example of scholarship on "Jewish-Christianity" may offer some cautions, in particular, concerning what was lost when certain Protestant Christian perspectives on the Jewish and Christian past came to be received as if "objective" or "neutral" – in this case, through the neglect of scholarship by and about Jews, particularly in the first half of the twentieth century in Germany. To the degree to which this neglect has skewed scholarship on the Pseudo-Clementines to this day, it stands as a "parade example" of the habits of forgetting that can be unintentionally reinscribed with the repetition of conventionalized accounts of the modern history of research. Studies of ancient sources like Acts and the Pseudo-Clementines have highlighted the power and limits of history writing, as a technology of memory shaped no less by the aim of accuracy of remembrance than by the inevitably situated (and often ideological) choices of structure, inclusion, and omission.[87] Much the same might be said, not just for ancient histories and modern retellings of ancient histories, but also for our own modern scholarly acts of tracing our academic lineages.

To the degree that the ancient sources that we call "Jewish-Christian" were themselves subject to overwriting, forgetting, and cultural amnesia, it is all the more pressing also to attend to what we ourselves may omit or forget when we also tell the tale of their modern "rediscovery." When we do so, new formative figures emerge, but also new vistas, comparanda, questions, and perspectives – especially concerning Jews and Judaism. These were avenues that were foreclosed by Baur and Harnack, and the continued emphasis on the foundational importance of Baur, in particular, has functioned to reinscribe and naturalize them, limiting the Jewishness of Christianity to Jesus and the apostolic age, and pressing "Jewish-Christian" sources like the Pseudo-Clementines into the service of specialist research on the New Testament.

The recovery of the contributions of Graetz and Neander, by contrast, helps to remind us that "Jewish-Christianity" is not necessarily or inevitably reduced to a matter of Christian Origins or New Testament exegesis. If we choose to treat sources like the Pseudo-Clementines as "Jewish-Christian," then we should also take seriously the possibility of using them as sources for the history of Jews and Judaism, as well as the prospect of bringing Jewish comparanda to bear upon their interpretation and contextualization. And even if current scholars may disagree with this or that interpretation of this or that text by these and other nineteenth-century Jewish thinkers, the engagement can nevertheless help us to bring the assumptions of early twentieth-century research into sharper relief and to tighten our own choices of questions, rubrics, and comparanda – perhaps even toward a renewed aim of revealing yet more of the overwritten Jewishness of Christian history.

---

[87] See Chapter Six in this volume and sources cited there.

After "Origins," Beyond "Identity," and Before "Religion(s)"*

The essays in this volume took form during dynamically productive years for scholarship on ancient identities. By means of conclusion, I would like to return to reflect on "Jewish-Christianity" in relation to scholarship on Jewish and Christian identities. I extend here some points in my discussion in the Introduction. I do so, however, with an eye to paths forward and outward, asking what questions can be put to rest, whether some frameworks may no longer be useful, and how new shifts in orientation might help us to move ahead. Lastly, having defended the provisional utility of the category "Jewish-Christianity" for the purposes of the present volume, I ask what the study of the main material conventionally categorized under this rubric might look like if pursued without it.

The first essay in this volume was initially published in 2003 in *The Ways That Never Parted*.[1] At the time, specialist critiques of the model of the "Parting of the Ways" were coalescing into a call for experimentation with new approaches to ancient Jewish and Christian identities, more apt for explaining the full range, complexity, and contexts of our sources. With that volume, my co-editor Adam H. Becker and I aimed foremost at a disciplinary intervention, highlighting some of the conceptual problems with the "Parting" model for the study of Late Antiquity and some of the practical consequences of its rise in popularity during the late twentieth century. Consistent with post-WWII trends in New Testament Studies, we noted how the "Parting" model departed from older supersessionist approaches by acknowledging Christianity's originary Jewishness. By virtue of focusing on the decisive moment when Christianity finally emerged as a separate "religion," however, the "Parting" model also functioned to *contain* this Jewishness, cordoning off the period of Christian Origins as distinct from the rest of Christian history. Following this model, pre-"Parting" Christianity can

---

* This essay has not been previously published or presented in any form. It owes much to conversations, bibliography, and feedback from Shaul Magid, Andrew S. Jacobs, James Carleton Paget, Matthew Chalmers, Phillip Fackler, Jae Han, Simcha Gross, Steven R. Reed, and Tariq al-Jamil.

[1] Adam H. Becker and Annette Yoshiko Reed, eds., *The Ways That Never Parted: Jews and Christians in Late Antiquity and the Early Middle Ages* (TSAJ 95; Tübingen: Mohr Siebeck, 2003).

(and perhaps should) be studied as a part of the history of Jews and Judaism. But post-"Parting," Christianity becomes distinct – by design, if not by definition.

The "Parting" model was founded on insights arising from the study of the New Testament and Second Temple Judaism, and its popularity further facilitated conversations between specialists in these areas. Yet it fostered quite the opposite for scholarship on Late Antiquity. To debate the moment of "Parting," after all, is simultaneously to mark a point *after which* any meaningful fluidity purportedly ceased – and, hence, in practice, to set a boundary for modern scholars too, marking the point *after which* historians of Christianity need not look to Jewish sources and historians of Judaism need not look to Christian sources. To the degree to which "Parting" is posited as the pivot on which Christian Origins gives way to Christian history, so it is also the pivot on which Jewishness is purported to shift – from the very ground of Christianity's growth to its defining "Other."

In framing Christian self-definition in this fashion, the "Parting" model grounds its plausibility in a distinctively late twentieth-century discourse about "identity."[2] Informed by Eriksonian psychological theories of individuation, this discourse treats the development of religious and other collective identities as akin to the process by which individual selfhood takes form in childhood and adolescence.[3] In both cases, the process is treated as the teleological emergence of a core self, constructed in consecutive stages that reach a climactic turning point, thereafter culminating in a distinct, bounded, and stable entity.[4]

When applied to the "origins" of "religions," this model of individuation thus naturalizes a narrative of inevitable development, from an early era characterized

----

[2] For a survey of the scholarly use of the term see Philip Gleason, "Identifying Identity: A Semantic History," *Journal of American History* 69 (1983): 910–31; Lewis D. Wurgaft, "Identity in World History: A Postmodern Perspective," *HT* 34 (1995): 67–85. Psychological models of individuation here loom large as do their transfer into Sociology, on which see further below. Notably, however, religion also played a part: "With Will Herberg's *Protestant-Catholic-Jew* (1955) we have turned a corner," Gleason notes, "Not only do the words recur again and again, but identity and identification are, in a sense, what the book is all about …. Religion, he said, had become the most satisfactory vehicle for locating oneself in society and thereby answering the 'aching question' of identity: 'Who am I?'" ("Identifying Identity," 912).

[3] I.e., especially influenced by Erik H. Erikson, *Childhood and Society* (New York: Norton, 1950). Erikson himself posited an overlapping of individual and collective identities; for him, for instance, the formation of identity is "a process 'located' in the core of the individual and yet also in the core of his communal culture, a process which establishes, in fact, the identity of those two identities"; *Identity: Youth and Crisis* (New York: Norton, 1968), 22.

[4] Gleason notes how Erikson "coined the expression identity crisis and did more than anyone else to popularize identity" ("Identifying Identity," 914). He summarizes the most enduring influential elements of Erikson's main model as involving "an interaction between the interior development of the individual personality, understood in terms derived from the Freudian id-ego-superego model, and the growth of a sense of selfhood that arises from participating in society, internalizing its cultural norms, acquiring different statuses, and playing different roles …. An identity crisis is a climactic turning point in this process; it is the normal occurrence of adolescence, but it can also be precipitated by unusual difficulties further along in the life cycle" (914). Notably, this model is far from uncontested even in Psychology.

by fluid undifferentiation, to some pivotal crisis point catalyzing self-definition, to what is thereafter framed as the inevitable emergence of "Christianity" as a bounded entity with a stable "core" forever after.[5] If fluidity and fuzziness are overemphasized in the period of "origins," crisis, contrast, and conflict are overemphasized thereafter. Accordingly, even as the narrative of the "Parting of the Ways" is predicated on Christianity's originary Jewishness, it simultaneously enables the treatment of Christianity and Judaism – after this moment of "Parting" – as two clear-cut and mutually exclusive "religions," which stand in a relationship of conflict thereafter, connecting only through discrete, exceptional, incidental, and largely unidirectional instances of "borrowing" or "influence."[6]

To the degree that the presumption of an early "Parting of the Ways" has thereby contributed to the habitual neglect of Jewish sources within the study of late antique Christianity, and to the habitual neglect of Christian sources within the study of late antique Judaism, the results have been somewhat tautological. The presumption of mutual isolationism between Jews and Christians by the second century CE has been mirrored in the mutual isolationism in the study of late antique Judaism and late antique Christianity. This isolationism, in turn, has functioned further to naturalize the notion of their inevitable separation as well as the scholarly habit of reading Jewish and Christian sources as each speaking to essentially self-contained entities with essentially self-contained histories.

It was this situation that Becker and I sought to address in *The Ways That Never Parted*. We asked what happens when one experiments with proceeding from the opposite premise – that is: reading Christian and Jewish sources from Late Antiquity, not in relative isolation or with the assumption of two increasingly divergent paths, but rather as intertwined histories, potentially overlapping and also reconnecting in new ways, long after Jesus, Paul, Bar Kokhba, and perhaps even Constantine. Proceeding from such a premise, what habituated blind spots might be exposed? What new vistas might come into view? And what might we see and notice about the past that isolationist disciplinary structures have occluded? With such questions of scholarly practice in mind, we stressed "the need to focus with renewed energy and intensity on *Jews* and *Christians* in Late Antiquity and the early Middle Ages, before settling on any new generalizations about *Judaism* and *Christianity* during this period."[7]

---

[5] On the approaches that seek to resolve evidence for continued inner-Christian difference within appeal to a "core" Christianity see, e.g., Karen King, "Factions, Variety, Diversity, Multiplicity: Representing Early Christian Difference for the 21st Century," *MTSR* 23 (2011): 216–37 at 221.

[6] Note also the shift from "origins" to "relations," on which see Andrew S. Jacobs, "The Lion and the Lamb: Reconsidering 'Jewish-Christian Relations' in Antiquity," in Becker and Reed, *The Ways that Never Parted*, 95–118.

[7] Annette Yoshiko Reed and Adam H. Becker, "Introduction: Traditional Models and New Directions," in Becker and Reed, *The Ways That Never Parted*, 24.

In the fifteen years since then, a growing number of scholars have set aside the traditional practice of refracting our literary and material evidence for pre-modern Jews and Christians through the lens of unilinear and monolithic "master narratives" about an early and singular separation of "Christianity" from "Judaism." Among the results has been a much richer body of research considering the relevance of Christian texts and traditions for studying post-Christian Judaism.[8] In addition, in the last fifteen years, it has become increasingly common for graduate training in Rabbinics and late antique Judaism to entail some attention to Patristics and Syriac Christianity and – albeit more gradually – even the converse.[9]

When the first article in this volume was initially published, for instance, it was still somewhat rare to read specialist studies in Rabbinics that adduced specific Christian intertexts.[10] Today, however, attention to Christian comparanda is increasingly taken for granted as part of the practice of scholarly training and research in late antique Judaism. The products of this shift, in turn, are increasingly aiding specialists in Patristics and late antique Christianity to begin to look to Rabbinic and other post-Christian Jewish materials in a manner not limited to the repetition of stereotypes and parallels from old handbooks.[11] Much remains

---

[8] Examples include Peter Schäfer, *Jesus in the Talmud* (Princeton: Princeton University Press, 2007); Schäfer, *Die Geburt des Judentums aus dem Geist des Christentums* (Tübingen: Mohr Siebeck, 2010); Ophir Münz-Manor, "Narrating Salvation: Verbal Sacrifices in Late Antique Liturgical Poetry," in *Jews, Christians, and the Roman Empire*, ed. Natalie Dohrmann and Annette Yoshiko Reed (Philadelphia: University of Pennsylvania Press, 2013), 154–66; Michal Bar-Asher Siegal, *Early Christian Monastic Literature and the Babylonian Talmud* (Cambridge: Cambridge University Press, 2013); Richard Lee Kalmin, *Migrating Tales: The Talmud's Narratives and Their Historical Context* (Berkeley: University of California Press, 2014); John G. Gager, *Who Made Early Christianity?: The Jewish Lives of the Apostle Paul* (New York: Columbia University Press, 2015); Miriam Benedikt, "The Letter that Lives: Mid. Ps. 29 as a Case Study of Anti-Christological Polemic," *JTS* 67 (2016): 38–76; Martha Himmelfarb, *Jewish Messiahs in a Christian Empire* (Cambridge, MA: Harvard University Press, 2017).

[9] It may be worth thinking more concretely about the place of scholarly practice (e.g., institutional contexts, pedagogical structures, patterns in doctoral training and faculty hiring) in informing the shifting questions about "identity" and difference here discussed – not least because these act of scholarly identity-formation are shaped by power-relations no less than their late antique counterparts.

[10] The most prominent exception, and a major catalyst for the above-noted developments, is Daniel Boyarin, *Dying for God: Martyrdom and the Making of Christianity and Judaism* (Berkeley: University of California Press, 1999). Specialist research on Rabbinics had been infamously inward-facing, although tending previously to cull comparanda instead from "pagan" and Greek elements of Roman culture, as in the work of Boyarin's teacher Saul Lieberman: *Greek in Jewish Palestine* (New York: Jewish Theological Seminary of America, 1942); Lieberman, *Hellenism in Jewish Palestine* (New York: Jewish Theological Seminary of America, 1950). On the more recent turn to Iranian contexts see note 135 below.

[11] It is perhaps telling in this regard, e.g., that Michael Satlow's review of the 2007 reprint of *The Ways That Never Parted* (*JAAR* 76 [2008]: 512–14) protested that the "master narrative" therein critiqued was no longer common – even despite its continued prominence within the

to be done to integrate Jewish sources further into the (still very Christocentric) study of Late Antiquity. That this integration is a desideratum, however, is increasingly acknowledged.[12]

The essays in the present volume extend this broader experiment in reorienting scholarly purviews and presumptions. My contention here has been that "Jewish-Christianity" can be analytically useful as a frame of analysis *precisely because* of its status as an anachronistically modern construction: it permits us to glimpse some of what is occluded when our present-day assumptions about Judaism and Christianity constrain our scholarly practices of reading late antique texts.

To the degree that modern notions of "religions" tend to reify the boundaries between traditions, for example, their retrojection risks predetermining an overemphasis on continuity when comparing inner-religious sources (however disparate in time and place) and an overemphasis on contrast and conflict when comparing interreligious sources (however proximate in time and place).[13] Such reading practices reflect and reinforce the disciplinary separation of specialist research on premodern Jewish and Christian literatures, while also fostering the neglect of textual and other materials that frustrate this binary or fall outside of it.[14] But what might we see when we look at Late Antiquity, instead, through

---

study of Christianity, in general, and Patristics, in particular. That said, other scholars of late antique Judaism have taken note of this imbalance and have sought to correct it by creating more accessible tools and introductions to Rabbinic and other late antique Jewish materials; so, e. g., Charlotte Elisheva Fonrobert and Martin S. Jaffee, eds., *The Cambridge Companion to the Talmud and Rabbinic Literature* (Cambridge: Cambridge University Press, 2007).

[12] See references and discussion in Annette Yoshiko Reed and Natalie Dohrmann, "Introduction: Rethinking Romanness, Provincializing Christendom," in Dohrmann and Reed, *Jews, Christians, and the Roman Empire*, 1–22.

[13] P. S. Alexander makes a parallel point in relation to Judaism and Islam in the Middle Ages, noting cases where "the changes which we find in the Islamic texts are *of precisely the same order* as those we find already *within* Jewish tradition," and "the traditions flow uninterrupted across the boundaries between the two religions" in a manner that makes a scholarly focus solely on their boundedness and boundaries potentially misleading; see, e. g., "Transformations of Jewish Traditions in Early Islam: The Case of Enoch/Idris," in *Studies in Islamic and Middle Eastern Texts and Traditions in Memory of Norman Calder*, ed. G. R. Hawting, J. A. Mojaddedi, and A. Samely (Journal of Semitic Studies Supplement 12; Oxford: Oxford University Press, 2000), 11–29.

[14] For the latter, note especially the case of Samaritans, on which see now Matthew Chalmers, "Thinking with Samaritans and Cynthia Baker's *Jew*," in *Forum on Cynthia Baker's Jew*, ed. Annette Yoshiko Reed and Shaul Magid (Los Angeles: Marginalia Review of Books, 2017, http://marginalia.lareviewofbooks.org/thinking-samaritans-cynthia-bakers-jew/; Chalmers, "The Samaritan Other: Rethinking Religious Difference in Late Antiquity" (Ph.D. dissertation, University of Pennsylvania, in progress). Material evidence, inscriptions, etc., are also illuminating in this regard. On Aramaic incantation bowls, see Shaul Shaked, "Popular Religion in Sassanian Babylonian," *Jerusalem Studies in Arabic and Islam* 21 (1997): 103–17; Michael G. Morony, "Religion and the Aramaic Incantation Bowls," *Religion Compass* 1 (2007): 414–29. On the challenges and opportunities of using inscriptional and archaeological materials as data for religious identities see, e. g., Leonard Victor Rutgers, "Archaeological

the lens of such marginalized sources – including but not limited to those that scholars have categorized as "Jewish-Christian," and thereby isolated from the modern study of both Judaism and Christianity? And what might we see when we also look back at the history of our scholarly practices and disciplines, asking why (and for whom) such compartmentalization was even necessary?

These are some of the aims, experiments, and questions that have shaped my inquiries in the present volume. Here at its end, I would like to reflect upon some possible paths ahead by looking to recent scholarly trends and trajectories in three related areas: [1] the "Parting of the Ways" and other scholarly narratives about the "origins" or "invention" of Christian identity, [2] the very notion of "identity," including critiques of its utility and the problematic place of alterity therein, and [3] the analytical limits of the category "religion(s)," including risks of anachronism and groupism. In addition to pushing on these three fronts, I shall conclude with another question thereby opened up: What might the study of what we now call "Jewish-Christian" materials look like if category-based correctives of this sort were no longer needed?

After "Origins"

As noted above, the notion of an early date of the "Parting of the Ways" has been much critiqued, with some notable ramifications for recent shifts in the practice of research on Late Antiquity, perhaps especially among scholars of Rabbinics and late antique Judaism. Nevertheless, even as the "Parting" model and its related "master narratives" have been increasingly abandoned, some lingering elements thereof continue to constrain the discussion. Most notable – I suggest – are those elements that reinforce longstanding practices and problems in scholarship on the "origins" of "religions" more broadly.[15]

Perhaps the most enduring component of the "Parting" model has been the very framing of the issue of Jewish and Christian difference in temporal terms – as a question of *when*.[16] The model's proponents debate the determinative moment of change in the first or second century CE, after which Christianity became irreversibly distinct from Judaism, both theologically and socially. Likewise,

---

Evidence for the Interaction of Jews and Non-Jews in Late Antiquity," *American Journal of Archaeology* 96 (1992): 101–18; Karen Stern, "Limitations of Jewish as a Label in Roman North Africa," *JSJ* 39 (2008): 1–34; Stern, "Opening Doors to Jewish Life in Syro-Mesopotamian Dura Europos," forthcoming in *JAJ*.

[15] On the broader issue, see esp. Tomoko Masuzawa, *In Search of Dreamtime: The Quest for the Origin of Religion* (Chicago: University of Chicago Press, 1993); Masuzawa, "Origin," in *Guide to the Study of Religion*, ed. Willi Braun and Russell McCutcheon (London: Cassell Academic, 1999), 209–24; Steven Weitzman, *The Origin of the Jews: The Quest for Roots in a Rootless Age* (Princeton: Princeton University Press, 2017), esp. 24–62.

[16] See Chapter Two in this volume.

most of the model's critics make a case for pushing the date of separation forward. But rather than only asking *when* "the ways parted" and answering first century, second century, fourth century, etc., we might do well to set aside this much-asked question – or, at the very least, to stop and ask *why* this temporal framing remains so appealing and *what* it assumes, forecloses, and effaces.

Only a small handful of our ancient and late antique Christian sources – and *none* of our ancient and late antique Jewish sources – frame Jewish/Christian difference in terms akin to "parting/parted ways."[17] The appeal of the "Parting" model does make sense, however, from a present-day purview in which "religions" are conceptualized as essentially separate entities with separate histories that might be likened to discrete and unilinear diachronic paths through time (which, in turn, are currently commonly studied by different scholars with different disciplinary training and distinctly delineated domains of academic expertise). It is from this present-day purview that it feels meaningful to frame Jewish/Christian difference in terms of the question of the precise moment *after which* we can speak of two separate paths that can be traced to our present, as understood in our terms, peering back in retrospect for that determinative moment when "Christianity" became a "religion" distinct from "Judaism."

When assessing recent debates about "Judaism," Seth Schwartz reflects upon the current scholarly attraction to the notion of "moments in which everything changed, in which social phenomena went from one pole in the binary system to the other; moments in which fundamental social or cultural phenomena were 'invented'":[18]

This intellectual style has the advantage of imposing clarity – and being provocative – and one can always maintain in its defense that everyone knows that the social realities were far more complex, in fact so much so as to be indescribable. ... But the tendency to think in binaries too often seems not an explanatory strategy but an intellectual style; its proponents seem to forget what they may claim to take for granted – that social realities were more complex – and they are too quick to relieve themselves of the responsibility to make sense of the social, political, and cultural dynamics of change. The need to produce a non-hyperschematized account is all the more urgent precisely when the evidence is poor (as it were, self-schematizing); in this case we must struggle to remember that the exiguous fragments of information that survive, which are sometimes easily reducible to simple patterns, do not tell the whole story, because they were necessarily produced by societies whose complexity is not reflected in the evidence.[19]

---

[17] For Justin, Tertullian, et al., the very point is that there is a single path: the church does not branch off from a Jewish past but is rather the sole culmination and continuation of the history of ancient Israel; to "Judaize," thus, is not to choose the wrong "religion," but rather to mistake past for present. See further discussion and references in my essay "Christian Origins and Religious Studies," *SR* 44 (2005): 307–19.

[18] Seth Schwartz, "How Many Judaisms Were There? A Critique of Neusner and Smith on Definition and Mason and Boyarin on Categorization," *JAJ* 2 (2011): 208–38 at 231.

[19] Schwartz, "How Many Judaisms Were There?," 231–32.

Some of the appeal of the "Parting" model can be explained along the same lines. Whether the dates proposed are early or late, what the participants in debates about the "Parting of the Ways" share is the habit of dramatizing change with appeal to a single pivotal moment, plotted along what is assumed to be a single diachronic line. Whatever date is deemed determinative (whether early or late), the very question of *when* serves tidily to collapse any local, geographical, social, ritual, doctrinal, or other specificities into the service of a monolithic narrative about two "religions" – whose distinction is thereby emblematized by the assertion of the divergent paths of their histories from that point until today.

Consistent with the longstanding fixation on "origins" in the discipline of Religious Studies – and also in keeping with the longstanding prominence of philology in both Classics and Patristics – much scholarly attention has focused on the task of identifying the oldest known examples of the uses of Greek terms etymologically related to our English words "Judaism" and "Christianity," especially when put in relation to one another.[20] The writings of Ignatius of Antioch have thus garnered much attention, and he is often heralded as marking or confirming the "Parting of the Ways."[21] Typically assumed in this equation is some degree of direct correspondence between this one author's polemical arguments about theological and exegetical difference, on the one hand, and the communal boundaries and social boundedness of Jewish and Christian groups in and beyond second-century Antioch, on the other. Ignatius's pleas about individual choices of affiliation, in effect, are read as if speaking to the differentiation of entire social groups and, indeed, entire "religions." And much of what enables this slippage is its presentist horizon: it is perhaps not coincidental that the first known attestations of the Greek term *Christianismos* have been read as if signaling a split that falls quite precisely along the lines of what is now commonly understood as Jewish/Christian difference – thereby conflating the theological and the social, the global and the local, the collective and the individual.

The very framing of the question thus encourages extrapolation from specific sources to globalizing conclusions about "religions" *writ large*. Below, I

---

[20] On the power and limits of this mode of philology see now Daniel Boyarin, *Judaism* (Key Words in Jewish Studies; New Brunswick: Rutgers University Press, forthcoming). On the prominence of word studies in specialist research on ancient Judaism and Christianity, and what it can hide, see also J. Barr, *The Semantics of Biblical Language* (Oxford: Oxford University Press, 1961) as well as W.A. Meeks on the *TDNT*: "A Nazi New Testament Professor Reads His Bible: The Strange Case of Gerhard Kittel," in *The Idea of Biblical Interpretation: Essays in Honor of James L. Kugel*, ed. H. Najman and J.H. Newman (JSJSup 83; Leiden: Brill, 2004), 513–44; cf. G. Kittel and G. Friedrich, eds., *Theologisches Wörterbuch zum Neuen Testament*, 10 vols. (Stuttgart, 1933–1979), translated into English as *Theological Dictionary of the New Testament* (Grand Rapids: Eerdmans, 1964–1976).

[21] To cite one recent example: Thomas A. Robinson, *Ignatius of Antioch and the Parting of the Ways: Early Jewish-Christian Relations* (Peabody: Hendrickson, 2009). For a detailed survey and critique of this line of scholarship, see Phillip Fackler, "Forging Christian Identity: Christians and Jews in Pseudo-Ignatius" (Ph.D. dissertation, University of Pennsylvania, 2017).

will reflect upon the ramifications in relation to the groupism that the rubric of "religion" can too often retroject. For now, it suffices to note the high degree of selectivity that this framing necessitates. As we have seen, there are a number of thinkers who were working to rethink and retheorize ritual and doctrinal difference in Late Antiquity.[22] Yet the scholarly discussion about the formation of Jewish and Christian identities nevertheless revolves around a very small handful of Greek (and some Latin) passages from Patristic literature that so happen to be explicit in framing difference in terms of the specific binaries "Jew"/"Christian" and "Judaism"/"Christianity."

Below, I shall return to consider the modern notions of "religion(s)" that undergird the plausibility of these scholarly modes of reading Jewish and Christian sources. For now, it suffices to signal some of what is missed, in the process, about Late Antiquity. As much attention has been given to the first attestations of terms like *Christianismos*, for instance, analysis of these attestations has been largely in isolation from their own literary contexts.[23] Even less attention has been paid to the usage of these terms thereafter – let alone to the limits of their influence and the continued cultivation of alternate terms and taxonomies.[24] It is typically assumed, rather, that to discover the earliest attestation of such terms suffices to establish the point *after which* the corresponding concepts *as we now know them* essentially came to prevail.[25] As in older treatments of "origins" as constituent of essence, temporality is telescoped, and synchronic variation is collapsed. Whether hailed as the moment of Christianity's "Parting of the Ways" with Judaism and/or as the construction of Christian identity and/or the invention of "Christianity" as "religion," the very act of pinpointing such a moment thus risks presentism, in practice, in a manner that conflates normative claims about the present with historical claims about the past.[26]

I do not mean to question the value of culling the past for precedents for those early modern modes of knowledge-ordering that came to inform our current notions of "Judaism," "Christianity," and "religions."[27] Much has been learned from recent work on their genealogies: such studies have proved particularly powerful for denaturalizing and historicizing these very notions, and they have

---

[22] See Chapter Two in this volume for detailed discussion of this point.

[23] On Ignatius, however, see now Fackler, "Forging Christian Identity."

[24] Notable, too, is the relative lack of scholarly attention to Josephus' use of *Christianoi* in *Ant.* 18.64 in the late first century in a manner that presumes their place within the history of *Ioudaioi*.

[25] My discussion here extends the similar point that I made in 2014 in "*Ioudaios* before and after 'Religion'" – reprinted as Appendix C in this volume.

[26] Perhaps needless to say, the choice of which/whose present counts as *telos* carries normative claims as well.

[27] See, e. g., T. Asad, *Genealogies of Religion* (Baltimore: Johns Hopkins University Press, 1993); J. Z. Smith, "Religion, Religions, Religious," in *Critical Terms for Religious Studies*, ed. M. C. Taylor (Chicago: University of Chicago Press, 1998), 269–84; D. Dubuisson, *L'Occident et la religion: Mythes, science et idéologie* (Bruxelles: Editiones Complexe, 1998).

also been an apt arena for scholars of Late Antiquity to contribute to broader conversations in Religious Studies and across the Humanities.[28] My point here, rather, is that this task should not be taken up as an end in itself, lest we replicate precisely the same problems with old "origins"-tracing that we say that we seek to avoid.[29] We should look, rather, to how such genealogies can also open up new vistas, taking us beyond the blinkered presentism of quests after "origins."[30]

Some Church Fathers – such as Ignatius, Tertullian, Epiphanius, and John Chrysostom – clearly contributed to the creation of conceptual taxonomies that define "Christian" and "Christianity" in contradistinction to "Jew" and "Judaism" in a manner that presages and perhaps even influences early modern articulations of the very notion of "religion(s)." To treat these particular Patristic sources as uniquely representative of their own time, however, risks eliding what we find familiar from our present with what we posit as the dominant approaches to partitioning social and lived realities in the past – or, in other words: mistaking our modern ways of organizing knowledge about antiquity for our reconstruction of ancient ways of organizing knowledge. The task of cultural history is thereby flattened into a simple narrative of before and after, and the past is construed as a reservoir of precedents for the presumed *telos* of our present (with whatever the presumed "our" thereby naturalized as inevitable if not normative). And, in the process, the treatment of such a selective set of sources as *uniquely* speaking to "Christianity," "Judaism," and "religion" distracts from the multiplicity of *other* late antique Christian experiments with retheorizing identity and difference, while also pressing late antique Jewish sources into those distinctively Christian frameworks that so happen most to resemble their modern Western scholarly heirs.

What is perhaps most misleading about such an approach, in my view, is what it forecloses – both diachronically and synchronically. From a diachronic perspective, such unilinear narratives of dramatic change treat "religions" in a manner akin to what Rogers Brubaker, when assessing scholarship on nationhood, calls a "developmentalist temporal register," wherein "the long-term formation of nations involves profound socioeconomic, political, and cultural transformations; but once formed, nations are treated as static, substantial entities."[31] In

---

[28] Boyarin, *Judaism*; Boyarin, "Semantic Differences; Or, 'Judaism/Christianity,'" in Becker and Reed, *The Ways that Never Parted*, 65–85; J. B. Rives, *Religion in the Roman Empire* (Malden: Blackwell, 2007), 1–53, 202–10; J. Schott, *Christianity, Empire, and the Making of Religion in Late Antiquity* (Divinations; Philadelphia: University of Pennsylvania Press, 2008); C. Barton and D. Boyarin, *Imagine No Religion: How Modern Abstractions Hide Ancient Realities* (New York: Fordham University Press, 2016); Cynthia Baker, *Jew* (Key Words in Jewish Studies; New Brunswick: Rutgers University Press, 2017).

[29] See further Reed, "Christian Origins and Religious Studies."

[30] So too Barton and Boyarin, *Imagine No Religion*.

[31] Rogers Brubaker, "Ethnicity, Race, and Nationalism," *Annual Review of Sociology* 35 (2009): 21–35 at 30.

scholarly narratives about the history of Christianity and other "religions," it is similarly the case that fluidity and dynamism are largely limited to a transformative period of "origins," which culminates in what is framed thereafter as forever bounded and set. For religion as for nationhood, however, the commensensical power of this diachronic narrative of identity-formation has not been borne out in analysis of actual examples; if anything, this narrative can be misleading, particularly for characterizing dynamics in those eras *after* the purported period of "origins" but *before* our present.[32]

When one finds early Patristic passages with special resonance with our present-day contrasts of Judaism and Christianity, for instance, it can be tempting to herald them as marking a point of "origin" (or "invention," "construction," etc.) after which their predominance to this day is treated as if instant and/or inevitable. As noted above, however, it is unclear just how representative these particular modes of knowledge ordering were in their own time. Nor is it clear that the *theological* claims of these particular authors necessarily reflected *social* realities in Late Antiquity – even in their own locales, let alone in any global sense across and beyond the Roman Empire.[33] Rather than continuing to debate the same sources, then, I wonder whether it might be worthwhile to step back and ask what has been missed in the very process. What is ignored and elided when we frame our analysis of ancient identity formation primarily in terms of the search for precedents for the terms and taxonomies most familiar to us today?

It is for this reason that I find the puzzling case of "Jewish-Christianity" so provocatively productive: it is exemplary of what must be ignored and elided to permit this particular presentism. The very term, as we have seen, was coined by modern thinkers to describe those premodern sources which have features of the sort commonly associated with Christianity's originary Jewishness but which date from *after* the period of "Christian Origins" (i.e., at a point when such Jewishness is deemed no longer simply in the continuum of "Christian").[34] Consequently, the materials that modern scholars have labeled as "Jewish-Christian" perhaps prove especially powerful for unsettling the very notion of a clear-cut *before/after* narrative of Christian identity-formation. To take such materials seriously, in this sense, is to be pushed to craft more sophisticated diachronic narratives about Jews and Christians, more attuned to the continued complexi-

---

[32] Such complexities are well known, of course, to scholars of the Middle Ages and on. My point here is that scholars of antiquity often tell dramatic narratives of "origins," "inventions," etc., that can assume a model of change that forecloses such medieval developments, treating ancient innovations as if leading directly to modern phenomena.

[33] What a focus on the earliest attestation of terms elides, in other words, is the question of when and how such sources may have had translocal impact, particularly due to their different positionings vis-à-vis imperial power: even if Ignatius is first to use *Christianismos*, for instance, the ramifications of his usage still differ dramatically from those of Eusebius, Epiphanius, et al.

[34] See Chapters One, Eight, and Eleven in this volume.

ties and creative interplay of identification evident in a number of late antique, medieval, and even modern sources.[35]

Perhaps no less poignant is the potential of this material to point us to some of what has been thereby overlooked in synchronic terms as well. However influential in the *longue durée*, after all, Patristic polemical passages contrasting *Ioudaismos* and *Christianismos* were only part of the picture in Late Antiquity. When one ceases to read these passages as if descriptive reportage or ethnographical survey, it is possible to see them as products of creative acts of categorization that formed part of a continuum of experimentation with different modes of categorizing difference in Late Antiquity. Some examples, as we have seen, can be found among those works that scholars now call "Jewish-Christian."[36] Yet they are hardly limited to such works. Long after Ignatius, Christians continued to experiment with other ancient binaries like "Israel"/"the nations," "Judaism"/"Hellenism," "Jew"/"Greek," and "barbarian"/"Greek" to make sense of the patterns of similarity and differences within their local and social worlds. Even Eusebius, for instance, frames the tale of the history of the church in terms of the conflict of Israel and the nations – with Christians now in the place of Israel and with "pagans" as *ta ethnē* (i.e., the Greek equivalent of Hebrew *ha-goyim*). And in this sense, he maps difference in a manner surprisingly similar to some of his Rabbinic Jewish contemporaries, among whom the contrast of "Israel"/"the nations" was being developed into a totalizing taxonomy in Late Antiquity as well.[37]

To use a small handful of Patristic passages as the lens through which to analyze and organize *all other* late antique materials pertaining to identity in our historical reconstructions, thus, is not just to retroject much of our own partitioning of religious difference into the past: it is also to distract from the much broader continuum of premodern approaches to ordering knowledge and classifying difference.[38] Much might be lost in the process. Without the context of this broader continuum, for instance, it is arguably difficult to understand the articulation and eventual dominance of now-familiar notions of Jewish/Christian difference. Furthermore, attention to the full range of what we know

---

[35] See, e.g., Shaul Magid, "Defining Christianity and Judaism from the Perspective of Religious Anarchy: Martin Buber on Jesus and the Ba'al Shem Tov," *JJTP* 25 (2017): 36–58, for an example of the types of much later "meaningful convergence" that scholarly narratives like the "Parting of the Ways" forget and foreclose. Magid notes too how such avenues of investigation are opened in part by "newer research [that] focuses on the local as opposed to the categorical, that is, what Jews and Christians may have thought about who they were and what they were doing instead of using categories that may have been foreign to them" (36).

[36] See Chapters Four, Five, and Six in this volume.

[37] Ishay Rosen-Zvi and Adi Ophir, "Goy: Toward a Genealogy," *Dine Israel* 29 (2011): 69–122. Their insights into the intensification of this development in Late Antiquity hold, even if we might wish to resist their impulse to try to pinpoint its moment of "invention."

[38] See now Todd Berzon, *Classifying Christians: Ethnography, Heresiology and the Limits of Knowledge in Late Antiquity* (Berkeley: University of California Press, 2016).

of this continuum can serve as a powerful reminder that our own second-order categories are neither natural nor inevitable: our own acts of classifying and theorizing difference are practices with precedents but alternatives too – looking backwards as well as forward.[39]

Beyond "Identity"

During the years covered by the articles in this volume, scholars of Judaism and Christianity largely took for granted that early Jewish and Christian texts were shaped foremost by a concern for constructing identity. In this, research in these areas followed broader trends across the Social Sciences and Humanities since the late twentieth century. Beginning in the 1960s – as Rogers Brubaker and Frederik Cooper note – "the notion of identification was pried from its original, specifically psychoanalytical contexts (where the term had been initially introduced by Freud) and linked to ethnicity on the one hand ... and sociological role theory and reference group theory on the other," and then, "in the 1980s, with the rise of race, class, and gender as the 'holy trinity' of literary criticism and cultural studies," spread further into the Humanities as well.[40] The latter was further shaped by the particular discourse about difference in the political, corporate, and academic cultures of North America, especially since the 1990s, wherein calls for "diversity" emblematized a push for the inclusion of ethnic and other "Others" under the ostensibly neutral canopy of (white) liberal multiculturalism.[41]

Throughout the late twentieth century and into the twenty-first, the general interdisciplinary interest in "identity" has been highly profitable for bringing questions of self-fashioning and communal differentiation to the fore of scholarly attention within research on Judaism and Christianity, especially in North America.[42] Likewise, the lionization of "diversity" fostered a cultural envi-

---

[39] Indeed, as Eviator Zerubbavel reminds us, "we tend to forget that language itself rests on social convention and to regard the mental divisions it introduces as real. When we label our world, we often commit the fallacy of misplaced concreteness .... It is important, therefore, to avoid the tendency to reify the conventional islands of meaning in which we organize the world in our minds"; *Social Mindscapes: An Invitation to Cognitive Sociology* (Cambridge, MA: Harvard University Press, 2009), 67.

[40] Rogers Brubaker and Frederik Cooper, "Beyond Identity," *Theory and Society* 29 (2000): 1–47 at 2–3. On the most influential forms of this psychological usage for this interdisciplinary conversation, see above.

[41] See further Olaf Kaltmeier and Sebastian Thies, "Specters of Multiculturalism: Conceptualizing the Field of Identity Politics in the Americas," *Latin American and Caribbean Ethnic Studies* 7 (2012): 223–40, as well as discussion below.

[42] Here and below, I focus on how shifts in the current cultural climate can help bring new questions to the fore of scholarly research on the past, so as to enable us to notice neglected dynamics in our ancient sources, etc., in a manner more complex than a simple presentism that

ronment conducive for historical efforts to recover lost and neglected voices from the Jewish and Christian past. Nevertheless, at this point, I suspect that both trends have largely run their course. We find ourselves at an intellectual moment where scholarly talk about "identity" has spread to the degree that the term has been evacuated of meaning. And – particularly in the United States in the wake of the 2016 presidential election and the rise of Trumpism – we also find ourselves at a political moment when the fissures in multiculturalism lie exposed, destabilizing its defining discourse about difference. As perhaps always in transitional moments, however, it is may be an apt time to consider what past trends effected and effaced, so as to chart new questions and perspectives to move ahead.

Since its emergence in the late 1950s, the scholarly discourse about identity has been articulated in interplay with a popular concern for identity in the United States in particular. Philip Gleason notes, for instance, how "the word identity was ideally adapted to talking about the relationship of the individual to society as that perennial problem that presented itself to Americans at midcentury," initially in the context of "national-character studies" and then in shifting ways as "the problem of the relation of the individual to society assumed new forms in the turmoil of the 1960s."[43] The more recent rise of multiculturalism and "identity politics" has been shaped, in particular, by "the most important legacy of the 1960s so far as usage of identity is concerned" – namely, the "revival of ethnicity" and the consequent "close connection between the notion of identity and the awareness of belonging to a distinctive group set apart from others in American society by race, religion, national background, or some other cultural marker."[44]

---

simply projects this or that "us" back into time and/or limits our curiosity about the past only to tales about the "origins" of our present. In the process, however, cultural historians may also have something to add to current discussions – such as concerning the pressing questions of alterity and difference noted below. Cornel West, for instance, posits that a "new cultural politics of difference faces three basic challenges – intellectual, existential, and political," and he frames the first (i. e., the intellectual challenge) as "how to think about representational practices in terms of history, culture, and society"; "The New Cultural Politics of Difference," *October* 53 (1990): 93–109 at 94. Discussions about ancient Jews and Christians might have something to contribute in that regard – not least because they have long shaped ideas about identity and difference in the West and thus may hold some power to reshape them as well. At the very least, with Karen King, "I regard historiography as a site for enlarging one's imaginative universe" ("Factions," 230), and as such, potentially a source for creativity in the present too – perhaps precisely when we permit our ancient sources to surprise and trouble us.

[43] Gleason, "Identifying Identity," 928. Brubaker and Cooper similarly note how "from the late 1960s on, with the rise of the Black Power movement, and subsequently other ethnic movements for which it served as a template, concerns with and assertions of individual identity, already linked by Erikson to 'communal culture,' were readily transposed to the group level" ("Beyond Identity," 3).

[44] Gleason, "Identifying Identity," 928.

During the late twentieth century, popular and scholarly appeals to "identity" proliferated, and so too did complaints about the lack of this term's specificity, clarity, and utility. Gleason's survey shows how the term "came into use as a popular social-science term only in the 1950s."[45] But already "by the early 1970s, Robert Coles could lament that the terms identity and identity crisis has become 'the purest of clichés.'"[46] Nevertheless, this trend was still so prominent in 1990s that Leon Wieseltier bemoaned how "in America, but not only in America, we are choking on identity."[47] And even as Wieseltier thus proclaimed it "an idea whose time has gone," it became extended and entrenched within popular and scholarly discourse. The same decades that saw academic interest in identity spread from the Social Sciences further into the Humanities, for instance, also saw public life in North America increasingly shaped by an "identity politics" grounded in the values of multiculturalism.

It is only in recent years that critiques of the category of "identity" have begun to come to a boiling point within scholarly circles, spurred especially by an essay that tackles head-on the problem of the blurring of its popular and scholarly usages. Published in 2000 and mounting in interdisciplinary influence in recent years, "Beyond Identity" by sociologists Brubaker and Cooper points to the contradictions and lack of conceptual clarity in the common notion of "identity." Brubaker and Cooper make the case that these problems stem from its simultaneous use as a "category of social and political *practice*" in contemporary America and as a "category of social and political *analysis*" for scholars of this and other societies:[48]

"Identity" is a key term in the vernacular idiom of contemporary politics, and social analysis must take account of this fact. But this does not require us to use "identity" as a category of analysis or to conceptualize "identities" as something that all people have, seek, construct, and negotiate. Conceptualizing all affinities and affiliations, all forms of belonging, all experiences of commonality, connectedness, and cohesion, all self-understandings and self-identifications in the idiom of "identity" saddles us with a blunt, flat, undifferentiated vocabulary.[49]

Among the problems with the concept – Brubaker and Cooper suggest – is an ambiguity that encompasses multiple conflicting meanings, including "a deep, basic, abiding, or foundational" core of a self, the "fundamental and consequential sameness of members of a group," "the processual and interactive development of collective self-understanding ... as the contingent product of social and political action," and "the evanescent product of multiple and competing

---

[45] Gleason, "Identifying Identity," 910

[46] Gleason, "Identifying Identity," 913.

[47] Leon Wieseltier, "Against Identity," *The New Republic*, November 27, 1994.

[48] Brubaker and Cooper, "Beyond Identity," 4.

[49] Brubaker and Cooper, "Beyond Identity," 2.

discourses ... unstable, multiple, fluctuating, and fragmented."[50] Rather than simply critique the category and its common usage, however, they attempt to "unbundle the thick tangle of meaning that have accumulated around the term 'identity' and to parcel out the work to a number of less congested terms."[51] Consequently, their essay has inspired new approaches to those issues conventionally clustered under the rubric of "identity," not just among sociologists, but increasingly among scholars across the Humanities as well.

Although Brubaker and Cooper focus upon race, ethnicity, and nationhood in the present, some of their insights may be profitable for rethinking scholarly approaches to "religions" in the past – and particularly for charting new approaches to Christian and Jewish identity-formation. For scholars of Late Antiquity, of course, identity is not a "category of social and political practice" in the cultures that we study. It remains, however, that research on late antique religions uses the idiom with much the same ambiguities as are common in the Social Sciences. Here too, for instance, one finds an "uneasy amalgam of constructivist language and essentialist argumentation" whereby "identity" is described as fluid, fragmented, invented, and multiple, *as per* scholarly conventions, even as specific identities (e. g., "Jew," "Christian") are treated in a reified or essentialist manner consistent with public discourse in the present (i. e., as if something set or stable that people "have").[52]

To some degree, as I noted above, scholarship on early and late antique Christianity has come to terms with this "uneasy amalgam" by mapping it onto the axis of time – with Christian identity characterized as fluid, fragmentary, and multiple in the originary past, but then posited to be constructed, and set and stable thereafter. In the "Parting" model and similar scholarly narratives, this mapping has largely been enabled by the doubled place of Judaism therein – as both fertile ground and defining foil. It is perhaps telling, then, that to the degree that recent critiques of the "Parting" model have been met with resistance, it has been largely from anxieties that abandoning such a model would necessitate reframing Christian (and/or Jewish) identities as forever trapped in a state of undifferentiated flux, as if remaining in the blur of infancy or the primordial ooze of precreation.

If we rethink "identity" with Brubaker and Cooper, however, we find ourselves with more analytical options – beyond the false dichotomy of the constructivist proclamation of the fluidity of all identities, on the one hand, and the presentist

---

[50] Brubaker and Cooper, "Beyond Identity," 8.

[51] Brubaker and Cooper, "Beyond Identity," 14.

[52] Brubaker and Cooper, "Beyond Identity," 6. They there note that "the problem is that 'nation,' 'race,' and 'identity' are used analytically a good deal of the time more or less as they are used in practice, in an implicitly or explicitly reifying manner, in a manner that implies or asserts that 'nations,' 'races,' and 'identities' 'exist' and that people 'have' a 'nationality,' a 'race,' and an 'identity'" (6). Much the same, as I note below, might be argued for "religion."

qua essentialist temptation to reify now-familiar identities, on the other. Above, I suggested that part of the problem with current debates about Jewish and Christian identities lies in the artificial bifurcation of Christianity's (Jewish) beginnings from its (non-/anti-Jewish) history, and I proposed the need for more sophisticated diachronic narratives about the continued interplay of Jewish and Christian identities. Perhaps useful, in this regard, is Brubaker and Cooper's call for a reorientation in how we even analyze identities: instead of focusing on "identity" (and thus debating how best to define specific identities, trace their "origins," organize them into subsets and systems, contest when they become set, etc.), we might better turn to focus on ongoing acts and processes of *identification*.

Not only does this approach defuse the danger of reifying identities, but it also counters the temptation to abstractify or globalize them. "'Identification,'" as Brubaker and Cooper note, "invites specification of the agents that *do* the identifying."[53] To forefront identification, moreover, is necessarily to attend to multiple sites and settings, since "how one identifies oneself – and how one is identified by others – may vary greatly from context to context: self- and other-identification are fundamentally situational and contextual."[54] Whereas a focus on "identity" can risk conflating different agents and contexts, a focus on identification further forces us to attend to the differences between acts of self-labeling as opposed to labeling others with exonyms as well as to the differences between personal acts of individuation and the authoritative imposition of more totalizing taxonomies. Or, as Brubaker and Cooper put it:

Self-identification takes place in dialectical interplay with *external identification*, but the two need not converge. *External identification* is itself a varied process. In the ordinary ebb and flow of social life, people identify and categorize themselves. But there is another key type of external identification that has no counterpart in the domain of self-identification: the formalized, codified, objectified *systems of categorization* developed by powerful, authoritative institutions.[55]

Attending to such distinctions may help us to see some of what our current concept of "identity" can hide when applied to Jews and Christians in Late Antiquity.[56] Today, for instance, we may take for granted that "Jew" functions as a

---

[53] Brubaker and Cooper, "Beyond Identity," 16.

[54] Brubaker and Cooper, "Beyond Identity," 14.

[55] Brubaker and Cooper, "Beyond Identity," 15. Self-identification includes how "to characterize oneself, to locate oneself vis-à-vis known others, to situate oneself in a narrative, to oneself in a category" (14). For this, Brubaker and Cooper make a notable distinction between "relative and categorical modes": positioning "in a relational web," on the one hand, and "by membership in a class of persons sharing some categorical attribute," on the other (15).

[56] I here consider internal and external identification with a focus on how Christians and Jews describe *one another*, but "pagan" Roman external identification of both is relevant as well. Some scholars, in fact, have suggested that Romans do not seem to associate Christians with Jews and have adduced this lack of association as proof that Jews and Christians "really" were "parted" by the late first or early second century, whatever some Jewish and Christian

term used by Jews for themselves, by Christians for them, and within scholarship in Religious Studies to classify people, texts, and history as belonging to one "religion" and not another. Cynthia Baker, however, has recently suggested that the label "Jew" and its equivalents were rarely used in premodern times by those whom we now call Jews.[57] Rather, the term functioned foremost as an exonym,

sources might themselves sometimes seem to suggest (e. g., Shaye Cohen, *From the Maccabees to the Mishnah* [3rd ed.; Louisville: Westminster John Knox, 2014], 231–58). This argument from silence is often made with specific reference to the *fiscus Iudaicus* – as most recently by Marius Heemstra, *The Fiscus Judaicus and the Parting of the Ways* (WUNT2; 277; Tübingen: Mohr Siebeck, 2010). Attention to Brubaker and Cooper's methodological cautions, however, should lead us to be a bit suspicious of taking such labeling at face value as if simply and directly descriptive of social realities. In the case of these early Roman examples, we might wish to be especially wary of naïvely treating such descriptions as if neutral reportage: after all, recent work in Classics has emphasized and explored the cultural and ideological work that Roman ethnography and Roman legal discourse does for Romanness and imperial ideology (see, e. g., Greg Woolf, *Tales of the Barbarians: Ethnography and Empire in the Roman West* [Malden: Wiley-Blackwell, 2011] and n. 101 below). And all the more so with our sources for Roman persecutions of Christians and Jews (e. g., as adduced by Cohen, *From the Maccabees*, 234–35), which have long been known to be problematic as direct historical data (see, e. g., Elizabeth Castelli, *Martyrdom and Memory: Early Christian Culture Making* [New York: Columbia University Press, 2004]; Candida Moss, *The Other Christs: Imitating Jesus in Ancient Christian Ideologies of Martyrdom* [Oxford: Oxford University Press, 2010]; Moss, *The Myth of Persecution* [New York: HarperOne, 2013]).

Even apart from such methodological issues, however, it strikes me as somewhat specious to cite the *lack* of Roman associations of Jews and Christians to argue for their "parting" by the late first century (as, e. g., Heemstra, *The Fiscus Judaicus*) when actually there are no Roman references to Christians until the second century. The relevant first-century evidence is from Josephus in his *Antiquities* (i. e., as completed in 93/94 CE; *Ant.* 20.267), written in Greek to a Roman audience: Josephus mentions Jesus, John the Baptist, and James – and even Jesus' followers who call themselves *Christianoi* in his own time – with no hint that they are *not* part of the history of *Ioudaioi* (*Ant.* 18.63–64; 18.109–19; 20.197). "Pagan" references to Christians are not found until almost twenty years later. In 111–12 CE, Pliny discusses *Christianoi* in his letter to Trajan, and a few years later (ca. 116 CE), Tacitus mentions those "called 'Chrestians' by the populace (*vulgus Chrestianos appellabat*)" in his *Annals* (15.44). During the reign of Hadrian (r. 117–38 CE) Suetonius writes *Lives of the Twelve Caesars* and similarly mentions a "Chrestus." The comments of Tacitus and Suetonius, moreover, are largely in keeping with Josephus' association of Jesus and *Christianoi* with *Ioudaioi* – a term which, at the time, could mean "Judaean" and/or "Jew": Tacitus explicitly associates "Chrestians" with Judaea, while Suetonius associates "Chrestus" with Jews/Judaeans in Rome (i. e., noting how Claudius "expelled the Jews/Judaeans from Rome, since they constantly made disturbances because of the instigator Chrestus [*Judaeos, impulsore Chresto, assidue tumultuantes Roma expulit*]"; *Claudius* 25.3–5). To be sure, Celsus' polemic against Christianity does draw out a contrast with Jews for the rhetorical force of undermining Christian claims to antiquity, but not until later in the second century – and, hence, hardly in a manner that can be directly correlated to the *fiscus Iudaicus*. Even the much-cited limitation of this Roman tax only to those "Jews who continued to observe their ancestral customs" comes from a source penned from a position of some retrospect – i. e., from Cassius Dio in the third century (*Hist. Rom.* 65.7.2), adding details not found in the more proximate report of Josephus, *War* 7.218.

[57] Baker, *Jew* – and for some of the rippling ramifications, see Reed and Magid, *Forum on Cynthia Baker's Jew*, http://marginalia.lareviewofbooks.org/introduction-forum-on-cynthia-baker-jew/.

defined and deployed by Christians in particular, especially in the context of interpreting the New Testament. "For most of two long millennia," Baker thus suggests, "the word *Jew* has been predominantly defined and delimited as a term for not-self":[58]

Prior to the advent of modernity, creation of knowledge about Jew(s) was, likewise, primarily a non-Jewish (and often an anti-Jewish) enterprise. Formulating meaning and content for the category Jew(s) had everything to do with constructing and sustaining collective identities that were "not that" (whatever "that" was construed to be). This long history of Jew as not-self, as dross to be purged in the refinement of (collective and individual) self, reached its devastating apogee in the twentieth century's Nazi war against the Jew(s). In the present era, by contrast, Jew has come more and more to be appropriated as a self-identification, a term by which "we Jews" speak about and represent "ourselves" in the common languages of "our" many homelands. Concomitantly, the last century, in particular, has also witnessed an explosion in the number of self-identified Jews contributing to discourses about (the) Jew(s).[59]

The very term "Jew" is a case, thus, in which "*self-identification* takes place in dialectical interplay with *external identification*" – eventually. Most of the term's history, however, is a parade example of how "the two need not converge."

The modern Jewish embrace of the identity label "Jew" can distract from the fact that it was the Christian sense of the term – as theologically-charged *external identification* – that shaped the place of "Judaism" in the *systems of categorization* that scholars of Religious Studies commonly take for granted as if a neutral, natural, and objective framework for the objective analysis of past and present alike (e. g., as one of many purportedly commensurate and nonoverlapping units within a totalizing taxonomy of "world religions").[60] Recently, Daniel Boyarin has further shown how "Judaism" does not function as a self-oriented term of Jewish collective identity in Late Antiquity and the Middle Ages, but rather and primarily as a Christian label for the superseded Christian past and/or Christological error.[61] As a result, it is especially misleading to read all premodern references to *Ioudaismos* as if directly equivalent to how "Judaism" is used in common parlance today – that is, as a "religion" contrasted with Christianity but still imagined to be essentially commensurate in form and structure.

Below, we will return to this question of what may have been skewed in the common framing of early Jewish/Christian relations as a matter of the "origins" and relations of "religions." For now, it suffices to note that most of what we know about the premodern equivalents of "Jew" and "Judaism" consists of their

---

[58] Baker, *Jew*, 4.

[59] Baker, *Jew*, 50.

[60] See further Tomoko Masuzawa, *The Invention of World Religions; Or, How European Universalism Was Preserved in the Language of Pluralism* (Chicago: University of Chicago Press, 2005). Here too, however, I personally am less interested in moment of "invention" and suspect that the fixation on "finding" such moments distracts from more interesting questions.

[61] Boyarin, *Judaism*.

usage as Christian polemical terms, used to conjure something more akin to a specter from the past, invoked as if by necromancy to serve as abject "Other" within inner-Christian debates about correct Christology and/or true Christianity. To note the premodern prominence of Christian uses and definitions of "Jew" is not just a signaling of anachronism: it has significant consequences for understanding what our evidence for the Patristic use of related Greek terms is even *evidence of.* Indeed, this is much of why it can also be so misleading to quote selective passages about *Ioudaioi* and *Ioudaismos* versus *Christianoi* and *Christianismos* from late antique Christian sources and to use them to make claims about the "origins" of what we now know as "Judaism," "Christianity," and Jewish/Christian difference today.

If the category "Jewish-Christianity" is surely anachronistic, then, it is perhaps in a manner that helps to expose what is also anachronistic about projecting our present sense of "Judaism" and "Christianity" back into the late antique past. After all, as we have seen, the very term "Jewish-Christian" signals the tensions between two different *systems of categorization*. The binary contrast "Jew"/"Christian" makes sense within a Christian theological framework, and it is in this context that "Jewish-Christian" is a heresiological term, marking some premodern articulations of Christianity as problematically retaining more or other features of the Jewish heritage of Christianity than present-day Christians now consider apt.[62] Inasmuch as "Jewish-Christian" is a modern neologism constructed in contrast to "Gentile-Christian," however, it also embeds another binary – that is, "Jew"/"Gentile." This binary recalls the pre-Christian Jewish approach to classifying human difference through the contrast of "Jew"/"Greek." But it also falls even closer to the biblically-based binary "Israel"/*ha-goyim*, which also lies at the heart of the dominant approach to classifying difference in Rabbinic literature, the major surviving corpus of Jewish writings from Late Antiquity.[63]

---

[62] I.e., as is the case made in Daniel Boyarin, "Rethinking Jewish Christianity: An Argument for Dismantling a Dubious Category (to which is Appended a Correction of my *Border Lines*)," *JQR* 99 (2009): 7–36.

[63] I.e., as shown in Rosen-Zvi and Ophir, "Goy." Their study is a superb example of the benefits of a shift from a focus on "identity"/identities to a focus on acts of identification. Rosen-Zvi and Ophir there note, for instance, how "much scholarship has been devoted to Jewish relations with and attitudes toward gentiles in different periods in, amongst other areas, halakha, philosophy, poetry, and literature"; what has been ignored in the process is that "such naming, partition, and structure is anything but self-evident, and was not always a part of the thought patterns and discursive practices of Jews" (69). The particular case that they make is that "the conceptual grid allowing for a stable, inclusive, and exclusive opposition between a universalized Goy and a particularized Jew first appeared in its crystallized form only in tannaitic literature" (69). However one might debate the precise timing of its emergence or the degree of its novelty vis-à-vis biblical and Second Temple Jewish grammars of difference, it remains that their focus on Rabbinic perspectives opens up a whole new set of questions – not least by reminding us that Church Fathers were not the only ones retheorizing difference in Late Antiquity.

That the two binaries do not align is clear already from the ancient debate that inspired the modern invention of the category of "Jewish-Christianity" in the first place – namely, the debate about Gentile inclusion in the Jesus Movement as reflected in Galatians 2, the Book of Acts, the *Epistle of Peter to James*, and the Pseudo-Clementine *Homilies*.[64] Paul's self-described conflict with Peter in Galatians 2 is predicated on the contrast between Jew/Israel/circumcised and Greek/*goyim*/uncircumcised – long prior to the articulation of the name "Christian" or the neologism "Christianity." It is because of the assumed incommensurability of Jew and Greek that non-Jewish interest in Jesus even posed a practical and social problem for the early Jesus Movement, as is clear from 1 Corinthians and Acts no less than from Galatians. As more non-Jews became persuaded that Jesus was the Jewish messiah predicted in the Jewish scriptures, it seems that practical questions arose among his Jewish followers. Many of these questions might be understood in halakhic terms as pertaining to the nature and degree of the inclusion in the people Israel of these particular non-Jews, who were marked separate from others by their interest in the Torah, Jewish monotheism, and the Jewish messiah. Idolatry and polytheism, for instance, were clearly proscribed to them. But questions arose about whether or not the men among them needed to be circumcised (cf. Gal 2:12; Acts 15:1–5) and which of the other laws of the Torah applied to them after baptism.

Likewise, Acts upholds the relevance to these non-Jews of Jewish laws against sexual impiety (*porneia*, i. e. *zenut*; Acts 15:20, 29; cf. Mark 7:21–22; Gal 5:19). And just as Paul holds non-Jews to the stricture against consuming meat associated with idolatrous rites (1 Corinthians 8), so Acts also maps out the continuum of other laws that govern their eating: Jesus-following Gentiles are here deemed exempt from those laws of *kashrut* whereby types of meat and fish are distinguished (Acts 10; cf. Mark 7:18–19) but remain bound by injunctions not to eat meat offered in sacrifice to idols, not to eat the blood even in other meat, and not to eat the meat of animals that have been strangled (Acts 15:20, 29).

Even apart from halakhic questions about individual practice and piety, one also glimpses new questions raised in relation to how the coming of Jesus as messiah affects the social separation of Jews and non-Jews. Some degree of social if not ontological separation is assumed already in Paul's own contention that God appointed separate apostles (i.e., Peter and himself) to go out to the circumcised and to the Gentiles (Gal 2:7–9). Yet already in Galatians, Paul also attests debates surrounding the propriety of Jewish and non-Jewish followers of Jesus eating meals together – which Paul himself accepts but presents James as eschewing, even as Peter vacillates (Gal 2:11–12; cf. Acts 10:28).

Pauline and Lukan approaches to such questions may have contributed to the eventual articulation of "Christian" as distinct from "Jew." Nevertheless, the texts

---

[64] See Chapters Eight and Eleven in this volume.

themselves speak to the situation prior to this mode of demarcation, when variations on the binary of Jew/non-Jew (e. g., Jew/Greek, Israel/*ta ethnē*) remained determinative for structuring social practice as well as halakhic and theological discourse among followers of Jesus, as for other Jews. It is in this sense that Ferdinand Christian Baur's enduring influence has been positive, serving as a reminder that the first century was not marked by debates about whether and how Jews, "Judaizing," or Jewish praxis have a place in Christianity, but rather by debates about whether and on what conditions non-Jews might have a place in Israel. Not only does the latter remain rooted in Jewish frameworks for understanding difference, but it points to some of what is at stake in this task of "thinking with Gentiles" – namely, the challenge of reinterpreting the laws of the Torah and rethinking halakhah when one believes that the messianic age has begun.

Nor is this issue settled in the first century or with the New Testament. Rather, as we have seen, the *Didascalia apostolorum* remains shaped by a framework that divides the world – and thus also the church – into "the People" (i. e., Israel) and "the nations," even as its authors reread the Torah in order to articulate a messianic-age halakhah for Jewish followers of Jesus.[65] And just as the *Didascalia apostolorum* does so by looking back to the Apostolic Council of Acts 15, so the *Epistle of Peter to James* claims to preserve the Petrine side of the story told by Paul in Galatians 2, and the Pseudo-Clementine *Homilies* argue for an even greater degree of Torah observance for non-Jews than Acts and the *Didascalia apostolorum*.[66] Here too, the texts themselves operate with binaries that are much closer in structure to the biblical and Rabbinic binary of Israel/*ha-goyim* than to Patristic or modern binaries of "Jew"/"Christian" (in this case: with the *Epistle of Peter to James* emphasizing Jewish/Gentile difference, even within the church, while the *Homilies* extends the construction of "Judaism" in contradistinction to "Hellenism").

Strictly speaking, only one of these perspectives was enshrined in what Brubaker and Cooper designate as "the formalized, codified, objectified *systems of categorization* developed by powerful, authoritative institutions" – that is the Christian heresiological taxonomy that distinguished "Christian," "Jew," "heretic," "Greek"/"pagan," etc., and was embraced in the legal codes of the Roman Empire in the course of its Christianization.[67] Nevertheless, prior to that development, heresiological classificatory schemes represent but one among many Christian approaches to organizing knowledge about ritual and doctrinal difference. Even afterwards, moreover, this taxonomy was clearly resisted in late antique Jewish approaches to difference as we know them from Rabbinic and related literatures.

---

[65] See Chapters Two and Three in this volume.
[66] See Chapters Six and Eight in this volume.
[67] See further Berzon, *Classifying Christians*.

Sources like the Mishnah, Tosefta, and Talmudim are rather exuberantly classificatory on multiple fronts. Yet terms that unequivocally denote "Christians" are rare and late, and we certainly do not find any definition of "Jew" or Israel that centers on the contrast with "Christian" and "Christianity" as defining. Scholars may debate when Rabbinic uses of *minim* and *minut* might come specifically to include Christians and Christianity, partly or prominently,[68] and we might also wonder whether and when the very lack of terms of this sort is a "deliberate silence," especially in sources from Roman Palestine after Constantine.[69] It remains, however, that Rabbinic concepts and systems of classification differ quite strikingly from the Christian-based concepts and systems still commonly used by scholars to describe and analyze the notions of "identity" therein. In fact, if Rosen-Zvi and Ophir are correct, there may have been some tannaim – precisely around the same time that Ignatius was coining the term *Christianismos* and Irenaeus was inaugurating Christian heresiological discourse – who were turning their attention to articulating a "concept of the *Goy* [that] divides humanity in a binary manner, separating Jews from all non-Jews, lumping the latter together into one group," and thereby enabling the classification of "both Jews and gentiles ... by rabbinic Judaism as part of a series of structural oppositions and relations."[70]

Scholarship on Late Antiquity would look very different indeed if we took *systems of categorization* from Rabbinic literature and read both Rabbinic and Patristic literature through their terms, principles, and guiding questions. But this should perhaps stand as a reminder that – in practice – we actually pretty much do the opposite. To go beyond a focus on Jewish and Christian identities and to follow recent sociological research in distinguishing between processes of *self-identification* and *external identification* within individual use and within *systems of classification*, thus, is to notice a stark incommensurability that has rarely been taken into full account in studies of Christian and Jewish identity-formation, precisely because Christian perspectives have been tacitly treated as central if not descriptively neutral.[71] Both this fiction of neutrality and the incommensurability that it masks, however, might be promising to plumb further.

If many of the debates in the subfield of early Jewish/Christian relations have begun to run in ever-tightening circles around the same texts and questions, it is perhaps partly because of this fundamental problem: its main categories, concepts, and concerns do not do justice to all of the evidence – not least because a

---

[68] See references and discussion in Chapter Five above.

[69] See, e. g., Joshua Levinson, "There is No Place Like Home: Rabbinic Responses to the Christianization of Palestine," in Dohrmann and Reed, *Jews, Christians, and the Roman Empire*, 99–120.

[70] Rosen-Zvi and Ophir, "Goy," 69.

[71] See Chapter Seven above for this point, especially with respect to messianism. For an attempt to center Rabbinic perspectives see now Joshua Ezra Burns, *The Christian Schism in Jewish History and Jewish Memory* (Cambridge: Cambridge University Press, 2016).

scholarly conversation that purports to be about Jews and Christians is actually largely about a discussion of Christians, told from Christian sources, from within Christian classificatory schemes, and with an eye to the rest of Christian history and scholarship.

Part of my experiment in the present volume has been asking whether "Jewish-Christian" sources might help us to open up the conversation in a manner that bridges onto a discussion of Jews, told from Jewish sources, from within Jewish classificatory schemes, and with an eye to the rest of Jewish history and scholarship. Moving ahead, I wonder if we can also do more to address this base problem by shifting our focus from the question of the differences and differentiation of Christian and Jewish *identities* to the differences in (and among) Jewish, Christian, and other *perspectives* and *positionings* in Late Antiquity.

It may be a timely moment to do so – I suggest – precisely because of shifts in the above-noted discourse about "identity." So far, following Brubaker and Cooper, I have focused on scholarly critiques that seek to separate out what popular usage typically conflates. I am not so sure, however, that the solution is quite so simple as severing our categories of scholarly analysis from our own cultural contexts. As much as historical inquiry should attempt not to retroject present-day norms or limit our curiosity about the past to the aetiology of our own lived experience, it remains that the shifting horizon of the present can proffer new lenses and new questions that help to highlight neglected elements in our sources. At times, moreover, shifts in the public imagination and political sphere can be useful for exposing and dislodging assumptions long taken for granted in scholarship. I suspect that we may well find ourselves at one of these times with respect to "identity," especially in relation to a trend that Brubaker and Cooper's seminal essay does not address head-on – that is, multiculturalism.

In the Americas, as Olaf Kaltmeier and Sebastian Thies note, "multiculturalism came into being when the surge of identity politics from a variety of ethnically defined subaltern groups and second-wave feminists joined with the politics of recognition devised by state institutions, academia and the juridical system."[72] Early multiculturalism was thus articulated within the bounds of nationalism, inasmuch as "the modern nation-state … in its integrative project, pretends to embrace all of its culturally heterogenous population."[73] Yet it has remained in tension with that very project, especially insofar as it has fostered

---

[72] Kaltmeier and Thies, "Spectres of Multiculturalism," 224, and on recent transnational shifts in this discursive field, see also O. Kaltmeier, S. Thies, and J. Raab, "Multiculturalism and Beyond: The New Dynamics of Identity Politics in the Americas," *Latin American and Caribbean Ethnic Studies* 7 (2012): 103–14. The scholarly literature on multiculturalism is obviously massive, and this is certainly not the place to engage it in full; my concern here is simply to draw out some of the dynamics that have echoes or effects on scholarship on Jewish and Christian difference in the past fifteen years, particularly in the North American milieux that most shaped the articles in the present volume.

[73] Kaltmeier and Thies, "Spectres of Multiculturalism," 236.

an "identity politics" that operates along a logic of "cultural belonging and cultural difference, which both exist outside the traditional conceptualization of the political constitution of liberal democracies as egalitarian, neutral and universal."[74] In practice, then, it rests precariously on a "radical asymmetry of power" whereby the state and elite institutions are positioned as those that recognize and include (and thus appropriate and order) the speech and claims of traditionally oppressed, underrepresented, and/or marginal groups.[75]

Kaltmeier and Thies are interested in mapping out these tensions in relation to what they analyze, with Pierre Bourdieu's field theory, as the "field of identity politics" and its shifting dynamics of social power and cultural capital in national and transnational spheres. For our purposes, however, their insights prove helpful inasmuch as they highlight some of the tensions within multiculturalism that are masked precisely by its dominant approach to difference – that is, its celebratory rhetoric of "diversity."

During the decades in which the essays reprinted in the present volume first took form, North American forms of multiculturalism were perhaps especially embedded within elite universities, together with this particular grammar of difference, which emphasizes representation and inclusion. Among the many positive effects on historical research – as noted above – was a push to rediscover "diversity" within the past, including within the histories of Judaism and Christianity.[76] Scholarship in these areas, in fact, may have especially benefited: both had been deeply structured by theological categories and apologetic and confessional concerns during their long histories, and both were perhaps especially enlivened by the infusion of fresh questions, categories, and concerns – as well as the prospect of new points of relevance to the present, beyond the narrow bounds of the confirmation, caretakership, or critique of their respective religious traditions. Even on strictly historicist grounds, the results have been

---

[74] Kaltmeier and Thies, "Spectres of Multiculturalism," 2226.

[75] Kaltmeier and Thies, "Spectres of Multiculturalism," 225. I.e., "it includes actors not only from the macro and meso levels of social interaction, but also, and perhaps most particularly, from the subaltern margins and everyday life. Although there are undeniably processes of professionalization within the field of identity politics, which are produced by the formation of new elites in cultural production, social movements or institutional politics of identity, they could hardly function without the continuous discursive reintegration of the field through the bottom-up transfer of authenticity" (227–28).

[76] Perhaps telling in this regard is the reception of Walter Bauer's *Rechtgläubigkeit und Ketzerei im ältesten Christentum* (Tübingen: Mohr, 1934), which was published in the 1930s but did not have a serious impact on scholarship until three decades later – i.e., when renewed interest in rethinking Christian difference inspired the production of the 1964 revised German edition by Georg Strecker, a year-long Philadelphia Seminar on Christian Origins (PSCO) dedicated to the book in 1966–1967, and the resultant English translation by Robert A. Kraft and Gerhard A. Kroedel, published in 1971. On its reception and the settings in which the book came to inspire a "new paradigm," see e.g., Robert L. Wilken, "Diversity and Unity in Early Christianity," *Second Century* 1 (1981): 101–10, as well as my discussion in Chapter Three above.

highly productive. Multiculturalist rhetoric of "diversity" has provided a handy vocabulary to argue for more comprehensive attention to the full range of surviving and available data for Late Antiquity, not constrained by canons or limited to what present-day religious traditions deem authentic and authoritative. Insofar as research into even seemingly arcane sources could be readily defended with appeal to the recovery of past "diversity" (and arguments thus made in an accessible fashion for research grants, conferences, and the publication of books and editions), the positive and rippling results for the study of Jews and Christians in Late Antiquity have been substantial.

Like the amorphous interdisciplinary enthusiasm around "identity" discussed above, however, the dominance of this sort of multiculturalism has perhaps reached a limit. Within American political life, in particular, the mounting backlash against "identity politics" reached a crescendo in the wake of the 2016 election.[77] The recognition of ethnic and other differences have been increasingly reframed, not as an assumed positive (e. g., as telegraphed by the celebration of "diversity") but rather as a demographic or even ontological threat to what has been asserted as a core American identity – whether framed in terms of an ostensibly colorblind liberalism, as especially on the left, or in terms of a national character or heritage often connected, especially on the right, tacitly or explicitly with whiteness.[78]

The very naming of this whiteness marks a striking change in the dominant discursive practices of identification in the United States, which have long been predicated on the privileging of the white majority as those with the unique right to self-identify only by their individual features (e. g., not as a "white professor" but just as a "professor"; not as a "white woman" but just as a "woman").[79] Yet

---

[77] For analyses of multiple European cases of the power and limits of multiculturalism, as well as an attempt to chart some of the common logics of backlash, see Steven Vertovec and Susanne Wessendorf, eds., *Multiculturalism Backlash: European Discourses, Policies and Practices* (London: Routledge, 2010). Here and below, I focus on cultural shifts in North America because that is the setting in which the essays in the present volume were written, and I am attempting here to historicize and situate myself no less than I have others throughout this volume. The results of these shifts have clearly rippled beyond North America, but I leave it to others to discuss how and with what results, ideally also in relation to specific settings.

[78] Examples of the former include white liberal critiques of identity politics, e. g., Mark Lilla, *After Identity Politics* (New York: Harper, 2017). With respect to the latter, Jason Mellard, for instances, notes the recent "surge of an explicit white nationalism into mainstream political discourse" and contrasts it with earlier calls for attention to multiple white ethnicities: "white nationalists have proclaimed *white itself* as a cultural identity that again subsumes the historical nationalisms of Pole, Italian, Irish, and Czech … The alt-right instead argues that white men are simply another interest group, aggrieved and forgotten in a liberal order that caters to ethnic minorities and women"; "1973 Redux: Revisiting Michael Novak and Agnes Moreland Jackson on White Ethnicity and National Belonging," *Soundings* 100 (2017): 222–33, italics mine.

[79] This linkage of majoritarian power with neutrality is well put by Richard Dyer: "There is no more powerful position than that of being 'just' human. The claim to power is the claim to speak for the commonality of humanity. Raced people can't do that – they can only speak for

it is perhaps not accidental that the discursive locus of whiteness is moving from personal to collective identification in an era when demographic shifts are threatening the traditional status of white Americans as a numerical majority. Some of those who self-identify as white now point to their exclusion from multiculturalist understandings of "diversity" and interpret this exclusion as the erasure of their identity *as a group*, thus arguing for recognition and inclusion with much the same rhetoric used by (other) minorities (e. g., "white lives matter"). Such shifts point to the limits of multiculturalism as a set of practical and rhetorical strategies for defusing social tensions in a society marked by long histories of both white supremacy and ethnic heterogeneity. But they also expose something of multiculturalism's silent workings: to the degree to which it has tended to structure difference in terms of the increased inclusion of various minorities under a single canopy, its efficacy has been predicated on what is invisibly outside that structure – that is, the benevolent gaze of a white *qua* neutral majority and a stable sense of an empowered white subject as assumed speaker, arbiter, and consumer of "diversity."[80]

The social, cultural, and political consequences remain unclear and fall well outside the bounds of the present inquiry. But what is interesting, for our purposes, is how such shifts have also made visible some of the structuring grammar and defining tensions of contemporary discourses about difference, more generally – and as such, may help us to rethink some of what has been taken for granted in much recent scholarship on early Jewish, Christian, and "Jewish-Christian" identities as well. As much as our historical scholarship has drawn profitably from the contemporary rhetoric of "diversity" and multiculturalism's social logic of inclusion, it might be an apt moment to stop and consider what this rhetoric and logic also mask and hide.[81]

---

their race"; "The Matter of Whiteness," in *White Privilege: Essential Readings on the Other Side of Racism*, ed. Paula Rothberg (2nd edition; New York: Worth Publishing, 2005), 10. That the 2016 election marked a shift in the discourse of whiteness in the American public sphere was widely noted even immediately in its wake; see, e. g., Laila Lalami, "The Identity Politics of Whiteness," *New York Times*, November 21, 2016; Toni Morrison, "Mourning for Whiteness," *The New Yorker*, November 21, 2016.

[80] On which see already Hazel V. Carby, "The Multicultural Wars," *Radical History Review* 54 (1992): 7–18. Notably, this may help to explain a pattern that bell hooks notes, i. e., "how amazed and angry white liberals become when attention is drawn to their whiteness"; *Black Looks: Race and Representation* (Boston: South End Press, 1992), 167.

[81] I here ask this question from an intellectual standpoint, but it can asked from a political standpoint as well. In Carby's prescient essay, for instance, her main point is less about academic discourse than about the political consequences: "Is the emphasis on cultural diversity making invisible the politics of race in this increasingly segregated nation, and is the language of cultural diversity a convenient substitute for the political action needed to desegregate?" ("Multicultural Wars," 13). Yet she does not isolate academic practice from the rest of public life – here asking, for instance, "at what point do theories of 'difference,' as they inform academic practices, become totally compatible with – rather than a threat to – the rigid frameworks of segregation and ghettoization at work throughout our society?" (12). Likewise, in a

Already in the 1990s, Hazel Carby noted how multiculturalism's "theoretical paradigm of difference is obsessed with the construction of identities rather than relations of power and domination, and in practice, concentrates on the effect of this difference on a (white) norm."[82] Accordingly, she suggested that "it is important to think about the invention of the category of whiteness as well as of blackness and, consequently, to make visible what is rendered invisible when viewed as the normative state of existence: the (white) point in space from which we tend to identity difference."[83]

Since then, this insight has been further honed and developed by critical race theorists who have critiqued multiculturalism from the left – including its effects on academic approaches to alterity. Frank B. Wilderson III, for instance, observes how "in sharp contrast to the late 1960s and early 1970s, we now live in a political, academic, and cinematic milieu which stresses 'diversity,' 'unity,' 'civic participation,' 'hybridity,' 'access,' and 'contribution'" to a degree that has largely served to domesticate "the radical fringe of political action" such that it "amounts to little more than a passionate dream of civil reform and social stability."[84] In conversation with Saidiya V. Hartman, Wilderson thus also lambasts the "sort of social sciences" that "is a kind of multiculturalism that assumes we all have analogous identities that can be put into a basket of stories … [that] can lead to similar interests."[85]

Multiple different stories and identities may appear to be embraced in their inclusion in a celebratory "diversity," but – as bell hooks cautioned already in the

---

pedagogical vein, she worries that "for white middle-class students in universities, these texts [of the multicultural curriculum] are becoming a way of gaining knowledge of the 'other': a knowledge that appears to satisfy and replace the desire to challenge exciting frameworks of segregation" (17).

[82] Carby, "Multicultural Wars," 12. See further now Sara Ahmed, "Declarations of Whiteness: The Non-Performativity of Anti-Racism," *Borderlands* 3 (2004); George Yancy, *Look, A White!: Philosophical Essays on Whiteness* (Philadelphia: Temple University Press, 2012) – both stressing, in different ways, how the invisibility of whiteness raises the question of invisible *to whom*, thereby pointing to black and other nonwhite perspectives as necessary for illumining the workings of whiteness. This is a "parade example" of the sort of critical difference in positionalities noted below.

[83] Carby, "Multicultural Wars," 12. In this sense, the liberal multiculturalism of a postmodern age might appear to counter the Eurocentrism of the Enlightenment, but it also functions to naturalize some of its base assumptions about power and knowledge.

[84] Frank B. Wilderson III, *Red, White, & Black: Cinema and the Structure of U.S. Antagonisms* (Durham: Duke University Press, 2010). Notably, Wilderson's critique of multiculturalism and white liberalism are far more scathing – and far more structurally and epistemologically destabilizing for academe – than these quotations convey.

[85] S. V. Hartman and F. B. Wilderson III, "The Position of the Unthought," *Qui Parle* 13 (2003): 183–201 at 184. Hartman thus also critiques "the kind of social revisionist history undertaken by many leftists in the 1970s, who were trying to locate the agency of dominated groups, resulted in celebratory narratives of the oppressed" (184); what she seeks, rather, is a manner of talking about racial difference that can be "about more than the desire for inclusion within the limited set of possibility that the national project provides" (184).

late 1980s – only to the degree to which "we are rewritten. We are 'other.'"[86] In her classic essay "Choosing the Margin as a Space for Radical Openness," hooks observes how "often this speech about the 'other' is also a mask, an oppressive talk hiding gaps, absences, that space where our words would be if we were speaking":

> Often this speech about the "other" annihilates, erases. No need to hear your voice when I can talk about you better than you can speak about yourself. ... I am still author, authority. I am still the colonizer, the speaking subject and you are now at the center of my talk.[87]

In response, hooks offers an intervention that consists not merely of "talking about the 'other'" or "even describing how important it is to be able to speak about difference" but rather of the challenge of embracing a perspectival shift, whereby one cedes the presumed right to speak for the "Other" and to rewrite their experiences in terms that make sense from the center.

At first sight, such discussions might seem irrelevant to historical scholarship on Judaism and Christianity. But just as our scholarly approaches to identity and difference have been so profitably seeded and cultivated by the multiculturalism of recent times, so we may perhaps also learn from attending to its present fissures and heeding its critics. All the more so – I would suggest – because it has been quite common in recent research on Jews and Christians in Late Antiquity *both* to use the celebratory rhetoric of "diversity" *and* to do so in a manner that presumes that there were "analogous identities that can be put into a basket of stories."[88] Too often we have done so, moreover, by virtue of a "theoretical paradigm of difference ... obsessed with the construction of identities rather than relations of power and domination."[89]

In a recent essay on ancient and modern approaches to inner-Christian difference, for instance, Karen King observes that "it is now a recognized commonplace in the field of ancient Christian historiography to speak of 'the diversity of early Christianity' and to characterize that diversity in terms of 'varieties' or even multiple 'Christianities.'" King marvels, in fact, at the "relative equanimity with which such characterizations are so widely embraced among academic scholars of otherwise quite different ideological persuasions and theological commitments."[90] In most of this research, moreover, such an approach to difference is simply presumed, and scholarly efforts thus focus instead on including, defining, and mapping the varieties therein: hence, as King notes, "scholars

---

[86] bell hooks, "Choosing the Margin as a Space for Radical Openness," *Framework* 36 (1989): 15–23 at 22–23.

[87] hooks, "Choosing the Margins," 22.

[88] I.e., as Wilderson notes for multiculturalism, on which see above.

[89] I.e., as Carby notes for multiculturalism, on which see above.

[90] King, "Factions," 216. For the Christian theological aims that this rhetoric can serve, see King's discussion there.

speak readily of Pauline or Johannine Christianity, Jewish Christianity and Gnosticism, and debate the precise contours of such groups, their practices, beliefs, and histories."[91]

Yet, as King further shows, this model of difference goes against the grain of our sources. Today "'diversity' ... frequently appears in a politics which applauds distinctiveness and individuality," but "the extant literature indicates that early Christians formulated the issue of difference less in terms of 'variety' or 'diversity' than as a problem of factionalism."[92] To the degree this problem was theorized by late antique Christians, the most influential approach was the binary of "orthodoxy" and "heresy," which structures difference in normative terms as a contrast between truth and falsehood and which entails "exertions of power that exclude and silence, even as they articulate the meaning of self in the face of 'otherness.'"[93]

At first sight, the recent scholarly emphasis on "the diversity of early Christianity" might seem to resist this polemical discourse and to redescribe the data in neutral, nonnormative terms. In practice, however, heresiological approaches to difference have often become reinscribed within scholarship precisely through the creation of classificatory systems that attempt to chart this "diversity":

Phenomenological-typological classification is widely used to group early Christian literature into set types. Each type is generally established by grouping a set of material together based on a limited number of similar features, describing their common essential characteristics, and then differentiating the resultant type from other types derived by the same means. This kind of method produced what became more or less standard conventions to characterize early Christian diversity. Divisions into basic types, such as Jewish, Gentile, or Hellenistic Christianity, Apocalypticism, or early Catholicism (e. g., "universalizing" Christianity), sometimes contrasted with their "excesses" in Ebionism, Gnosticism (Sethianism, Valentinianism, Marcionism), or Montanism pervade discussions of the varieties of early Christianity.[94]

Such scholarly practices of typology, taxonomy, and classification are framed as a neutral and objective alternative to the normative and polemical discourse of these late antique Christians. King, however, makes the case that this line of modern scholarship nevertheless mirrors elements of late antique Christian heresiological discourse. It is not just that it necessarily draws much data from the heresiological writings by Irenaeus, Epiphanius, et al.; it also coins new categorical terms that reinscribe the binary logic therein, distinguishing between groups that are mainstream and marginal, between "proto-orthodox" and "lost Christianities" and the like. King thus shows how – in practice – "the terms to

---

[91] King, "Factions," 216.

[92] King, "Factions," 217–18.

[93] King, "Factions," 218.

[94] King, "Factions," 218.

describe early Christian diversity often fit all too neatly into the old bifurcating frame … even if there is no apparent interest in setting normative boundaries."[95]

King here highlights a common pattern in scholarship on "the diversity of early Christianity" whereby "many historians – and even critics of normative identity projects ('orthodoxies') can fall into oppositional strategies that merely reproduce the terms of the problem as defined by ancient polemics."[96] I find her argument both convincing and compelling.[97] To her point, however, I would add that if these two seemingly conflicting discourses of difference so readily dovetail, it is perhaps because they share a grammar of difference. The temptation to slip into "the old bifurcating frame" is perhaps not accidental but rather reflects what our contemporary notions of "diversity" have in common with late antique Christian heresiology: in both cases, difference is reduced to a series of "analogous identities" that can be tidily sorted into a single taxonomic system, and what permits this classificatory move is precisely what stands invisibly yet necessarily outside of that system – namely, the gaze that is thereby authorized and naturalized as its neutral and objective arbiter.[98]

In the case of multiculturalist discourses about difference as "diversity" in the United States, the ostensible neutrality of this gaze is predicated on what Richard Dyer has described as "the invisibility of whiteness as a racial position in white (which is to say dominant) discourse," which has enabled whites "not to be represented to themselves as whites but as people."[99] If "whiteness never has to speak its name, never has to acknowledge its role as an organizing prin-

---

[95] King, "Factions," 221–22.

[96] King, "Factions," 220.

[97] Whereas I here focus on how King's insights can help us expose theories of difference that tacitly underlie much scholarly discussions of Jewish and Christian identities, it is notable that part of her concern is also with recovering the creative and ethical power of difference itself: "When the 'diversity of early Christianity' has become comfortable, it might be just the time to ask how we have managed to domesticate the salutary capacity of our differences to disturb complacencies, expose unseen complexities, or feed the possibilities of imaginative vision, and to wonder if we have whittled unsettling indeterminacies and provocations into convenient and comfortable tools that obfuscate or authorize rather than illumine or heal. It is here that properly historical methods can impose a profitable discipline upon the imagination that, at its best, grounds thinking and acting more firmly in grim and gracious reality, with all its unsettling truths, instabilities, and grief-laden limitations"; King, "Factions," 230–31.

[98] I focus here on the white gaze that brings coherence to this particular system of ordering "Others" so as to highlight the somewhat parallel place of a Christian gaze in the heresiological systems of ordering "Others" that still shape and constrain modern scholarly discourse about the Jewish and Christian past. It might also be worth wondering about better ways of thinking about how alterity here functions too – perhaps, e. g., following Homi Bhabha's insight that "it is only by understanding the ambivalence and the antagonism of the desire of the Other that we can avoid the increasingly facile adoption of the notion of a homogenized Other for a celebratory, oppositional politics of the margins or minorities"; *The Location of Culture* (London: Routledge, 1994), 75.

[99] Dyer, "Matter of Whiteness," 11.

ciple in social and cultural relations" – as George Lipsitz similarly notes – it is because it largely functions as the "unmarked category against which difference is constructed."[100]

One might see something similar at play in late antique Christian heresiology: its particular grammar of difference presumes (and thereby elevates and authorizes and hides) a particular speaker.[101] Part of what is so powerful about its approach to difference is thus what it takes from Greek ethnography and Roman imperialism – that is, the projection of a very specific self into the position of ordering knowledge about "Others" and the claim to do so in a totalizing manner from which only this self is excluded – always subject, never object.[102] Hence, for Irenaeus, it is possible to chart Christian difference as multiplicity, even while positing the authentic apostolic tradition as a stable unity untouched by any such division, and for Epiphanius, it is possible to write a history of the proliferation of "heresies" even while positing Christian truth as standing wholly outside of time and history.[103]

The self-effacing efficacy of such strategic moves is perhaps part of the reason it has been so difficult for scholars to escape the pull of heresiology's orchestrating logics, even when we attempt to do so. When dealing with sects that our sources call "heretics," for instance, it is now conventional to counter this negative judgment. If scholars nevertheless often reinscribe the heresiological assumption that the act of classification suffices to explain such sects, however, it is perhaps – at least in part – because of an approach to difference akin to multiculturalism's social logic of inclusion: we are accustomed to thinking of a positive approach to difference as one in which more and more different identities can be added to the same overarching structure, but we sometimes do not notice how debate is thereby displaced away from that structure (and its workings vis-à-vis knowledge and/as power) and onto questions of how best to define or delineate this or that element therein, whether new elements are necessary to add, and so on.

What might be effaced by the fixation on attempting to narrow the best definition for a term like "Jewish-Christian," for instance, or debating whether this-or-

---

[100] George Lipsitz, *The Possessive Investment in Whiteness* (Philadelphia: Temple University Press, 2006).

[101] Carby notes, e.g., how "processes of racialization, when they are mentioned at all in multicultural debate, are discussed as if they were the sole concern of those particular groups perceived to be racialized subjects" ("Multicultural Wars," 12).

[102] For the power dynamics of classification in relation to Roman imperial power see Woolf, *Tales of the Barbarians*; T. Murphy, *Pliny the Elder's Natural History: The Empire in the Encyclopedia* (Oxford: Oxford University Press, 2004); J. König and T. Whitmarsh, ed., *Ordering Knowledge in the Roman Empire* (Cambridge: Cambridge University Press, 2007). For the connections with Christian heresiology see most extensively now Berzon, *Classifying Christians*.

[103] See further Berzon, *Classifying Christians*; J. Schott, "Heresiology as Universal History in Epiphanius's *Panarion*," *Zeitschrift für Antikes Christentum* 10 (2007): 546–63.

that sect or source fits therein? What might we learn by taking seriously, instead, just how different the religious landscape of Late Antiquity looks when viewed from the positions and perspectives articulated within "Jewish-Christian" sources, and how they might challenge and enrich our understandings of "Christianity," "Judaism," and "religion"? What might we see of those particular Christian approaches to difference that have been privileged as if neutral, and what might we see of those particular Jewish approaches to difference that have often been ignored as a result?

These are some of the questions that I have experimentally explored throughout this volume within the small crucible of the particular test case of "Jewish-Christianity." What I wonder, however, is whether the historiography of Judaism and Christianity might also profit more broadly from additional acts of reorientation. Above, I suggested that much could be gained if we shift our focus from discussing or delineating different *identities* to considering acts of *identification* and their agents. But we also might wish to take more seriously the different *positionings* of those acts, attempting to shift our own gaze to try to look upon the past from multiple different *perspectives* as well.[104]

The case of late antique Judaism and Christianity is actually a "parade example" of the differences that can be made precisely by different positionings. Much scholarly effort has been spent on the project of enumerating differences between Jews and Christians and speculating about which of these differences were supposedly so insurmountable that "Judaism" and "Christianity" could not but become separate "religions." In addition, as we have seen, much effort has also been spent puzzling over the so-called "Jewish-Christian" materials that undermine this project by drawing attention to the fact that Jewish criteria of who counts as a "Jew" (e. g., matrilineal descent, circumcision, Torah observance) do not overlap with Christian criteria of who counts as a "Christian" (e. g., belief in Jesus, baptism, proper Christology). Rather than bracketing the cases that point to the ease with which such identities could be simultaneous or complementary, it may be worth attending to the very fact that Patristic and Rabbinic sources configure "religious" affiliation in such different terms. What we might wish to take more seriously, in effect, is the possibility that we may not be dealing with "analogous identities" *per se* – or, at the very least, that our analysis may be skewed when we assume the commensurate character of what scholars today commonly sort and study as the identities attached to "religions."

---

[104] Or, as Bhabha puts it in a different but related context, an approach in which "what is interrogated is not simply the image of the person, but the discursive and disciplinary place from which questions of identity are strategically and institutionally posed"; *Location of Culture*, 68.

Before "Religion(s)"

Today, "Judaism" and "Christianity" are widely perceived as neutral, objective, and thus simply descriptive terms. Accordingly, it can be tempting to imagine Jewish/Christian differentiation as always and everywhere symmetrically mirrored, equal in agency, and on the same terms. This is the modern context, for instance, that makes possible a pat chiasm such as Eliezer Berkovitz's dictum that "Judaism is Judaism because it rejects Christianity, and Christianity is Christianity because it rejects Judaism."[105] But within late antique contexts – as we have seen – the very practice of sorting ideas and practices as "Jewish" or "Christian" is a *distinctively Christian* practice, unparalleled within Jewish sources.[106] To the degree that scholars engage in this practice without self-consciousness of other perspectives and possibilities, we thus risk unidirectionally imposing (certain) Christian regimes of knowledge and power onto those thereby sorted and labeled into what became an increasingly totalizing imperial Christian system of classification.

In the Introduction to this volume, I noted how the category "Jewish-Christianity" often functions in modern scholarship to cordon off those sources that cannot be readily sorted into this now-naturalized binary of "Judaism"/"Christianity." To this, we might add that such sources also point to the problems in imposing a single classification scheme uniformly across our premodern sources; in late antique context, this binary is far from neutral, and it is also not the only organizing principle at play. From the standpoint of Christian theological discourses that privilege Christology as the main criterion for "orthodoxy," for instance, a belief in Jesus as messiah may appear to be the line that marks where Judaism ends and Christianity begins.[107] From the standpoint of

---

[105] Eliezer Berkovitz, "Judaism in the Post-Christian Era" [1966], reprinted in *Disputation and Dialogue: Readings in the Jewish-Christian Encounter*, ed. Frank E. Talmage (New York: Ktav, 1975), 291.

[106] I do not mean to imply that Jewish sources have no engagement with Christian traditions, but rather that this engagement is not expressed through the categorical practice of labeling this or that (Christian and/or Jewish) group or idea as "Christian" vs. "Jewish." Even the dominant classificatory terms for error and difference that we find in Rabbinic literature (e.g., *minut*, *goyim*) leave Christianness notably unmarked – and certainly do not deploy it as *the* major point of contrast for Jewish self-definition in a manner akin to how Jewishness functions within Christian self-definition. Explicit polemics are relatively rare and tend to pinpoint Jesus rather than projecting a contrast with "Christianity" writ large. For examples of the range of engagement in Late Antiquity see footnote 7 above, and for medieval and modern examples see Ellen Haskell, *Mystical Resistance* (Oxford: Oxford University Press, 2016); Shaul Magid, *Hasidism Incarnate* (Stanford: Stanford University Press, 2014).

[107] So, e.g., Larry Hurtado, *Lord Jesus Christ: Devotion to Jesus in Earliest Christianity* (Grand Rapids: Eerdmans, 2005), but contrast now Daniel Boyarin, *The Jewish Gospels* (New York: New Press, 2012); Matthew V. Novenson, *The Grammar of Messianism: An Ancient Jewish Political Idiom and Its Users* (Oxford: Oxford University Press, 2016) – and see further discussion in Chapter Nine.

Rabbinic halakhah, however, belief in this-or-that Jewish messiah has no bearing whatsoever on a person's status vis-à-vis Jewishness and inclusion in the people Israel.[108] To describe this belief as if an objective boundary between "religions" is thus to impose a distinctively *Christian* notion of identity and difference upon Jewish and other sources.[109]

If we treat Jewishness and Christianness as "analogous identities," commensurate in shape and contrastive in character, this difference might seem puzzling, and the very existence of "Jewish-Christian" sources might appear paradoxical. But it might be more illuminating (and more interesting) to approach this seeming puzzle and this apparent paradox as an invitation to take positionality seriously – not least as a challenge to our usual assumptions about what "religions" are, how they relate to one another, and how to study them.

Across the discipline of Religious Studies, it is now commonplace to acknowledge that "religion" itself is a modern construct, for which there is no precise premodern counterpart. Its status as a modern neologism, in fact, has been so widely repeated that articles and books on the specific moment(s) and setting(s) of its invention have become virtually a subfield in their own right.[110] To this conversation, scholars of Late Antiquity have richly contributed both by confirming that the features of human practice and experience that we now cluster under the rubric "religion" were not readily separable in premodern times from politics, economics, law, "magic," "science," etc., and by excavating premodern literature to discover precedents for some elements in the eventual evolution of the modern notion. Many of my insights, both here and above, build upon these lines of critical self-reflection in Religious Studies as well as research on related acts of theorizing among late antique Jews, by scholars like Daniel Boyarin, and among late antique Christians, by scholars like Todd Berzon and

---

[108] One finds a partial exception in Maimonides, *Laws of Idolatry* 9:4, which defines Christianity as idolatry, which in turn is contrasted to Jewishness. On the intricacies of Maimonides' assessment of Christianity, however, see David Novak, *Jewish-Christian Dialogue* (Oxford: Oxford University Press, 1992), 57–67.

[109] See further Chapter Seven in this volume.

[110] W. C. Smith, *The Meaning and End of Religion* (New York: Macmillan, 1963); T. Asad, *Genealogies of Religion* (Baltimore: Johns Hopkins University Press, 1993); R. T. McCutcheon, *Manufacturing Religion* (New York: Oxford University Press, 1997); Smith, "Religion, Religions, Religious"; D. Dubuisson, *L'Occident et la religion: Mythes, science et idéologie* (Bruxelles: Editiones Complexe, 1998); B. Nongbri, *Before Religion: A history of a modern concept* (New Haven: Yale University Press, 2013); Barton and Boyarin, *Imagine No Religion*. For other examples see R. T. McCutcheon, "The Category 'Religion' in Recent Publications: Twenty Years Later," *Numen* 62 (2015): 119–41. I discuss the repetition that marks this discourse in "Partitioning 'Religion' and its 'Prehistories': Reflections on Categories, Narratives, and the Practice of Religious Studies," forthcoming; see also Aaron W. Hughes, "Haven't we been here before? Rehabilitating 'Religion' in light of Dubuisson's Critique," *Religion* 36 (2006): 127–31 at 128–29.

Jeremy Schott.[111] A focus on "Jewish-Christianity," however, opens up some different lines of inquiry, oriented less toward the question of the prehistory and invention of our concept of "religion" and more toward the question of what has been omitted as a result – and how such omissions, moreover, might skew our understanding of Late Antiquity more broadly.

As with the term "Jewish-Christianity" itself, one might readily proclaim the concept of "religion" to be an anachronistically modern invention. We might wish to be wary, however, of the temptation to make such proclamations about "religion" while also continuing to discuss specific religions (e. g., "Judaism," "Christianity") as if self-evident and stable units from antiquity until today. This tendency mirrors what we noted above as Brubaker and Cooper's critique of the scholarly tendency to proclaim the fluidity and constructedness of "identity" even while reifying specific identities; here too, the contradiction may root in the blurring of scholarly terms of analysis with popular terms of practice. What they note there with respect to nations and races might be similarly said of religions:

One does not have to take a category inherent in the practice of nations – the realist, reifying conception of nations as real communities – and make this category central to the theory of nationalism. Nor does one have to use "race" as a category of analysis – which risks taking for granted that "race" exists – to understand and analyze social and political practices oriented to the presumed existence of putative "races."[112]

Elsewhere, Brubaker further develops this line of thought into a critique of what he terms "groupism" – that is, "the tendency to take discrete, sharply differentiated, internally homogenous and externally bounded groups as the basic constituents of social life, chief protagonists of social conflicts, and fundamental units of social analysis."[113] In relation to the study of ethnicity, race, and nationalism, he calls for "the development of a set of analytical resources for studying the *ways* ethnicity, race, and nation *work* in social, cultural, and political life without treating ethnic groups, races, or nations as substantial entities, or even taking such groups as units of analysis at all."[114] What might our analyses of what we now study as "religion" look like if we took a similar approach? And what might it mean further to resist "even taking such groups as units of analysis at all" in

---

[111] Schott, *Christianity, Empire*; Berzon, *Classifying Christians*; Daniel Boyarin, *Border Lines* (Divinations; Philadelphia: University of Pennsylvania Press, 2004).

[112] Brubaker and Cooper, "Beyond Identity," 6.

[113] Rogers Brubaker, "Ethnicity without Groups," *European Journal of Sociology* 43 (2002): 163–89 at 164. For a thoroughgoing attempt to apply this critique of "groupism" to late antique Christianity, see Éric Rebillard, *Christians and their Many Identities in Late Antiquity: North Africa, 200–450 CE* (Ithaca: Cornell University Press, 2012). Notably, Rebillard there focuses on one element thereof not discussed here, namely, the problem of the "internal plurality" of identification within the individual.

[114] Brubaker, "Ethnicity, Race," 28, italics mine.

the case of those times and places where the concept of "religion" is never or not yet a dominant frame for human experiences of community, piety, ritual, etc.?[115]

In my view, the case of "Jewish-Christianity" is particularly telling in this regard. It is impossible to understand the need for the category apart from the work that religion does in *modern* "social, cultural, and political life." But it may be quite possible (and quite interesting) to consider the *late antique* data categorized therein without taking "Judaism," "Christianity," or "religion" as our defining and constraining "units of analysis."

Throughout this volume, I have noted repeatedly how the very need for the term "Jewish-Christianity" stands as a reminder of the limits of our present notions of "Judaism" and "Christianity" to describe our premodern data pertaining to Jews and Christians. That "religion" is ultimately at stake in the modern category of "Jewish-Christianity" is clear when we compare its usage to the usage of two related terms: Ebionite and "Judaeo-Christian." The former is the term found in late antique heresiology that most closely corresponds to "Jewish-Christian" in the sense of describing a sect that combines Jewish and Christian features in ways that some Christians judge to be improper, thereby rendering them neither Jew nor Christian. In nineteenth-century research, "Ebionism" was thus often used where we might use "Jewish-Christianity" or interchangeably. To be sure, there are reasons not to use this term, not least because it is far from clear that any single sect produced all the material now clustered under the rubric "Jewish-Christianity." Yet insofar as "Jewish-Christian" is still often used in much the same manner, it may be telling that no specialists (at least to my knowledge) have suggested just eschewing the endless debate over how best to define "Jewish-Christianity" and just using "Ebionite" instead. What's at stake in this category for modern scholarship is not mapping a point of inner-Christian difference, as for Epiphanius et al., but rather drawing a border between "Judaism" and "Christianity."

---

[115] I do not mean here to narrow the options as much as to raise questions in the hopes of hearing from others and proceeding in conversation and collaboration. What I personally see as some possibilities, however, include a local focus (on which see Chapter Two and below) and/or a focus on the movement of traditions in space or time within *and* across what we are accustomed to distinguish as "religions." For a focus on movement in space, one good model is Indian Ocean Studies (e.g., Markus P. M. Vink, "Indian Ocean Studies and the 'New Thalassology,'" *Journal of Global History* 2 [2007]: 41–62), and one useful source of theoretical grounding is Histoire Croisée (e.g., Michael Werner and Bénédicte Zimmerman, eds., *De la Comparison à l'histoire croisée* [Paris: Seuil, 2004]; Werner and Zimmerman, "Beyond Comparison: Histoire Croisée and the Challenge of Reflexivity," *HT* 45 [2006]: 30–50; Annette Yoshiko Reed, "Beyond the Land of Nod: Syriac Images of Asia and the Historiography of 'the West,'" *History of Religions* 49 (2009): 48–87; Paul C. Dilley, "Religious Intercrossing in Late Antique Eurasia: Loss, Corruption, and Canon Formation," *Journal of World History* 24 [2013]: 25–70). For movement in time, Reception Studies, Book History, and Manuscript Studies are among the vital options; see, e.g., Brennan Breed, *Nomadic Text: A Theory of Biblical Reception History* (Bloomington: Indiana University Press, 2014); Eva Mroczek, *The Literary Imagination in Jewish Antiquity* (Oxford: Oxford University Press, 2016).

The work that this modern hybrid does is to make a buffer precisely to hide the overlaps resulting from the lack of symmetry and commensurability between Jewish and Christian approaches to identity and difference. The ways that this is done become clear when we compare another modern hybrid term that sounds similar but functions quite differently – namely, "Judaeo-Christian." In some senses, "Judaeo-Christian" does the opposite work as "Jewish-Christian": it serves to hail what is normative rather than mark what is marginal *qua* "heretical," and it evokes a shared present rather than the lost past.

In some nineteenth- and early twentieth-century Anglophone scholarship, "Judaeo-Christianity" was sometimes used where we now use "Jewish-Christianity" – on analogy with the Francophone use of *Judéo-christianisme* and hence with reference to ancient expressions of Christianity's originary Jewishness. This practice has largely been discontinued, however, in part because "Judaeo-Christian" has come to mean something quite different in North America. Since the 1950s, the term has been used to telegraph those commonalities between Judaism and Christianity that are said to underpin American culture, in particular, and it has appeared in such prominent public settings as US presidential speeches.[116] When used in this sense and these settings, the adjective tends to modify words like "tradition," "culture," "civilization," "ethics," "morals," or even "the West" – but rarely "religion."[117] On that front – as Shaul Magid notes – the hyphen does as much to divide as to unify and may ultimately be "more illustrative of anxiety, or difference, than comradery ... a reiteration of the exceptionalism of both through the prism of the other."[118]

If "Jewish-Christian" evokes a past when the boundaries between two religions were not yet clear, "Judaeo-Christian" evokes a present in which the two retain some commonality, albeit firmly predicated on what is nevertheless maintained as their ultimate structural antagonism. "The Judaeo-Christian tradition" has been typically invoked in contrast to Communism and other specters of secularism. Nevertheless, it is often questioned or rejected precisely in those

---

[116] See further Mark Silk, "Notes on the Judeo-Christian Tradition in America," *American Quarterly* 36 (1984): 65–85. Early uses tended to focus on the threat of Communism; some, such as J. B. Matthews, went so far as to proclaim that "the international Communist conspiracy aims at the total obliteration of Judeo-Christian civilization"; "Reds and Our Churches" [1953], reprinted in *A Documentary History of Religion in America Since 1877*, ed. Edwin S. Gaustad and Mark A. Noll (Grand Rapids: Eerdmans, 2003), 486. More recent approaches include Steve Bannon's evocation of the "Judaeo-Christian West" in contrast to Islam and China – on which see Shaul Magid, "Jew, Christian, and the Judeo-Christian: Thinking with Cynthia Baker's Jew," in Reed and Magid, *Forum on Cynthia Baker's Jew*, http://marginalia.lareviewofbooks. org/jew-christian-judeo-christian-thinking-cynthia-bakers-jew/.

[117] Mario Cuomo, for instance, even took pains to emphasis that this commonality is anything but religious: "A Judeo-Christian moral tradition is not a Judeo-Christian religion. A moral tradition is part of a religion but by no means the whole of it; nor, especially in Christianity, is it the most important part"; *Documentary History*, 685.

[118] Magid, "Jew, Christian, and the Judeo-Christian."

cases where the claim of cultural or civilizational common ground might seem to challenge the assumption of the defining difference between Judaism and Christianity *as religions*.[119]

Perhaps tellingly, concerns of the latter sort have been expressed mostly from Jewish perspectives. Magid notes that Trude Weiss-Rosmarin's *Judaism and Christianity* in 1943 "may have been the first to argue 'Judaeo-Christian' was a form of erasure threatening the survival of *Judaism* in a society where the rights of *Jews* were legally assured"; in this, she presages Arthur Cohen who "viewed the American Judaeo-Christian tradition as a guise for the erasure of *Judaism* at the price of the survival of the *Jew*."[120] Such critiques make clear that "Judaeo-Christian tradition" is a rubric that makes sense only from within a Christian frame of reference: it marks and claims only those parts of Jewishness (e. g., monotheism, the Ten Commandments) that Christians deem unproblematically integrated into Christianity – with no threat of erasing any originary split with Judaism.

What is interesting, for our purposes, is what these three terms thus reveal about the cultural work done by the very notion of *religions* in relation to the relationship of Judaism and Christianity. In late antique Christian heresiology, the term "Ebionite" – as Daniel Boyarin, Andrew S. Jacobs, and others have noted – serves a function similar to our present-day term "Jewish-Christian" in invoking and constructing a heretical hybrid so as to assert two pure and otherwise separate entities (i. e., "Jew," "Christian").[121] Yet – I would add – what results from heresiological discourse about Ebionites are not two entities that are commensurate in the sense that we now think of "religions." If Ebionism is reduced to a Christian

---

[119] It is perhaps telling, e. g., that even arguments for "Judaeo-Christian culture" begin by acknowledging Jewish/Christian *religious* difference. Even while arguing that Jewish survival might hinge on the degree to which "the Gentile world comes to see in truer perspective the vital part the Jews constitute in the total pattern of Judaeo-Christian world culture," for instance, Carl Friedrich found it necessary to address such questions: "What justifies the expression Judaeo-Christian culture? Are not Judaism and Christianity fundamentally opposed to one another?"; "Anti-Semitism: Challenge to Christian Culture," in *Jews in a Gentile World*, ed. Isacque Graeber and Stewart Henderson Britt (New York: Macmillan, 1942), 7–8, cited after Silk, "Notes," 66.

[120] Magid, "Jew, Christian, and the Judeo-Christian," here engaging Trude Weiss-Rosmarin, *Judaism and Christianity: The Differences* (New York: Jewish Book Club, 1943), and Arthur A. Cohen, "The Myth of the Judeo-Christian Tradition," *Commentary*, 1 November 1969 (italics mine). Cohen here, in fact, begins by evoking the ancient points of contact between Judaism and Christianity as they contrast with what he presents as the reality of Jewish/Christian difference: "How can it be that Christianity, regarding itself the successor and completion of Judaism, should have elected to take into itself the body and substance of that Jewish teaching which it believed to be defective, which it regarded itself as having in measure rejected, in measure transformed, in measure repaired and fulfilled? How can it be that Judaism, the precedent in principle and progenitor in history of Christianity, should have remained not only independent of but unassimilated by the doctrinal vision and historical pressure of Christianity?"

[121] Boyarin, *Border Lines*, 207–14; Andrew S. Jacobs, *Epiphanius of Cyprus: A Cultural Biography of Late Antiquity* (Berkeley: University of California Press, 2016), 91–92.

"heresy" by Epiphanius, it is only because Judaism is too: both become named and told as part of genealogy of error in which *Ioudaismos* is positioned as exemplary of one pole of Christian error (i. e., with *Hellenismos* at the other).

At first sight, the modern neologism "Jewish-Christian" might appear to neutralize this asymmetry. Its limits, however, are exposed by the contrast with "Judaeo-Christian": if the "Jewish" of "Jewish-Christian" serves to mark those aspects of Jewishness that are deemed problematic when absorbed into Christianity (e. g., circumcision, Torah observance), the "Judaeo-" of "Judaeo-Christian" marks those deemed unproblematically Christian (e. g., monotheism, sexual and other ethics, the Tanakh/Old Testament); what the latter marks, in effect, are those elements of Christianity's originary Jewishness that were claimed as "Christian" in Late Antiquity with the rhetoric of supersessionism. Even as the discourse around both appears to be about two religions, its grammar of difference actually bifurcates one (i. e., Judaism) in the service of the self-understanding of the other (i. e., Christianity). In effect, then, both of these modern hybrid terms are anxious echoes of Christianity's own Jewishness and point to the limits of imagining this Jewishness as only a matter of Christianity's "origins."

Attention to these hybrids further points us to the problem with framing the relationship of Judaism and Christianity as if self-evidently a matter of the relationship between two religions – or, at least to the degree that "religions" are now commonly imagined to be completely separate entities of commensurate shape, potentially originating from one another but defined by their differences thereafter (e. g., as commonly imagined also for Hinduism and Buddhism). This, to my view, is also the base problem with analyzing late antique Jewish, Christian, *and* "Jewish-Christian" sources with "religions" as the main units of analysis. It is not simply that the concept of "religion" is anachronistic when applied to Late Antiquity (which is not necessarily a problem in its own right, depending on the purpose of the inquiry at hand). Rather, to approach this material only or mainly through the lens of questions about "Judaism" and "Christianity" is to risk reification, abstractification, and groupism of the sort noted above. Given the late antique Christian prehistory and modern European genealogy of our current notions of "religions," it is also to script the story of Jewish/Christian relations in a crypto-theological manner that frames Jewish/Christian difference in Christian terms and from a Christian perspective.

In the course of his methodological critique of "groupism," Brubaker calls for "distinguishing consistently between categories and groups" so as to be able to "ask about the degree of groupness associated with a particular category in a particular setting and about the political, social, cultural and psychological processes through which categories get invested with groupness" and also "ask how people – and organizations – *do* things with categories."[122] Such questions would

---

[122] Brubaker, "Ethnicity without Groups," 169.

be interesting to open up for Late Antiquity but are among what gets foreclosed when scholars read even early references to *Christianismos*, for instance, as evidence for what is clustered under our current understanding of "a religion" as combining a cohesive theological core, a socially separate community or set of communities, and a collective identity to which individuals affiliate in a manner that is both exclusive of other "religions" and central to their personal sense of self in a manner that trumps all other affiliations (e. g., ethnic, local, civic, political, philosophical).

If the groupism of modern assumptions about "religions" thus distracts from more fine-grained analysis of our evidence for late antique Christian identification and its effects, it is perhaps all the more skewing for their late antique Jewish counterparts. Studies of late antique "Judaism" and "Christianity" tend to treat these abstractions as the main "units of analysis" (to use Brubaker's terms), and it is typically assumed that the two are categories of the same sort. Both assumptions perhaps owe less to ancient polemics or late antique heresiology than to the system of categorization that undergirds the modern scholarly discipline of Religious Studies. Just as "religion" is defined in distinction from "science," "magic," politics, economics, and so on, "religions" are also assumed to be mutually-exclusive entities of similar shape and structure. In practice, moreover, they have been modeled foremost on Protestant Christianity, thereby privileging interiorized personal belief and theological doctrine while downplaying ritual, ethnicity, and law. "The modern concept of religion," as Leora Batnitzky reminds us, "is not a neutral or timeless category but instead a modern, European creation, and a Protestant one at that."[123] If this specificity is now invisible, moreover, it is largely because of a dynamic similar to what we noted above for late antique heresiology and contemporary American multiculturalism – that is, the presumption of the neutrality, universalism, and objectivity of the specific (in this case, modern European) perspective from which this particular system of theorizing difference is constructed.[124]

Scholars of Religious Studies have longed noted the deleterious effects upon the study of South and East Asian traditions.[125] But even as the modern European taxonomy of "religions" has a long prehistory in Christian reflection on Jews, the corollary "Judaism" has never neatly fit into the resultant system of categoriza-

---

[123] Leora Batnitzky, *How Judaism became a Religion* (Princeton: Princeton University Press, 2011), 1.

[124] Masuzawa, *Invention of World Religions*.

[125] E. g., L. M. Jensen, *Manufacturing Confucianism: Chinese Traditions & Universal Civilization* (Durham: Duke University Press, 1997); R. King, "Orientalism and The Modern Myth of 'Hinduism'," *Numen* 46 (1999) 146–86; N. J. Girardot, "Finding the Way: James Legge and the Victorian Invention of Taoism," *Religion* 29 (1999): 107–21; J. Ā. Josephson, "When Buddhism Became a 'Religion': Religion and Superstition in the Writings of Inoue Enryō," *Japanese Journal of Religious Studies* 33 (2006): 143–68; Josephson, *The Invention of Religion in Japan* (Chicago: University of Chicago Press, 2012).

tion either. This is not to suggest that there is no "groupness" to Jewry in a sense of a collective with social cohesion across time and space and a history that can be told:[126] it is only to resist its conflation with the category of "Judaism" as one of multiple non-overlapping components within a modern European Christian taxonomy of "religions."

Indeed, if anything, Jewish examples and perspectives have consistently served to expose the internal contradictions and epistemological limits of what purports to be a totalizing classificatory rubric – perhaps in the case of modern scholarship in Religious Studies no less than in the case of late antique Christian heresiology. Rabbinic narratives of difference, as Boyarin has shown, bear some parallels with Christian heresiology but ultimately resist "religion."[127] And, on some level, this situation might be said to hold up until modern times. Susannah Heschel makes a persuasive case, for instance, that the very notion of "Judaism" as a "religion" akin to "Christianity" is essentially a nineteenth-century invention:

Judaism as a religion is a modern invention, developed in mimicry of Christianity; pre-modern Jewish texts speak instead of Torah and mitzvot. "Judaism" was invented by nineteenth-century Protestant theological discourse as a religion of legalism, literalism, and an absence of morality, and was made to function discursively as the abject of the Christian West.[128]

To be sure, just as "Jew" eventually came to be appropriated as self-label, so "Judaism" and "religion" came to be productive categories within modern Jewish thought.[129] Nevertheless, if Heschel is correct, it remains that the construction of "Judaism" as "religion" is actually contemporaneous with what we have seen above as the modern invention of "Jewish-Christianity."[130] The dynamics of their interplay may be interesting to investigate further. For now, it suffices to note how the Jewishness both within and beyond Christianity resists easy reduction to "religion" – perhaps even in modern times, but certainly in Late Antiquity.

Such categories are so entrenched in our own culture that it can be difficult even to imagine excising them. How, then, might we investigate their patterns

---

[126] I.e., in Brubaker's sense of "group" as a "mutually interacting, mutually recognizing, mutually oriented, effectively communicating, bounded collectivity with a sense of solidarity, corporate identity and capacity for concerted action"; "Ethnicity without Groups," 169.

[127] Boyarin, *Border Lines*.

[128] Susannah Heschel, "Revolt of the Colonized: Abraham Geiger's *Wissenschaft des Judentums* as a Challenge to Christian Hegemony in the Academy," *New German Critique* 77 (1999): 61–85. See now Boyarin, *Judaism*, on early modern development presaging this move – especially with Martin Luther.

[129] Batnitzky, *How Judaism*, 1 – there making a case that "it is the clash between the modern category of religion and Judaism that gives rise to many of the creative tensions in modern Jewish thought."

[130] See Chapters Seven, Eight, and Eleven in this volume.

of similarity and differences that we find in our late antique sources? One avenue, as noted above, may be to reorient our analyses to think about Jewish and Christian positionalities; in this, we might begin by charting what we know of the different ways that our sources themselves theorize difference – ideally including "Jewish-Christian" options, so as to resist reinscribing a binary of Jewish/Christian difference, but also other sources from other perspectives, such as from Neoplatonists, Samaritans, and Manichees.

Another avenue may be to shift our units of analysis so as to avoid the pitfalls of groupism – and hence away from Judaism and Christianity. In this, it may be useful to follow the lead of recent research on inner-Christian difference that has resisted heresiological models, not least by showing how misleading it can be to treat different "varieties" of Christianity as if stable entities.[131] Contrary to what is typically assumed in the framing of questions about the "diversity of early Christianity," for instance, David Brakke reminds us that "no forms of Christianity that existed in the second and third centuries have survived intact today."[132] Accordingly, it does not suffice to identity "varieties" and ask which failed and which prevailed:

If we are to appreciate truly the diversity of early Christianity and not dissolve that diversity into a soup of hybridity, we still need to make distinctions among forms of Christian life. ... Our goal should be to see neither how a single Christianity expressed itself in diverse ways, nor how one group of Christians emerged as the winner in a struggle, but how multiple Christian identities and communities were continually created and transformed.[133]

In the above-noted essay, King builds upon Brakke's insight, cautioning about the degree to which "divisions into fixed types of early Christianity can function to script the narrative of church history as a battle or horse race between those who won and those who lost."[134] It is not the valuation of this or that type that is ultimately misleading, but rather the very framing in terms of types: "it is not that the orthodox won and the heretics lost (as their own rhetoric declares), but that what variously constitutes Christianity is always in the on-going process

---

[131] There is also an ample literature on inner-Jewish diversity – including recent debate about what has been taken for granted of this "diversity." I deal in more detail with that conversation, as well as different models of inner-Jewish difference, in A. Y. Reed, "Old Testament Pseudepigrapha and post-70 Judaism," in *Les Judaïsmes dans tous leurs etats aux Ier–IIIe siecles*, ed. S. C. Mimouni, B. Pouderon, and C. Clivas (Turnhout: Brepols, 2015), 117–48. For important methodological comments in relation to Jewish Studies more broadly see R. S. Boustan, O. Kosansky, and M. Rustow, eds., *Jewish Studies at the Crossroads of Anthropology and History: Authority, Diaspora, Tradition* (Philadelphia, University of Pennsylvania Press, 2011), 1–30.

[132] D. Brakke, *The Gnostics: Myth, Ritual, and Diversity in Early Christianity* (Cambridge, Mass., Harvard University Press, 2010), 136.

[133] Brakke, *Gnostics*, 15.

[134] King, "Factions," 222–23.

of formation, deformation, and reformation; constituted of the plural voices, practices, and possibilities of tradition past and present."[135]

It remains to be seen whether approaches of this sort can also be applied across the bounds of "religions" as well.[136] Perhaps profitable in this regard, however, is one of the suggestions that King makes about moving ahead. She suggests that "a particularly good approach to mapping differences in my view are studies which focus upon writing local histories of Christianity."[137] Throughout the present volume, our discussions of "Jewish-Christianity" have centered on third- and fourth-century Syria. We might wish to ask, however, whether instead of telling a story about "Jewish-Christianity" in which Syria is the main backdrop it might be possible (also or instead) to tell a story about late antique Syria in which "Jewish-Christian" sources are one element.[138]

---

[135] King, "Factions," 222–23.

[136] King herself addresses this question only indirectly in this essay – albeit precisely in reference to "Jewish-Christianity." She cites "Jewish-Christianity" as exemplary of how "typology has also been used to address problems for which it is not suited methodologically," noting how this category "bundles together what are quite distinct literary phenomena that point toward different histories, types of social formation, practices, and theological views" ("Factions," 223). In this context, she suggests that "while it is clear that ancient Christians defined themselves in a wide variety of ways with regard to (other) Jews and Judaism, and indeed that they defined 'Judaism' in various ways so as to make it into a entity usable for their own self-definition and boundary setting, to reduce such attempts into reified groups (Christians, Jews, Jewish Christians) is now widely recognized as highly problematic. Not only is the constructed character and rhetorical utility of all three of these categories obscured by naturalizing them as distinct social groups, but the complexity of social-intellectual strategies and the real practices and problematics on the ground can become oversimplified" (224). King concludes, however, by returning to the realm of inner-Christian differences, asserting that "it would be more accurate to speak of a variety of *Christian* positionalities than a single monolithic entity. Or rather I should say, than three monolithic entities, since the frequent division of earliest *Christianity* into Jewish Christianity (too much, too positive a relation to Judaism), Gnosticism (too little, too negative), and proto-orthodox Christianity (just right) also naturalizes the "proper" (i.e., historically dominant) solution to this problem – and it does so definitionally rather than by engaging the much more messy perspectives of the literature" (224; italics mine). In the process, she thus largely reinscribes the common tendency to treat "Jewish-Christianity" simply as a variety of Christianity. The challenge of extending her methodological insights in light of the discussions in the present volume, thus, is to be able to take Jewish positionalities into account here as well.

[137] King, "Factions," 223. Within Jewish Studies, this has been done most richly in the recent turn to explore the Sasanian context of the Talmud Bavli; see, e.g., Schäfer, *Jesus in the Talmud*; Yaakov Elman, "Middle Persian Culture and Babylonian Sages: Accommodation and Resistance in the Shaping of Rabbinic Legal Traditions" in *Cambridge Companion to Rabbinic Literature*, ed. Charlotte Fonrobert and Martin Jaffee (Cambridge: Cambridge University Press, 2006), 165–97; Richard Kalmin, *Jewish Babylonia between Persia and Roman Palestine* (Oxford: Oxford University Press, 2006); Shai Secunda, *The Iranian Talmud: Reading the Bavli in its Sasanian Context* (Philadelphia: University of Pennsylvania Press, 2014); Jason Mokhtarian, *Rabbis, Sorcerers, Kings, and Priests: The Culture of the Talmud in Ancient Iran* (Oakland, CA: University of California Press, 2015). On the methodological challenges posed by contextualizing without reifying Persianness or Jewishness see now Simcha Gross, "Haughty Rabbis: Reconsidering the place of the Babylonian Rabbis in their 'Iranian' Context," forthcoming in *JAJ*.

[138] See Chapter Two, Three, and Ten in this volume.

Interestingly, new insights into "Jewish-Christian" sources may be what enables such a tale to be told across the lines of "religions." Recently, for instance, F. Stanley Jones has offered a fresh reading of the *Book of Elchasai* "as an important witness to a possibly distinct brand of Christianity that developed beyond the eastern border of the empire." By his reading, the *Book of Elchasai* dates from 116–117 CE and is not a "strange aberration in early Christianity" or a "bizarre unicum" but rather "a founding document of early Syrian Christianity" and "chronologically the earliest identifiable witness to Christianity" in Mesopotamia.[139] If so, it is culturally proximate to Bardaisan of Edessa (154–222 CE), and closely linked in a chain of influence both with the Pseudo-Clementines (i.e., beginning with the Basic Writing, ca. 220 CE) and with Mani (ca. 216–274 CE).

Seen from the perspective of late antique Roman Syria, much of what modern scholars define as "Jewish-Christianity" is revealed not to be a single line with a trajectory of decline with dwindling influence after 70 CE. Rather, it centers on a cluster of sources that emerges from a vital conversation over a century later, when some Syrians sought to answer the "direct and aggressive assault on [their] understanding of Jewish heritage … from Marcionite Christianity."[140] Far from an archaizing perspective silenced by the success of Paul's Gentile mission, it reflects a textualization of tradition sparked "into defensive and creative activity" by the encroachment of Marcionism into Syria with its "denial of the creator god, of the goodness of creation, and of the goodness of marriage and childbearing."[141]

Jones stresses the need to read our evidence for Syro-Mesopotamia without "foist[ing] upon it a definition of Christianity that might have been applicable in other parts of the Roman empire."[142] And to his argument, we might add the importance of situating what has been compartmentalized as "Jewish-Christian" in relation to Jewish conversations about topics like the Torah, prophets, *minut*, and *goyim*,[143] but also in relation to "pagan" philosophical discussions about topics like prophecy, prediction, and the contrast between Greek and "barbarian" wisdom among Syrian Neoplatonists like Porphyry and Iamblichus.[144] If it is not clear that our reading of sources like the *Didascalia apostolorum* and Pseudo-Clementines benefits from compartmentalization under modern European definitions of "Jewish-Christianity," it is also not clear that it is entirely useful to cordon them off with the label "Christian."

---

[139] Jones, *Pseudoclementina*, 199, 434, 473.

[140] Jones, *Pseudoclementina*, 205.

[141] Jones, *Pseudoclementina*, 206.

[142] Cf. Jones, *Pseudoclementina*, 397

[143] See Chapters Five, Six, and Nine in this volume.

[144] See Chapters Two and Ten in this volume, and further now Jae Han, "Rethinking Prophecy in Late Antique Syria" (PhD dissertation, University of Pennsylvania, 2018) as well as Nathanael Andrade, *Syrian Identity in the Greco-Roman World* (Cambridge: Cambridge University Press, 2013).

If Jones is correct, "the history of how Jewish-Christians came to be heretics has not yet been fully written."[145] It is clearly misleading, however, to retroject that later marginalization back onto the Pseudo-Clementines, which are themselves – as we have seen – much more heresiological in stance than "heretical." The self-presentation embedded therein, moreover, pertains as much to Jewish identification as to Christian identification. To the degree that the *Homilies* writes the memory of the apostolic past, it does so in a manner that combines a commitment to the chosenness of Israel and the Oral Torah given to Moses on Mt. Sinai, with a conviction of Jesus' special role in enabling the salvation of non-Jews. As such, it does not reflect debates of the sort that we find discussed by Paul three centuries earlier. Rather, it resonates with Jewish and Christian responses to Marcionism in Roman Palestine, Syria, and Mesopotamia. The results form part of a continuum with translocal efforts to rethink Christianity's Jewishness at the cusp of the Christianization of the Roman Empire. Yet, at the same time, they stand in continuum with contemporaneous Jewish concerns for retheorizing the *Goy*. And they also engage and extend Jewish, Christian, and "pagan" concerns to rethink Greekness and Hellenism from the perspective of the Roman Near East. Their theorization of identity and difference, thus, is far from a fossilized relic of first-century debates that ostensibly concluded with Galatians and Acts. What it reflects, rather, is the creative ferment among Syrians in the late second and third centuries, as received and reshaped into the fourth and fifth.

Despite their apparent awareness of Rabbinic traditions and overlaps with Hekhalot traditions, the reception of such efforts among non-Christian Jews remains unknown. Yet the reception among later Christians is notable: the *Didascalia apostolorum* and John Chrysostom speak to varying degrees of local Syrian anxieties over the popularity of such approaches in the third and fourth centuries, and Epiphanius, writing in Roman Palestine, may attempt to marginalize them from the broader project of Christian identification via "guilt through association" with Ebionites.[146] It remains, however, that the Pseudo-Clementines themselves have a rich history of transmission and translation into the Middle Ages – far beyond the bounds of Roman Syria. To understand the context of their formation, it is useful to reorient our lens onto Late Antiquity away from what has been presumed to be a Roman center and onto what has been treated as a Syrian periphery. To focus on the local, however, is not to cordon off this one particular region as somehow "more Jewish" or "essentially Semitic," nor to limit our understanding of the relevance of its literary products. Such a focus, rather, can serve as an invitation also to see Late Antiquity from a different per-

---

[145] Jones, *Pseudoclementina*, 523.
[146] Jones, *Pseudoclementina*, 516–31.

spective, relativizing the traditional presumption of a Roman center, Western trajectory, and European *telos*.[147]

Looking Ahead

Writing of race in America, George Lipsitz stresses that "the significance of marginalized peoples to cultural studies does not lie in their marginality, but rather in the role that marginalization (not to mention oppression and suppression) plays in shaping intellectual and cultural categories that affect everyone."[148] Throughout this volume, I have tried to make a similar case for a certain set of marginalized texts, arguing that the sources traditionally studied under the rubric of "Jewish-Christianity" have much to tell us about Jews and Christians in Late Antiquity.

Too often, as King notes, "the 'varieties of Christianity' are deployed precisely to categorize, and thereby to sequester, contain, and control the plethora of undomesticated things people imagine, say and do."[149] Many of our sources, however, resist such modes of control:

With their multi-voiced diversity, ambiguities, and transgressive interconnections, the ancient texts constantly resist and spill across the boundaries that attempt to fix their meanings. They impossibly complicate neat categories and test assumptions.[150]

I have here suggested that "Jewish-Christian" sources are especially rich in such fascinating and challenging complication. And, accordingly, they may be especially profitable to plunder for understanding their own times and also for rethinking the modern categories and metanarratives that we often take for granted when studying Judaism and Christianity. New approaches to familiar sources are certainly illuminating, but perhaps only go so far.

To the degree that insights thereby garnered might be brought to bear on our understanding of Late Antiquity and "religion" more broadly, I hope that it is not just to add a footnote to the usual story of Christian Origins or even to invert the heroes and villains, winners and losers, of that well-worn tale. My aim, rather,

---

[147] Indeed – as Peter Brown reminds us – "the Christianity of what we now call Europe was only the westernmost variant of a far wider Christian world, whose center of gravity lay, rather, in the eastern Mediterranean and in the Middle East"; *The Rise of Western Christendom: Triumph and Diversity, A. D. 200–1000* (rev.ed.; Oxford: Blackwell, 2003), 2. Brown thus calls for a shift away from the notion of a single Roman center, and towards a concern for "a constellation of centers," each shaped by simultaneous impulses towards universalism and localization, and each in interaction with others through the exchange of goods and ideas (15–16). For more on this broader point with respect to Syria and Mesopotamia, see Reed, "Beyond the Land of Nod."

[148] Lipsitz, *Possessive Investment in Whiteness*, 180.

[149] King, "Factions," 234.

[150] King, "Factions," 234.

is to have shown something of the value of laboring to see the past through the lens of such marginalized sources. In the case of "Jewish-Christianity," the reorientation of centered locales, positions, and perspectives may be particularly useful for experimenting with fresh approaches to "identity" and difference in late antique Christian, late antique Jewish, and modern scholarly approaches to the Jewish past. Other marginalized sources may be useful on other fronts too.

Throughout this volume, I have emphasized the importance of historicizing modern scholarship no less than late antique literature, and within this Epilogue, in particular, I have also proposed the need for sharper attention both to different positionings and to specific locales. Accordingly, I have tried throughout this Epilogue to resist falling into the conventional tone and stance of theoretical and methodological reflections of this sort, which tend to totalize about scholarly trends in the present, even when calling for less generalizing about the past. I have thus self-consciously focused my comments upon those North American settings that shaped the articles reprinted in this volume – penned, as they were, from 2003 to 2017, during my time at Princeton University, McMaster University, and the University of Pennsylvania. In this, I have tried to take seriously the challenge of historicizing myself and reflecting upon my own positioning. For the present no less than the past, we can often get so accustomed to generalizing that it can be tempting to consider any emphasis on the situatedness of a dynamic to imply that it is less significant or influential (i. e., "*only* local"). I would suggest, however, that we might do well to resist the temptation to totalize on both fronts: like local trends in Late Antiquity, local trends in current scholarship are no less telling, influential, or constitutive for their locality, not least because of their exportation, spread, and transformation along the constellations of translocal networks of knowledge.

In this Epilogue, I have called for setting aside simplistic temporal models of Christian and Jewish self-definition, and I have suggested that it might be more profitable to shift from classifying identities to analyzing practices of identification with more fine-grained attention to specific agents, settings, power relations, and social ramifications. I have questioned the selectivity of a focus on "origins," and I have argued for attention to a broader range of late antique sources, attending especially to how some sources might theorize "identity" or categorize difference in ways that surprise or puzzle us. I have critiqued the conflation of groups and categories, especially with respect to how we habitually frame our inquiries in terms of "religion(s)." I have proposed that new theories about "identity" – as well as attention to shifting cultural circumstances – might aid us in bringing new questions to our sources, revealing elements therein that have been previously neglected. In addition, I have asked what might be gained by framing the questions that we bring to our late antique sources without "Judaism" and "Christianity" as our main units of analysis. Following King and Jones, I raised the possibility of locality as one possible focus to foreground. To this, we might also add the possibility of focusing on interactions and transmission of traditions across space (e. g., in a manner akin to how early modernists study transnationalism or trade networks) or across time (e. g., drawing upon interdisciplinary conversations such as Reception Studies, Memory Studies, Manuscript Studies, and the History of the Book).[151] To the degree that I have here sketched some possible paths ahead, however, my hope is not to narrow any options but rather to help spark further and broader conversations.

Both in and beyond North America, the past fifteen years have been a period with notable changes in the multiple subfields touched by the topic of the present volume – including but not limited to the exploration of the ramifications of earlier "paradigm shifts" like the rereading of New Testament sources as sources for Second Temple Judaism, the emergence of new critical approaches to Rabbinic literature, the rise of a line of theoretically sophisticated scholarship on Patristic literature, the renaissance of research on Hekhalot literature and the consequent diversification of sources consulted for late antique Judaism, and the intensified questioning of the core categories in Religious Studies and Jewish Studies alike. For moving ahead, it is hoped that our attention can go beyond the critique of the metanarratives of past research or their reversal into revisionist narratives, to inspire new conversations. As much has been learned from critiquing old models like the "Parting of the Ways," we might wish to strive now, also or instead, towards a more capacious vista onto Late Antiquity, heeding what Homi Bhabha reminds us of the limits and power of postmodernism:

If the interest in postmodernism is limited to a celebration of the fragmentation of the "grand narratives" of postenlightenment rationalism then, for all its intellectual excitement, it remains a profoundly parochial enterprise. The wider significance of the postmodern condition lies in the awareness that the epistemological "limits" of those ethnocentric ideas are also the enunciative boundaries of a range of other dissonant, even dissident histories and voices.[152]

To do so, in my view, is not to be set adrift, so much as to be freed to look anew to our literary and material sources – both familiar and neglected – so as to hear their own acts of theorizing "identity" and categorizing difference, heed the multiple perspectives that they reveal, glimpse the worlds that they see and make from their particular positionings, and attend to the creativity with which late antique authors rewrote their present with their past in ways that both dovetail and depart from our own.

---

[151] I discuss these further in Reed, "Beyond the Land of Nod"; Reed, *Fallen Angels and the History of Judaism and Christianity: The Reception of Enochic Literature* (Cambridge: Cambridge University Press, 2005); Reed, "Categorization, Collection, and the Construction of Continuity: *1 Enoch* and *3 Enoch* in and beyond 'Apocalypticism' and 'Mysticism,'" *MTSR* 29 (2017): 268–311. See further references also in note 114 above.

[152] Bhabha, *Location of Culture*, 6.

Timeline of Key Texts, Figures, and Events

ca. 67/68 CE	Traditional date of the death of the apostle Peter in Rome
ca. 68/75–116 CE	Life of Ignatius, bishop of Antioch
66–72 CE	First Jewish Revolt against Rome, culminating with the Roman destruction of the Second Temple in 70 CE
ca. 70–90 CE	Gospels of Mark, Matthew, Luke, and John, and the Book of Acts, now part of the New Testament
ca. 70–220 CE	Tannaitic period of Rabbinic history
ca. 85–160 CE	Life of Marcion
90 CE	Traditional date for so-called "Council" of Yavneh
ca. 90–99 CE	Traditional date for Clement of Rome's tenure as bishop of Rome
81–96 CE	*4 Ezra* (Palestine)
ca. 100 CE?	*Didache* (Palestine? Syria?)
second century	Proposed era for the formation of the *Testaments of the Twelve Patriarchs* (i.e., prior to Justin's *Dial.*), *Apocalypse of Peter* (i.e., in the wake of the Bar Kokhba Revolt), and *Protevangelium of James* (i.e., late second or early third), as well as for the possibly Syrian Jewish work behind *Homilies 4–6*
116–117 CE	F. Stanley Jones' suggested date for the *Book of Elchasai*
ca. 120–180 CE	Life of Tatian
132–135 CE	Bar Kokhba Revolt
fl. ca. 138–165 CE	Justin Martyr (b. Samaria; fl. Ephesus, Rome)
ca. 130–200 CE	Life of Irenaeus (b. Smyrna; fl. Lyons)
154–222 CE	Life of Bardaisan, a Syrian Christian whose teachings were recorded in *The Book of the Laws of the Countries*, which was used as a source both by Eusebius (esp. *Praep. ev.* 6.10) and the Pseudo-Clementines (esp. *Rec.* 9.19–29)
ca. 165–175 CE	fl. Hegesippus (b. Palestine?)
ca. 195–225 CE	fl. Tertullian (fl. North Africa)
ca. 200 CE	Date posited by F. Stanley Jones for the hypothetical source behind Ps.Clem. *Rec.* 1.27–72
ca. 200–250? CE	*Didascalia apostolorum* (Syria)
ca. 200–220 CE	Redaction of the Mishnah
ca. 203–254 CE	fl. Origen (fl. Alexandria, Caesaria)
ca. 216–274 CE	Life of Mani
218–222 CE	Reign of the Syrian Elagabalus as Roman emperor
ca. 220 CE	Date posited by F. Stanley Jones for the Pseudo-Clementine *Grundschrift*

ca. 220–500 CE	Amoraic period of Rabbinic history
ca. 220–350 CE	Redaction of the Tosefta
ca. 222–236 CE	fl. Hippolytus (fl. Rome)
ca. 230?	*Didascalia apostolorum*
ca. 232–305 CE	Life of Porphyry
ca. 240–325 CE	Life of Iamblichus
270–345 CE	Life of Aphrahat (fl. Mesopotamia)
ca. 290–312 CE	Commonly posited date range for first edition of Eusebius' *Ecclesiastical History* (books 1–7)
306–373 CE	Life of Ephrem
313 CE	Traditional date of so-called "Edict of Milan"
ca. 313–324 CE	Eusebius' *Praeparatio evangelica* and *Demonstratio evangelica*
ca. 320–324 CE	Pseudo-Clementine *Homilies*
325 CE	Council of Nicaea
325–380 CE	Range of dates commonly suggested for the Pseudo-Clementine *Recognitions*, which tends to be placed later than the *Homilies* and post-Nicaea
ca. 350–403 CE	fl. Epiphanius of Salamis; his heresiological opus *Panarion* (ca. 374–376 CE) mentions two otherwise non-extant sources used by the Ebionites, which may bear some connection to the Pseudo-Clementines: *Periodoi Petrou*, a Clementine pseudepigraphon about Peter (*Pan.* 30.15), and *Anabathmoi Jakobou* (*Pan.* 30.16)
ca. 360–420 CE	fl. Jerome (fl. Palestine)
ca. 380 CE	Proposed date for the *Apostolic Constitutions*
ca. 400? CE	Era of the redaction of the Talmud Yerushalmi and *Bereshit Rabbah* in Roman Palestine
406/407 CE	Date of Rufinus' translation of the Pseudo-Clementine *Recognitions* into Latin, which survives in approximately 115 manuscripts
411 CE	Date of British Museum Additional 12,150, the earliest manuscript preserving the Syriac version of the Pseudo-Clementines (cf. *Rec.* 1–4.1 + *Hom.* 10–12.24, 13–14.12); F. Stanley Jones suggests its origins in the School of Persians in Edessa
fifth/sixth century?	Approximate date of "E," a Greek epitome of Pseudo-Clementine *Homilies*. This epitome was revised in the tenth century by Symeon Metaphrases, resulting in a second epitome that scholars designate as "e"
early sixth century	Beginning of the era of the redaction of the Talmud Bavli in Sassanian Babylonia
587 CE	Date of another important manuscript of the Syriac version of the Pseudo-Clementines, British Museum Additional 14,609
857–886 CE	fl. Photius (Constantinople), whose comments on materials attributed to Clement of Rome in his *Library* seem based in knowledge of the *Recognition(s)*, *Homilies* (under the title *Klementia*, as in the manuscripts), and the Pseudo-Clementine epitome "E"
tenth century	Probable era of origin of Codex Parsinus gr. 930 ("P"), which preserves the Pseudo-Clementine *Homilies* (albeit breaking off in 19.14)

1504	First printing of Rufinus' Latin translation of the Pseudo-Clementine *Recognitions*, in Jacques Lefèvre d'Étaples' *Pro piorum recreations. Et in hoc opere contenta. Epistola ante indicem. Index contentorum. Ad lectores. Paradysus Heraclidis. Epistola Clementis. Recognitiones Petri apostoli. Complementum epistole Clementis. Epistola Anacleti* – an anthology that also features two letters from the *Decretales Pseudo-isidorianae*, including the *Epistle of Clement to James* (i.e., a letter typically prefaced instead to the *Homilies*). Consistent with the *Recognitions'* wide circulation in the Latin West, its second printing was soon thereafter (i.e., by Johannes Sichard in Basel in 1526)
1562–1564	Date of one of the two known Greek manuscripts containing the *Homilies*, Codex Vaticanus Ottobonianus gr. 443 ("O") – initially dated by Albertus R.M. Dressel to the fourteenth century but more recently shown by F. Stanley Jones to be later in date: written by Nikolaos Turrianos and others in Trient or Venice, this manuscript seems to have been owned and used by the Spanish Jesuit Hellenist Francisco Torres (a.k.a. Franciscus Turrianus; 1504–1584) long prior to its much-celebrated "discovery" by Dressel in 1837
1672	First printing of the *Homilies*, by virtue of the inclusion of this lesser-known version of the novel and associated letters in Codex Parsinus gr. 930 ("P") within Jean Baptiste Cotelier's collection of "Apostolic Fathers" (*SS. Patrum qui Temporibus Apostolicis floruerunt, Barnabae, Clementis, Hermae, Ignatii, Polycarpi opera edita et inedita, vera, et suppositicia; una cum Clementis, Ignatii, Polycarpi actis atque martyriis*) alongside the *Recognitions*, Epitome, and other materials associated with Clement of Rome
1718	Publication of John Toland's *Nazarenus, or Jewish, Gentile, and Mahometan Christianity*, which marks the earliest known attestation of the term "Jewish-Christianity" in the sense that the term is used today
1818	Publication of August Neander's *Genetische Entwickelung der vornehmsten gnostischen Systeme* (Berlin, 1818) – the first systematic treatment of *Gnosis*, but also the first extensive attempt to analyze the Pseudo-Clementines (esp. *Homilies*) as "Jewish Christian" sources – and to do so in relation to both Jewish and Christian literature (pp. 361–421); within Neander's overarching argument for categorizing all types of *Gnosis* as Jewish vs. anti-Jewish, the Pseudo-Clementines are adduced as an example of an anti-gnostic Jewish-Christian/Ebionite text that preserves information about the anti-Jewish gnosis to which Rabbis also respond. These ideas are also repeated within Neander's more synthetic surveys of church history, published from the 1830s to 1850s, and widely reprinted in both German and English translation for use as popular handbooks, etc.
1831	Publication of Ferdinand Christian Baur's seminal article on "Die Christuspartei in der korinthischen Gemeide, der Gegensatz des petrinischen and paulischen Christentums in der alten Kirche, der Apostel Petrus in Rom," which remains the most influential articulation of Baur's theory of apostolic history as marked by the struggle of Petrine "Jewish-Christianity" and Pauline "Gentile-Christianity" – often credited as marking the beginning of the modern discussion of "Jewish-Christianity"
1837	Date of Albertus R.M. Dressel's "discovery" of Codex Vaticanus Ottobonianus gr. 443, which preserves the Greek of the *Homilies* – which he soon after published, with Latin translation, in *Clementis Romani quae feruntur Homilae viginti nunc prinum integrae* (Göttingen, 1853)

1841	Discovery of manuscript containing Books 1 and 4–10 of Hippolytus' *Refutation of all Heresies* at Mount Athos (published by Emmanuel Miller under the title *Philosophumena* [Oxford: Clarendon, 1851] and originally attributed to Origen)
1846	Publication of Heinrich Graetz's dissertation, *Gnosticismus und Judenthum*, which is dedicated to Rabbi Samson Raphael Hirsch, builds especially on Neander, and includes a discussion of the Pseudo-Clementines that presages some of his description of Ebionites and "Jewish-Christians" in his famous historical writings
1853	First edition of Graetz, *Geschichte der Juden*, vol. 4: *Vom Untergange des jüdischen Staates bis zum Abschluss des Talmud* – which includes an extensive treatment of "Jewish-Christianity" (ch. 5), drawing especially on the Pseudo-Clementines and extending Neander's readings thereof no less than Baur's ideas about "parties"
1854	First edition of the *Didascalia apostolorum* published by Paul Anton Lagarde (i.e., *Didascalia apostolorum syriace* [Leipzig: Teubner, 1854])
1856	First edition of Graetz, *Geschichte der Juden*, vol. 3: *Von dem Tode Juda Makkabis bis zum Untergang des jüdischen Staates* – published without the chapter on Christian Origins due to concerns of the publisher about the controversial character of his claims about Jesus and Christianity
1861	First edition of the Syriac version of the Pseudo-Clementines published by Paul Anton Lagarde (i.e., *Clementis Romani Recognitiones Syriace* [Leipzig: F.A. Brokhaus, 1861]), consisting of transcriptions of both major manuscripts
1863	Second edition of the third volume of Graetz's *Geschichte der Juden* – which includes the chapter on Christian Origins omitted from the first edition
1867	Publication of English translations of the Pseudo-Clementine literature by Thomas Smith, Peter Peterson, and James Donaldson as part of Alexander Roberts and James Donaldson, eds., *Ante-Nicene Christian Library* (10 vols.; Edinburgh: T&T Clark, 1867). The *Recognitions* was published in Volume 3, together with works of Tatian and Theophilus. The translator's preface notes "the importance attached to these strange and curious documents by one school of theologicals" (3:137), quoting Adolf Hilgenfeld's assertion that "there is scarcely a single writing which is of so great importance for the history of Christianity in its first stage and which has already given such brilliant discourses at the hands of the most renowned critics in regard to the earliest history of the Christian Church as the writings ascribed to the Roman Clement, the *Recognitions* and *Homilies*" (*Die clementinischen Recognitionen und Homilien nach ihrem Ursprung und Inhalt dargetellt* [Leipzig: J.G. Schreiber, 1848], 1). The *Homilies*, together with the *Epistle of Peter to James*, *Contestation*, and *Epistle of Clement*, does not appear until Volume 17, where it is rendered alongside the *Apostolic Constitutions*. These translations are still widely used today by virtue of their reprinting in revised and rearranged form in the American *Ante-Nicene Fathers* series
1870	First edition of Graetz, *Geschichte der Juden*, vol. 11: *Vom Beginn der Mendelssohnschen Zeit (1760) bis in die Neueste Zeit (1848)* – which includes a reference to Neander, in context of 1840 Damascus Affair and the defense of Jews against charges of blood libel

1883	Publication of the only known complete manuscript of the *Didache* (Hierosolymitanus 54; 1056 CE), discovered in Constantinople by Philotheos Bryennios
1885	Publication of the first volume of Adolf von Harnack's *Lehrbuch der Dogmengeschichte* (Freiburg: Mohr Siebeck, 1885), which includes a complete dismissal – explicitly countering Ferdinand Christian Baur – of the relevance of both "Jewish-Christianity" and the Pseudo-Clementines for Christian history
1886	Reprinting of Pseudo-Clementine translations from Volumes 3 and 17 of the *Ante-Nicene Fathers Library* together in Volume 8 of the *Ante-Nicene Fathers* (Buffalo: The Christian Literature Company, 1886) – a project headed by Cleveland Cox, the Episcopal bishop of Western New York, reprinting and rearranging the texts printed by T&T Clark in the 1860s with his own comments interspersed (and apparently without permission, at least initially). Cox's introduction to Volume 8 explains that "the Apocryphal works of the Edinburgh collection have been here brought together" and frames this material as the work of "fraudulent imitators and corruptors" (p. v). Whereas the earlier version of the translation of the *Recognitions* was prefaced by comments by the translator explaining the place of the Pseudo-Clementines in specialist scholarship on Christian history, the American reprint includes an "Introductory Notice to the Pseudo-Clementine Literature" by M.B. Riddle, positing that "the entire literature is of Jewish-Christian, or Ebionitic, origin" (p. 69)
1890	Publication of a seminal article by Charles Biggs establishing the fourth-century Syrian provenance of the Pseudo-Clementine *Homilies*, on the basis of apparent familiarity with the Arian controversy and the occurrence of certain Syriac words therein ("The Clementine *Homilies*," in *Studia biblica et ecclesiastica*, vol. 2, ed. Samuel R. Driver, Thomas Killiam Cheyne, and W. Sanday [Oxford: Clarendon, 1890], 191–92, 368–69). The fourth-century provenance of the *Recognitions* was established soon after by Hans Waitz (see *Die Pseudoklementinen: Homilien und Rekognitionem: Eine quellenkritische Untersuchung* [TU 10.4; Leipzig: Hinrichs, 1904], 372)

Annotated Bibliography on "Jewish-Christianity"

"Jewish-Christianity" is a modern scholarly category. In nineteenth- and early twentieth-century scholarship, this and related terms (e. g., *Juden-Christentum*, Judéo-christianisme, Judaeo-Christianity) were popularized particularly in discussions of the apostolic Jerusalem Church led by Peter and James, the traditions about them preserved in the Pseudo-Clementine literature, and the Ebionites and Nazoraeans mentioned in Patristic catalogues of "heresies." To this day, most research on "Jewish-Christianity" continues along these same lines.

With the flowering of scholarship on Jewish/Christian relations after World War II, however, the topic has also attracted fresh interest. Special attention has been given to the possible place of "Jewish-Christians" as early agents or targets of anti-Jewish polemics, as well as to the fate of "Jewish-Christianity" and its consequences for the history of Jewish/Christian relations. In addition, the scope of materials brought to bear on the study of "Jewish-Christianity" has been expanded to include a varied range of archaeological, documentary, and literary data that might attest the combination of "Christian" beliefs with "Jewish" identity and practice – whether in direct continuity with the apostolic Jerusalem Church or in other expressions of Christianity's Jewish heritage. At the same time, increased attention to the Jewish cultural matrix of the Jesus movement and early Christianity has contributed to heated debates about the definition of "Jewish-Christianity" and its heurism as a category. More recently, evidence for "Jewish-Christianity" has played an important part in studies of Christianity's so-called "Parting of the Ways" with Judaism, and the topic has been richly discussed in relation to hybridity, heresiology, the dynamics of religious self-definition, and the challenges of constructing modern categories for the study of ancient identities. Although the study of "Jewish-Christianity" was traditionally a domain of New Testament Studies, it thus increasingly occurs at the intersection of multiple other subfields as well – including Patristics, Rabbinics, and Late Antiquity.

The following annotated bibliography is not meant as a comprehensive list of all published works on the topic.[1] Rather, I here compile a selection of major

---

[1] This bibliography is a revised version of Annette Yoshiko Reed, "Jewish Christianity," in *Oxford Bibliographies Online, Biblical Studies*, ed. Christopher Matthews (August 2011; http://www.oxfordbibliographies.com, DOI: 10.1093/OBO/9780195393361–0032), and it is reprinted here with permission from Oxford University Press. The online version includes links to

tools and influential, accessible, and representative studies, with the aim of providing a "roadmap" for navigating developments and debates that shape current specialist research on "Jewish-Christianity." Whereas much of the present volume focuses on literary evidence from Late Antiquity, the following bibliography thus encompasses a broader range of relevant textual as well as material data.

General Overviews

Scholarship on "Jewish-Christianity" is notorious for inspiring confusion, owing to both definitional issues and the complex, fragmented, and indirect character of the relevant ancient data. Clear introductions to the topic are thus invaluable for beginner and specialist alike. Among these, James Carleton Paget's 1999 survey article and Simon Claude Mimouni's 1998 monograph still provide the best starting points. For brief, up-to-date introductions to the topic in the wider context of Christian origins and early Jewish/Christian relations, see the below-listed articles by Stephen Wilson and Charlotte Fonrobert – both of which are also accessible enough to be useful for undergraduate teaching. Important introductions to the topic that focus on issues of methodological concern include two 1992 articles by John Gager and Alan Segal.[2] For an introduction to the broad range of potentially relevant data, see the below-listed volumes by Frédéric Manns and Simon Claude Mimouni.[3]

Manns, Frédéric. *Essais sur le Judéo-Christianisme.* Studium Franciscanum Biblicum Analecta 12. Jerusalem: Franciscan Printing Press, 1977.
    Collection of Mann's inquiries into New Testament, Patristic, Rabbinic, and archaeological data for "Jewish-Christianity," representative of the maximalist perspective associated with the Studium Franciscanum Biblicum in Jerusalem (see "Archaeological Evidence" below) and covering a broad range of potentially relevant sources.
Gager, John G. "Jews, Christians, and the Dangerous Ones in Between." In *Interpretation in Religion*, ed. Schlomo Biderman and Ben-Ami Scharfstein, 249–57. Philosophy and Religion 2. Leiden: Brill, 1992.
    Eloquent essay on "Jewish-Christians" as excluded from memory by the "winners of history" – the Jews and Christians who promoted views of their respective traditions as mutually exclusive, who shared their discomfort with those who felt otherwise, and who came to shape the notion of what is "orthodox" and "authentic" in each tradition.

---

electronic resources not reproduced here as well as listings of other tools and links to e-books. This version has been updated, revised, and restructured to fit the present volume, and it has also been extended further beyond the scope of Biblical Studies, e. g., to include a section on Islam. In addition, I have rearranged the bibliographical listings within each section chronologically rather than alphabetically.

[2] See also the works listed in the below section on "Debates over Definition."

[3] See also below section on "Collected Volumes."

Segal, Alan F. "Jewish Christianity." In *Eusebius, Christianity, and Judaism*, ed. Harold Attridge and Gohei Hata, 326–51. Studia Biblica 42. Detroit: Wayne State University Press, 1992.
> Chronological survey and assessment of literary and historical evidence for apostolic and post-apostolic "Jewish-Christianity," distinguished by its focus on primary sources, equal attention to New Testament (especially Pauline) and later (especially Rabbinic) sources, and clarity of prose and arrangement.

Wilson, Stephen G. "Jewish Christians and Gentile Judaizers." In *Related Strangers: Jews and Christians 70–170* CE, 143–68. Minneapolis: Fortress, 1995.
> Brief and accessible introduction to the sources, figures, groups, and issues traditionally studied under the rubric "Jewish-Christianity," drawing the common distinction from those called "Judaizers" (i. e., individual followers of Jesus from non-Jewish backgrounds with more occasional and selective adoption of Jewish practices).

Mimouni, Simon Claude. *Le judéo-christianisme ancien: Essais historiques*. Patrimoines. Paris: Cerf, 1998.
> This collection provides a representative selection of Mimouni's wide-ranging articles on "Jewish-Christianity." It also represents the most extensive recent survey of materials relevant to the topic (especially after 135 CE) and is recommended for both its comprehensiveness and its care in treating complex issues of interpretation.

Carleton Paget, James. "Jewish Christianity." In *The Cambridge History of Judaism*, vol. 3: *The Early Roman Period*, ed. William Horbury, W. D. Davies, and John Sturdy, 733–742. Cambridge: Cambridge University Press, 1999.
> A comprehensive, evenhanded, and widely cited survey of scholarship on "Jewish-Christianity," which includes an unusually lucid treatment of the problem of definition, particularly as debated in the second half of the twentieth century.

Fonrobert, Charlotte Elisheva. "Jewish Christians, Judaizers, and Christian Anti-Judaism." In *Late Ancient Christianity*, ed. Virginia Burrus, 234–54. A People's History of Christianity 2. Minneapolis: Fortress, 2005.
> Brief and accessible introduction to the topic, distinguished by methodological caution with regard to assumptions about ethnicity and by sophistication in treating notions of self-representation and communal identities. Here, as elsewhere, Fonrobert situates "Jewish-Christianity," etc., within the history of Judaism as well as within the history of Christianity.

Classic Works

Although interest in "Jewish-Christianity" arose already in the eighteenth century with John Toland, the modern study of the phenomenon is commonly traced to Ferdinand Christian Baur. Baur's classic 1831 article largely set the parameters for the study of Peter, James, and the Jerusalem Church in terms of "Jewish-Christianity" as well as popularizing the use of the Pseudo-Clementine literature as later witnesses to this same stream of tradition.[4] With the increased

---

[4] See below on "Early 'Jewish-Christianity'" and the "Pseudo-Clementine Literature" respectively.

interest in the history of Jewish/Christian relations in the wake of World War II, as inspired and inaugurated by Marcel Simon, "Jewish-Christianity" also became a key focus for considering Christianity's Jewish roots and eventual self-definition as distinct from Judaism. Hans Joachim Schoeps built on Baur to try to tell the full history of "Jewish-Christianity" from early apostles to late antique Ebionites, while Jean Daniélou sought to reconstruct its parallel "orthodox" history, particularly in relation to the development of Christian theology; the latter entailed expanding the definition of "Jewish-Christianity" to include *any* expression of early Christianity (i. e., prior to the second century) in Jewish "thought-forms." Critics of Simon and Schoeps raised questions concerning the fate of "Jewish-Christianity" and the continuity between its apostolic and post-apostolic varieties.[5] Daniélou's notion of Judéo-Christianisme became a focus for heated debates over the definition of the term and the delineation of the phenomenon and its sources. The relevant monographs by Schoeps and Daniélou were important catalysts for scholarly discussion of "Jewish-Christianity" *both* in the immediate wake of their publication *and* also, again, with their availability in English in the 1960s, which also saw the publication of the second edition of Simon's *Verus Israel*. At the same time, Georg Strecker's studies established the centrality of the Pseudo-Clementine literature for the study of "Jewish Christianity," especially through source-critical efforts to recover earlier sources therein. For other early and influential studies, the reader is referred to the helpful surveys of Bruce Malina and Frédéric Manns.

Baur, Ferdinand Christian. "Die Christuspartei in der korinthischen Gemeide, der Gegensatz des petrinischen and paulischen Christentums in der alten Kirche, der Apostel Petrus in Rom." *Tübinger Zeitschrift für Theologie* 4 (1831): 61–206.
Classic article applying the Hegelian dialectic to apostolic history, arguing that early Christianity was forged in the conflict between the "Jewish-Christian" party of Peter, James, and the Jerusalem Church, and the party of Paul and his Gentile mission; Baur is frequently (although not entirely accurately) credited with inaugurating the study of "Jewish-Christianity" as we now know it.

Simon, Marcel. *Verus Israel: Étude sur les relations entre Chrétiens et Juifs dans l'empire romain (135–425)*. Bibliothèque des Écoles Françaises d'Athènes et de Rome 166. Paris: de Boccard, 1948.
Work widely credited with marking the beginning of current scholarly discussion of early Jewish/Christian relations and serving as an important catalyst for scholarship on "Jewish-Christianity." Simon tackles questions concerning its definition, fate, diversity, and secondhand sources for it. The second edition (1964), which includes a postscript engaging Schoeps and Daniélou, forms the basis for the English translation by Henry McKeating: *Verus Israel: A Study of the Relations between Christians and Jews in the Roman Empire, AD 135–425* (London: Littman Library of Jewish Civilization, 1986).

---

[5] See below on "Post-Apostolic 'Jewish-Christianity.'"

Schoeps, Hans Joachim. *Theologie und Geschichte des Judenchristentums.* Tübingen: Mohr Siebeck, 1949.

Attempt to reconstruct a synthetic history of "Jewish-Christianity," as predicated on the posited connection between the Jerusalem Church and the Ebionites mentioned in Patristic literature. It has been critiqued for its assumption of the singularity of "Jewish-Christianity" and for its lack of sensitivity to the literary complexities of the sources.

Daniélou, Jean. *Théologie du Judéo-Christianisme.* Histoire des Doctrines Chrétiennes avant Nicée 1. Paris: Desclée, 1958.

Thoroughgoing attempt to reconstruct "Jewish-Christianity" as a theological system, based on first- and second-century materials deemed to stand in continuity with Jewish "thought-forms" (especially apocalyptic). Although widely critiqued, it remains a poignant demonstration of Christianity's debts to multiple forms of Second Temple Judaism. English translation by John A. Baker: *Theology of Jewish Christianity* (London: Darton, Longman & Todd, 1964).

Strecker, Georg. "On the Problem of Jewish Christianity" (1964). In Walter Bauer, *Orthodoxy and Heresy in Earliest Christianity*, ed. and trans. R.A. Kraft and G. Kroedel, 241–85. 2nd ed. Philadelphia: Fortress, 1971.

First published in German in 1964, this essay was added as an appendix to the second edition of Walter Bauer's seminal corrective on "orthodoxy" and "heresy," and it considers "Jewish-Christianity" from the perspective of the diversity of early Christianity; Strecker focuses on what he calls "legalistic Jewish Christianity situated in Greek-speaking Syria," for which he considers the *Didascalia apostolorum* and Patristic reports about the Ebionites as indirect evidence, and the *Kerygmata Petrou* (a hypothetical source of the hypothetical *Grundschrift* shared by the Pseudo-Clementine *Homilies* and *Recognitions*) as firsthand evidence.

Schoeps, Hans Joachim. *Jewish Christianity: Factional Disputes in the Early Church*, trans. D. Hare. Philadelphia: Fortress, 1969.

Revised English version of *Theologie und Geschichte des Judenchristentums*; a shorter and more accessible account.

Malina, Bruce J. "Jewish Christianity: A Select Bibliography." *Australian Journal of Biblical Archaeology* 2 (1972): 60–65.

Brief bibliography of influential early studies.

Manns, Frédéric. *Bibliographie du Judéo-Christanisme.* Studium Biblicum Franciscanum Analecta 13. Jerusalem: Franciscan Printing Press, 1979.

Extensive bibliography including almost two thousand entries, albeit with somewhat confusing arrangement. The work of scholars of the Studium Franciscanum Biblicum in Jerusalem is particularly well represented.[6]

Strecker, Georg. *Das Judenchristentum in den Pseudoklementinen.* TU 70. 2nd ed. Berlin: Akademie-Verlag, 1981.

The most comprehensive and detailed survey and analysis of the question of the "Jewish-Christianity" of the Pseudo-Clementine literature (see further below), especially as considered with the aim of source-critically recovering earlier sources therein.

Fiano, Emanuel. "The Construction of Ancient Jewish Christianity in the Twentieth Century: The Cases of Hans-Joachim Schoeps and Jean Daniélou." In *Patristic Studies in the Twenty-First Century: Proceedings of an International Conference to Mark the 50th*

---

[6] See below on "Archaeological Evidence."

Anniversary of the International Association of Patristic Studies, 279–97. Turnhout: Brepols, 2015.
Insightful reassessment of the classic works of Schoeps and Daniélou, reflecting on their continued relevance for the study of "Jewish-Christianity."

Collected Volumes

Research on "Jewish-Christianity" crosses multiple subfields (e. g., New Testament Studies, Jewish Studies, Patristics, Rabbinics, Church History, Late Antiquity) as well as national and linguistic boundaries. Accordingly, international colloquia and collected volumes have been especially important for advancing scholarship on the topic. Such volumes are also ideal as entry-points into current discussion. Jackson-McCabe's 2007 volume both surveys and advances research on "Jewish-Christianity," particularly in the context of Christian Origins, apostolic history, and New Testament literature, while Mimouni and Jones' 2001 volume and Tomson and Lambers-Petry's 2003 volume are critical to consult for up-to-date and incisive assessments of post-apostolic texts and figures – including late antique, medieval, and even contemporary movements. Jones' 2012 volume is an intervention into the history of scholarship on the topic, which has tended to begin with Baur and thus to neglect the rich early modern discussion. Although Skarsaune and Hvalvik's 2007 volume has been critiqued for its lack of engagement with recent theoretical debates and definitional discussions, it has a broad scope and includes some important pieces as well as some useful surveys of potentially relevant data.

Mimouni, Simon Claude, and F. Stanley Jones, eds. *Le Judéo-Christianisme dans tous ses états*. Paris: Cerf, 2001.
Collection of twenty-two specialist articles in French and English, based on papers delivered at a 1998 conference in Jerusalem. This volume gathers experts in the full range of relevant subfields – including apostolic and post-apostolic "Jewish-Christianity," as well as New Testament literature, Palestinian archaeology, Rabbinic literature, and contemporary messianic Judaism.

Tomson, Peter J., and Doris Lambers-Petry, eds. *The Image of the Judaeo-Christians in Ancient Jewish and Christian Literature*. WUNT 158. Tübingen: Mohr Siebeck, 2003.
Collection of sixteen specialist articles in English, German, and French, based on papers delivered at a 2001 colloquium at the Institutum Iudaicum of Belgium. The focus is on post-apostolic "Jewish-Christianity," including analyses of Patristic, Rabbinic, "gnostic," Pseudo-Clementine, and archaeological materials, as well as articles on contemporary messianic Judaism and Christian missions to Jews.

Skarsaune, Oskar, and Reidar Hvalvik, eds. *Jewish Believers in Jesus: The Early Centuries*. Peabody, MA: Hendrickson, 2007.
Wide-ranging surveys of figures and groups commonly associated with "Jewish-Christianity," framed in terms of an attempt to recover the history of ethnic Jews with faith commitments to Jesus (Torah-observant and otherwise) in continuity with

present-day missionizing concerns. Although it has been critiqued for its unevenness, particularly in relation to methodological problems and lack of engagement with recent scholarship, it includes some important pieces.

Jackson-McCabe, Matt, ed. *Jewish Christianity Reconsidered: Rethinking Ancient Groups and Texts*. Minneapolis: Fortress, 2007.

Collected volume distinguished by its methodological sophistication, with the editor's introduction and subsequent articles pushing questions of definition, interpretation, and methodology in new directions. It focuses mainly on apostolic history (Jerusalem Church, Paul and his opponents) and New Testament materials ("Q," Gospel of Matthew, Gospel of John, Letter of James), but also includes important articles on later materials.

Jones, F. Stanley, ed. *The Rediscovery of Jewish Christianity: From Toland to Baur.* History of Biblical Studies 5. Atlanta: Society of Biblical Literature, 2012.

Collection of seven essays based on presentations in the Society of Biblical Literature "Jewish-Christianity/Christian Judaism" Section revisiting the question of the previous origins of the modern category of "Jewish-Christianity," looking to scholars before Baur, and revealing a fascinating and forgotten lineage of thought leading back to the eighteenth-century freethinker John Toland; the volume also includes a reprint of the relevant sections of Toland's 1718 *Nazarenus*.

Debates over Definition

One's definition of "Jewish-Christianity" will depend on how one defines "Jewish," "Christian," and the relationship between them. Accordingly, debates over the scope and delineation of the category have been a particularly fruitful arena for interrogating broader scholarly assumptions about the historiography of Christian self-definition in relation to Jews and Judaism. If one places the origins of Christianity within Judaism, how is "Jewish-Christianity" distinct from any other form of Christianity during the early period? When does this early period come to a close, and what does it mean for a work or group to be "Jewish-Christian" thereafter? And, in light of the diversity of both ancient Judaism and ancient Christianity – as Bob Kraft has stressed – is it reasonable to assume only a single "Jewish-Christianity" with a single theology and history? Can the term be used in a manner that reflects the fluidity, subjectivity, and local variation of Jewish and Christian self-definition, specifically, and religious identity formation, more generally? Or is the category so problematic that it should be abandoned or replaced, as Joan Taylor and Daniel Boyarin suggest? Despite active discussion of such questions, particularly since the 1970s, no consensus has been reached. Nevertheless, the issue of definition continues to be debated in fruitful and illuminating fashion. For the full history of the definitional discussion, see the below-listed essays by Carsten Colpe and James Carleton Paget.

Simon, Marcel. "Problèmes du judéo-christianisme." In *Aspects du Judéo-Christianisme: Colloque de Strasbourg, 23–25 avril 1964*, 1–18. Paris: Presse Universitaires de France, 1965.

Exploration of the problem of definition, extending and tightening earlier comments in his classic monograph *Verus Israel* (see above) and stressing the importance of practice as a criterion.

Kraft, Robert A. "In Search of 'Jewish Christianity' and Its 'Theology': Problems of Definition and Methodology." *RSR* 60 (1972): 81–96.

Influential discussion of the array of issues involved in isolating and defining "Jewish-Christianity," drawing out the assumptions behind Daniélou's delineation of "Judéo-Christianisme" in terms of "thought-forms" and periodization (see above), as they speak to broader methodological issues involved in the study of Christianity and Judaism.

Murray, Robert. "Jews, Hebrews and Christians: Some Needed Distinctions." *NovT* 24 (1982): 194–208.

Article using definitional problems raised by the category of "Jewish-Christianity" to expose terminological and taxonomical issues with respect to common usages of "Jew," "Christian," "Judaism," and "Christianity" in the study of antiquity.

Brown, Raymond. "Not Jewish Christianity and Gentile Christianity but Types of Jewish/Gentile Christianity." *CBQ* 45 (1983): 74–79.

Article questioning the adequacy of a simple contrast between "Jewish-Christianity" and "Gentile Christianity" for understanding first-century materials, and suggesting instead a continuum of positions promoted by "Jewish Christians" and their Gentile converts.

Colpe, Carsten. "Das deutsche Wort 'Judenchristen' und die ihm entsprechende historische Sachverhalte." In *Das Siegel der Propheten: Historische Beziehungen zwischen Judentum, Judenchristentum, Heidentum und fruhen Islam*, ed. Colpe, 38–58. Arbeiten zur Neutestamentlichen Theologie und Zeitgeschichte 3. Berlin: Institut Kirche und Judentum, 1989.

Survey of treatments of German *Judenchristen* and *Judenchristentum*, which illumines the context and concerns that shaped the emergence of the modern study of "Jewish-Christianity," as well as raising important methodological points concerning the criteria by which one judges the heurism of modern categorical constructs of this sort.

Taylor, Joan. "The Phenomenon of Early Jewish-Christianity: Reality or Scholarly Invention?" *VC* 44 (1990): 313–34.

Critical assessment of scholarship on "Jewish-Christianity," marked by skepticism both about the heurism of the category for historical description and about common scholarly assumptions of continuity between what has been treated as its apostolic and post-apostolic forms.

Carleton Paget, James. "The Definition of the Terms Jewish Christian and Jewish Christianity in the History of Research." In *Jewish Believers in Jesus: The Early Centuries*, ed. Oskar Skarsaune and Reidar Hvalvik, 22–52. Peabody, MA: Hendrickson, 2007.

Judicious survey of the history of research, distinguished by its inclusion of important studies prior to those of Ferdinand Christian Baur. The piece ends with an important question about the heurism of the term: "Why not simply settle on a term like 'Torah-observant' and then introduce categories like Ebionite, Elchasaite, etc.?"

Boyarin, Daniel. "Rethinking Jewish Christianity: An Argument for Dismantling a Dubious Category (to Which Is Appended a Correction of My Border Lines)." *JQR* 99 (2009): 7–36.
> Thoughtful and provocative review essay of Jackson-McCabe's *Jewish Christianity Reconsidered* and Skarsaune and Hvalvik's *Jewish Believers in Jesus* (see above), which proposes, among other things, that "Jewish-Christianity" is a heresiological and polemical category not apt for scholarly usage.

Early "Jewish-Christianity"

In the history of research on the New Testament and Christian origins, discussions of early "Jewish-Christianity" have focused mostly on the attempt to reconstruct the beliefs, practices, and history of Peter, James, and the Jerusalem Church, primarily by reading the Book of Acts "against the grain" and in concert with the Pauline Epistles (especially Galatians 2 versus Acts 10–15) and early strata of the Pseudo-Clementine tradition. More recently, this and related rubrics (e.g., "Christian Judaism") have been applied to other New Testament texts and related materials, particularly in discussions of the Jesus movement's place within Judaism and the process by which some Christ-believers came to articulate and promote a self-definition as distinct. For this, the Gospel of Matthew has been central. Inquiries into Jewish identity and practice have been used also to shed new light on a range of other New Testament texts, including the Epistle of James, Epistle to the Hebrews, and Revelation.

Peter, James, and the Jerusalem Church

The New Testament Book of Acts preserves references to followers of Jesus who required circumcision of Gentile converts (15:1–6), and it associates James and Peter with the view that Jewish followers of Jesus must maintain ritual purity through separation from Gentiles, particularly at meals, even as it posits Peter's later change of heart (10–11; 15:6, 20). Particularly since the influential theories about the conflicts between Petrine and Pauline "parties" popularized by Ferdinand Christian Baur (see above), these references have been commonly read as clues to a conflict that is largely suppressed in Acts, but apparent in Paul's letters (especially Galatians 2:11–14) and perhaps also in traditions preserved in the Pseudo-Clementine literature (e.g., *Epistle of Peter to James*): Acts is shaped by attempts to promote a view of apostolic harmony, whereby the authority of the Jerusalem Church is paired with that of Paul and his mission. To reconstruct apostolic history, it is necessary to set aside Acts's image of apostolic harmony and read its account critically; when one does, it might be possible to glimpse something of the older "Jewish-Christian" perspectives here suppressed in favor of Pauline ideas about Christ devotion and Torah observance. Although few have adopted Baur's dichotomous view of apostolic history as characterized by the conflict between a singular "Jewish-Christianity" and a singular "Gentile Christianity," Petrine and anti-Pauline traditions have remained a topic of interest. On the one hand, many still approach Peter and James as emblematizing a form of apostolic religion close to the Jewish roots of Christianity, and there remains much research focused on these apostles in relation to Jewish tradition. On the other hand, the critical questioning of the account of apostolic history in Acts has extended even to its depiction of the Jerusalem Church.

Longenecker, Richard N. *The Christology of Early Jewish Christianity*. Studies in Biblical Theology 2.17. London: SCM, 1970.
Attempt to reconstruct a "Jewish-Christian" Christology from a variety of New Testament traditions posited to stand in a "conceptual frame" of Judaism, to exhibit non-Pauline ideas about Jesus, and to attest perspectives related to the apostolic Jerusalem Church.

Buchanan, George W. "Worship, Feasts, and Ceremonies in the Early Jewish-Christian Church." *NTS* 26 (1980): 279–97.
One of the few focused investigations of early "Jewish-Christianity" in terms of practice, with particular attention to the festal calendar and evidence for observance of Sabbath, Passover, and Pentecost.

Lüdemann, Gerd. *Paulus, der Heidenapostel*, vol. 2: *Antipaulinismus im frühen Christentum*. Forschungen zur Religion und Literatur des Alten und Neuen Testaments 130. Göttingen: Vandenhoeck & Ruprecht, 1983.
Seminal monograph, surveying New Testament, Patristic, and other traditions relevant to "Jewish-Christianity" through the lens of anti-Paulinism, thus sidestepping some of the problems of scope and definition noted above. The revised English edition was published as *Opposition to Paul in Jewish Christianity* (Minneapolis: Fortress 1989).

Smith, T. V. *Petrine Controversies in Early Christianity: Attitudes towards Peter in Christian Writings of the First Two Centuries*. WUNT2 15. Tübingen: Mohr Siebeck, 1985.
A counterpart to Lüdemann's inquiries into anti-Paulinism, revisiting Baur's theories in light of more recent evidence and understandings of the New Testament and early Christianity – in this case, with a focus on the texts and traditions surrounding the apostle Peter.

Bauckham, Richard. *James: Wisdom of James, Disciple of Jesus the Sage*. London: Routledge, 1999.
Monograph exploring the Epistle of James from the perspective of Palestinian "Jewish-Christianity."

Chilton, Bruce, and Craig A. Evans, eds. *James the Just and Christian Origins*. NTSup 98. Leiden: Brill, 1999.
Collection of essays on James, particularly rich in exploring his relationship to the Judaism of his time.

Cameron, Ron, and Merrill P. Miller, eds. *Redescribing Christian Origins*. SBLSymS 28. Atlanta: Society of Biblical Literature, 2004.
Collection of papers based on the work of the Society of Biblical Literature's Seminar on Ancient Myths and Modern Theories of Christian Origins, including a number of essays questioning traditional scholarly assumptions about the Jerusalem Church.

Myllykoski, Matti. "James the Just in History and Tradition: Perspectives of Past and Present Scholarship (Part I)." *CBR* 5 (2006): 73–122 + "James the Just in History and Tradition: Perspectives of Past and Present Scholarship (Part II)." *CBR* 6 (2007): 11–98.
A detailed two-part survey of the history of research on James the brother of Jesus and the rich traditions surrounding him, including analyses of both New Testament and later evidence.

The Gospel of Matthew and the Didache

Already in Late Antiquity, readers noticed the Gospel of Matthew's marked connections with the Judaism of its time; Eusebius, for instance, preserves speculations that Matthew's own native language was Hebrew and that he composed his gospel specifically for Jewish converts (*Hist. eccl.* 3.24.5–6; 5.10.3; 6.25.4; see also John Chrysostom, *Homilies on Matthew* 1.7; Jerome, *On Illustrious Men* 3). The gospel's place in "Jewish-Christian" belief and practice, moreover, is suggested by its early and persistent association with the Ebionites (e. g., Irenaeus, *Adv. haer.* 1.26.2; 3.11.7, 3.21.1; 5.1.3) and by the exegetical engagement with Matthean traditions in the Pseudo-Clementine *Homilies* and *Recognitions*. Similarly, in modern research, this gospel has been central for the reassessment of anti-Judaism in the New Testament, particularly after World War II (i. e., as *intra muros* versus *extra muros*), and for the exploration of Jewish forms and ideas in the first-century writings that would eventually become enshrined as Christian Scripture. A number of recent studies follow critiques of the use of the term "Jewish-Christianity" in an early period and, consequently, adopt terms such as "Christian Judaism" or "Matthean Judaism" to describe the gospel and its community (e. g., Anthony J. Saldarini, David Sim; cf. Anders Runesson). Some of its traditions are paralleled in the *Didache*, an early rule book that has been similarly central for explorations of "Jewish-Christian" or "Christian Jewish" piety, halakhah, and community structures. Investigations of both texts, and their connections, have helped to illumine the sociohistorical contexts for the flourishing of forms of Christ-devotion developed with a continued commitment to the importance of the Torah and against the background of competing claims (Pharisaic and/or Rabbinic) to its proper interpretation and practice.

Saldarini, A. J. *Matthew's Christian-Jewish Community*. Chicago Studies in the History of Judaism. Chicago: University of Chicago Press, 1994.
Seminal study of the Judaism of the Gospel of Matthew, the community in which it was formed, and its relationship to emergent Rabbinic Judaism. Emphasis is here placed on the gospel's points of continuity with the Hebrew Bible and post-biblical Judaism, while anti-Jewish statements are explained in terms of inner-Jewish debates wherein the gospel's "Pharisees" encode rabbis of the late first century.

Draper, Jonathan A., ed. *The Didache in Modern Research.* Arbeiten zur Geschichte des Antiken Judentums und des Urchristentums 37. Leiden: Brill, 1996.

Invaluable guide to scholarship on the *Didache*, featuring an extensive survey of recent scholarship by the editor, together with classic articles. The latter include English translations of pieces originally published in French, German, Hebrew, and Italian, and feature a number of discussions relevant to the question of whether and how the *Didache* might attest early "Jewish-Christian" praxis.

Sim, David C. *The Gospel of Matthew and Christian Judaism: The History and Social Setting of the Matthean Community.* Studies of the New Testament and Its World. Edinburgh: T&T Clark, 1998.

Another major attempt to situate the Gospel of Matthew's relationship to Judaism in historical context, albeit with a more critical and cautious use of Jewish parallels, more attuned to current research on the early Rabbinic movement.

Van de Sandt, Huub Maria, ed. *Matthew and the Didache: Two Documents from the Same Jewish-Christian Milieu?* Minneapolis: Fortress, 2005.

Collection of twelve essays from a 2004 conference in Tilburg, The Netherlands, exploring the parallels between the Gospel of Matthew and the *Didache* as a starting point for exploring the texts' social contexts and relationships to Judaism.

Viviano, Benedict T. *Matthew and His World: The Gospel of the Open Jewish Christians: Studies in Biblical Theology.* Novum Testamentum et Orbis Antiquus 61. Göttingen: Vandenhoeck & Ruprecht, 2007.

Collection of classic and new essays on the Gospel of Matthew by one of the scholars most involved in exploring its connections to Jews and "Jewish Christians."

Van de Sandt, Huub Maria, and Jürgen K. Zangenberg, eds. *Matthew, James, and Didache: Three Related Documents in Their Jewish and Christian Setting.* SBLSymS 45. Atlanta: Society of Biblical Literature, 2008.

Collection extending van de Sandt's *Matthew and the Didache*, with reference to the Epistle of James and including an impressive array of international scholars. For a thoughtful reflection on whether and how these newer lines of research relate to the older Petrine, Jacobite, Ebionite, etc., foci of research on early "Jewish-Christianity" and the past debates over its definition, Joseph Verheyden's piece (pp. 123–38) is highly recommended.

Runesson, Anders. "Rethinking Early Jewish–Christian Relations: Matthean Community History as Pharisaic Intragroup Conflict." *JBL* 127 (2008): 95–132.

Recent article on identity in the Gospel of Matthew, integrating extensive references to relevant studies.

Other New Testament Texts

The move away from monolithic understandings of "Jewish-Christianity" has opened the way for the study of multiple early sources as evidence for possible expressions of (or reactions to) devotion to Christ in continuity with Jewish identity and practice. At the same time, the increased scholarly awareness of the diversity of the Second Temple Judaism in the wake of the discovery and publication of the Dead Sea Scrolls has enabled the identification of such parallels and continuities in a broad range of New Testament texts – not limited to those traditionally discussed as "Jewish" or "Jewish-Christian." Scholars continue to study the Epistles of James, Jude, and Hebrews from the perspective of their resonances with Second Temple Judaism and the early Jerusalem church, for instance, and such approaches have also yielded rich results, more recently, with respect to the Book of Revelation. Even some authors traditionally deemed exemplary of "Gentile Christianity," such as Paul and Luke, have been reconsidered from the perspective of the variety of types of Jewish devotion to Jesus that shaped early Christianity.

Jervell, Jacob. "The Mighty Minority." *Studia Theologica* 34 (1980): 13–38.
 Provocative essay on the importance of "Jewish-Christians" for understanding the Gospel of Luke and Book of Acts, contrary to the traditional view of Luke-Acts as a fundamentally "Gentile-Christian" work.

Marshall, John W. *Parables of War: Reading John's Jewish Apocalypse*. Studies in Christianity and Judaism 10. Waterloo, Ontario, Canada: Wilfrid Laurier University Press, 2001.
 Groundbreaking analysis of the New Testament Book of Revelation as a Jewish work.

Frankfurter, David. "Jews or Not? Reconstructing the 'Other' in Rev 2:9 and 3:9." *HTR* 94 (2001): 403–27.
 Important article on Revelation as a work reflecting a Jewish self-definition, particularly in relation to ritual purity.

Goulder, Michael. "Hebrews and the Ebionites." *NTS* 49 (2003): 393–406.
 Interpretation of the aim and audience of the Epistle to the Hebrews in light of Patristic evidence (especially Irenaeus) for the Ebionites.

Bauckham, Richard. *Jude and the Relatives of Jesus in the Early Church*. London: T&T Clark, 2004.
 Monograph on the Epistle of Jude, although largely exploring the role of the family of Jesus in leading and shaping "Palestinian Jewish Christianity in the period of the New Testament."

Donaldson, Terence L. "Jewish Christianity, Israel's Stumbling and the *Sonderweg* Reading of Paul." *JSNT* 29 (2006): 27–54.
 Article exploring the place of "Jewish Christians" within Paul's thought (especially in the Epistle of Romans), as approached from the perspective of the "two-track" soteriology posited by Lloyd Gaston, John G. Gager, and Stanley Stowers, whereby Jews can be saved as Jews, and the message about Jesus is pointed particularly to Gentiles.

Witherington, Ben. *Letters and Homilies for Jewish Christians: A Socio-Rhetorical Commentary on Hebrews, James and Jude*. Downers Grove, IL: IVP Academic, 2007.
 Recent "socio-rhetorical" commentary on the Epistle of Hebrews, James, and Jude in their Jewish contexts.

Archaeological Evidence for "Jewish-Christianity"

Discussion of possible archaeological evidence for "Jewish Christians" has been highly polarized. Bellarmino Bagatti, Emanuele Testa, and other scholars associated with the Studium Franciscanum Biblicum in Jerusalem have produced a

rich body of studies of sites and symbols, and they have largely adopted maximalist positions, identifying a broad range of materials from Roman Palestine
with Jewish Christians, speculating about early "Jewish-Christian" iconography
and devotional practices, and positing that the Christianization of the Holy Land
after Constantine stood in continuity with earlier Jewish-Christian veneration of
sites associated with the life of Jesus and his family. Many interpretations and
theories of the "Franciscan school" have been criticized as highly speculative –
most concertedly, by Joan Taylor, who has argued for minimalist readings of
the archaeological data, as well as questioning literary evidence adduced for
continuity between the apostolic Jerusalem Church and later Jewish Christians.
Others, such as Bargil Pixner and Zeev Safrai, have attempted to chart some
middle ground between these positions.

Testa, Emanuele. *Il Simbolismo dei Giudeo-Cristiani*. Pubblicazioni dello Studium Biblicum Franciscanum, Collectio Maior 14. Jerusalem: Franciscan Printing Press, 1962.
   Monograph interpreting a series of symbols as markers of "Jewish-Christianity" and
   speculating as to the ideas that they might encode. Although highly hypothetical, Testa's
   theories have shaped the identification of specific sites and form an important part of
   the Franciscan school's argument for the survival and thriving of "Jewish-Christianity"
   up to and beyond the fourth century.
Bagatti, Bellarmino. *The Church from the Circumcision: History and Archaeology of the
   Judaeo-Christian*. Studium Biblicum Franciscanum, Collectio Minor 2. Jerusalem:
   Franciscan Printing Press, 1971.
   Monograph by the scholar often credited as the founder of the Franciscan school,
   synthesizing theories about the archaeological remains of Christian sites in Roman
   Palestine as reflecting "Jewish-Christian" devotion even prior to the beginning of the
   Christianization of the Holy Land under Constantine.
Pixner, Bargil. *Wege des Messias und Stätten der Urkirche: Jesus und das Judenchristen-
   tum im Licht neuer archäologischer Erkenntnisse*. Studien zur biblischen Archäologie
   und Zeitgeschichte 2. Giessen: Brunnen, 1991.
   Pixner generally advances an approach to the archaeological search for "Jewish-
   Christian" remains that is less maximalist than the Franciscan school; his bold attempts
   to read remains on Mount Zion in terms of Josephus's reference to the "gate of the
   Essenes" (*War* 5.145) and evidence from the Dead Sea Scrolls to posit connections
   between Jesus and the Essenes, however, have not been widely accepted.
Taylor, Joan E. *Christians and the Holy Places: The Myth of Jewish Christian Origins*.
   Oxford: Clarendon, 1993.
   Critical assessment of the identification of Christian sites in Roman Palestine with early
   "Jewish Christians," which mounts a sustained attack on the "Bagatti-Testa hypothe-
   sis," synthesizes earlier critiques, and expresses skepticism concerning the "Jewish-
   Christian" (as opposed to "pagan") prehistories of sites that became associated with
   Jesus' life during the Christianization of the Holy Land beginning in the fourth century.

Safrai, Zeev. "The House of Leontis 'Kaloubas' – A Judaeo-Christian?" In *The Image of the Judeo-Christians*, ed. Peter J. Tomson and Doris Lambeers-Petry, 245–66. WUNT 158. Tübingen: Mohr Siebeck, 2003.
Article follows Joan Taylor in critiquing the Franciscan school, but makes a cautious attempt to posit a "Jewish-Christian" identification of archaeological finds with the house of Leontis at Beth Shean as a fascinating "test case."

"Jewish-Christian" Gospels

Based primarily on the evidence of Patristic quotations (see below), scholars have also adduced the existence of lost gospels associated with "Jewish-Christian" sects. Relevant quotations have been associated with three hypothetical lost works – the *Gospel of the Nazoraeans*, *Gospel of the Ebionites*, and *Gospel of the Hebrews* – which are all commonly dated to the first half of the second century. For instance, A. F. J. Klijn posits that the *Gospel of the Ebionites* is based on New Testament materials, while *Gospel according to the Nazoraeans* and *Gospel of the Hebrews* preserve something of the early fluidity of gospel traditions in the second century. Recently, the heurism of this category has come under question.

Klijn, Albertus Frederik Johannes. *Jewish-Christian Gospel Tradition*. VCSup 17. Leiden: Brill, 1992.
Comprehensive edition of quotations from Patristic and medieval authors relevant for the reconstruction of "Jewish-Christian gospels," with parallel materials juxtaposed for handy consultation and analysis.
Vielhauer, Philipp, and Georg Strecker. "Jewish-Christian Gospels." In *New Testament Apocrypha*, vol. 1: *Gospels and Related Writings*, ed. Wilhelm Schneemelcher, 134–78. Translated by R. McL. Wilson. Rev. ed. Cambridge: James Clark, 1992.
English translation of a German translation and reconstruction of "Jewish-Christian Gospels" in a widely used collection of apocryphal literature; although handy for consultation and as an introduction to these materials, it is best used together with Klijn's volume.
Gregory, Andrew. "Hindrance or Help: Does the Modern Category of 'Jewish-Christian Gospel' Distort Our Understanding of the Texts to Which It Refers?" *JSNT* 28 (2006): 387–413.
Detailed, critical reassessment of evidence for "Jewish-Christian" gospels, questioning the heurism of the category for the study of the excerpts in question.
Luomanen, Petri. *Recovering Jewish-Christian Sects and Gospels*. VCSup 110. Leiden: Brill, 2011.
Monograph synthesizing the results of Luomenen's research on early "Jewish-Christians," first by revisiting Patristic reports about Nazarenes and Ebionites and then by reconsidering evidence for "Jewish-Christian" gospels like the *Gospel according to the Hebrews*; Luomanen here focuses on evidence outside of the New Testament, and he applies Jonathan Z. Smith's notions of polythetic classification to outline a profile of "Jewish-Christian" and to determine multiple indicators for categorizing gospels in these terms.

The Pseudo-Clementine Literature

Particularly since the influential work of Ferdinand Christian Baur (see above), the Pseudo-Clementine literature has been central for attempts to bridge the gap between apostolic and post-apostolic evidence for "Jewish-Christianity," and to recover firsthand accounts of "Jewish-Christian" beliefs and practices, owing to its concern for Peter and James, promotion of Torah observance, and parallels with Patristic accounts of the Ebionites. This literature consists of two parallel fourth-century novels about Clement of Rome and the apostle Peter – the *Homilies* and the *Recognitions* – together with the Petrine and Clementine epistles transmitted with them. The two novels are thought to draw on a shared third-century source (commonly called *Grundschrift* or "Basic Source") and have been posited as preserving even earlier, lost sources from the second century, such as the *Kerygmata Petrou* and *Anabathmoi Jakobou.*

Editions and Translations of the Pseudo-Clementines

Owing to the complex textual situation and source-critical theories surrounding the Pseudo-Clementine literature, reliable critical editions and translations are invaluable. The editions by Bernard Rehm remain authoritative for the Greek of the *Homilies* and the Latin of the *Recognitions*. There is no adequate English translation; the translations in the nineteenth-century *Ante-Nicene Fathers* collection are widely used but provisional and should be used with caution. In addition, some passages from the Pseudo-Clementine *Homilies* and *Recognitions* are also among the works in the English edition of Schneemelcher's *New Testament Apocrypha*; although convenient and widely cited, this translation renders only selective passages. Fortunately, however, recent and reliable translations of the full corpus are now available in French. In addition, there is now a new translation of the Syriac version by F. Stanley Jones, soon to be accompanied by a new edition in place of the old Syriac edition by Wilhelm Frankenberg. For other editions and translations, see Jones' survey of the history of research there.

Smith, Thomas, trans. "The *Recognitions* of Clement" and "The Clementine *Homilies*." In *Ante-Nicene Fathers*, vol. 8, ed. A. Roberts and J. Donaldson, 73–346. London: T&T Clark, 1886.
The only full English translation of the Pseudo-Clementine literature is the provisional translation in the late nineteenth-century Ante-Nicene Fathers collection. This translation is in the public domain and widely available online. Although handy for quick consultation and searching, it should be used with care.
Frankenberg, Wilhelm *Die syrischen Clementinen mit griechischen Paralleltext: Eine Vorarbeit zu dem literargeschichtlichen Problem der Sammlung.* TU 48.3. Leipzig: Hinrichs, 1937.
Edition of the Syriac version of the Pseudo-Clementines, which includes parts of *Recognitions* 1–4 and *Homilies* 10–14, and which is attested in the oldest surviving Syriac

manuscript (i.e., British Library Additional 12,150; 411 CE); this edition is based on this manuscript together with British Museum Additional 14,609 (587 CE) but does not take additional fragments into account, and it also includes a somewhat speculative retrojection into Greek.

Rehm, Bernard. *Die Pseudoklementinen*, vol. 1: *Homilien*. Rev. ed. GCS 42. Berlin: Akademie-Verlag, 1969.

Critical edition of the Pseudo-Clementine *Homilies*, which survives in Greek, is probably earlier than the *Recognitions*, and is generally viewed as containing more "Jewish-Christian" features.

Rehm, Bernard. *Die Pseudoklementinen*, vol. 2: *Rekognitionen in Rufins Übersetzung*. GCS 51. Berlin: Akademie-Verlag, 1969.

Critical edition of the Pseudo-Clementine *Recognitions*, which is preserved in Rufinus's Latin translation of 406 CE. This version is better attested than the *Homilies*, surviving in more than one hundred manuscripts; Rehm's edition is based on about twenty manuscripts.

Irmscher, Johannes, and Georg Strecker, eds. and trans. "The Pseudo-Clementines." In *New Testament Apocrypha*, vol. 2: *Writings Relating to the Apostles, Apocalypses and Related Subjects*, ed. W. Schneemelcher, trans. R. McL. Wilson, 482–541. Rev. ed. Cambridge: James Clark, 1992.

Translation of selected passages from the Pseudo-Clementines, including some that are presented as possibly having belonged to the *Kerygmata Petrou*, a hypothetical source for the putative *Grundschrift* of the two novels. Some care should be exercised in the use of this translation, due to the selectivity of passages chosen and their abstraction from their literary contexts.

Le Boulluec, Alain, Marie-Ange Calvet, Dominique Côté, Pierre Geoltrain, Bernard Pouderon, and André Schneider, trans. "Roman Pseudo-Clémentin: Homélies." In *Écrits apocryphes chrétiens*, vol. 2, ed. Pierre Geoltrain and Jean-Daniel Kaestli, 1193–589. Bibliothèque de la Pléiade 516. Paris: Gallimard, 2005.

Most recent and reliable translation of the *Homilies* into a modern European language.

Cirillo, Luigi, and André Schneider, trans. "Roman Pseudo-Clémentin: Reconnaissances." In *Écrits apocryphes chrétiens*, vol. 2, ed. Pierre Geoltrain and Jean-Daniel Kaestli, 1593–2003. Bibliothèque de la Pléiade 516. Paris: Gallimard, 2005.

Most recent and reliable translation of the whole of the *Recognitions* into a modern European language.

Jones, F. Stanley, trans. *The Syriac Pseudo-Clementines: An Early Version of the First Christian Novel*. Apocryphes 14. Turnhout: Brepols, 2014.

A new translation of the Syriac version of the Pseudo-Clementines, based on a fresh consideration of the full range of manuscript evidence (including fragments manuscripts and Jones' forthcoming edition of the text); the volume includes a succinct and accessible introduction to the Pseudo-Clementines (pp. 13–48) as well as a comprehensive bibliography guide to past editions and translations (pp. 49–56), and it builds on Jones' seminal research establishing the importance of this version.

Studies on the Pseudo-Clementines

For more than a century, source-critical approaches have dominated research on the Pseudo-Clementine literature; scholars have sought, in particular, to reconstruct second-century sources thereof that might stand in continuity with Peter, James, and the Jerusalem Church. In this, much attention has focused on the first book of the *Recognitions*, which contains traditions that resonate with Epiphanius's description of the Ebionites in *Panarion* 30 – including anti-Paulinism and polemics against animal sacrifice, as well as an account of the martyrdom of James that echoes elements in the non-extant Ebionite *Anabathmoi Jakobou* described in *Pan.* 30.16.6–9. Some studies of the "Jewish-Christianity" of the Pseudo-Clementines have focused on reconstructing this and other second-century sources (e. g., *Kerygmata Petrou*), which might shed light on the *Nachleben* of the early "Jewish-Christianity" of the Jerusalem Church. More recently, the study of the Pseudo-Clementines has also been marked by renewed concern for its late antique forms and contexts, as well as connections with Rabbinic Judaism. For the full history of research, the reader is directed to Jones' 1982 survey of the history of the research, and for a survey of recent developments, including its concern with philosophy and "paganism," see Amsler's 2008 volume.

Bergman, J. "Les éléments juifs dans les Pseudo-Clémentines." *REJ* 46 (1903): 89–98.
An early exploration of parallels between the Pseudo-Clementines and a range of post-biblical Jewish traditions; although representative of the "parallelomania" of its time, this article remains useful for its learned collection of potentially relevant materials.

Strecker, Georg. *Das Judenchristentum in den Pseudoklementinen.* TU 70. 2nd ed. Berlin: Akademie-Verlag, 1981.
The most extensive and detailed treatment of the question of the "Jewish-Christianity" of the Pseudo-Clementine literature as considered from the perspective of source-critical analysis. A brilliant monograph that remains necessary to consult for any inquiry into the Pseudo-Clementine literature, source critical or otherwise.

Jones, F. Stanley. "The Pseudo-Clementines: A History of Research." *Second Century* 2 (1982): 1–33, 63–96.
An invaluable guide to the history of scholarship on the Pseudo-Clementine *Homilies*, *Recognitions*, and related materials by one of the leading authorities on these works. It includes an accessible summary and assessment of source-critical discussions and debates, as well as a survey of assessments of whether these works and/or their sources can be deemed "Jewish-Christian." Reprinted in Jones, *Pseudoclementina Elchasaiticaque inter Judaeochristiana,* 50–113.

Van Voorst, Robert E. *The Ascents of James: History and Theology of a Jewish-Christian Community.* SBL Dissertation Series 112. Atlanta: Scholars Press, 1989.
Prominent example of an attempt to use Pseudo-Clementine evidence to reconstruct and situate the *Anabathmoi Jakobou,* a lost work mentioned by Epiphanius in the context of his description of the Ebionites (*Pan.* 30.16.6–9).

Jones, F. Stanley. *An Ancient Jewish Christian Source on the History of Christianity: Pseudo-Clementine Recognitions 1.27–71.* Texts and Translations 37, Christian Apocrypha Series 2. Atlanta: Scholars Press, 1995.
Major monograph, which seeks to reconstruct the early source embedded in the first book of *Recognitions* through internal criteria. On this basis, Jones argues that *Recognitions* 1.27–71 preserves a "Jewish-Christian" source written in Roman Palestine

around 200 CE. He provides a helpful parallel translation of Latin, Syriac, and Armenian witnesses, and also demonstrates the importance of the Syriac version for study of the text.

Côté, Dominique. *Le thème de l'opposition entre Pierre et Simon dans les Pseudo-Clémentines*. Études augustiniennes série antiquités 167. Paris: Études augustiniennes, 2001.

Study of the depiction of Peter and Simon Magus in the Pseudo-Clementine novels; in contrast to approaches influenced by Ferdinand Christian Baur, which have read descriptions of conflicts between Peter and Simon as evidence for the conflict between Petrine and Pauline positions, Côté here considers their literary, rhetorical, and discursive functions in their late antique contexts, particularly with reference to Christian attitudes toward philosophy.

Amsler, Frédéric, Albert Frey, Charlotte Touati, and Renee Girardet, eds. *Nouvelles intrigues Pseudo-clémentines: Plots in the Pseudo-Clementine Romance*. Publications de l'Institut romand des sciences bibliques 6. Lausanne: Zèbre, 2008.

Multilingual collection featuring thirty-seven essays on the Pseudo-Clementine literature. This rich and varied volume provides a "snapshot" of the present state of international discussion of this important corpus.

Reed, Annette Yoshiko. "Heresiology and the (Jewish-)Christian Novel: Narrativized Polemics in the Pseudo-Clementines *Homilies*." In *Heresy and Identity in Late Antiquity*, ed. Eduard Iricinschi and Holger Zellentin, 273–98. TSAJ 119. Tübingen: Mohr Siebeck, 2008.

Article exploring aspects of the Pseudo-Clementine *Homilies* in relation to Patristic heresiology as well as Rabbinic tales of disputations with *minim*, exploring the possibility that the fourth-century authors/redactors of the novel had some awareness of contemporaneous Jewish (especially Rabbinic) traditions. Reprinted in the present volume in revised and expanded form as Chapter Five.

Jones, F. Stanley. *Pseudoclementina Elchasaiticaque inter Judaeochristiana: Collected Studies*. Orientalia Lovaniensia Analecta 203. Leuven: Peeters, 2012.

Reprint volume collecting over thirty years of essays and reviews from among the foremost specialists in the Pseudo-Clementines; the two-thirds of the volume is dedicated to this corpus, including previously unpublished material such as a detailed introduction (pp. 7–49) as well as an compilation of wide-ranging articles, especially invaluable for as a basis for research on the *Grundschrift* (pp. 114–16) and its formation in a third-century Syro-Mesopotamian cultural context that can be reconstructed with appeal to Elchaasai, Bardaisan, Mani, transcredal debates about astrology, and a concern "Jewish-Christian" reaction against Marcionism.

Côté, Dominique. "Le problème de l'identité religieuse dans la Syrie du IVe siècle. Le cas des Pseudo-Clémentines et de l'Adversus Judaeos de S. Jean Chrysostome." In *La croisée des chemins revisitée: Quand l'Église et la Synagogue se sont-elles distinguées?*, ed. Simon Claude Mimouni and Bernard Pouderon, 339–70. Patrimoines Judaïsme antique. Paris: Cerf, 2012.

Article exploring the redacted forms of the Pseudo-Clementines in their fourth-century Syrian contexts, presenting them in counterpoint to John Chrysostom's infamous polemics against Judaizers in Antioch.

Carlson, Donald H. *Jewish-Christian Interpretation of the Pentateuch in the Pseudo-Clementine Homilies.* Minneapolis: Fortress, 2013.
   Dissertation-based monograph focusing on the "doctrine of the false pericopes" in the *Homilies*, here analyzed in exegetical terms and treated as witnessing to a third- and fourth-century tradition with earlier "Jewish-Christian" roots.
Ruffatto, Kristine J. "Moses Typology for Peter in the *Epistula Petri* and the *Contestatio*." *VC* 69 (2015): 345–67.
   Article exploring anti-Paulinism and the exemplary modeling of Peter after Moses in the much-understudied epistolary material prefaced to the Pseudo-Clementine *Homilies*.

Other "Christian Apocrypha" and "Old Testament Pseudepigrapha"

Questions about "Jewish-Christianity" have also been profitably explored in relation to a range of noncanonical sources. Among the so-called Old Testament Pseudepigrapha, for instance, are a number of works that scholars have long debated as either "Jewish" or "Christian" in provenance (especially *Testaments of the Twelve Patriarchs*) – some of which might be better understood as meaningfully both; other cases of the Christian reception and transmission of pre-Christian Jewish writings may be best understood in this manner as well. A number of so-called New Testament Apocrypha – such as the *Apocalypse of Peter*, *Protevangelium of James*, and Ethiopic *Book of the Cock* – have also been illumined with reference to Jewish identities and traditions.

Bauckham, Richard. "The *Apocalypse of Peter*: A Jewish Christian Apocalypse from the Time of Bar Kokhba." *Apoc* 5 (1994): 7–111.
   Article arguing for a Palestinian "Jewish-Christian" provenance for the *Apocalypse of Peter* as a "rare example of an extant work deriving from a Palestinian Jewish Christianity" of the second century and suggesting that its imagery preserves reactions to martyrdoms of "Jewish Christians" as well as other Jews during the Bar Kokhba Revolt (132–135 CE).
Bauckham, Richard. "Jews and Jewish Christians in the Land of Israel at the Time of the Bar Kochba War, with Special Reference to the *Apocalypse of Peter*." In *Tolerance and Intolerance in Early Judaism and Christianity*, ed. Graham N. Stanton and Guy G. Strousma, 228–38. Cambridge: Cambridge University Press, 1998.
   Whereas most treatments of the fate of early "Jewish-Christianity" have rehashed the same limited set of Patristic and other sources, this article builds on Bauckham's earlier work to offer a fresh consideration of the fate of "Jewish Christians" in the land of Israel in the period between the two revolts against Rome.
Piovanelli, Pierluigi. "Exploring the Ethiopic *Book of the Cock*, an Apocryphal Passion Gospel from Late Antiquity." *HTR* 96 (2003): 427–54.
   Discussion of the apocryphal *Book of the Cock*, preserved in Ethiopic and featuring anti-Pauline traditions of possible "Jewish-Christian" origin.

Frankfurter, David. "Beyond 'Jewish Christianity': Continuing Religious Sub-cultures of the Second and Third Centuries and Their Documents." In *The Ways That Never Parted: Jews and Christians in Late Antiquity and the Early Middle Ages*, ed. Adam H. Becker and Annette Yoshiko Reed, 131–44. TSAJ 95. Tübingen: Mohr Siebeck, 2003.
Article exploring the *Ascension of Isaiah*, *5* and *6 Ezra*, and the *Testaments of the Twelve Patriarchs* as possibly products of "continuous communities of halakhically observant Jewish groups, perhaps of a sectarian nature, that incorporated Jesus into their cosmologies and liturgies while retaining an essentially Jewish, or even priestly, self-definition." Frankfurter here argues against the label "Jewish-Christian" as traditionally conceived.

Horner, Timothy. "Jewish Aspects of the *Protevangelium of James*." *JECS* 12 (2004): 313–35.
Article considering the oldest apocryphal work on Mary in relation to early Rabbinic traditions. Although resisting the label "Jewish-Christian," Horner places the work's "initial author and audience within the milieu of Christian Judaism ... loosely defined as those Christians who maintained that Jesus was the prophetic Messiah but also saw no reason to reinterpret the Torah and its incumbent practices."

Piovanelli, Pierluigi. "The *Book of the Cock* and the Rediscovery of Ancient Jewish-Christian Traditions in Fifth-Century Palestine." In *The Changing Face of Judaism, Christianity and Other Greco-Roman Religions in Antiquity*, ed. Ian H. Henderson and Gerbern S. Oegama, 308–22. Judische Schriften aus Hellenistisch-Romischer Zeit 2. Gütersloh: Gütersloher, 2006.
Article exploring the implications of Piovanelli's earlier work on the topic, particularly with reference to fifth-century Ebionites in Roman Palestine.

Winter, Michael M. "Theological Alterations in the Syriac Translation of Ben Sira." *CBQ* 70 (2008): 300–12.
Article proposing that the Syriac version of the Wisdom of ben Sira was originally translated by an Ebionite.

Post-Apostolic "Jewish-Christianity"

Early research (see above) largely assumed the continuity between the apostolic Jerusalem Church and so-called heterodox, post-apostolic "Jewish-Christian" sects such as the Ebionites – the latter of which were seen as "survivals" of the former, rendered "heretical" by the success of "Gentile/Pauline Christianity" and the resultant "Parting of the Ways." Central to these connections was the assumption of the historicity of the accounts of the flight of members of the Jerusalem Church to Pella during the first Jewish Revolt (66–70 CE) by Eusebius (*Ecclesiastical History* 3.5.3) and Epiphanius (*Pan.* 1.29.7–30.7; *Weights and Measures* 15). Some, however, have taken a more skeptical approach, both to the question of continuity (e. g., Johannes Munck) and to the Pella tradition (e. g., Gerd Lüdemann), concurrent with broader critiques of the treatment of "Jewish-Christianity" as a single movement with a single theology and with more critical

approaches to the historical value of the reports of Epiphanius and other heresiologists. Others have pointed to apparent evidence for the continuation of such
traditions into Late Antiquity and beyond, even after the rise of Islam.

Munck, Johannes. "Primitive Jewish Christianity and Late Jewish Christianity: Continuation or Rupture?" In *Aspects du Judéo-Christianisme: Colloque de Strasbourg, 23–25
avril 1964*, 77–94. Paris: Presse Universitaires de France, 1965.
Critical assessment of the scholarly assumption, common in research at the time (and
today), that late antique reports about Ebionites and other "Jewish-Christians" refer to
the direct heirs of the Jerusalem Church of apostolic times.

Klijn, Albertus Frederik Johannes. "The Study of Jewish Christianity." *NTS* 20 (1974):
419–31.
Reflection on the historiography of "Jewish-Christianity," focusing on its post-apostolic forms. Countering efforts to reconstruct a single "Jewish Christian" theology or history, Klijn stresses diversity; he suggests that it is more apt to discuss the
"Jewish-Christianity" of a text or author, and to allow for different forms of "Jewish-
Christianity" in interaction with different forms of Judaism, including but not limited
to Syro-Palestinian traditions.

Lüdemann, Gerd. "The Successors of Pre-70 Jerusalem Christianity: A Critical Evaluation
of the Pella Tradition." In *Jewish and Christian Self-Definition*, vol. 1: *The Shaping of
Christianity in the Second and Third Centuries*, ed. E. P. Sanders, 161–173, 245–254.
Philadelphia: Fortress, 1980.
Perhaps the most influential of a spate of articles in the 1980s and 1990s questioning
the historicity of traditions about the Jerusalem Church's departure from Jerusalem for
Pella during the first Jewish Revolt (66–70 CE), by revisiting the relevant passages from
Eusebius and Epiphanius.

Reed, Annette Yoshiko. "'Jewish Christianity' after the 'Parting of the Ways': Approaches
to Historiography and Self-Definition in the Pseudo-Clementines." In *The Ways That
Never Parted: Jews and Christians in Late Antiquity and the Early Middle Ages*, ed.
Adam H. Becker and Annette Yoshiko Reed, 189–231. TSAJ 95. Tübingen: Mohr
Siebeck, 2003.
Consideration of how assumptions about the "Parting of the Ways" have shaped the
history of research on post-apostolic "Jewish-Christianity," in general, and on the
Pseudo-Clementine literature, more specifically – arguing for the importance of con-
sidering the present form of the *Homilies*, in particular, as evidence for late antique
"Jewish-Christianity." Reprinted as Chapter One in the present volume, with minor
bibliographical updates.

Boyarin, Daniel. *Border Lines: The Partition of Judeo-Christianity.* Divinations. Philadelphia: University of Pennsylvania Press, 2004.
While considering the role of heresiology in producing Jewish/Christian difference,
Boyarin draws attention to the discursive function of "Jewish Christians," namely, as hybrids constructed to reaffirm the purported purity of the parts imagined to be combined.
He thus proposes that "the ascription of existence to the 'hybrids' assumes (and thus
assures) the existence of nonhybrid 'pure' religions (i. e., Judaism and Christianity)."

Patristic Evidence for "Jewish-Christianity"

The study of the post-apostolic fate of "Jewish-Christianity" has traditionally revolved around Patristic reports about Ebionites, Nazoraeans, and other sects, noted in catalogues of "heresies" for their Torah observance, low Christologies, and/or closeness to Judaism (especially Epiphanius, *Panarion* 28–30). Although such reports were often taken at face value in early research, recent studies have become increasingly attuned to their indirect character, polemical aims, and largely heresiological contexts and the challenges thus posed for their use for historical reconstruction.

In early research, the accounts of "Jewish-Christianity" by Patristic authors such as Irenaeus, Origen, Epiphanius, Eusebius, and Jerome were largely read as accurate reports, despite their polemical aims and heresiological contexts. Critical reassessments of this material began in the 1970s – particularly with the publication of Albertus Frederik Johannes Klijn and Gerrit J. Reinink's 1973 sourcebook. Klijn and Reinink offer a comprehensive collection of excerpts of relevant passages from the writings of Irenaeus, Origen, Epiphanius, Jerome, and other early and late antique Christian writers concerning the Ebionites, Nazoraeans, and other groups considered "Jewish-Christian" in modern research; this volume is thus an ideal starting point for research. It is also advisable, however, to consider the meaning of these and other excerpts in their original literary and rhetorical settings. More recently, a number of studies have attempted to understand references to these and other "Jewish-Christian" sects in their literary and discursive contexts, as well as revisiting the full range of evidence.

Klijn, Albertus Frederik Johannes, and Gerrit J. Reinink. *Patristic Evidence for Jewish-Christian Sects.* NovTSup 36. Leiden: Brill, 1973.
> The core of this invaluable resource is a collection of excerpts. The accompanying analysis is incisive, not least due to the authors' care in weighing the historical value of these indirect reports against their largely polemical literary settings. The authors, for instance, question the overconfidence with which some scholars reconstruct the beliefs and practices of Ebionites and Nazoraeans.

Barthelemy, Dominique. "Qui est Symmaque?" *CBQ* 36 (1974): 451–65.
> Consideration of Patristic traditions identifying the second-century Greek biblical translator Symmachus as a "Jewish Christian."

Testa, E. "La Grande Chiesa e le minoranze giudeo-cristiane nell'ultimo scorcio del IV secolo." *Studii Biblici Franciscani Liber Annuus Jérusalem* 28 (1978): 24–44.
> Attempt to map the range of attitudes toward "Jewish Christians" among fourth-century Christians, ranging from the "traditionalist" position of Epiphanius and Jerome, to the views of Antiochenes and Origenists.

Jones, F. Stanley. "Hegesippus as a Source for the History of Jewish Christianity." In *Le Judéo-Christianisme dans tous ses états*, ed. Simon Claude Mimouni and F. Stanley Jones, 201–12. Paris: Cerf, 2001.
> Judicious reassessment of the evidence for the lost *Hypomnemata* of the second-century Hegesippus (cf. Eusebius, *Hist. eccl.* 2.23; 4.8; 4.11) as a reliable source for details

about the life and death of James and Jesus' other relatives, the succession of bishops of Jewish ancestry in the Jerusalem Church, and other important elements in the history of "Jewish-Christianity." Reprinted in Jones, *Pseudoclementina Elchasaiticaque inter Judaeochristiana,* 456–66.

Verheyden, Joseph. "Epiphanius on the Ebionites." In *The Image of the Judaeo-Christians in Ancient Jewish and Christian Literature,* ed. Peter J. Tomson and Doris Lambers-Petry, 182–208. WUNT 158. Tübingen: Mohr Siebeck, 2003.

Incisive essay situating Epiphanius's comments on the Ebionites in *Panarion* 30 within the heresiologist's own context and concerns, and discussing methodological issues related to the heavy scholarly dependence on these and other traditions from Epiphanius for reconstructing "Jewish-Christianity."

Reed, Annette Yoshiko. "'Jewish Christianity' as Counter-history? The Apostolic Past in Eusebius' *Ecclesiastical History* and the Pseudo-Clementine *Homilies.*" In *Antiquity in Antiquity: Jewish and Christian Pasts in the Greco-Roman World,* ed. Gregg E. Gardner and Kevin L. Osterloh, 173–216. TSAJ 123. Tübingen: Mohr Siebeck, 2008.

Comparison of Eusebius's representations of Judaism, Peter, Paul, the Jerusalem Church, and "Jewish Christians" with those in the Pseudo-Clementine *Homilies,* considering the two as competing fourth-century attempts to articulate true belief and practice, each with appeal to its own selections of received traditions about the apostolic past. Reprinted in the present volume as Chapter Six.

Ebionites, Nazoraeans, and Elchasaites

The Ebionites were a mainstay of Christian heresiological literature since Irenaeus's *Against Heresies* in the second century CE (e. g., 1.26.2; 3.11.7; 21.1; 5.1.3), and Patristic references to them form the heart of the secondhand evidence for "Jewish-Christianity" after the apostolic age. The Nazoraeans, although not as well attested, have gained attention owing to accounts of their combination of Torah observance with "orthodox" Christology. The Elchasaites and other groups have also been studied in relation to post-apostolic "Jewish-Christianity."

Pritz, Ray A. *Nazarene Jewish Christianity: From the End of the New Testament Period until Its Disappearance in the Fourth Century.* StPB 37. Leiden: Brill, 1988.

Attempt to reconstruct the history of the Nazarenes/Nazoraeans, a group discussed in detail by Epiphanius (*Panarion* 29) as Torah-observant with an "orthodox" Christology. Owing to the dearth of evidence, its reconstruction remains highly speculative, and its utility has been critiqued on these grounds. It remains an interesting effort, however, to disentangle the history of the Nazarenes/Nazoraeans from that of the much-discussed Ebionites.

Lichtenberger, Hermann. "Syncretistic Features in Jewish and Jewish-Christian Baptism Movements." In *Jews and Christians: The Parting of the Ways AD 70 to 135,* ed. James Dunn, 85–97. WUNT 66. Tübingen: Mohr Siebeck, 1992.

Interesting treatment of some "Jewish-Christian" sects with a focus on practice and in relation to a continuum of practices related to ritual ablution by the Qumran community, John the Baptist, Jesus Movement, and Mandaeans.

Bauckham, Richard. "The Origin of the Ebionites." In *Image of the Judeo-Christians*, ed. Peter J. Tomson and Doris Lambeers-Petry, 162–81. WUNT 158. Tübingen: Mohr Siebeck, 2003.
  Positive reassessment of evidence related to the Ebionites, primarily on the basis of Patristic reports about them.
Mimouni, Simon Claude. "Les elkasaïtes: États des questions et des recherches." In *The Image of the Judeo-Christians*, ed. Peter J. Tomson and Doris Lambeers-Petry, 209–29. WUNT 158. Tübingen: Mohr Siebeck, 2003.
  Helpful, up-to-date guide to research on the Elchasaites – another sect discussed by Patristic heresiologists, sometimes described as "Jewish-Christian," and particularly significant in relation to the background of Mani. The article includes a survey of the recent debate over the genre of the *Book of Elchasai* (i. e., as Jewish apocalypse versus early Church order).
Manns, Frédéric. "Le judéo-christianisme nazoréen: Sources et critique des sources: Réalité ou fiction?" *Estudios bíblicos* 63 (2005): 481–525.
  Positive reassessment of evidence for Nazorenes from Patristic reports about them as well as Rabbinic references to *notzrim*.
Jones, F. Stanley. "The Book of Elchasai in Its Relevance for Manichaean Institutions with a Supplement: The *Book of Elchasai* Reconstructed and Translated." *ARAM* 16 (2004): 179–215.
  Most extensive articulation of Jones' important argument that the *Book of Elchasai* is not an apocalypse but rather an early church order, dating from 116–117 CE and thus "chronologically the earliest identifiable witness to Christianity" in Syro-Mesopotamia. By Jones' reading, the *Book of Elchasai* emerges "as an important witness to a possibly distinct brand of Christianity that developed beyond the eastern border of the [Roman] empire." Reprinted in Jones, *Pseudoclementina Elchasaiticaque inter Judaeochristiana*, 359–97, alongside his other discussions of this text as well as articles that explore themes showing its cultural proximity to Bardaisan, the Pseudo-Clementine *Grundschrift*, and Mani.

"Jewish-Christianity" in Syria and Egypt

Although most research on "Jewish-Christianity" has centered on Roman Palestine, some attention has been given to Syria and Egypt, particularly as centers for the flourishing of its postapostolic forms. Syrian Christianity has long been associated with Judaism, not just because of older assumptions about the "Semitic" character of its Syriac expressions, but also because of the association of the *Didascalia Apostolorum* and Pseudo-Clementines with this region and the richness of the relevant data for interactions between Jews, "Jewish Christians," "Judaizers," and varieties of other Christians – particularly in Antioch but perhaps also in Edessa and its environs. The discussion of possible Egyptian "Jewish Christianities" has similarly helped to highlight the need to consider Hellenistic Judaism and the diaspora when mapping the range of early Christian continuities with "Jewish" identities, ideas, and practices.

Drijvers, Han Jan Willem. "Edessa und das jüdische Christentum." *VC* 24 (1970): 4–33.
Detailed, critical assessment of the association of Edessa and Syriac Christianity with the survival of an older "Jewish/Semitic Christianity" generally supplanted in the Roman Empire by "Gentile/Hellenistic Christianity."

Grant, Robert McQueen. "Jewish Christianity at Antioch in the Second Century." *RSR* 60 (1972): 97–108.
Seminal article on evidence for "Jewish Christians" in Antioch, important for its adoption of a geographical focus for the inquiry into "Jewish-Christianity" and for drawing on sources that help to bridge between the New Testament and Patristic evidence. Grant suggests that "many of the most important aspects of Christian and Gnostic history at Antioch in the second century can be explained in relation to the continued presence of 'Jewish-Christianity' there."

Klijn, Albertus Frederik Johannes. "Jewish Christianity in Egypt." In *The Roots of Egyptian Christianity*, ed. Birger Albert Pearson and James E. Goehring, 161–75. Studies in Antiquity and Christianity. Philadelphia: Fortress, 1986.
Survey of evidence for "Jewish-Christian" traditions attested in early Egyptian materials, notable for its expansion of the term with reference to Hellenistic Judaism.

Dorival, Gilles. "Un groupe judéo-chrétien méconnu: Les Hébreux." *Apoc* 11 (2000): 7–36.
Whereas most studies of "Jewish-Christian" groups have focused on Syro-Palestine, this article considers references to "the Hebrews" by Clement of Alexandria, Origen, and Didymus in terms of a Jewish-Christian group current in second-century Egypt.

Fonrobert, Charlotte Elisheva. "The *Didascalia Apostolorum*: A Mishnah for the Disciples of Jesus." *JECS* 9 (2001): 483–509.
Sophisticated analysis of the third-century Syrian *Didascalia Apostolorum* in terms of the differing "Jewish-Christian" perspectives of its author(s) and opponents, particularly in relation to *deuterosis*, exegesis, and menstrual purity. In the process, Fonrobert makes a number of important methodological points with regard to "Jewish-Christianity" in general.

Zetterholm, Magnus. *The Formation of Christianity in Antioch: A Social-Scientific Approach to the Separation between Judaism and Christianity.* London: Routledge, 2003.
Recent consideration of the development of "Christian" self-definition in Antioch, focusing on first- and second-century sources (e. g., Galatians 2; letters of Ignatius) and positing the importance of a split between "Jesus-believing Jews" and "Jesus-believing Gentiles" in the city.

Romeny, Bas ter Haar. "Hypotheses on the Development of Judaism and Christianity in Syria in the Period after 70 CE" In *Matthew and the Didache: Two Documents from the Same Jewish-Christian Milieu?*, ed. Huub Maria van de Sandt, 13–33. Minneapolis: Fortress, 2005.
Recent article reassessing Drijvers' conclusions about Edessa, particularly with reference to the possible Jewish or "Jewish-Christian" origins of the Peshitta version of the Old Testament (i. e., the Syriac translation of the Hebrew Bible).

"Jewish-Christianity" and Post-Christian Judaism

Traditionally, "Jewish-Christianity" has been studied primarily by specialists in the New Testament and Christianity. It is still most often treated as a variety of Christianity, rather than as a variety of Judaism. Perhaps partly as a result, scholarship on the topic has suffered from a lack of engagement with research on post-Christian Judaism, in general, and Rabbinic Judaism, in particular. One notable example is the older tendency to read all references to *minim* ("heretics") in the classical Rabbinic literature as referring to Christians. Nevertheless, the study of possible Rabbinic references to "Jewish-Christians," as well as Rabbinic parallels to "Jewish-Christian" materials, remains a promising avenue for exploring the transmission of traditions across creedal boundaries, especially when considered in terms of the methodological caveats in more recent research. Less studied, but also suggestive, are parallels with Jewish mystical and esoteric traditions.

Marmorstein, A. "Judaism and Christianity in the Middle of the Third Century." *HUCA* 10 (1935): 223–63.

An early exploration of possible evidence for awareness of Christianity, and "Jewish-Christianity" in particular, among Rabbinic Jews in third-century Roman Palestine, collecting a wealth of intriguing possible parallels with Pseudo-Clementine and other traditions.

Kimelman, Reuven. "*Birkat ha-minim* and the Lack of Evidence for an Anti-Christian Jewish Prayer in Late Antiquity." In *Jewish and Christian Self-Definition*, vol. 2: *Aspects of Judaism in the Graeco-Roman Period*, ed. E. P. Sanders, Albert I. Baumgarten, and Alan Mendelson, 226–44. Philadelphia: Fortress, 1981.

Classic article questioning the common understanding of the historicity of the *birkat ha-minim* in research on the New Testament and early Christianity, as referring to a systematic early expulsion of "Jewish-Christians" from synagogues.

Fossum, Jarl E. "Jewish-Christian Christology and Jewish Mysticism." *VC* 37 (1983): 260–87.

Learned reflection on possible evidence for connections between Christology and varieties of "mystical" traditions within Judaism (especially *merkavah, Shiur Qomah*) via "Jewish-Christianity," arguing that "the Jewish mysticism which was centered on the man-like figure upon the heavenly throne was influential in shaping the saviour image in the first centuries of our era."

Visotzky, Burton L. "Prolegomenon to the Study of Jewish-Christianities in Rabbinic Literature." *AJS Review* 14 (1989): 47–70.

Programmatic essay outlining methodological guidelines for exploring Rabbinic references to "Jewish Christians" without "parallelomania." The piece makes a number of important points about the topic in general, including the observation that it is best to allow for multiple "Jewish Christianities," rather than imagining a singular "Jewish-Christianity" occupying the space between a singular "Judaism" and a singular "Christianity."

Baumgarten, Albert. "Literary Evidence for Jewish Christianity in the Galilee." In *The Galilee in Late Antiquity*, ed. Lee I. Levine, 39–50. New York: Jewish Theological Seminary of America, 1992.

Influential article for drawing attention to parallels with Rabbinic traditions about the Oral Torah found in the Pseudo-Clementine literature.

Kalmin, Richard. "Christians and Heretics in Rabbinic Literature of Late Antiquity." *HTR* 87 (1994): 155–69.

Seminal article on the shifting meanings of *minim* in Rabbinic literature, tracing differences in tannaitic and amoraic materials, and in Palestinian and Babylonian materials, and providing a nuanced perspective on whether and when traditions about *min* and *minut* might be relevant for the study of Rabbinic encounters with Christians.

Reed, Annette Yoshiko. "Rabbis, Jewish Christians and Other Late Antique Jews: Reflections on the Fate of Judaism(s) after 70 CE." In *The Changing Face of Judaism, Christianity and Other Greco-Roman Religions in Antiquity*, ed. Ian H. Henderson and Gerbern S. Oegama, 323–46. Judische Schriften aus Hellenistisch-Romischer Zeit 2. Gütersloh, Germany: Gütersloher, 2005.

Brief survey of evidence for the continued diversity of Judaism even after the Second Temple period, reflecting on the possibility that some "Jewish-Christian" sources may provide evidence for the post-70 diversity of non-Christian Judaism.

Wolfson, Elliot. "Inscribed in the Book of the Living: *Gospel of Truth* and Jewish Christology." *JSJ* 38 (2007): 234–71.

Consideration of Christological materials in the *Gospel of Truth* that may preserve an ancient "Jewish-Christian" tradition which, in turn, sheds light on the relationship between Jewish and Christian esoteric discourses in Late Antiquity.

Côté, Dominique. "La forme de Dieu dans les Homélies Pseudo-clémentines et la notion de Shiur Qomah," in *"Soyez des changeurs avisés": Controverses exégétiques dans la littérature apocryphe chrétienne*, ed. Gabriella Aragione and Rémi Gounelle, 69–94. Cahiers de Biblia Patristica 12. Strasbourg: Université de Strasbourg, 2012.

Article surveying and revisiting early theories about parallels between the Pseudo-Clementines and early Jewish mysticism, triangulating the "pagan" philosophical discourse shaping the former's representation of the divine.

"Jewish-Christianity" and Early Islam

Debates about Islamic Origins form an important, if overlooked, part of the historiography of "Jewish-Christianity." This line of discussion – as Guy Stroumsa has recently shown – illuminates wider trends in the shifting place of "Jewish-Christianity" in the academic study of religions. Nineteenth- and early twentieth-century discussions of Islam's relationship to Judaism, Christianity, and "Jewish-Christianity" tended to focus on the question of "origins" and to adduce parallels to depict Islam as purportedly derivative. Specialists in Islamic Studies, thus, largely set aside this lines of discussion in the late twentieth century. More recently, however, parallels have been revisited in relation to new concerns to situate the Qur'ān in its late antique contexts – especially following the lead of Patricia Crone. In turn, John Gager has appealed to Crone's discussions of "Jewish-Christianity" to support his contention of the continued survival of "Jewish-Christian" perspectives for many centuries after the rise of Christianity. The value of this enterprise for the study of Islam remains sharply debated, and its many methodological pitfalls are outlined by Guillaume Dye.

Toland, John. *Nazarenus, or Jewish, Gentile, and Mahometan Christianity*. London, 1718.
Often credited as the earliest known thinker to use the English term "Jewish-Christianity" and the first to present it as key to recovering the most ancient form of Christianity, Toland here develops this idea concurrently in relation to Islam by virtue of his appeal to the *Gospel of Barnabas* alongside Pseudo-Clementine and other Christian apocrypha.

Crone, Patricia. "Islam, Judeo-Christianity, and Byzantine Iconoclasm." *Jerusalem Studies in Arabic and Islam* 2 (1980): 59–95.
Picking up on a suggestion by Shlomo Pines contested by Samuel Stern, this article argues that materials from the tenth-century Islamic author ʿAbd al-Jabbār draw on "Jewish-Christian" traditions from the fifth and sixth centuries, adducing additional evidence for the survival of Jewish-Christianity up to and even after the seventh century.

Gager, John G. "Did Jewish Christians See the Rise of Islam?" In *The Ways That Never Parted: Jews and Christians in Late Antiquity and the Early Middle Ages*, ed. Adam H. Becker and Annette Yoshiko Reed, 361–72. TSAJ 95. Tübingen: Mohr Siebeck, 2003.
Survey and reassessment of the scholarly debate over the possibility that "Jewish-Christian" traditions are preserved in the writings of the tenth-century Islamic author ʿAbd al-Jabbār, exploring the consequences for the history of Jewish/Christian relations.

Zellentin, Holger M. *The Qurʾān's Legal Culture: The Didascalia Apostolorum as a Point of Departure*. Tübingen: Mohr Siebeck, 2013.
Study highlighting points of parallel between the legal discourse of the Qurʾān and a "Judaeo-Christian" legal tradition reconstructed from the *Didascalia apostolorum* and Pseudo-Clementines, in conversation with recent discussions of the Qurʾān's late antique contexts.

Stroumsa, Guy G. "Jewish Christianity and Islamic Origins." In *Islamic Cultures, Islamic Contexts: Essays in Honor of Professor Patricia Crone*, ed. Asad Q. Ahmed, Behnam Sadeghi, Robert G. Hoyland, and Adam Silverstein, 72–96. Leiden: Brill, 2014.
Erudite and engaging survey of the intellectual history and scholarly discourse about the relationship of "Jewish-Christianity" to Islam from John Toland to Patricia Crone.

Crone, Patricia. "Jewish Christianity and The Qurʾān (Part One)." *Journal of Near Eastern Studies* 74 (2015): 225–53 + "Jewish Christianity and The Qurʾān (Part Two)." *Journal of Near Eastern Studies* 75 (2016): 1–21.
Detailed two-part article drawing on materials traditionally studied under the rubric of "Jewish-Christianity" (here loosely defined as "a wide variety of Christians who did not think of Christianity as a religion that abrogated Judaism") to revisit the question of its possible impact on early Islam. Against Sidney Griffith's denial of a connection, Crone argues that some points in the Qurʾān are "are extremely hard to explain without recourse to the hypothesis of a Jewish Christian contribution," including but not limited to ideas that "the Qurʾānic Jesus is a prophet sent to the Israelites, not to the gentiles; the Israelites appear to include Christians; the Messenger sees Jesus as second in im-

portance to Moses and as charged with confirmation of the Torah and insists that Jesus was only a human being, not the son of God."

Dye, Guillaume. "Jewish Christianity, the Qur'ān, and Early Islam: Some Methodological Caveats," In *"Jewish Christianity" and Early Islam: Papers Presented at the Eighth Annual ASMEA Conference*, ed. Francisco del Rio Sanchez, 11–28. Turnhout, Brepols, 2017.

In contrast to Crone, Dye cautions against the tendency to "use 'Jewish Christian' in a strict sense and … look for specific communities or groups" in a manner that "imagine(s) Arabia as a kind of Jurassic Park for ancient 'heresies.'" Nevertheless, Dye admits the very minor heurism of a looser sense of the term, concluding that "even if … fancying Jewish Christian groups behind the rise of Islam was too speculative (and unnecessary), one can concede that there is something that might be called a 'Jewish Christian sensitivity' in the Qur'ān." In his view, this reflects "the concrete religious situation of the Late Antique Middle East," in which "confessional loyalties were much more in flux than we generally believe" and "ordinary Christians had certainly other interests than border policy."

Ioudaios before and after "Religion"*

When did the Greek term *Ioudaios* come to mean "Jew"? The debate surrounding this question exposes the gaps separating contemporary English speakers from the ancient Greek writings that preserve so much of our evidence for formative periods of Judaism and Christianity. Difference in language is compounded by distance of time, but also by varying approaches to defining and distinguishing identities. In the case of *Ioudaios*, there is much at stake for scholars who study the New Testament, Flavius Josephus, and early Judaism and Christianity. Even beyond the bounds of Biblical Studies, however, this case may offer an instructive example of how modern assumptions about "religion" can pose challenges for understanding premodern texts, terms, and taxonomies.

Among specialists in Biblical Studies, the debate surrounding the translation of *Ioudaios* was reinvigorated by the new Brill translation of the writings of Josephus, the first-century Jewish author to whom we owe most of our knowledge of the history of Jews under Roman rule.[1] That translation rendered some occurrences of *Ioudaios* as "Judaean," and Steve Mason defended the decision by tracing a trajectory in the term's meaning – from the geographically rooted origins of *Ioudaios* (i. e., "Judaean" as a resident of Judah/Yehud/Judaea) to its early Christian reinterpretation as a religious affiliation (i. e., "Jews" as an adherent of Judaism).[2] By this logic, all first-century uses of the term retain an

---

* This piece first appeared in Timothy Michael Law and Charles Halton, eds., *Jew and Judean: A Forum on Politics and Historiography in the Translation of Ancient Texts* (Los Angeles: Marginalia Review of Books, 2014), http://marginalia.lareviewofbooks.org/ioudaios-religion-annette-yoshiko-reed/; it is reprinted here with permission from the Marginalia Review of Books.

[1] Steve Mason, gen. ed., *Flavius Josephus: Translation and Commentary* (Leiden: Brill, 2008–); so far, seven of the planned ten volumes have been published.

[2] Steve Mason, "Jews, Judaeans, Judaizing, Judaism: Problems of Categorization in Ancient History," *JSJ* 38 (2007): 457–512. See also Mason, "Ancient Jews or Judeans? Different Questions, Different Answers," in Law and Halton, *Jew and Judean,* http://marginalia.lareviewofbooks.org/ancient-jews-judeans-different-questions-different-answers-steve-mason/. For further discussion of the question see Shaye J. D. Cohen, *The Beginnings of Jewishness: Boundaries, Varieties, Uncertainties* (Berkeley: University of California Press, 1999); Daniel R. Schwartz, "Judaean or Jew? How Should We Translate *Ioudaios* in Josephus?," in *Jewish Identity in the Greco-Roman World,* ed. Jörg Frey, Daniel R. Schwartz, and Stephanie Gripentrog (Ancient Judaism and Christianity 71; Leiden: Brill, 2007), 1–28; Seth Schwartz, "How Many Judaisms Were There? A Critique of Neusner and Smith on Definition and Mason and Boyarin on Categorization," *JAJ* 2 (2011): 208–38; David M. Miller, "The Meaning of *Ioudaios* and its Relationship to Other Group Labels in Ancient 'Judaism,'" *CBR* 9 (2010): 98–126; Miller,

ethno-political sense – not yet religious. Adele Reinhartz agrees, but she suggests rendering even first-century uses of *Ioudaios* as "Jew," in part by adducing examples from the Gospel of John and their afterlife in Christian anti-Judaism; she draws attention to the contemporary ethical consequences of a scholarly practice that results in "the growing invisibility of Jews and Judaism in English translations of ancient texts and scholarship about them."[3]

At first sight, the debate might seem to pivot on the choice between Mason's search for the most accurate English equivalent of the term's meaning in the first century and Reinhartz's concern to tailor its translation to the understanding (and potential misunderstandings) of present-day readers. Yet the ramifications are also much wider. Just as Mason shows how the translation of a single term can engage the very nature of identity in the ancient world, so Reinhartz also calls us to critical reflection concerning the degree to which modern historical research can be isolated from its own historical contexts. Rather than arguing for one side or another, I would thus like to push further on both fronts – in part by asking what we miss when we plot the different meanings of *Ioudaios* along a straight line towards the concept of "Judaism" as "religion."

When did the Greek term *Ioudaios* shift in meaning from "Judaean" to "Jew"? There are telling assumptions embedded in the very question. First is the assumption that the one-to-one choice of an English equivalent might suffice to solve the challenges that we face when trying to describe ancient identities in modern terms. Second is the assumption that shifts in the conceptualization of identity can be tidily mapped onto the axis of time, such that we would be able to translate *Ioudaios* accurately if only we could determine *when* its meaning shifted. To be sure, I doubt that any of the scholars involved in the debate would defend such assumptions when stated quite so starkly. But this makes it all the more telling that the framing of the main question nevertheless presumes and reinforces them.

The focus on word-level translation reflects a longstanding tendency in Biblical Studies to treat the etymologies and histories of specific words as direct windows onto ancient thought – with the first known occurrence of a word *in writing* too often conflated with the birth of a concept.[4] If such approaches feel natural, even despite their bizarre atomization of language, it is in part because modern scholars of ancient *Ioudaioi* have long delighted in quests for the "origins" or "invention" of concepts now common in the West. Teleology, of course,

---

"Ethnicity Comes of Age: An Overview of Twentieth-Century Terms for *Ioudaios*," *CBR* 10 (2012): 293–311; Cynthia Baker, *Jew* (Key Words in Jewish Studies; New Brunswick: Rutgers University Press, 2017).

[3] Adele Reinhartz, "The Vanishing Jews of Antiquity," in Law and Halton, *Jew and Judean*, http://marginalia.lareviewofbooks.org/vanishing-jews-antiquity-adele-reinhartz/.

[4] Malcolm Lowe, "Concepts and Words," in Law and Halton, *Jew and Judean*, http://marginalia.lareviewofbooks.org/concepts-words-malcolm-lowe/. See also my discussion in the Epilogue above.

makes for poor history, and presentism courts anachronism. Yet their enduring power may help to explain the appeal of reducing the meaning of *Ioudaios* to a question of *when*. To assert a moment *before which* a word bore a now-familiar meaning, after all, is also to evoke the point *after which* we might confidently presume what it means to us today.

For the limits of such approaches, we need look no further than to the use of the English term "Jew." Those who prefer to translate first-century uses of *Ioudaios* as "Judaean" argue that "Jew" is a religious affiliation and therefore anachronistic prior to the Christian invention of "religion" in the third or fourth centuries. But this line of reasoning, as Reinhartz notes, presumes that "Jew" denotes a religious affiliation for "us" – an assumption not all English speakers who self-identify as Jews today share, as 2013 Pew polls made dramatically clear.[5] The persistence of multiple meanings can be seen even in the scholarly debate about *Ioudaioi*. If anything, the debate demonstrates how the term "Jew" can seem self-evidently *religious* to some people from the very same time and culture (and even the same profession and similar education) as others who understand it as self-evidently ethnic, political, cultural, or otherwise *not* or *not just* religious. It is not simply that the history of the meaning of *Ioudaios* might be told differently if we chose a different end point, such as the modern equivalents in Hebrew or Japanese or German. Even the English term "Jew" resists reduction to a single meaning at the end of a single story.

Something may be lost when the different senses of *Ioudaios* are collapsed into a series of points along one straight line to one present-day meaning. In focusing on changes in its meaning before and after "religion," for instance, there is some risk in reifying what came before. It can be tempting to imagine pre-Christian collective identities as all stable and of the same sort – devoid of the cult so often adhering to culture, the ritual practice so often tied to place, and the inextricability of so many local lineages and landscapes of memory from devotion to deities. That such elements have been habitually neglected in scholarly disciplines like Classics makes it all the more pressing not to write them out of history just because we cannot find a Greek or Latin term directly equivalent to "religion." Brent Nongbri is surely right to remind us of the dangers of universalizing a modern sense of "religion" as "a kind of inner disposition and concern for salvation conceived in opposition to politics and other 'secular' areas of life."[6] Yet one need not posit Jewish exceptionalism to recognize that different ancient identities (and a good many modern ones) cut differently across the lines of what we are now accustomed to compartmentalizing as "geographical," "ethnic," "political," and "religious."

---

[5] Reinhartz, "The Vanishing Jews"; "A Portrait of Jewish Americans," *Pew Forum*, 1 October 2013, http://www.pewforum.org/2013/10/01/Jewish-american-beliefs-attitudes-culture-survey/.

[6] Brent Nongbri, *Before Religion: A History of a Modern Concept* (New Haven: Yale University Press, 2013), 1.

The ancient Mediterranean world was hardly a realm of clear-cut bounded lands occupied only by autochthonous peoples. The same centuries that biblical scholars study as the Second Temple period (538 BCE–70 CE) saw the consolidation of forms of education whereby even elites with no connection to Greece could become "Greeks" and also the articulation of new spatial ideologies whereby Macedonians like the Seleucids could redefine what it meant to be "Syrian." Greek terms for peoplehood like *ethnos* may remind us of our words for ethnicity, but the etymological connection should not lead us to treat them as identical to what we now categorize as race or nationality.[7] At times, Greek historians and Roman jurists may use terms of this sort when trying to impose order on the sprawling diversity of the ancient Mediterranean world. Nevertheless, labels for different *ethnoi* do not necessarily denote stable entities of the same sort.[8] Even under the Roman Empire, there was no static sense of land-bound or genealogical identity from which Jews might be posited as the sole exception – or against which Christians might be heralded as the only agents of change. The second and third centuries might see the beginnings of a Christian discourse rereading "Jewishness" (*Ioudaismos*) as an entity more comparable to "Christianity" (*Christianismos*) than "Hellenism" (*Hellenismos*), but in these same centuries, Lucian could call himself "Greek" or "Syrian" depending on the point he wished to make; even Bardaisan could be variously described as "Christian," "Parthian," "Mesopotamian," "Babylonian," and "Armenian."[9] Despite the tendency in Biblical Studies for scholars to describe even Paul as self-evidently "Christian," even this label is not "religious" in any manner always and everywhere distinct from ethnic reasoning; not unlike *Ioudaioi*, the Greek term *Christianoi* and its cognates continued to be reinterpreted in creative and productive ways into Late Antiquity and well beyond.[10] We may wish to be wary, thus, lest we refract the differences between ancient *Ioudaioi* and modern Jews

---

[7] Jonathan M. Hall, *Ethnic Identity in Greek Antiquity* (Cambridge: Cambridge University press, 1997),

[8] Greg Woolf, *Tales of the Barbarians: Ethnography and Empire in the Roman West* (Malden: Wiley-Blackwell, 2011); Benjamin Isaac, *The Invention of Racism in Antiquity* (Princeton: Princeton University Press, 2006).

[9] See further Nathanael J. Andrade, *Syrian Identity in the Greco-Roman World* (Cambridge: Cambridge University Press, 2013); William A. Adler, "The Kingdom of Edessa and the Creation of a Christian Aristocracy," in *Jews, Christians, and the Roman Empire: The Poetics of Power in Late Antiquity*, ed. Natalie B. Dohrmann and Annette Yoshiko Reed (Philadelphia: University of Pennsylvania Press, 2013), 43–62; cf. Adam H. Becker, "The Ancient Near East in the Late Antique Near East: Syriac Christian Appropriation of the Biblical East," in *Antiquity in Antiquity: Jewish and Christian Pasts in the Greco-Roman World*, ed. Gregg Gardner and Kevin Osterloh (TSAJ 123; Tübingen: Mohr Siebeck, 2008), 394–415.

[10] Aaron P. Johnson, "Identity, Descent, and Polemic: Ethnic Argumentation in Eusebius' *Praeparatio Evangelica*," *JECS* 12 (2004): 23–56; Denise Buell, *Why This New Race? Ethnic Reasoning in Early Christianity* (New York: Columbia University Press, 2005).

through the lens of a misleadingly static concept of "Christianity" as inventor and exemplar of "religion."

There is a compelling case to be made that early Christians like Ignatius and Tertullian innovated a new sense of Jewishness by reducing *Ioudaismos* to the Christian past and by redefining *Ioudaios* as a term of Christological error. These particular senses of "Judaism" and "Jew" would have a long afterlife in medieval and modern Christian polemical discourse – with dire consequences for European Jewry in particular. Looking back, we may glimpse some modes of categorization akin to our current taxonomic practice of distinguishing "religions." But in their own contexts, many of these cases might be better explained as the use of *Ioudaios* and related terms as negative *exempla* of Christianness. Nor are Jews the sole focus for such efforts; rather, as Douglas Boin reminds us, the meanings of *Christianoi* and its cognates were negotiated through multiple contrasts with constructed categories of various sorts (e. g., Greek *Hellenismos*, *haeresis*; Latin *paganus*).[11] Likewise, our sense of the development of ancient identities may be skewed when we globalize those patterns that so happen to be attested in Greek and Latin literary evidence. These patterns are partly a result of accidents of preservation: the later in time, the greater percentage of surviving Greek and Latin writings that are Christian. Would our picture of the changing meanings of *Ioudaioi* and *Ioudaismos* look different, for instance, if there were more surviving literary evidence for Greek-speaking Jewry in Late Antiquity and the Middle Ages?[12] We certainly find different self-designations and other approaches to categorizing identity and difference in the premodern Jewish writings richly preserved in Hebrew, Aramaic, and Arabic – although these have been comparably neglected by modern scholars and only rarely (if ever) culled for evidence for dramatic narratives of "invention" of the sort commonly told from Greek and Latin sources.

Mason and Reinhartz both present the problem of translating first-century *Ioudaioi* as a matter of defining identity before the rise of "religion," and they look to a late antique horizon when Christian discourses of difference constructed both "religion" and "Judaism" as we now know them. In this, they follow Daniel Boyarin's influential argument for the fourth century as a determinative era for the disembedding of "religion" from ethnic, political, geographical, and

---

[11] Douglas Boin, "Hellenistic 'Judaism' and the Social Origins of the 'Pagan-Christian' Debate," *JECS* 22 (2014): 167–96.

[12] On what we do know, see Nicholas De Lange, *Greek Jewish Texts from the Cairo Genizah* (Tübingen: Mohr Siebeck, 1996); De Lange, "Hebrews, Greeks or Romans? Jewish Identity in Byzantium," in *Strangers to Themselves: The Byzantine Outsider*, ed. Dion C. Smythe (Aldershot: Ashgate, 2000), 105–18; De Lange, "Research on Byzantine Jewry: The State of the Question," in *Jewish Studies at the Central European University IV, 2003–2005*, ed. András Kovács and Michael L. Miller (Budapest: Central European University, 2006), 41–51.

other elements of ancient identity.[13] Boyarin's argument has important ramifications for understanding the Roman Empire in Late Antiquity. Yet it remains that late antique shifts did not suffice to produce "religion" as we now know it. The genealogy of our current system of categorizing "religion" and "religions" owes more to modern European colonial and related contexts – as Talal Asad, Daniel Dubuisson, Tomoko Masuzawa, and others have variously demonstrated.[14]

If scholars can defend different moments of "invention," moreover, it is in part because none of them was ever quite complete. Just as Boyarin himself points to the Rabbinic resistance of "religion" in Late Antiquity, so Leora Batnitzky has shown how the reduction of "Judaism" to "religion" continued to remain contested well into modernity; "Judaism" has never fit neatly only in the category "religion," and this very misfit, in fact, has spurred much creativity within Jewish thought.[15] Seen from this perspective, it is not surprising that the twenty-first-century English term "Jew" is no more static, set, or stable than the first-century Greek term *Ioudaios*; like many terms of communal identity, they have been continually constituted as relevant in part through creative contestation.

That "Jew" becomes a category that is both opposite and equivalent to "Christian" is an axiom of much modern research on the New Testament, Christianity, and even Jewish/Christian relations. This contention, however, may tell us as much about the modern histories of these academic subfields as about premodern trajectories in the meanings of Greek *Ioudaios* and its cognates. Susannah Heschel, for instance, emphasizes the influence of nineteenth-century German Protestant theologians on modern ideas about "Judaism" as a category akin to "Christianity."[16]

It is perhaps not surprising that the results can seem natural or invisible nonetheless – especially to scholars who study early Judaism and Christianity; after all, this particular image of "Judaism" was forged within the same settings that were also formative for the modern Western discipline of Biblical Studies. Indeed, this is part of the reason that Mason's intervention was so powerful. The

---

[13] Daniel Boyarin, *Border Lines: The Partition of Judaeo-Christianity* (Philadelphia: University of Pennsylvania Press, 2004).

[14] Talal Asad, *Genealogies of Religion: Discipline and Reasons of Power in Christianity and Islam* (Baltimore: Johns Hopkins University Press, 1993); Daniel Dubuisson, *L'Occident et la religion: Mythes, science et idéologie* (Paris: Editiones Complexe, 1998); Tomoko Masuzawa, *The Invention of World Religions: Or, How European Universalism Was Preserved in the Language of Pluralism* (Chicago: University of Chicago Press, 2005).

[15] Leora Batnitzky, *How Judaism Became a Religion: An Introduction to Modern Jewish Thought* (Princeton: Princeton University Press, 2011).

[16] Susannah Heschel, "Revolt of the Colonized: Abraham Geiger's *Wissenschaft des Judentums* as a Challenge to Christian Hegemony in the Academy," *New German Critique* 77 (1999): 61–85. See further now Daniel Boyarin, *Judaism* (Key Words in Jewish Studies; New Brunswick: Rutgers University Press, forthcoming) as well as discussion and references in the Epilogue to this volume.

new Brill translation unsettled a longstanding tendency in Biblical Studies by challenging us to reread Josephus's representation of his people's history anew, apart from older assumptions about the narrowly religious nexus of Jewish peoplehood. As effective as this intervention has been, however, it makes a bit less sense outside of this one specific context – as Reinhartz has shown.[17]

The debate over the translation of *Ioudaios* has been valuable in opening up a broader perspective and bringing insights from the study of Late Antiquity and Religious Studies to bear on the often isolationist study of Josephus and the New Testament. But the more we delve into the complexity of ethno-political discourse in the ancient Mediterranean world, the long and winding prehistories of modern Western notions of "religion," and the tenacious multiplicity of identity labels like "Christian" and "Jew," the less it seems plausible to solve the problem of anachronism just by choosing one or another rote translation depending on the date of the text in question. Even the challenge of translation might be better understood on the level of sentences or paragraphs or texts or corpora rather than single words interpreted in isolation.

As this particular example becomes more widely discussed, it also becomes increasingly feasible just to transliterate *Ioudaios* in those cases where rendering "Jew" might seem unduly misleading. If our aim is to avoid anachronism, it might be better to begin by historicizing our own scholarly habits, diagnosing our blind spots, and avoiding presentist narratives that uncritically reinforce them. However one translates *Ioudaios*, it remains misleading to trace a thin line in the development of Jewish/Judaean identities that flattens their ancient Mediterranean contexts and ignores their manifold afterlives outside of Greek, Latin, and Christian literature. The very challenge of translating ancient *Ioudaioi* into modern terms points to the power and limits of categorizing "religions" – in antiquity and modernity alike.

---

[17] Reinhartz, "The Vanishing Jews."

"Jew" and the Making of the Christian Gaze*

It is a potent time to rethink identity. Much of the twenty-first century had been marked by scholarly proclamations of its demise. Already by the close of the twentieth century, scholars had long noted how modern nation-states are "imagined communities,[1] and the reminder of the constructed character of national origin myths, civic religions, and patriotic emblems had been repeated and repeated again. During the 1980s and 1990s, it similarly became commonplace for historians to trace how this or that religious and/or ethnic "identity" was created through the mirror of the Other (which was thereby constructed, and so forth). Such tropes became so widespread that Rogers Brubaker and Frederick Cooper declared the discussion done in 2000.[2] Precisely because of the promiscuous proliferation of assertions about "identity" as "fluid, constructed, and multiple," Brubaker and Cooper suggested that the idea had been evacuated of all meaning: "If identity is everywhere, it is nowhere."[3] And as within academe, so too within some sectors of American culture. For many white liberals, the Obama years marked the age when the United States finally became postracial and postethnic.[4] For many white conservatives, it was an era no longer in need of an "identity politics" emblematized by the political correctness of the 1990s. Leon Wieseltier thereby proclaimed it "an idea whose time has gone."[5]

What seemed increasingly irrelevant with certain circles at the dawn of the twenty-first century, however, was rather abruptly demonstrated to be a major factor, at least within American political life. Among the surprises of the 2016 presidential election was the importance of identity in mobilizing and collectiv-

---

* This piece first appeared in 2017 in Annette Yoshiko Reed and Shaul Magid, eds., *Forum on Cynthia Baker's Jew* (Los Angeles: Marginalia Review of Books, 2017), http://marginalia.l areviewofbooks.org/jew-making-christian-gaze/; it is reprinted here with permission from the Marginalia Review of Books.

[1] Benedict Anderson, *Imagined Communities: Reflections on the Origin and Spread of Nationalism* (London: Verso, 1983).

[2] Rogers Brubaker and Frederik Cooper, "Beyond Identity," *Theory and Society* 29 (2000): 1–47. See further discussion in the Epilogue of this volume.

[3] Brubaker and Cooper, "Beyond Identity," 1.

[4] David A. Hollinger, *Postethnic America: Beyond Multiculturalism* (New York: Basic, 2006).

[5] Leon Wieseltier, "Against Identity," *The New Republic*, 27 November 1994.

izing a set of voters who had not previously been understood in those terms –
namely, those self-identifying as white.

Since at least 2012, census data signaled demographic shifts rendering whites
no longer a numerical majority in the United States. Nevertheless, in public
discourse, whiteness remained framed as a neutral and unstated norm, devoid of
ethnic particularity, exemplifying radical individualism, embodying the Amer-
icanness to which minorities aimed or feared to assimilate. During the 2016
presidential campaign, and now in the wake of the election of Donald Trump,
however, this demographic shift has begun to be matched by a shift in public
discourse. "The president-elect," as Laila Lalami noted, "earned the votes of a
majority of white people while running a campaign that explicitly and consistently appealed to white identity and anxiety."[6] In political speech, whiteness has
shifted from unstated norm to named particularity; the white voter is now polled
and labeled, and whiteness is increasingly framed as an "identity" in the same
sense that term is used of (other) minorities.

What makes this shift so striking is its departure from the longstanding pattern, noted by Richard Dyer and others, whereby "the invisibility of whiteness
as a racial position in white (which is to say dominant) discourse" has enabled
whites "not to be represented to themselves as whites but as people."[7] Now,
however, positions once whispered at the margins are becoming positions increasingly voiced in the public square, with white supremacy rebranded as alt-
right ethno-nationalism, and some thinkers retheorizing whiteness precisely by
redeploying the same rhetoric of collective identity commonly used by Jewish
and other minorities (cf. "white Zionism"). The range of acceptable public discourse is being reconfigured under Trumpism, and among the results is a shift
in what is even spoken of as "identity": the locus of whiteness can move from
personal to collective identity – from "who am I?" to "who are *we*?"

Cynthia Baker's *Jew* could not have appeared at a more timely moment.[8] This
concise and engaging book takes up the task of "tracking the term *Jew* through
diverse eras, contexts, and genres" so as to "provide a way of seeing – with
depth and nuance – the ongoing construction and negotiation of 'the West' and

---

[6] Laila Lalami, "The Identity Politics of Whiteness," *New York Times*, 21 November 2016.
See also, more recently, Perry Bacon Jr., "Charlottesville and the Rise of White Identity Politics," *FiveThirtyEight*, 14 August 2017, https://fivethirtyeight.com/features/charlottesville-an
d-the-rise-of-white-identity-politics/. Note also recent polls on perceptions of discrimination of
whites, e. g., Robert Jones, "Republicans More Likely to Say White Americans – Rather Than
Black Americans – Face Discrimination," *Public Religion Research Institute*, 2 August 2017,
https://www.prri.org/spotlight/republicans-white-black-reverse-discrimination/.

[7] Richard Dyer, "The Matter of Whiteness," in *White Privilege: Essential Readings on the
Other Side of Racism*, ed. Paula Rothberg (2nd ed.; New York: Worth, 2005), 11. See further
discussion in the Epilogue of this volume.

[8] Cynthia Baker, *Jew* (Key Words in Jewish Studies; New Brunswick: Rutgers University
Press, 2017).

of the westernized self."[9] In the process, Baker provides a model for how we can discuss "identity" anew, taking seriously the above-noted critiques of the idea but also taking seriously the enduring power of naming to shape groups, make differences, and motivate collective action. Baker does not analyze *Jew* as an "identity," in the sense of a stable category or condition in which people participate to greater or lesser degrees; what she tracks is some of the "complex (and often ambivalent) processes" of identification that constitute *Jew*, heeding Brubaker and Cooper's call "to specify the agents that do the identifying."[10] Rather than just asking *when* the term *Jew* came to take on this or that meaning (e. g., ethnic, religious, racial, cultural), she considers *who* makes and takes its meanings.

Historians of ancient Judaism have hotly debated the question of precisely *when* the Greek term *Ioudaios* came to mean "Jew" in a religious sense rather than "Judaean" in a geographical or ethnic sense. That the translation of this term has ethical as well as historiographical consequences became richly clear in our 2014 Marginalia forum on the topic.[11] By shifting our focus from *when* to *who*, Baker draws out dynamics in the debate itself. She notes the oddity of "the compulsion to provide two distinct categories and names – 'ethnic' Judaeans versus 'religious' Jews – by which to translate identical terms (whether *yehudim*, *yehuda'i*, *Ioudaioi*, or *Ieudei*) from ancient linguistic cultures that display no inclination to such bifurcation."[12] If this compulsion makes little sense in the ancient cultural contexts of the texts in question, it fits well within the modern cultural contexts that have shaped our scholarship: "Modern scholarship on the terms *yehudim*, *Ioudaioi*, and their cognates was, from its inception and until very recent generations, the purview of Christian philologists, homilists, and biblicists."[13] The very question presumes and reinscribes a distinctively Christian gaze:

Although content, context, and rationale differ significantly among those who adopt the bifurcated terminology Judaean/Jew, what persists, as noted above, is the division between elements that are currently assembled under the rubric ethnicity (nation, genealogy, nature, tribe) versus those gathered under religion (profession, adherence, faith, belief). Part and parcel of this dualism is the implication or assertion that the former represents a given or inherited condition whereas the latter involves choice and, more than that, aspiration (realizable through fundamental transformation or conversion) to a higher, more developed, and enlightened level of individual and/or collective being. In this respect, ethnicity versus religion shares a great deal with such other dualisms as outward versus

---

[9] Baker, *Jew*, 10.

[10] Brubaker and Cooper, "Beyond Identity," 14; Baker, *Jew*, 76.

[11] Timothy Michael Law and Charles Halton, *Jew and Judean: A Forum on Politics and Historiography in the Translation of Ancient Texts* (Los Angeles: Marginalia Review of Books, 2014), http://marginalia.lareviewofbooks.org/jew-judean-forum/.

[12] Baker, *Jew*, 21.

[13] Baker, *Jew*, 21.

inward, letter (or flesh) versus spirit, worldly versus heavenly, and particular/local versus universal, which come to shape Christian rhetoric and worldview. It appears, then, that our modern sociological/anthropological dualism ethnic versus religious, which is commonly presented as objective, neutral, and rationally secular description when invoked in social-scientific analyses, may nonetheless be as deeply rooted in a Christian Western worldview as are the more theologically explicit dualisms to which it so closely conforms. Indeed, the patterns of correspondence ethnicity=flesh/particular and religion=spirit/universal are as consistent and striking in recent academic studies of the origins of Jews as are historicized narratives of cultural transformation.[14]

What appears to be neutral is crypto-theological: "Rather than displacing theological and imperialist paradigms with neutral social-scientific descriptors, Judaean as 'earlier ethnic group' paired with Jew as 'later adherent of a religion' (or 'ethno-religion' or 'race religion') only serves to reinscribe these paradigms still more firmly and subtly while obscuring their association with anti-Jewish discourses."[15]

In the assumptions undergirding the current scholarly debate about *Jew*, we thus find reflected part of the very history of *Jew*: "For most of two long millennia, the word *Jew* has been predominantly defined and delimited as a term for not-self… often signif[ying] an absolute other, the very antithesis of the Western Christian self."[16] And among the effects of the Christian construction of *Jew* – as Baker deftly shows – is the naturalization of this hierarchicalized bifurcation of "ethnicity" and "religion," in which is also embedded an assumed narrative of development:

Not only do the terms "ethnicity" and "religion" come down to us through the prism of early Christian discourse about the Jews, but the narrative of progress from ethnicity to religion itself resembles an explicitly Christian historiography – one that morally subordinates ethnicity (as primitive and particular) to religion (as universal aspiration), much as it morally subordinates Judaism and Jew (as limited and superseded) to Christianity and Christian (as universal apex of human attainment).[17]

This framework is now so naturalized as to be invisible and unintentionally reinscribed – even by those academics working in self-consciously non-confessional domains of historical scholarship on ancient Judaism. Accordingly, as Baker notes, one finds even Jewish historians of Judaism such as Shaye Cohen posing the question of the beginnings of Jewishness in these very terms – as the story of how "religion overcame ethnicity."[18]

---

[14] Baker, *Jew*, 25.

[15] Baker, *Jew*, 42.

[16] Baker, *Jew*, 4.

[17] Baker, *Jew*, 41.

[18] Shaye J. D. Cohen, *The Beginnings of Jewishness* (Berkeley: University of California Press, 1999), 340.

For Baker, this insight clears the way for her story about the "centuries-long process" by which the Christian construction of *Jew* as exonym became inverted with "the historically recent appropriation of *Jew*, in dominant Western vernaculars, as a term of self-identification."[19] Far from any simple arithmetic of alterity that mirrors Self and Other, Baker's study thus embodies what can be done when one heeds Juliet Steyn's corrective concern to "rethink identity as something made, as a process, as something that can never be complete, that is always becoming and contingent."[20] Baker shows how *Jew* is not simply appropriated from premodern Christian gaze to modern Jewish self-empowerment: "Currently, Jew conveys neither a simple sense of abject otherness nor one of secured selfhood," and "just as the Jew is 'proximate other' (in the apt phrase of Jonathan Z. Smith) and repressed self of Christian/Western articulations of identity, so, too, the Jew has become, in many respects, a kind of proximate other and repressed (or celebrated, excavated, or memorialized) self to modern articulations of Jewish identity."[21] Here too, a focus on identification opens the way for understanding what might otherwise seem like strange or surprising twists in the expression of identity.

My question here, however, is about what is thereby rendered invisible – that is, the Christian ownership of an ostensibly neutral gaze and objective perspective. What did the Christian making of *Jew*, as abject and exonym, also make of the *Christian*? And what was lost, erased, constrained, or forgotten in the process? This is another story, and it is a story perhaps all the more pressing to ponder now, since it is part of the story of how whiteness came to be constructed as invisible – part of the Western making of a mirage of neutrality whereby white/Christian has been framed as a human norm rather than a marked "identity." Baker's book may open up a new window onto this story too.

To the degree that Baker traces the genealogy of the totalizing Christian gaze that constructs *Jew*, it is with appeal to Eusebius. Like Justin Martyr and Tertullian before him, Eusebius resigns Jewishness to the Christian past – a move that empties *Jew* to serve thereafter as a protean imagined Other. But this move also empties "Christian" to serve as a stable imperial stance from which one might claim to categorize and organize the ethnic and cultural difference of other Others as well. The latter is the stance that can adopt the universalizing epistemological pretensions of Greek ethnography – as Todd Berzon shows of Epiphanius and others – so as to classify Christian "heretics" alongside Jews, Samaritans, and Greeks.[22] If these acts of knowledge ordering do not tell us as much as we might like about "heretics," Jews, Samaritans, and Greeks, they do

---

[19] Baker, *Jew*, 9.

[20] Baker, *Jew*, 76; Juliet Steyn, *The Jew: Assumptions of Identity* (London: Cassell, 1999).

[21] Baker, *Jew*, 77.

[22] Todd Berzon, *Classifying Christians: Ethnography, Heresiology, and the Limits of Knowledge in Late Antiquity* (Berkeley: University of California Press, 2016).

tell us about those particular Christians who claimed the authority to order such knowledge, and they also tell us something about what was erased of Christianness in the course of their totalizing claims.

Perhaps most notable are those positions that modern scholars call "Jewish-Christian" – that is, those positions that frustrate both ancient and modern Christian projects of framing *Jew* as a model for difference-making. Precisely in the fourth century, contemporaneous with Eusebius, for instance, one finds quite a different use of "Jew" in the Pseudo-Clementine *Homilies*, here placed in the mouth of the apostle Peter. Peter here claims that no Jews suffer the diseases caused by demons, thereby occasioning an explanation of what he means by *Jew*:

But no one of us [i. e., Jews] can suffer such a thing; they themselves [i. e., demons] are punished by us, when, having entered into anyone, they entreat us so that they may go out slowly. Yet, someone will perhaps say: "Even some of the God-fearers fall under such sufferings [i. e., diseases caused by demons]." I say that is impossible! For I speak of the God-fearer who is truly God-fearing, not one who is such only in name, but one who really fulfills the commandments of the Law that has been given him. If anyone acts impiously, he is not pious. And, hence, if a foreigner keeps the Law/Torah, he is a Jew, but he who does not is a Greek. For the Jew, believing in God, keeps the Law/Torah. But he who does not keep the Law/Torah is manifestly a deserter through not believing God. And thus – as no Jew, but a sinner – he is on account of his sin brought into subjection to those sufferings that are ordained for the punishment of sinners. (Ps.-Clem. *Hom.* 11.16)

Here, the opposite of Jew is not Christian but rather Greek and sinner, and the criterion is one's adherence to "the Law that has been given him" – a criterion that the Pseudo-Clementine *Homilies* later explains to mean the teachings of Moses for Jews and the teachings of Jesus for Gentiles (both of which are asserted to be essentially the same). Accordingly, when the "pagan" Clement of Rome comes to follow the apostle Peter, Pseudo-Clementine *Homilies* do not describe his change of affiliation as "conversion to Christianity"; rather, Clement here says that he "took on the holy God and Law of the Jews, putting my faith in the well-assured conclusion that the Law has been assigned by the righteous judgment of God" (4.22). He does so, moreover, after realizing that "the whole learning of the Greeks is a most dreadful fabrication of a wicked demon," choosing instead to embrace "the doctrine of the supposedly barbarian Jews" as the "most pious, introducing One [God] as the Father and Creator of all this world, by nature good and righteous – good, indeed, as pardoning sins to those who repent; but righteous, as visiting to every one after repentance according to the worthiness of his doings" (4.12).

What is absent and unnamed is "Christian." The term, in fact, occurs nowhere in the Pseudo-Clementine *Homilies*. The world is here split into Jews and Greeks/Gentiles, and what we might call "Gentile Christians" (i. e., non-Jewish followers of Jesus and his apostles) are here categorized as "Jews" and/

or "God-fearers," in contrast to Greeks, sinners, and "heretics." "Christian" is subsumed into "Jew," and authentically apostolic truth is defined by analogy to Judaism but in contradistinction to Greek *paideia*.

The contrast with Eusebius is notable. But this is not the only possible comparison. Baker notes how the Hebrew and Aramaic equivalents of *Jew* "rarely appear in midrash or Talmud."[23] This is also the case for the name "Christian" and, indeed, for any framework in which this pair of labels might even make sense. To the degree that late antique Rabbis partition the world, it is into Israel and *goyim*,[24] and whether intentionally or not, this bifurcation subverts any claim for "Christian" as a taxonomically meaningful "identity." So too for the Pseudo-Clementine *Homilies*. The text is often called "Jewish-Christian," but from its own perspective, the designation is meaningless: there are no "Jewish-Christians" or "Gentile-Christians," just Jews and Greeks, Israel and the nations. Nor is the distinction merely abstract or rhetorical: the former are on the side of God, while the latter are infested by demons. As with Eusebius and Epiphanius, their position has precedents (in this case: in what is noted of *Ioudaioi* by authors like Philo and Josephus, and in what is noted of *Hellênes* by authors like Tatian). As in the Mishnah and other Rabbinic literature, moreover, Jewishness is less of a "religious identity" than the gaze and framework for organizing knowledge about particularity and difference in the rest of the world – albeit, for the Pseudo-Clementine *Homilies*, grappling in particular with those new sorts of particularity and difference posed by non-Jews who accept Jesus as the Jewish messiah proclaimed in the Jewish Scriptures.

It may be significant that such perspectives were voiced even as late as the fourth century (and circulating widely thereafter) – not least because they point to some of what was lost *within* Christianity during the course of the process charted by Baker. The construction of a totalizing and imperial Christian gaze by Eusebius, Epiphanius, and others, with *Jew* as Other, also resulted in the reduction of the Jewishness of Christianity to the Jewishness of Christian Origins. In the perceived need for a hybrid term like "Jewish-Christianity," no less than in the puzzling retention of "Judaeo-" in "Judaeo-Christian," one might glimpse some anxiety about forgetting (and the impossibility of forgetting) this very Jewishness. It may not be coincidental, as Baker notes, that "almost all modern Western forms of the word – *Jew, Jude, juif, Judío, giudeo, jood, Zsidó,* etc. (and even the Yiddish word *yid*) – came into being in decidedly Christian-dominant societies and geopolitical contexts, and, with the exception of *yid*, they seem often to have taken their earliest written form in commentaries, translations, and sermons on the New Testament."[25]

---

[23] Baker, *Jew*, 3.

[24] Ishay Rosen-Zvi and Adi Ophir, "Goy: Toward a Genealogy," *Dine Israel* 29 (2011): 69–122.

[25] Baker, *Jew*, 4.

For Christians to think with *Jew* is also to think about Christian Origins that are never just origins, as embodied in those Jewish writings that became Christian Scripture but remain trenchantly Jewish all the same. These generative tensions may be controlled by the creation of a totalizing Christian gaze exemplified by the Christian discourse about *Jew*, but they are never wholly erased – as perhaps clear from the relentlessly repeated remembering and forgetting and remembering of even Jesus' identity as *Jew*. In this sense, Jewishness functions for Christianness perhaps akin to what Frank B. Wilderson III notes of blackness with respect to "the racial labor that Whiteness depends on for its unracialized 'normality'": it is the particularity without which a claim to universality cannot be articulated.[26] And, as with blackness for whiteness, this claim is precarious, even when it is invisible, and especially when it is finally seen.

Instead of asking only how the Self is constructed with the Other, we might instead wish to ask: *Who* gets to construct an Other, and with what consequences to the Self? And which of these constructions of difference do and do not get to inform those systems of classification that we treat as neutral and natural, not least through the questions and categories that we use in our scholarship? Current events suggest that such questions may prove increasingly pressing in the coming years, especially as the dominance of whiteness (and white Christianness) in the United States shifts from demographic fact to discursive identity claim. After all, as Michel Foucault has taught us, claims about knowledge are always, or mostly, claims to authority and power. In this respect, it is significant that Baker is self-conscious about her participation in a process whereby Jewish Studies lays claim to a scholarly stance on Jews and Judaism that has been traditionally monopolized by Christians. "Scholarship on the *Jew*, as a kind of 'cottage industry' within Jewish studies," Baker notes, "has served not only as a locus for exploring all of the important subjects and dynamics enumerated in the titles of the books and articles produced under this rubric, but also as a workshop for constructing, deconstructing, examining, and critiquing ideas about *Jew* as self."[27] And, precisely because of this perspectival shift, we might wonder whether Baker's project can also tell us something about the Self more broadly, especially in an age now in need of rethinking "identity."

---

[26] Frank B. Wilderson III, *Red, White & Black: Cinema and the Structure of US Antagonisms* (Durham: Duke University Press, 2010), 250.

[27] Baker, *Jew*, 77.

Index of Sources

1. Biblical literature

Genesis
1:1 169–70
1:26 169–70, 324, 355–57
1:27 170
2:17 171
2:20 171
2:21–22 169
3:1–5 171
3:22 168, 324
3:6 168
6:1–4 33
6:6 168n83, 171–72
8:21 168
9:6 355
11:5 172
11:7 171, 324
15:13 171
18:1 188
18:18 195
18:21 168, 324
22:1 168
49:10 188–89, 192

Exodus
14:31 39
20:1 169
32 75

Leviticus
12–15 70
15:19 78
18:24–30 234n55
19:17 351n85
19:31 234n55
20:1–3 234n55
26:46 163

Numbers
11 173, 271

11:16–25 105, 173n91, 191, 193, 258, 323
24:17 228n34

Deuteronomy
4:32 170
18:15–18 236n63
21:23 226
23:3 234n55
32:7 191, 322
33:10 163

2 Kings
17 72

Isaiah
2:1–4 226n26, 244n96
3:9–11 315
7:14 98
19:24–25 244n96
42:6 246n107
45:22–23 226n26
49:5–6 180n22, 226n26, 315
52:5 315
56:6–7 226n26

Micah
4:1–3 224n96

Zechariah
9:1–7 244n96

Psalms
8:4 357

Proverbs
8:22–31 169

Song of Songs
6:8–9 152n39

2. *"Old Testament Pseudepigrapha" and Second Temple Jewish Literature*

3. New Testament, Apostolic Fathers, and Christian Apocrypha

4. Pseudo-Clementine Literature

5. Early and Late Antique Christian Literature

6. Late Antique Jewish Literature

7. *Other Literature*

Author Index